ROMAN CASTLEFORD

Excavations 1974-85
Volume III
The Pottery

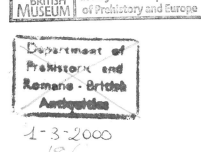

by

Peter Rush, Brenda Dickinson, Brian Hartley and K.F. Hartley

Principal Illustrator

Kath Keith

West Yorkshire Archaeology Service

ISBN   1 870453 23 9
ISSN   0959-3500

Edited by: C. Philo and S. Wrathmell
Published by: West Yorkshire Archaeology Service, on behalf of West Yorkshire
                    Joint Services
Typeset by: West Yorkshire Archaeology Service
Printed by: Short Run Press, Exeter

This publication has been made possible by a grant from English Heritage

Yorkshire Archaeology
Series Editor: Stuart Wrathmell

Available from West Yorkshire Archaeology Service, West Yorkshire Joint Services, Nepshaw
Lane South, P.O. Box 5, Morley, Leeds LS27 OQP
For more information about our publications, visit our web site at http://www.arch.wyjs.org.uk

Cover: Design from samian vessel No. 1013
Cover design and photography by Paul Gwilliam

Contents

List of Figures

List of Tables

Acknowledgements

This volume, the final monograph in the 'Roman Castleford' series, is devoted to the Roman pottery assemblages recovered during the West Yorkshire Archaeology Unit's excavations of 1974 to 1985. The excavation and post-excavation projects were supervised by P. Abramson, S.A. Moorhouse and A.B. Sumpter, under successive County Archaeologists P. Mayes and J.D. Hedges. Co-ordination of the pottery cataloguing and reporting was in the hands of J.C. Clarke, J.J. Marriott and P. Rush. P. Allon, S.J.N. Tomson, B. Lowe, K. Keith and J. Heron all assisted in sorting and recording the ceramic material. Figures 1, 2 and 82-86 were drawn by M.R. Fossick, the samian from Site 1(74) was drawn by A. Newland J. Heron helped with the course ware drawings, and C. Philo helped with the mortaria drawings; the rest was drawn by Kath Keith. Other contributions to this report are acknowledged on the title page and at the heads of chapters.

C. Wood undertook the initial typing of the report, a role later taken on by A. Whawell who also assisted in the sub-editing process. Sub-editing and typesetting were carried out by C. Philo, with technical support provided by D. Berg and P. Gwilliam. The West Yorkshire Archaeology Service gratefully acknowledges the work of the project staff, and the assistance given by Pam Judkins, Keeper of Archaeology, Wakefield Museums and Arts, and by successive English Heritage Inspectors, Andrew Davison and John Etté.

The pottery described in this volume has been deposited with Wakefield Museum, along with the full catalogues and other documentation.

Part One

Introduction

by Peter Rush

1 The Excavations at Castleford

The town of Castleford in West Yorkshire (SE 426 257) has long been identified with the Roman site of *Lagentium* mentioned in the *Antonine Itinerary* and the *Ravenna Cosmography* (Rivet and Smith 1979, 383). It lies 16km south-east of Leeds and 32km south-west of York, immediately below the confluence of the rivers Aire and Calder, and on the south side of the River Aire. Between 1974 and 1985 redevelopment of the town allowed extensive archaeological investigations to be undertaken (Figs 1 and 2). The twenty major trenches and 37 minor trenches and sondages revealed the remains of two successive forts occupied during the later 1st century and a contemporary *vicus* which continued to be a centre of activity into the mid-2nd century. Later Roman occupation in the vicinity was also attested by a perimeter wall and ditch system and a few late artefacts, but the main focus of the settlement had clearly moved away from the area of the modern town by the 4th century. Table 1 records the phasing that has been established across all of the sites. This has been derived principally from the study of coins and pottery in undisturbed contexts, and two sequences of phasing have been identified. One relates to sites within the fort area and is designated by Roman numerals as Phases I, II, III and IV. The other is for the sites in the *vicus* area and is designated by Arabic numerals as Phases 1 to 4.

The two previously published volumes on Roman Castleford have dealt with the Small Finds (Cool and Philo 1998), and with the Structural and Environmental Evidence (Abramson *et al.* 1999). As acknowledged in the first of these, the post-excavation analysis was lengthy and poorly co-ordinated: specialists worked largely in isolation, with outline phasing data to help them but without benefit of the kind of information and ideas exchange which would now be required of any post-excavation programme (Cool 1998a, 1). The effects of this have been mitigated in two ways. In the first place, two of the contributors read all the draft reports, and were thereby able to synthesise the data and provide a measure of general interpretation (Cool 1998b; 1999a; Bishop 1999). Secondly, concordances have been included in each volume to enable readers with sufficient interest or need to regroup material by context and phase (Cool and Philo 1998, 375-93; Cool 1999b). The Appendix in this volume completes the series, and allows users to reconstitute stratigraphic associations between small finds, potsherds and environmental data, according to trench, phase and context. As far as the pottery is concerned, it should be noted that references to vessels represented by several sherds from different contexts has been selective: only the first context recorded in any catalogue entry has been cited.

2 The Roman Pottery

The reports presented in this volume are devoted to the samian (Part Two), the coarse wares (Part Three) and the mortaria (Part Four) from the fort and *vicus* sites. They have been prepared at different times by different specialists, and an indication of the chronology of report preparation and revision is given at the start of the relevant part or section. There are also differences in the levels to which these varying assemblages have been published.

The samian reports in Part Two focus primarily upon the decorated vessels and the potters' stamps, although the overall quantification table of vessels by form, for both the forts and the *vicus*, include the plain samian (Tables 2-5 and 8-11) The report of the samian from the earliest excavations in the *vicus*, Site 1(74), is comprehensive, but those for the forts and *vicus* Trench 10 are selective: full lists have been incorporated in the Archive, which is in the care of Wakefield Museum.

The coarse ware reported in Part Three was quantified according to estimated vessel numbers and sherd counts, and so in this respect it has a measure of presentational compatibility with the samian. The detailed coarse ware methodology is discussed in Part Three.

The pottery from some of the minor trenches has not been included because of its unstratified nature and numerical insignificance. The pottery from Sondage 23 (Fig. 2), however, was one of the more important assemblages from the site, containing the latest stratified group of Roman pottery from the Castleford excavations (of later 4th-century date). The coarse ware from the Site 1(74) excavations has also been treated differently from the rest of the pottery, as the recording system used for this excavation unfortunately does not allow the pottery to be linked directly to the contexts from which it was recovered. As a result there was little to be gained from including the bulk of the material from this site except for that which related to a large deposit of burnt and unused vessels, forming part of what came to be referred to, as the 'pottery shop' assemblage. The only other vessels

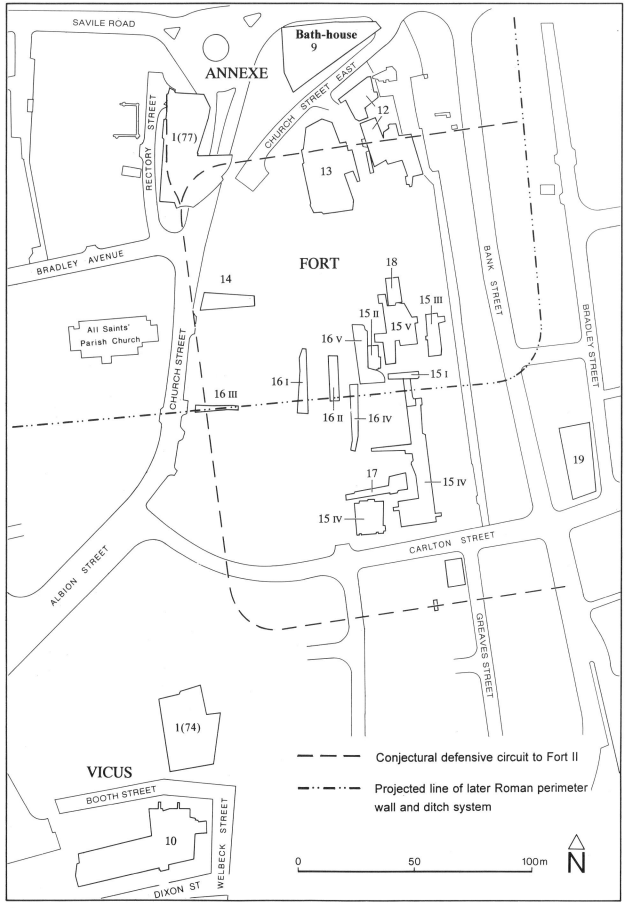

Fig. 1. Location plan of major excavation trenches investigated 1974-85.

Table 1. Phases of occupation in the fort and *vicus* at Castleford.

Fort	Vicus
Phase I: *c.* AD 71/4 - *c.* AD 86 (Fort I)	Phase 1: *c.* AD 71/4 - *c.* AD 86 (*Vicus*)
Phase II: *c.* AD 85-90 - *c.* AD 95-100 (Fort II)	Phase 2: *c.* AD 85-90 - *c.* AD 135-40 (*Vicus*)
Phase III: *c.* AD 100 - 250 (Abandoned/rubbish disposal)	Phase 3: *c.* AD 140 - *c.* AD 180 (*Vicus*)
	Phase 4: *c.* AD 180+ - *c.* 400 (Abandoned)
Phase IV: *c.* AD 250 - 400 (Late Roman occupation)	

included are those which provide the best or only examples of particular types, and which appear in the 'drawn pottery' section of the coarse ware report.

The mortarium report was written some four years after the coarse ware report had been completed, and as a result it has been possible to present the mortarium types as a continuation of the coarse ware fabric series. The method of quantification between these two reports, is also consistent.

As far as possible, sherds from coarse ware and mortarium vessels were grouped together. This not only formed part of the quantification process but also allowed problems of residuality and redeposition to be investigated. The methodology is explained fully in the introduction to the coarse ware report. This work showed, importantly, that very little pottery was recovered from the location where it was originally discarded. The distribution of pottery across the sites cannot, therefore, be interpreted meaningfully in terms of the various activities that may have taken place in different areas of Roman Castleford.

An exception to this generalisation may be the 'pottery shop' assemblage noted above. The assemblage consisted of a large amount of burnt and unused pottery including Central Gaulish samian, mortaria of a distinctive type and jars, bowls and dishes of black-burnished ware type 1 from Dorset. The original discovery of this material was in the 1974 *vicus* excavations, but subsequently a further part of the assemblage was discovered in Trench 10; further related pottery has also been recovered from a watching brief carried out in 1989 in Dixon Street. The nature of this pottery suggested that it had come from a shop or store that had been destroyed by fire. The recording system used in 1974, does not, however, permit the exact structures associated with the assemblage to be identified, since excavation was carried out on the basis of arbitrary 'spits' or levels, rather than by stratigraphic units. A further result of the recording method was that a small amount of colour-coated fine ware, that may have belonged to this group, could not be ascribed to it with certainty (see The Coarse Wares, this volume).

The presence of 'pottery shop' material in the southern half of Site 1(74), in Trench 10 and in a trench immediately south of Trench 10 suggests that the assemblage had been subject to post-destruction movement. Nevertheless, the dating of this material, its formal character and its general location, all point to an association with the suggested 'ritual complex' which may have occupied *vicus* Trench 10 during the mid-2nd-century (Cool 1999a).

Finally, in the catalogues that follow, illustrated sherds are indicated by an asterisk following the catalogue number. The contextual and other details of the sherd are given in italics following the catalogue entry thus:

101 T14; SF97; IIa

The first element consists of the context number and trench (T) or sondage (Sg.) number (see Figs 1 and 2). The second element is the small find number issued at the time of excavation. The fourth element is the phase (see Table 1). In Part Four: The Mortaria other information is included in the catalogue entries as follows:

Stamp No. 4; (40 and 83); 170 Site 1(74); 3

The first element indicates that the stamp appears in the stamp catalogue. The numbers in brackets are the archive identification numbers marked on the sherds. In the mortaria stamp catalogue the drawing number of the vessel appears in place of the stamp number.

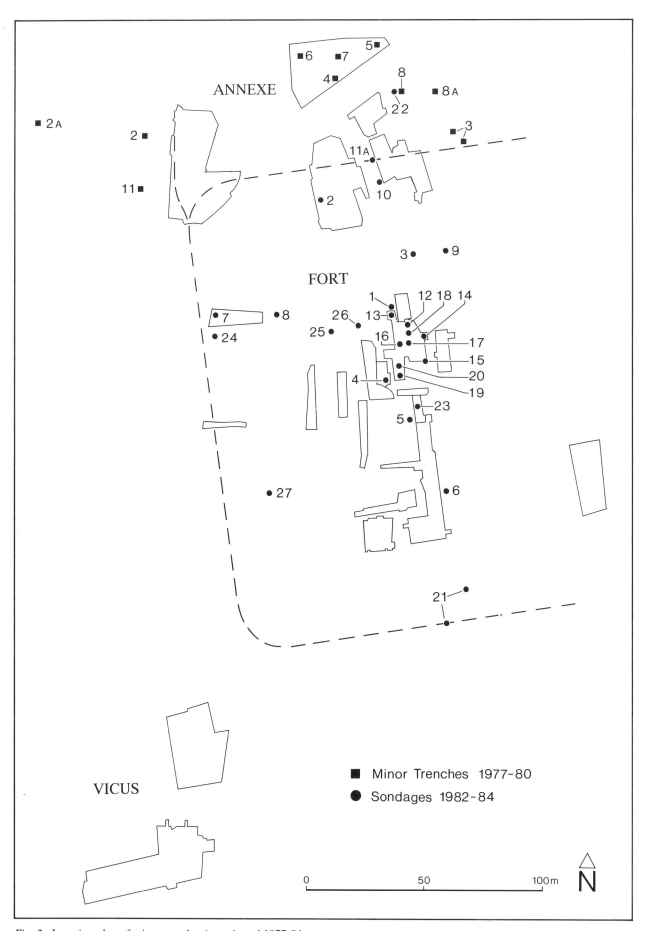

Fig. 2. Location plan of minor trenches investigated 1977-84.

Part Two
The Samian

by Brenda Dickinson and Brian Hartley

3 Decorated Samian Ware and Potters' Stamps from the Forts

This report was written in 1985/90 and the final revisions were made in 1999.

Introduction

The following catalogue of decorated samian is confined to those vessels which have been illustrated for publication. A full listing of the unpublished material is held in the Research Archive. The published catalogues of decorated samian and stamps are followed by a summary discussion of the fort samian as a whole: the accompanying quantification tables include plain as well as decorated samian.

Site 1(77)

The unstratified material ranges from the late Neronian or early Flavian period to the late 2nd or early 3rd century, mainly Central Gaulish, with some South Gaulish and a little East Gaulish ware. It includes decorated bowls in the styles of Iustus i of La Graufesenque, Cettus of Les Martres-de-Veyre and the Lezoux potters Casurius ii, Cinnamus ii, Paternus iv, X-5, X-6, Rogers's P-15 and members of the Cerialis ii-Cinnamus ii and Paternus v groups. There are also stamps of Paternus v (No. 103, on form 37), Primulus i (No. 114), Reburrus ii (No. 121) and Taurinus.

Worthy of separate note are:

1* Form 37, South Gaulish. A small bowl, with internal groove at the level of the top of the ovolo, as normally on form 30 and occasionally on earlier examples of form 37. The sherd shows a saltire between panels with corner-tassels, one containing a triple medallion with a goose (Hermet 1934, pl. 28, 30). The ovolo is on signed bowls of Memor from the Pompeii Hoard of AD 79 (Atkinson 1914, nos 73-4) and was also used by Mommo and a potter whose name begins in Trim-/Prim. The upper and lower elements of the saltire and the leaves used as corner tassels are on a form 29 from the Pompeii Hoard, with basal stamp of Mommo (Atkinson 1914, no. 13). The basal wreath of trifid motifs and the medallion (used as a festoon) are on a signed bowl of Trim-/Prim from Camelon. c. AD 70-90. *U/S Site 1(77); SF130*

2* Form 37, Central Gaulish. The lavish use of the trifid motif Rogers G29 is paralleled on bowls from Housesteads (Bosanquet 1904, 294) and Corbridge, whose styles suggest Hadrianic-Antonine date. *U/S Site 1(77); SF334*

Context 049

Material ranging from the Neronian period to AD 135 or later, including a Central Gaulish form 37 by a member of the Cerialis ii-Cinnamus ii group.

Worthy of separate note are:

3* Form 29, South Gaulish. The upper zone has triple festoons, containing large rosettes and separated by tassels. The leafy scroll in the lower zone has crossed leaf-tendrils in the upper concavities, in the manner of Neronian bowls stamped by such potters as Crestio, Gallicanus and Modestus i. cf. Wild 1985, D.10 for a similar lower zone on a bowl from the Gloucester Kingsholm site. *c.* AD 50-65. *049 Site 1(77); SF1158,* with *115 Site 1(77); SF870, 115/2 Site 1(77); SF826, and 992 T9; II*

4* Form 37, slightly burnt, South Gaulish. The upper zone includes a kneeling Cupid (Hermet 1934, pl. 18, 35) and an adjacent panel of arrowheads. The scroll in the lower zone has identical upper and lower concavities, each with a small spiral, a large, tightly-wound spiral and a bifid tendril. The basal wreath consists of chevrons. The general style recalls Calvus i, who used chevron wreaths in several sizes and favoured zonal decoration on form 37. The Cupid and arrow-head are on bowls in his style from Vindonissa and Caerleon, respectively. *c.* AD 70-90. *049 Site 1(77); SF692,* with *006/1 Site 1(77); SF468, 006/6 Site 1(77); SF865, 010 Site 1(77); SF184, 026 Site 1(77); SF581 and T7; SF113; II*

Context 052

(Comprising 052, 052/1-3 and Tr. 13 Site 1(77))
Material ranging from the Flavian to the late Antonine period or the early 3rd century. It includes a dish stamped by Peculiaris i (No. 105) and Central Gaulish decorated bowls in the styles of Criciro v, Docilis i, Pugnus ii and the Cerialis ii-Cinnamus ii and Quintilianus i groups.

Also worthy of note are:

5* Form 29, South Gaulish. The scroll in the upper zone has astragulus bindings, large and small spirals, the latter ending in eleven-petalled rosettes, and striated spindles. The upper concavity of the lower zone scroll has a webbed leaf (Hermet 1934, pl. 6, 32), between similar, larger leaves. The motif in the lower concavity has a four-bladed plant at the bottom (Hermet 1934, pl. 14, 50) with four tendrils springing from its stem, each with the small leaf of the upper concavity. Scrolls in both zones of form 29 are more typical of the pre-Flavian period than later, though a few were probably made in the early 70s. The small leaf occurs on bowls from Vindonissa, stamped by M. Crestio (Knorr 1919, Textbild 17), and London, stamped by Modestus i (formerly Guildhall Museum), Niger ii (British Museum) and Primus iii - Sco- (formerly London Museum). *c.* AD 60-75. *052 Site 1(77); SF715,* with *U/S Site 1(77); SF962 and SF970; II*

6* Form 37, Central Gaulish, with small mould-stamp of Cinnamus ii (No. 76) in the decoration. The panels include: 1) A seated Apollo? (D.52?) and eight-petalled rosette (Rogers C53). 2) A draped

Fig. 3. Decorated samian from Site 1(77). Scale 1:2

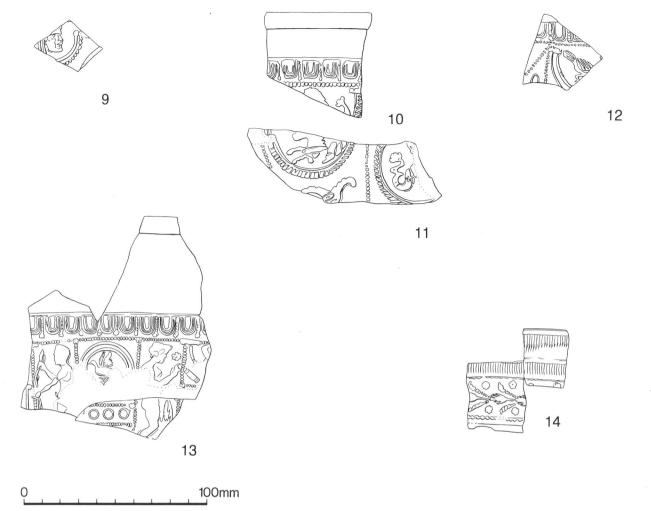

Fig. 4. Decorated samian from Site 1(77). Scale 1:2

figure? A lozenge (Rogers U36) joins a leafy spray (Rogers M31) to the basal ridge. 3) Another figure. Cinnamus's bowls with small mould-stamps are rather earlier than those with his large label-stamps. *c.* AD 140-60. *052 Site 1(77); SF1076,* with *Level + Site1(77); SF228; II*

7* Form 37, Central Gaulish. A bowl in the style of Paternus v (Rogers's Paternus II), with a ring-tongued ovolo (Rogers B105) and a scroll with a peacock (D.1027) in the upper concavity. *c.* AD 160-95. *052 Site 1(77); SF1120; II*

8* Form 37, Central Gaulish. A bowl in the style of Banuus, with ovolo Rogers B136 and panels: 1) a Pudicitia (D.547). 2) A single festoon. The upper border is unusual in having square beads above panel 1 and ovoid beads over panel 2. The vertical border has rhomboidal beads. *c.* AD 160-200. *052 Site 1(77); SF639; II*

9* Form 37, Central Gaulish. The decoration includes a festoon with beaded outer border (Rogers F61) containing a mask, as on a bowl from Corbridge in the style of Do(v)eccus i (S. & S. 1958, pl. 151, 58). There is also a medallion. *c.* AD 165-200. *052/1 Site 1(77); SF417; II*

10* & 11* Form 37, burnt, Central Gaulish. A bowl in the style of Casurius ii, with adjacent panels containing the motif Rogers F38, used first as a festoon and then as a medallion. The festoon contains a sea-horse (D.33) and the medallion a triton (D.16). Below the festoon is an acanthus in a cup (S. & S. 1958, pl. 133, 14). The ovolo is Rogers B208. *c.* AD 160-190. *052/1 Site 1(77); SF 439* joining *Level 5 Site1(77); SF477; II*

12* Form 30, Central Gaulish. A bowl in the style of Criciro v, with his single-bordered ovolo (Rogers B12) and panels: 1) a saltire. 2) A double festoon with bird to right (0.225OA). The decoration is paralleled on a signed bowl from Cardurnock (S. & S. 1958, pl. 117, 2). *c.* AD 135-65. *127 Site 1(77); SF606; II*

13* Form 37, Central Gaulish. The panels include: 1) Diana (D.65). 2) A double medallion containing a bird (D.1011), over a central row of rings. 3) Man with *chlamys* (D.344) and a seven-beaded rosette. 4) (Upper part) A single festoon with bird to left, looking back, and astragalus across the corner. The medallions, rings, astragalus and blobs joining the borders all suggest the Large-S Potter, but he is not known to have used the figure-types, and the ovolo (Rogers B231) is more typical of Cinnamus ii and the Sacer i group. Hadrianic date is almost certain, however. *c.* AD 125-140. *140 Site 1(77); SF658; ?*

14* Form 29, South Gaulish. The straight wreath in the upper zone is composed of overlapping trifid motifs (Hermet 1934, pl. 14, 69) and rows of rosettes. This is exactly paralleled on a bowl in the Pompeii Hoard, stamped by Mommo (Atkinson 1914, no. 18). A similar wreath appears on a bowl from Vechten, stamped by Manduilus (Knorr 1919, Taf. 55E). *c.* AD 60-80. *156 Site 1(77); SF1097 (2),* with *156/1 Site1(77); SF1084 (2); I*

Trench 9

15* Form 37, Central Gaulish, with a rosette-tongued ovolo (Rogers B24) and festoon in a panel. Probably by Docilis i. *c.* AD 125-60. *706 Site1(77); SF1046* (joining a sherd in *986 T9,* see Archive Report context *986,* ii); *II*

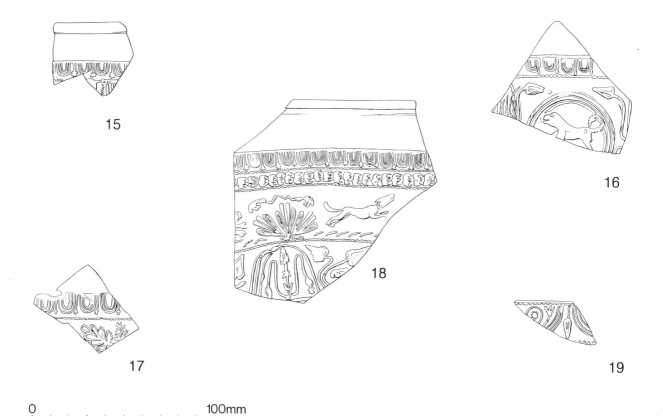

15

16

17

18

19

0   100mm

Fig. 5. Decorated samian from Trench 9. Scale 1:2

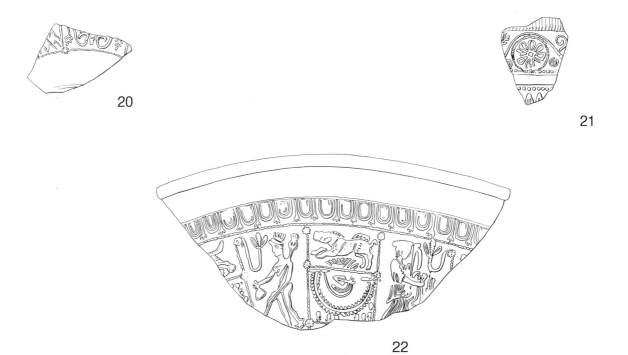

20

21

22

0   100mm

Fig. 6. Decorated samian from Trench 12. Scale 1:2

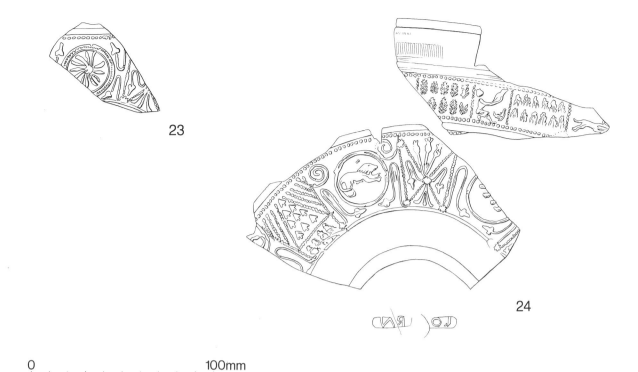

23

24

0   100mm

Fig. 7. Decorated samian from Trench 13. Scale 1:2. Stamp (No. 24) 1:1

Context 931

Late Neronian or early Flavian to Antonine. The
material includes:

16* Form 37, South Gaulish. The ovolo was used by M. Crestio
(Dickinson 1984, D9, from Verulamium) and C. Valerius Albanus.
One panel has corner-tassels with heart-shaped leaves and a triple
medallion containing a dog to left. *c.* AD 80-110. *931 T9; II*

17* Form 37, South Gaulish, probably with scroll decoration. The
ovolo and small leaf are on stamped bowls of M. Crestio from
Mainz (Knorr 1952, Taf. 19A, B respectively). The seven-lobed
leaf (Hermet 1934, pl. 10, 4) is not known for him. *c.* AD 75-100.
931 T9; II

18* Form 37, South Gaulish. The ovolo, with narrow core and four-
pronged tongue, occurs fairly often in Scotland. The wreath of
leaves below it is probably on a bowl from Newstead. The
freestyle upper zone includes a hare, Nile geese (Hermet 1934, pl.
28, 68) with an eel and a dog (Hermet 1934, pl. 26, 18?). The fan-
shaped plant (composed of three impressions of a smaller version
of Hermet 1934, pl. 14, 49) is on form 37s from Verulamium (on a
bowl with the same ovolo: Hartley 1972a, D44) and Newstead. The
scroll in the lower zone has heart-shaped leaves with fringed
borders in the upper concavity, with the Nile goose to left. The
composite motif in the lower concavity is closely paralleled on
form 29 from Valkenburg ZH, stamped by Meddillus. *c.* AD 75-90.
931 T9; SF1079, with 701 T9; SF900, T9 702; SF925, SF901; II

19* Form 29, South Gaulish. Triple festoons in the upper zone are
separated by a tassel with a lanceolate leaf. One festoon contains a
spiral ending in a rosette and a tendril with trifid motif. Neither of
these types of motif is common in festoons, being more normally
used in scrolls. The festoons suggest a date. *c.* AD 70-85. *931 T9*
(with *950 T9); II*

Trench 12

20* Form 37, South Gaulish. The surviving panels contain: 1) rows of
pointed leaf-tips. 2) Tendrils with bud-clusters, springing from the

base of a fan-shaped motif (Knorr 1919, Taf. 28, 25). Probably by
M. Crestio, who regularly used the fan-shaped motif. *c.* AD 75-95.
070 T12; ?

21* Form 29, South Gaulish. The scroll in the upper zone has feathery
plants and spirals in the upper concavity and a toothed medallion
between roundels and containing an eight-petalled rosette in the
lower concavity. The lower zone has a series of palisades. The
decoration is exactly matched on a bowl stamped by Carillus, in a
group of samian believed to be from a pottery shop outside the
legionary fortress at Nijmegen (Morren 1966, 225). The group is
dated to the 70s. *c.* AD 65-80. *316 T12; Med.*

22* Form 37, South Gaulish. The trident-tongued ovolo, also present
on Archive Report 019 T17, is known for Albanus iii, Bassinus i
and Litugenus i. It occurs on several bowls from the Domitianic
foundation at Wilderspool. The panels contain: 1A) a dog? to left
(Hermet 1934, pl. 26, 39?); 1B) a chevron festoon. 2) Mercury
(Hermet 1934, pl. 18, 47). 3A) Boar to left (0.1672), over a grass
tuft; 3B) a chevron festoon, containing a stirrup-leaf, over leaf-
tips. There is another section of panel below this. 4) Diana and
hind (Hermet 1934, pl. 18, 6). Panels 2 and 4 have trifid corner-
tassels. There are no close parallels for the decoration as a whole,
but the Mercury and Diana are on a bowl from London (Bank of
England) with a cursive signature Gra..., retrograde (Knorr 1952,
Taf. 29A). *c.* AD 80-100. *322 T12* (joining *305/2 T12); Ib*

Trench 13

23* Form 29, South Gaulish. The lower zone has a panel with corner-
tassels of elongated, heart-shaped leaves and a medallion with a
cross of trifid motifs. The saltire in the adjacent panel also has the
leaves and trifid motif. All the details are on bowls in the Pompeii
Hoard stamped by Mommo (Atkinson 1914, nos 13, 18, 19). The
trifid motif is on two bowls from a group of samian of the 70s from
Nijmegen, thought to be from a pottery shop (Morren 1966, 229,
7, 8). Both have internal stamps of Vanderio and illiterate or
cypher mould-stamps in the decoration. The leaf is on a bowl from
the same group, also stamped by Vanderio (Morren 1966, 227, 5).
c. AD 70-85. *011 T13; III*

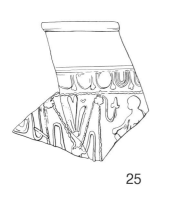

25

26

27

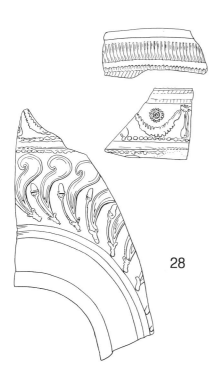

28

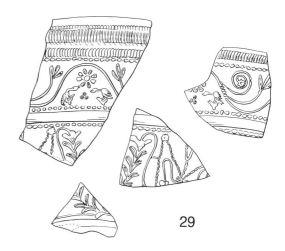

29

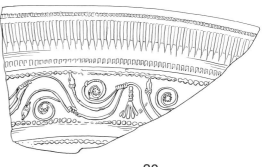

30

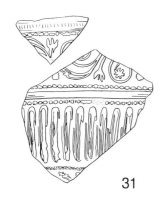

31

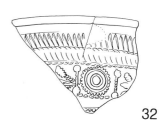

32

0   100mm

Fig. 8. Decorated samian from Trench 14. Scale 1:2

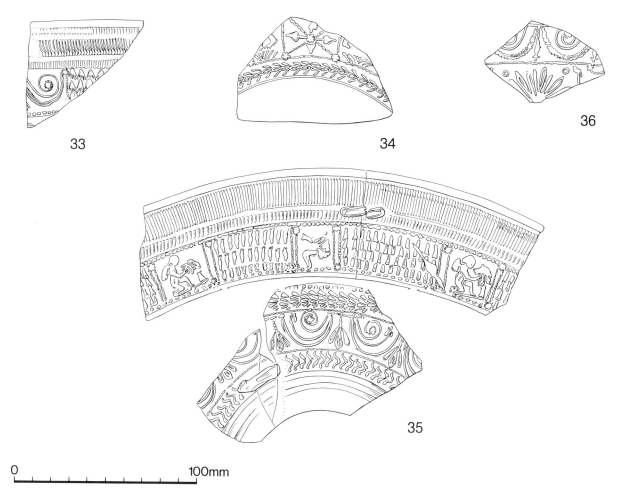

33   34   36

35

0 _____ 100mm

Fig. 9. Decorated samian from Trench 14. Scale 1:2

24* Late Neronian to Flavian, including: SF183 form 29, South Gaulish, with internal stamp LOGIRN retrograde (No. 91). Four sherds, with others in 181 T12 and 302 (3), 303/3C, 338 (2), 343, 345, 378 (4) T13. The upper zone has panels with a bird-catcher (Hermet 1934, pl. 23, 268) and dog to right, chasing a hare, between panels with rows of rounded and pointed serrated leaves. Alternate panels in the lower zone have tendrils in the bottom corners and spirals in the top corners. One medallion has a lion (Hermet 1934, pl. 25, 25); another perhaps has a goose to left. The intervening panels consist of a triangle of arrow-heads flanked by diagonal wavy lines, over a row of pointed, serrated leaf-tips, and a saltire. There are several parallels on form 29s with the IIVST label stamp of Iustus i, namely the leaf in the medallion panels (Rome), the poppy-heads in the saltire (Valkenburg ZH) and the arrow-heads (de Meern). The trifid motif in the saltire is on an unprovenanced bowl in Iustus's style in Scarborough Museum and on form 29 from Strasbourg with internal stamp of Logirnus. Logirnus made moulds at Montans but probably not at La Graufesenque, where he is more likely to have bought them from other potters. Iustus may have been one of his suppliers, though the overall style is not entirely convincing for him. *c.* AD 65-80. *385 T13; IIb*

Trench 14

25* Flavian-Trajanic to the second half of the 2nd century. The material includes a Central Gaulish form 37 in the style of Criciro v, two sherds from a South Gaulish bowl in 207 T14 and two which might possibly belong to it (one 002, the other 007 T14). These show the ovolo (Knorr 1919, Taf. 57, 19), plant in the top of the saltire (Knorr 1919, 11) and heart-shaped leaf on the corner-tassel (Knorr 1919, 15), all used by Mercator i, who almost

certainly made the bowl. The figure-types are a Jupiter? (Hermet 1934, pl. 18, 2?) and a man with a scroll (Hermet 1934, pl. 20, 133). *c.* AD 80-110. *002 T14; Med.*

26* Early Flavian to Antonine, including form 29, South Gaulish. The scroll in the upper zone has triple(?) poppy-heads in the lower concavity, between bottle-buds. The bud recurs in the upper concavity of the scroll in the lower zone. The lower concavity contains a griffin (Hermet 1934, pl. 25, 6, with a spindle on the end of its tail), over arrow-heads in a chevron(?) festoon. The arrangement of this concavity is paralleled on a bowl from Lisieux with an internal stamp of Severus iii, which may have the same festoon and arrow-heads. *c.* AD 70-85. *027 T14; Med.*

27* Two fragments of form 29, South Gaulish. The lower zone includes unusual S-shaped gadroons, over a series of elongated, heart-shaped leaves. The latter are of a type much used in the early Flavian period. *c.* AD 70-85. *108 T14; Ic*

28* Form 29, South Gaulish. The leafy festoon in the upper zone is on form 29 from Gloucester stamped by Matugenus ii. The rosette is a pre-Flavian type. The nautilus gadroons in the lower zone are perhaps Oswald 1951, 153, 44, on a stamped bowl of Murranus from Boulogne. This is one of the earliest pieces from Castleford. *c.* AD 50-65. *108/A T14 (with sherds in 108/B1, 108/B2 (3), 108/C (5), 112 (2), 203, 206, 220 (5), 226, 301, 308, 318 T14); Ic*

29* Form 29, South Gaulish. The scroll in the upper zone has spirals and trifid motifs (Knorr 1919, Taf. 65, 18) in the upper concavities and an eight-petalled rosette (Knorr 1919, 21), over a triangle of rings between a pair of Nile geese (Hermet 1934, pl. 28, 68) in the lower concavities. The lower zone has leafy festoons with tendrils attached at the top and saltire panels with trifid motifs (Knorr

11

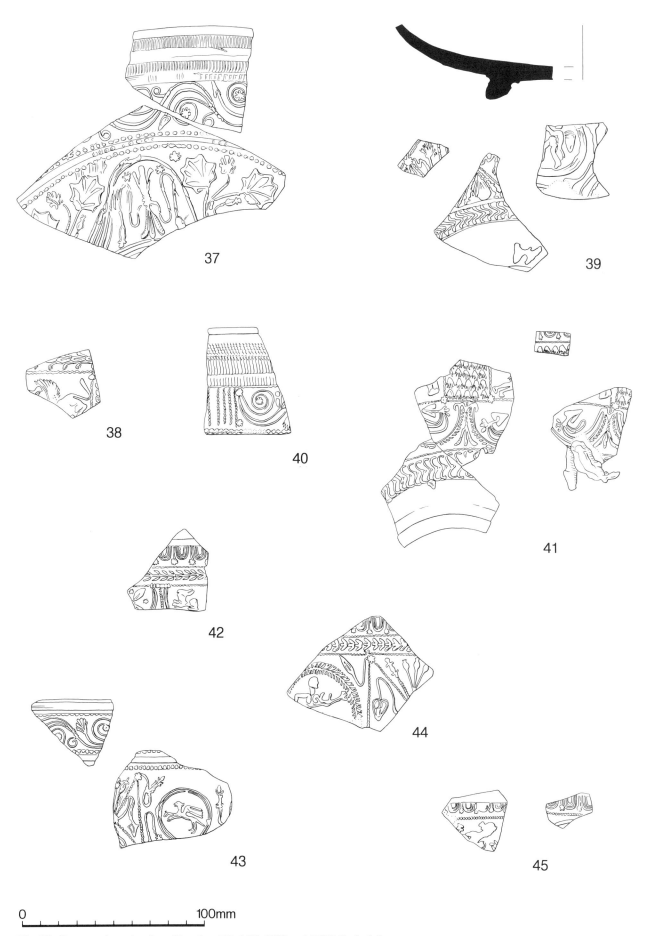

37

39

38

40

41

42

44

43

45

Fig. 10. Decorated samian from Trenches 15I, 15II, 15III and 15IV. Scale 1:2

1919, Taf. 65, 19) in the top quadrants and small leaves (Knorr 1919, 17) at the sides. Both trifid motifs, the five-beaded scroll binding, the leaves, the spirals and the rosette joining the diagonals of the saltire are all on form 29 from Mainz stamped by Primus iii (Knorr 1919, Taf. 66B). The trifid motif and rosette in the upper zone are on another bowl from Mainz (Knorr 1919, J), with the same stamp, which comes from one of Primus's later dies. The geese are on a Primus bowl with a different stamp from Silchester (May 1916, pl. VII, A). *c.* AD 55-65. *108/B2 T14 (*with sherds in *108/C, 112, 147, 172, 179, 220 T14); Ic*

30* Form 29, South Gaulish. The scroll in the upper zone has spirals with ten-petalled rosettes, tendrils with acorns and six-beaded bindings. A five-bladed plant is used as a space-filler in one of the lower concavities, where the scroll comes back on itself and there is no room for the spiral and tendril. All the motifs except the last are on form 29 from Bonn stamped by Labio (Knorr 1919, Taf. 44A), and this is on a bowl with the same stamp from Rheingönheim (Knorr 1952, Taf. 32C). It is also on a bowl from Hofheim stamped by Matugenus ii (Knorr 1919, Taf. 53). *c.* AD 55-75. *108/B2 T14 (*with sherds in *147, 149, 183, 194 (2), 408 T14); Ic*

31* Form 29, South Gaulish. The upper zone consists of a scroll, with spirals and trifid tendrils in both concavities and blobby rosettes in the lower concavities. The lower zone has straight gadroons over a wreath of trifid motifs. The upper zone is closely paralleled on a bowl from Nijmegen stamped by Coelus (Knorr 1919, Taf. 24D). He was perhaps involved earlier in the Bassus ii-Coelus firm, which used the motif in the basal wreath (Knorr 1919, Taf. 13, 4). *c.* AD 65-85. *108/C T14 (*with *232 T14); Ic*

32* Form 29, South Gaulish. The upper zone includes a panel with concentric medallions, between panels with trifid motifs (Hermet 1934, pl. 14, 36) impressed sideways. This zone is unusually shallow, perhaps suggesting a small bowl. The rouletting on the rim is very coarse and the central moulding is barely rounded. The fabric is overfired. This bowl is not necessarily from La Graufesenque, but its provenance remains uncertain, in the absence of parallels for the decoration. *c.* AD 75-90/95. *179 T14 (*with sherds in *135, 158, 216, 220 (2) T14); Id*

33* Form 29, South Gaulish. The upper zone is unusual in having panels divided by fine beads, instead of wavy lines. These include triple-bordered festoons with spirals and rows of pointed leaf-tips. *c.* AD 55-70. *206 T14 (*with *232 T14); Ic*

34* Form 37, South Gaulish. The panels contain: 1) a figure (to left?), over a partly impressed grass-tuft (Knorr 1919, Taf. 57, 13). 2) (Lower half) A saltire, with heart-shaped leaves (Knorr 1919, 15) in all four quadrants. 3) A figure (to right?), over a grass-tuft, as in 1. The motifs were used by Mercator i, who almost certainly made this bowl. The basal wreath of trifid motifs is on a bowl in his style from Southwark. See context 002 for a description of two other sherds which may come from this bowl. *c.* AD 80-110. *207 T14 (*with *002 (2?) and perhaps *007 T14); II*

35* Form 29, South Gaulish. The panels in the upper zone contain: 1) rows of elongated, heart-shaped leaves. 2) A kneeling Cupid (Hermet 1934, pl. 18, 36). 3) Rows of poppy heads. 4) A seated man (Hermet 1934, 52). 5) = 1. The lower zone contains a wreath of fan-shaped plants, over a zone of festoons with spirals and tendrils ending in tulip leaves. The festoons are separated by trifid tassels. The basal wreath consists of recurving chevrons, of a type common in the early Flavian period. The leaf-tips and Cupid are on a bowl from Bonn, stamped by Cotto ii (Knorr 1919, Taf. 27) and another of his bowls, from Wroxeter, has the leaf-tips. The tassel motif is on bowls stamped by Rufinus iii (London, formerly Bethnal Green Museum) and Pass(i)enus (Aislingen: Knorr 1912a, Taf. IX, 1). The double panel borders in the upper zone are on a bowl from Leicester with a stamp of Monti-Cres-. *c.* AD 65-85. *220 T14 (*three sherds, with others in *313 (3) and 318 T14); Ic*

36* Form 37, South Gaulish, perhaps going with the base in 313. The decoration includes a zone of chevron festoons containing spirals and separated by bottle buds. The lower zone has a fan-shaped plant composed of trifid motifs (Hermet 1934, pl. 14, 47), the tail of a lion (Hermet 1934, pl. 25, 12), small rings and a tendril attached to the upper border by a rosette. The upper zone is exactly paralleled on a bowl in 012 T16II from a mould with a signature of Meddillus, inscribed after firing, like all his signatures recorded so far. The trifid motif is on bowls with his interior stamp, from London (formerly Guildhall Museum) and Alchester. Meddillus was not necessarily a mould-maker, and the style of his bowls suggests that he may have bought moulds from other potters, such as Calvus i, Iustus i and Vitalis ii, the last of whom used the fan-shaped plant, the tendril and perhaps the wreath, on a bowl from Mainz (Knorr 1919, Taf. 84F). *c.* AD 70-90. *232 T14; Ic*

Trench 15I

37* Form 29, South Gaulish. The bowl was taken from the mould while the clay was too wet, so that the decoration is blurred and distorted in places. The scroll in the upper zone has spirals and lanceolate leaves in both concavities. The scroll in the lower zone has upper concavities with small leaves and bottle-buds, alternating with polygonal leaves. The composite motifs in the lower concavities include trifid motifs (Hermet 1934, pl. 14, 46) and larger bottle-buds. The lanceolate leaf is on a bowl from Mainz stamped by Cabucatus (Knorr 1919, Taf. 19A, under Carugatus), and the zone as a whole is similar to one on a bowl from Rottweil, stamped by Secundus ii (Knorr 1919, Taf. 74E). The smaller leaf in the lower zone was used by Calvus i and Patricius i, among others. It occurs on an unprovenanced bowl in Utrecht Museum, stamped by Cosius Rufinus, and the double trifid motif is on a bowl with the same stamp, from Rheingönheim (Knorr 1952, Taf. 16B). *c.* AD 70-85. *023 15I (*two sherds, with others in *017 T15I, 957 T15V, 211 T14, 212 T14); Ib*

38* Form 37, South Gaulish. A panel, with trifid wreaths above and to one side, contains a griffin (Hermet 1934, pl. 25, 2). The motif in the horizontal wreath is on a bowl in the style of Calvus from Burgh-by-Woodbridge. The vertical wreath is on No. 44, below. *c.* AD 70-90. *025 15I; Ib*

Trench 15II

39* Form 37, South Gaulish. Part of a signature,]M below the decoration, from a mould inscribed after firing, almost certainly belongs to Meddillus, who may have bought moulds from other potters and put his name on them. The surviving panels show: 1) corner-tassels of fringed plants and a triple medallion, with Cupid (0.435?). 2) A saltire, with fan-shaped plant at the bottom, between bottle-buds and fringed plants (as in 1) at the sides. The bottle-bud and fan-shaped plant are on a bowl from Nijmegen (Knorr 1952, Taf. 40A) and the chevron basal wreath and fringed plant are on another, from Wroxeter. Both have signatures of Meddillus. The unusual footring is only slightly worn, and the profile of the bowl resembles a cross between forms 29 and 37. *c.* AD 70-90. *064 15II (*four sherds, with others in *053 T15II and 704 T16V); Ic*

40* Form 29, South Gaulish. One panel in the upper zone consists of vertical wavy lines. The adjacent panel has a spiral and tendril with trifid motif (a smaller version of Hermet 1934, pl. 13, 38), attached to a rosette. The third tendril may be part of a scroll, as on a bowl from La Graufesenque in the style of Germanus i (Hermet 1934, pl. 102, 41). Short stretches of scroll in panels are one of the features of his style. The decoration is also closely paralleled on a bowl in his style in a group of samian of the AD 70s from Nijmegen, thought to be from a pottery shop (Morren 1966, 226, 3). The Nijmegen bowl, in turn, has similarities with one from Nanstallon, a site probably evacuated by *c.* AD 75 (Hartley 1972c, 100, 4). *c.* AD 65-80. *080 T15II; Ia*

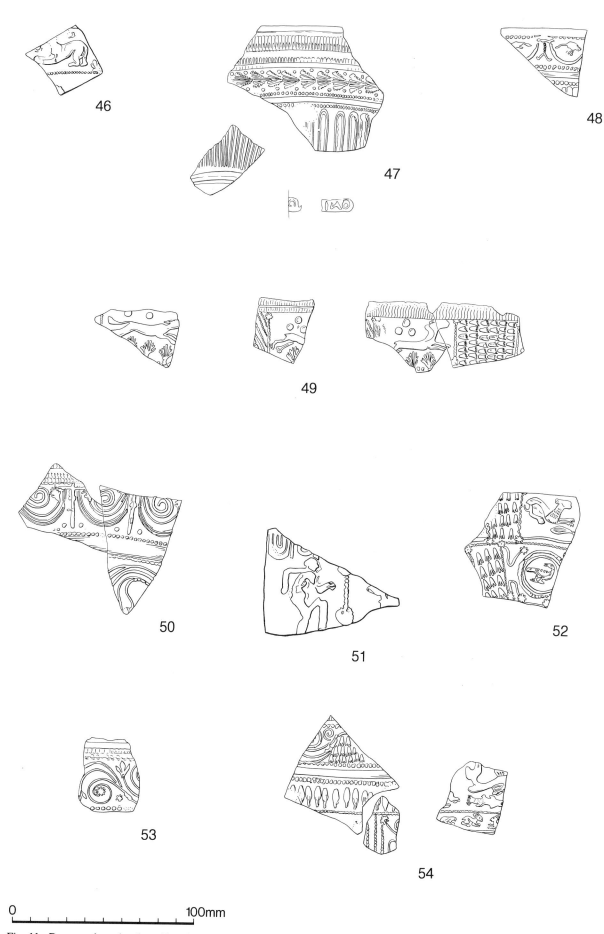

Fig. 11. Decorated samian from Trenches 15IV and 15V. Scale 1:2. Stamp (No. 47) 1:1

14

Trench 15III

41* Form 37, mended with lead rivets and with a very worn footring, South Gaulish. The trident-tongued ovolo is on an unstamped bowl in the Pompeii Hoard (Atkinson 1914, no. 76) and a stamped bowl of Mommo from Winchester. The upper zone includes panels with rows of pointed leaf-tips and others with hares to right. The lower zone has festoons containing stirrup-leaves, alternately to right and left. The festoons are joined by recurving chevrons, which also form the basal wreath. The pendants between the festoons end in trifid motifs. Three of the motifs are on bowls stamped by, or in the style of, Mommo. The pendant and chevron are on forms 29 and 37 in the Pompeii Hoard (Atkinson 1914, nos 3 and 68, respectively) and the leaf-tips are on form 29 from La Graufesenque (Rodez Museum). *c.* AD 70-85. *268 T15II (with sherds in 075 T15II; 932, 1115, 1120/B (4), 1132 (3), 1133, 1141 (2), 1145 (3) T15V); Id*

42* Form 37, South Gaulish. The rosette-tongued ovolo is on form 37 variant from La Graufesenque, with cursive signature, Calvo, in the decoration and a plainware stamp of Patricius i on a handle. The signature almost certainly belongs to Calvus I, to judge by details on other bowls with the same ovolo which also appear on his form 29s. The Castleford bowl has a wreath of trifid motifs below the ovolo, over a zone of double festoons joined by an astragalus, with a pendant below. One festoon has a rosette motif (similar to Hermet 1934, pl. 15, 100), the other has a hare (Hermet 1934, pl. 26, 72?). *c.* AD 70-90. *295 T15III (joining a sherd in 258/2 T15III); Ib*

43* Form 29, South Gaulish. The lower zone has a saltire with bottle-buds flanking a motif in the top quadrant and tendrils with lozenges (as on Archive Report, 317, i T14) at the sides. The adjacent panel has corner-tassels and a double medallion containing a griffin (similar to 0.882). The medallion, griffin, lozenge and perhaps bottle-bud are on a bowl from Chester stamped by Silvanus i (Newstead and Droop 1939, pl. VI, 1). The sherd of upper zone has a scroll with spirals and fan-shaped plants. *c.* AD 60-80. *300 15III (probably from the same bowl as 304 Sg. 26 to judge by the curious ridgy finish on the inside); Ic*

44* Form 37, South Gaulish, with rosette-tongued ovolo, wreath of trifid motifs and panels: 1) a man with a trident (Hermet 1934, pl. 21, 149), in a chevron arcade, and a lanceolate leaf, used as a corner-tassel. 2) A saltire, with triple poppy heads at the top, flanked by bottle-buds, and almond leaves at the sides. The ovolo occurs on bowls in the style of Calvus i and appears with the lanceolate leaf, arcade and top quadrant of the saltire on a bowl from London (Museum of London). The almond leaf is on a bowl from Wanborough with ovolo as on No. 42, above. The wreath is on No. 38, above. *c.* AD 70-90. *302 T15III; Ib*

Trench 15IV

45* Form 37, Central Gaulish, with a small, rosette-tongued ovolo used by Criciro v and Sacer i (Rogers B14) and, probably, a draped figure. *c.* AD 125-160. *567/A T15IV; II*

46* Form 37, Central Gaulish. The panther (0.1566), in the upper part of the upper concavity of a scroll, was used by Attianus ii and Drusus ii. *c.* AD 125-145. *586/A T15IV; II*

47* Form 29, South Gaulish, stamped QVINTIIO Quintio i of La Graufesenque, Die 1a' (No. 119). The upper zone is composed of a straight wreath of unusual trifid motifs (Hermet 1934, pl. 14, 19). The lower zone consists of straight gadroons. The beads bordering the central cordon are unusually small for form 29. Few bowls stamped by this potter are known, but see No. 120 for another, stamped with a different die. *c.* AD 70-85. *634/B T15IV (3 sherds, with others in 556, 581/3 (4), 618, 624, 660 15IV); Id*

48* Form 29, South Gaulish, with very overhanging rim. Small, single-bordered festoons in the shallow upper zone contain Nile geese to right and left (Hermet 1934, pl. 28, 68), with a curious bifid tassel between. The festoons appear on bowls stamped by Censor i (Knorr 1919, Taf. 22, 11). *c.* AD 70-85. *670 T15IV; Ia*

49* Form 29, South Gaulish. Panels in the upper zone include: 1) a dog (Hermet 1934, pl. 26, 18), over fan-shaped plants. 2) (Not necessarily following 1) Diagonal wavy lines. 3) A stag (Hermet 1934, pl. 27, 15 or 16), over plants, as in 2. 4) Rows of pointed leaf-tips, impressed sideways. The rings in panels 1 and 3 were used by Iustus i and occur on a bowl in his style from Archive Report 119, i Site 1(77). The plants are on a stamped Iustus bowl from Framlingham, Suffolk. *c.* AD 70-85. *680/2 15IV (with sherds in 551, 634/B, 683, 705 (2) T15IV); Ia*

Trench 15V

50* Form 29, South Gaulish. The elliptical, triple-bordered festoons in the upper zone contain spirals and feathery fronds and are separated by vertical rods, topped by small leaves. The lower zone contains a winding scroll. *c.* AD 70-85. *985 T15V (three sherds, with others in 049/1 Site 1(77); SF532 and 318 T14); Ib*

51* Form 37, East Gaulish. A panelled bowl, from one of the East Gaulish factories in the Argonne. The ovolo is on an unprovenanced bowl in Reims Museum. Bowls from the Saalburg feature the naked figure (Ricken 1934, Taf. XIII, 42) and (different) rosettes across the borders (Ricken 1934, 52). Probably Antonine. *1032 T15V; IV*

52* Form 37, South Gaulish. The upper surviving zone of decoration has a narrow panel with rows of leaf-tips, between panels with horizontal corner-tendrils. One tendril ends in a lanceolate leaf, below a crouching lion (Hermet 1934, pl. 25, 23). The lower zone has a similar panels of leaf-tips; the adjacent panel has corner-tassels ending in rosettes and a double medallion with a bird (Hermet 1934, pl. 28, 41?). *c.* AD 70-90. *1070 T15V; II*

53* Form 29, South Gaulish. The scroll in the upper zone has spirals and trifid motifs in both concavities. The trifid motifs are on a form 29 from Corbridge, stamped by Calvus i (Simpson 1953, fig. 13 1). *c.* AD 70-85. *1107 T15V (with 1146 T15V and 032 T18); Id*

54* Form 29, South Gaulish. The upper zone has an infilled scroll, with spirals in the upper concavity. Below the central cordon is a zone of palisades. The zone below this has a panel of vertical wavy lines and another with corner spirals. The sherd in 318 T14 has a dolphin (0.2388) and fish (0.2411), over a zone of hares, alternately to left and right. *c.* AD 70-85. *1107 T15V (three joining sherds, one burnt, and a sherd in 318 T14 which probably belongs to this bowl); Id*

55* Form 37, South Gaulish. The trident-tongued ovolo is on a stamped bowl of Mommo from Winchester and on an anonymous bowl in the Pompeii Hoard (Atkinson 1914, no. 76). The panels include: 1) a stag (Hermet 1934, pl. 27, 16). 2) A triangle of heart-shaped leaves, flanked by diagonal wavy lines. This panel is closely paralleled on form 29 stamped by Vanderio, in a group of samian from Nijmegen, thought to be from a pottery shop or store (Morren 1966, 227, 5). *c.* AD 70-90. *1120/B T15V (five sherds, with two in 1145 T15V and one with no recorded context); Id*

56* Form 29, South Gaulish. The scroll in the upper zone has stirrup-leaves to right and small spirals in both concavities. The lower zone consists of short straight gadroons over a zone of chevron festoons with spirals and bottle-bud pendants. This zone is almost exactly paralleled on form 37 in 012 T16I, from a mould belonging to Meddillus, and the gadroons appear on form 29 from Mainz, with an internal stamp of Meddillus (Knorr 1919, Taf.55B). *c.* AD 70-85. *1115 T15V (with 920, 1134 (2), 1145 T15V); Id*

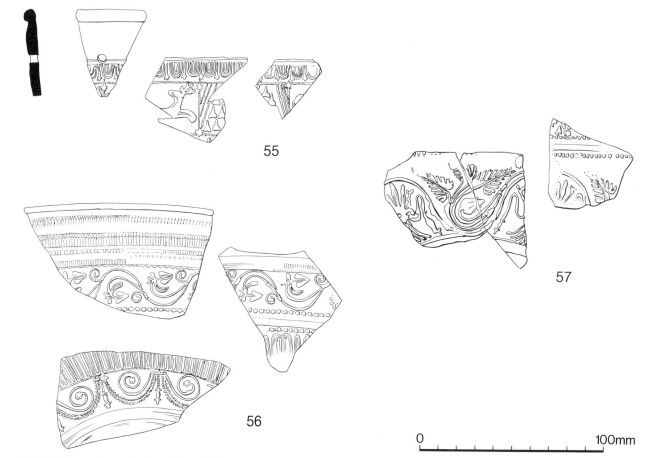

55

57

56

0   100mm

Fig. 12. Decorated samian from Trench 15V. Scale 1:2

57* Form 29, South Gaulish. One of the panels in the upper zone consists of rows of arrow-heads. The lower zone has a winding scroll, with triangular, ribbed leaves in the lower concavities, alternating with fan-shaped motifs and tulip leaves. The lower concavities contain composite motifs, involving trifid plants at the top, between bifid tendrils, bottle-bud tendrils at the sides and grass-tufts at the bottom. This is a typical bowl of the early Flavian period. *c.* AD 70-85. *1145 T15V (with 607, 612/B T15IV; 608 T16V); Ic*

Trench 16I

58* Form 37, South Gaulish. The cursive signature, Medi[(with barred D), inscribed below the decoration after firing, belongs to Meddillus. The upper surviving zone of decoration includes four-bladed plants (Knorr 1919, Taf. 18, 41, under Calvus i) and a blurred, six-petalled rosette. The basal zone is identical to the one on No. 36, above. The bottle-bud pendants are probably on a bowl from 'near Nijmegen' (Museum Kam), with a similar signature. The rosette and festoon are on two different form 29s from London (formerly Guildhall Museum), both with basal stamps of the same potter. All the cursive signatures of Meddillus known to us were cut in the moulds after firing, so it is by no means certain that he was a mould-maker. Stylistic similarities with Calvus i, Iustus i and Vitalis ii have been noted. *c.* AD 70-90. *012 T16I; IIa*

Trench 16II

59* Form 37, with stamp IIVST in the decoration: Iustus i of La Graufesenque (No. 88). The same trident-tongued ovolo occurs on an unstamped bowl in 010. The scroll in the upper zone has bottle-buds (Hermet 1934, pl. 44, 4), stirrup-leaves and spirals in the

upper concavities. The lower concavities each have a row of pointed leaf-tips with an animal above, including a dog to right (Hermet 1934, pl. 26, 31) and hare to left. Wreaths of large and small chevrons enclose a basal zone of short, straight gadroons. The larger of the chevron wreaths and the stirrup-leaf are on form 29 with the same stamp from Koenigshoffen (Strasbourg Museum). The lower concavities of the scroll are similarly treated on form 29 from London (formerly Guildhall Museum) with basal stamp of Meddillus. *c.* AD 70-90. *303 T16II (SF84 and a sherd in 307 T16II); IIa*

Trench 16V

60* Form 29, South Gaulish. The upper zone includes an eight-petalled rosette (Hermet 1934, pl. 15, 50), between palisades on beaded stalks. The lower zone is a scroll, with a ribbed, triangular leaf in the upper concavity and a striated medallion with a bird in the lower. Bowls stamped by Celadus have the palisades, without beads (Longthorpe), medallion and rosette (Verulamium). The palisades with beads are on a bowl from Asberg, stamped by Matugenus ii (Vanderhoeven 1976, Taf. 44, 325). The triangular leaf is on bowls from Tiddington and Mainz in the style of Calvus i. *c.* AD 60-80. *720 T16V (with 701 T16V); Ic*

61* Form 29, South Gaulish. The lower zone has a wreath of polygonal leaves below the central cordon, with a bead-row below it. Cogged medallions alternate with triple vertical bead-rows, topped by astragali. The medallions contain alternate centaurs(?) and dogs (0.1697?). The medallion is on bowls in Hermet's Canrucatus-Vegenus style (i.e. Cabucatus and Regenus; pls 103-5) and occurs on one example with the dog (pl. 105, 55). Beaded borders are unusual within the zones of form 29s. *c.* AD 65-80. *720 T16V (five sherds, with others in 743 (2), 704 T16V); Ic*

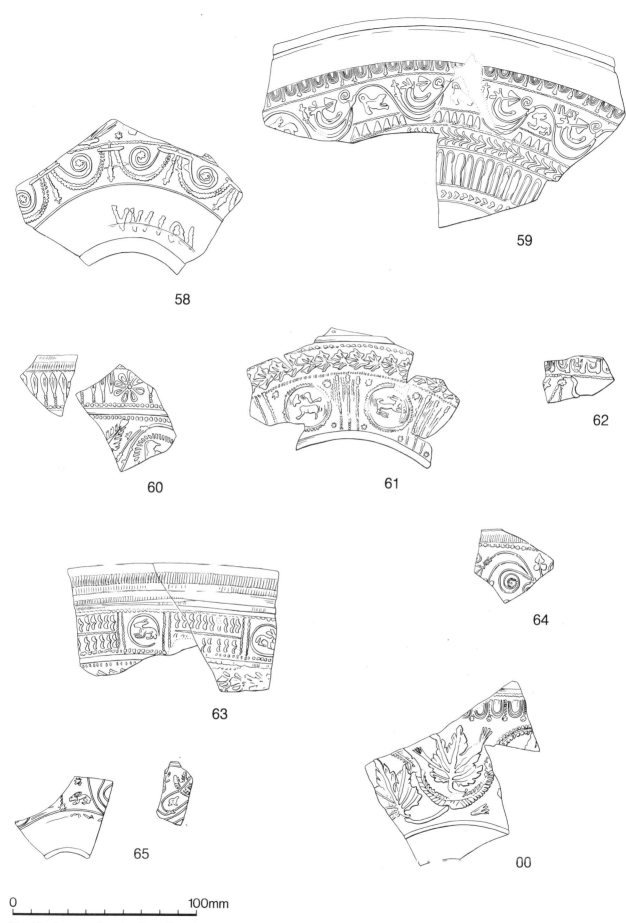

58

59

60

61

62

63

64

65

00

0   100mm

Fig. 13. Decorated samian from Trenches 16I, 16II, 16V and 17. Scale 1:2

17

62* Form 37, South Gaulish. A saltire panel has a bottle-bud at the top, impressed diagonally. The adjacent panel probably contains a lion to right. No parallel has been found for the trident-tongued ovolo. *c*. AD 75-95. *721 T16V; II*

63* Form 29, South Gaulish. The double-bordered panels in the upper zone include double rows of chevrons with wavy-line border between and single medallions with hares alternately to right and left. The wreath below the central cordon consists of fan-shaped leaves. (Different) chevrons are similarly used on bowls from Nijmegen (Morren 1966, 228, 6) and the Pompeii Hoard (Atkinson 1914, no. 15), stamped by Vanderio and Mommo, respectively. The medallion is on a bowl from Vechten, stamped by Coelus (Knorr 1919, Taf. 24E). *c*. AD 65-80. *735 T16V (with 719/B T16V and 070/C (2), 086 T15II); Ic*

64* Form 29, South Gaulish. The scroll in the upper zone probably has identical upper and lower concavities, each with a small spiral, large spiral with many-petalled rosette and leaf (similar to Hermet 1934, pl. 11, 8). The small spirals are attached to the scroll with butterfly bindings. *c*. AD 55-65. *743 T16V (three sherds, with another in 111/2 Site 1(77); SF525); Ib*

65* Form 67, South Gaulish. The fragmentary cursive signature, upside-down below the decoration, almost certainly belongs to Vitalis ii. It gives the bottom halves of the letters]alis and comes from a mould signed before firing. The upper concavity of a scroll includes a bud-cluster, a leaf (similar to Hermet 1934, pl. 8, 6, but much smaller) and a small bird. The lower concavity has a central vertical motif, probably separating a pair of hares, facing each other. There is also a six-petalled rosette, which is on form 29 from La Graufesenque (Millau Museum) with basal stamp of Vitalis ii. The scroll is bound with a tiny butterfly tie. Signatures on form 67 are excessively rare. *c*. AD 70-90. *743 T16V; Ib*

Trench 17

66* Form 37, Central Gaulish. The ovolo (Rogers B231) is chiefly associated with Cinnamus ii, but was used at Les Martres-de-Veyre in the Trajanic period by potters who supplied moulds to Medetus and Ranto and at Lezoux in the Hadrianic period by the Sacer i group. The unusual scroll, made up of chevron festoons (Rogers F41), impressed first one way up and then the other, has leaves (Rogers H13) and four-bladed motifs in both upper and lower concavities. Some connection with Medetus is suggested by the use of a bead-row above, but not below, the ovolo. The bowl may be from a mould made at Les Martres-de-Veyre, though the fabric belongs to the Lezoux range. Almost certainly Hadrianic. *002 T17; Mod.*

Stamps from the fort trenches

The samian stamps listed below are from all of the fort trenches, but have not been illustrated.

Each entry gives: potter (i, ii, etc. where homonyms are involved), die number, form of vessel, reading, published example (if any), pottery of origin and concludes with contextual information.

a, b and c after the place of manufacture indicate:
(a) A stamp attested at the pottery in question.
(b) A stamp not attested at the pottery in question, though the potter is known to have worked there.
(c) A stamp assigned to the pottery on the evidence of fabric and/or distribution.

67 Albanus ii 1b 27g ꓕFA.BNI (Hartley 1972a, fig. 81, S6) La Graufesenque a. Most of Albanus's output is Flavian, though he occasionally made forms 24 and Ritterling 8 and a few of his stamps turn up in pre-Flavian contexts. The die was modified, after wear or fracture, in the pre-Flavian period. This stamp, from the original die, will belong to the AD 60s, at the latest, though it is not closely datable within the decade. *701 T9; SF909; II*

68 Albanus ii 1b' 27g ꓕFA.BAꓕI (Durand-Lefebvre 1963, 8, 23) La Graufesenque a. Stamp from the modified version of Die 1b, above. There are two examples from the (mainly) pre-Flavian cemeteries at Nijmegen. *c*. AD 65-90. *158 Site1(77); SF867; II*

69 Albus i 3b 27g OFALBI (Ettlinger 1978, Taf. 1, 1) La Graufesenque a. One of his later stamps, noted from Chester (2), the Nijmegen fortress and York. Others occur in a group of samian of the AD 50s from La Graufesenque, and on forms 24, Ritterling 8 and Ritterling 9. *c*. AD 60-70. *1146 T15V; SF840; Ic*

70 Aucella 1a 33 AVCELLA·F Lezoux a. A stamp noted on forms 31, 33 and (once) on form 80. Antonine, probably *c*. AD 150-180. *705 T9; SF906; II*

71 Aucius 1a 18 [oΛV]Clo La Graufesenque a. There is no site dating for this potter, but his forms and fabrics suggest a date *c*. AD 50-70. *108/B2 T14; SF282; Ic*

72 Bio or Bionis 2c 27g BIOFECI(T) retrograde (Hartley 1972a, fig. 81, S66) La Graufesenque a. Bio or Bionis's output is almost certainly all pre-Flavian, though his stamps turn up occasionally at Flavian foundations. His plain forms include 24, Ritterling 5 and Ritterling 8. *c*. AD 45-65. *984 T15V; SF856; Ib*

73 Briccus 6b 18/31R [BRIC]CI Lezoux a. One of Briccus's stamps is noted from Mumrills. His forms include 18/31, 27, 31R, 38 and 80. *c*. AD 140-170. Burnt. *072 Site 1(77); SF543; ?*

74 Capellianus 1a 33 CAPELLIANI Lezoux b. All the stamps noted from this die are on form 33, and include examples from Halton Chesters (2) and South Shields. Another stamp occurs on form 80. *c*. AD 150-190. *054/2 Site1(77); SF465; IV*

75 Cerotcus 1a 31 CE[ROTCIM] Lezoux a. A stamp noted from the fort at Wallsend and on forms 31 and 33. Antonine. *001 T18; Mod.*

76 Cinnamus ii 5e, 18/31 (Tq), 37 CINNAM[I]; CINN[retrograde, Lezoux b. The dish is Hadrianic in form and the bowl is decorated in one of his earlier styles. *c*. AD 135-155. *052 Site1(77); SF1076; II. 129 T10; SF570; 3*

77 Cobnertus iii 1a 18/31R [COBNE]RTI·M Lezoux a. This stamp occurs in groups of samian of *c*. AD 150-60 and 170 from Alcester (Hartley, Pengelly and Dickinson 1994, 109, S130) and Tác (Hungary), respectively. It is common on form 18/31R. *c*. AD 150-180. *312 T14; SF112; II*

78 Comitialis 5d 37 [C]OMITI[ΛLISF] retrograde (Ludowici 1927, 240, e), Rheinzabern a. A stamp from one of his less-common dies. Comitialis's decorated bowls occur at sites founded in the late 2nd century, such as Holzhausen and Niederbieber. *c*. AD 180-220. *202 T15III; SF33; IV*

79 Cosius Rufinus 4b 18R COSIRFN La Graufesenque a. A stamp noted from Caerleon, Chester (2) and the Nijmegen fortress. His other stamps occur at Camelon, Newstead and the main site at Corbridge, and on early Flavian form 29s. *c*. AD 70-90. *1107 T15V; SF811; Id*

80 L. Cosius Virilis 6b 18/31 [OF·LCOSV]RIL La Graufesenque b. A potter whose stamps turn up at Domitianic foundations. The decoration of his form 29s suggests that he did not begin work before *c*. AD 80. *c*. AD 80-110. *015 T17; SF25; IIb*

81 Crestio 17c 15/17 or 18 CRES[TI] (*ORL* B62a, Taf. 16, 5) La Graufesenque a. Most of Crestio's output is pre-Flavian, though he may still have been at work in the early AD 70s. This particular stamp is noted from Malton. *c.* AD 50-70. *031 T13; SF170; IIb*

82 Crestus 3a 18 [O]Γ˙CRES (Nash-Williams 1930, fig. 1, 30) La Graufesenque b. The site record for this stamp is mainly Flavian, but one example is noted from the mainly pre-Flavian cemeteries at Nijmegen. *c.* AD 65-90. *080 T15II; SF139; Ia*

83 Felicio i 5a 15/17 or 18 FELI[CIO] La Graufesenque b. There is no dating evidence for this particular stamp. His other stamps occur at Baginton (after *c.* AD 61), Chester and Hofheim. He occasionally stamped decorated bowls of form 29, and these seem to be pre-Flavian. *c.* AD 55-70. *553/B T15IV; SF459; Id*

84 Felix i 1a 15/17 or 18 OFFELICISΛ retrograde, La Graufesenque b. Felix i's output is mainly Neronian, though his wares turn up occasionally at Flavian foundations. There is no internal dating for this particular stamp, but his general range was *c.* AD 50-70. *1169 T15V; SF890; Ib*

85 Gallus ii 10a 27g GAL[LIM] La Graufesenque a. Gallus's stamps, though not from this particular die, occur in groups of samian of *c.* AD 50-60 from La Graufesenque and Narbonne, La Nautique. *c.* AD 45-65. *302 T15III; SF450; Ib*

86 Gratus ii 1a 33 GRATI·M (S. & S. 1958, pl. 68, 7) Lezoux b. This stamp occurs on a stamped bowl of Quintilianus i, to which it was applied after moulding (S. & S. 1958, pl. 63, 7). It occurs also on form 33 from South Shields. Both this cup and the Castleford one have grooves above and below the external junction of base and wall, and these suggest a date *c.* AD 125-40, though the die probably continued in use for several more years. *909 T15V; SF541; III*

87 Ingenuus ii 21g' 27g <I>NGENV<I> La Graufesenque a. A stamp from a broken die, which was used on form 24. Ingenuus ii stamped form 29s whose decoration suggests a date *c.* AD 45-65. *116 Site 1(77); SF953; I*

88 Iustus i 15a 37 IIVST , from a mould stamped in the decoration (Mees 1995, Taf. 95, 8) La Graufesenque a. This stamp was used in the Flavian period on moulds for both forms 29 and 37. *c.* AD 70-90. *303 T16II; SF84; IIa*

89 Labio 1a 15/17 or 18 OF·LABIO[NIS] (Hermet 1934, pl. 111, 72) La Graufesenque a. A stamp occurring mainly on Neronian form 29s. The site record includes Chester, Carlisle, York and the Nijmegen fortress, however. *c.* AD 50-70. *301 T12; SF185; Mod.*

90 Labio 7a 18 OF.LABE (Hermet 1934, pl. 111, 72b) La Graufesenque a. A stamp noted at Chester, Caerleon and the Nijmegen fortress. *c.* AD 50-70. *126 Site 1(77); SF999; II*

91* Logirnus 12a 29 LOGIRN retrograde, La Graufesenque b. There is no site dating for this stamp, but the decoration of the bowl suggests a date *c.* AD 65-80. See Fig. 7, 24. *385 T13; SF183; IIb*

92 Logirnus 5a 18 (2) [LO]GIRNI; LO[(Dickinson 1986b, 190, 3. 79) La Graufesenque a. This stamp is noted from Camelon (2) and in the Inchtuthil Gutter (4) (Hartley 1985, fig. 90, 6-7), but an example on form 24 suggests that the die was first used in the pre-Flavian period. *c.* AD 65-85. *321 T16II; SF75; Ib. Level 7 Site 1(74); I*

93 Martinus iii 7a 33 Μ·ΛRTIΜ (Durand-Lefebvre 1963, 143, 437) Lezoux b. A stamp used on forms 79, 79R and 80 and noted at Bainbridge, Catterick and Brancaster. *c.* AD 160-200. *203 T15III; SF81; IV*

94 Meddillus 5a 29 ΜΕ⊕[ILLVS] La Graufesenque a. A decorated bowl with this stamp occurs in the Boudiccan destruction material from Verulamium (Hartley 1972a, fig. 81, 2), but this must mark

the very beginning of his career, as the stamp is much more common at Flavian foundations. The fabric of the Castleford piece suggests such a date. *c.* AD 70-85. *108/B T14; SF4; Ic*

95 Mommo 14a 33? OΜOΜ (Simon 1978, 250, C766) La Graufesenque a. A stamp noted from Aislingen and Oberstimm (both before *c.* AD 75) and also from Chester. The die continued in use after fracture, and stamps from this secondary version (14a') occur at Segontium and Binchester and in a pit at Verulamium filled *c.* AD 75. *c.* AD 60-75. *108/C T14; SF305; Ic*

96 Montanus i 1a 15/17 or 18 OFMONΛNI La Graufesenque b. Stamps from this die occur in the Inchtuthil Gutter and at Caerleon, Carmarthen and Nijmegen (Ulpia Noviomagus). *c.* AD 70-90. *310 T16II; SF62; IV*

97 Monti- Cres- 6a 15/17 or 18 (the one from Trench 14 is burnt)]ONTC] (2); [OFΜ]ONTC (Durand-Lefebvre 1963, 157, 480) La Graufesenque a. The site evidence for this stamp is entirely Flavian, but it occurs once on a Neronian-Flavian form 29. *c.* AD 65-85. *108 T14; SF55; Ic. 931 T9; II. 1073 T15V; SF700; IIa*

98 Namilianus 3b 31 NAΜILI[ΛNI] Lezoux b. A stamp noted from northern forts in Britain re-occupied *c.* AD 160, and in the group of late-Antonine samian from Pudding Pan Rock. It was used on forms 31R and 79. *c.* AD 160-200. *202 T15III; SF19; IV*

99 Ovidius 1a 27 (2) ˒VIDI[Μ];; ˒VIDI·Μ (Glasbergen 1955, 142, 292) Les Martres-de-Veyre a. The forms and fabrics associated with this stamp suggest that Ovidius was not one of the earliest potters at Les Martres, though it has been noted from the London Second Fire groups. *c.* AD 110-30. *008/A T17; SF19; II. 255 T10; SF1068; 3*

100 Pass(i)enus 5a 29 (2) OFPΛ22ENI;]FPΛ22ENI (Durand-Lefebvre 1963, 177, 547) La Graufesenque a. This stamp occurs only on form 29. Many of the bowls are early Flavian, though some could belong to the 60s. This is borne out by the site record, which includes Aislingen, Burghöfe, Carlisle and Caerleon. *c.* AD 65-80. *177 T14; SF234; Ic. 006 Site 1(77); II*

101 Pass(i)enus 12b 27g OFPAS retrograde, La Graufesenque a. Only one other example of this stamp has been noted by us, possibly from York. *c.* AD 60-75. *1095 T15V; SF719; IIa*

102 Pass(i)enus 33a 15/17 or 18 [PA·S]SFN (Durand-Lefebvre 1963, 175, 541) La Graufesenque a. This stamp occurs at Baginton (after AD 61) and in a group of burnt samian of the early 60s from Oberwinterthur (Switzerland), but also on Flavian sites such as the fortresses at Chester and Nijmegen. *c.* AD 60-80. *219 T14; SF203; Ic*

103 Paternus v 7a 37 with the usual, large, ligatured and retrograde stamp used on his decorated ware (S. & S. 1958, pl. 169). Lezoux a. This stamp, which may be taken as PΛ≥NI≥ retrograde occurs at northern forts re-occupied *c.* AD 160 and in the Wroxeter Gutter, but is entirely absent from Scottish forts with a normal Antonine occupation. *c.* AD 160-195. *Level 1 Site 1(77); SF70; ?*

104 Patricius i 13e 27g PATRI[CI] La Graufesenque a. The site record for this stamp is entirely Flavian or late 1st century and includes Holt and Binchester. The final I often does not register (cf. Walke 1965, Taf. 43, 284) *c.* AD 75-100. *U/S T9*

105 Peculiaris i 5a 18/31 ⊊ECVLI[Я·F] (Curle 1911, 238, 72) Lezoux a. This stamp was used on both forms 27 and 80, but more often on form 27. Examples are noted from Carzield, Newstead and Wallsend. *c.* AD 140-160. *U/S Site 1(77); SF962*

106 Perrus i 12d' 27g NERRVSI La Graufesenque a. A stamp from a recut die which originally gave PERRVSF. The original die was used on form Ritterling 9, and stamps from the recut version occur at Carlisle and the Nijmegen fortress. *c.* AD 65-80. *214 T14; SF142; Ie*

107 Pontheius 1a or a' 15/17 or 18 OFPOI∕∓EI (Hermet 1934, pl. 112, 125) La Graufesenque a. Die 1a was used on early Flavian form 29s and a stamp from it occurs at Inchtuthil. A stamp from the broken die (1a') comes from the main site at Corbridge. *c.* AD 75-90. *108/C T14; SF338; Ic*

108 Pontus 5a 15/17 or 18 OFPONTI∕∖∕ La Graufesenque a. A stamp sometimes used on early Flavian form 29s. *c.* AD 70-90 or, more probably, 70-85. *305 T12; SF214; I/III*

109 Pontus 8a 15/17 or 18 OF·PONTI La Graufesenque a. There is no evidence for dating this stamp closely within the general range for Pontus, i.e. *c.* AD 65-95. *115/2 Site 1(77); SF855; III*

110 Pontus 8h 27 OI∕∿ONTI (Dickinson 1986b, 193, 154) La Graufesenque a. Like the last, no closer dating than AD 65-95 is possible. *1146 T15V; SF846; Ic*

111 Pontus Incomplete 1 15/17 or 18 OI∕∿PONT[La Graufesenque b. No other examples of this stamp have been noted by us. *c.* AD 65-95. *232 T14; SF196; Ic*

112 Primulus i 4h 27g PRI∕∖∕L[I] (Durand-Lefebvre 1963, 189, 584) La Graufesenque a. There is no dating evidence for this particular stamp. Primulus i's output is mainly Flavian, but he occasionally made forms 24 and Ritterling 8. *c.* AD 60-90. *984 T15V; SF853; Ib*

113 Primulus i 4j 15/17 or 18 PRIT∕∖∕[LI] (*sic*) (May 1930, 238, 50) La Graufesenque b. A stamp noted from Rheingönheim, Carlisle, Chester (2) and York. *c.* AD 70-90. *302 T14; SF17; ?*

114 Primulus i 9c 15/17 or 18 [P]RI∕∖∕VL La Graufesenque a. Stamps from this die occur at Chester and York. *c.* AD 70-90. *Level + Site 1(77); SF578; Mod.*

115 Primus iii 3a 15/17R or 18R OFIC·PRIM[I] (Ritterling 1913, 242, 235) La Graufesenque a. Form 29s stamped with a broken version of this die are rather later than Primus's usual decorated ware, and a few turn up at Flavian foundations. The original die, therefore, will fall within the range *c.* AD 60-70. *025 T16I; SF66; IIa*

116 Primus iii 21b' 27g (2) OFPRIM La Graufesenque a. The original version of this die was used on forms 24 and Ritterling 8. Stamps from the modified die occur at York and the Nijmegen fortress, and in the Boudiccan burning at Colchester. *c.* AD 60-70. *124/1 Site 1(77); SF724; IV. 992 T9; ?*

117 Primus iii 22g 27g OFPRI La Graufesenque a. This stamp, used only on cups, occurs at the Nijmegen fortress. *c.* AD 50-75. Slightly burnt. *151 Site 1(77); SF809; IV*

118 Quartus iii 5a 27 QVARTI·O La Graufesenque b. Quartus iii's earliest stamps turn up in Claudio-Neronian groups from La Graufesenque and Narbonne and one comes from Velsen (before AD 47?). This one is rather later, and is noted from Caerleon and Carlisle. *c.* AD 50-70. *931 T9; II*

119* Quintio i 1a' 29 QVI∕∖∕TIIO (Rouquette *et al.* 1990, fig. 6, 102) La Graufesenque a. This stamp is from a die which, before it was damaged, gave QVI∕∖∕TIO It occurs at Chester and Cardiff. *c.* AD 70-85. See Fig. 11, 47. *634/B T15IV; SF484; Id*

120 Quintio i 1b 29 QVINTIO (Nieto 1989, no. 40. 1) La Graufesenque a. Several stamps from this die occur at Flavian foundations, such as York, Chester and the Nijmegen fortress. They appear occasionally on early Flavian form 29s. *c.* AD 70-85. *313 T14; SF180; Ic*

121 Reburrus ii 4a 33 REBV[RRI∆ON] (Hartley 1972a, 256, S151-3) Lezoux a. A stamp used on forms 18/31R, 27, 79 and 80. It occurs at Great Chesters and in the Verulamium Second Fire groups. *c.* AD 140-170. *Level + Site 1(77); SF578; Mod.*

122 Severus iii 71 15/17 or 18 [OFSE]∖∕ERI La Graufesenque a. Severus iii's output is mainly Flavian, but some of his stamps, including this one, turn up on pre-Flavian forms. It occurs at the Nijmegen fortress (3) and Risstissen (before *c.* AD 75). *c.* AD 65-85. *1161 T15V; SF884; Ib*

123 Severus iii 7e' 15/17 or 18 OF·SEVER† La Graufesenque b. The frame of this stamp was originally rectangular (7e), but slight swallow-tails were later cut into the ends (7e'). The site record for 7e' includes many Flavian foundations, one of which is the main site at Corbridge. *c.* AD 70-90. *931 T9; II*

124 Sissus i-Pr- 1a 18/31 SISSVSPR retrograde Lezoux c. This stamp probably represents an association of two potters. Sissus i made forms 18/31 and 27 and his decorated ware is connected stylistically with the Quintilianus i group. The name of the other potter is not obvious. *c.* AD 125-145. *717 T9; SF926 and SF942; II*

125 Virthus 2a 15/17R or 18R VIRⱵ[VSFEC╀] La Graufesenque a. A stamp noted in period IIA at Verulamium (after AD 75; Hartley 1972a, fig. 81, S56) and at the Nijmegen fortress. One of his others is said to have occurred in period I at Valkenburg ZH, though that may seem a little unlikely, if period I has the date-range suggested by the excavators. The frame of the Castleford stamp is worn, so that the usual swallow-tail at the beginning is lost. *c.* AD 55-75. *706 T15IV; SF611; Ia*

126 Virtus i 1a 29 OFVIRTVTIS (Knorr 1907, Taf. XXXII, 292) La Graufesenque a. Virtus i's career seems to have been divided equally between the Neronian and Flavian periods. This particular stamp occurs mainly on form 29s of *c.* AD 70-85. *310/5C T13; SF192; IIa*

127 Virtus i 8a 15/17 or 18 ·VIRT[VTIS] (Nieto 1989, fig. 7 bis, 6.1) La Graufesenque a. Probably one of his later stamps, since it occurs at Rottweil. *c.* AD 70-90. *1033 T15V; SF705; IV*

128 Virtus i 8b (probably), 29 VIRTVTIS (?) La Graufesenque b. A stamp noted from Caerleon, Camelon and Chester. *c.* AD 70-85. *997 T15V; SF623; Ic*

Illiterate Stamps
129]V†, IAN†·on form 27g (2), South Gaulish. Flavian. *108/B2 T14; SF298; Ic. 220 T14; SF295; Ic*

130 ⅂θI.[on form 33, South Gaulish. Flavian. *318 T14; SF240; Ic*

131 NI on form 27g, South Gaulish. Flavian. *665 T15IV; SF406; II*

132 IIIⱯ∕I on form 27g, South Gaulish. Flavian. *984 T15V; SF850; Ib*

133 ∕∖∕ƛ\XI on form 15/17 or 18, South Gaulish. The stamp occurs at Carlisle. Flavian. *995 T15V; SF634; Ic*

134]\/Ʌ on form 18, South Gaulish. Flavian. *997 T15V; SF866; Ic*

135 ·AIꟼLII \ on form 27g, South Gaulish. Flavian. *1105 T15V; SF768; Id*

136]III on form 27g, South Gaulish. Flavian. *1173/B T15V; Ib*

Unidentified
137 OFRV[(?) on form 29, South Gaulish. Almost certainly a stamp of Rufinus iii. *c.* AD 70-85. *313 T12; SF203; IIa*

138 ⎨ on form 15/17 or 18, South Gaulish. Flavian. *112 T14; SF250; Ic*

139]VITIV on form 27, South Gaulish. Flavian. *201/B T14; SF114; III*

140 A[on form 15/17 or 18, South Gaulish. Flavian. *302 T15III; SF449; Ib*

141 O[(?) on form 15/17R or 18R, South Gaulish. Flavian. *568 T15IV; SF536; Ic*

142 OF/\[on form 27(?), South Gaulish. Flavian. *1145 T15V; SF829; Ic*

143 An illegible stamp on form 27, South Gaulish. Flavian. *551 T15IV; SF186; IV*

144]FECI on form 31, Central Gaulish, Antonine. *Tr. 15 Site 1(77); SF29*

Cursive signatures

145 Meddillus: on form 37, South Gaulish. Medi[retrograde, upside-down below the decoration, La Graufesenque a. Signatures of Meddillus appear occasionally on bowls of both form 29 and 37. They are always inscribed in the mould after firing, and so do not necessarily indicate manufacture by Meddillus. See No. 58, above, for the decoration. *c.* AD 70-90. *012 T16I; IIa*

146]alis(?) on form 67, South Gaulish. The jar is from a mould signed, upside-down, below the decoration. Almost certainly by Vitalis ii. See No. 65, above. *c.* AD 70-85. *743 T16V; Ib*

147 C[retrograde, on form 37, Central Gaulish from a mould signed, before firing, below the decoration. Hadrianic or early Antonine. *924 T15V; IV*

Summary of the samian pottery from the forts

The excavations of the fort at Castleford in 1977-84 produced large quantities of samian, the bulk of which is 1st century. Tables 2 to 5 provide a quantification of plain as well as decorated samian by form and phase. The histogram in Figure 14, based on the average annual loss of stamped vessels and stratified decorated ware, shows the fluctuations in the amounts of samian deposited on the site over a period of 150 years or so, which, in the 1st century at least, will have been pottery used in the fort.

The samian is dominated by South Gaulish ware, almost certainly all from La Graufesenque, with moderate quantities of Central Gaulish ware from Lezoux and less from Les Martres-de-Veyre. The few pieces of East Gaulish ware come from a restricted number of sources. The Hadrianic-Antonine factory of La Madeleine is scarcely represented, though its products occur in significant quantities elsewhere in the province (Dickinson and Hartley 1971, 132) and particularly towards the east coast. The rest of the East Gaulish ware, all after AD 150 or 160, consists of material from Rheinzabern and the Argonne, with single sherds from Trier and, perhaps, Heiligenberg.

The presence of moderate quantities of pre-Flavian and Neronian-Flavian material and the abundance of early Flavian samian suggest that the fort was founded in the early to mid-70s. Thirty of the stamps belong to potters whose careers were largely or partly pre-Flavian and nearly all the Flavian potters represented sometimes stamped the carinated bowl, form 29. The relative frequencies of form 29 and form 37, which eventually replaced it, are also significant. Form 29 had virtually gone out of production at La Graufesenque by AD 85, and form 37, though first produced there *c.* AD 70 or slightly earlier, was slow to overtake it. In Scotland, on sites occupied for only a few years in the 80s, the numbers of form 29 and 37 are roughly equal. By contrast, at Newstead which was first occupied for twenty years or so, down to AD 105, the ratio of form 29 to 37 is 1:3. The Castleford fort, which would have been receiving South Gaulish decorated ware for twenty years or more, produced forms 29 and 37 in a ratio of 5:6, reinforcing an early Flavian foundation date. This must surely have been in the early to mid 70s, probably under Cerialis rather than Frontinus. A comparison of the ratios of form 29 to 37 in Phases I and II can be used to date the start of Phase II. In Phase I the ratio is 3:1; in Phase II it is 9:14, with the implication that the second fort dates from the second half of the 80s, when the quantities of form 29 still in use were beginning to decrease.

The relative amounts of 1st and 2nd-century samian in this collection suggest that the second fort was abandoned, or the garrison reduced, *c.* AD 95. However, the lack of firm dating evidence for the early 2nd-century samian industry introduces a complication. It is not unusual for British sites occupied continuously from the 1st century to produce comparatively little Trajanic samian. The date for the end of export of South Gaulish (i.e. La Graufesenque) ware to Britain, normally thought to be *c.* AD 110, cannot be pushed much later, in view of the relatively small quantities present on Hadrian's Wall. This would have left Les Martres-de-Veyre as the main source of samian in the Trajanic period, and it seems to have been unable to supply the province with the same quantities as La Graufesenque, unless some parts of Britain received less than others. Certainly, the potters' stamps from York (Dickinson and Hartley 1971, 129), Colchester and Leicester show this 'Trajanic gap', as do the decorated ware and stamps from Alcester. If one accepts that the drop in the quantities of discarded material in the Trajanic period relates to the history of the site, Phase II should not have gone into the 2nd century. If, however, Castleford, along with many other sites in Britain, was simply unable to obtain as much samian in the early 2nd century as it had done before, then there is theoretically no reason why Phase II should not go through to AD 160, or beyond. The latest decorated ware assigned to this phase includes bowls in the styles of Banuus, Casurius ii, Do(v)eccus i and Paternus v, all mid to late-Antonine potters.

Nevertheless, it would be very difficult to justify a full occupation of Fort II down to the late 2nd century on the evidence of the samian. Such a fort ought to have produced at least as much Antonine Lezoux ware as 1st-century La Graufesenque ware, if it was serving a full unit. Indeed the proportion of Antonine material should be considerably higher than the South Gaulish (cf. Dickinson and Hartley 1971, 129). The histogram on p. 22 clearly demonstrates the anomaly. It is hard to imagine that Castleford differed from the rest of the province in its

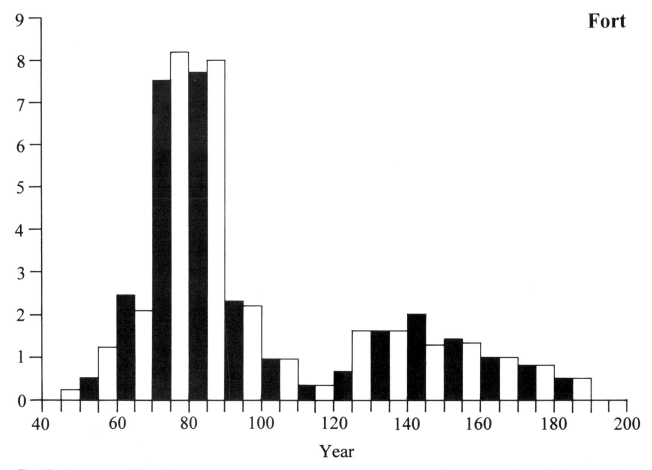

Fig. 14. Average annual loss of decorated and stamped samian vessels in terms of dates of manufacture, from AD 45 to AD 200.

use of table ware, but other factors, such as the erosion of the upper levels of the site, or a change in the system of rubbish disposal might account for the comparative lack of 2nd-century samian. It is far more likely, however, that there was no fort on the site after the 1st century.

It will be seen that the Hadrianic-Antonine decorated ware from the fort is very similar in character to the 'pottery shop' material. Many of the same potters are involved, such as Acaunissa, Drusus ii, Geminus iv, Paternus iv, X-5, members of the Sacer i and Quintilianus i groups, and others. It must be said, however, that not much of this material is demonstrably burnt. As in the 'pottery shop' and the *vicus* as a whole, there are more decorated bowls by the Cerialis ii-Cinnamus ii group than by any single potter or other group of potters. This group has been dated *c*. AD 135-70, though there is a strong suspicion that it did not survive much beyond AD 160. Therefore, to reduce any undue distortion in the statistics, these bowls have been given a date range *c*. AD 135-65 for the purposes of the histogram.

The similarities between the Hadrianic-Antonine material from the fort and *vicus* are scarcely enough in themselves to cause comment, as the fort could have been supplied partly or wholly by the 'pottery shop' in the *vicus*. However, though the quantities of samian deposited within the area of the fort rise somewhat in the Hadrianic and early Antonine periods, they never reach the level which would be expected on a site with flourishing Hadrianic and Antonine occupations, when Lezoux ware was plentiful throughout Britain. Therefore, as the 2nd-century samian recovered from the fort would scarcely be enough to supply a full, or even reduced garrison, it is more likely that the fort was unoccupied for most of the century, and that samian was being dumped in it from elsewhere. The most obvious place would be from the adjacent *vicus*, where some sort of activity in the mid-2nd century is certain. The unusual peak on the histogram for the fort at *c*. AD 140-45, which shows in the same place in the histogram for the *vicus* (see Figure 42) is almost certainly caused by the wide dispersal of the material from the 'pottery shop', after its destruction by fire at that time.

Most of the excavated areas produced small quantities of samian later than *c*. AD 160, usually with some going down to the first half of the 3rd century. The greatest concentration of this material comes from Trench 15. No large quantities are involved, but there is nevertheless an indication of activity of some kind either within the fort itself, or nearby, from the later 2nd century onwards.

Phase I, on the evidence of the samian, starts in the early to mid-70s and continues until the mid-80s. The problems of dating the end of Phase II are discussed above, but there is no reason to doubt that it began in the later 80s and is likely to have ended *c*. AD 95. The samian contributes nothing to the dating of Phase IV, not being exported to Britain after the middle of the 3rd century.

Table 2.: Distribution of the fort samian by phase: South Gaul.

Form	Phase I	Phase II	Phase III	Phase III/IV	Phase IV	Total
Ritt. 1	1	-	-	-	-	1
Ritt. 9	1	-	-	-	-	1
Ritt. 12	1	-	-	-	-	1
Ritt. 13	-	-	-	-	1	1
15/17	16	7	2	-	2	27
15/17R	1	1	-	-	2	4
15/17 or 18	60	36	6	2	10	114
15/17R or 18R	7	3	1	2	-	13
16	-	-	-	1	-	1
18	121	60	32	1	24	238
18R	10	8	5	1	6	30
18/31	-	1	1	1	1	4
24	1	-	-	-	-	1
27g	22	5	2	-	2	31
27	101	40	24	2	31	198
29	101	46	15	-	12	174
30	6	4	2	-	5	17
30 or 37	6	11	4	-	4	25
33a	1	2	1	-	1	5
33	2	1	-	-	-	3
35	4	1	2	-	-	7
35 or 36	1	-	-	-	-	1
36	1	-	-	-	2	3
37	36	67	38	3	28	172
42	-	-	1	-	-	1
67	6	7	-	-	6	19
78	-	-	-	-	1	1
Curle 11	3	1	1	-	3	8
Curle 15	1	-	-	-	1	2
Dish	2	6	3	-	2	13
Dish or bowl	1	2	-	-	3	6
Bowl	-	1	-	-	-	1
Decorated bowl	2	1	1	-	1	5
Cup	7	2	2	-	6	17
Jar	-	2	-	-	1	3
Total	**522**	**315**	**143**	**13**	**155**	**1148**

Table 3. Distribution of the fort samian by phase: Central Gaul (Les Martres-de-Veyre).

Form	Phase I	Phase II	Phase III	Phase III/IV	Phase IV	Total
18/31	-	5	2	-	2	9
18/31 or 31	1	-	-	-	-	1
18/31R	1	-	1	-	-	2
27	1	1	-	-	-	2
30 or 37	-	3	-	-	1	4
33	-	-	-	-	1	1
37	-	3	2	-	1	6
Curle 11	-	1	-	-	-	1
Dish	-	1	-	-	-	1
Dish or bowl	-	1	-	-	1	2
Cup	-	1	-	-	-	1
Total	**3**	**16**	**5**	**-**	**6**	**30**

Table 4. Distribution of the fort samian by phase: Central Gaul (Lezoux).

Form	Phase I	Phase II	Phase III	Phase III/IV	Phase IV	Total
15/31	-	-	-	-	1	1
18/31	-	9	-	2	7	18
18/31 or 31	-	4	6	-	18	28
18/31-31	-	1	-	-	-	1
18/31R	-	2	3	-	5	10
27	-	2	2	-	2	6
30	-	1	1	-	1	3
30 or 37	-	9	14	-	5	28
31	1	10	7	1	22	41
31R	-	2	-	-	5	7
33	2	13	6	1	17	39
35	-	-	-	-	2	2
35 or 36	-	-	1	-	-	1
36	-	2	1	-	4	7
37	1	31	22	1	25	80
38	-	-	-	-	2	2
38 or 44	-	1	-	-	2	3
80	-	-	-	-	1	1
Curle 11	-	-	1	-	1	2
Curle 15	-	1	-	-	2	3
Curle 15 or 23	-	1	1	-	-	2
Dish	-	-	-	-	3	3
Dish or bowl	-	1	1	-	1	3
Bowl	-	-	1	-	2	3
Cup	-	1	-	-	-	1
Jar	-	-	-	-	2	2
Total	**4**	**91**	**67**	**5**	**130**	**297**

Table 5. Distribution of the fort samian by phase: East Gaul.

Form	Phase I	Phase II	Phase III	Phase III/IV	Phase IV	Total
18/31	-	1	-	-	-	1
31	-	1	-	-	4	5
33	-	-	1	-	-	1
37	-	-	2	-	3	5
45	-	-	1	-	-	1
Total	-	2	4	-	7	13

The East Gaulish ware includes vessels from:

Argonne: 2   La Madeleine: 1   Rheinzabern: 1   Trier: 1

4   Decorated and Plain Samian, and Potters' Stamps from the Castleford *Vicus* Site 1(74)

This report was written in 1982 and revised in 1999.

Introduction

Originally, we based the scheme of phases on information which we were given in 1974 for the Castleford *vicus* Site 1(74). In the subsequent post-excavation analysis it was determined that the structural differences between Phases 1 and 2 in the original scheme were unwarranted. In this report these have been amalgamated as Phase 1. One result of this is a greater degree of compatability between the phases of the *vicus* Site 1(74) and the adjacent Trench 10 (see below).

A brief discussion of the dating-evidence derived from the samian follows each section. A general discussion of the economic evidence is given at the end.

The decorated ware is described for each phase and the potters' stamps follow in a separate section afterwards. We were not asked to report on the unstamped plain samian, except for the material from the 'pottery shop', nor, with the same exception, did we see the samian in groups after the initial appraisal on the site. The plain samian has, however, been included in the quantification tables which record form by phase (Tables 8-11). These appear at the end of this part.

The lower case letters appended in footnote style to the names of potteries indicate: (a) that stamps from the die in question have been recorded there; (b) that other stamps of the same potter are known there and (c) that the stamp is assigned to that pottery on the evidence of associated fabrics and distribution.

It will be observed that in all phases after the initial one, there is an appreciable proportion of residual samian.

This is listed, since it should serve as a guide to the proportions of other residual material to be expected.

It should be noted that all the samian from Phases 1 and 2 is South Gaulish, and almost certainly from La Graufesenque, unless otherwise stated.

Phase 1

148*A substantial fragment of form 29. The wreath of the upper zone is identical to ones on bowls from Carthage (Knorr 1952, Taf. 15C) and Longthorpe (Hartley 1974, 91), both stamped CELADI·MAИ (Die 5a) by Celadus of La Graufesenque. The die was evidently one of his earlier ones. Identical wreaths also occur on bowls from Baginton and London stamped respectively by Fedotus and Murranus (Knorr 1952, Taf.15D). The overlapping leaf-tips of the lower zone are on another bowl stamped by Fedotus at London (unpublished), though he is unlikely to have been the mould-maker, Celadus being a more likely candidate. The association with these potters and the Longthorpe and Baginton evidence make certain of a date *c.* AD 55-70. *Level 10 Site 1(74); 1*

149*A fragment from the lower zone of form 29, burnt. The decoration is a continuous scroll of triple leaves as on a bowl from Aislingen (Knorr 1913, Taf.III, 13). The composite decoration with spirals is unusual and no precise parallel has been found, though Hermet 1934, pl. 12, 57 and 76 show generally similar schemes. Pre-Flavian manufacture is certain, probably *c.* AD 55-65. *Level 9 Site 1(74); 1*

150*Four fragments of a bowl of form 29. The scroll of the upper zone is closely paralleled on a bowl stamped by Meddillus (5a) from London (British Museum). Another London bowl (formerly Guildhall Museum) with the same stamp has the overlapping leaf-tips. For the leaf in the scroll in use as late as AD 79 in the Pompeii Hoard see Atkinson 1914, no.55 and cf. No. 171, below. The associations with Meddillus and the style both suggest a date *c.* AD 60-75. *Level 7 Site 1(74); 1*

151 Two fragments from the lower zone of form 29. Panels with saltire and medallion probably alternated. A galloping horse (Hermet 1934, pl. 26, 54) is on a bowl from Rome stamped by Gallicanus of La Graufesenque (Knorr 1952, Taf.26B). A hare is probably Hermet 1934, pl. 26, 54 and a rosette at a panel corner was used on bowls stamped by Modestus i (Knorr 1919, Taf.58A). Used half-impressed, as a festoon, the medallion appears in the work of Frontinus (Atkinson 1942, pl. 68), though similar, smaller ones were used by Modestus, and by Mommo in the Pompeii Hoard (Atkinson 1914, no.15). *c.* AD 55-75. *Site 1(74); 1*

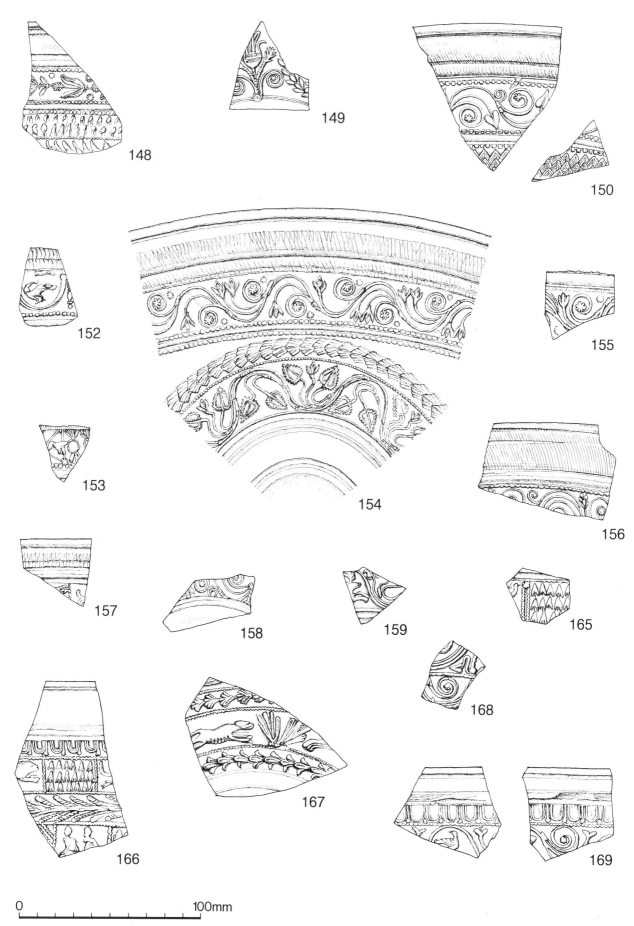

148 149 150 152 153 154 155 156 157 158 159 165 168 166 167 169

0   100mm

Fig. 15. Decorated samian from Site 1(74), Phase 1. Scale 1:2

152*A fragment from the upper zone of form 29. The bird in the elliptical festoon is Hermet 1934, pl. 28, 40. An identical scheme of decoration is on bowls from Vindonissa stamped, after moulding, by Carus i (Knorr 1919, Taf.20F) and Chester stamped by Rufinus iii (Newstead 1928, pl. II, 1). *c.* AD 60-75. *Level 7 Site 1(74); 1*

153*A fragment from the upper zone of form 29. No parallel has been noted for the unusual style, though the bird (Hermet 1934, pl. 28, 67) and the composite motif (Hermet 1934,. pl. 17, 33) are both known from La Graufesenque. Probably *c.* AD 65-80. *Level 7 Site 1(74); 1*

154*A complete bowl of form 29, in fragments. In the base is an illiterate stamp IИI\Iʌ (see No. 536). This bowl is of unusual interest technically as the mould had a false setting-out line for the continuous scroll approximately 180° out of phase with the final version. The problem of spacing the scroll correctly evidently led to the unusual variation in the numbers of leaves in the concavities, the complete scheme being:
\2/2\2/2\2/1\1/1\1/1\1/2\1\2\2/2\2/1\2/2\2/2\1/2\.

An almost identical scroll is on an unpublished bowl from Rheingönheim stamped internally by Meddillus and on bowls at Rottweil (Knorr 1912, Taf.V, 2 and Knorr 1919, Taf.94A). The Rheingönheim bowl also has a similar scroll to the Castleford one in the lower zone, including the same leaf, which recurs in the Pompeii Hoard (Atkinson 1914, no.43). In view of the parallels, this bowl must be dated *c.* AD 65-80. *III Site 1(74); 1*

155*A sherd of form 29 with a common type of scroll, similar to one used on a bowl stamped internally by Coelus (Knorr 1919, Taf.24D). The same style appears at Rottweil (Knorr 1912b, Taf.VIII, 2). *c.* AD 65-80. *Level 10 Site 1(74); 1*

156*A fragment from the upper zone of form 29. Generally similar scrolls were used on bowls stamped internally by Iustus i at Nijmegen, Manduilus at London (Knorr 1952, Taf.33), Masclus i at London (Knorr 1952, Taf.36D), and Matugenus ii at Aislingen (Knorr 1952, Taf. 38B). *c.* AD 65-80. *Level 7 Site 1(74); 1*

157*A small fragment from the upper zone of form 29. The surviving horizontal leaf will have been repeated to fill the panel, in the manner of Murranus and his contemporaries (Knorr 1952, Taf.44C). The other panel has the hindquarters of a dog (cf. Hermet 1934, pl. 26, 9). This general style just survived in use into the early Flavian period, as at Malton (Museum 30.234). *c.* AD 60-75. *Level 7 Site 1(74); 1*

158*A fragment from the lower zone of form 29. Winding scrolls of spirals, closely similar in type, were used in the upper zones of bowls from London, stamped by Masc(u)lus i (Knorr 1952, Taf.36D), and Aislingen, stamped by Matugenus (Knorr 1913, Taf.IV, 3). But a similar one also occurs in the lower zone of form 29 at Richborough with the stamp of Frontinus (1a) in the base, so a range *c.* AD 60-85 must be allowed for. *Level 9 Site 1(74); 1*

159*A fragment from the lower zone of form 29. The stag (Hermet 1934, pl. 27, 11) is on a bowl stamped by Vitalis ii at Clermont-Ferrand. The tulip-shaped leaf is also on bowls with his stamp from London (Knorr 1952, Taf.62C) and in the Pompeii Hoard (Atkinson 1914, no.29). *c.* AD 70-85. *Level 7 Site 1(74); 1*

160 A single fragment from the lower zone of form 29 with straight gadroons. Although the general style tends to be Neronian, the poor moulding may suggest the use of an old mould and perhaps Flavian date. *Site 1(74); 1*

161 A single sherd from the lower zone of form 29. Straight gadroons are here used over a continuous wreath in the manner of such potters as Iucundus iii, Meddillus, Pontus and Vitalis ii, or Crestio in his later work (cf. Hartley 1972a, D15). *c.* AD 60-80. *Site 1(74); 1*

162 A fragment from the upper zone of form 29 showing a panel with a large dog (Hermet 1934, pl. 26, 39), as on a bowl of form 37 from Camelon with a ovolo used by Memor of La Graufesenque. *c.* AD 75-85. *Site 1(74); 1*

163 A fragment from the lower zone of form 29. Both a heart-shaped leaf and a conventional plant on this bowl (Hermet 1934, pl. 14, 89) are on vessels stamped by Rufinus iii of La Graufesenque, the former at Chester (Newstead 1928, pl. II, 1), the latter at London (formerly London Museum). The plant, and probably also the leaf are on a bowl from Bonn stamped by Calvus (Knorr 1919, Taf.17B). Some connection with Rufinus and, or, Calvus is likely for the Castleford piece. *c.* AD 70-85. *Site 1(74); 1*

164 A small fragment from the lower zone of form 29 with scroll decoration. This piece cannot be closely dated, though in view of the form it must be earlier than AD 85. *Site 1(74); 1*

165*A fragment from the upper zone of form 29. The panel of leaf-tips is typical of many bowls in the Pompeii Hoard (Atkinson 1914, nos 5, 8, 9 and 12), where there are several stamped by Mommo of La Graufesenque. Multiple borders of the sort used here are not very common, but they were used by Mommo and Rufinus (Atkinson 1914, 15 and Knorr 1919, Taf.85c). *c.* AD 70-85. *Level 7 Site 1(74); 1*

166*Two joining sherds of form 37, grooved internally well above the level of the ovolo, a feature only found in the earliest bowls of this form from La Graufesenque. The ovolo, leaf-tips, and bitch (Hermet 1934, pl. 26, 25) were used at La Graufesenque by Memor and are on bowls from his signed moulds at Mandeure and in the Pompeii Hoard (Atkinson 1914, nos 73-4). The lion (Hermet 1934, pl. 25, 25) is on bowls at Pompeii stamped by Mommo (Atkinson 1914, nos 6 and 17). For the wreath, on form 29 stamped by Meddillus, see Knorr 1919, Taf.55F. The figures at the bottom have not been identified. This bowl is probably by Memor, but in any event the connections suggest a date *c.* AD 70-85. *Level 10 Site 1(74); 1*

167*A substantial sherd of form 37 with four zones of decoration. It is likely that the zone below the ovolo was entirely composed of double-bordered festoons. The plant forming the wreath in the next zone is on bowls stamped by Cosius Rufinus at Vechten (Knorr 1919, Taf.24B) and Vitalis ii at Kettering (unpublished?). In the next zone is a freestyle scene with bitch (Hermet 1934, pl. 26, 25) and hare (Hermet 1934, 56, 62 or 63) which occur on bowls in the Pompeii Hoard (Atkinson 1914, nos 9, 31, 40, 42, 48, 95). The plant was in common use at La Graufesenque in the Flavian period and was often used by Mercator i (Knorr 1919, Taf.57G, H). The final zone has an unusual wreath which we have not seen on stamped bowls. *c.* AD 75-95. *Site 1(74); 1*

168*A single fragment of form 37. The triple medallion and flanking tendrils with leaves are typical of such Flavian potters of La Graufesenque as C. Iulius Sabinus, Iustus i, C. Valerius Albanus and Vanderio, and they occur frequently in the Pompeii Hoard (e.g. Atkinson 1914, nos 3, 5, 60, 78). *c.* AD 75-95. *Level 6 Site 1(74); 1*

169*Three fragments of form 37. The single-bordered ovolo, the chevron in the scroll and the bird (Hermet 1934, pl. 28, 39), were used with beaded-borders, unusual for La Graufesenque, by a potter who did not stamp such products, but who was closely connected with, or even identical to, Severus iii. His bowls are known from the period 2 construction at Fishbourne (Dannell 1971, no.41) and period II at Verulamium (Hartley 1972a, D41). A date *c.* AD 70-85 is, therefore, likely. *Level 9 Site 1(74); 1*

170*Many fragments of a large bowl of form 37. The ovolo, the leaf in the festoons, the festoon pendant and the composite plant all appear on a bowl from Camelon (*c.* AD 83-7) and most are also on a bowl in the Pompeii Hoard (Atkinson 1914, no. 57). Another bowl in the Hoard with a cursive signature of Mommo probably

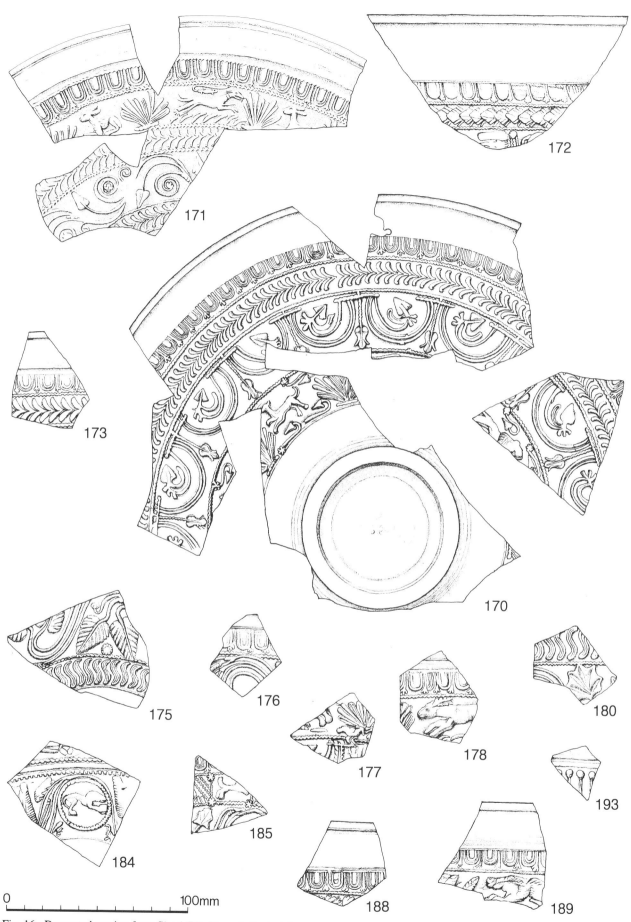

Fig. 16. Decorated samian from Site 1(74), Phase 1. Scale 1:2

has the same ovolo (Atkinson 1914, 54), which was used by several Flavian potters at La Graufesenque, including Cobnithus and Severus iii. Similar zones of festoons are very common in the Flavian period. The bottom zone, very similar to the upper zone of No. 171, contains a dog used on bowls stamped internally by Meddillus (London, British Museum), Mommo and Manduilus (in the Pompeii Hoard: Atkinson 1914, nos 10 and 32). The lion (Hermet 1934, pl. 25, 8A) may be the one on another Mommo bowl in the Pompeii Hoard (Atkinson 1914, no.2), and another animal (not on the drawing) is very probably the dog to right also on the same bowl at Pompeii. The associations and dated contexts point to manufacture *c.* AD 75-90. *Site 1(74); 1*

171* Several fragments of form 37 with zonal decoration. The upper zone is similar to No. 170, and the bowls share the same ovolo and fan-shaped plant. The dog and hare do not seem to have exact equivalents on stamped bowls, but very similar ones (Hermet 1934, pl. 26, 18 and 66 respectively) are very common both on form 29 and form 37 in the Flavian period. The small leaf in the upper zone was used by too many potters to be diagnostic. For the leaf in the continuous scroll see No. 150. The composition recalls some bowls by Frontinus, who often used similar chevron wreaths. *c.* AD 75-95. *Levels 6 and 7 Site 1(74); 1*

172* Two joining fragments of form 37. Unfortunately the ovolo is too blurred for identification. The wreath below is made from partial impressions of a leaf found on bowls stamped internally by Censor i and Coelus, but it was also used in the manner of the Castleford bowl by C. I(ulius) Sa(binus?) on a bowl from La Graufesenque (Hermet 1934, pl. 82, 7). *c.* AD 75-95. *Level 7 Site 1(74); 1*

173* A single fragment of form 37. The ovolo is on a bowl with the cursive signature of Mommo in the Pompeii Hoard (Atkinson 1914, no.59). The wreath occurs on form 37 at Bainbridge and Rottweil (Knorr 1912b, Taf.XXIII, 4 and 8). *c.* AD 75-95. *Level 7 Site 1(74); 1*

174 A single fragment of form 37 with the same ovolo as No. 171. A wreath of trifid motifs below the ovolo was used by Calvinus at La Graufesenque. *c.* AD 75-95. *Site 1(74); 1*

175* A single fragment of form 37. The leaves in the scroll were used by several Flavian potters of La Graufesenque and appear at Mandeure on a bowl with a cursive signature of Memor, at Nijmegen on form 29, stamped internally by Vanderio, and at Strasbourg, associated with a stamp of Carillus on a bowl of form 29 which also has the small rosettes in the field (Knorr 1952, Taf.74D). The gadroons were in common use in the Flavian period and are frequent in the work of Mercator i. *c.* AD 75-95. (cf. Nos 176 and 208, which could be from the same bowl.) *Level 7 Site 1(74); 1*

176* A single fragment of form 37, possibly from the upper part of the same bowl as No. 175 (and cf. No. 208). The ovolo was used at La Graufesenque by M. Crestio and is on one of his stamped bowls from London (ex-Guildhall Museum). M. Crestio may have begun work after AD 80 (cf. Hartley 1985, 322), though to be on the safe side should perhaps be dated *c.* AD 75-95. *Level 7 Site 1(74); 1*

177-8* Three sherds, two joining, of form 37. The ovolo, conventional plant and grass-blades were used on a bowl from Rottweil (Knorr 1912b, Taf. XVIII, 2). Two other bowls from Rottweil (Knorr 1912b, 7 and 8) apparently have the same zone of festoons with triangular leaves. No. 207, below, is another piece of this bowl, adding a dog (Hermet 1934, pl. 26, 46), and No. 211 may possibly belong to it, too. *c.* AD 80-95. *Level 7 Site 1(74); 1*

179 A small, single fragment of form 37, probably with a panelled zone, above a basal chevron wreath. The panelled zone has decoration common at La Graufesenque in the Flavian period, with triple medallions flanked by elongated, heart-shaped leaves on the ends of tendrils. The basal wreath is not assignable to a particular potter. *c.* AD 75-95. *Site 1(74); 1*

180* A single sherd of form 37. The central zone of S-shaped gadroons and the leaf in the scroll of the lower zone were both in use at La Graufesenque in the Flavian period. *c.* AD 75-90. *Level 9 Site 1(74); 1*

181 A single fragment of form 37, with a winding scroll having a bird and palm in the lower concavity. Both of the motifs were used by Mercator i of La Graufesenque on a bowl at London (British Museum), and the bird (Hermet 1934, pl. 28, 39) occurs on a form 29 with his stamp at Besançon Museum. The plant was used by several other potters of La Graufesenque, including Cotto (Knorr 1919, Taf.27, 5), M. Crestio (Knorr 1919, Taf.28S), Crucuro (Knorr 1919, Taf.29, 13) and Memor in the Pompeii Hoard (Atkinson 1914, no.61). *c.* AD 75-100. *Site 1(74); 1*

182 A single fragment of form 37, with panelled decoration. The style of decoration, with one panel having triangles of leaf-tips contained by diagonal wavy lines, and the other with leaf tendrils (presumably flanking a medallion) occurs on bowls from La Graufesenque in the Pompeii Hoard (Atkinson 1914, nos 10, 11, 60). *c.* AD 75-90. *Site 1(74); 1*

183 A single fragment of form 37 with a basal wreath of S-shaped gadroons of the type used at La Graufesenque by Mercator i and his associates. The other decoration is not identified. *c.* AD 75-100. *Site 1(74); 1*

184* A sherd of form 29. The bilobed leaf in the upper zone was used by Germanus i at La Graufesenque (Knorr 1919, Taf.35, 61) and the large, pointed leaf in the scroll is on one of his bowls from Richborough. The chevron-medallion with lion (Hermet 1934, pl. 25, 25) appears on bowls stamped by several potters, including Coelus, L. Cosius, Memor, Mommo and Rufinus iii. The birds in the scroll are Hermet 1934, pl. 28, 65 and 68, the former recurring on stamped sherds of Germanus at Nijmegen.

The general style is more typically Neronian than Flavian, but it was used as late as AD 79, in the Pompeii Hoard (Atkinson 1914, passim). In view of the characteristic motifs, the bowl is likely to have been made by Germanus, but in his early days before his workshop had developed its own peculiar style. *c.* AD 60-75. *Level 6 Site 1(74); 1*

185* A single fragment of form 37 with zonal decoration. The dog (Hermet 1934, pl. 26, 12) and the rosettes on the junctions are on a bowl in the period 2 construction levels at Fishbourne (Dannell 1971, no. 42). Scrolls below panels on zonal bowls are never common, but they are more typical of the range *c.* AD 70-85 than later. *Level 6 Site 1(74); 1*

186 A large, single sherd of form 37 with zonal decoration in the style of Germanus i. For the basal zone of chevron festoons see Hermet 1934, pl. 101, 32 and for conventional rocks like those in the next zone, Hermet 1934, pl. 100, 9-10. Bowls in this style often occur at sites founded around AD 70-85. *Site 1(74); 1*

187 Two sherds of form 37 in the style of Mercator i of La Graufesenque. The arrangement in the top zone of festoons alternating with a composite plant, is on bowls stamped by Mercator from Epinal and Poitiers. cf. Knorr 1919, Textbild 47 for the type of plant, but the Castleford bowl has grass-tufts (Knorr 1919, Taf.57, 13 in full impression) at the sides. A 'butterfly' tie to the continuous scroll below is typical of Mercator, though also used by several of his contemporaries. *c.* AD 80-110. *Site 1(74); 1*

188* This sherd of form 37 has an ovolo used by Patricius i and by Mercator i at La Graufesenque. No precise parallel for the wreath has been noted, however. *c.* AD 85-110. *Level 6 Site 1(74); 1*

189* A single sherd of form 37. In Britain trident-tongued ovolos were current at Agricolan sites in Scotland, but this particular one does not occur, and it should therefore be later than AD 85, and probably later than AD 90. The boar (O.1672) is only recorded for

Pass(i)enus, but this bowl is too late to be his work. *c.* AD 85-110. *Level 7 Site 1(74); 1*

190 A small fragment of form 37 with an ovolo used by Frontinus (Atkinson 1942, pl. 68, 36A) and Paullus iii. *c.* AD 75-100. *Site 1(74); 1*

191 A sherd of form 37 with a basal wreath of short, slightly sinuous gadroons of the kind used by Frontinus of La Graufesenque. They also occur at Newstead on a bowl with an ovolo common to Frontinus and Paullus iii (see No. 190). *c.* AD 80-100. *Site 1(74); 1*

192 Two small fragments of form 37, one with a panel of overlapping leaf-tips, the other with part of a large, unidentified rosette. The sherd is not closely datable, though it must be Flavian or early-Trajanic, as it is certainly from La Graufesenque. *Site 1(74); 1*

193* A fragment of form Déchelette 67 with a widely-spaced palisade of a simple kind. Both decoration and fabric point to La Graufesenque as the source. *c.* AD 70-100. *Level 6 Site 1(74); 1*

Discussion of Phase 1

All the samian ware from Phase 1 is South Gaulish and all almost certainly comes from La Graufesenque. Theoretically it might be possible to postulate a pre-Flavian origin for Castleford, however, the samian from the *vicus* does not include anything like enough pre-Flavian material to justify such a suggestion. On the other hand the presence of some definitely pre-Flavian bowls, taken with the appreciable quantity of Neronian-Flavian samian, is clear evidence of pre-Agricolan foundation. The choice between Cerialis or Frontinus is less easy, and theoretically either would be possible on historical grounds, though with some bias in favour of the former. The position for the samian is the same: it slightly favours the earlier date, and the establishment of the site in AD 71, or very soon after, seems increasingly likely. That is not to say necessarily that the *vicus* was set up then, as rubbish from forts was, of course, regularly dumped in areas later occupied by *vici*.

The latest material from Phase 1 is Flavian in date, with two sherds definitely later than AD 80 (Nos 187 and 191) and two later than AD 85 (Nos 188-9). In view of the small quantity of material which must be later than AD 80, it seems reasonable to suppose that Phase 1 ended in or soon after AD 85.

Phase 2

194 A fragment of form 29 with an upper zone of corded festoons and poppy-head tassels of the kind used by Frontinus of La Graufesenque (Knorr 1952, Taf.25A). *c.* AD 70-90. *Site 1(74); 2*

195* A small, burnt, piece of form 29. Similar arrangements of gadroons are on bowls stamped by Albus i, Germanus i, Meddillus and Primus iii at La Graufesenque. In view of this, attribution to any potter would be unwise, though the date is likely to be *c.* AD 55-75. *266 Site 1(74); 2*

196 A small fragment from the lower zone of form 29 with badly moulded and blurred decoration. Probably Neronian or early Flavian. *Site 1(74); 2*

197 A piece of form 29 with a continuous scroll in the upper zone. A closely similar scroll using the same ties is on a bowl from Bregenz stamped by Calvus (Knorr 1919, Taf.18D). The leaf in the scroll of the Bregenz bowl reappears at Castleford, used in a continuous wreath below the cordon. A rosette in the upper zone is on a stamped bowl of Calvus from La Graufesenque. *c.* AD 70-85. *Site 1(74); 2*

198 A small sherd from the upper zone of form 29, with a band of single-bordered festoons, as on a bowl of Pass(i)enus from Bonn. A bird in the festoon (Hermet 1934, pl. 28, 40) was used by many Neronian-Flavian potters at La Graufesenque. *c.* AD 60-75. *Site 1(74); 2*

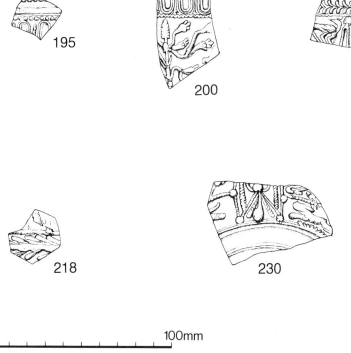

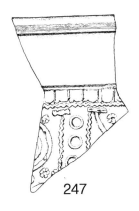

Fig. 17. Decorated samian from Site 1(74), Phase 2. Scale 1:2

0   100mm

199 A single fragment of form 37 with a continuous scroll over a chevron-wreath. This wreath was used on a bowl at Mainz stamped by Meddillus, and a bird in the scroll (Hermet 1934, pl. 28, 68) is on some of his stamped bowls, too. A tie on the scroll, although not clear, is probably also a detail used by Meddillus. *c.* AD 70-85. *Site 1(74); 2*

200*A single fragment of form 37 with a freestyle scene including a tree approximating to one used by Germanus and his circle. Instead of the trunk being incised with a stylus in the mould, a formal ornament, which appears on bowls stamped by Cosius Rufinus, Cotto and Iustus (Knorr 1919, Taf.27, 6) was used. The ovolo occurs on other bowls in the Germanus tradition. (cf. 206, which may be from the same bowl.) *c.* AD 80-100. *Site 1(74); 2*

201 A single fragment of form 37 with zonal decoration. The short S-shaped gadroons were used on two bowls in the Pompeii Hoard (Atkinson 1914, no.54 and 61). The chevron-wreath above the gadroons is common in the same hoard. *c.* AD 75-90. *Site 1(74); 2*

202 A single fragment of form 37 with several zones of decoration. The top surviving zone has an animal, perhaps the stag Hermet 1934, pl. 27, 6. The next zone consists of short, vertical spindles like ones on a bowl from Malton (Corder 1930, fig. 18, 3). The basal wreath is also on another Malton bowl with an ovolo which first appears at sites founded in the 80s under Agricola. *c.* AD 80-110. *Site 1(74); 2*

203 A single fragment of form 37 having a freestyle zone with a stylised tree flanked by two birds. This arrangement was undoubtedly used by many potters (cf. Knorr 1912b, Taf. XXII, 7 for a bowl from Baden-Baden stamped inside by L. Cosius Virilis). The stag (Hermet 1934, pl. 27, 15) was used by potters represented in the Pompeii Hoard. *c.* AD 75-95. *Site 1(74); 2*

204 A single fragment of form 37 with a trident-tongued ovolo of the period *c.* AD 75-95, but not assignable to particular potters. *Site 1(74); 2*

205*A single fragment of form 37 with panelled decoration. The ovolo was largely planed off in finishing the rim, but appears to have had a single border. Although the style is Flavian, no close parallels are known. The bird is Hermet 1934, pl. 28, 39. Probably *c.* AD 70-90. *64 Site 1(74); 2*

206*A single fragment of form 37 with a stag (Hermet 1934, pl. 27, 8), as on a bowl from the Bregenz Cellar (Jacobs 1913, Taf.1,t3), which probably has the same ovolo. The general style is derived from the work of Germanus, and the piece could be from the same bowl as No. 200. *c.* AD 80-100. *53, 54 and 55 Site 1(74); 2*

207 See No. 177. *Site 1(74); 2*

208 A fragment of form 37 with scroll decoration. The ovolo is on a bowl from London stamped by M. Crestio of La Graufesenque. Numbers 175 and 176 could possibly be from the same bowl. *c.* AD 75-95. *Site 1(74); 2*

209 Four pieces of form 37 with the same ovolo as the last and also with a continuous scroll. The leaves are smaller versions of Hermet 1934, pl. 9, 39 (pointing to the right) and pl. 9, 10. The larger was used by M. Crestio (Knorr 1919, Taf.28, 14), although neither the smaller leaf nor the Nile goose (Knorr 1919, pl. 28, 68, facing right) used as a filler, seems to be attested for him. *c.* AD 75-95. *Site 1(74); 2*

210 A single fragment of form 37 having zonal decoration, and with an ovolo (Knorr 1919, Taf.57, 19) used by Mercator i at La Graufesenque, as on one of his stamped bowls from Silchester. A four-petalled motif, used to form a continuous wreath, is not known to us on a stamped bowl. *c.* AD 80-105. *Site 1(74); 2*

211 A sherd from the basal zone of form 37, conceivably from the same bowl as No. 177 *q.v.* for the festoons, leaves and bird. A heart-shaped leaf used as the festoon pendant appears on bowls from Rottweil (Knorr 1912, Taf. XVIII). *c.* AD 80-95. *Site 1(74); 2*

212 Three sherds from a bowl of form 37 with a continuous scroll divided horizontally in the lower concavities. The workmanship is poor. The large, four-pronged ovolo and the closing wreath were both used by Sabinus iv on bowls from Cannstatt (Knorr 1909, Taf. III, 1) and London (British Museum). Confirmation of date comes from the presence of his work at Saalburg (Ricken 1934, Taf.13, 14). Bowls with this ovolo were also produced at Espalion, as M. J.-L. Tilhard tells us. *c.* AD 85-110. *Site 1(74); 2*

213 A single fragment of form 37, with a winding chevron-scroll reminiscent of Germanus i of La Graufesenque and his associates. The animal(?) in the lower concavity of the scroll has not been identified, but may be a small boar. The tendril in the upper part ends in a bud, probably used by the Germanus group. *c.* AD 70-85. *Site 1(74); 2*

214 A small fragment of form 37 with traces of a chevron-festoon or wreath similar to 213. Probably by Germanus or one of his successors. Flavian or early-Trajanic. *Site 1(74); 2*

215 A small sherd with a carelessly-impressed basal wreath between bead rows (cf. No. 169). A wreath of trilobed buds is of a type used by several potters in the late Neronian or early Flavian period. *c.* AD 65-80. *Site 1(74); 2*

216 A single fragment of form 37, probably with a freestyle zone over a basal wreath. The details of the freestyle scene are not clear, though a leaf tendril recalls a bowl of Vitalis ii from Bregenz (Knorr 1952, Taf.61). The wreath is the same as on No. 210. *c.* AD 75-95. *Site 1(74); 2*

217 A single sherd of form 37 with a continuous scroll over a basal wreath. A hare, leaf, grass tufts (Knorr 1919, Taf.57, 13) and leaf tips all occur on a bowl of form 29 from Besançon stamped by Mercator i of La Graufesenque. A wreath of trifid motifs (Knorr 1919, 12) was commonly used by Mercator, but it has also been noted on a form 29 stamped by Pontus. *c.* AD 80-105. *Site 1(74); 2*

218*A small, single fragment of form 37 with a wreath as on No. 217, though more carelessly impressed. The details of the zone above cannot be restored. *c.* AD 85-110. *Site 1(74); 2*

219 A small fragment of form 37 with an ovolo used by Frontinus and Paullus iii at La Graufesenque (see No. 190). There are traces of a chevron-wreath below the ovolo which suggest the former. *c.* AD 75-100. *Site 1(74); 2*

220 A single fragment of form 37 with panelled decoration, one panel having a simple saltire of Flavian or Flavian-Trajanic type. See Knorr 1912b, Taf.XXVI, 1 and 2 and Taf.XXVII for similar designs at Rottweil, and cf. Nos 221 and 226-8. *c.* AD 85-110. *Site 1(74); 2*

221 A fragment of form 37 with what is probably the same ovolo as the last. Since there is also a poppy-head which may be from a saltire like No. 220's, it is possible that the sherds are from the same bowl. *c.* AD 85-110. *Site 1(74); 2*

222 A single fragment of form 37 with a panelled zone over a zone of unusually elongated leaves arranged in a palisade. Somewhat similar leaves were used by Frontinus on a bowl from Richborough and on a bowl stamped after moulding by Iucundus iii at Günzburg. A lion (Hermet 1934, pl. 25, 25) was used at La Graufesenque by several potters and is on bowls stamped by Mommo in the Pompeii Hoard (Atkinson 1914, no. 6 and 13). *c.* AD 70-90. *Site 1(74); 2*

223 A single piece of form 37 with the same lateral plant as 187. The adjacent panel contains a festoon. The ovolo is one used in the Pompeii Hoard (Atkinson 1914, 63). *c.* AD 80-105. *Site 1(74); 2*

224 A single fragment of form 37 with an arcade in the only surviving panel. A Cupid (Hermet 1934, pl. 18, 33) is on a bowl in the style of Mommo in the Pompeii Hoard (Atkinson 1914, no. 60) and on bowls stamped by Vitalis ii (Knorr 1919, Taf.83). At La Graufesenque arcades were used mainly in the later Flavian and Trajanic periods (cf. Hermet 1934, pl. 86). c. AD 90-110. *Site 1(74); 2*

225 A single piece of form 37 with a panelled zone above a chevron wreath. One panel has a Venus (Hermet 1934, pl. 18, 18), the other has a ribbed leaf, perhaps one on a bowl from Vechten stamped by Meddillus. The basal wreath is on other stamped bowls by him at Mainz and Bregenz (Knorr 1952, Taf.39D). c. AD 75-85. *Site 1(74); 2*

226 A fragment of form 30 with panelled decoration, one panel containing a Victory (Hermet 1934, pl. 86, 13). The other panel has a saltire, possibly identical to the one on No. 227, which could be from the same bowl. The Victory is on a stamped bowl of L. Tr-Masculus at Cannstatt (Knorr 1910, Taf.XI, 1) and occurs several times in the Bregenz Cellar (Jacobs 1913, Taf.II, 13 etc.). The associations of this piece thus suggest a date c. AD 90-110, which fits with the coarse rope-like borders. *Site 1(74); 2*

227 A single fragment of form 37 with a saltire similar to the last, and no doubt of the same date. *Site 1(74); 2*

228 A piece of a panelled form 37. The ovolo and a trilobed plant in a saltire were used by Sabinus iv on a bowl from Cannstatt (see No. 212). The Castleford ovolo has had the tongues partly removed by the border below it. c. AD 90-110. *Site 1(74); 2*

229 A single fragment of form 37 with panelled decoration. One panel has a *bestiarius* (Hermet 1934, pl. 23, 253) used on a stamped bowl of Mercator i from York. The plant (Knorr 1919, Taf.57, 11) was used by many potters at La Graufesenque, including Mercator i. The S-shaped gadroons occur several times in the Pompeii Hoard (Atkinson 1914, nos 37, 39 etc, once with a signature of Mommo no. 61). The leaf-tendril in an adjacent panel is unusual, but the bowl may be dated c. AD 80-100. *Site 1(74); 2*

230* Two joining fragments of form 37 with panelled decoration. Alternate panels are divided horizontally. The animal (dog?) in the bottom half of one panel has not been identified, otherwise all the features have parallels in the work of Mercator i of La Graufesenque. An identical saltire is on a stamped bowl of his from Vechten, the hare on stamped bowls from Croft Ambrey and Silchester. The lion (D.747) above the hare is on one of his stamped bowls at York. c. AD 90-110. *Site 1(74); 2*

231 A small, single fragment of form 37 with an ovolo typical of Germanus i of La Graufesenque (Hermet 1934, pls 99-102). A similar sherd came from period II at Verulamium (Hartley 1972a, D83). c. AD 70-85. *Site 1(74); 2*

232 A single fragment of form 37 with decoration of panels divided horizontally. One has a bird to right (cf. Atkinson 1914, no.3 stamped by Mommo). A chevron-festoon and its pendants are identical to ones on a bowl of form 29 in the British Museum stamped by L. Cosius Virilis. c. AD 75-100. *Site 1(74); 2*

233 A small fragment of form 37 with a single-bordered ovolo (Rogers B28) used in Central Gaul by many potters, but with wavy-line borders, as here, characteristic of X-2 of Les Martres-de-Veyre. c. AD 100-120. *Site 1(74); 2*

234 Six fragments, some joining, of form 37. The ovolo (Rogers B44), fan-shaped plant (Rogers J17), tree, made from Rogers U283, and partly impressed acanthuses (Rogers J2) are on a bowl at London by the Potter of the Rosette (S. & S. 1958, pl. 25, 308). A lioness is on one of his bowls from Silchester (S. & S. 310). c. AD 100-120. *Site 1(74); 2*

235 A small, burnt fragment of form 37 of unusual style, but undoubtedly Central Gaulish. A voided saltire and rosette are reminiscent of the 'Ioenalis' style, though the beads of the borders are too large for his mould-makers. The use of a beadrow at the bottom of the decoration suggests Trajanic or Hadrianic date. Probably from Les Martres-de-Veyre. *Site 1(74); 2*

236 A fragment of form 37 with freestyle decoration. Both a zone of beaded circles replacing the ovolo and a spiral below it were used at Les Martres-de-Veyre by Drusus i (S. & S. 1958, fig. 4, 3 and 5). He is also known to have used the tree (Rogers N4). An animal is probably the bear (O.1597) used on his bowls at London and Brecon (S. & S. 1958, pl. 14, 173, 175). c. AD 100-120. *Site 1(74); 2*

237 A small piece of form 37 with a basal wreath used at Les Martres-de-Veyre by a mould-maker associated with Ioenalis (S. & S. 1958, pl. 40. 462 etc.). For the rest, a spindle and trilobed bud used by this potter may be involved. c. AD 100-125. *Site 1(74); 2*

238 A piece of form 37 with panelled decoration. A sole surviving figure, an Abundance (D.472, variant), is on a bowl at London in the style of a man who worked for, or sold moulds to, Donnaucus of Les Martres-de-Veyre (S. & S. 1958, pl. 48, 574). A rosette on the Castleford bowl is blurred, but may be one on the London bowl. c. AD 100-125. *Site 1(74); 2*

239 A small piece of form 37, with tree branches and acanthus used by one of the mould-makers who worked for, or sold moulds to, Donnaucus and Ioenalis at Les Martres-de-Veyre (S. & S. 1958, pl. 47, 555 and fig. 42, 15). c. AD 100-125. *Site 1(74); 2*

240 A fragment of form 37 with panelled decoration and arcades of the kind used at Les Martres-de-Veyre by mould-makers associated with Medetus and Ranto (S. & S. 1958, pl. 30), but who worked later at Lezoux. c. AD 110-135. *Site 1(74); 2*

241 A small piece of form 30 with a Cupid (D.236) used at Lezoux by Drusus ii. It is on a signed bowl at Verulamium and also on a bowl in his style from the first destruction of the Wroxeter forum (Atkinson 1942, pl. 36, H61). A naked figure (not in D. or O.) is on an unsigned bowl in Drusus style from Great Chesterford. c. AD 125-140. *Site 1(74); 2*

242 A small piece of form 37 with alternating wide and narrow panels. The only figure (O.293A) is on a bowl from Alchester in the style of Avitus of Lezoux. The use of rosettes in vertical series is characteristic of Avitus and his associates, though this rosette does not seem to have been recorded for them. c. AD 120-145. *Site 1(74); 2*

243 A small fragment of form 37 with the single-bordered ovolo (Rogers B28) used both at Les Martres-de-Veyre and Lezoux. A fragmentary athlete (D.378) is on a bowl in the style of Quintilianus at Lezoux, and as he used the ovolo, the bowl is probably by one of his circle, though a small cup used as a filler is only assigned to one of the early Secundini by Rogers (U67). c. AD 125-145. *Site 1(74); 2*

244 A fragment of form 37 with an ovolo (Rogers B31) and ribbed leaf (Rogers J33), used at Lezoux by X-5 (S. & S. 1958, pl. 67, 4). A spindle on this piece was constantly used by him, though usually as a mask for the panel junctions, but a double festoon in the next panel does not seem to be known for him. c. AD 125-145. *Site 1(74); 2*

245 A single, large fragment of form 37 with panelled decoration and the distinctive ovolo (Rogers B144) of the Cerialis-Cinnamus style (see No. 295). All the details of this piece, including the Vulcan (D.14), Minerva (D.77), warrior (D.614), boar (O.1666), astragalus (S. & S. 1958, fig. 50), and 'buds' (Rogers J178, with only the end impressed) occur constantly in this style. For further discussion see No. 295.

The problem of date is crucial for this piece, since, if the stratification of this bowl is secure, the style must have been introduced before the collection in the 'pottery shop' of Phase 3 was formed. It has been shown that the style must have been current by AD 145 at the latest (Hartley 1972b, p. 34-5), and there is no reason why it should not have been introduced by AD 140. The question is whether a slightly earlier date is possible. It must be said at once that there is no certain instance of its occurrence in a definitely Hadrianic context, either in this country (at sites like Melandra or Slack evacuated *c.* AD 140), or in Germany (in the Erdkastell at Saalburg, for instance). There are, however, at least five bowls in Cerialis-Cinnamus style at Holt, where early to mid-Antonine samian is virtually completely absent. At Lezoux the style occurs in groups which are broadly Hadrianic-Antonine, but there is no means of being sure that any were formed before AD 140. Indeed, the only group at Lezoux known to us with early Cinnamus products which we may be reasonably certain belongs to the 130s does not have bowls in the Cerialis style, but rather in the quite different styles associated with Cinnamus's own cursive signature. On the whole, then, it looks as if this bowl points to the end of phase 2 coming about AD 140. If the Holt evidence is to be stressed, then AD 135 might possibly be invoked as the appropriate *terminus post quem*, however. *Site 1(74); 2*

246 A substantial fragment of form 37 in the style of Cettus of Les Martres-de-Veyre. A lioness (D.805), double ring across a bead-row (S. & S. 1958, pl. 142, 24-5), large, single festoon and small leaf (S. & S. 1958, 42, 4) are all common in his work, though a lozenge (Rogers U5?) does not seem to be known for him. For the date see Hartley 1972b, p. 34. *c.* AD 135-160. *Site 1(74); 2*

247* A fragment of form 37 of poor workmanship with alternating wide and narrow panels. All the details are characteristic of Tetturo of Lezoux (S. & S. 1958, pl. 131) and the ovolo (Rogers B247, but often with a straight tongue) and six-petalled rosette (Rogers C125) were also used by a related potter who signed Immuni. There is no entirely satisfactory site evidence for either's date (S. & S. 1958, p.233). However, we may note a bowl from Holt, where the samian is predominantly pre-Antonine (Grimes 1930, fig. 45, 119). Another sherd, from Carzield, should be Antonine I (Birley 1946). Tetturo's stamps on plain samian are frequently on form 27, and there would be nothing surprising in an activity beginning around AD 140, or even a trifle earlier. Both Immunus and Tetturo certainly worked at Lezoux, as their stamps or signatures have either been found there on decorated and, or, plain samian or occur on vessels in Lezoux fabric. But decorated bowls from moulds signed by Tetturo, or in his style, were also produced at Toulon-sur-Allier, by potters such as Albinus v and Paullus vi. *c.* AD 135-160. *Level 4 Site 1(74); 2*

248 A fragment of form 37 with alternate wide and narrow panels. The style is close to the last and it must also be assigned to either Tetturo or Immunus, although the ovolo has not previously been recorded for them. It is similar to one used by Mapillus and Pugnus of Lezoux (Rogers B41), but the core may be slightly wider and the tongue seems to be attached to the left side of the egg rather than the right. See No. 247 for the date and No. 249 for another sherd possibly from this bowl. *Site 1(74); 2*

249 A sherd which may be from the same bowl as the last. The same small, rosette in a single festoon is diagnostic for Tetturo (or Immunus?). *Site 1(74); 2*

Discussion of Phase 2

The South Gaulish samian ware of Phase 2 includes much which is residual or had survived long in use, but there is an appreciable quantity of material not made before AD 85 or 90, as well as the earliest products of Les Martres-de-Veyre. A starting date in the late 80s would fit the evidence.

The end date for Phase 2 is determined by the bowls in the styles of Cerialis-Cinnamus (No. 245), Cettus (No. 246) and Tetturo-Immunus (Nos 247-9). The dates of these bowls are discussed under their entries above, the result being that the earliest possible date for the end of the period is AD 135, though AD 140 may be thought to be more likely. The potters' stamps are consistent with this dating.

Phase 3, excluding the 'pottery shop'

Numbers 250-84 are all residual or survival pieces in Phase 3, or are apparently unburnt, and so not definitely to be assigned to the 'pottery shop'. They may be dealt with summarily. Stamps 556-8 are unburnt and, though not likely to be residual, cannot be shown to have belonged to the 'pottery shop'. They are, therefore, dealt with separately.

250 Form 29, South Gaulish, with two panels in the upper zone divided by double wavy lines, as sometimes in the Pompeii Hoard (cf. Atkinson 1914, 2 and 15). *c.* AD 70-85. *Site 1(74); 3*

251 A large fragment of form 37 with a winding scroll. The ovolo, used by Calvus and, later, by Mercator i (Knorr 1919, Textbild 47), a small heart-shaped leaf and the basal chevron wreath all occur on bowls at La Graufesenque found in a large group from the Calvus workshop. A fan-shaped leaf (Knorr 1919, Taf.54, 17) is on bowls stamped by Meddillus, who probably bought moulds from Calvus. A wreath below the ovolo is on an unstamped bowl from Camelon. *c.* AD 70-95. *Site 1(74); 3*

252* A fragment of form 37 with the same ovolo as the last. The closest parallel is a bowl from Valkenburg ZH from a mould signed]BINI below the decoration (Glasbergen 1948, Afb.61, 3). Whether Albinus or Sabinus, the piece is clearly Flavian. *49 Site 1(74); 3*

253 A fragment of form 37 with an ovolo (Knorr 1919, Taf.57, 19) and Minerva head (D.659) used by Mercator i of La Graufesenque. *c.* AD 85-110. *Site 1(74); 3*

254 A fragment of form 37 with festoon and pendant identical with those on No. 186, to which this sherd probably belongs. *Site 1(74); 3*

255* A fragment of form 37 with freestyle zone, including a tree and a doe (D.881), over a basal wreath. The style is derived from Germanus bowls. cf. Grimes 1930, fig. 37, 42 for a bowl from Holt with similar decoration. *c.* AD 80-110. *Site 1(74); 3*

256 A fragment of form 30 with panelled decoration, South Gaulish. A Victory (Hermet 1934, pl. 86, 13), borders and tassels are like those of No. 226, and of similar date, though the bowls are different. *Site 1(74); 3*

257* A small fragment of form 37, South Gaulish, with blurred, badly-moulded decoration. The herringbone wreath at the bottom is unusual. Workmanship, fabric and glaze all suggest Flavian-Trajanic date. *49 Site 1(74); 3*

258 A fragment of form 67, South Gaulish. The surviving motif is a hare (O.2102). *c.* AD 70-100. *Site 1(74); 3*

259* A fragment of form 37 with an ovolo, tree, lion and griffin all used at Les Martres-de-Veyre by the potter X-2 (S. & S. 1958, pl. 9, 114 and 116). *c.* AD 100-120. *Site 1(74); 3*

260 A small fragment of form 37 in the style of Drusus i of Les Martres-de-Veyre. All the details are common in his work (S. & S. 1958, fig. 4). *c.* AD 100-120. *Site 1(74); 3*

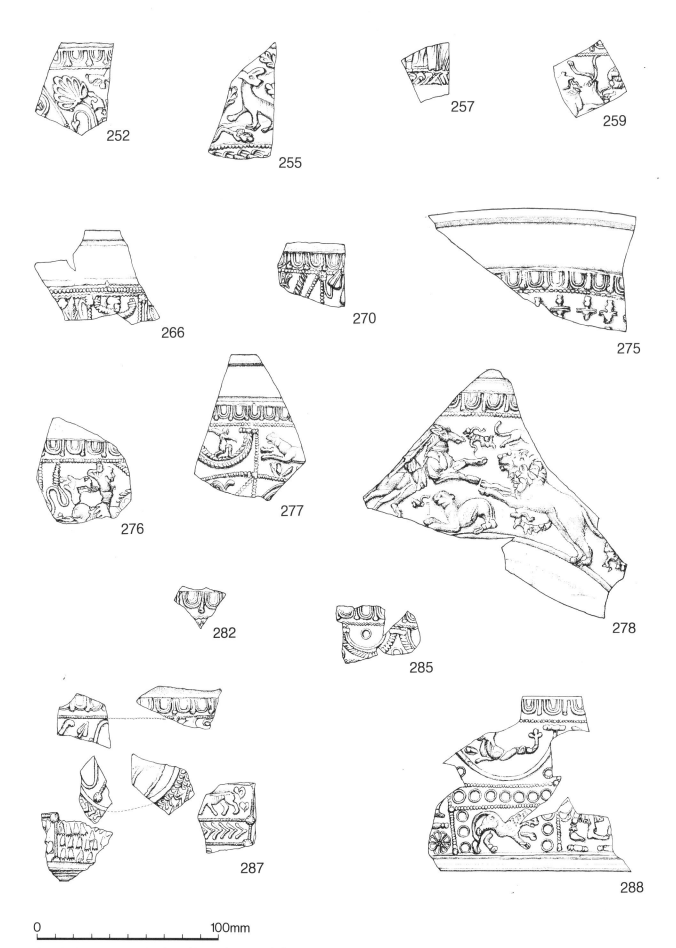

252

255

257

259

266

270

275

276

277

278

282

285

287

288

0   100mm

Fig. 18. Decorated samian from Site 1(74), Phase 3. Scale 1:2

261 Another fragment of form 37 in the style of Drusus i. Once more, all the details are known for him, though a Cupid is uncommon (Terrisse 1968, pl. XII, 10135). *c.* AD 100-120. *Site 1(74); 3*

262 A small fragment of form 30. The only identifiable decoration is a narrow vertical panel of rings, but it, and the associated zig-zag lines, are characteristic of Igocatus (X-4) of Les Martres-de-Veyre (cf. S. & S. 1958, pl. 18, 223). *c.* AD 100-120. *Site 1(74); 3*

263 A fragment of form 37 with panelled decoration in the style of the Potter of the Rosette, who sometimes used beaded borders, as on this bowl. *c.* AD 100-120. *Site 1(74); 3*

264 A fragment of form 37 with a large, winding scroll over a chevron wreath. The general style suggests Les Martres-de-Veyre as the source. *c.* AD 100-130. *Site 1(74); 3*

265 A fragment of form 37 with panelled decoration and a basal chevron wreath. Most of the details are known for the Potter of the Rosette, who also used an unusual grazing animal (D.969 bis) on this piece (Terrisse 1968, pl. XVIII, 1059). A hare (O.2084) in an adjoining panel is on a bowl at Colchester stamped after moulding by Ioenalis of Les Martres-de-Veyre (S. & S. 1958, pl. 35, 412). *c.* AD 100-120. *Site 1(74); 3*

266* Two burnt fragments from a bowl of form 30, ostensibly from the level over the 'pottery shop', may be treated here, since they were presumably burnt in the general fire, though then residual. There is no ovolo, and probably never was, as the surviving top of the decoration has a row of large beads between wavy lines. The opposed cornucopiae forming a festoon match a bowl stamped after moulding by Ioenalis of Les Martres-de-Veyre (S. & S. 1958, pl. 35, 412), though the corner tassel and leaf in the other panel seem to be unparalleled. The head in the festoon is probably a bear's (cf. S. & S. 1958, pl. 44, 509). *c.* AD 100-130. *Level 3 Site 1(74); 3*

267 An unburnt fragment of form 37 with arcades containing a Diana (D.67) in the style of a potter who signed moulds with a name beginning in D. Whether there was any direct connection with Medetus and Ranto is less than certain, though they almost certainly used his moulds at Les Martres-de-Veyre before his probable migration to Lezoux. *c.* AD 115-35. *Site 1(74); 3*

268 A small, unburnt fragment of form 37. The ovolo, seven beaded rosette and *pelta* (Rogers U129) were all used by a mould-maker whose moulds reached Medetus and Ranto (S. & S. 1958, fig. 9, 1). *c.* AD 110-130. *Site 1(74); 3*

269 A single fragment of form 30 with the same ovolo as No. 268. This has a dancer (D.217) and a festoon (S. & S. 1958, pl. 31, 366) both used by the maker of the mould for the last. *c.* AD 110-130. *Site 1(74); 3*

270* An unburnt fragment of form 37. A closely similar bowl from London has all the same elements of decoration (S. & S. 1958, pl. 44, 513). The mould-maker worked for, or sold moulds to, Donnaucus of Les Martres-de-Veyre, but his style was very close to that of Sacer i, who may have begun work at Les Martres, but whose main activity was at Lezoux. This piece is certainly from Les Martres, however. *c.* AD 110-25. *Site 1(74); 3*

271 A small, unburnt fragment of form 37 with an ovolo and pelta (Rogers U129) both used at Les Martres-de-Veyre. The connections are with the same mould-maker as No. 270. *c.* AD 110-25. *Site 1(74); 3*

272 A small, unburnt piece of form 37 with an ovolo (Rogers B114) used by Butrio, Austrus and several later potters at Lezoux. Presumably here we are dealing with one of the earlier two, and a date *c.* AD 120-145. *Site 1(74); 3*

273 An unburnt fragment of form 37 in the style of X-5 of Lezoux. Almost identical scrolls are known from Caersws and London (S. & S. 1958, pl. 67, 12). *c.* AD 120-40. *Site 1(74); 3*

274 A single fragment of form 37, probably with freestyle decoration. An eagle (D.987) flanked by small vine-scrolls (Rogers M18) and a zone of rings below the decoration hint at links with the Quintilianus-Bassus Group of Lezoux, Paterclus perhaps being the likely candidate (S. & S. 1958, pl. 72, 35). *c.* AD 125-45. *Site 1(74); 3*

275* An unburnt fragment of form 37 with an ovolo (Rogers B35) and a zone of 'dumb-bells' used at Lezoux by X-6 (Rogers Q89). *c.* AD 125-45. *Level 3 Site 1(74); 3*

276* A unburnt fragment of form 37 with panelled decoration. The ovolo (Rogers B321) was used by Sacer of Lezoux, and later by Cinnamus. But the style is the former's and the tendrils and spindles may be compared with S. & S. 1958, pl. 83, 11. The horseman in the panel is an uncommon type, later used by Secundus v of Lezoux. *c.* AD 125-145. *Level 3 Site 1(74); 3*

277* An unburnt fragment of form 37 with subdivided panels. All the motifs and figures may be matched on stamped or signed bowls of Attianus and Sacer of Lezoux. The Cupid (D.245), dog (D.930) and the characteristic partial impression of a grass-tuft (Rogers L19) are common to several members of their circle. *c.* AD 125-45. *Level 3 Site 1(74); 3*

278* A large, unburnt fragment of form 37 with freestyle decoration. The ovolo (S. & S. 1958, fig. 23, 4), horse and rider (D.158), lion (D.1450) and serpent on rock (D.960 bis) were all used at Lezoux on stamped bowls of Attianus ii. A bowl from Verulamium (S. & S. 1958, pl. 86, 12) has most of the details and also a small lion to right which may be the same as one on the Castleford bowl, but a panther (D.969 ter) is not known on stamped bowls. *c.* AD 125-50. *Level 3 Site 1(74); 3*

279 A small, unburnt piece of form 37 with the same grass-tuft as No. 277. Fabric and glaze suggest a source at Lezoux, probably with one of the Sacer Group. *c.* AD 125-50. *Site 1(74); 3*

280 A small, unburnt fragment of form 37 with badly damaged decoration. The only recognisable motif is a bunch of grapes used by Cettus of Les Martres-de-Veyre (S. & S. 1958, pl. 144, 51). cf. 246. *c.* AD 135-60. *Site 1(74); 3*

281 A small piece of form 37 with rosettes characteristic of Tetturo and Immunus of Lezoux (Rogers C125). An acanthus on this piece is known from some of their unsigned bowls. This bowl adds to the increasing evidence for a pre-Antonine start for their work (cf. D.100-2). *c.* AD 135-60. *Site 1(74); 3*

282* A small unburnt sherd from form 37 with an ovolo used by Sissus ii of Lezoux on bowls at Hardknott, Leicester and Wilderspool. Sissus is well-represented in Scotland, but he almost certainly began work before AD 140, and the Hardknott bowl should be Hadrianic rather than after AD 158. *c.* AD 130-50. *Level 3 Site 1(74); 3*

283 Two unburnt pieces of form 37 with large, winding scroll. The fabric appears to be East Gaulish and the ovolo is closely similar to, though not identical with, one on an unpublished bowl from Rottweil from a mould stamped by Ciriuna of Heiligenberg. The beaded border below the ovolo is typical of that centre, where the leaf of the scroll was also used (Forrer 1911, Taf.29, 8). Although Heiligenberg products in general are rarely well-dated, they are on the one hand absent from the Erdkastell at Saalburg, but on the other some of the potters who had worked there were among the earliest active at Rheinzabern. A date *c.* AD 140-60 seems required. *Site 1(74); 3*

284 A small unburnt piece of form 30 with an ovolo having a tongue ending in a circle. The ovolo is not otherwise known, but is more probably Hadrianic-Antonine than Antonine. *Site 1(74); 3*

Phase 3, the 'pottery shop' samian

The rest of the material from Phase 3 forms a large, homogeneous group of fragments, many joining, from decorated bowls and plain samian, all more or less heavily burnt. This collection is the most important group of 2nd-century samian to have been found in this country since the discovery of the Wroxeter Gutter Group in the 1923-7 excavations (Atkinson 1942, p. 127ff). Fortunately it is earlier in date than the Wroxeter group and adds much to our information about Central Gaulish ware of the Hadrianic-Antonine period. The collection is also much larger than the Wroxeter one (of 13 decorated and 210 plain vessels). However, the Castleford bowls were rarely anything like as complete as the Wroxeter ones, and it is evident that the debris from the shop was scattered and levelled after the conflagration. We deal first with the decorated ware, Nos 285-525, adding a general discussion (p. 52). We then summarise the types of plain samian (pp 52-5) and finally, there is a summary of the group and discussion of its date (p. 55). The potters' stamps on plain samian (Nos 559-996) are catalogued in a section below and the comparative material and the dating (pp 63-4) are discussed after the stamp catalogue.

285* Three burnt pieces of form 30 with zonal decoration. The ovolo, striated festoons (Rogers F70) containing circles, and the astragalus were all used by a potter (Rogers's X-9) who supplied Medetus and Ranto with moulds (S. & S. 1958, pl. 32, 347). Because of the burning, it is impossible to decide whether this bowl was made at Les Martres-de-Veyre or Lezoux, and hence whether it was residual or an oldish piece in stock. c. AD 110-30. *Level 3 Site 1(74); 3*

286 Two burnt fragments of form 30 with panelled decoration, but with several of the same features as the last. Perhaps residual in the 'shop'. c. AD 110-30. *Level 3 Site 1(74); 3*

287* Six burnt pieces from form 30 with panelled decoration of an unusual kind. The ovolo is blurred, but is probably one used by a potter (Rogers's X-12) selling moulds to, or otherwise providing them for, Ioenalis of Les Martres-de-Veyre (S. & S. 1958, fig. 10, 2). All the other details of this bowl occur on pieces with similar connexions with Ioenalis (S. & S. 1958, fig. 10 has most).

Bowls with generally similar arrangements of scrolls and panels occur at Les Martres-de-Veyre (Terrisse 1968, pl. 41, 1062) and at Corbridge (S. & S. 1958, pl. 41, 480), and the same arrangement for the scroll is on an unpublished bowl from Little Chester which has the DD monogram.

It is likely that the mould for this bowl was made at Les Martres-de-Veyre, but, because of the burning, we cannot judge whether the bowl itself was made there or at Lezoux, since some bowls found at the latter in local fabrics typical of the Flavian-Trajanic period were certainly made in moulds originating at Les Martres. However, since the bowl was fractured in or after the fire, it cannot easily be explained as residual, and it could have been long in stock. c. AD 100-125. *Level 3 Site 1(74); 3*

Numbers 288-417 are all bowls (some of form 30) in what one of us once called the 'Cinnamus-Paullus' style, but which has subsequently come to be known as the 'Cerialis-Cinnamus' style. This style always involves a particular ovolo (Rogers B144) which, although it is found on moulds stamped by Sacer, Anunus, Paullus iv and Cinnamus, is constantly associated with mould signatures of Cerialis ii, who evidently produced moulds for Cinnamus early in the latter's career. Cinnamus also signed moulds, but they are in a very different style, sometimes, though not invariably, close to the one used by Attianus. It is curious that the 'standard' Cinnamus style, which had emerged by AD 150 at the latest, is closer to Cerialis-Cinnamus than to the original Cinnamus style, but it is known that bowls in Cerialis-Cinnamus style were also still being made after AD 150, when Paullus was certainly stamping similar moulds. It should be made clear, however, that very few of the bowls in this style are from stamped or signed moulds. (For discussions of the style see Hartley 1961, 103; 1972, 34-5; Simpson and Rogers 1969.)

We have been very selective in choosing bowls in this style for illustration, especially as most of the panelled ones are very stereotyped. All the bowls have the same borders of rounded beads and a restricted range of figure-types and motifs here listed under Nos 295-337, 338-45, 346-87 and 392-417. Apart from the ovolo, the most characteristic motif is the use of a 'bud' (apparently an impression of the end of a leafy frond (Rogers J178) as a space-filler). This occurs on many signed bowls of Cerialis and also (with fuller impression) on a signed bowl of Cinnamus from Heronbridge (S. & S. 1958, pl. 165, 1).

288* Form 30 in panelled style. The sea cow (D.29) was used by Paullus iv on a bowl with mould-stamp from Richborough, and the leopard (D.798) on his stamped or signed bowls at York and Leicester (S. & S. 1958, pl. 165, 3 and 4) and on a signed bowl of Cerialis ii at Silchester (S. & S. 1958, pl. 164, 4). The Diana with hind (D.64) was in common use at Lezoux in the Hadrianic and Antonine periods and is on other illustrated bowls in this group (Nos 290 and 293), as well as on several not drawn. *Level 3 Site 1(74); 3*

289* Form 30 with panelled decoration. The Venus is the D.176 type, but larger. A smaller version was also used by this Group on bowl No. 290. At least three versions of the figure therefore existed, the largest and smallest being used by the Cerialis-Cinnamus Group. The smaller versions were produced by *surmoulage*. The characteristic buds (from Rogers J178) are here used very liberally on each side of the Venus. The winged centaur (a blurred version of O.735A: see No. 292 for a clearer impression) is on a stamped bowl of Paullus at Wroxeter (S. & S. 1958, pl. 165, 1). The large rosette (Rogers C2) was used on bowls in the style of Pugnus ii at Southampton (Rogers and Laing 1966, fig. 4, 76) and also by Rentus on an unpublished bowl at Lezoux. The small double-medallion is one of the most characteristic motifs separating this style from the later Cinnamus one. *Level 3 Site 1(74); 3*

290* A fragment of form 30 with panelled decoration. For the Diana cf. bowls Nos 288 and 293. The Venus is a smaller version of D.176 (cf. bowl No. 289). *Level 3 Site 1(74); 3*

291* Several pieces of form 30 with free figures separated by arcades. One arcade contains a blurred impression of the seated Apollo (D.52), used by many Lezoux potters, including Cinnamus. The man holding the adze-hammer is on a bowl at Castleford in the style of Drusus ii, without the hammer (D.1103), which occurs separately on a mould at Lezoux. The partially-impressed dolphin (D.1058) was used by Cinnamus ii at Lezoux, but the figure in the other arcade has not been identified. Similar arcades and pillars occur on bowls from Mumrills and London (S. & S. 1958, pl. 159, 32 & 161, 49). *Level 3 Site 1(74); 3*

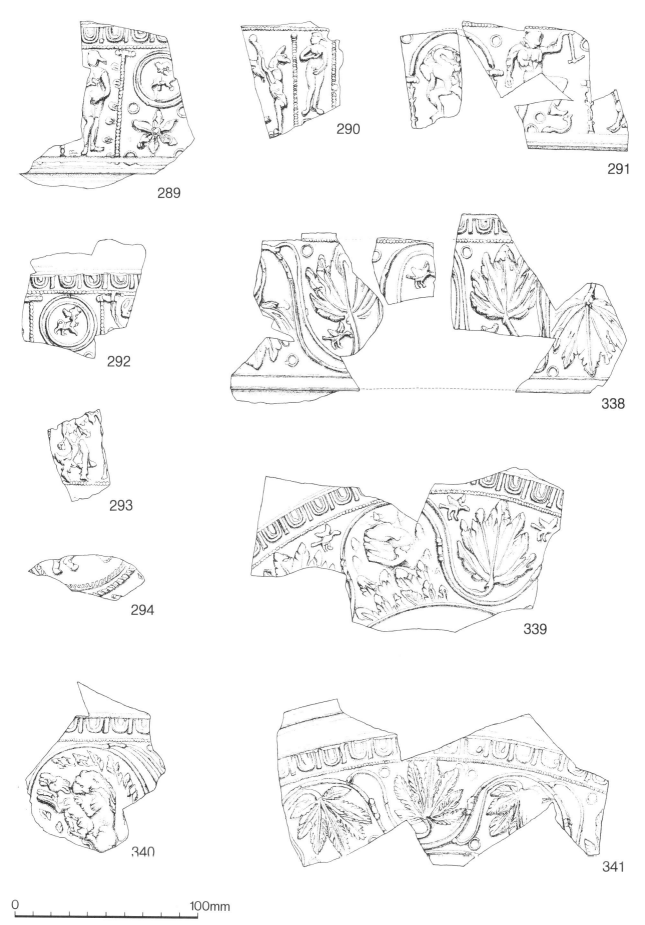

289 290 291 292 338 293 294 339 340 341

0   100mm

Fig. 19. Decorated samian from Site 1(74), Phase 3. Scale 1:2

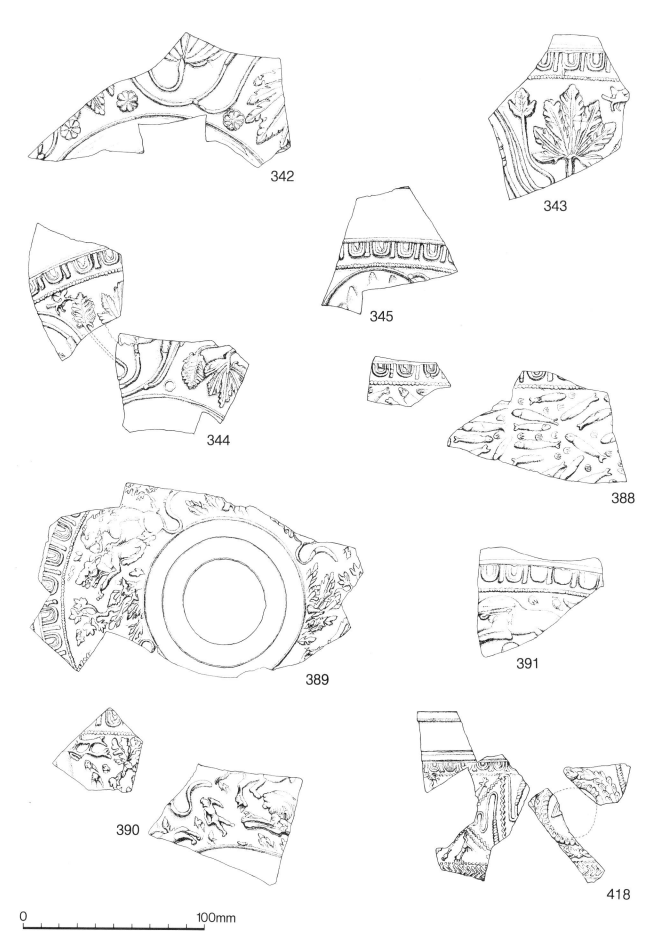

342

343

345

344

388

389

391

390

418

0   100mm

Fig. 20. Decorated samian from Site 1(74), Phase 3. Scale 1:2

38

292* A fragment of form 30 with panels. The medallion and centaur are as on bowl No. 289. The leopard (D.799) was used by Sacer i, Cinnamus ii and Paullus iv (on a bowl from Camelon: S. & S. 1958, pl. 165, 2). *Level 3 Site 1(74); 3*

293* A fragment of form 37 with a Diana and hind (D.64). *Level 3 Site 1(74); 3*

294* A fragment of form 37 with panelled decoration. The compound festoon (Rogers F11) is one used on large bowls in the Cerialis-Cinnamus style, occasionally with small Cinnamus mould-stamps. It occurs several times on bowls in the 'pottery shop'. The leopard is probably D.798, as on bowl No. 288. *Level 3 Site 1(74); 3*

295-337 These are all different panelled bowls assigned to the Cerialis-Cinnamus style (see the note after No. 287). Most of the figure types are already known to have been used by Cinnamus ii, Cerialis or Paullus iv.

Figure-types used on this series of bowls are: a sea-cow (D.29), Vulcan (D.42, attested both with and without implements), Diana (D.64), a kilted warrior (D.86), Perseus (D.146), Apollo (O.84 variant with a lozenge replacing the chair leg), dancers (D.175 and a variant of the type), Venuses (D.176, 176 variant and 185), Mercury (D.290a), a man with cloak and staff (D.338), satyrs (D.354, 358), a naked man similar to, but smaller than D.403, centaurs (D.434 and O.735a), Victory (O.819A), a seated figure (D.490), sphinxes to right and left (D.496, 497, 497 variant and O.857 variant), a philosopher (D.523), a warrior with a shield and dagger (D.614), a mask (D.683), a bust (O.1261?), a lion to right (of the general type O.1512-16), bears to left (D.775, 775 variant and 817), panthers to right and left (D.799 variant and 805), boars to right and left (D.823 and 834), a kneeling stag to right (D.847), hares to left and right (D.950a and O.2057?),an eagle (D.981), birds to right (D.1001, 1038), a bird to left (O.2298).

Motifs include: leaf (Rogers J153), vine-scroll (Rogers M2), leafy scroll (Rogers M31), cup (Rogers T25), lozenge (Rogers U36), dolphins on basket (Rogers Q58). *Level 3 Site 1(74); 3*

338* Several fragments of form 30 with large vine-scroll. The leaf (Rogers H22) was used by Sacer (S. & S. 1958, pl. 83, 8) and by Cinnamus ii in his standard style (Karnitsch 1959, Taf.72, 1, with a rim-stamp of Amenus), but it is common on bowls in the Cerialis-Cinnamus style (cf. No. 339). The bird is D.1038, commonly used by Cinnamus ii. *Level 3 Site 1(74); 3*

339* Form 37 with scroll involving figures in the lower part. The leaf is probably Rogers H22 as on the last bowl, but here it is also used partly impressed as a space-filler, as often in this style, presumably because it was to hand and saved finding the usual filler. (Paullus iv used the same dodge.) The bear, also partly impressed is O.1633I, used on a bowl of Paullus iv at York. For the bird cf. the last bowl. The astragalus is one normally used on bowls in the Cerialis-Cinnamus style. *Level 3 Site 1(74); 3*

340* Form 37 with decoration of the same type as the last, but with the lion-attacking-boar type (D.778) in the lower part. There is an almost identical bowl at Stockstadt (*ORL* B33, Taf.XVIII, 6), also with the bird (O.2239B, used by Cinnamus ii) and the tips of Rogers H22, as on the last bowl. *Level 3 Site 1(74); 3*

341* Form 37 with a plain scroll using Rogers H37 and the standard astragalus used for scrolls in the Cerialis-Cinnamus style. *Level 3 Site 1(74); 3*

342* Form 37 with a scroll incorporating Rogers H22, as on Nos 338-9 and a large rosette (Rogers C53) used on a Cerialis-Cinnamus bowl at Chester and at Lezoux, by Cinnamus ii (S. & S. 1958, pl. 162, 60) amongst others. *Level 3 Site 1(74); 3*

343* Form 37 with scroll decoration incorporating two different leaves. The larger leaf (Rogers H51) is apparently on a London bowl in standard Cinnamus style and with his late CINNAMIⱵ stamp

(S. & S. 1958, pl. 162, 58). The smaller leaf (Rogers H99) was also used by Cinnamus ii (S. & S. 1958, fig. 47, 31), but on the Castleford bowl it is not fully impressed and appears shorter. For the bird (D.1038) see No. 239 below. Had it not been for the ovolo, this bowl might well have been assigned to the standard Cinnamus style. It is certainly closer to that than any other bowl in the burnt group. *Level 3 Site 1(74); 3*

344* Form 37, apparently with three leaves in the scroll. The smaller (Rogers J105) is probably on a bowl in Cerialis-Cinnamus style stamped after moulding by Aventinus ii (S. & S. 1958, pl. 156, 3). The larger leaves are Rogers H22 and H76; the bird is D.1038. A bowl from Schleitheim may be from the same mould as the Castleford piece (S. & S. 1958, 8). *Site 1(74); 3*

345* A fragment of form 37 using leaf-tips as a filler, as on Nos 339-40, but the leaf is not the same and has not been identified. *Level 3 Site 1(74); 3*

346-87 See the general note after No. 287. These are all bowls with large winding scrolls of the same general category as Nos 338-45, and like them have a very limited range of leaves and figures comprising: lion and boar (D.778), birds (D.1009, 1038, O.2239B, 2298), leaves (Rogers H22, 37, 51, 99, J105, 178), rosette (Rogers C53) and tree (Rogers N2). *Site 1(74); 3*

388* Form 30 with freestyle decoration. This amusing decoration was used occasionally in the Cerialis-Cinnamus Group, but never, so far as we know, by others. The fish are apparently O.2412 and 2419. One is, it seems, on a bowl probably from Lezoux (S. & S. 1958, pl. 157, 7) which has the same decoration as a mould at Lezoux with a cursive signature of Cerialis ii. The fillers on the Castleford bowl are the usual ones derived from Rogers J178, but here even less than usual was impressed in the mould. *Level 3 Site 1(74); 3*

389* Form 37 with freestyle decoration of an economic turn, with the lion and boar (D.778) and leaf tips, impressed overlapping (Rogers H22). The tree Rogers N2 is the only part of the repertoire not figured before. It occurs on bowls in standard Cinnamus style, e.g. at Southampton (Rogers and Laing 1966, fig. IV, 74), but also in the Cerialis-Cinnamus style (Kenyon 1948, fig. 8, 6). *Level 3 Site 1(74); 3*

390a & b* Two fragments of form 37, one with the ovolo and a large stag (D.867), used by the Sacer Group and Illixo, but also on a Cerialis-Cinnamus bowl at Cambridge. The latter also has the bear to left (D.820), as on the other sherd, and the tree (Rogers N4). The lion and boar (D.778), lion (D.766), horseman (O.251), warrior (D.614) and leaf-tips (from Rogers H22) are all attested for the Sacer Group, Cinnamus ii or for the Cerialis-Cinnamus style. *Level 3 Site 1(74); 3*

391* Form 37, freestyle with a blurred impression of the lion to left (D.766; cf. the last bowl) and the characteristic Cerialis- Cinnamus buds, probably with the shield of the same horseman (O.251) as the last just showing. *Level 3 Site 1(74); 3*

392-417 The remaining freestyle bowls, mainly of form 37, but with a few more examples of form 30, add a considerable number of figure-types to those already attested on Nos 388-91. Almost all have either buds (from Rogers J178) or leaf-tips (from Rogers H22) as fillers. The figure-types are: sea-cow (D.29), Vulcan without tools (D.42), naked man (D.103), horse and rider (D.157), satyr (D.354), naked man (D.403, but smaller), centaur (D.431), pygmy with spear (D.439), sphinx (O.871A), warrior (D.614), bestiarius (D.627A), mask (D.719), lions to left and right (D.775 variant and O.1497G), lion attacking boar (D.778), lioness (D.793), leopard to right (D.798), leopard (of the D.799 type, but smaller), bears to right and left (D.808? and 817), lion to left (O.1633H), boars to right (D.823, 826?), stag kneeling to right (D.845 variant), stag to left (D874), dogs to right and left (D.913? and O.1989A). The only additional motif is the adze-hammer (D.1103). *Site 1(74); 3*

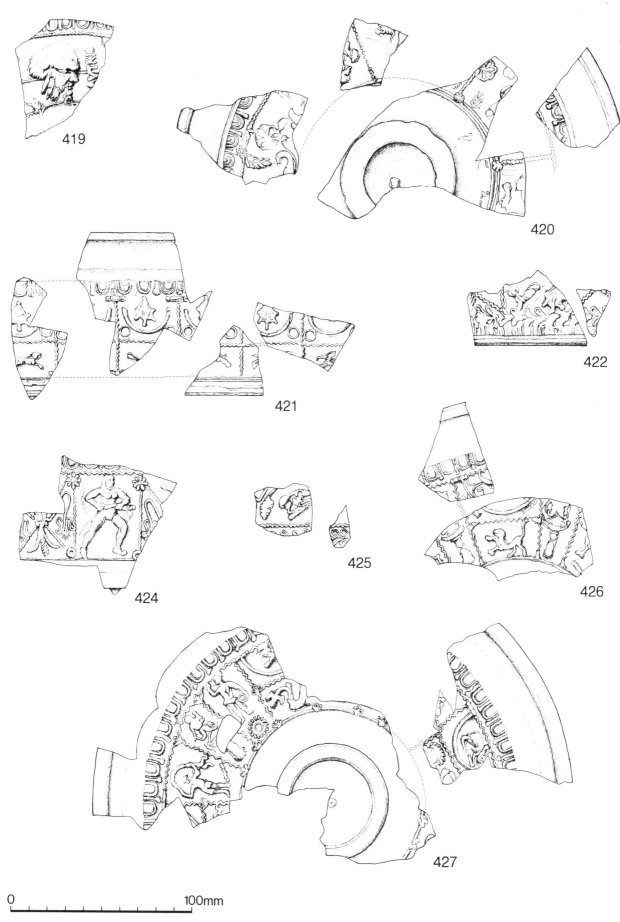

419

420

421

422

424

425

426

427

0   100mm

Fig. 21. Decorated samian from Site 1(74), Phase 3. Scale 1:2

418* Several fragments of form 30 with panels divided both by horizontal beadrows, under the ovolo and above the basal wreath, and by zig-zag lines elsewhere. The small ovolo with forked tongue appears at Lezoux in Trajanic-Hadrianic contexts in 'pre-export' styles and fabrics (Potter P-3 in Rogers's classification). The type in the medallion was winged, presumably either a Cupid or an eagle. No stamped or signed bowls in this style are known, but the style is not normally found in Britain, which implies a date before AD 125 or so. This bowl could either be from an old mould or possibly had a long 'shelf-life.' The fragments are all burnt, however, and the former explanation is perhaps likely. *Level 3 Site 1(74); 3*

419* A single fragment of form 37, from a mould stamped by Butrio of Lezoux (Die 1a). The ovolo (Rogers B213), leafy frond (Rogers J160) and mask (a larger version of D.692) are all already known for him. As often with Butrio's work a setting-out line is still visible. See stamp catalogue No. 600. *Level 3 Site 1(74); 3*

420* Several fragments of a poorly-moulded form 37 with an ovolo (Rogers B114) used by several Lezoux potters, including Butrio and Austrus. The latter also used a large rosette, possibly as here (perhaps Rogers C52, the blurred moulding making identification difficult). The leafy frond (Rogers J160) was a Butrio type, later used by others. A fragmentary figure is a Bacchus (D.534). On balance this bowl is likely to have been one of Butrio's. *Level 3 Site 1(74); 3*

421* Several fragments of form 30. The ovolo, very poorly impressed, is one used by X-6, with the signature Catull- (Rogers B35). The small festoon and leaf (Rogers J91) were both used by Vegetus iii (S. & S. 1958, pl. 62, 2), as was the astragalus (Rogers R6). The use of wavy-line borders without junction masks is uncommon, but is known for Vegetus's associate Avitus (S. & S. 1958, pl. 63, 12). None of the small animals in the lower panels is certainly identifiable. This bowl is most likely to have been made by Vegetus, but if so he must have used the Catull-ovolo. *Level 3 Site 1(74); 3*

422* Several fragments of form 30 of exceptionally bad workmanship. The panel next to the saltire contains an acanthus (Rogers K18?) assigned to one of the early Secundini. However, the leaf (Rogers J91) and the wreath both appear on a stamped bowl of Vegetus iii from Chester (S. & S. 1958, pl. 62, 2). The unusual zone below the wreath is almost certainly a series of overlapping impressions of the Avitus-Vegetus ovolo (Rogers B228) upside down, and it seems highly likely that the bowl was from a Vegetus mould. *Level 3 Site 1(74); 3*

423 A small fragment of form 30. Traces of a guide-line used in setting out the ovolo would normally point to Avitus-Vegetus or one of the Quintilianus Group, but the ovolo here (Rogers B76) was used by Arcanus and Geminus iv. The remaining decoration is an unidentified trilobed leaf. *Site 1(74); 3*

424* Several fragments of form 30. The ovolo (Rogers B228) was used by Avitus-Vegetus and by Bassus iv. The 'tulip' flower (Rogers G137), rosette and ovolo are all on a bowl in the style of Avitus iv (S. & S. 1958, pl. 64, 20), but the small rings are characteristic of the style of Bassus ii and the warrior (D.111) and ovolo are on a bowl at London from a mould signed by him (S. & S. 1958, pl. 73, 41). There was clearly some connection between the work of all the potters named above. *Level 3 Site 1(74); 3*

425* Two small fragments of form 30. The squirrel to right (related to O.2142) was used by Sissus ii, and probably by Pugnus ii. The wreath is the one on No. 422, and suggests origin with Avitus or Vegetus for this bowl. *Level 3 Site 1(74); 3*

426* Fragments of form 37 in one of the styles used by Geminus iv. The ovolo is Rogers B28, always associated in his work with this particular style. The details are a triton (D.20), pedestal (Rogers P80), leafy motif (Rogers M35), lion (D.765 bis) and figure (D.611?). The style is the same as the next bowl. *Level 3 Site 1(74); 3*

427* Several fragments of form 37 with the same ovolo, triton and pedestal as the last bowl and with Geminus's characteristic trilobed motif (Rogers G112) and double astragalus (Rogers R91). The scarf-dancer (D.212) is on a signed bowl in his other style (S. & S. 1958, pl. 65, 1), as is the hare to left (a smaller version of D.950a), which is on a signed bowl from Le Mans and an unsigned bowl from Camelon. The beaded ring (Rogers C294) and dolphin to left (O.2394) are on a signed bowl in his usual style from Chesters (S. & S. 1958, pl. 90, 3). The decoration also includes a warrior (D.106), dolphin to right (O.2385) and hare to right (presumably the counterpart of D.950a). *Level 3 Site 1(74); 3*

428* Form 37 with an unusually clear impression of Geminus iv's commonest ovolo (Rogers B76, which really has a tongue ending in a small, round bead over a small oval one). The spiral plant (Rogers M35) is on a signed bowl of Geminus from York (S. & S. 1958, pl. 65, 1). The urn (D.1075) and column of cups (similar to Rogers Q49 upside down) are on a signed bowl from Vichy at Saint-Germain-en-Laye. The toothed ring (Rogers E75) and trilobe (Rogers G112) are on a signed bowl from Berghausen (S. & S. 1958, pl. 66, 200). Although Geminus used a festoon of the same general type as the medallion on this bowl, the medallion has a smaller diameter and is not in Rogers. *Level 3 Site 1(74); 3*

429* Seven fragments of form 30 with the single-bordered ovolo (Rogers B28) and guide-line of the Quintilianus Group. All the elements of decoration are known to have been used by the Group. They include: Neptune (D.14, without chlamys), Jupiter (D.1), ram's horn motifs (Rogers G359, 361) and eight-beaded rosette (Rogers C281). *Level 3 Site 1(74); 3*

430* Two joining fragments of form 37 with the same ovolo and rosette as the last. These, the bird (O.2296) and the festoon are all on a stamped bowl of Quintilianus i from Dorchester, Dorset (S. & S. 1958, pl. 68,3). *Site 1(74); 3*

431* A sherd of form 37 with the same ovolo as the last. The pygmy (D.440) is on the Dorchester bowl mentioned under No. 430. The top part of the composite motif is Rogers G333, now firmly assignable to the Quintilianus Group. *Level 3 Site 1(74); 3*

432 A sherd of form 37 with the same ovolo as the last three bowls and with traces of a guide-line below it. One of the vertical borders continues into the ovolo, as often in the work of Quintilianus and his associates. *Site 1(74); 3*

433* Two small fragments of form 37 with freestyle decoration. The stag with broken right antler does not appear either in Déchelette or Oswald. The trilobe is on a bowl from Littleborough, Notts in the style of Quintilianus i. *Level 3 Site 1(74); 3*

434 A fragment of form 30, with a saltire panel. A six-petalled rosette at the intersection of the diagonals is on a Quintilianus style bowl at Chester, but two leaves used in the saltire are attested for Tittius or Tittius-Cassia: they are Rogers H109 (?) and H73. However, there are no saltires on the Tittius-Cassia bowls known to us and the attribution of this piece must be left open. *Site 1(74); 3*

435* Several fragments of form 37 with freestyle decoration. The band of spirals replacing the ovolo is on a bowl from Aldborough from a mould stamped by Docilis i and might be thought to be diagnostic of that potter. The tripod is Rogers Q21 upside down, but the lion to left and the griffin have not been identified. The potter cannot yet be named, but was probably related to Docilis or Pugnus ii. *Level 3 Site 1(74); 3*

436* Several fragments of form 30. The ovolo (Rogers B49) has been noted on some unsigned bowls, including one from Cardurnock (Birley 1948, fig. 6, 5) which define the style of an anonymous potter of Lezoux (Rogers's P-14). The trilobe (Rogers G176) and astragalus (Rogers R22) are attested for this potter, but the figure (O.633A) is not, and nor is there a parallel for the use of a freehand arcade formed with a wavy line, though Pugnus ii's associates used one. *Level 3 Site 1(74); 3*

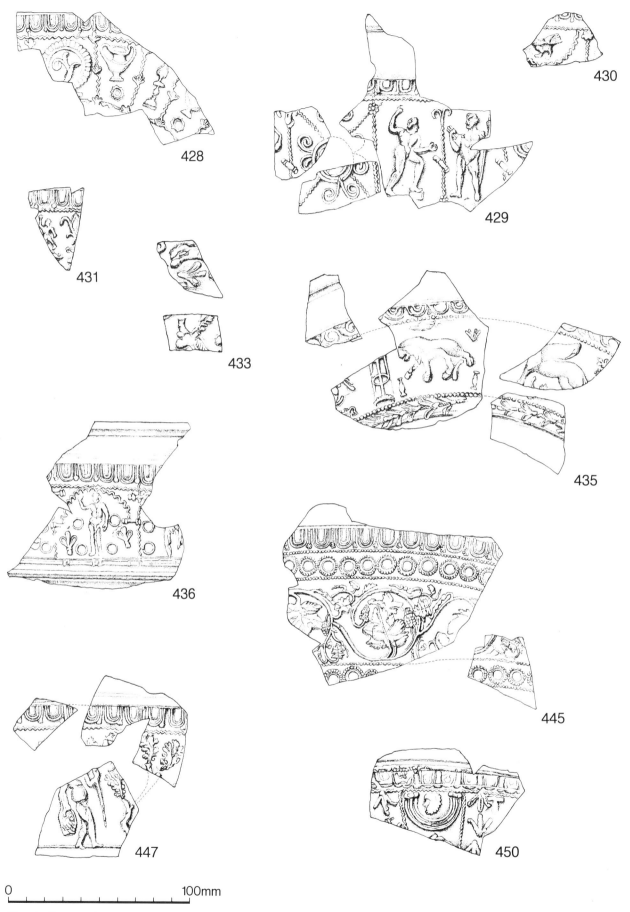

428

430

429

431

433

435

436

445

447

450

0   100mm

Fig. 22. Decorated samian from Site 1(74), Phase 3. Scale 1.2

42

437 A fragment of form 30 with the same ovolo as the last. A freestyle scene includes a bird to left (O.2263B) and a tree as on No. 447 below. Perhaps by P-14 or Pugnus ii. *Site 1(74); 3*

438 A fragment of form 30 with the same ovolo as Nos 436-7. The decoration includes a single-bordered festoon not divided from an adjacent saltire by a border. The astragalus from which the festoon is suspended was used by Vegetus iii (S. & S. 1958, pl. 62, 2 and 4), as was a spiral in the saltire (S. & S. 1958, pl. 63, 11). *Site 1(74); 3*

439 A fragment of form 30 with the same ovolo as Nos 436-8 and a naked male figure (O.676A). *Site 1(74); 3*

440 A fragment of form 30 with the same ovolo as Nos 436-9. An athlete (D.378) recurs on a stamped bowl of Vegetus iii and on a bowl in Quintilianus style, both from Lezoux. There is also a small cup (unidentified) to the left of the figure. *Site 1(74); 3*

441 Two joining fragments of form 30 with the same ovolo as Nos 436-40. The decoration is probably freestyle and includes a deer (a larger version of D.884), and a spiral similar to the one on 438. *Site 1(74); 3*

442 A sherd of form 30 with the same ovolo as Nos 436-41 and part of an unidentified figure. *Site 1(74); 3*

443 Two fragments of form 30 with the same ovolo as Nos 436-42, but without a border underneath. A standing figure as on No. 436 (O.633A) is over a horizontal trilobe attached to an astragalus. To the left of the figure is a leaf on a tendril. In another panel the same figure is between two rings. Presumably by P-14 again. *Site 1(74); 3*

444 A small fragment of form 30 with the same ovolo as Nos 436-43. *Site 1(74); 3*

445* Several fragments of form 37 with an ovolo (Rogers B20) and vine-scroll (Rogers M1), as on a bowl from Nursling from a stamped mould of Secundinus ii (Rogers's Secundinus I: Rogers and Laing 1966, fig. III, 59). Both of these occur, together with the wreaths of beaded rings (Rogers C293) on an unstamped bowl from Carzield (Birley 1946) with virtually the same decoration as the Castleford bowl. *Level 3 Site 1(74); 3*

446 A fragment of form 30 with an ovolo (Rogers B35) occurring on a bowl from Lezoux in one of the styles usually assigned to X-6, but with a cursive signature reading Catull[below the decoration in the mould. A trilobe (Rogers G117?) is probably on a bowl from Chester with a different ovolo of X-6. A fragmentary astragalus is perhaps one used by X-6 on a bowl at Birdoswald (S. & S. 1958, pl. 75, 14). *Site 1(74); 3*

447* Fragments of form 30 with freestyle decoration. The ovolo (Rogers B233) was used by Pugnus ii and his associates. The tree is made up by impressions of separate poinçons (cf. Rogers N5 and bowl No. 437 above). The slave with basket is a variant of D.321. *Level 3 Site 1(74); 3*

448 A sherd of form 30 with the same ovolo as No. 447, but without a border below. A naked man (O.570), here in a single-bordered medallion or arcade, is on a bowl from Lancaster from a mould signed by Drusus ii (S. & S. 1958, pl. 88, 5). *Site 1(74); 3*

449 A sherd from a badly moulded bowl of form 30 with the same ovolo as Nos 447-8 and with no border below it. A figure is too blurred for identification. *Site 1(74); 3*

Numbers 450-55 and 457-9 are all bowls of form 37 with the same ovolo (Rogers B35) as No. 446.

450* Two joining fragments in one of the typical styles of X-6, who used the trilobe (Rogers G32), the triple festoon (Rogers F83) and the mask (O.1213A). cf. No. 457, which may be from the same bowl. *Level 3 Site 1(74); 3*

451* Several fragments from a bowl which probably has alternating wide and narrow panels. The griffin is not known to Déchelette or Oswald. The goose (D.1013) is not otherwise known for X-6, but its counterpart to left is on bowls in his style from Lezoux with a different ovolo (S. & S. 1958, pl. 76, 27) and from Leicester. The blurred figure is Neptune (D.14, without chlamys), also on the Leicester bowl. The pygmy (D.437) is on a bowl from London with this ovolo (S. & S. 1958, pl. 74, 5) and also on No. 453 below. The eagle (D.982) and trilobe are not known for X-6. *Level 3 Site 1(74); 3*

452* Several fragments of form 37 apparently with alternating wide and narrow panels. The figures are: a partly impressed leopard (D.799), the head of a lion (from O.1640?), a bear (not in D. or O., but see Karnitsch 1959, Taf.54, 7) impressed vertically beside a tree (not in Rogers, but used on bowls in Mapillus-Pugnus style). The small trifid is Rogers G29 (used by Cinnamus, Pugnus, in one of his his later styles, and X-6), the large one in the saltire is perhaps his G65, which was used on bowls in the styles of Mapillus, Pugnus and X-6. The beadrows do not have the irregular rectangular beads which go with ovolo B35 in the X-6 style, but regular oval ones, as on a bowl in Mapillus-Pugnus style from Nettleton Scrubb also with this ovolo (Simpson 1982, pl. 69, 77). *Level 3 Site 1(74); 3*

453* Several fragments of form 37 with wavy line borders like the usual X-6 ones, but which do not usually go with this ovolo. The pygmies are D.437 and 439, the latter used by Catull-, the dolphins are not in D. or O., but seem to have been used at Les Martres-de-Veyre (S. & S. 1958, pl. 31, 373). The trifid is Rogers G32, commonly used by X-6, but also by Pugnus and Tittius. *Site 1(74); 3*

454* Several fragments of form 37, with wavy line borders. The boar is D.826 (used by X-6 with a different ovolo). For the large festoon, containing a dolphin, and the larger trifid see No. 453. The smaller trifid is similar to Rogers G97 and G99, but may not be identical to either. See No. 455. *Level 3 Site 1(74); 3*

455 This bowl is from the same mould as No. 454. *Site 1(74); 3*

456 A fragment of form 37, perhaps divided into panels in the same way as Nos 454-5 and with the same large festoon and smaller trifid. A hare (O.2136?) is also on bowls with X-6 ovolos (S. & S. 1958, pl. 75, 20, 22). *Site 1(74); 3*

457 A fragment of form 37 with similar details to No. 450, and perhaps from the same mould. *Site 1(74); 3*

458* Several fragments of form 37 with ovolo as No. 446 and wavy-line borders. The geese (D.1013 and its reverse) are on other bowls from the Group in X-6 style, as are the boar (D.826) and the large festoon. The larger trifid is Rogers G32, the smaller one, at the top of the border, is incomplete and blurred and has not been identified. *Level 3 Site 1(74); 3*

459 A fragment of form 37 with the same ovolo, double festoons, bird to left and trilobe as the last, and possibly from the same mould. *Site 1(74); 3*

460* Two fragments of form 37 with birds as on bowls Nos 451, 458 and 459, but with the ovolo sheared off. The small astragalus across the borders is too blurred for comment, but the general style suggests, in this context, the work of X-6. *Level 3 Site 1(74); 3*

461 Two fragments of form 37 with ovolo as No. 446. A double festoon with mask (D.700) was used by X-6 on several bowls (S. & S. 1958, pl. 75, 13, 18 and 20). An astragalus from which the festoon hangs is probably one known for X-6, though here and elsewhere it is very blurred. *Site 1(74); 3*

462 A fragment of form 37, with a small double festoon or medallion over a wreath of trilobes (Rogers G175?). Almost certainly by a potter associated with X-6 or Pugnus ii. *Site 1(74); 3*

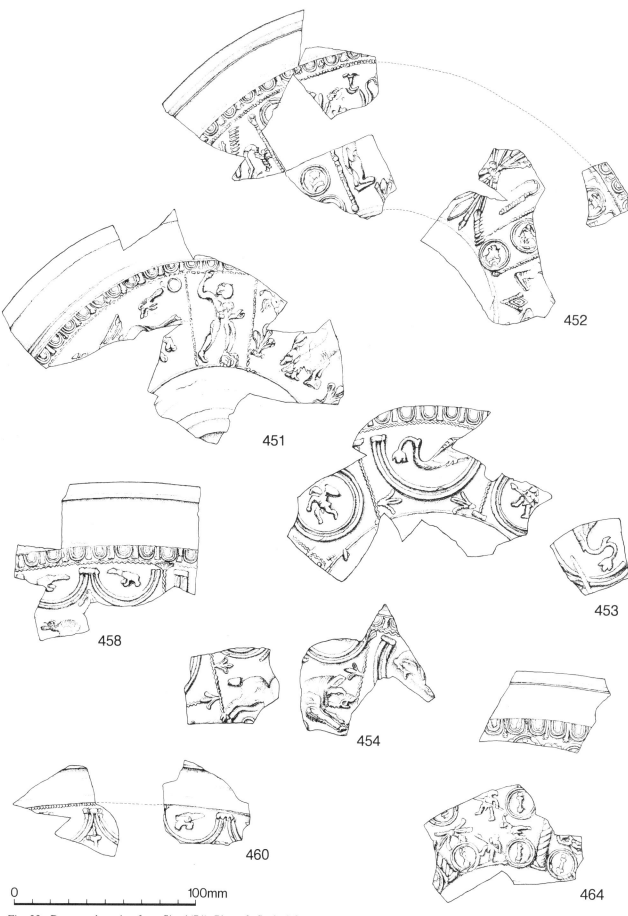

452

451

453

458

454

460

464

0   100mm

Fig. 23. Decorated samian from Site 1(74), Phase 3. Scale 1:2

44

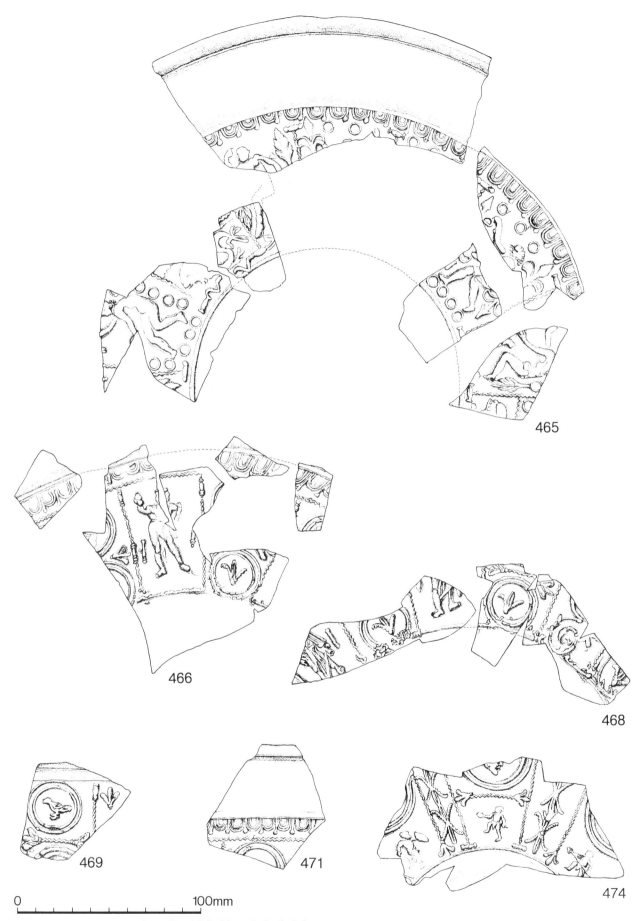

465

466

468

469

471

474

0   100mm

Fig. 24. Decorated samian from Site 1(74), Phase 3. Scale 1:2

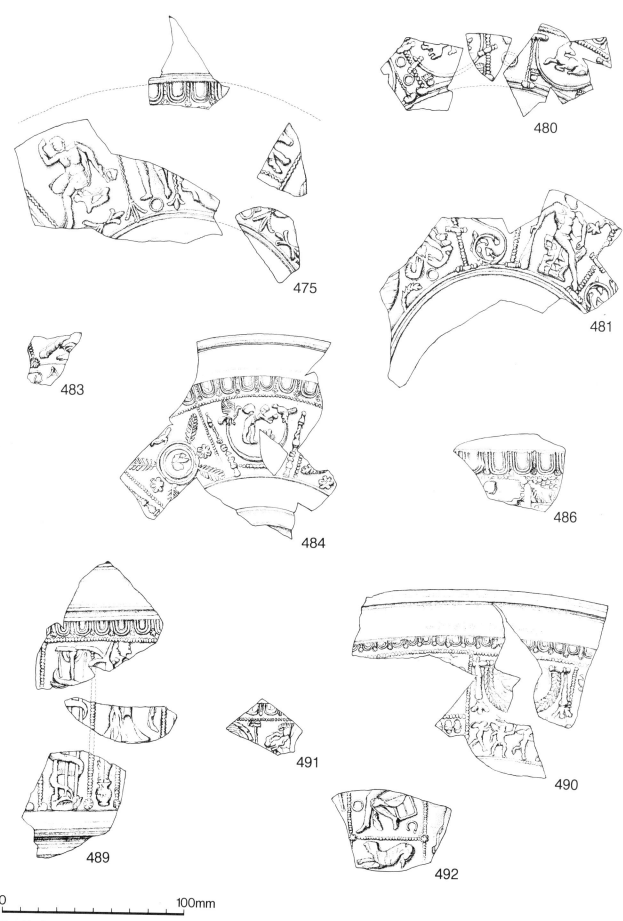

480

475

481

483

484

486

489

491

490

492

0   100mm

Fig. 25. Decorated samian from Site 1(74), Phase 3. Scale 1:2

463 A fragment of form 37 with the same ovolo as No. 446. The decoration was probably panelled, with the borders topped by the trifid plant used on Nos 454-5. A hare (D.950a variant) was used by too many Lezoux potters to be useful. *Site 1(74); 3*

464* Several fragments of form 37 with an ovolo used at Lezoux by Cassia-Tittius, X-6 and probably Pugnus ii (Rogers B32). The trilobed plant (Rogers G32), column (Rogers P66), astragalus (Rogers R22) in small medallions and the pygmy with spear (D.439) were used on bowls with this ovolo at Lezoux and Augst (S. & S. 1958 pl. 75, 18 and 22). The dancing pygmy (D.442) is on a bowl at Chesters with X-6's ovolo 3 (S. & S. 1958, pl. 76, 25). This bowl has stylistic connections with the work of both Pugnus ii and X-6. *Level 3 Site 1(74); 3*

465* Numerous fragments of form 37 with a fragmentary cursive signature, possibly an M, below the decoration. The ovolo (Rogers B233) without a border below, leaf (Rogers H105), chevron (Rogers G283) and round-ended astragalus are on a signed, unpublished bowl of Pugnus ii from Carlisle. Although the figures in the panels are repeated, the fillers in the fields vary from repeat to repeat. The dancer is O.361A (variant without scarf). The dolphin may be O.2394, used by Silvius ii (S. & S. 1958, pl. 77, 2) and on bowls in the style of X-6. The remaining figure is the seated Bacchus (D.534). The other astragalus (like Rogers R63) is on a bowl at Saalburg (Ricken 1939, Taf.28, 17) which has many elements in common with Pugnus. The fleur-de-lys (Rogers G88) was used by X-5, but is not on signed or stamped work of contemporary potters.

Although the style of the Castleford bowl is somewhat unusual, there are enough links with Pugnus, including the profusion of circles in the decoration, to justify the suggestion that it came from his workshop. There is a Pugnus cursive signature]GNIM, with part of the M missing, on a burnt fragment from Castleford (T 45) and, though it cannot be from this bowl, it has the same type of wavy line as here, and also the round-ended astragalus. *Site 1(74); 3*

466* Several fragments of form 37 with badly moulded panelled decoration. This bowl is one of several in the Castleford Group with distinctive style, all using the same ovolo, small double medallions and an astragalus impressed vertically on the borders. (cf. Nos 467-72). The workmanship of all the bowls is astonishingly poor. The ovolo, here impressed diagonally, is Rogers B228, used by Avitus-Vegetus, Bassus iv, and probably other members of the Quintilianus Group, as well as Birrantus and Paullus. The laterally impressed trilobe (Rogers G175) and the one in the medallion (Rogers G32) both occur on X-6 bowls (S. & S. 1958, fig. 18, 10 and 13). The Perseus (D.146) was used by several potters, including Caletus, Cinnamus ii and Secundus v. The astragalus with thin shaft is probably one used by X-6 (S. & S. 1958, fig. 18, 18). For the one on the border, and the general style, cf. three bowls from London (S. & S. 1958, pl. 154, 17-19) related to X-6, Pugnus and Rogers's P-14. *Level 3 Site 1(74); 3*

467 Two sherds of form 37, perhaps from the same mould as No. 468. The bowl is related to No. 466 etc. and has the same small double medallion with trilobe, a horizontal trilobe (Rogers G175), an exceptionally badly moulded Perseus (D.146) and astragali along the borders. A philosopher (D.523) is on one of the London bowls - attributed to Pugnus ii (S. & S. 1958, pl. 154, 19). *Site 1(74); 3*

468* Several fragments of form 37 possibly from the same mould as the last bowl. Most of the details are as on No. 467, but this adds the astragalus flanking the philosopher (cf. S. & S. 1958, fig. 18, 18) and a panel of spirals with a trilobe, as on bowl No. 478, but here impressed vertically. The spiral is on a Birdoswald bowl in X-6 style with ovolo Rogers B32. *Level 3 Site 1(74); 3*

469* Several fragments of form 37 in the same style as No. 466 etc. The double medallion here encloses a bird to left (apparently not in Déchelette or Oswald) which also appears on the next bowl. *Level 3 Site 1(74); 3*

470 Two joining fragments of form 37 with a bird in a double medallion, as on No. 469, and a trilobe on the end of the panel border, as in No. 466. *Site 1(74); 3*

471* A fragment of form 37 with ovolo and double medallion as on No. 466. *Level 3 Site 1(74); 3*

472 A single fragment of form 37 with astragalus impressed vertically along the panel border, as on No. 466 etc. The surviving panel has a vertical column of trilobes (Rogers G32). *Site 1(74); 3*

473 A fragment of form 37 with panelled decoration. One panel is divided by a horizontal band of trilobes (Rogers G97), cf. Nos 454-5 and 463. In the lower half of the panel is an unidentified detail. An adjacent panel may have a gladiator's helmet, but it is not in D. or O., if so. A panel junction is masked by a vertical astragalus as on No. 466 etc. *Site 1(74); 3*

474* Several fragments of form 37, some joining. All the details occur on bowls assigned to X-6 and recur on other bowls in this Group. The pygmies are D.437 and 439. The trilobes are Rogers G32 and G97 and the mask is D.700. Bowls Nos 453-7 offer several parallels for the details and layout. *Level 3 Site 1(74); 3*

475* Several fragments of form 37 with ovolo Rogers B32, used by X-6, Tittius-Cassia and Pugnus ii. The figures are Jupiter (D.1, with only the legs left), Bacchus (D.534), part of a horse belonging to an Amazon (D.153) and dolphin (O.2394). The trilobes are Rogers G32 and G97. cf. No. 465 for the dolphin and No. 474 for the trilobes. Two other undrawn sherds joining each other and probably from this bowl have a goose to right (D.1013) in a narrow panel with trilobes Rogers G32 and G97 at the top of the left and right borders, respectively (cf. No. 479 for the same arrangement at the bottom of a panel and No. 474, where trilobes and horizontal astragali occur at opposite sides of the same panel). *Level 3 Site 1(74); 3*

476 Two sherds of form 37 with a trilobe (Rogers G32) upside down in a narrow panel with horizontal astragali at the bottoms of the borders. The adjacent panel has the seated Bacchus (D.534) as on No. 475, but here with the left foot projecting below the basal ridge. Another panel has a pygmy with shield (D.437) in a double medallion (cf. No. 453 etc.). *Site 1(74); 3*

477 Two fragments of form 37 with panels, one with a vertical series of fleurs-de-lys (Rogers G88) impressed alternately the right way up and reversed. cf. No. 465 for this motif. The adjacent panel, divided horizontally, has a lion looking backwards, as on a bowl in the style of X-6 (S. & S. 1958, pl. 76, 23). *Site 1(74); 3*

478 A fragment of form 37 with a spiral and reversed trifid (Rogers G32), probably part of a symmetrical arrangement with the spiral repeated, laterally inverted, on the other side. No. 479 has the same device. *Site 1(74); 3*

479 A fragment of form 37 with a double basal ridge. One panel has a dolphin to left, as on No. 453. The next one has a spiral and trifid as on the last bowl. The trilobe on the bottom of the vertical wavy border is Rogers G97, as on No. 454 etc. *Site 1(74); 3*

480* Several fragments from a small bowl of form 37. The ovolo (Rogers B114) was used by several Lezoux potters, including Austrus. The double-D ornament (Rogers U181) at the bottom of the borders, the astragali across them, and the distinctive cups (not in Rogers, and not as in S. & S. 1958, fig. 25, 6, but well-attested on bowls at Lezoux) are diagnostic for Austrus. The animals are a leopard (O.1554) and a kneeling doe (a larger version of O.1752). The double ridge below the decoration on this and No. 482 is almost invariably present on his bowls. *Level 3 Site 1(74); 3*

481* Several fragments of form 37. For the astragali across the borders cf. No. 480. The first panel probably has a boat (D.574) alongside the triton (D.18) and leafy spray (Rogers J167). The vine-scroll is Rogers M23, the Hercules is a larger version of D.450 and the ivy-leaf is Rogers J143. Style of Austrus. *Level 3 Site 1(74); 3*

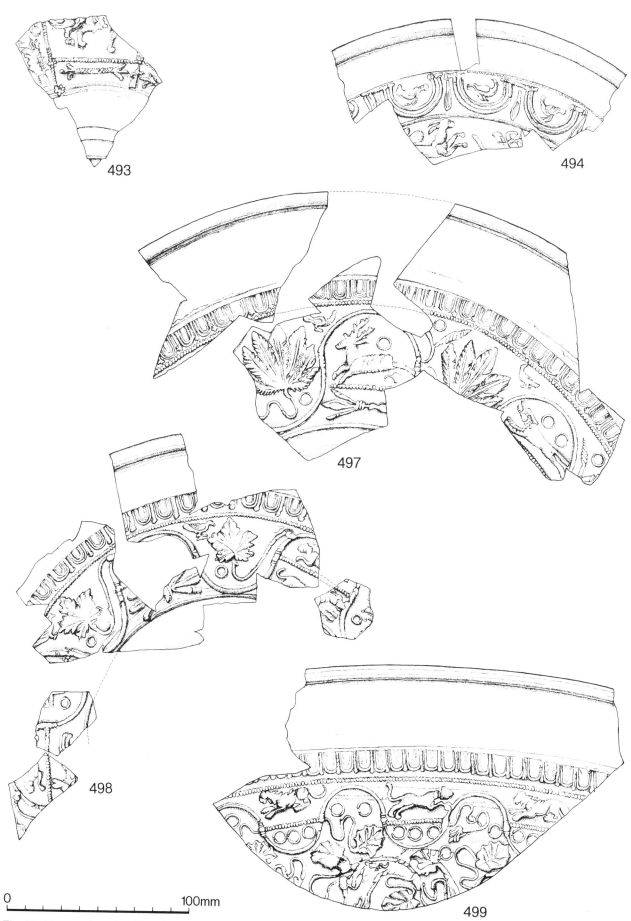

493

494

497

498

499

0   100mm

Fig. 26. Decorated samian from Site 1(74), Phase 3. Scale 1:2

482 A sherd of form 37 with Austrus's vine-scroll, as on No. 481. *Site 1(74); 3*

483* A small fragment of form 37, from a mould signed ACA[, retrograde, below the decoration. This is part of the longer signature used by Acaunissa. The rosette is Rogers C249, the figures are a pygmy, impressed horizontally (D.442), and probably the boar D.833. See stamp catalogue No. 559. *Site 1(74); 3*

484* Several fragments of form 37 with Acaunissa's smaller ovolo (Rogers B22) and many details used by him, including birds O.2278 and a smaller version of O.2317, a poorly impressed mask (also on a bowl from London in a panel with the same arrangement as this: S. & S. 1958, pl. 79, 3), rosette (Rogers C30), leaf (Rogers J121), and composite column (cf. S. & S. 1958, pl. 80, 18-20). The Cupid in the festoon is not known to D. or O. and we have not seen it before on Acaunissa bowls. The suspension of the festoon from birds is an unusual feature. *Level 3 Site 1(74); 3*

485 Several fragments of form 37 with the same ovolo as the last bowl. The scheme of decoration is a zone of festoons (suspended from birds as on No. 484) containing the vine-scroll Rogers M14 over a series of medallions (Rogers E30) separated by short bead rows ending in rosettes (Rogers C249) and containing the rosette Rogers C30. Acaunissa was more original in his schemes of decoration than most of his contemporaries, and there is no precise parallel to this piece, though some of the same general ideas occur on S. & S. pls 79-80. *Site 1(74); 3*

486* A sherd of form 37, with Acaunissa's larger ovolo (Rogers B5), the dancer (D.188), the tripod-with-basket (Rogers Q1) and his small rosette (Rogers C429). *Site 1(74); 3*

487 Two joining fragments of form 37. A large cogged medallion (Rogers E6) containing an Amazon (D.155) and a kilted warrior (D.102) are on a bowl from London in the style of Acaunissa (S. & S. 1958, pl. 81, 24). The Amazon is on a signed bowl from Lincoln (S. and S. 1958, 22). *Site 1(74); 3*

488 A fragment of form 37 with Acaunissa's smaller ovolo (Rogers B22). One panel contains part of a triangular leaf (Rogers J137). *Site 1(74); 3*

489* Several fragments of form 30. The ovolo is Rogers B16, (used by Sacer i and Rogers's P-9), the tripod is Rogers Q14, the Apollo is D.55, the caryatid D.656 and the fragmentary skirted figure is a Minerva D.77. The cornucopia used as a filler is Rogers U248, and the rosette on the borders is Rogers C175. The general style and the potters known to have used the various figures and motifs suggest that this is the work of one of the Sacer Group. *Level 3 Site 1(74); 3*

490* Several fragments of a bowl of form 37 with Rogers B14 as ovolo. The festoon and the trilobe pendant are not in Rogers, though the festoon is on a stamped bowl of Sacer from Dragonby (May 1996, 593 no. 45). The Cupids are D.247 and 249. The so-called DD monogram, really just an ordinary motif, was used at Les Martres-de-Veyre but, more importantly for our purposes, also on a stamped bowl of Sacer from Besançon (unpublished?). As the ovolo was used by Sacer, and the Cupids by Sacer and Attianus respectively, this bowl should be by Sacer or a close associate. *Level 3 Site 1(74); 3*

491* A small sherd of form 37. The ovolo (Rogers B74) was used by several Lezoux potters, including Butrio (a mould at Lezoux), Anunus i, Quintilianus i and Senila. The gladiator is D.587. The beads definitely exclude some of the potters who used the ovolo. Attribution is best left open. *49 Site 1(74); 3*

492* A fragment of form 30 with the Jupiter D.4 and a leopard, a variant of O.1566. The rosettes on the junctions suggest Attianus ii, and the leopard is on a bowl in his style from Wroxeter (Atkinson 1942, pl. 41, H55) and was also used by Drusus ii. This is clearly by a member of the Sacer Group. *Level 3 Site 1(74); 3*

493* Three fragments of a bowl of form 37 from a worn mould. The griffin (cf. O.866 and bowl No. 500 below) was originally used at Les Martres-de-Veyre, but later transmitted to Lezoux, where it was used on bowls in the style of Sacer i (Hartley 1957, fig.14). The caryatid is O.1207A, the trifid is not in Rogers (but cf. his G89-123). The rosette in Rogers C280. We suspect origin with one of the Sacer Group. *Level 3 Site 1(74); 3*

494* Several fragments of form 37 whose ovolo has been cut away. It is a standard bowl in the zonal style of Sacer with birds (D.1019 and O.2298), goat (O.1842) and tree (Rogers N16). *Level 3 Site 1(74); 3*

495 A sherd of form 37, possibly from the same bowl as the last, showing the festoon in the upper zone and a dog (O.2039N), used by Sacer, in the lower zone. There is a double ridge, such as Sacer occasionally used, below the decoration. *Site 1(74); 3*

496 A sherd of form 37, perhaps belonging to No. 494, with ovolo cut away and the same upper zone. *Site 1(74); 3*

497* Fragments giving about half of a bowl of form 37. The ovolo is Rogers B17, used by Attianus. The leaf is Rogers H58, the trifid Rogers G76, the birds D.1019 and O.2298, as on No. 494. The stag is D.874 and the dog O.20390. All the details were used by Sacer and Attianus, the precise style here suggesting the latter. *Level 3 Site 1(74); 3*

498* Several fragments of form 37 in the style of a potter who used the cursive signature Paternus in his moulds, and is labelled Paternus iv in the Index of Potters' Stamps. The double trifid is on a signed bowl from Barnsley Park villa (Hartley 1983, 171, 9 but with the relevant sherd missing from the drawing). The ovolo is Rogers B231, frequently used by Cinnamus, but the leaf (similar to Rogers H74) is only known on this man's work and appears on another bowl from Barnsley Park (Hartley 1983, 171, 10) with the panther of this bowl (D.805). The bird is O.2239C, the hare is D.952, but the dog has not been identified. cf. Nos 499 and 519 for other bowls by this potter. *Level 3 Site 1(74); 3*

499* Several, large joining fragments giving the greater part of a bowl of form 37. All the motifs occur on other bowls with the same ovolo (Rogers B77) with details used by Paternus iv. The panther is O.1512, the lion is probably O.1423 or 1424. Neither the leaf, nor the bud is illustrated by Rogers. The rings, the larger of two sizes used by Paternus, are on a bowl from the Gorhambury villa in his style (Dannell 1990, 199, 31). The complicated design with a double layer of scroll is an unusual feature, unparalleled in the work of other potters, though there is another similar (unprovenanced) bowl probably by this man.

An added detail which helps to confirm the attribution to Paternus, is the presence of horizontal striations in the mould, a feature often occurring in this man's work. *Site 1(74); 3*

500 Two fragments of form 37 with the same ovolo as the last. The decoration is probably freestyle and has parts of two dolphins, a harpy (O.863B?) and the head of a griffin, close to O.866, or perhaps the one on No. 493, if that is different. Too many potters used this ovolo for attribution to be possible. *Site 1(74); 3*

501 A fragment of form 37 with an ovolo used by Sacer and his associates (Rogers B18). The decoration includes a bird to left (O.2298). *Site 1(74); 3*

502* Two fragments of form 37 with the same ovolo as the last. The types are: a stag (D.867), lion (D.766), lioness (D.793), tree made up of individual branches (Rogers U281), tufts (Rogers L19) and an acanthus (Rogers K2 partly impressed). All are on stamped or signed bowls of Sacer or Attianus, and there is part of the first letter of a signature, almost certainly an S, below the decoration, so presumably this is a Sacer bowl. *Level 3 Site 1(74); 3*

503 A fragment of form 37 with the same tufts as No. 502, and possibly from the same bowl. *Site 1(74); 3*

502

505

514

515

516

517

518

519

521

0   100mm

Fig. 27. Decorated samian from Site 1(74), Phase 3. Scale 1:2

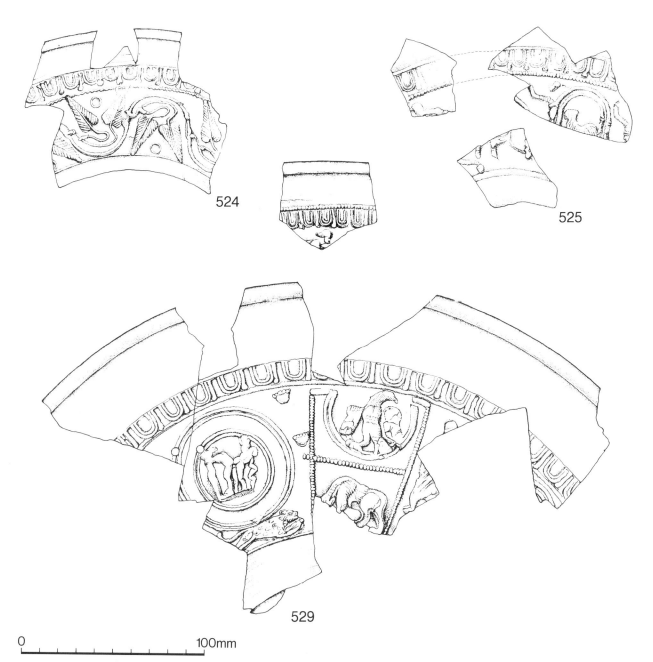

524

525

529

0 ⊢———————————— 100mm

Fig. 28. Decorated samian from Site 1(74), Phase 3. Scale 1:2

504 A fragment of form 37 with the same ovolo as No. 501 and a vine-leaf (Rogers H23) partly impressed, as on signed bowls of Sacer (S. & S. 1958, pl. 83, 9, 11 and 12). *Site 1(74); 3*

505* Two fragments of form 37 with ovolo Rogers B204, used by Attianus and Criciro. The lion, probably O.1424, is on a signed bowl of Criciro at Chester (S. & S. 1958, pl. 117, 5) and a slightly smaller version is on a stamped Attianus bowl from Middlewich. *Level 3 Site 1(74); 3*

506 A fragment of form 37 with the same stag and acanthus (here fully impressed) as No. 502 above. *Site 1(74); 3*

507-13 Fragments of eight bowls, all showing only Sacer's smallest ovolo (Rogers B14). *Site 1(74); 3*

514* A fragment of form 30 with an ovolo (Rogers B36) used by Drusus ii. The head in the first panel belongs to a tambourine dancer (D.210) and it and the six-beaded rosette (Rogers C278) are typical of Drusus. The leaf impressed over the vertical border is part of a baluster-like ornament, a smaller version of Rogers Q5, known on a bowl in Drusus style from Ambleside. *Level 3 Site 1(74); 3*

515* A fragment of form 37 with the same ovolo as the last. The upraised arm is part of a slave, a larger version of D.374. The lion is O.1403A in the festoon Rogers F41, and the Cupid is D.236. All the motifs are known on signed bowls of Drusus, apart from the lion, which occurs on a bowl in his style at Silchester (S. & S. 1958, pl. 89, 15). *Level 3 Site 1(74); 3*

516* A fragment of form 30 with a finely beaded vertical border typical of one of Drusus ii's styles. The slave, a larger version of D.374 (cf. the last bowl), is on a signed Drusus bowl from Doncaster (Dickinson 1986a, p. 133, 29) and the leaf (Rogers G200) is on a bowl in his style from Utrecht (S. & S. 1958, 89, 13). *Level 3 Site 1(74); 3*

517* Several fragments of form 30 with the same ovolo as No. 514. The Abundance (O.800) was used on a bowl at Wroxeter with a cursive signature almost certainly Drusus ii's (Atkinson 1942, pl. 41, H60). The junction-mask is also almost certainly his six-beaded rosette (Rogers C278). Neither the naked man (D.393), nor the eagle in the next panel, is known to have been used by Drusus. Nevertheless this must be his work, as it is evidently from the same mould as No. 518. *Level 3 Site 1(74); 3*

51

518* Several fragments of form 30, probably from the same mould as the last, and with the same naked man and eagle. The lantern (Rogers Q65) and Cupid are both on a signed Drusus bowl from Lancaster (S. & S.1958, pl. 50, 593). The small athlete is probably a version of D.403 and the large rosette (Rogers C87) is typical of Drusus, as are the scattered rings in the field. *Site 1(74); 3*

519* Many fragments of form 37 which could be from the same mould as a bowl from the Barnsley Park villa with a signature in the nominative of Paternus iv of Lezoux (Hartley 1983, 171, 9, but with some of the decoration missing from the drawing). Only the acanthus and ram's horn of this piece are missing at Barnsley Park. The details are Venus (D.175), stag (O.1704A), trifid (Rogers G76), large rosette (Rogers C62?), seven-beaded rosette, acanthus (Rogers K22), and ram's horn (falling between Rogers G365 and 368). *Level 3 Site 1(74); 3*

520 A fragment of form 37 with one of the ovolos of Criciro v (S. & S. 1958, fig. 33, 1). *Site 1(74); 3*

521* Several fragments of form 37 in the style of the Large-S Potter, whose work is distinct from X-6's. The ovolo is Rogers B24. The panels have: a captive (D.642 bis), birds (D.1038, 1019), stag (D.854), Venus (D.176), man with staff (D.338) and trilobe (Rogers G233). *Level 3 Site 1(74); 3*

522 A fragment of form 37 with the same medallions as the last bowl, one containing the bird D.1038 and with a ring between it and the next medallion. This could perhaps be from the same bowl as the last. *Site 1(74); 3*

523 A fragment of form 37 with parts of three panels, but with only a trilobe (Rogers G233) and a lion (O.1404) identifiable in one of the panels. This is in the style of the Large-S Potter. *Site 1(74); 3*

524* Several fragments of form 37, giving the complete scheme of decoration. The ovolo (Rogers B233), leaf (Rogers J33), rings and wavy line were all used on bowls in a Pugnus-Mapillus style (S. & S. 1958, pl. 153), which can be difficult to split into the work of the individual potters. *Level 3 Site 1(74); 3*

525* Several fragments of form 37. Other pieces of the same bowl were found in Trench 10, some 15 yards away (see No. 1005). The ovolo (Rogers B231) was used by Cinnamus, Paternus iv (see No. 498), Sacer, X-7 and, perhaps, Pugnus ii. The unusual decoration of this piece, with festoons put together to form oval medallions, seems to rule out all these potters, except Paternus iv and Pugnus, both of whom used unconventional decoration sometimes. The small bobbin-like filler (Rogers U59) was used by Paternus, but the cornucopia (Rogers U245) occurs on a bowl assigned to Pugnus by Rogers. The cockerel (D.1026) does not help with attribution. *Level 3 Site 1(74); 3*

General comments on the samian from the 'pottery shop'

The quantity of burnt fragments of samian ware found in Level 3, or in later layers derived from it, was so large that there is no doubt that it came from a wholesaler's store, or more probably, in view of the nature of the structures on the site, a shop or shops selling pottery, perhaps together with other goods. We have used the term 'pottery shop' as a convenient label. That one or the other interpretation must be right is clear from the burnt state of the whole collection, combined with the unworn state of the footrings and the presence of the sandy grit used to prevent fusion of stacked pots in the kiln inside many of the bases. Such grit normally disappeared rapidly when

samian was used and washed. While the shop must have been in the area excavated, or close to it, material derived from the deposit became widely scattered. Many individual sherds of the same nature have been found in the fort, though comparatively few were demonstrably burnt. Part of another substantial deposit of burnt samian of the same kind was cut through by a service trench in Dixon Street, about 65m to the south.

Decorated ware

One general point must be made first: namely, that a very high proportion of the decorated bowls are either from more-or-less worn moulds or were blurred in removal from their moulds. The implication seems to be either that Castleford was landed with a batch of near-seconds, or that, if we are truly dealing with a shop, the better bowls of the batch had sold readily and the shelves were left stocked with the poorer specimens. It would be interesting to know if this happened regularly in the *vici* of forts in frontier provinces, but so far as we know, no-one has tested the matter.

Apart from a few bowls apparently in the styles of potters who worked at Les Martres-de-Veyre (Nos 285-7), all the material is by potters of Lezoux. Without prejudging the fine detail, we can say that all students of samian ware would agree that the range of the material as a whole must fall within the late-Hadrianic to early Antonine period. It may be helpful first to list the quantities of bowls in each of the main styles reasonably securely identified.

Acaunissa	6	Pugnus ii or associates	6
Avitus-Vegetus	2 + 1?	Pugnus ii/X-6/Cassius	15
Austrus	3	Quintilianus Group	6
Bassus iv	1	Sacer Group	20
Butrio	2	Secundinus ii	1
Catul-including X-6	12	A-10	1
Cerialis-Cinnamus	129	P-14*	9
Criciro	1	X-9	2
Drusus ii	5	X-12	1
Geminus iv	3	Large-S Potter	2
Paternus iv	3	*Now known to be Pugnus ii	

Some twenty potters supplied about 230 decorated bowls, though it will be noted that the Cerialis-Cinnamus contribution just outweighs all the rest put together. The average of 11.5 bowls per potter is obviously misleading, since if we leave the Cerialis-Cinnamus bowls aside the average is about five pots per maker. (The corresponding figures for identified stamps on plain ware are: 55 potters making 410 pots, i.e. almost eight pots per man.)

The plain samian

The range of the plain samian was not great, and for most of the forms there is surprisingly little variation in detail and proportions between vessels, especially in view of the number of potters involved, attested by 425 identified stamps, two of them illiterate, from 70 different dies. It is impossible to estimate the total number of vessels

Table 6. Forms used by 'pottery shop' potters.

Potter	Die	30	37	18/31	18/31R	27	31	33	38	42	44	79/80	44/81
Acaunissa	Curs.		*										
Agedillus ii	2a			*	+	+		*		+			*
Ambitotus	1a			*	*	*	*	*	*?				
Attianus ii	7a			*	*	*	*	+	+				*
Atticus ii	2a			*	+	*	*	*	*	+		+	
Banvillus	2a			*	*	*	*	*	*				
Banvillus	Inc. 1			*	+	+	+	+	+				
Beliniccus i	9d			*	*	+	+	*					
Biturix	1f			*	+	*	*	*		+			*
Borillus i	10a			*	*	+	+	*	+			+	
Burdo	6a			+	+	*	+	*	+			*?	
Butrio	1a	*	*										
Calava	2b			*	*	*	*	*	*				
Caratedo	1a			*	*			*					
Caratillus	1a												
Cassius i	Inc. 1		+	*		*		*					
Cassius i	Inc. 2		+	*		+		+					
Cerialis ii	2a		+	*	*	*	*	*	*?			+	
Cerialis ii	9a/a'		+	*	*	*	*	*				+	
Cerialis ii	Inc. 1		+	*	+	+	+	+				+	
Cintusmus i	4a			*	*	*	*	*	*?	*		+	
Cracissa	4a			+	*	*	*	*	*	*			
Cracuna i	2a			*		*	*	*	*				
Dagomarus	11a			*	+	+							
Divicatus	3a			*	*	*	*	*	+		*	+	+
Divicus	1e			+		+	*	+					
Doccalus	4a		+	*	+	*	+	*					+
Doccalus	5c		+	+	*	*	*	*					
Episus	1a					*		+					*
Felix ii	2a			*	*	*	*	+	+?				
Felix ii	2d			*	+	+	*	*	+?				
Geminus vi	6c			*	+	+	+	+	+				
Gnatius ii	4a			*		*	+	*	+				*
Littera i	1b			*	*	*		*	*				
Lupoisucus	1a							*					*
Maiudilus	3a			*	*	*		*					
Malliacus	3h			*	*	*	*	*	+			+?	
Mallus	2b			*	*	*		+	+				
Muxtullus	1b			*	*	*	*	*	+				
Muxtullus	5a			*	+	*	+	*	+				
Pateratus	1a			*	*	*	*	*					*
Paternus iii	2b	+	+	*	+	*	*	*	+				
Paullus iv	3b	+	+	+	+	*	+	*				+	
Paullus iv	3g	+	+	*	+	*	*	*	+			+	
Primigenus ii	3a			*			+						
Priscinus	1d		+	+	+	*	+	*		+		+	
Pugnus ii	1b	+	*	+	+	*	+	*	+			+	

53

Table 6 continued. Forms used by 'pottery shop' potters.

Potter	Die	30	37	18/31	18/31R	27	31	33	38	42	44	79/80	44/81
Pugnus ii	Inc. 2	+	+	*	+	+	+	+	+			+	
Putrimus	1a			*		*		*	*				
Quintilianus i	1b	+	+	*	*	+	+	+	+				
Roppus ii	1a			*	*	*							
Ruffus ii	1a			*	*	*	*	*	+				
Sacisamo	1a							*					
Sacr(i)emus	1a			*		*							
Sacroticus	1a		+	*	+	*	+	*	+			+	+
Secundus v	5a		+	*	*	*	*	*	*			+	*
Secundus v	Inc. 2		+	+	*	+	+	+	+			+	+
Severus v	1b			*	+	+	+	*	*	+			
Severus v	2a			*	*	*	*	*	+	+			
Severus v	6e			+	+	*	+	*	+	+			
Sextus ii	2b			+		*		*	*				
Sollemnis i	5a	*		*	*	*	*	*					
Sollemnis i	Inc. 1			+	*	+	+	+	+				
Sulp-Certus	2a												
Suservio- Cer-	1a			*			*						
Tertullus ii	Uncertain 1												*
Tintirio	4a			*	*	*	+	+	+			+	
Tittius	4b		+	+	*	+	+	+					
Vespo	1a			*	*	*	*	*	*?	+			*

* indicates the same die; + another die of the same man

represented by the fragments, but a minimum number may be deduced from the potters' stamps, which will also serve as a guide to the approximate proportions of the different forms. It need scarcely be stated that the deposit excavated only contained part of the burnt material, which was widely scattered. The total of identified stamps was distributed between the main forms as follows: 18/31 - 140; 18/31R - 26; 27 - 119; 33 - 110; 44/81 or 81 - 17. In addition there were many bowls of Curle (1911) form 11, all unstamped, as usual, a few examples of form 35/36, almost always unstamped in Central Gaul, and of form 38 (with no certain stamps). A conservative estimate of the minimum number of plain vessels in the group would therefore be of the order of 500-600, with the probability that the true number would be considerably higher.

Form 18/31, with 34% of the stamped vessels, was the single most popular form; the shallower variant was by far the most common. The forms invite comparison with the Birdoswald Alley group of period Ia (before AD 139), but may also be matched in Antonine contexts in Scotland.

Form 18/31R was relatively uncommon, with only 6% of the stamped pieces. Again the form, which is characteristic of the Hadrianic-Antonine period, is paralleled both at Birdoswald and in Scotland.

Form 27 had almost 29% of the stamps, thus being scarcely less frequent than form 18/31 and with almost the same proportion as form 33, a fact which is clearly significant for the date of the group. There was little variation in the precise form, or indeed in the size. The very high flat upper wall characteristic of the latest varieties is absent, but flat upper walls are normal.

Form 33, with 26.5 % of the stamps, showed much more variation than form 27. The wide range in size (with some very large examples by such potters as Cerialis and Vespo) was coupled with variation in form, some examples being reminiscent of the older South Gaulish type and its copies at Les Martres-de-Veyre, particularly seen in the internal moulding at the junction of wall and base. Two or three others had the slightly beaded lip which occasionally appears in the mid-2nd-century.

Form 35/36 (always unstamped) was rare, and always appeared to belong to the true intermediate 35/36 type rather than to forms 35 and 36. One or two examples may possibly not have had barbotine leaves on the rim.

Form 38 was uncommon, and none of the walls could certainly be associated with a stamped base. The variant with bead lip was used, the flanges being noticeably rounded. Although form 38 is typically Antonine, examples noted at Lezoux in contexts demanding late Hadrianic date also have rounded flanges.

Form 44/81 and form 81 were surprisingly frequent in the group and it is interesting that no fewer than a third of the potters represented at Castleford are attested as making it. It emerged in Central Gaul under Trajan or early under Hadrian and may be taken as characteristic of the period 120-55. The cordoned variety 44/81 seems always to have been stamped in the base, the one with thickened upper wall, form 81 proper, was stamped on the collar, but sometimes in the base as well, though no example certainly with two stamps was in the group.

Form Curle 11 (1911) was surprisingly common in the shop, where the examples all have a large, strongly down-turned flange and stand typologically at the end of the series. The rarity of such bowls in Antonine contexts could be taken as significant for dating the Castleford group.

The remaining forms comprised at least two inkwells, one or two examples of Curle 23 (1911) in typologically early variants, and a few jars approximating to Déchelette 72, but without any decoration.

Taking the plain ware as a whole, the only surprises are the relative commonness of forms 44/81, 81 and Curle 11 (1911), but if the context was truly a shop or a wholesaler's store, this may simply reflect some degree of unpopularity with customers.

For the range of plain forms associated with stamps, see Table 6.

The date of the group

The plain ware is in general Hadrianic-Antonine and most of the forms are very close to those in the Birdoswald Alley group (Birley 1930), and to the typologically early pieces in the Antonine Scottish forts. More cannot be said.

The decorated ware obviously tells the same tale, though it is noticeable that some bowls are from moulds which must have been made in the earlier 120s at the latest. Apart from the Cerialis-Cinnamus bowls, practically all the pieces could be from moulds made in the Hadrianic period, though they would be at home in the early years of the Scottish occupation, too.

The negative evidence of the absence of the standard Cinnamus style, and of the work of other common potters who began production around AD 150, such as Albucius or Divixtus, shows that the fire must have happened before AD 150. The crucial bowls for dating are the Cerialis-Cinnamus ones, however. The evidence has already been discussed in connection with No. 245, above, and it will be enough to quote the conclusion here, namely that there is no reason why such bowls should not have been in production by AD 140, and it is possible that they appeared a little before that. The trend of the evidence from the decorated ware is clear. The fire must have been between AD 140 and 150, probably nearer the former date.

Phase 3, later than the 'pottery shop'

The following pots come from Phase 3, but from contexts later than the 'pottery shop'. They are unburnt.

526 A fragment of form 37 with a vine-scroll (Rogers M2) in a large double medallion. This is likely to belong to a bowl in the standard style of Cinnamus (cf. S. & S. 1958, pl. 160, 41). *c.* AD 150-80. *Site 1(74); 3*

527 A fragment of form 37 with Cinnamus's ovolo 1 (Rogers B231) and a winding scroll. *c.* AD 150-80. *Site 1(74) ; 3*

528 A fragment of form 37 with a panel containing a large double medallion. A small double medallion in a double festoon in the adjacent panel and the hollow bead on the end of the border are both on a stamped bowl of Divixtus i from Cirencester. An astragalus (S. & S. 1958, fig. 33, 1) is on a stamped bowl from Corbridge (S. & S. 1958, pl. 115, 7). *c.* A.D. 150-80. *Site 1(74); 3*

529* Several fragments of form 37, drilled for riveting. The ovolo (Rogers B231) and all the figures were used by Cinnamus, but not with a straight line below the ovolo. The concentric medallions and a different ovolo with a similar straight line are on a stamped bowl of Secundus v from Great Chesterford (Simpson and Rogers 1969, 6, 4), and the bowl must be attributed to him. The figures are the erotic group (O. B), philosopher (D.523), leopard (D.787), eagle (D.981) and bear (D.817). *c.* AD 150-80. *Site 1(74); 3*

Phase 4, later than the 'pottery shop'

The following pots came from excavated Levels 1 and 2 which sealed the 'pottery shop' levels:

530 Five fragments from a panelled bowl of form 37. The ring-tongued ovolo (Rogers B105) was used by Paternus v and many of his associates. The sequence of panels is: i) Cupid with torches (D.265); ii) a warrior (D.177); iiia) a dolphin to right (D.1050) in a single-bordered festoon; iiib) a dolphin to left (O.2393). A rosette used at the top of the vertical borders (S. & S. 1958, fig. 30, 26), an astragalus (S. & S. 1958, 12) and rhomboidal beads suggest that this is the work of Paternus himself. *c.* AD 160-95. *Levels 1-2 Site 1(74); 4*

531 A fragment from a panelled bowl of form 37. A combination of horizontal and vertical astragalus borders was used by Censorinus ii, as was an Apollo (O.91B). The adjacent panel perhaps includes a dolphin. *c.* AD 160-90. *Levels 1-2 Site 1(74); 4*

532 A fragment of form 37. Although residual, and a very small fragment, this piece is of particular interest, as it is the only decorated ware from Castleford in the early Cinnamus style which at Lezoux is associated with his plain ware stamps in the nominative. Elsewhere, it goes with his cursive signature inscribed below the decoration of moulds. The ovolo of this piece (not in Rogers) occurs in a pit at Lezoux with the Cinnamus stamps referred to above and also with the work of Sacer and Attianus. Some of the Lezoux pieces are without a border below the ovolo, but have one above it, as here. The fragmentary figure appears to be a sphinx to right. *c.* AD 130-40. *Levels 1-2 Site 1(74); 4*

Discussion of samian later than the 'pottery shop'

It is remarkable that the samian from those parts of the *vicus* dealt with here scarcely includes any of the standard Antonine decorated ware of the second half of the 2nd century. Either there was little or no occupation of the area, or the levels containing later material have been totally removed. It will be observed, however, that if there was later occupation, it cannot have involved the presence of pits filled with discarded rubbish.

The sources of the samian ware

The pattern of supply to the areas of the *vicus* included here is very clear. All the 1st-century material is South Gaulish and it is virtually certain that all is from La Graufesenque. Some of the earliest 2nd-century samian will also be from La Graufesenque, but export from that centre to the Province ended about AD 110, and its place was taken to some extent in Britain in general by Les Martres-de-Veyre. But Les Martres wares are not conspicuously common in Phase 2 (cf. Nos 233-45 and stamp No. 551). The same applies to other parts of the *vicus*, and also to the fort, whatever the reason.

The groups from the 'pottery shop' are dominated completely by Lezoux ware, even though one or two of the decorated bowls may have been made at Lezoux in moulds manufactured at Les Martres (Nos 285-7). The very sparse samian later than the 'shop' is also all from Lezoux, and none is necessarily later than AD 160.

The East Gaulish samian kilns are only represented by one decorated bowl (No. 283), almost certainly from Heiligenberg.

Samian ware from Dixon Street, 1989

Observation of service trenches by Mr A. Sumpter on a site about 55m from the area of the 'pottery shop' produced a quantity of samian which was nearly all burnt and which was in general remarkably similar to the material from the 'shop'.

The decorated ware was nearly all by potters represented in the 'shop', and comprised bowls in the styles of Acaunissa, Paternus iv (2 or 3), Pugnus ii or associates (at least 4), the Sacer i group (5), Secundinus ii (2?), Sissus ii, Tetturo, Vegetus iii or Avitus iv and X-6 (at least 5). Not represented before were Cinnamus ii in his earliest style and Doccalus (2, one with a signature, but no surviving decoration). There were one or two bowls in the style of Senila, who was not represented in the 'shop' assemblage, though a stamped bowl of his, heavily burnt, occurred in the material from Trench 10. Bowls by the Cerialis ii-Cinnamus ii group accounted for as much as the rest of the decorated ware put together, thus paralleling the assemblage from the 'shop'.

The stamps on plain ware, all burnt, comprised:

1   Granio 1a on form 18/31. Also noted from Trench 10 (unburnt).

2-3 Patricius ii 8b on form 33 (2). No stamps from this die have been recorded for Castleford before, but one from another die occurred in Trench 10 (unburnt).

4   Sedatus iv 2c on form 18/31. Also noted from Trench 10 (unburnt).

The plain ware comprised forms 18/31 or 31 (4), 18/31R (2), 27 (1), 38 or 44 (1) and many examples of forms 33 and 81. There were surprisingly few dishes of forms 18/31 and 18/31R or cups of form 27, though all were common in the material from the 'shop'. However, form 81, which is not a particularly common form, occurred in considerable quantity both in the 'shop' and at Dixon Street.

In view of the large number of parallels with the 'pottery shop' material and the closeness of Dixon Street to the area where it was found, it would be very surprising if this small group of samian did not come from the same source.

Stamps from Site 1(74)

Phase 1

533 ONCPA on form 27g. A curious stamp (Die 1a), known from La Graufesenque, conceivably illiterate, though perhaps more probably concealing an association of two potters (Oswald's suggestion of Nicius and Patricius is very uncertain, however). It is not common, is always on form 27, and occasionally appears at Flavian foundations, such as Chester and the Nijmegen fortress. It was, therefore probably current in the 70s. *c*. AD 60-80. *Level 7 Site 1(74); 1*

534 [P]RIMVL[I] on form 15/17 or 18. A stamp of Primulus i (Die 4b) of La Graufesenque. It is in period II at Zwammerdam (i.e. before AD 70), but also from many Flavian foundations, including Corbridge and the Nijmegen Ulpia site. *c*. AD 65-85. *Levels 9-10 Site 1(74); 1*

535 OFVIT[AL‹IS› on form 29 without decoration surviving. This is a stamp of Vitalis ii of La Graufesenque from a die which originally gave OFVITALIS (4b), but the die was broken and later gave OFVITAL (4b'). As the Castleford stamp is itself broken, we cannot be sure which version it belongs to, but since the original version is rare, b' is more likely. The later version is known from Caerleon, Gauting, the Nijmegen fortress (3), and Rottweil, so we can be sure that it was mainly Flavian, *c*. AD 65-85. *Level 11 Site 1(74); 1*

536 IΛΙ\IΛ on form 29 (Illiterate No. 138). La Graufesenque. See No. 154. The dating of this stamp depends largely on its presence at Catterick (probably AD 79+), and the Epfach Dorf. Probably *c*. AD 65-85, though this particular one cannot have quite so late a terminal date, and in view of the associated decoration must be put *c*. AD 65-80. *111 Site 1(74);1*

537 °F\IO ‹I·› on 27g. La Graufesenque. We take this as a stamp of a Vonus (1a'), though it may possibly be illiterate. This stamp occurs twice in the Nijmegen fortress, so it was evidently current in Flavian times. The first version (1a) is on form 29s of Flavian type, so this version should fall *c*. AD 70-90. *111 Site 1(74); 1*

538 ALBINI on form 15/17 or 18. Albinus iii of La Graufesenque (Die 9a). This Albinus was a basically Neronian potter with almost no records from Flavian contexts. A stamp from this die comes from Dramont Wreck G, which belongs to the 60s or, just possibly, the early 70s of the 1st century. *c*. AD 55-70. *Level 6 Site 1(74); 1*

539 OF·CALV[I] on form 18R. One of the later dies of Calvus of La Graufesenque (5ff), since it occurs at Camelon, Newstead and the later fort at Corbridge. Unusually for Calvus, this stamp is more often on rouletted than unrouletted dishes. *c*. AD 75-90. *Level 9 Site 1(74); 1*

540 [LO]GIRNI on form 18. A stamp (5a) of Logirnus of Montans and La Graufesenque attested at many Flavian foundations, including Camelon, and Heddesdorf and also in the dumped material from

the Inchtuthil Store (4 examples, cf. Hartley 1985, 315, S5-8). It was clearly current in the 80s of the 1st century, but it was perhaps also used slightly earlier, especially as there is one record on form 24 at La Graufesenque. However, the form is present in the Cala Culip iv wreck of the mid-70s (Nieto 1989, 131), and was stamped occasionally by Flavian potters who were supplying the North African market, where the form was still in demand. *c.* AD 75-90. *Level 7 Site 1(74); 1*

541 OFSECVND on form 29 (without decoration). Secundus ii of La Graufesenque (Die 8b). Another, fragmentary example came from a post-Roman context. This stamp is usually on form 29, though occasionally on dishes. Three examples came from a pottery shop of the 70s outside the Flavian fortress at Nijmegen (Morren 1966, 230-31), and it is relatively common at early Flavian foundations among which Brough-on-Humber, Rottweil-Hochmauren and York may be noted. *c.* AD 65-80. *Level 6, Level 7 Site 1(74); 1*

542 OF·M[on form 27g. This stamp has not been identified, though the details of the form suggest Flavian date. *Level 7 Site 1(74); 1*

543 I·III[on form 27g. A fragmentary, illiterate stamp for which we have no parallel. The form of the cup suggests late Neronian or early Flavian date. *Level 11 Site 1(74); 1*

544 [OF·RVF]NI on form 18. A stamp (Die 3a) of Rufinus iii of La Graufesenque with records from Chester, the Hayton fort, Malton and other early Flavian foundations. An example from period 3 of the fort at Valkenburg ZH (Glasbergen 1972, 109) should also be noted, as it means that the stamp was in use before AD 70. *c.* AD 65-80. *Level 6 Site 1(74); 1*

Phase 2

545 ALBINVS·F on form 18/31R. Die 7b of Albinus iv of Lezoux. This stamp is common in the Rhineland, which suggests a date before AD 150 for a Lezoux potter. The forms suggest Hadrianic-Antonine date, *c.* AD 125-155. *Level 4 Site 1(74); 2*

546 [OFC]ALVI on form 15/17 or 18. Die 5m of Calvus of La Graufesenque. A residual piece of *c.* AD 70-90. *Site 1(74); 2*

547 GRA[NIOM] retrograde on form 18/31. Die 1a of Granio of Lezoux. On the associated forms this stamp should be Hadrianic-Antonine, and that agrees with his other rather more common die, which is represented on wasters at Lezoux from a pit of the 130s, in association with the earliest work of Cinnamus. *c.* AD 125-45. *Level 5 Site 1(74); 2*

548 [OF·IV]CVN on form 18. Die 5f of Iucundus iii of La Graufesenque. Residual here, since the dating evidence points to the period AD 70-85. *Level 5a Site 1(74); 2*

549 ƆFPASS[E] on form 15/17 or 18. Die 9a' of Pass(i)enus of La Graufesenque. This stamp, always on dishes, occurs in its later variants at several sites founded in the early or mid-70s, but also at Camelon. Residual here and *c.* AD 70-80. *Site 1(74); 2*

550 [P]ATER·F on form 18/31. Die 2a of Pater ii of Lezoux. This stamp is known from the Erdkastell at Saalburg (Schönberger and Hartley 1970, 30, 47) and on a very large form 33, like the ones from the Castleford 'pottery shop', in the same pit at Lezoux as No. 547 above. But it also occurs twice at Newstead. *c.* AD 130-45. *Level 5 Site 1(74); 2*

551 PATERNVSF on form 27. Die 2a of Paternus ii, who may have moved from Les Martres-de-Veyre to Lezoux. The forms and distribution suggest an early 2nd-century *floruit,* and this piece is in Les Martres fabric. *c.* AD 100-120. *Level 4 Site 1(74); 2*

552 SECVND on form 33 (slightly burnt). Die 7a of a Secundus of Lezoux, possibly Secundus v. There is no independent evidence for the date of this stamp, and in view of the uncertainty about which of the Secundi it belonged to, the matter is best left open. *Level 4 Site 1(74); 2*

553 OFSVL[PICI] on form 18. Die 1b of Sulpicius of La Graufesenque. Sulpicius was a Flavian-Trajanic potter, though there is no precise evidence for the date of this particular stamp. *Level 4 Site 1(74); 2*

554 [T]ARVILLIM on form 27. Die 1a of Tarvillus of Lezoux, whose stamps are uncommon, though always on Hadrianic or early Antonine forms. *Level 5b Site 1(74); 2*

555 ////ND on form 15/17 or 18. This stamp has not been identified, but the fabric is South Gaulish and the dish probably Flavian and certainly residual in this context. *Site 1(74); 2*

Phase 3, excluding the 'pottery shop'

556 MALLVROF on form 33. Die 3f of Malluro of Lezoux. This stamp has not been recorded elsewhere, but the general record for Malluro shows that he was basically an early to mid-Antonine potter. It is not unlikely, however, that he began work slightly before the Antonine period, as there is a stamp of his on form 18/31 from Halton Chesters. This is much more likely to have got there under Hadrian than after AD 158. *c.* AD 135-55. *6 Site 1(74); 3*

557 NATONVSГ on form 27. Die 1a of Natonus, whose workplace is not known, though the fabrics of his relatively few vessels suggest that Les Martres-de-Veyre is perhaps the most likely source. A short period of work within the Trajanic-Hadrianic range is suggested. *Site 1(74); 3*

558 [SV]OBNI·ᴧ on form 31. Die 5a of Suobnus of Les Martres-de-Veyre, where he was one of the later group. The final letter was probably meant to be M, but the cutter perhaps ran out of space on the die. Suobnus's work is regularly on Hadrianic-Antonine forms and occurs in Antonine Scotland, where this stamp has been recorded at Mumrills. *c.* AD 130-55. *154 Site 1(74); 3*

Phase 3, potters' stamps and signatures from the 'pottery shop'

We list here the potters' stamps and signatures from the 'pottery shop' which are on burnt vessels, or on pots stamped with dies known on some of the burnt material. We then add a list of stamps from Level 3 which are only known on unburnt pots. We have not dated individual stamps, since the evidence needs to be considered as a whole (see Table 7 and pp 63-4).

559 Acaunissa, cursive signature, form 37, from a mould signed before firing, below the decoration, Aca[, retrograde, Lezoux. See No. 483 in the drawn samian from Site 1(74). *Level 3 Site 1(74); 3*

560-62* Agedillus ii 2a 33 (3) AGƎ[I]LLI Les Martres-de-Veyre, Lezoux. *Level 3 Site 1(74); 3*

563-75* Ambitotus 1a 18/31 (2), 18/31R (7), 81 (4) ᴧMBITOVMᴧ Lezoux. *Level 3 Site 1(74); 3*

576-81* Attianus ii 7a 18/31-31, 44/81 (6) ᴧTTIANIM Lezoux. *Level 3 Site 1(74); 3*

582-7* Atticus ii 2a 27 (6) ᴧTTICI·M Lezoux. *Level 3 Site 1(74); 3*

588-90* Banvillus 2a 18/31 (3) [BAN]VILLIM Les Martres-de-Veyre, Lezoux. *Level 3 Site 1(74); 3*

591* Banvillus Incomplete 1 18/31 BᴧN[Les Martres, Lezoux. *Level 3 Site 1(74); 3*

592* Beliniccus i 9d 18/31 BELIN[ICCIM] Lezoux. *Site 1(74); 3*

593-4* Biturix 1f 18/31(?), 81 [BITV]RIX·F Lezoux. *Site 1(74); 3*

561-62

563-75

576-81

582-87

588-90

591

592

593-94

595-96

597-99

601-11

612-14

615

616

617

618-21

622

623-24

625-26

627

628-30

631-32

633-52

653

654-79

680-90

691-93

694

695

696-98

699-772

773-79

0　　　　　　　　　　　50 mm

Fig. 29.　Samian stamps from Site 1(74). Scale 1:1

595-6* Borillus i 10a 18/31R (2) BOR[ILL]IM Lezoux. *Site 1(74); 3*

597-9* Burdo 6a 33 (3) BVꟼDOF Lezoux. *Level 3 Site 1(74); 3*

600 Butrio 1a 37, stamped in the mould, BVTRIO Lezoux. See No. 419 in the drawn samian from Site 1(74). *Level 3 Site 1(74); 3*

601-11* Calava 2b 18/31 (11) CALAVA·F Lezoux. *Level 3 Site 1(74); 3*

612-14* Caratedo 1a 18/31 (3)CΛRΛTEDOFELezoux. *Level 3 Site 1(74); 3*

615* Caratillus(?) 1a(?) 27 [C]ΛRΛ[TILLIM] Lezoux. *Level 3 Site 1(74); 3*

616* Cassius i Incomplete 1 18/31 CΛSS[IΛOF] Lezoux. *Site 1(74); 3*

617* Cassius i Incomplete 2 18/31 [CΛSSI]ΛOF Lezoux. *Level 3 Site 1(74); 3*

618-21* Cerialis ii 2a 33 (4) CERIALI·M Lezoux. *Level 3 Site 1(74); 3*

622* Cerialis ii 9a or 9a' 18/31 [C]ERIAL·F, with or without decorative ends, Lezoux. *Site 1(74); 3*

623-4* Cerialis ii Incomplete 1 (probably a surmoulage of 9a) 18/31 (2) CER[Lezoux. *Level 3 Site 1(74); 3*

625-6* Cintusmus i 4a 18/31, 18/31R [C]INVSMϜ Lezoux. *Site 1(74); 3*

627* Cracissa 4a 33CRACISM Lezoux. *Level 3 Site 1(74); 3*

628-30* Cracuna i 2a 18/31 (3) CRACVNAϜ Lezoux. *Site 1(74); 3*

631-2* Dagomarus 11a 18/31 (2, but perhaps from the same pot) DΛGOMRI Lezoux. *Level 3 Site 1(74); 3*

633-52* Divicatus 3a 18/31 (20) DIVICATVS Lezoux. *Level 3 Site 1(74); 3*

653* Divicus 1e 33 DIVICIM Lezoux. *Site 1(74); 3*

654-79* Doccalus 4a 18/31, 27 (22), 33 (3) DOCCΛLIϜ Lezoux. *Site 1(74); 3*

680-90* Doccalus 5c 33 (11) DOCCALI Lezoux. *Level 3 Site 1(74); 3*

691-3* Episus 1a 27, 44/81 (2) EPISIM Lezoux. An uncommon potter, who presumably only worked for a short time. The only other known stamps come from Carlisle (1b) and Bavai (1-). *Level 3 Site 1(74); 3*

694* Felix ii 2a 18/31 [ꟼFELIX]FꞰ Lezoux. *Level 3 Site 1(74); 3*

695* Felix ii 2d 18/31 FELIX[·F] Lezoux. *Site 1(74); 3*

696-8* Geminus vi 6c 18/31 (3) GEMINIM Lezoux. This is a previously unrecorded die. *Level 3 Site 1(74); 3*

699-772* Gnatius ii 4a 18/31, 27 (24), 33 (49) GNⱯIVS Lezoux. *Level 3 Site 1(74); 3*

773-9* Littera i 1b 18/31R (7) LITTERAϜ Lezoux. *Level 3 Site 1(74); 3*

780-81* Lupoisucus (or Lupot-?) 1a 33, 44/81 LVPOISVC retrograde Lezoux. A new potter, whose work has only otherwise been recorded at Chester (three examples). *Level 3 Site 1(74); 3*

782-5* Maiudilus 3a 18/31 (4) MAIVƁILV[S] Lezoux. *Level 3 Site 1(74); 3*

786-9* Malliacus 3h 18/31 (2), 27 (2) MALLIACI Lezoux. *Level 3 Site 1(74); 3*

790-93* Mallus 2b 18/31 (3), 18/31R MΛⱩⱩIM Lezoux. *Level 3 Site 1(74); 3*

794-806* Muxtullus 1b 18/31 (13) MVXTVLLIM Lezoux. *Level 3 Site 1(74); 3*

807-8* Muxtullus 5a 18/31 (2) [MV]XTVLLVS Lezoux. *Site 1(74); 3*

809-11* Pateratus 1a 18/31 (3) ·PΛTERΛTIOF Lezoux. *Level 3 Site 1(74); 3*

812-16* Paternus iii 2b 18/31 (2), 27 (3) PATERNI Lezoux. *Level 3 Site 1(74); 3*

817* Paullus iv 3b 27 PAⱯ[LIM] Lczoux. *Level 3 Site 1(74); 3*

818-30* Paullus iv 3g 18/31 (12), 18/31R PΛVLLI·M Lezoux. *Level 3 Site 1(74); 3*

831-3* Primigenius ii 3a 18/31 (3) PRIMIGENIM Lezoux. *Level 3 Site 1(74); 3*

834* Priscinus 1d 27 PRIS[CINIM] Lezoux. *Level 3 Site 1(74); 3*

835* Pugnus ii 1b 44/81 [P]VGNI·[M] Lezoux. *Level 3 Site 1(74); 3*

836 Pugnus? cursive signature below the decoration 37 [PVGNI]M retrograde Lezoux. See No. 465. *Level 3 Site 1(74); 3*

837* Pugnus ii Incomplete 2 18/31 (2) PVG/[Lezoux. *Level 3 Site 1(74); 3*

838* Putrimus 1a 18/31 ·PVTRIMI· Lezoux. *Level 3 Site 1(74); 3*

839-42* Quintilianus i 1b 18/31 (4) QVINTIⱠi[ANIM] Lezoux. *Site 1(74); 3*

843-4* Roppus ii 1a 18/31 (2) RO[PP]VSFE Les Martres-de-Veyre, Lezoux. *Site 1(74); 3*

845-7* Ruffus ii 1a 27, 33 (2) RVFFI·MA Lezoux. *Level 3 Site 1(74); 3*

848 Sacer? cursive below the decoration 37 S[ACRIO?] retrograde Lezoux. See No. 502. *Site 1(74); 3*

849* Sacisamo 1a 33 [SΛC]ISΛMO retrograde Lezoux. An uncommon potter only otherwise known from another example from the Castleford *vicus* (p. 00) and a form 33 at York. *Level 3 Site 1(74); 3*

850-51* Sacr(i)e(mus?) 1a 27 (1 + 1?) SΛCR·EⱮ Lezoux. *Site 1(74); 3*

852-66* Sacroticus 1a 18/31 (2), 27 (8), 33 (4 + 1?) SΛCROTICIM Lezoux. *Level 3 Site 1(74); 3*

867* Secundus v 5a 18/31R [S]ECVNDMLezoux. *Site 1(74); 3*

868* Secundus v Incomplete 2 18/31R [SEC]VNꝺF Lezoux. *Site 1(74); 3*

869* Severus v 1b 18/31 S[E]VERIⱮ Lezoux. *Level 3 Site 1(74); 3*

870-75* Severus v 2a 18/31 (5 + 1?) SEVERI·MI Lezoux. *Site 1(74); 3*

876-913* Severus v 6d 27 (38) ƧEVERVƧI'Lezoux. *Level 3 Site 1(74); 3*

914-20* Sextus ii 2b 27 (5), 33 (2) SEXTIM Lezoux. *Level 3 Site 1(74); 3*

Fig. 30. Samian stamps from Site 1(74). Scale 1:1

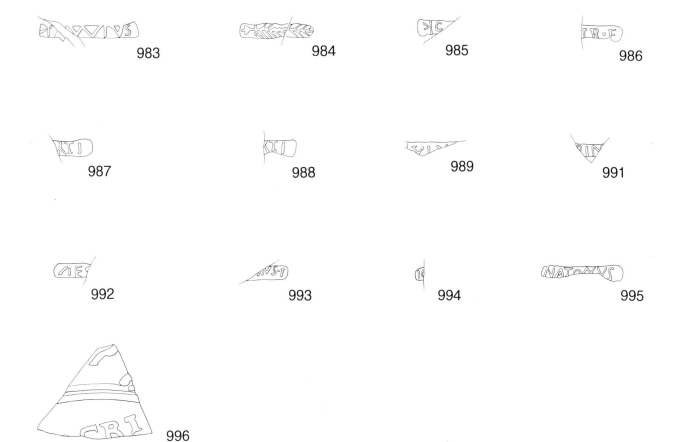

Fig. 31. Samian stamps from Site 1(74). Scale 1:1

921-40* Sollemnis i 5a 33 (20) SOLIIMNI Lezoux. *Site 1(74); 3*

941* Sollemnis i(?) Incomplete 1 18/31 SOLI[Lezoux. *Level 3 Site 1(74); 3*

942-3* Sulp-Certus 1a 18/31 (2) [SVLP·CERTI Lezoux. *Site 1(74); 3*

944-54* Suservio- Cer- 1a 18/31 (11) SV·SERVIO·CER Lezoux. *Site 1(74); 3*

955* Tertullus ii Uncertain 1 81 TER[Lezoux. *Level 3 Site 1(74); 3*

956-70* Tintirio 4a 18/31 (3), 18/31 or 18/31R, 18/31R TINTIRI[M] Lezoux. *Level 3 Site 1(74); 3*

971-3* Tittius 4b 18/31R (3) TI[TT]IVS Lezoux. *Level 3 Site 1(74); 3*

974-82* Vespo 1a 18/31 (3), 18/31 or 18/31R, 33 (4), 44/81 VESPONI Lezoux. *Level 3 Site 1(74); 3*

In addition to the legible potters' stamps there are some illiterate stamps and many very fragmentary ones. We now list the identified illiterate stamps, and the fragmentary ones which may possibly be identifiable eventually.

983* ƆII꒐RIVS Illiterate 147 18/31 (2). Lezoux. *Site 1(74); 3*

984* Herringbone pattern 5 18/31 (2). Lezoux. *Level 3 Site 1(74); 3*

985* C[18/31, perhaps another stamp of Cerialis ii with decorative end like Nos 622 and 623 above. Lezoux. *Level 3 Site 1(74); 3*

986*]IR F 18/31. Lezoux. *Level 3 Site 1(74); 3*

987*]RTI-:18/31. Lezoux. cf. Sercertus 869, above, perhaps the same die, but the characters after the I only show on this. *Site 1(74); 3*

988*]RTI 18/31. Lezoux. *Level 3 Site 1(74); 3*

989*]VIII[18/31. Lezoux. *Level 3 Site 1(74); 3*

990*]CVS 18/31. Lezoux. *Site 1(74); 3*

991*]PII[18/31 or 18/31R. Lezoux. *Level 3 Site 1(74); 3*

(For tables showing distribution of forms for the identified stamps, and parallels in dated or semi-dated contexts see pp 53 and 62.)

The stamps listed below are from the same contexts as the 'pottery shop' ones, but are unburnt. Some are residual.

992* Aestivus 3a 33 AES[TIVM] Lezoux a. Although this die was used on form 27, it also appears on Ludowici form Tx, so it could scarcely have been in use before AD 160. *c.* AD 160-185. *Level 3 Site 1(74); 3*

61

Table 7. The occurrence of 'pottery shop' stamps in dated and significant contexts.

Potter	Die	HWB	HW	AS	Rhine	LF	VF	HF	WG	PPR	Comments
Acaunissa	Curs.	*			*						
Agedillus ii	2a				+	+					
Ambitotus	1a			+	*						
Attianus ii	7a		+	*	+						
Atticus ii	2a				*						
Banvillus	2a			*	*						
Banvillus	Inc. 1			*	+						
Beliniccus i	9d		+	+	+	+					
Biturix	1f		+		*			*			
Borillus i	10a			+	+						
Burdo	6a				*						In the Bregenz shop of c. 140-55*
Butrio	1a				*						
Calava	2b		*	*							
Caratedo	1a										
Caratillus	1a										
Cassius i	Inc. 1			+							Cassius made decorated ware with Tittius below
Cassius i	Inc. 2			+							
Cerialis ii	2a		*	*	*		+	+			
Cerialis ii	9a/a'		+	+	+		+	+			
Cerialis ii	Inc. 1		+	+	+		+	+			
Cintusmus i	4a		+	+	*		+	+	+		
Cracissa	4a		*		*			*			
Cracuna i	2a		*	*	*						
Dagomarus	11a	+	+		*						
Divicatus	3a			+	+						
Divicus	1e				+						
Doccalus	4a		+		+						
Doccalus	5c		+		*						
Episus	1a										A new man also known at Carlisle
Felix ii	2a			+							
Felix ii	2d			+	*						
Geminus vi	6c			+	+						
Gnatius ii	4a			+	*						
Littera i	1b				*	+		*			
Lupoisucus	1a										A new man, otherwise only at Chester
Maiudilus	3a										
Malliacus	3h			+	*						
Mallus	2b	+			*						
Muxtullus	1b		+	*	+			+	+		
Muxtullus	5a		+	+	*			+	+		
Pateratus	1a		*	*	*						

Table 7 continued. The occurrence of 'pottery shop' stamps in dated and significant contexts.

Potter	Die	HWB	HW	AS	Rhine	LF	VF	HF	WG	PPR	Comments
Paternus iii	2b			*	*	*					
Paullus iv	3b	+		+					+		
Paullus iv	3g	+		+					+		
Primigenus ii	3a			*	+						
Priscinus	1d		+		*						
Pugnus ii	1b		+	+					+		
Pugnus ii	Inc. 2		+	+					+		
Putrimus	1a										
Quintilianus i	1b		*	*	*						
Roppus ii	1a			*	*						
Ruffus ii	1a		+		+			*			
Sacisamo	1a										
Sacr(i)emus	1a	*									
Sacroticus	1a		+		*						
Secundus v	5a		*	+							
Secundus v	Inc. 2		+	+							
Severus v	1b	+		+	*			+			
Severus v	2a	+		+	*			*			
Severus v	6e	+		+	*			+			
Sextus ii	2b				*						
Sollemnis i	5a	*	+		*			*			
Sollemnis i	Inc. 1	+	+		+			+			
Sulp-Certus	2a										
Suservio- Cer-	1a			*							
Tertullus ii	Uncertain 1										
Tintirio	4a		+		+						
Tittius	4b		*	+	+						
Vcspo	1a			*	+						

*		the same,	LF		London Fire *c.* 120
+		a different die	VF		Verulamium Fire of *c.* 155-60
HWB:	Hadrian's Wall (Birdoswald Alley)		HF		Hinterland forts
HW		Hadrian's Wall	WG		Wroxeter Gutter Group
AS		Antonine Scotland	PPR		Pudding Pan Rock
Rhine		Rhineland			

993* Dagomarus 4c 18/31R   [DAGOΛΛ]R/S·F   Les Martre-de-Veyre b, c, Lezoux b, c. This example, on an unused dish, appears to be from Les Martres. There is little evidence of date for this die, but the potter had probably moved to Lezoux by AD 125, so it should be Trajanic or early Hadrianic. *Level 3 Site 1(74); 3*

994* Ioenalis i 2a 18/31R   IO[ENΛLIS]   Les Martres-de-Veyre b, c. This stamp is known from the Second Fire of Roman London. *c.* AD 100-125. *Site 1(74); 3*

995* Natonus 1a 27   NΛTONVSF   Les Martres-de-Veyre c. The stamp is always on form 27, and its presence at Corbridge and Maryport suggests that it is probably Trajanic. *171 Site 1(74); 3*

996* Sacer i 1a 37   [OFI2A]CRI   Lezoux a. The general evidence for Sacer suggests a date *c.* AD 125-145. *Level 3 Site 1(74); 3*

Discussion of the 'pottery shop' potters' stamps

In discussing the date of the potters' stamps from the 'pottery shop', occurrences on dated sites elsewhere have to be given priority. Some semi-dated contexts are also relevant, such as the presence of particular stamps in the Rhineland, where Lezoux wares are extremely rare after AD 150. (Table 7 gives a convenient pictorial indication of links elsewhere.)

Unfortunately there is only one major group of samian assignable to period IA of Hadrian's Wall (i.e. before AD 139), namely the pots from the Birdoswald Alley (Birley 1930). The links with that are, however, interesting, particularly in view of the small total of stamps at Birdoswald. Of the seven potters there represented by stamps or a signature, six recur at Castleford, though only thrice with the same die or signature (Acaunissa, Sacr(i)emus and Sollemnis). Occurrences of stamps from the same dies in Antonine Scotland are naturally more prolific, 21%, rising to 57% when other dies of the same potters are taken into account. The corresponding figures for Corbridge AD 125-39 (unoccupied in the main, it is usually argued) are 24% and 52%. These figures suggest that the Castleford fire happened during the Antonine occupations of Scotland and Corbridge, but with the weight of the Birdoswald evidence allowed for, it is clear that the range AD 140-50 is certain and that the first half of that range is likely. Confirmation of this comes from the very high proportion of form 27 still in use (and cf. Table 6), as well as the astonishingly high percentage in common with the Rhineland, where 44% of the Castleford dies are attested, and where Central Gaulish ware was very rare after AD 150.

Negative evidence is provided by the (unsurprising) lack of links with the Pudding Pan Rock collection, with only one potter (Cintusmus) in common with the Castleford 'shop', but the die is different. Even the Wroxeter Gutter Group has only three potters in common with Castleford. They are represented by six dies, none in the Castleford 'shop'. Two of the three potters (Paullus and Pugnus) certainly began work under Hadrian, and only Muxtullus remains doubtful as a Hadrianic starter. Similarly, there are no links with the main series of Hinterland forts of Hadrian's Wall, only with Binchester and Piercebridge, where there must always have been some occupation in the 2nd century, even when the forts were not garrisoned.

There is no need to expound on the relationship of the Castleford stamps to forms, as they are summarised in Table 6.

We may now finally reiterate our opinion that the burning at Castleford took place in the decade AD 140-50, and almost certainly AD 140-45.

Phase 4 Stamps
The following stamps came from layers above the 'pottery shop'.

997 Attianus ii 3a 27? [ATTIA]N·O Lezoux a. A stamp which occurs on Hadrianic and early Antonine decorated bowls. There is one example from Newstead. *c.* AD 125-45. *Level l Site 1(74); 4*

998 Calvinus ii lb 33 CΛlVIΛ/lo Lezoux a. A stamp used on forms 18/31, 27 and 42. He also made forms 38 and 80. His range is therefore *c.* AD 135-65, with 135-60 for Die lb. *Level l Site 1(74); 4*

999 Urbicus ii la 31R VR[BI-CVS] Rheinzabern a. There is no site dating for this potter, but his forms suggest late 2nd or 3rd-century date. *125 Site1(74); 4*

5 Decorated Samian Ware and Potters' Stamps from the Castleford *Vicus* Trench 10

This report was written in 1985 and revised in 1999. The following illustrated catalogue entries have been extracted from the main Trench 10 Archive Report, to which there may be references. This is available on request from the WYAS.

Unstratified
Material ranging from the early Flavian period to the late 2nd or early 3rd century, but decreasing in quantity in the Antonine period. The forms represented are:

South Gaulish: 15/17R, 15/17R or 18R, 18 and 29.
Central Gaulish: 18/31, 18/31R, 27, 31, 31R, 33, 36, 37, 42, 81, Curle 11, 21 and 23 and Bushe-Fox 82, etc.
East Gaulish: 43 or 45.

The plain ware includes stamps of Attillus iii, Buccula, Iullinus ii and Taurianus (Nos 1059, 1062, 1086 and 1142 in the stamp list).

The decorated ware includes a stamped bowl of Sacroticus (see No. 1006 and No. 1126 in the stamp list) and bowls in the styles of Acaunissa (burnt), Advocisus, Albucius ii (see No. 1041), Avitus iii, Cettus (several), the Cerialis ii - Cinnamus ii group (several, including sherds in other deposits), Criciro v, Drusus ii, Pugnus ii (see No. 1027), the Large-S Potter, X-5 (see No. 1031), X-6 and X-8.

Worthy of separate note is:

1000* Form 37, Central Gaulish, A bowl in the style of Do(v)eccus i, with a Cupid (D.282), rosette (Rogers C170) and leaf (Rogers H134). cf. S. & S. 1958, pl. 151, 54, from Lancaster. *c.* AD 165-200. *U/S T10*

Context 005
Much of the material is Hadrianic-Antonine, but there are some quite weathered Antonine pieces, including a heavily burnt form 31 with a high basal kick, which could be late in the period.

The plain ware comprises forms 18/31 or 31 (3, one burnt), 27 (burnt), 33 (3) and many scraps. Two dishes from Les Martres-de-Veyre are probably Trajanic.

The decorated ware includes bowls in the styles of Cerialis ii - Cinnamus ii group (2), Criciro v (see Archive Report U/S ii) and the Quintilianus i group (with contexts 083 and 121, Archive Report).

Worthy of separate note is:

1001* Form 37, Central Gaulish. A very small bowl, over-fired and with unworn footring and kiln-grit inside the base, has cursive signature, Sissus (retrograde), upside-down below the decoration, from a mould signed before firing. There is a double ridge below the decoration and double finely beaded borders separate the panels. This is the work of Sissus ii, a Lezoux potter who seems to

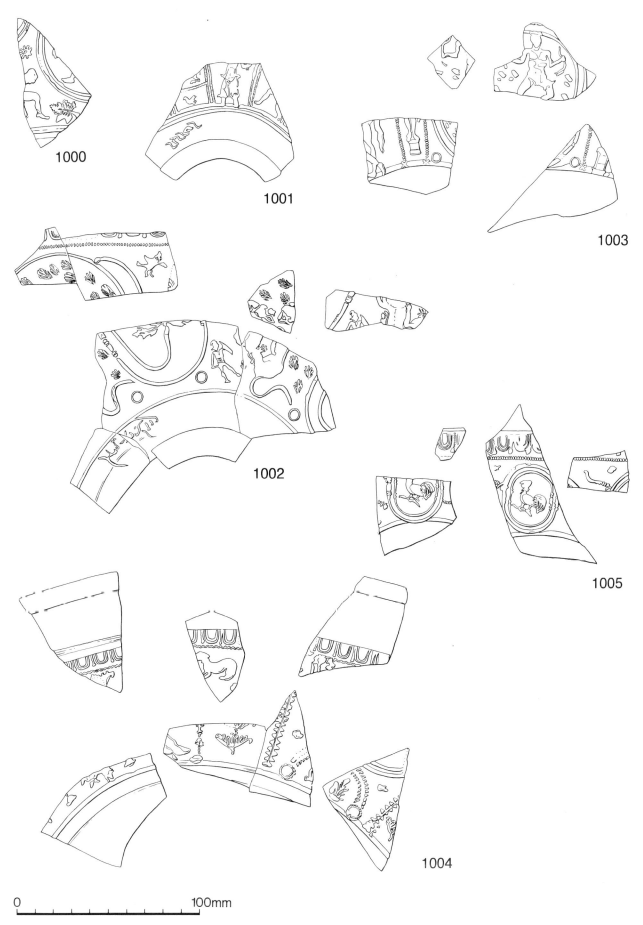

1000

1001

1002

1003

1004

1005

0   100mm

Fig. 32. Decorated samian from Trench 10. Scale 1:2

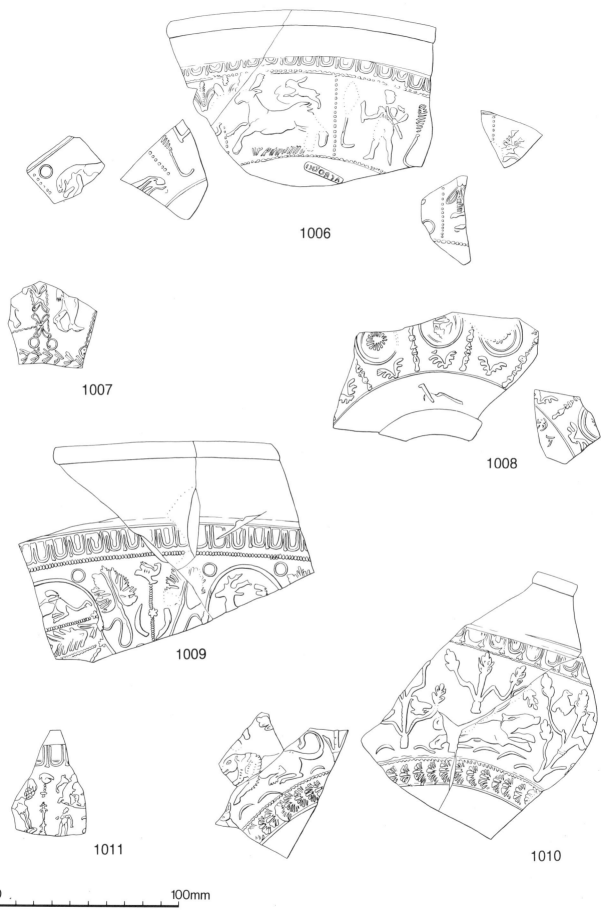

1006

1007

1008

1009

1011

1010

Fig. 33. Decorated samian from Trench 10. Scale 1:2

have used a variety of styles, so that it is not easy to distinguish his wares without the aid of a signature. The tiny bird is on a bowl from Dorchester, Dorset, with a motif used by Sissus. The dancer (D.202), used by Curmillus, is on a bowl from Wanborough (Wilts), with motifs which were probably also used by Sissus and Priscinus. These three potters seem to have been connected in some way and may have shared an ovolo, one used by Sacroticus (see No. 1006, below), who may be a member of the group. *c.* AD 130-60. *005 T10; Mod.*

Context 024
Worthy of separate note are:

1002* Form 37, Central Gaulish, with cursive signature of Cerialis ii, Ciirialis retrograde, below the decoration. The ovolo is the one most commonly used by Cerialis and his associates (Rogers B144). The upper concavity of the scroll contains a large leaf (Rogers H24). The lower concavities contain a warrior (D.614) and a lion attacking a boar (D.778). The buds are partial impressions of a leafy spray (Rogers J178). See Stamp No. 1175. *c.* AD 135-70. *024 T10 (two sherds, with 4 in 028 T10 and 3 in a trial trench); 3*

1003* Form 37, Central Gaulish, made in a cracked mould. The panels include: 1) man with *chlamys* (O.576A). 2) Figure on a pedestal (perhaps the Venus D.199). 3) Double medallion and corner rings. In another panel the medallion contains a Hercules with snakes (D.464) and partly impressed acanthi. The adjacent panel has a larger pedestal than in 2). There are connections with Criciro (the Hercules and acanthus tips) and Advocisus, who used the beads and, occasionally, the crosses. The Hercules is also on a bowl from London in the style of Divixtus i. The decoration as a whole is not typical of any of these potters, however, and the bowl cannot be closely dated. *c.* AD 140-80. *024 T10 (with 028 (3) and 027 T10); 3*

Context 028
Almost certainly an early Antonine group, most of it burnt. The plain ware, of Hadrianic and early Antonine date, comprises forms 18/31 (4), 18/31R (1 or 2), 18/31 or 31 (a maximum of 14), 27 (2), 33 (a maximum of 8), 38 (2), 38 or 44 (3), 81 and 14 scraps.

The decorated ware includes sherds from four bowls in context 174 (Nos 1014-17), two in 024 (Nos 1002 and 1003) and one in 027 (Archive Report). There are also the following:

1004* Form 37, Central Gaulish. The single-bordered ovolo (Rogers B77), acanthus (Rogers K6), leaf (Rogers G205) and divider (Rogers P71) are all on bowls stamped by, or in the style of, Priscinus of Lezoux. The decoration also includes a panther (0.1566), a Victory? (D.474?), an arcade (Rogers F43?), a rosette and a tier of cups. *c.* AD 125-50. *028 T10 (three sherds, with others in 080, 099 (2) and 157 T10); 3*

Context 056
Worthy of separate note is:

1005* Form 37, Central Gaulish. A small bowl, with an ovolo used chiefly by Cinnamus ii (Rogers B231, or a variant of it). It occurs also on bowls in the style of a Lezoux Paternus (iv), who signed moulds in the nominative. The design was perhaps intended to be a scroll, but the double festoons which would have formed it have been joined by vertical astragali to form medallions. One of the spaces between the medallions is divided horizontally by beads. The cockerel is D.1026. Paternus iv, though clearly connected with the Sacer i group, seems not to have been exactly contemporary, probably working in the period *c.* AD 135-55. *056/1 T10 (a burnt fragment with another burnt, in Phase 2 and two unburnt in 121 T10. Also sherds, burnt (No. 525 in Level 3 Site 1(74)); 3*

Context 058
Material ranging from the pre-Flavian period to the mid-2nd century. It includes Central Gaulish decorated bowls in the styles of Attianus ii? (2: see Archive Report contexts 026 and 285), Cettus of Les Martres-de-Veyre, Drusus i (X-3: 2 bowls, one from Les Martres, the other in Lezoux fabric), Geminus iv (see No. 1022), the Quintilianus i group (2, one from a bowl in Archive Report context. 028, i, *q.v.*), X-5, X-6 (Archive Report context 301) and the Cerialis ii - Cinnamus ii group (4, one with other sherds in Archive Report context 129, iii). There are also stamped vessels of Gnatius, Paullus iv, Sacroticus (see below) and Senila (see No. 1012).

Worthy of separate note are the following Central Gaulish bowls:

1006* Form 37, with mould stamp S CROTICI (retrograde) below the decoration: Sacroticus of Lezoux (see stamp No. 1126). The single bordered ovolo (Rogers B77), trilobed motif (Rogers G153) and 'whip' (Rogers S73) are all known for Curmillus, and Priscinus used the ovolo and, probably, the 'whip'. The panels are unusually wide and their sequence is not entirely clear. The figure-types, all facing left, include a warrior, large and small stags, a hare and a lion or bear. The panels containing the larger stag have striated columns, impressed horizontally. Borders of separate beads (Rogers A5) define the panels and the upper and lower limits of the main zone of decoration. There are no parallels for any of the figure-types in Déchelette or Oswald except for the smaller stag, which may be O.1788, and the column is not illustrated by Rogers. No other stamped decorated ware of Sacroticus is known, but an unstamped fragment of form 37 from Leicester could be from the same mould. There are many of his stamps, probably from a different die, on plain forms in the large group of burnt samian from Site 1 (74). Plain ware stamps from Birdoswald and Ambleside may be from the same die as this decorated bowl. This evidence, together with parallels in the decorated ware of Curmillus, Priscinus and, probably, Sissus ii suggests a date *c.* AD 130-155. *058 T10 (with Phase 2 (2), 012 (2), 078 (2) and 081/4 (2) T10, some joining); Mod.*

Context 078
Material ranging from the pre-Flavian period to the mid-2nd century. It includes Central Gaulish decorated bowls in the styles of Albucius ii (see No. 1041) Attianus ii? (2: see Archive Report context 026, iii and No. 1020), Cettus of Les Martres-de-Veyre, Drusus i (X-3: 2 bowls, one from Les Martres, the other in Lezoux fabric), Geminus iv (see No. 1022), the Quintilianus i group (2, one from a bowl in Archive Report context 028, i, *q.v.*), X-5, X-6 (see Archive Report context 301, iii) and the Cerialis ii - Cinnamus ii group (4, one with other sherds in Archive Report context 129, iii). There are also stamped vessels of Gnatius, Paullus iv, Sacroticus (see below) and Senila (see No. 1012).

Worthy of separate note is the following Central Gaulish bowl:

1007* Form 37. The bifid motifs (Rogers G282) are on a bowl from Cardurnock in the style of Rogers's potter P-14 (Birley 1947, fig. 6, 5) and he used the rings in the same way on a bowl from Chester. The element of the basal wreath (Rogers G328), perhaps a partial impression of a leaf, was used by X-6. No parallels have been found for the figure-types. Hadrianic-Antonine. *078 T10; 4*

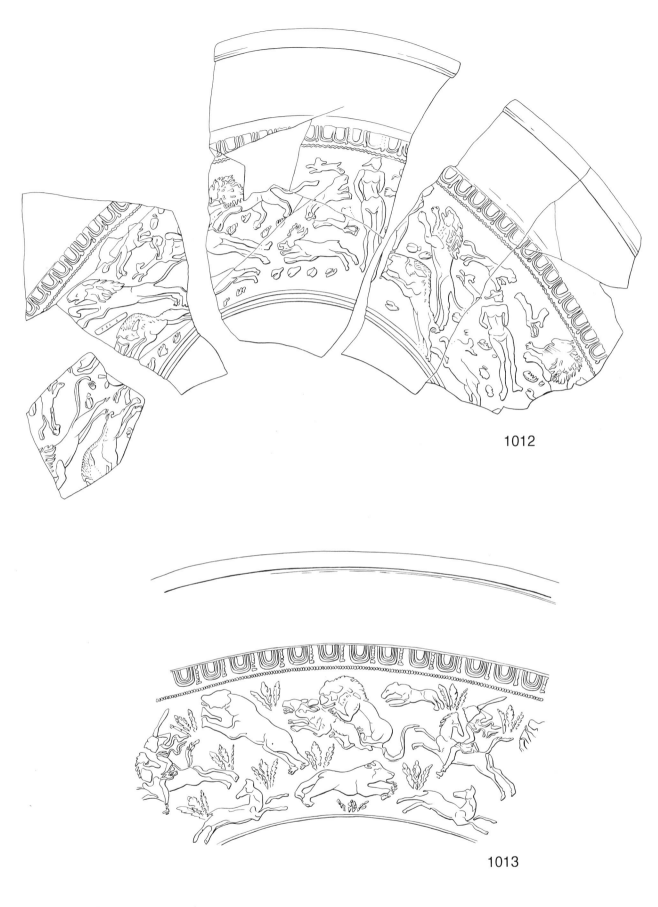

1012

1013

0   100mm

Fig. 34. Decorated samian from Trench 10. Scale 1:2

Context 079

Material ranging from the Flavian period to the late 2nd or early 3rd century. Most of it is Hadrianic-Antonine, but there are several sherds which will not be before *c*. AD 160, at the earliest. These comprise forms 31R (4), 37, in the style of Paternus v and 45 from Central Gaul and forms 31R and 37 from East Gaul. There are also a stamped vessel of Felix ii (No. 1077) and Central Gaulish decorated bowls in the styles of Albucius ii (see No. 1041), Medetus-Ranto (2: context 400A also see Archive Report context 448, ii), X-5 (see No. 1031), X-6 (2 or 3, including a sherd from a bowl in Archive Report context 301, iii *q.v.*) and the Cerialis ii - Cinnamus ii group (with context 472). Form 37, South Gaulish, is in the style of L. Cosius (see No. 1029). Form 30, from Les Martres-de-Veyre is by a predecessor of Sacer i (with context 472 T10).

Also worthy of note are:

1008* Form 37, Central Gaulish, with cursive signature of Acaunissa below the decoration Aca[, retrograde. The panels are apparently identical, with 15-petalled rosettes (Rogers C241?) in double medallions, over acanthi (one of the series Rogers K16-35), with tiers of cups between. There is a graffito, Fr? below the decoration, from a mould inscribed after firing. Mentioned in stamp text catalogue No. 1174. *c*. AD 125-45. *079 T10 (SF361*, joining *472* and with *013 T10); 4*

1009* Form 37, Central Gaulish. The single bordered ovolo (Rogers B77) occurs on bowls in a wide variety of styles. This one is probably by a member of the Sacer i - Attianus ii group, to judge by the lion (O.1424), stag (D.874?), leaf (Rogers H72) and partly-impressed acanthus. The chevron is probably Rogers G289 and the leafy spray is Rogers J177. The bird is not in Déchelette or Oswald and the rosette is too blurred for identification. A similar bowl (No. 499) occurs in the large group of burnt samian from *Level 3 Site 1(74)*. *c*. AD 125-45. *079 T10* (two sherds, with three in *097 T10*, some joining)*; 4*

Context 092

Worthy of separate note is:

1010* Form 37, South Gaulish. The trident-tongued ovolo is on a signed bowl of Albanus iii (from La Graufesenque), but was almost certainly used by other potters. It occurs on several bowls from the Domitianic foundation at Wilderspool (Dickinson and Hartley 1992, fig. 14, 37; 16, 52). The dog (O.1914B) and the lion, or one very similar, were used at Banassac, but probably also at La Graufesenque. The five-lobed leaf is on a La Graufesenque bowl from the Flavian-Trajanic Bregenz Cellar hoard (Jacobs 1913, no. 23), but also on a Banassac bowl from Arles. The element in the basal wreath originated at La Graufesenque in the Flavian period. The fork of the tree branches is a striated chevron and the base and lower part of the trunk are made from a motif normally used as a tassel between festoons. *c*. AD 80-110. *092 T10* (with *129*, *226* (2) and *448 T10*, some joining)*; 3*

Context 097

Material ranging from the Flavian period to the late 2nd century or 3rd century. It includes sherds from bowls in the styles of Avitus iii (with context 056/A), Albucius ii (see No. 1041), Butrio, the Cerialis ii - Cinnamus ii group (3, one with context 080) and the Sacer i group (see No. 1009). The latest piece is form 31, East Gaulish, probably from Trier. The dish is the size and shape of form 31R, but without rouletting. A groove marks the internal junction of the base and wall.

Worth separate note is:

1011* Form 37, Central Gaulish. The single-bordered ovolo (Rogers B77) is impressed over a straight line. The figure-types include a harpy (O.863B), Cupid (D.274 variant) and a standing figure (not in D. or O.). The composite motif is Rogers Q11 with the addition of a cup at the top. The ovolo was occasionally used by potters in the Quintilianus i group, and the use of a guide-line below it strengthens the attribution. *c*. AD 125-50. *097 T10; 4*

Context 127

Worthy of separate note is:

1012* Form 37, perhaps slightly burnt, Central Gaulish, with mould-stamp of Senila (No. 1130). The freestyle scene includes lions (O.1459 and one not in D. or O.), stags (D.860 and O.1822N), a panther (D.790?), a horse (D.909 variant), a boar (D.835A) and a captive (D.642 variant). The lion O.1459, a variant of the other lion and the panther are all on a stamped Senila bowl from Rouen. His style connects him with the Quintilianus i group. The single-bordered ovolo (Rogers B74) is on a stamped mould of Quintilianus from Lezoux and he, and his associates, regularly used double ridges below the decoration. *c*. AD 125-50. *127 T10* (fourteen fragments, with *058* (2), *078*, *146* (5), *169* (8), *286*); *3*

Context 162

Worthy of separate note is:

1013* Form 37, Central Gaulish, in the style of Cinnamus ii. The ovolo (Rogers B145) is one of his less-common ones. The freestyle scene includes a horseman (D.152a), lion attacking a boar (D.778), doe (D.878), bears to left (D.820 and O.1633H) and right (O.1588), and trifid motifs (Rogers H109). *c*. AD 150-180. *162 T10; 3*

Context 174

Much of the samian from this context is burnt. Worthy of separate note are:

1014* Form 37, burnt, Central Gaulish. Over half of a bowl with ovolo (Rogers B114), beads and double ridge below the decoration typical of the style of Austrus. The panels include: 1) a seated Apollo (D.52) between Cupids (D.247, 245). 2) An athlete (D.394). The mask is on a stamped bowl from Caistor-by-Norwich. He is also known to have used the leafy spray (Rogers J167?), rosette (Rogers C54) and one of the Cupids (D.245). *c*. AD 125-40. *174 T10* (eighteen sherds, most joining, with others in *028* and *169 T10*); *3*

1015* Form 37, almost two-thirds complete, Central Gaulish. A bowl in the style of the Large-S Potter, with his distinctive S-motif in some of the panels and his rosette-tongued ovolo (Rogers B24). Each alternate panel contains a tripod (Rogers Q21). Other panels contain a warrior (D.614), gladiators (D.852), a winged centaur (O.735A), a bird (D.1038) and a tiny Venus with a mirror. The ovolo, warrior and gladiator panel are on another bowl of this potter from Castleford (museum) and the bird and tripod are on bowls in his style from East Studdal, Kent (British Museum) and Wilderspool (Grosvenor Museum, Chester), respectively. *c*. AD 125-40. *174 T10* (many fragments, most burnt, with others in *027*, *028*, *058* and *472*); *3*

1016* Form 30, burnt, Central Gaulish. The decoration includes a rosette-tongued ovolo (Rogers B14), Diana (D.67), Bacchus (O.566), panther (D.799), bird (O.2315A), lion (not in D. or O.), Hercules (O.784), acanthus (Rogers K2) and partly-impressed acanthi (Rogers K10 or 11). The arrangement of the panels is not entirely clear. Most of the details were used by X-13, a potter who supplied moulds to Donnaucus at Les Martres-de-Veyre, and the

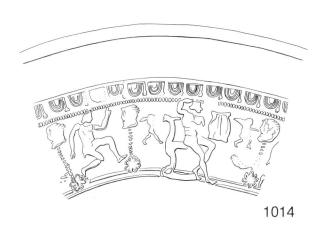

1014

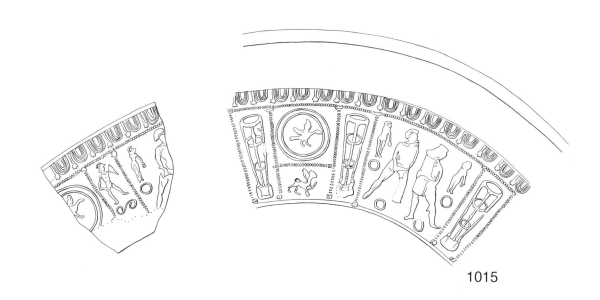

1015

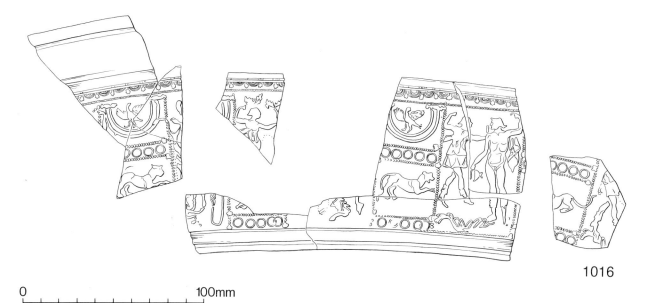

1016

0 ⊢————————————————⊣ 100mm

Fig. 35. Decorated samian from Trench 10. Scale 1:2

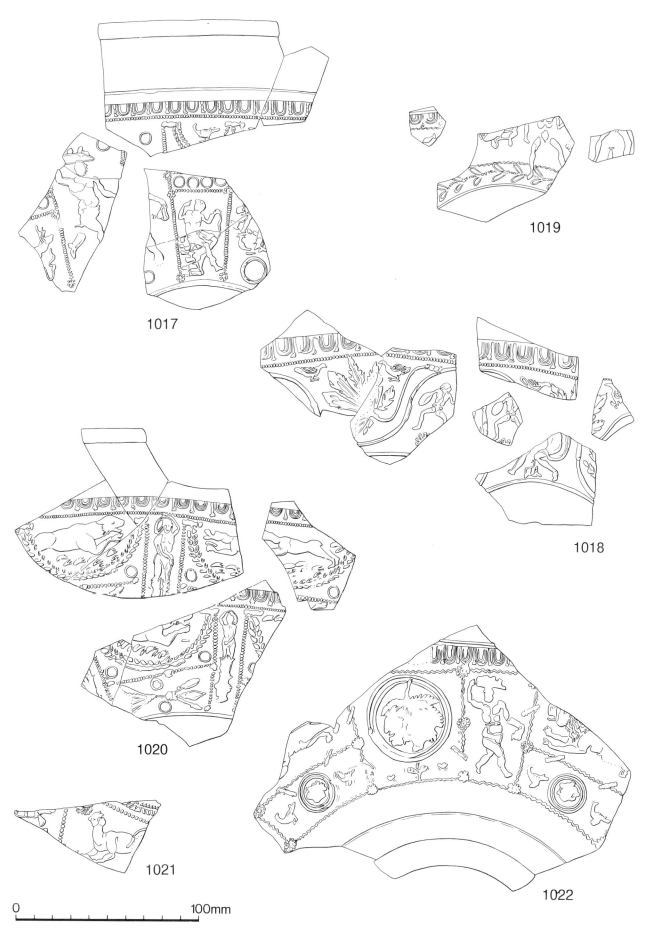

1017

1019

1018

1020

1021

1022

0   100mm

Fig. 36. Decorated samian from Trench 10. Scale 1:2

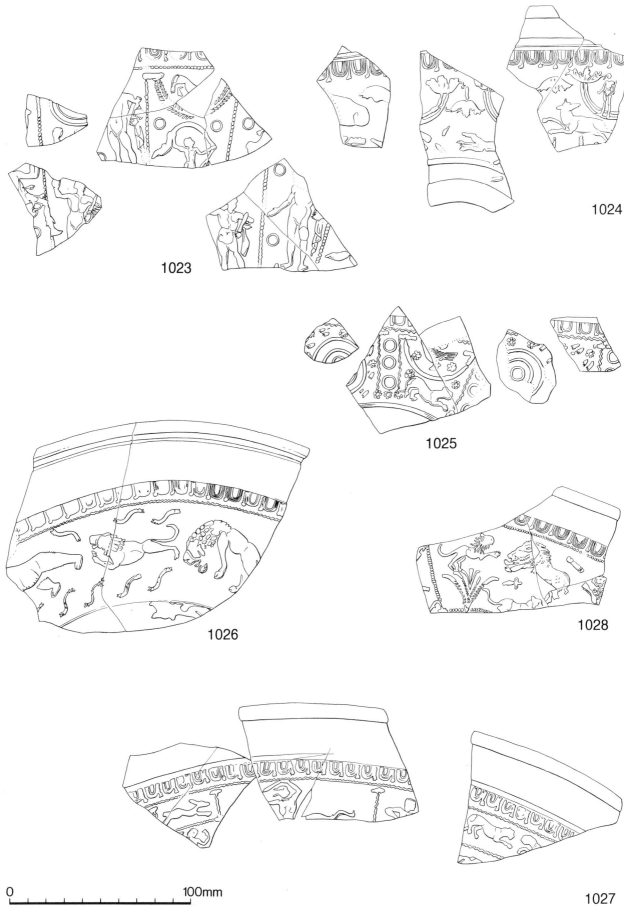

1023

1024

1025

1026

1028

1027

0   100mm

Fig. 37. Decorated samian from Trench 10. Scale 1:2

general arrangement and use of rings is consistent with his style (S. & S. 1958, pl. 46, 533, 544). Sacer i, who almost certainly began his career at Les Martres, occasionally produced bowls in this style at Lezoux, where this piece was made, and he is known to have used the ovolo, spindle and panther. The Hercules is on a bowl in his style from Scole, Norfolk. *c.* AD 125-40. *174 T10* (eight sherds, with *028* (6) and *010 T10*); *3*

1017* Form 37, Central Gaulish. The decoration consists of a single-bordered ovolo (Rogers B12) and four repeated panels: 1) a row of rings over an erotic group (a smaller version of Oswald 1936-7 pl. XC, B). 2) A slave (D.322). 3) A row of rings over a seated figure (D.68). 4) Diana with hind (D.64) over a small, double medallion. One sherd, probably with the top part of panel 3, has a bird (O.2298) in a chevron festoon (Rogers F56). The beaded junction masks are diagnostic of Criciro v and many of the details, including the ovolo, are on signed bowls from Wels; cf. Karnitsch 1959, Taf, 58, 4 for the erotic group, seated figure, festoon and rings and Taf. 59, 1 for the Diana. One of the sherds (unburnt, in context 080) has a possible cursive signature, which should belong to Criciro, rather than Divixtus, though one of his styles is very similar and he is known to have used the medallion. *c.* AD 135-55. *174 T10* (six fragments, with 11 in *010* and *028* and 3 in *080 T10*, most burnt); *3*

Context 239
Worthy of separate note is:

1018* Form 37, Central Gaulish. The ovolo (Rogers B231, or a variant), is on a bowl from the Barnsley Park villa in the style of a Lezoux Paternus (iv), who signed bowls in the nominative, and the rosette (Rogers C56?) is on a signed bowl of the same potter from the same site. No close parallels have been found for the warrior, scarf-dancer, bird or leaf, but the warrior and ovolo are on a bowl in his style from Carlisle (May and Hope 1917, pl. IV, 43). Another of his bowls is in the group of burnt samian from Site 1(74). *c.* AD 135-65. *239 T10* (three fragments, with *259* (2), *301* and *056A T10*); *3*

Context 254
Worthy of separate note is:

1019* Form 37, Central Gaulish. A freestyle bowl, with an athlete (O.676A) and crane (D.1001). The ovolo is not in Rogers, but the astragalus (Rogers R63) and trifid motif in the wreath (Rogers G172) were both used by his potter P-8, who may have made the bowl. *c.* AD 125-45. *254 T10* (with *198 T10*); *3*

Context 285
Worthy of separate note is:

1020* Form 37, Central Gaulish. Each alternate panel contains a caryatid (D.655). The other panels have chevron festoons (Rogers F8) over trifid motifs (Rogers G76), back to back. The festoons contain alternately panthers to right (O.1504, incompletely impressed) and bears to left (D.818 bis), both amid acanthus-tips (Rogers K22, partly impressed). All the details, apart from the ovolo, caryatid and panther appear on signed or stamped bowls of Attianus ii. For the ovolo see a bowl from Doncaster (Dickinson 1986, 133, no. 31). *c.* AD 125-145. *285 T10* (*058* (5), *129* (2), *286*, *293*, *299* and *623 T10*, some joining); *3*

Context 298
Worthy of separate note is:

1021* Form 37, burnt, Central Gaulish. The panels include: 1) Minerva (D.77). 2A) A chevron festoon (Rogers F12); 2B) a panther (D.804) and leaf (Rogers H167). The heavy beads and all the other details were used by Casurius ii, but it should be noted that his panther normally only has the stump of the tail (S. & S. 1958, pls 136, 51 and 137, 60). The tail here seems to have been added,

perhaps soon after it was broken, and may indicate one of Casurius's earlier products. Even so, it will scarcely be earlier than AD 160 and could be considerably later in the 2nd century. *298 T10; 3*

Context 299
Worthy of separate note is:

1022* Form 37, Central Gaulish. A badly-made bowl, with a groove between the bottom of the decoration and the (unworn) footring. The ovolo (Rogers B76) and zig-zag borders with astragali placed diagonally across them and rosettes (as Rogers C297, but with 10 petals) are typical of bowls by Geminus iv, divided by S. & S. into G.I. Vibius and Gelenus (1958, pls 65, 1 and 66, 16). The other details include a slave (D.322), a mask (not in D. or O.), a lion (D.767), a bird (not closely identifiable), a leaf (not in Rogers), a double medallion and two trifid motifs (Rogers G112 and 173). This is from the same mould as an unsigned (unpublished) bowl from Wroxeter. *c.* AD 125-45. *299 T10* (with *058*, *239* (2), *301*, *457*, *474*, *448* (2) and *952 T10*); *3*

Context 318
Worthy of separate note is:

1023* Form 37, Central Gaulish, with panels: 1) A warrior. 2) A double medallion over a Perseus (D.146). 3) Man with *chlamys* (O.96). 4) Panther (D.799) in a chevron festoon (Rogers F41), over a scarf-dancer. 5) Warrior, as in 1, or a Diana. The ovolo, an unusually clean impression of Rogers B144, is on early bowls of Cinnamus ii and he regularly used the Perseus, panther and festoon. A smaller version of O.96 is on a stamped bowl from Cologne (Rheinisches Landesmuseum, Bonn) and the full-sized version is on two bowls in his style with identical decoration from Corbridge (Simpson 1953, fig. 17, 40) and Les Martres-de-Veyre. The coarse fabric and orange glaze are not typical of Cinnamus's later work, but the glaze appears on his early wares and those of potters such as Cerialis ii and Paullus iv. *c.* AD 140-60. *318 T10* (three fragments, with *U/S* (2), *219* and *464 T10*); *3*

Context 332
Worthy of separate note is:

1024* Form 37, Central Gaulish. The ovolo (Rogers B233) was used by Pugnus ii and X-6, among others. The freestyle scene includes a small figure (not in D. or O.), stag (D.884), dog (D.934) and acanthus (Rogers K12?). This style makes use of suspended festoons, as on a bowl from Margidunum (Oswald 1948, pl. XXXVI, 1). The festoons either do not go all the way round the bowl or are arranged in pairs. *c.* AD 130-50. *332 T10* (with *535*, *900A* and *909 T10*); *4*

Context 342
Worthy of separate note is:

1025* Form 37, Central Gaulish. The small, beaded rosettes (Rogers C120) are diagnostic of Tetturo and he used multiple medallions (though slightly different ones) on signed bowls from Camelon and Verulamiun. The panther (D.799), vertical series of rings and single festoon are on a bowl in his style from West Stow, Suffolk. The ovolo (not in Rogers) is on a bowl in his style from Camelon. The bird is perhaps O.2267A and the space-fillers are partly impressed acanthi. *c.* AD 130-60. *342 T10* (4 fragments, with *081/4*, *146* and *152 T10*); *?*

Context 440
Worthy of separate note is:

1026* Form 37, Central Gaulish. The ovolo (S. & S. 1958, pl. 29, 344) was used at Les Martres-de-Veyre and also at Lezoux, where this was made. It occurs on a bowl from Bannaventa, possibly in the

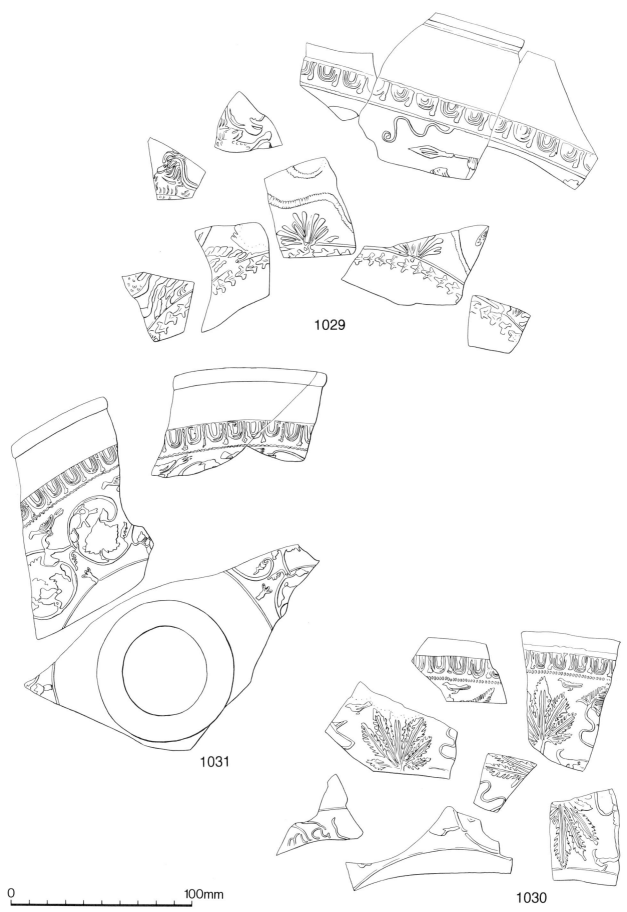

1029

1031

1030

0   100mm

Fig. 38. Decorated samian from Trench 10. Scale 1:2

style of Cassius ii, with a mould-signature]ssi, retrograde, below the decoration (signed in the mould after firing). This bowl also shows possible traces of a signature,]ss[, retrograde. The freestyle scene includes two lions (D.769 and O.1497E), a bear and serpentine motifs. Hadrianic, probably after AD 130. *440 T10* (with *455* (4) and *301 T10); 2*

Context 448

Mixed in with 448 are sherds from contexts 129, 164, 361, 449 and 474.

Of separate note are:

1027* Form 37, Central Gaulish. The sequence of panels is not clear, but the decoration includes panthers (D.799 and 805), a warrior on a horse (O.263), Perseus (D.145), Venus (D.175), a lion? (D.767?) and a hare (not in D. or O.). The ovolo (Rogers B41) suggests an early bowl of Pugnus ii. The thin brown glaze has worn off in many places, revealing a cream slip. *c.* AD 125-50. *448 T10* (ten fragments, with *U/S* (2), *129*, *455* (2) and *483 T10*, some joining); *3*

1028* Form 37, Central Gaulish. The ovolo (not in Rogers) is occasionally on bowls by a Hadrianic potter who did not often use ovolos. He also used the lion to right (O.1404) and panther (O.1519). The decoration also includes another lion (D.753), a boar (not in D. or O.) a fan-shaped motif (Rogers G8) and a 'dagger' (Rogers G219), the last mainly associated with Pugnus ii. *c.* AD 125-140. *448 T10* (three fragments, with *462* (2) and *472 T10*, some joining); *3*

Context 472

Material ranging from the Flavian-Trajanic period to the 3rd century. It includes stamped vessels of Anaillus, Silvinus iii and Calendio (Nos 1055, 1139, 1066-7) and a signed form 37 of Acaunissa (see No. 1008). The decorated ware also includes bowls in the styles of Attianus ii (see Archive Report context 445, iii), Drusus i (with context 452), Drusus ii (with Archive Report context 445, iv), Cettus, Geminus iv, X-5 or Sissus ii, the Large-S Potter (6, including a sherd from context 174, No. 1015), Sacer i (from Archive Report context 535, v), the Cerialis ii - Cinnamus ii group (2, one with context 079) and an anonymous Hadrianic potter (see No. 1028). The latest piece is a stamped form 31 of Severianus ii of Rheinzabern (No. 1132).

Worthy of separate note are:

1029* Form 37, South Gaulish. The ovolo, basal wreath and probably the fan-shaped plant (Hermet 1934, pl. 14, 49?) are on a signed bowl of L. Cosius from the Saalburg (Ricken 1934, Taf XIV, 11) and the wreath is on two of his bowls from La Graufesenque. The rocks are on a signed bowl from Rottweil (O. & P. 1920, pl. XIX, 6). The decoration also includes a *bestiarius* (Hermet 1934, pl. 24, 281), snake winding round the bowl, lion and tree. The bowl may depict the Labours of Hercules, a favourite theme of this potter. *c.* AD 90-110. *472 T10* (three sherds, with others in *079*, *097* (2), *473*, *535*, *908* (3), *909* (2) and *900 T10); 4*

1030* Form 37, Central Gaulish, with mould-signature of Drusus ii,]rususf (retrograde), below the decoration. The ovolo (Rogers B61) is on another signed bowl, from Doncaster (Dickinson 1986, 133, 29). The scroll includes a vine-leaf (Rogers H58) and triangular leaf (not in Rogers) and two birds to left (not closely identifiable). *c.* AD 125-45. *472 T10* (three sherds, with others in *078*, *115*, *445*, *448* (2), *517*, *688*, *900* and *909 T10); 4*

Context 495

Worthy of separate note is:

1031* Form 37, Central Gaulish. The ovolo (Rogers B233), used by Pugnus ii and his associates, is on a signed Pugnus bowl from Carlisle (publication forthcoming), together with a (different) trifid motif on an astragalus. The bird, perhaps O.2270A, is on bowls from Braughing and Towcester, in the style of X-5. The vine-scroll is Rogers M10. The footring is hardly worn. *c.* AD 130-50. *495 T10* (three sherds, with *298, 452* (2) and *U/S T10); 2*

Context 589

Worthy of separate note is:

1032* Form 37, South Gaulish. Wide panels alternate with narrow ones containing birds to right, looking back, in single medallions. The other figures are a mounted warrior (Hermet 1934, pl. 23, 233), lion (Hermet 1934, pl. 25, 22?) and bear (Hermet 1934, pl. 26, 4). The basal wreath consists of rosettes. The trident-tongued ovolo and birds are on a stamped bowl of Crucuro i from Colchester. The bear is on a bowl from the Bregenz Cellar (Jacobs 1913, Taf. 5, 34), which has a basal wreath of (larger) rosettes. The lion is on a stamped bowl of Sabinus iv from London (British Museum). *c.* AD 80-110. *589 T10* (two sherds, with *872* (4), *040 and 019 T10); 2*

Context 605

Worthy of separate note is:

1033* Three fragments of form 37, Central Gaulish. The ovolo is the same as on No. 1028 and the bowl is almost certainly by the same potter. The panels include a trumpet-player (D.311), a tier of cups (Rogers Q77?), topped by a ram's-horn motif (Rogers G380), a naked man (O.633A), a bird (D.1038), a cup (Rogers U67?), an acanthus (Rogers K11?) and a beaded rosette (Rogers C280). The potter has connections with Secundinus ii (Rogers's Secundinus I) and, apparently, with Pugnus ii (cf. No. 1028). Almost certainly Hadrianic. *605 T10; 3*

Context 620/A

Worthy of separate note is:

1034* Form 29, South Gaulish. The leaf in the upper zone scroll is on bowls from Valkenburg ZH and Alchester stamped by Meddillus. No parallel has been found for the six petalled rosettes. *c.* AD 70-85. *620/A T10* (two sherds, one joining *495 T10); 2*

Context 628

Worthy of separate note is:

1035* Form 37, South Gaulish. The single-bordered ovolo is on form 37 in the Pompeii Hoard (Atkinson 1914, no. 81), but was more normally used on form 30. The arrangement of the decoration is unusual, with some of the panels having double borders. One wide panel contains a detached triple festoon with internal and external tendrils and an eagle (not in Oswald) on top of a wavy line. Other motifs include triple dots, striated spindles and bifid buds. The ovolo, dots and sharpness of the borders suggest early Flavian date. *c.* AD 70-85. *628 T10* (three sherds, with *620A, 739, 1173* (2) and *872 T10); 2*

Context 796

Worthy of separate note is:

1036* Form 37, Central Gaulish. A freestyle (?) bowl in the style of the Rosette Potter of Les Martres-de-Veyre, with fan-shaped motif (Rogers J17), partly-impressed acanthi (Rogers K2), a trifid motif (Rogers G121), a panther (a larger version of O.1500) and a series of rings. cf. S. & S. 1958, pl. 25 for similar bowls. *c.* AD 100-125. *796 T10; 2*

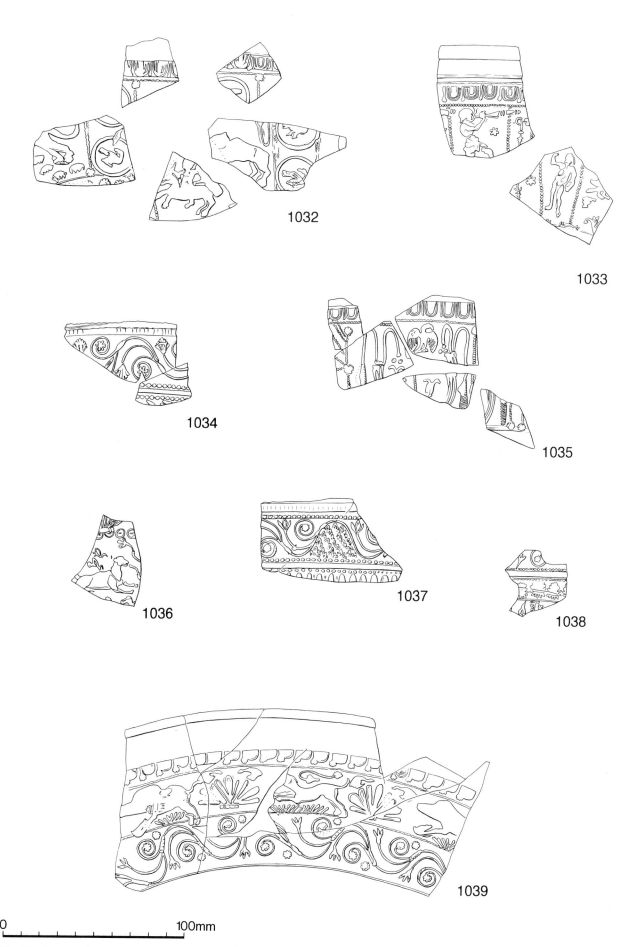

1032

1033

1034

1035

1036

1037

1038

1039

0   100mm

Fig. 39. Decorated samian from Trench 10. Scale 1:2

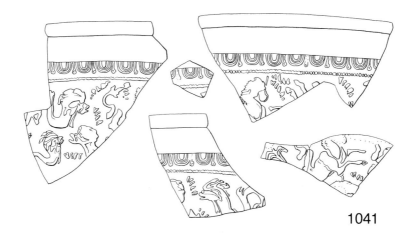

1041

1040

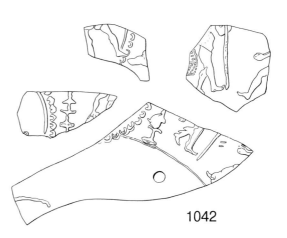

1042

1043

0   100mm

Fig. 40. Decorated samian from Trench 10. Scale 1:2

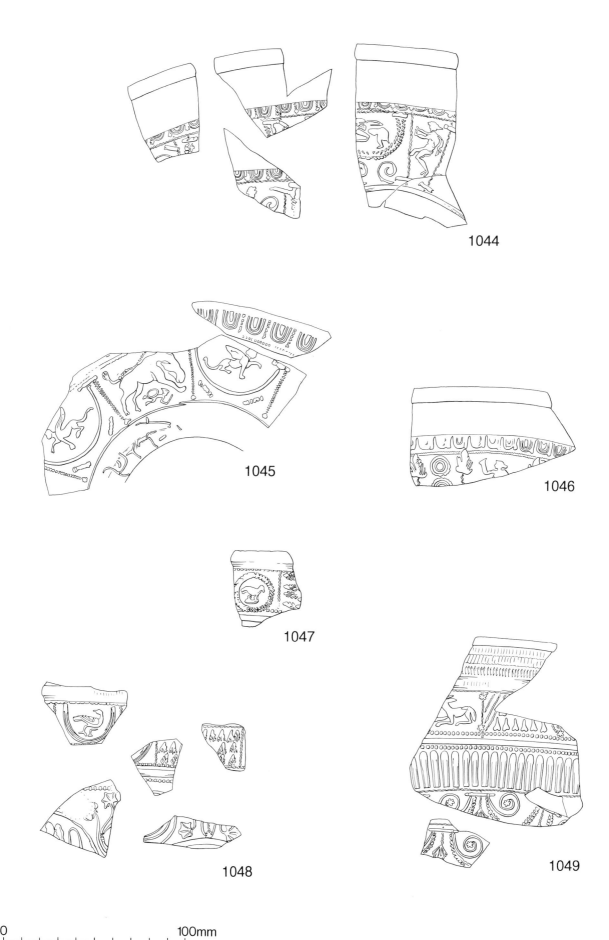

1044

1045

1046

1047

1048

1049

0   100mm

Fig. 41. Decorated samian from Trench 10. Scale 1:2

Context 822

Worthy of separate note is:

1037* Form 29, South Gaulish. The scroll in the upper zone has trifid motifs and spirals in the upper concavities and perhaps in some of the lower concavities, though one of these has rows of pointed leaf-tips. The lower zone contains straight gadroons. The trifid motif occurs on form 29s with internal stamps of Coelus, Meddillus and Pudens (Knorr 1919, Taf. 24C, D; 55J and 68, respectively). It is also on form 37 in the Pompeii Hoard (Atkinson 1914, no. 44). *c*. AD 60-80. *822 T10* (with *757* (joining) and *824 T10*); *2*

Context 824

See context 822.

Context 872

Worthy of separate note are:

1038* Form 29, South Gaulish. The unusual lower zone includes a wreath of rosettes below the central cordon. The zone below this apparently has a chevron festoon, containing the same leaf as the scroll in the upper zone. cf. the so-called Canrucatus-Vegenus style for the fine beads bordering the cordon and the straight line below the rosettes (Hermet 1934, pls 103-105). The line is on a stamped 'Canrucatus' (i.e. Cabucatus) bowl from Vechten. *c*. AD 65-80. *872 T10* (joining *129 T10*); *1*

1039* Eight joining fragments of form 37 (including one in context 056), South Gaulish. A bowl with Mercator i's rosette-tongued ovolo (Knorr 1919, Textbild 47). The upper, freestyle zone includes a dog (Hermet 1934, pl. 26, 40), boar (Hermet 1934, pl. 27, 42), fan-shaped plant (with Hermet 1934, pl. 57, 42) and partly-impressed grass-tuft (Hermet 1934, 13). The scroll in the lower zone has identical upper and lower parts, each with a trifid motif, spiral and blurred rosette. *c*. AD 80-110. *872 T10*; *1*

Context 908

Worthy of separate note are:

1040* Form 37, in the style of Cettus of Les Martres-de-Veyre. The ring-tongued ovolo is Rogers B97. The Cupid (O.419) is in a double festoon, suspended from three rosettes. The leaf below it is not known to Rogers. The leaf in the adjacent panel (Rogers H59) is next to Cettus's familiar small double medallion. The rosettes are on a bowl in his style from Carlisle. *c*. AD 135-60. *908 T10; 3*

1041* Form 37, Central Gaulish. A bowl in the style of Albucius ii, with one of his ring-tongued ovolos (Rogers B107). The freestyle marine scene includes two pairs of dolphins (D.1052, 1050 and O.2394A, 2384), a pair of sea-horses (D.35 and its reverse) and partly-impressed leaves (from Rogers J146). cf. a similar bowl, from Corbridge (S. & S. 1958, pl. 121, 8). *c*. AD 150-80. *908 T10* (three sherds, with machine trench (3), *075*, *078* (2), *079* and *097 T10*); *3*

Context 909

Worthy of separate note is:

1042* Form 37, Central Gaulish. The decorative medallion (Rogers E1) contains a figure, probably a boxer, viewed from the back. The same figure recurs in the field. The other figure is a slave with basket (D.321). The divider is not known to Rogers. Sissus ii and X-5 used the medallion, but there are no other parallels with named potters. There is a signature below the decoration, C[, retrograde, from a mould signed before firing. This could be part of a signature of Cassius i; cf. S. & S. 1958, pl. 174, 5 for a bowl from Strasbourg with a signature Cassi retrograde, which looks to have been inscribed after the mould was fired. Similar signatures in]ssi retrograde, from Baldock (Dannell 1986, p. 221, D56) and Bannaventa were originally assigned to Sissus ii, but they might

really belong to Cassius, particularly as they were almost certainly inscribed in the mould after firing. On the decoration of these and the Strasbourg bowl, there may be some stylistic similarities between the two potters, but too little is known about Cassius's work to be sure. *c*. AD 130-60. *909 T10* (with *908* (2 sherds, one bored for riveting) and a burnt sherd in *910 T10*); *3*

Context 910

Worthy of separate note is:

1043* Form 37, Central Gaulish, with stamp ALBVCI in the decoration (No. 1052-3). The five panels, repeated, contain: 1) A Venus (D.204), over a horizontal column (Rogers similar to P3). 2) An erotic group (Oswald 1936-7, pl. XC, L). 3) A Cupid with torches (a reduced version of D.265). 4) Cupid (D.242), bird (D.1011) and seated figure (not in D. or O.). 5) Erotic group (a reduced version of Oswald 1936-7, pl. XC, H). Some of the panels have partly-impressed leaves (Rogers J146) used as space-fillers. A bowl from Clermont-Ferrand (Collection Souchon) is apparently from the same mould. *c*. AD 150-80. *910 T10; 3*

Context 951

Worthy of separate note are:

1044* Form 37, Central Gaulish. The ovolo (Rogers B19), chevron festoon (Rogers F42), spirals and wavy-line border were used by Rogers's potter P-16, whose bowls occur in Scotland, at Camelon (3) and Inveresk (2). Another bowl from Inveresk, apparently in the style of Illixo, who has some motifs in common with P-16, has the festoon and horizontal astragli. The figure in Phrygian cap and the hare are not known to Déchelette or Oswald. *c*. AD 130-150. *951 T10* (two sherds, with *952* (5) and *932 T10*); *3*

1045* Form 37, almost complete, Central Gaulish. A bowl by a member of the Cerialis ii - Cinnamus ii group, with panels: 1) A single festoon with sphinx to left (D.496). 2) A boar to right (D.823), over a pygmy (O.696A). 3) A sphinx to right, in a single festoon (D.497). 4) = 2). 5) = 1). 6) = 2). 7) = 3). 8) = 2). The cursive signature, Cer---s, retrograde, from a mould signed before firing, belongs to Cerialis ii. *c*. AD 135-165. *Stamp No. 1176; 951 T10* (with 4 sherds in *950 T10*); *3.*

Context 1170

Worthy of separate note is:

1046* Form 37, Central Gaulish. The ovolo (Rogers B229), horizontal border of tiny beads (Rogers A1, here blurred), leaf (Rogers G205) and, probably, the beaded circles in the narrow panel (Rogers C295?) and the zig-zag vertical border (Rogers A23) were used by Priscinus. The figure-type is an Amazon (D.154). *c*. AD 130-60. *1170 T10; 1*

Context 1173

Worthy of separate note are:

1047* Form 29, South Gaulish. A fragment of the upper zone, with a bird (Hermet 1934, pl. 28, 67) in a chevron medallion and an adjacent panel with rows of serrated leaf-tips, impressed sideways. All the details are on bowls with internal stamps of Pass(i)enus, the bird and medallion on one from Alésia, the leaves on another, perhaps from Bingerbrück (Knorr 1952, Taf. 48A). The leaves are also on bowls with mould-stamp of Murranus from London (formerly Guildhall Museum) and internal stamp of Celadus from Mainz (Knorr 1919, Taf. 21B). *c*. AD 60-80. *1173 T10* (joining *147 T10*); *1*

1048* Form 29, South Gaulish, with panelled upper zone and winding scroll in the lower zone. The festoon and bird (Hermet 1934, pl. 28, 39) in the upper zone are on a bowl from Bonn stamped by Pass(i)enus. The serrated leaf-tips are on a bowl from Bingerbrück, also stamped by him (Knorr 1952, Taf. 48A). The ivy leaf in the scroll is perhaps one used by Calvus i (cf. Knorr 1919, Taf. 18D) and later by Mercator i. *c.* AD 65-80. *1173 T10 (twelve sherds, some joining, including one in 872 T10); 1*

1049* Form 29, South Gaulish. The hare (Hermet 1934, 1934 pl. 26, 66), panel of leaves and diagonal wavy lines, tassel in the lower zone and, probably the short straight gadroons are on form 29s with mould stamps of Iustus i (IIVST), the first two from York, the tassel from de Meern (Utrecht Museum) and the gadroons from La Graufesenque (1978 excavations). Bowls with internal stamps of Calvus i, Meddillus, Pass(i)enus and Vitalis ii also have many of the details. cf. Knorr 1919, Taf. 54, 9 (Meddillus) and Knorr 1952, Taf. 48A (Pass(i)enus and Vitalis ii) for the festoons; Knorr 1952, 40B (Meddillus) for the tassel; the same bowl for the gadroons and also Knorr 1919, Taf. 83D (Vitalis ii), which has similar, but longer gadroons. Bowls with stamps of Calvus i from La Graufesenque have the hare, tassel motif and gadroons. An unprovenced bowl of his, in Clermont-Ferrand Museum, has the festoons. *c.* AD 65-80. *1173 T10 (five joining sherds, and one in 056/B); 1*

Stamps from Trench 10

Each entry gives: potter (i, ii, etc. where homonyms are involved), die number, form of vessel, reading, pottery of origin followed by the context information.

a, b and c after the place of manufacture indicate:
(a) A stamp attested at the pottery in question.
(b) A stamp not attested at the pottery in question, though the potter is known to have worked there.
(c) A stamp assigned to the pottery on the evidence of fabric and/or distribution.

1050 Aelianus i 6b 18/31 ΛIIΚIΛNVS Lezoux c. Aelianus's fabrics suggest that he worked at both Les Martres-de-Veyre and Lezoux. This piece is in Lezoux fabric. His output includes dishes of form 15/17 in Les Martres fabric which are Trajanic or early Hadrianic. His Lezoux output, therefore, probably falls within the range *c.* AD 125-40. *908 T10; SF2717; 3*

1051 Albinus iv 8b 18/31 ALBINVS (Walke 1965, Taf. 40, 59) Lezoux a. The form of this dish and the occurrence of the stamp at Chesterholm suggest Hadrianic date, though a vessel from Castlecary, with another of his stamps, shows that he was probably still working in the Antonine period. *c.* AD 130-50. *091 T10; 3*

1052-3 Albucius ii 6h 37 (2) AL] and ALBVCI (S. & S. 1958, pl. 120, 1) Lezoux a. Decorated bowls with this stamp occur on Hadrian's Wall and in Antonine Scotland. There is also one from the Wroxeter Gutter. *c.* AD 150-180. *910 T10; SF2109; 3. 004 T10; SF263; Mod.*

1054 Ambitotus 1a 18/31 [ΛMBIT]OVMΛ (Dickinson 1990, fig. 183, 1) Lezoux a. A stamp noted on forms 18/31R and 27. There are nine examples from the 'pottery shop'. *c.* AD 130-55. *445 T10; SF1494; 3*

1055 Anaillus 2a 33 ΛNΛILLF (Durand-Lefebvre 1963, 11, 34) Lezoux a. The use of this stamp on forms 18/31, 18/31R and 27, and its occurrence at Rhineland forts, suggest a range *c.* AD 125-145. *147 T10; SF558; 3. 472 T10 SF1780; 4*

1056 Anaillus 4a 27 ANAILLVS Lezoux b. The dating evidence for this stamp is the same as for No. 1055, above. *457 T10; SF1433; 3*

1057 Annius ii 2a 18/31R ΛΛΙ[ΜΙοF] (Hartley 1972a, fig. 82, 91) Lezoux a. This stamp occurs in period IIC at Verulamium (*c.* AD 140-50) and one of his others is in a late-Hadrianic context on Hadrian's Wall (Birley 1930, 186, no. 6). *c.* AD 130-50. *174 T10; 3*

1058 Arcanus 5a 27 ARC Lezoux b. No other examples of this stamp have been noted by us. His decorated ware is mostly Hadrianic and his plain forms include dishes of forms 18/31 and 18/31R. His vessels turn up at Rhineland forts. *c.* AD 125-45. *264 T10; 3*

1059 Attillus iii 4a 33 ATTILLVS La Graufesenque c. A stamp noted on form 27 from Catterick. Flavian, but not closely datable within the period. *U/S T10; SF1465*

1060 Attius ii 5b 18/31 ATTIVS·FE Lezoux b. A stamp noted in the Rhineland and on forms 18/31R and 27. *c.* AD 135-50. *688 T10 SF2276; 2*

1061 Attius ii 6a 18/31 ΛTTIVƧ·EF Lezoux b. A stamp from this die at South Shields could be either Hadrianic or Antonine, since Attius's occasional use of forms 79 and 80 shows that he was still at work in the 160s. *c.* AD 135-65. *952 T10 SF1838; 3*

1062 Buccula 3a 33 BVCCVΚM retrograde. Buccula's fabrics suggest that he worked at both Les Martres-de-Veyre and Lezoux, and this particular die may have been used at both centres. The stamp occurs on forms 27 and 80. The Castleford piece is in Les Martres fabric. Hadrianic. *U/S T10; SF1943*

1063 Butrio 1a 37 BVT[RIO] (Walke 1965, Taf. 39, 8) Lezoux a. The decorated bowls with this stamp are mainly Hadrianic, though a few pieces in his style from Scotland suggest that he was still at work in the early 140s. There is a burnt example from the 'pottery shop'. *c.* AD 125-45. *952 T10; 3*

1064 Calava 2b 18/31 [CALA]VA·F (Walke 1965, Taf. 40, 102-3) Lezoux a. A stamp noted from Camelon, Chesters and Rhineland forts. There are eleven examples from the 'pottery shop'. *c.* AD 125-50. *452 T10; SF1474; 3*

1065-7 Calendio 4a 27(2), 18/31 KAL·EN[; KAL·ENDIO ;]NDIO (Nash-Williams 1930, fig. 1, 45) Lezoux a. A stamp used on forms 18/31, 18/31R, 27 and 81. One of his other stamps appears on the rims of decorated bowls in the styles of Cinnamus ii, Laxtucissa and, probably, the Large-S Potter. *c.* AD 135-160. *508 T10; 4. 472 T10; SF1469 and SF1472; 4*

1068 Calenus 2a 27 CALENVS bE Lezoux a. A stamp used on forms 18/31, 18/31R, 27, 81 and (once) 80. It occurs at Rhineland forts. *c.* AD 130-165. *448 T10; SF642; 3*

1069 Cerialis ii 9a 33 ϽCERIAL·FΚ Lezoux b. A stamp used on forms 18/31, 18/31R and 27. A stamp from this die, or its broken version, comes from the 'pottery shop'. *c.* AD 135-65. *453 T10; SF1391;?*

1070 Cinnamus ii 9a 33 CINNΛ retrograde, Lezoux b. No other examples of this stamp have been noted by us. The left-hand end of the frame is diagonal, suggesting that the die may have been re-used after fracture. *c.* AD 140-60. *258 T10; SF932; 3*

1071 Criciro v 1a 33 CR-CIR·O·OFI (Walke 1965, Taf. 41, 145) Lezoux b. Criciro v's stamps, including this one, occur in Antonine Scotland. The die was used on forms 18/31 and 27. *c.* AD 135-65. *952 T10; SF1501; 3*

1072 Dagomarus 13a 18/31 DΛGOMΛ (Ludowici 1927, 213) Lezoux a. Dagomarus worked at Les Martres-de-Veyre in the Trajanic period and at Lezoux under Hadrian. This particular stamp occurs in the Birdoswald Alley. *c.* AD 125-40. *267A T10; 4*

1073 Docilis i 2a 37 [D]OCILISF[E] retrograde, below the decoration (S. & S. 1958, pl. 92, 16) Lezoux a. This stamp was also used on plain forms, including 27 and 31. Docilis's decorated bowls turn up both on Hadrian's Wall and in Antonine Scotland. *c.* AD 130-50. *908 T10; 3*

1074 Donatus ii 1b 31 DONATI·M Lezoux a. The occurrence of this stamp in the Rhineland and its use on forms 18/31 and 27 suggest that it was in use before *c.* AD 150, though a stamp from another die on form 80 extends his career beyond AD 160. *c.* AD 130-60. *452 T10; SF1484; 3*

1075 Fabianus ii 2a 33 [FABIA]NIM retrograde Lezoux a. Only one die is recorded for Fabianus. All the stamps noted are on form 33, apart from one example on form 31R. Antonine, continuing after AD 160. *081 T10; 3/4*

1076 Falana 1a 27 Mᴧᴧᴧᴧᴧ retrograde (Hartley 1970, 26, 46) Lezoux c. All the examples noted are on form 27 and all are from either Britain or the Rhineland. One comes from the Saalburg Erdkastell (before AD 139). *c.* AD 125-50. *219 T10; SF930; Mod.*

1077 Felix ii 2d 18/31 [FELI]XF Lezoux c. Two of Felix's stamps, including one from this die, occur in the 'pottery shop'. This stamp appears also in the Rhineland, and there are others from Newstead and Carzield. *c.* AD 140-60. Slightly burnt. *079 T10; SF406; 4*

1078 Frontinus 18b 15/17 or 18 [OFR]ON retrograde, La Graufesenque a. Frontinus's wares appear frequently at Flavian foundations. This particular stamp, from one of his less-common dies, occurs at Rottweil. *c.* AD 75-95. Burnt. *739 T10; 2*

1079 Fuscus ii 8d 18/31 FV[SCI] La Graufesenque a. A stamp noted from Holt and the Saalburg (2). It occurs on both forms 18 and 18/31, and will have been in use *c.* AD 80-110. *234 T10; SF853; 3*

1080 Gnatius ii 4a 33 GNᴧIVS Les Martres-de-Veyre c, Lezoux c. Though Gnatius may have worked at Les Martres, this piece seems to be in Lezoux fabric, as are the many vessels with this stamp from the 'pottery shop'. One of his other stamps occurs in the Rhineland. *c.* AD 130-55. Burnt. *058 T10; SF132; Mod.*

1081 Gongius 2a 33 GONGI·M (Ettlinger 1978, Taf. 1, 45-6) Lezoux c. A stamp used on forms 18/31, 18/31R, 27 and 31R (one example only). It occurs twice at Camelon, once in Antonine I or the Antonine II construction levels. *c.* AD 140-70. *155 T10; SF673; 3*

1082 Icttiama 1a 18/31R ICTTIAMᴧ (de Schaetzen and Vanderhoeven 1964, pl. VII, 1) Lezoux a. Only one die is recorded for this potter, who used it on forms 18/31R, 31, 31R and 33. His stamps occur at Bainbridge, Benwell and Bewcastle. *c.* AD 155-85. *145 T10; 4*

1083 Iucundus iii 3a 15/17 or 18 [OFI]VCVNDI La Graufesenque a. A stamp often used on form 29. It occurs at Elginhaugh, Rottweil, the York fortress (Dickinson and Hartley 1993, fig. 283, 2757) and the Nijmegen Ulpia Noviomagus site. *c.* AD 70-90. Burnt. *389 T10; SF1848; 2*

1084 Iulius ii 13a 27 IVLI· (Hermet 1934, pl. 111, 70a) La Graufesenque a. Much of this potter's output is Flavian, but the occurrence of this stamp at Sels and the early cemeteries at Nijmegen suggests that the die was first used in the Neronian period. *c.* AD 60-90. *749 T10; 2*

1085 Iullinus i 3c 15/17 or 18 [IVLↃ]IMI La Graufesenque b. A stamp noted from Chester, Köngen (Simon 1962, 40, 389) and Rottweil-Hochmauren. Stamps from other dies occur at Newstead and Inchtuthil. *c.* AD 70-100. *389 T10; SF1799; 2*

1086 Iullinus ii 1a 33 IVLLI[NI·OF] Lezoux a. Iullinus ii's stamps occur on Hadrian's Wall and in groups of samian from the Wroxeter Gutter and Pudding Pan Rock. This particular stamp appears at Catterick. *c.* AD 160-90. *U/S T10; SF1315*

1087 Littera i 1d 18/31 LITTERA·F Lezoux b. This stamp occurs, burnt, in the London Second Fire groups and a stamp from a different die comes from the 'pottery shop'. *c.* AD 120-45. *T10 197: 3*

1088 Lollius ii 2a 33 LOLLI·M (Walke 1965, Taf. 42, 196) Lezoux a. This stamp was used on a wide variety of forms, including 27 and

79, in roughly equal proportions. It occurs at Camelon and in an early Antonine pit at Castor. *c.* AD 140-70. Burnt. *002 T10; SF154; Mod.*

1089 Macrinus ii 3a 18/31 MᴧCRIᴧVSF Lezoux b. This potter's stamps turn up in the Rhineland and in Hadrianic or early Antonine contexts at Lezoux. His forms include 18/31R and 27. *c.* AD 125-50. *043 T10; SF1566; 4*

1090 Malliacus 3h 18/31 MᴧLLIACI Lezoux b. A stamp used on forms 18/31 and 18/31R. There are several examples from the 'pottery shop'. *c.* AD 130-60. Burnt. *174 T10; 3*

1091 Marcus v 9d 33(2) [M]ᴧRCI:, MᴧRCI: Lezoux b. Marcus v's wares come from late-Antonine kilns at Lezoux. His stamps occur at Pennine forts and in the samian from Pudding Pan Rock. *c.* AD 160-200. *952 T10; SF570; 3*

1092 Maternus iii 2a 33 NᴧT·ERN (Dickinson 1990, fig. 183, 94) Lezoux b. This stamp was used on forms 18/31 and 18/31R. Both it and some of his other stamps occur in the Rhineland, suggesting activity before the middle of the 2nd century. *c.* AD 125-50. Burnt. *267/A T10; SF944; 4*

1093 Mettius la' 33 METTI·Aᴧ Lezoux c. A stamp from a broken die, which originally had ansate ends to the frame. It occurs at Mumrills, Newstead (Curle 1911, 238, 64) and Corbridge. One of his other stamps comes from the Saalburg Erdkastell (before AD 139). *c.* AD 135-60. *952 T10; SF1518; 3*

1094 Miccius la 18/31R MICCIVS[F] (Dannell 1971, 310, 65) Lezoux a. The occurrence of this stamp in the Rhineland, together with its occasional use on forms 31R and 79 suggests a range *c.* AD 140-70. *129 T10; SF886; 3*

1095-6 Modestus i 9a' 27g (2) ƆFMOI (Laubenheimer 1979, fig. 11, 135) La Graufesenque a. This stamp comes from a broken die which originally gave OFMOD·. The broken version was used occasionally on forms 24 and Ritterling 8, but the stamp occurs so often at Flavian foundations (including Ebchester and Broomholm) that it was almost certainly still in use in the 70s. By this time it probably belonged to one of Modestus's associates, or successors. *c.* AD 60-75. *480 T10, SF1816; 2. 985 T15V; SF630; 1b*

1097 Mon-ii la' 27ƆFNOV(Walke 1965, Taf. 43, 256) La Graufesenque a. A stamp from a die which continued in use after fracture. The full die was first used in the Flavian period and a stamp from the broken version occurs at the Saalburg. *c.* AD 80-100. *448 T10; SF1500; 3*

1098 Monti- Cres- 3a 18[OFM]ONˇCR (Ulbert 1959, Taf. 41, 39) La Graufesenque a. A stamp recorded from Burghöfe, Chester and the Nijmegen fortress. It appears occasionally on form 29s, some with decoration suggesting that the die was first used in the pre-Flavian period. *c.* AD 65-80. *017 T10; SF2162; 3*

1099-1100 Murranus 6a 27g (2) [OF]MRAↃI; ƆFMRAↃI (Hartley 1972a, fig. 81, S79) La Graufesenque a. Most of Murranus's output is Neronian. This stamp is from one of his latest dies, noted from sites such as Chester, the Nijmegen fortress and Rottweil, but also on form 24. *c.* AD 60-75. *628 T10 SF2025; 2. 421 T10; SF1313; 3*

1101 Muxtullus 1b 18/31R MVXTVLLIM (Walke 1965, Taf. 43, 262) Lezoux a. There are many examples of this stamp from the 'pottery shop', all on form 18/31. It occurs also at Camelon (3) and in a pit of the AD 150s at Alcester. *c.* AD 140-60. *267 T10; 4*

1102 Nicephor ii 3a 27 [Ↄ]ICIIPHOR Lezoux b. Nicephor ii's stamps turn up in the Rhineland. His range of forms includes 18/31, 18/31R, 27, 42 and 80. *c.* AD 140-65. *147 T10; 3*

1103-4 Ovidius 1a 27 (2) : see *Fort Stamps*, No. 99 above.

1105 Pacatus iii 1a 33 PΛCΛTVSI Les Martres-de-Veyre c. The fabric of this piece and the characteristic shape of the U suggest origin at Les Martres. Hadrianic, to judge by the form. *448 T10; SF1342; 3*

1106 Pass(i)enus 33a or a' 27 PA·SSE(N) or PA·SSE[N] La Graufesenque a. 33a occurs in both Neronian and Flavian contexts (see No. 103, above). Stamps from 33a' (Die 33a with the N recut), have not provided any additional dating evidence. *c.* AD 60-80. *118 T10; SF284; 3*

1107-8 Pateratus 1a 18/31R (2) ·PΛTERΛTIOF (Walke 1965, Taf. 43, 277-9) Lezoux a. (Both almost complete, in fragments, but with worn footrings.) There are two examples of this stamp from the 'pottery shop'. The die was used on forms 18/31, 27 and 81. *c.* AD 135-55. *910 T10; SF2112 and SF2118; 3*

1109 Paterclus ii 10a 18/31 PΛTERCL[OSFE] (Allgaier 1992, no. 78) Les Martres-de-Veyre a. Die 10a was modified twice, and stamps from the latest version occur in the London Second Fire groups (four times) and at Corbridge (2), Nether Denton and Chesterholm. The Castleford dish is one of the few vessels to have been stamped with the die in its original state and so should belong to the period *c.* AD 100-110. *389 T10; SF1813; 2*

1110 Patricius i 3h 15/17 or 18 [OFPΛ]RIC(I) (Laubenheimer 1979, fig. 10, 170) La Graufesenque a. A stamp noted from the Burghöfe Geschirrdepot of AD 69, but also at Camelon. It appears occasionally on early Flavian form 29s. *c.* AD 65-85. *237 T10; SF1979; 3*

1111 Patricius i 5a 15/17 or 18 OFPΛTRC (Laubenheimer 1979, fig. 11, 165) La Graufesenque a. One of this potter's commonest stamps, noted at Flavian foundations in Britain, and also at Butzbach and the Saalburg. *c.* AD 75-100. *255 T10; SF1089; 3*

1112 Patricius ii 6a 38 or 44 [PΛ T·]RI·CIMΛ (Juhász 1935, pl. XLVII, 214) Lezoux b. Patricius ii's stamps turn up in the Rhineland, suggesting that he was at work before *c.* AD 150, but examples are also known from the Wroxeter forum destruction and the Verulamium Second Fire deposits. *c.* AD 140-70. *708 T10; 2*

1113-15 Paullus iv 7a 27 (3) PAVL[IF];]AVLIF;]VLIF Lezoux b. One of Paullus iv's less-common stamps, noted on forms 27 (8) and 33 (1). It occurs in the Verulamium Second Fire deposits (Hartley 1972a, fig. 82, S149, tentatively read PAULL.M, *c.* AD 140-60. *081 T10; SF377; 3. 198 T10; 3. 301 T10; 3*

1116 Paullus iv 10a 18/31 PΛVI·VS[M] retrograde (de Schaetzen and Vanderhoeven 1964, pl. X, 13) Lezoux b. An earlier stamp than the last, noted from the Hadrianic group in the Birdoswald Alley. *c.* AD 130-50. *124 T10; 4*

1117 Pinna 2a 33 PINNΛFE Lezoux c. A stamp noted from a pit of the 140s at Castor. It occurs in roughly equal proportions on forms 27 and 79/80. *c.* AD 135-65. *118/2 T10; SF334; 3*

1118 Primulus i-Pater 1a 15/17R or 18R PRIMM·PATER (Knorr 1913, Taf. XIV, 87) La Graufesenque a. The style of lettering on this stamp shows that the die belonged to the maker of Nos 112-14, above, presumably in association with another potter. Examples are noted from Camulodunum, Aislingen and the Nijmegen fortress. *c.* AD 60-80. *1067 T10; SF2285; 1*

1119 Pugnus ii 1b 33 [P]VGNI·MΛ Lezoux b. This stamp occurs on form 81(?) from the 'pottery shop'. It appears also on decorated bowls, one of which is from a pit of the AD 150s at Alcester. (Hartley *et al.* 1994, fig. 50, 274) *c.* AD 130-60. Burnt. *174 T10; 3*

1120 Pugnus ii 2a 33PVΠMIM Lezoux b. This die originally gave PVΠMIM, but was damaged in the centre, so that some stamps from it look like the Castleford one. It is not possible, however, to date the two stages of the die separately. *c.* AD 130-60. *118/2 T10; SF335; 3*

1121-2 Regullus 2a 18/31(2) (Vanderhoeven 1975, 112, 594) REGVLLVSF. This stamp is from a die used at both Les Martres-de-Veyre and Lezoux. It appears on form 18/31 from both centres and on form 80 from Lezoux. The Castleford dishes are in Lezoux fabric and will fall within the range *c.* AD 130-50. *908 T10; SF2092; 3. 910 T10; SF2119; 3*

1123 Regulus 9a 27 REGVLV2[F] Lezoux b. All the examples noted of this stamp, including one from Benwell, are on form 27. Regulus also made forms 18/31, 15/31R and 80 and his wares turn up in the Rhineland. His range will be *c.* AD 140-170, with 140-160 for Die 9a. *078 T10; SF286; 4*

1124 Restutus 3a 31R RIIS[LLVLVSL] (Ludowici 1927, 228, a) Rheinzabern a. There is no site dating for this potter, but his forms, mainly 31R and 32, suggest late 2nd or early 3rd-century date. *004 T10; SF64; Mod.*

1125 Sacisamo 1a 33 SΛCISΛMO retrograde, Lezoux c. The only other examples of this stamp noted by us are from the 'pottery shop' and York(?), both on form 33. Hadrianic or early Antonine. *258 T10; SF936; 3*

1126 Sacroticus 2c 37 SΛCROTICI retrograde, Lezoux c. This stamp provides the first evidence that Sacroticus made decorated ware. It is just possible that it comes from the die which was used on his plain forms from the 'pottery shop'. The style of decoration suggests a date *c.* AD 125-50. See No. 1006 for a discussion of this bowl. *U/S T10; SF35*

1127 Secundus v 2a 18/31R(?) [SIIC]VDIM (Durand-Lefebvre 1963, 212, 660) Lezoux a. Stamps from two of this potter's dies occur on heavily-burnt vessels from Castleford, which are probably from the 'pottery shop', and his decorated ware is related to that of Cinnamus ii. This gives him a range *c.* AD 140-75, though this dish, if it is really form 18/31R, is unlikely to be later than *c.* AD 160/165. *141 T10; SF988; 3*

1128-9 Sedatus iv 2c 18/31; 33(2) S[; S ƎΛTI·M (Walke 1965, Taf. 44, 341) Lezoux a. A heavily-burnt vessel with this stamp from Gauting is perhaps from the Hadrianic fire there. It occurs in the Rhineland and on forms 18/31 and 27, also on a jar mould signed by Paullus iv. *c.* AD 130-60. *083 T10; 3. Level 2 Site 1(74); 4*

1130 Senea or Senila 3a 37 SENILA·F (Hartley and Dickinson 1981, 266, 13) retrograde, Lezoux c. The L is uncertain and may really be the second half of an archaic E. This stamp was used mainly on plain ware, including forms 18/31 and 27, but one other example has been noted on form 37, from Rouen. Both bowls are related stylistically to Quintilianus i and his associates. *c.* AD 125-50. *146 T10; 4*

1131 Senilis ii 1a 18/31 [ː SE]NILIM·ː Lezoux a. This stamp occurs in Hadrianic-Antonine groups at Lezoux. *c.* AD 130-50. Burnt. *174 T10; 3*

1132 Severianus ii 3e 31 (without rouletting, but 31R in form) 2IIVII[RIΛNV2F] (Ludowici 1927, 229, d) Rheinzabern a. Severianus ii's decorated ware suggests that he was one of the later Rheinzabern potters, almost certainly working only in the 3rd century. *472 T10; SF1583; 4*

1133 Severus iii 7q 29 ⊙FS[EVERF] (Guéry 1979, no. 196) La Graufesenque b. This stamp occurs at Newstead and in a grave at Winchester with vessels stamped by potters whose careers extended into the Flavian-Trajanic period. *c.* AD 70-100. *440 T10; SF1942; 2*

1134-5 Severus v 6d 27 (2) 2E[VE\R]V2I'; 2EV[(Knorr 1907, Taf. XXXI, 94) Lezoux b. There are many examples of this stamp from the 'pottery shop'. It occurs also at Rhineland forts. *c.* AD 130-50. *075 T10; 3. 127 T10; SF604; 3*

1136 Sextus v 2c 38 or 44(?) SEXTI·MN Lezoux b. Sextus v's stamps occur on Hadrian's Wall and in the group of late-Antonine samian from Pudding Pan Rock. This particular stamp appears at Benwell. *c*. AD 160-200. *908 T10; SF2085; 3*

1137 Sextus v 5b 38 SIIXTI·M (Knorr 1907, Taf. XXXI, 274) Lezoux a. A stamp used on forms 31R and 79, and very rarely on form 27. *c*. AD 160-200. *908 T10; SF2212; 3*

1138 Silvanus iv 2a 18/31 (Tq) SILLVANI·M. All the other examples of this stamp noted by us come from the kilns at Toulon-sur-Allier, but the Castleford piece is almost certainly in Lezoux fabric. Hadrianic-Antonine, on the form. *908 T10; SF2093; 3*

1139 Silvinus iv 2c 27 [SILVI]NI Les Martres-de-Veyre b. A stamp used on forms 18/31 and 27. Other stamps of this potter occur on form 46 and in the groups from the London Second Fire. *c*. AD 115-35. *475 T10; SF1582; 2*

1140 Silvius ii 1g 27 SILVI·OF Lezoux b. A stamp recorded from Rhineland forts and on form 18/31R. His decorated ware suggests a range *c*. AD 125-45, which would fit well with the evidence of the plain forms. Burnt. *244 T10; SF1134; 3*

1141 Tasgillus ii 11a 18/31 [T]ASCI[LLIFE] . Tasgillus ii worked both at Les Martres-de-Veyre and Lezoux. This stamp seems to have been used only at Lezoux, to judge by the associated fabrics. It occurs in the Rhineland. Other stamps used at Lezoux turn up on Hadrian's Wall and in Antonine Scotland. *c*. AD 125-40. *613 T10; SF2006; 4*

1142 Taurianus 1a 18/31R TAVRIANI (Dickinson 1994, 510, 19) Lezoux c. There is no site dating for Taurianus, but the form of this dish suggests the period *c*. AD 130-150. *U/S T10; SF49*

1143 Taurinus 1a 18/31 TAVRINI·M (Nash-Williams 1930, fig. 3, 102) Lezoux c. A stamp used on forms 18/31 and 27. It occurs at Rhineland forts. *c*. AD 125-50. *457 T10; SF1513; 3*

1144-5 Taurinus 2a 33; 18/31R TAVRINI (Baatz 1973, Abb. 41, 64) Lezoux c. For Taurinus's date, see no. 181, above. *267C T10; SF982; 4. Level + Site 1(77); SF338; Mod.*

1146 L. Ter-- Secundus 5b 27g L∃R[SECW]. This stamp occurs in a group of Flavian-Trajanic samian from La Graufesenque (Vernhet 1981, 34, 17) . Some of his others turn up at Domitianic foundations, such as Butzbach, Cannstatt and the main site at Corbridge. *c*. AD 80-110. *062 T10; SF13; 2*

1147 Tittius 2a 33(?) TITTIV[SFE] (Walke 1965, Taf. 44, 366-7) Lezoux a. A stamp noted from Newstead and Rhineland forts. One of his others comes from the 'pottery shop'. *c*. AD 130-60. Burnt. *136 T10; SF490; 3*

1148 Viducus ii 5a 18/31 [VIDVC]VSF (Vanderhoeven 1975, 134, 752) Les Martres-de-Veyre a. A stamp noted from the London Second Fire groups, also from Malton and Birrens. *c*. AD 110-30. *800 T10; SF2005; 2*

Illiterate Stamps
1149 XIXIIIN on form 33, South Gaulish. Flavian. *579 T10; SF1885; 2*

1150 VIIWΛ on form 27, South Gaulish. Flavian. *952 T10; SF1368; 3*

1151 IXIMI on form 27, South Gaulish. Flavian-Trajanic. *078 T10; SF288. 4. 068 T10 SF658; 4*

1152]/Wı on form 27, slightly burnt, from Les Martres-de-Veyre. Trajanic. *078 T10; SF445; 4*

1153 LVIL[on form 27, heavily burnt. Probably from Les Martres-de-Veyre and Trajanic. *267/B T10; 4*

1154 ΛΗ·ΙΗ·ΙΗ on form 33, Central Gaulish. Hadrianic or early Antonine. *079 T10; SF1013; 4*

1155]ΛΛ Λ[(?) on form 33, burnt, Central Gaulish. Hadrianic-Antonine. *471 T10; SF1626; 1*

1156 ΝΙΙΝΙ∨ on form 18/31, Central Gaulish. Hadrianic-Antonine. *028 T10; SF430; 3*

1157 ΛΛΙΙ[on form 18/31 or 31, Central Gaulish. Hadrianic or Antonine. *U/S T10*

1158 ∙IHΛˑNI∆ on form 31R, Central Gaulish. Mid to late-Antonine. *482 T10; SF1577; 4*

Unidentified
1159]PR[(?) on form 15/17R or 18R, South Gaulish. Flavian. *444 T10; Mod.*

1160 ..ΛΙΛ.. on form 27, South Gaulish. Flavian. *495 T10; SF1733; 2*

1161 RΛX[or MX[on form 27g, South Gaulish. Flavian. *825 T10; SF2158; 2*

1162 OI[or]IO (in a frame with a swallow-tail end) on form 18, South Gaulish. Flavian. *1075 T10; 2*

1163 ϽFALB[(?) on form 27, South Gaulish. Flavian. *495 T10; SF1733; 2*

1164 ΛI[or]IV on form 15/17 or 18, South Gaulish. Flavian or Flavian-Trajanic. *226 T10; 3*

1165 VI[or]IΛ on form 27, South Gaulish. Flavian or Flavian-Trajanic. *472 T10; SF1471; 4*

1166 S[or]S on form 27, from Les Martres-de-Veyre. Trajanic. *303 T10; SF1157; 3*

1167 An illegible stamp on form 27, from Les Martres-de-Veyre. Trajanic. *688 T10; SF2280; 2*

1168 C[on form 33, Central Gaulish. Hadrianic. *079 T10; SF403; 4*

1169]IM. on form 18/31, Central Gaulish. Hadrianic or early Antonine. *U/S T10; SF38*

1170]M (in an ansate frame) on form 18/31R, Central Gaulish. Hadrianic or early Antonine. *124 T10; SF1270; 4*

1171 An illegible stamp on form 18/31, Central Gaulish. Hadrianic or early Antonine. *688 T10; SF2280; 2*

1172]MA on form 18/31R, Central Gaulish. Hadrianic-Antonine. *U/S T10; SF34*

1173 An eight-petalled rosette on form 46, with rim as on form Curle 23 (1911). The cup has scarcely been used. Hadrianic-Antonine. *276 T10; SF1042; 3*

Cursive signatures
1174 Acaunissa: on form 37.Aca[retrograde, from a mould signed below the decoration, before firing, Lezoux a. See No. 1008 for a discussion of the decoration. Signed bowls of Acaunissa occur at Birdoswald, Corbridge and the Saalburg. There is also one from the 'pottery shop'. *c*. AD 125-45. *472 T10; 4*

1175 Cerialis ii: on form 37. Cerialis retrograde, from a mould signed below the decoration, before firing, Lezoux a. This signature often appears on bowls with small label-stamps of Cinnamus ii, decorated in one of his earlier styles. See No. 1002 for a discussion of the decoration of this bowl. *c*. AD 135-65. *028 T10; SFs 223 and 320; 3*

1176 Cerialis ii: on form 37. Cer....s retrograde, from a mould signed below the decoration, before firing, Lezoux a. See No. 1045, above, for dating. *951 T10; 3*

1177 Cerialis ii?: on form 37, Central Gaulish. C[, retrograde, from a mould signed below the decoration, before firing. Almost certainly a signature of Cerialis, from the decoration. *c.* AD 135-60. *075 T10; 3*

1178 Criciro v: on form 37.]iciro, retrograde, from a mould signed below the decoration, before firing, Lezoux a. This signature occurs on several bowls from Antonine Scotland. There is also an example from the Aquincum Hoard which may, or may not, be residual. *c.* AD 135-70. Burnt. *010 T10; Mod.*

1179 Drusus ii: on form 37.]rususf retrograde, from a mould signed below the decoration, before firing, Lezoux a. Decorated bowls in the style of Drusus ii turn up on Hadrian's Wall and, less frequently, in Antonine Scotland. *c.* AD 125-45. *472 T10; 4*

1180 Mommo: on form 37. Of Mom retrograde, from a mould signed below the decoration, before firing, La Graufesenque a. Signatures of Mommo occur on bowls in the Pompeii Hoard, once on form 29 and twice on form 37. *c.* AD 70-90. *1087 T10; 1*

1181 Sissus ii: on form 37. Sissus, retrograde, from a mould signed below the decoration, before firing, Lezoux a. The style of this potter's decorated bowls suggests Hadrianic-Antonine date. There is another signed one from Castleford, in Sheffield Museum. *c.* AD 130-60. *005 T10; SF75; Mod.*

1182 Form 37, Central Gaulish, from a mould signed, after firing, below the decoration. The bowl is by a member of the Cerialis ii-Cinnamus ii group, but the signature reads A C or V C, retrograde. *c.* AD 135-70. *118 T10; 3*

1183 Form 37, Central Gaulish. C[retrograde, from a mould signed below the decoration, before firing. For discussion of the decoration, see No. 1042. *909/C T10; 3*

Summary of the samian pottery from the *vicus* Trench 10

The sources of supply for Trench 10 are, not surprisingly, much the same as for the fort. Nearly all the South Gaulish ware comes from La Graufesenque, but one vessel appears to be in 2nd-century Montans fabric. There is also a sherd of 1st-century Lezoux ware which, it is becoming clear, was not confined to the south and west of the province, as was previously thought. It is now known from Doncaster and is recorded as far north as Strageath, with several examples from Lowland Scottish forts. The Central Gaulish ware is dominated by Lezoux, but the small amount of Trajanic material comes from Les Martres-de-Veyre. A substantial contribution to the Hadrianic-Antonine decorated ware is made by the Les Martres potter, Cettus. Only one Central Gaulish potter's stamp is necessarily later than *c.* AD 160, but some of the decorated and unstamped plain ware clearly is. This includes bowls in the styles of Advocisus and Casurius ii, the dish forms 31R and 79 or Ludowici Tg and a gritted samian mortarium. Two bowls of Albucius ii and one by Divixtus i may also belong to the later Central Gaulish material. Like the fort, Trench 10 produced a little East Gaulish ware, most of it after AD 160. The potteries mainly involved are Rheinzabern, which almost certainly

produced the bulk of the East Gaulish ware, the Argonne and, probably, Trier. Surprisingly, as in the fort, there is only one sherd of La Madeleine ware, though it is not uncommon in eastern Britain.

Trench 10 produced rather less pre-Flavian samian than the fort. This is reflected in the stamped material, where the proportion of early Flavian potters to those working wholly, or entirely, under Nero is greater than at the fort. Nevertheless, there is nothing to suggest that the fort and *vicus* were not founded at much the same time, in the early to mid-70s.

As the histogram Figure 42 shows, a peak in the quantities of samian deposited in the *vicus* occurs *c.* AD 85-90, with a subsequent falling off until the Hadrianic period. The ratio of form 29 to 37 in the *vicus* is approximately 1:3, as against 5:6 in the fort. This may imply both that in the first few decades of occupation this part of the *vicus* was slower to develop than the fort, and that it was receiving South Gaulish samian for rather longer. The same 'Trajanic gap' is displayed here as in the fort, when Castleford seems to have received very little samian from Les Martres-de-Veyre.

In contrast to the fort, the greatest quantities of samian recovered from the *vicus* are Hadrianic-Antonine. The sharp rise in the histogram at *c.* AD 140, noted to a lesser degree in the histogram for the fort, is almost certainly to be accounted for by the scattering of the damaged and burnt 'pottery shop' material over a wide area. Like the contemporary material from the fort, there is a marked similarity to the samian from the shop and, indeed, there are sherds from one of the 'pottery shop' bowls in the material from Trench 10. Further evidence is supplied by the fact that much of the Hadrianic-Antonine samian from the site is burnt. There are also parallels in the potters' stamps and the decorated ware. Some of the stamps belong to the same potters and a few come from the same dies as those from the 'pottery shop'; a few others are burnt. The decorated ware is again dominated by the Cerialis ii-Cinnamus ii group and many of the other potters involved are the same. There is also a high proportion of decorated vessels by Cettus, one of the later potters at Les Martres-de-Veyre, and the Large-S Potter, who are both represented to a lesser degree in the 'pottery shop'. A little of this material is burnt and could have been damaged in the destruction of the 'shop'.

The samian from Trench 10 goes beyond AD 160 and almost certainly into the 3rd century, on the evidence of the Rheinzabern ware. This later material, and a comparable collection from the fort, can only have been used in the fort or the *vicus* itself, though what sort of activity it was associated with is not clear. The proportion of decorated to plain samian had not changed, which might suggest that a reasonable standard of living was being maintained.

The samian from Phase 1 contexts certainly ranges from the early 70s to the early 2nd century, but there is also a small quantity of Hadrianic-Antonine decorated ware of 'pottery shop' type. This seems to come mainly from pits, and might have sunk into tops of the fillings.

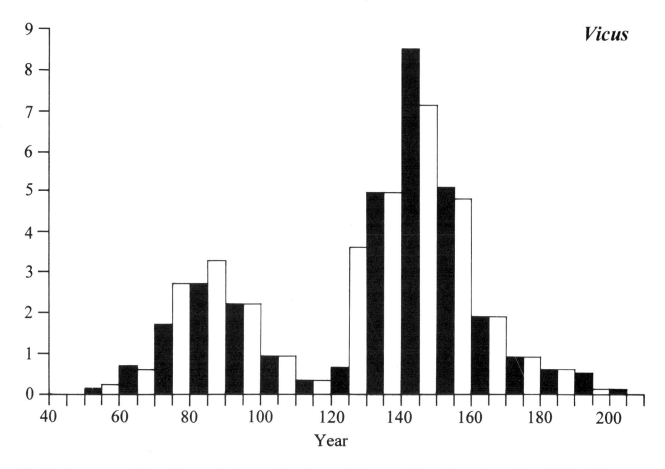

Fig. 42. Average annual loss of decorated and stamped samian vessels in terms of dates of manufacture, from AD 50 to 200.

There is very little samian from Phase 2 as a whole, and only a few pieces which are post-Trajanic. None of them is necessarily later than the 130s and it seems from the samian that this phase was relatively brief.

Phase 3 produced large quantities of decorated ware of the type found in the 'pottery shop', including some burnt sherds. In theory, some of the bowls by the Cerialis ii-Cinnamus ii group could go down to AD 165/170, but the rest of the Central Gaulish ware could scarcely be later than AD 150, with the possible exception of a bowl of Paternus iv. A problem remains with the single East Gaulish decorated bowl, which is almost certainly after AD 160. However, layers associated with the post-*vicus* period contain some of the latest samian from the site, and some of this, in theory, could belong to Phase 3.

Otherwise the later 2nd-century Central Gaulish decorated ware and plain forms not made before *c.* AD 160 come from post-*vicus* layers. There is also a Comitialis-Latinnus bowl from Rheinzabern. These are all more likely to belong to Phase 4.

Phase 4 produced a stamped Rheinzabern dish, of the late 2nd or first half of the 3rd century.

If one accepts the explanation for the small quantities of samian deposited in the Trajanic period, discussed in the summary of the material from the fort, there is no

reason to suppose that occupation of Site 10 was interrupted, or even reduced, before the early Antonine period. The fire which destroyed the 'pottery shop' would clearly have caused an upheaval, and there may have been a period of a few years when the area was unoccupied, until some sort of activity was resumed in the later 2nd century. How long this went on cannot be determined from the samian.

Quantification of decorated and plain samian from the *vicus*

The following Tables 8-11, recording forms by phase, demonstrate the bias towards the first half of the 2nd century. This is made particularly clear by the ratios of forms 18/31 (Hadrianic and early Antonine) to 31 (mainly Antonine, Central Gaulish production going down to the end of the 2nd century) and 18/31R (Hadrianic to mid-Antonine) to 31R (*c.* AD 160 onwards). Similarly, cups of form 27, a form which had gone out of production in Central Gaul by *c.* AD 160, feature prominently. In contrast, some of the commoner later 2nd-century forms, such as 79, 80 and 45 scarcely appear.

Table 8. Distribution of the *vicus* samian by phase: South Gaul.

Form	Phase 1	Phase 2	Phase 3	Phase 4	Total
Ritt. 13	-	1	2	-	3
15/17	2	2	9	4	17
15/17R	1	2	1	3	7
15/17 or 18	8	15	15	-	38
15/17R or 18R	1	1	4	1	7
18	24	46	53	6	129
18R					
18/311	13	3	6	4	26
22	-	2	-	-	2
24	-	-	1	-	1
27g	1	6	9	-	16
27	19	32	66	12	129
29	22	16	24	1	63
30	2	4	1	3	10
30 or 37	5	10	18	6	39
33a	-	2	3	3	8
33	-	1	4	1	6
35	1	6	2	-	9
35/36	-	6	-	-	6
35 or 36	-	1	-	-	1
36	2	5	6	-	13
37	14	66	81	15	176
46	1	1	1	-	3
67	2	9	4	2	17
78	-	-	1	-	1
Curle 11	1	7	8	-	16
Curle 15	-	2	-	-	2
Dish	2	2	3	-	7
Dish or bowl	-	2	3	-	5
Decorated bowl	-	-	-	1	1
Bowl	-	1	5	-	6
Cup	1	1	5	1	8
Total	**122**	**252**	**335**	**63**	**772**

Table 9. Distribution of the *vicus* samian by phase: Central Gaul (Les Martres-de-Veyre)

Form	Phase 1	Phase 2	Phase 3	Phase 4	Total
15/17	-	2	-	-	2
15/17 or 18/31	-	2	-	-	2
18/31	1	11	38	-	50
18/31 or 31	-	-	2	-	2
18/31R	-	-	9	-	9
27	3	4	35	-	42
30 or 37	-	-	4	-	4
36	-	-	3	-	3
37	2	9	26	-	37
46	-	1	1	-	2
81	1	1	2	-	4
Curle 11	1	2	5	-	8
Dish	-	-	1	-	1
Bowl	-	-	1	-	1
Cup	-	1	3	-	4
Total	**8**	**33**	**130**	**-**	**171**

Table 10. Distribution of the *vicus* samian by phase: Central Gaul (Lezoux).

Form	Phase 1	Phase 2	Phase 3	Phase 4	Total
18/31	1	13	115	49	178
18/31 or 31	1	2	42	50	95
18/31-31	-	-	1	-	1
18/31R	-	3	55	36	94
18/31R or 31R	-	-	3	1	4
18/31R-31R	-	-	7	3	10
27	1	11	110	46	168
30	-	1	10	2	13
30R	-	-	3	-	3
30 or 37	2	8	47	11	68
31	-	-	11	7	18
31R	-	-	4	8	12
33a	-	-	2	-	2
33	1	7	176	86	270
35	-	-	1	-	1
35/36	-	-	1	-	1
36	-	1	7	3	11
37	1	22	219	68	310
37R	-	-	1	-	1
38		-	9	4	13
38/44	-	-	7	-	7
44	-	-	3	-	3
44/81	-	-	1	-	1
45	-	-	1	1	2
46	-	-	5	1	6
72	-	-	2	-	2
79 or Tg	-	-	1	-	1
81	-	1	4	1	6
Curle 15	-	-	2	-	2
Curle 15 or 23	-	-	1	1	2
Curle 23	-	-	3	-	3
Ritt. 13	-	-	3	-	3
Dish	-	-	13	-	13
Dish or bowl	-	-	5	1	6
Bowl	-	-	4	-	4
Flanged bowl	-	-	3	-	3
Cup	-	1	9	-	10
Mortarium	-	-	2	-	2
GSM	-	-	1	-	1
Jar	-	1	4	-	5
Total	**7**	**73**	**911**	**385**	**1376**

Table 11. Distribution of the *vicus* samian by phase: East Gaul.

Form	Phase 1	Phase 2	Phase 3	Phase 4	Total
18/31	-	-	1	-	1
27	-	-	-	2	2
31	-	-	-	3	3
31R	-	-	1	2	3
32	-	-	-	1	1
33	-	-	-	1	1
37	1	-	-	2	3
45	-	-	-	1	1
Tb	-	-	-	1	1
Dish	-	-	2	-	2
GSM	-	-	-	1	1
Total	**1**	**-**	**4**	**14**	**19**

Abbreviation

GSM   gritted samian mortarium

The East Gaulish ware includes vessels from:

Argonne   3?
La Madeleine   1
Rheinzabern   3
Trier   1?

Part Three
The Coarse Wares

by Peter Rush

This report was written in 1990 and amended in 1995.

6 Introduction

This report deals with all the Roman pottery from the Castleford excavations excluding the mortaria and the samian ware. Unfortunately the amount of time available resulted in some of the unstratified material not being examined in detail. For a similar reason the Site 1(74) material, which had been recorded during excavation in such a way that pottery of different phases could not be reliably distinguished and the relationship of the pottery to excavated contexts was largely indeterminate, has not been included in this report except for the important 'pottery shop' group and for some drawn examples.

Methodology

The methodology applied to the assemblage is based on that developed for medieval pottery by S. Moorhouse, the most detailed overview of which is given in Moorhouse (1986).

As far as possible all sherds were reassembled into the vessels from which they were originally derived, using both conjoining sherds and occasionally, where a distinctive characteristic of a vessel made it possible, non-conjoining sherds. Where this process involves sherds from separate contexts it is referred to as cross-matching in this report. The size of the assemblage and the space available for laying out sherds limited examination to pottery from one trench at a time. In general this meant that only cross-matches between sherds from the same trench could be obtained, although in a small number of cases it did prove possible to link sherds from separate trenches suggesting, as might be expected, that other similar cross-matches have been missed.

Cross-matching helped to identify residual and intrusive material where sherds were linked to vessels in phases other than the one in which they occurred. Cross-matches of material in contexts of the same phase also meant that in some cases the fill of different features could be shown to have the same source, indicating redeposition or re-use of accumulated rubbish deposits for the levelling of ground surfaces.

Quantification

The methods of quantification used in this report, sherd counts and numbers of vessels, follow directly from the approach outlined above. The numbers of vessels were obtained by simply counting the number of groups of sherds produced by reassembling the sherds into their original vessels. Statistically neither of these methods is particularly reliable (Orton 1975) but together they do enable the further manipulation of the data to reduce the effect of post-depositional movement on the quantified results.

Using the information provided by the process of cross-matching, all sherds were reassigned to their parent vessel's context of earliest occurrence. This reduces the level of residual material present in each context but does not necessarily guarantee that the sherds are reallocated to their original discard locations. In order that a sherd is reassigned to its original and earliest archaeological context a number of conditions must be met:-

1. The original context must not have been destroyed by subsequent activity and must also have been recovered during excavation.

2. Part of the vessel to which the sherd belongs must survive within the original context.

3. The cross-match between the sherd and the vessel in the original context must be made.

Clearly these conditions will not always be met and reassigned pottery may still occur as residual material. However, this process does reduce the level of residuality and usually appears to reallocate pottery to its original phase if not its original discard location. The presence of intrusive material can cause problems for this method but where apparent this can be dealt with by reassignment of sherds in the opposite direction.

In general ceramic vessels should become more fragmentary and abraded and have fewer surviving sherds as they undergo more post-depositional movement and disturbance. Based on this, the quantifications of the pottery assemblage produced by the techniques outlined previously were modified to reduce further the effect of residuality and post-depositional movement on the data for some analyses. Vessels with a sherd to vessel ratio of less than 6:1 were disregarded (i.e. those vessels consisting of 5 sherds or fewer). This was an arbitrary level chosen to eliminate as much of the residual and redeposited material as possible and yet still leave sufficient data to analyse. Obviously the method is not completely reliable but in practice appears to work well, the data producing results that match the pottery whose nature and condition suggests that it has suffered the least post-depositional movement. The data produced by the technique is referred to as filtered elsewhere in this report. Complete vessels, which are usually likely to be recovered from their original discard locations, are missed by this method but their small number at Castleford makes this an insignificant problem.

A number of factors make it unlikely that any quantification method would produce a result that accurately reflected the amounts of the different types of pottery originally deposited on the site. After deposition the pottery is subject to various chemical and physical processes (for instance the effects of acidic soil and post-depositional movement) which may cause it to decay or fragment and, perhaps, become effectively irrecoverable (Schiffer 1987, 158-62). Different types of pottery are affected to different extents by these post-depositional processes; clearly samian, with its well fired, hard fabric, tends to survive better than pottery like Dales ware with its abundant soluble shell inclusions, particularly in acidic conditions.

The process of excavation may also alter the apparent quantities of pottery types present as the recovery rate from an archaeological context will depend on the method of excavation and the visibility of the pottery. Smaller sherds and those whose colour is similar to the surrounding matrix of the context will tend to have lower recovery rates.

Fabric identification

The assemblage was classified into a series of fabrics macroscopically and by examination of freshly broken sections at x30 magnification. Examples of each newly differentiated fabric were retained separately to ensure consistency in the classification. Unfortunately it was not possible to separate completely all the coarse ware fabrics, as a result of which some of the fabrics listed in the Type Series should, in fact, be considered as groups of fabrics with overlapping characteristics.

In addition the pottery was examined for evidence indicative of the way in which it was utilised.

7   The Type Series

Introduction

The identified fabrics have been used as the basis of the type series and where possible references to previously published descriptions of the wares have been given. The forms and decorative features listed here for each fabric do not necessarily cover the full range that has been found elsewhere. In some cases, however, decorative features associated with particular wares have enabled the discrimination of types with apparently identical fabrics.

More detailed descriptions of the amphora wares can be found in Peacock and Williams (1986). Some of the amphora body sherds may be from forms not listed but it is improbable that these would be numerically significant.

1 South Spanish (Baetican) amphorae
Fabric: Quite variable but usually has a rough surface, sometimes whitened externally, and is buff, red-brown or grey. The inclusions are quartz, feldspar, limestone and other rock fragments.

Forms: Mainly Dressel 20, of which the usual contents were olive oil.

Source: Baetica, Southern Spain.

Drawing Nos: 144, 233-4, 378, 524 and 560-66.

2 Southern Spanish amphorae
Fabric: Slightly rough and sandy with obvious pieces of red iron ore. Red, red-buff or yellow in colour.

Forms: Dressel 38 appears to be the most common but Camulodunum 186A also occurred on the site. Beltran IIB amphorae are also possible in this fabric although none of these was identified in the Castleford assemblage. These types of amphorae are usually assumed to have been used for transporting garum and similar fish products.

Source: The coastal region of Southern Spain.

Drawing Nos: 4, 145, 239 and 420.

3 Carrot amphorae
Fabric: Hard, red and very rough, containing quartz and limestone inclusions.

Forms: Camulodunum 189 (Hawkes and Hull 1947).

Source: Possibly from the Mediterranean area.

Drawing No.: None.

4 Campanian amphorae
Fabric: Hard, light-brown fabric containing many augite grains which appear as 'black sand' (Peacock 1971). A darker, red, coarser variant also occurs.

Forms: Dressel 2 to 4. The original contents were probably wine.

Source: Campania, Italy.

Drawing No.: 240.

5 South Gaulish amphorae
Fabric: A range of fine grained fabrics of buff, red and cream colour. They can sometimes be quite micaceous.

Forms: Pelichet 47 (Pelichet 1946) and Dressel 28 are the dominant forms in this fabric. One Gauloise 5 amphora was identified. All these forms were generally used for wine.

Source: Southern Gaul.

Drawing Nos: 1, 2, 3, 142, 235, 236 and 237.

6 Catalonian amphorae
Fabric: Hard, red with large inclusions of quartz, feldspar and some mica.

Forms: Dressel 2 to 4. Used for transporting wine.

Source: Catalonia, Spain.

Drawing No.: None.

7 Buff amphora ware
Fabric: Hard, pale buff with abundant coarse quartz and frequent fine iron ore inclusions. This fabric is similar to Fabric 56.

Forms: The only identifiable sherd is a handle fragment probably from an amphora of Dressel 2 to 4 form.

Source: Possibly from Brockley Hill/Verulamium (Castle 1978).

Drawing Nos: None.

8 Lyon ware
Greene 1978; 1979.
Fabric: Moderately hard, pale cream, often with a slight green tinge.

Decoration: Colour-coated usually in a glossy, dark brown. On some examples this has worn to leave the appearance of a very thin brown wash. All of the Castleford vessels are rough cast with sand on the outside of the body only. Horizontal grooves are also present.

Forms: Beakers and small, hemispherical cups.

Source: Lyon, South Gaul.

Drawing Nos: 28, 29, 383 and 414.

9 Nene Valley colour-coated ware
Anderson 1980, 38; Howe *et al.* 1981.
Fabric: Generally off-white containing a mixture of quartz and iron rich inclusions.

Decoration: Slipped in a range of colours: black, dark-brown and red-brown being the most usual. The surface is often matt. Other decoration includes barbotine, rouletting, white paint and grooving.

Forms: Variety of different beakers, bowls and flagons.

Source: Nene Valley.

Drawing Nos: 354, 382, 430, 431, 433, 434, 439-40, 444-5, 479, 498, and 526-7.

10 Lower Rhineland fabric 1
Anderson 1980; Anderson *et al.* 1982.
Fabric: Indistinguishable from Nene Valley products (see Type 9).

Decoration: As for Fabric 9 with the addition of clay particle rough casting.

Forms: Beakers.

Source: Lower Rhineland.

Drawing Nos: 151, 204, 272 and 276.

This ware can only reliably be separated from Nene Valley material on the basis of chronology or if rough casting is present. The majority of the pre-3rd-century material is most likely to be from the Lower Rhineland.

11 Glossy metallic colour-coated ware
Fabric: Similar to Nene Valley material but darker and coarser.

Decoration: Brown colour coat with a metallic lustre. Barbotine work including scales and animal figures.

Forms: Flanged bowls and beakers.

Source: This is possibly a variant of Fabric 9 and so may be from the Nene Valley area.

Drawing Nos: 432, 529 and 545.

12 Colour-coated white ware
Fabric: Hard, white containing a few small quartz grain inclusions.

Decoration: Usually matt-black colour coat. Barbotine, rough casting with clay particles, rouletting and grooving present.

Forms: Beakers.

Source: Probably the Lower Rhineland region.

Drawing Nos: 274, 277, 280, 435 and 437-8.

13 Argonne? colour-coated ware
Anderson 1980, 28 (see North Gaul fabric 1); Symonds 1987.
Fabric: Red or orange, sometimes with a grey core. Hard when in good condition. Inclusions of quartz and fine black iron ore are visible at x30 magnification.

Decoration: Colour-coated, usually dark brown but can be black or red-brown. Horizontal grooving, clay rough casting and occasionally barbotine decoration also occur.

Forms: Beakers.

Source: The majority of this material is probably from the Argonne region of France. Other Continental areas and Colchester are also possible production sites.

Drawing Nos: 267, 269, 275 and 436.

14 Colchester colour-coated ware
Anderson 1980.
Fabric: Very similar to Fabric 13 but generally contains more quartz and the small black inclusions are often absent.

Decoration: Similar to Fabric 13.

Forms: Beakers

Source: Most of this material was probably produced in Colchester.

Drawing Nos: 205, 264, 268, 273, 278-9, 442-3 and 446.

15 Coarse rough-cast ware
Fabric: Soft, brown with inclusions of quartz, iron rich material and occasional large calcareous pieces easily visible.

Decoration: Low gloss brown colour coat, large clay particle rough casting and grooving.

Forms: Large beakers and jars.

Source: Uncertain but, perhaps, fairly local.

Drawing Nos: 271 and 469.

16 Buff rough-cast ware
Fabric: Moderately hard, buff containing occasional small inclusions of quartz, ironstone and calcareous material.

Decoration: External slip which is often very close in colour to that of the fabric but can be darker. The surface has a matt finish and clay pellet rough casting is always present.

Forms: Beakers.

Source: Uncertain.

Drawing Nos: 265, 384, 447 and 528.

17 Fine brown ware
Fabric: Hard fine brown fabric with no inclusions visible to the unaided eye. At x30 magnification some quartz, mica and iron flecks can be seen in a fresh section.

Decoration: Highly burnished externally.

Forms: Beakers.

Source: Uncertain but probably not local.

Drawing Nos: 43 and 208.

18 Red colour-coated ware
Fabric: Hard, red with sparse inclusions of quartz, iron rich and calcareous material.

Decoration: Colour coat varying from matt to slightly glossy and from a thin red-brown to dark brown. Other decoration includes rouletting, multiple grooving and white barbotine applied prior to colour coating.

Forms: Beakers.

Source: Imported, possibly from the Rhineland or Central Gaul.

Drawing No.: 44.

19 Buff colour-coated ware
Fabric: Hard, usually buff with inclusions of calcareous material, mica, fine quartz and small black nodules visible under the microscope.

Decoration: Dark brown colour coat with a slightly metallic lustre. Clay particle rough casting is evident on some vessels.

Forms: Beakers.

Source: Uncertain.

Drawing No.: 27.

20 Rhenish ware
Greene 1978.
Fabric: Fine, very hard, red fabric often with dark grey layers just beneath the surface.

Decoration: Glossy, metallic, dark-brown or black slip. Rouletting, grooving and barbotine also occur.

Forms: Beakers.

Source: The most likely source for all the Castleford examples is Trier.

Drawing No.: 441.

21 Green glazed ware, type 1
Fabric: Hard, grey with moderate amounts of fine quartz and iron ore inclusions.

Decoration: Green glaze with vitreous lustre.

Forms: Only 1 vessel occurred in this fabric; a very small dish.

Source: Uncertain.

Drawing No.: 359.

22 Green glazed ware, type 2
Fabric: Hard, black with pale grey surface. Inclusions of very fine quartz and occasional fine ?grog particles.

Decoration: As above with the addition of shallow grooves below the glaze.

Forms: None identifiable.

Source: Uncertain.

Drawing No.: 374.

23 Oxfordshire red colour-coated ware
Young 1977, 123.
Fabric: Medium, hard, orange-red with flecks of mica and occasional iron rich pieces visible.

Decoration: Red slip with dots of white paint and rouletting.

Forms: Bowls and jars.

Source: Oxford region.

Drawing Nos: 486 and 521.

24 African red-slipped ware
Hayes 1972.
Fabric: Hard, red-orange fabric with moderate amounts of quartz, iron ore and calcareous inclusions.

Decoration: Slightly glossy red slip, rouletting and grooves.

Forms: Bowls.

Source: North Africa.

Drawing No.: 475.

25 Fine red-brown ware
Fabric: Hard, red-brown with infrequent inclusions of very fine quartz and fine iron ore.

Decoration: Red-brown slip and burnishing.

Forms: Small bowls or cups.

Source: Uncertain.

Drawing No.: 497.

26 Pompeian red ware
Peacock 1977.
Fabric: Buff, usually with much mica visible at the surface. It has inclusions of small quartz grains and occasional dark brown or red fragments. This is probably Peacock's fabric 3.

Decoration: Thick red colour coat on the interior and over the top of rim. On most of the sherds this has almost completely worn off. A thin red-brown wash is present on the exterior of some of the vessels.

Forms: Platters.

Source: Auvergne, central France is probable.

Drawing Nos: 231, 368, 369 and 508.

27 Buff-slipped ware
Fabric: Hard buff with no inclusions visible. However, at x30 magnification, sparse quartz, orange fragments and some mica can be seen.

Decoration: Red-brown dots of barbotine and thin orange-brown slip.

Forms: Flagons and jars.

Source: Uncertain.

Drawing Nos: 61 and 456.

28 Grog tempered white ware
Fabric: Hard, white to cream with frequent large red-brown grog fragments which contains frequent quartz inclusions.

Decoration: Deeply incised lattice pattern.

Forms: Uncertain.

Source: Uncertain.

Drawing Nos: None.

29 Red-painted cream ware
Fabric: Medium hard, cream buff containing sparse quartz grains and very occasional iron-rich fragments.

Decoration: Red painted lattice pattern and burnishing.

Forms: Bowls.

Source: Uncertain.

Drawing Nos: None.

30 Fine cream ware
Fabric: Hard, cream with moderately smooth surface. It has inclusions of quartz and occasional orange fragments.

Decoration: Red and brown paint, external red slip barbotine and grooves.

Forms: Bowls, flagons, *unguentaria*, cheese presses and beakers.

Source: Uncertain.

Drawing Nos: 33 and 282.

31 Red-painted cream ware
Fabric: Hard, cream and slightly micaceous with small orange inclusions.

Decoration: External red painted lattice. The paint tends to be thicker and wider spaced than that on Type 25.

Forms: Bowls and flagons.

Source: Uncertain.

Drawing Nos: 127, 320 and 541.

32 Coarse grey-white ware
Fabric: Hard grey-white with inclusions of quartz and red-brown of black iron rich fragments. It has a slightly rough surface texture.

Decoration: Grooving, rouletting, slip and barbotine.

Forms: Flagons, jars, lids, tazze, beakers and cheese presses.

Source: Uncertain.

Drawing Nos: 8, 13, 35, 37, 134, 139, 152, 173, 185, 219, 224, 241, 243-5, 249, 252, 259, 358, 388, 405, 421-2, 426, 512 and 544.

33 Self-slipped cream ware
Fabric: Cream, pink-cream or off-white with a smooth surface. Inclusions consist of sparse quartz and red-brown grains.

Decoration: Often self slipped. Red-brown painted patterns, rough-cast decoration and grooving also occur.

Forms: Bowls, flagons and beakers.

Source: Uncertain.

Drawing Nos: 24, 32, 38, 50, 62, 113, 116-19, 133, 206, 225, 257, 270, 292, 327, 403, 477 and 517.

34 Cream ware
Fabric: Similar to Type 33 but harder and with slightly more quartz inclusions.

Decoration: Grooving and burnishing.

Forms: Bowls and flagons.

Source: Uncertain.

Drawing Nos: 153, 196, 212, 232, 299, 300, 311, 348, 392 and 476.

35 Fine white ware

Fabric: Thin, hard, finely sandy fabric. Usually white but can be grey or cream tinged.

Decoration: Rouletting, grooves and vertical lines of brown or red-brown barbotine.

Forms: Butt and biconical beakers.

Source: Uncertain.

Drawing Nos: 23, 26, 30-31 and 45-6.

36 Coarse grey-white ware

Fabric: Very hard, grey-white with frequent, well-rounded quartz inclusions.

Only four sherds were recovered and no other details of this ware can be ascertained.

37 Crambeck buff ware.

Fabric: Hard, buff, sometimes with a pale orange core and very frequent medium-sized quartz inclusions.

Decoration: Red painted designs.

Forms: Bowls and platters.

Source: Almost certainly Crambeck, North Yorkshire.

Drawing Nos: 546 and 550.

38 Coarse cream ware

Fabric: Cream or buff, hard, containing much quartz and large red-brown inclusions.

Decoration: Plain.

Forms: Large flagons or, perhaps, small flat-bottomed amphorae.

Source: Uncertain.

Drawing No.: None.

39 Cream ware

Fabric: Hard, cream or cream-brown with inclusions of iron ore, quartz and mica.

Decoration: Grooves and burnishing.

Forms: Flagons, lids and bowls.

Source: Uncertain.

Drawing Nos: 98, 223, 246, 248, 250 and 255.

40 Fine painted cream ware

Fabric: Fine, hard, cream or cream-orange. Flecks of mica are visible on the surface and occasional quartz and red-brown grains can be seen in section.

Decoration: Polished surfaces painted with red-brown lattice patterns.

Forms: Bowls.

Source: Uncertain.

Drawing No.: None.

41 Oxidised wares

Fabric: Consists of a range of fabrics. Usually hard, orange, red or orange-brown and sometimes with a grey core. Inclusions are quartz and iron rich fragments in varying amounts.

Decoration: A wide range of decorative techniques are evident on these wares. They include white slip, rouletting and mica dusting.

Forms: Bowls, flagons, beakers, jars, tazze, dishes and lids.

Source: Probably more than one production area. Most of the material was presumably produced within the local region.

Drawing Nos: 9-12, 14- 21, 36, 53, 72, 95, 101-102, 106, 112, 120-26, 131, 137, 141, 147, 149-50, 154, 158, 169, 175, 177, 179-80, 184, 186, 189, 190-95, 200, 203, 211, 222, 226, 229-30, 242, 251, 253-4, 258, 260-61, 266, 284, 293, 301, 314-16, 324, 326, 329-31, 333, 338, 349-50, 357, 360, 367, 371-3, 379-80, 385, 400, 404, 411, 416, 419, 423-4, 429, 448, 454, 466, 470, 472-3, 478, 480, 499, 500, 507, 515, 525, 537, 539, 542 and 552.

42 Yorkshire red-painted ware

Keen 1970.

Fabric: Included within the range of Type 41. Orange-brown, usually with a grey core.

Decoration: Grooves and lines and dots of red paint.

Forms: Bowls.

Source: The distribution of this ware suggests a source within Yorkshire.

Drawing Nos: 412, 427 and 538.

43 Brown ware

Fabric: Hard, light-brown with a moderate amount of quartz and occasional iron ore inclusions.

Decoration: Grooves, burnished areas.

Forms: Bowls, flagons, jars and cheese presses.

Source: Uncertain.

Drawing Nos: 7, 74, 181, 471 and 494.

44 Coarse buff ware

Fabric: Buff or orange, sandy fabric, often with a grey core. Many red-brown fragments and few pieces of mica are easily visible on the surface and throughout the fabric in section.

Decoration: Grooves and white or cream slip.

Forms: Bowls, flagons, jars and tazze.

Source: Uncertain.

Drawing Nos: 163, 195, 197, 247, 328 and 355.

45 Sandy oxidised ware
Fabric: Hard, sandy, orange to orange brown with darker bands sometimes present beneath the surface. Contains abundant, small quartz grains, some mica and small sandstone fragments.

Decoration: External white slip and grooving.

Forms: Flagons.

Source: Uncertain.

Drawing No.: None.

46 Coarse brown ware
Fabric: Rough, red-brown with a grey core. Inclusions are frequent white, calcareous and red-brown fragments.

Decoration: Plain.

Forms: Jars

Source: Uncertain.

Drawing No.: None.

47 Orange-slipped ware
Fabric: Buff or buff-orange, hard containing fragments of red iron ore and quartz.

Decoration: External orange slip.

Forms: Small bowls or cups.

Source: Uncertain.

Drawing No.: 115.

48 Hard brown ware
Fabric: Very hard brown with inclusions of iron ore and quartz.

Decoration: Plain.

Forms: Jars

Source: Uncertain.

Drawing Nos: 96, 214 and 553.

49 Sandy brown ware
Fabric: Moderately hard, fine sandy fabric varying in colour from brown to orange-brown with a grey core. Flecks of mica and small iron ore fragments are visible on the surface.

Decoration: Grooves.

Forms: Beakers.

Source: Uncertain.

Drawing No.: 47.

50 Mica dusted ware
Fabric: Hard, fine with thin mid-brown surface layers and a black core. At x30 magnification it can be seen to be packed with small quartz grains. The fabric closely resembles Pompeian Red Ware fabric 6 (Peacock 1977, 155).

Decoration: External, highly micaceous slip and wide shallow grooves. One example has a red-external slip similar to that of Pompeian Red Ware.

Forms: Bowls and beakers.

Source: Possibly from the same production source as Pompeian Red Ware fabric 6 for which West Flanders, Belgium has been suggested (De Laet and Thaen 1969).

Drawing No.: 168.

51 Red-slipped oxidised ware
Fabric: Hard, dark orange with a smooth surface. Inclusions visible at x30 are iron ore fragments and fine quartz grains.

Decoration: Slip, grooves and mica dusting.

Forms: Bowls, flagons and jars.

Source: Uncertain.

Drawing Nos; 6, 256, 425 and 459.

52 Coarse oxidised ware
Fabric: Rough, orange to brown with calcareous, iron ore, quartz and a few mica inclusions.

Decoration: Slip and burnishing.

Forms: Beakers, bowls, dishes and lids.

Source: Uncertain.

Drawing Nos: 296, 351, 509, 513 and 551.

53 Red brown ware
Fabric: Hard, brown exterior, red core and grey interior. Contains large amounts of fine quartz grains, some mica and occasional iron ore fragments.

Decoration: External brown slip.

Forms: Flagons.

Source: Uncertain.

Drawing No.: None.

54 Coarse dark brown ware
Fabric: Rough, moderately hard, dark brown with frequent glossy, quartz inclusions.

Decoration: Plain.

Forms: None identifiable.

Source: Uncertain.

Drawing No.: None.

55 Coarse brown ware
Fabric: Hard, brown with a lighter exterior and black interior. Large inclusions of calcite, 'pebbles' and other smaller fragments of quartz and red-brown material.

Decoration: Plain.

Forms: Jars.

Source: Possibly local.

Drawing Nos: 157 and 213.

56 Coarse sandy oxidised ware

Fabric: Hard, orange to buff, with frequent quartz and less common iron ore inclusions. Reduced examples occasionally occur.

Decoration: Grooving.

Forms: Bowls, flagons, jars and lids.

Source: Some of this ware may derive from the Brockley Hill/Verulamium area.

Drawing Nos: 5, 52, 54, 129, 148, 183, 199, 201, 215-16, 238, 263, 347, 356, 381, 389-91, 393, 402, 408 and 418.

57 Hard-fired cream ware

Fabric: Very hard, cream with a grey core. The section at x30 has a vitrified appearance and contains only very occasional inclusions of black iron ore and quartz.

Decoration: Generally plain.

Forms: Flagons.

Source: Uncertain.

Drawing Nos: None.

58 Hard-fired grey ware

Fabric: Very similar to Fabric 56. Grey with a lighter grey core.

Decoration: Grooving.

Forms: Jars.

Source: Uncertain.

Drawing Nos: None.

59 Hard-fired black ware

Fabric: Very hard black fabric, usually with a red-brown core. The section has a vitrified lustre and inclusions of a few quartz grains.

Decoration: Grooving and rouletting.

Forms: Jars, beakers, bowls.

Source: Uncertain.

Drawing Nos: 42, 56 and 97.

Types 57-9 may be overfired versions of other types and may not, therefore, be distinct wares.

60 Terra Nigra

Fabric: Hard, fine, black with a grey or grey-brown core. Flecks of mica are visible at the surface. At x30 the section appears granular and contains much fine quartz and some mica.

Decoration: Highly burnished.

Forms: None identifiable.

Source: Uncertain.

Drawing No.: None.

61 London ware

Marsh 1978.

Fabric: Moderately hard, fine, smooth, slightly micaceous fabric. At x30 magnification occasional quartz and mica pieces are visible. The fabric is generally black with a slightly coloured core.

Decoration: Geometric groove patterns.

Forms: Bowls.

Source: Similar material was produced at a variety of places including London and probably also others as yet undiscovered.

Drawing Nos: 334 and 540.

62 Fine micaceous grey ware

Fabric: Moderately hard, light grey or grey-brown with darker surfaces. Sparse inclusions of quartz and more common mica.

Decoration: Grooving, burnishing and rouletting.

Forms: Beakers and jars.

Source: Uncertain.

Drawing Nos: 76, 174 and 207.

63 Fine grey ware

Fabric: Hard, light grey with darker grey surfaces. Smooth with occasional black inclusions.

Decoration: Grooves, cordons, burnishing and rustication.

Forms: Jars, beakers and bowls.

Source: Uncertain.

Drawing Nos: 25, 51, 65, 75, 83, 86-7, 130, 166, 323, 387, 467, 530 and 557-8.

64 Micaceous grey ware

Fabric: Fairly soft, grey with a slightly, rough sandy surface. It has inclusions of fine quartz, mica and black particles.

Decoration: Often plain but burnishing and barbotine dots occur.

Forms: Flagons and large beakers.

Source: Uncertain.

Drawing No.: 294.

65 Hard grey ware

Fabric: Hard, dark grey with lighter core. Rough surface and inclusion of rounded quartz grains, calcareous material and occasional iron ore fragments.

Decoration: Grooves.

Forms: Jars, beakers.

Source: Uncertain.

Drawing Nos: 453 and 506.

66 Sandy grey ware

Fabric: Hard, grey with abundant very fine quartz inclusions. The fabric has a fine sandy surface texture. It is very similar to the fabric used for the spoon moulds.

Forms: None identifiable.

Source: Possibly local.

Drawing Nos: None.

67 Grey wares

Fabric: Moderately hard to hard grey, sometimes with a darker exterior. Frequent inclusions of quartz and less common black iron rich fragments.

Decoration: Grooves, various rustication patterns, burnishing, rouletting, barbotine and incised decoration.

Forms: Jars, beakers, bowls, dishes and lids.

Source: Probably produced in a number of different areas including South Yorkshire and the local region.

Drawing Nos: 22, 34, 39-40, 48, 57-60, 63-4, 66-7, 71, 73, 77, 79, 81-2, 84-5, 88-94, 105, 114, 128, 132, 138, 143, 156, 160-61, 164-5, 167, 178, 188, 209-210, 220-21, 227-8, 283, 285-7, 295, 312, 322, 352, 386, 394, 397-9, 413, 428, 449, 455, 457-8, 466, 474, 483, 487-8, 493, 496, 503-5, 511, 514, 516, 519, 522, 534, 536, 543 and 547-8.

68 Hard-fired reduced ware

Fabric: Very hard, dark grey or black with a slightly rough surface. At x30 the section has a vitrified appearance and frequent quartz grains can be seen.

Decoration: Grooves, incised cross-hatching.

Forms: Jars and beakers.

Source: Uncertain.

Drawing Nos: 68, 451, 460 and 468.

69 Slipped grey ware

Fabric: Dark grey, slightly rough and with only a very few iron ore inclusions and a number of voids.

Decoration: Light grey slip.

Forms: Beakers.

Source: Uncertain.

Drawing No.: None.

70 Grey ware

Fabric: Hard, grey, slightly rough with inclusions of frequent small, angular quartz grains and sparse red to brown iron ore particles.

Decoration: Burnishing and grooves.

Forms: Jars.

Source: Uncertain.

Drawing No.: None.

71 Coarse dark grey ware

Fabric: Hard, dark grey with black surface containing abundant quartz grains and occasional black iron ore fragments.

Decoration: Burnishing and grooves.

Forms: Jars.

Source: Uncertain.

Drawing No.: 104.

72 Grey ware

Fabric: Hard, light grey with abundant rounded quartz and occasional red iron rich inclusions.

Decoration: Burnishing, grooves and rouletting.

Forms: Jars.

Source: Uncertain.

Drawing Nos: 41, 69 and 80.

73 Coarse black ware

Fabric: Hard, black, sometimes with a red brown core. Contains abundant quartz and occasional calcareous fragments. It can have the appearance of wheel made black-burnished ware type 1.

Decoration: Burnishing, grooves and cross-hatched patterns.

Forms: Jars.

Source: Uncertain.

Drawing Nos: 55, 159, 520 and 532.

74 Coarse black ware

Fabric: Moderately hard, brown or orange-brown with black surfaces and sometimes a grey core. Granular surface and inclusions of quartz and iron ore.

Decoration: Rustication, grooves, burnishing and rouletting.

Forms: Jars.

Source: Uncertain.

Drawing Nos: 218, 317, 325, 415, 417, 495 and 510.

75 Coarse sandy grey ware

Fabric: Hard, grey sometimes with a red-brown core. Inclusions of abundant, rounded quartz, giving the surface a coarse sandy texture.

Decoration: Burnishing, grooves and cross-hatching.

Forms: Jars, bowls and dishes.

Source: Similar to material produced in the Doncaster, South Yorkshire area.

Drawing Nos: 290, 305, 406, 410, 461 and 554.

76 Coarse grey ware
Fabric: Rough, hard, light grey with a darker core. Inclusions of rounded quartz, occasional calcareous fragments and sometimes mica.

Decoration: Grooves.

Forms: Jars.

Source: Probably a variety of fairly local sources. The Doncaster area is a possibility for some of it.

Drawing Nos: 353, 535 and 559.

77 Coarse grey ware
Fabric: Hard, grey with darker surfaces. Inclusions of quartz and calcareous fragments.

Decoration: Burnishing, grooves and cross-hatching.

Forms: Bowls, jars, lids and beakers.

Source: Uncertain.

Drawing Nos: 49 and 99.

78 Castleford grey ware
Fabric: Hard, grey with inclusions of abundant medium and coarse sized quartz and moderately frequent calcareous fragments up to 3 or 4mm across. The calcareous material is possibly derived from magnesian limestone.

Decoration: Burnishing and lattice decoration presumably in imitation of black-burnished ware.

Forms: Small and medium sized jars.

Source: Most of the vessels recovered in this fabric are probably wasters suggesting manufacture at Castleford.

Drawing Nos: 297-8, 302, 310 and 531.

79 Black-burnished ware type 1
Fabric: Generally black, sometimes red-brown margins beneath the surface. Heavily quartz tempered.

Decoration: Burnishing, grooves, cross-hatching, intersecting arc and other incised decoration.

Forms: Beakers, bowls, lids, jars and jugs.

Source: Poole, Dorset or Rossington Bridge, Doncaster. Material from these sources is effectively indistinguishable.

Drawing Nos: 262, 281, 288-9, 291, 303-4, 306-9, 318-19, 321, 335-7, 339-46, 361-6, 370, 375-7, 395, 409, 450, 452, 462-5, 481-2, 490-92, 501-2 and 549.

80 Black-burnished ware type 2
Fabric: Hard, dark grey or black usually with a black surface. Abundant quartz inclusions.

Decoration: Burnishing and lattice patterns.

Forms: Bowls and jars.

Source: Produced at Colchester and in Kent.

Drawing Nos: 396 and 484-5.

81 Coarse ware
Fabric: Hard, rough, dark grey to black with inclusions of quartz, sedimentary rock and occasional pieces of grog.

Decoration: Burnishing and grooves.

Forms: Jars, bowls and dishes.

Source: Possibly local.

Drawing Nos: 100, 103, 108-111, 135-6, 155 and 187.

82 Grey ware with calcareous inclusions
Fabric: Hard, grey, slightly rough with inclusions of quartz, iron ore and calcareous material.

Decoration: Grooves, burnishing, cordons and cross-hatching.

Forms: Jars and bowls.

Source: Uncertain.

Drawing Nos: 107, 172, 313 and 489.

83 Shell-gritted ware
Fabric: Moderately hard, dark grey or black with inclusions of shell and quartz.

Decoration: Grooves.

Forms: Jars.

Source: Uncertain.

Drawing No.: 70.

84 Coarse grog-tempered ware
Fabric: Moderately hard, rough, black with grey or brown core. Inclusions of large pieces of red-brown grog, iron ore and quartz.

Decoration: Grooves.

Forms: Jars.

Source: Uncertain.

Drawing No.: 162.

85 Dales ware
Loughlin 1977, 85-146
Fabric: Rough, dark grey or brown, often with internal red-brown layers. Obvious frequent shell fragments and some quartz inclusions.

Decoration: Plain.

Forms: Jars and cheese presses.

Source: Probably North Lincolnshire or Humberside.

Drawing Nos: 518 and 523.

86 Huntcliff ware
Fabric: Grey or black, with frequent calcite fragments and quartz inclusions.

Decoration: Grooves.

Forms: Jars.

Source: Production of this ware has been suggested at Crambeck, North Yorkshire and at Norton, East Yorkshire (Swan 1984, 111).

Drawing No.: 533.

87 Coarse millstone grit ware

Fabric: Hard, black or dark grey fabric sometimes with a brown core. Inclusions of frequent millstone grit and large quartz grains.

Decoration: Grooves.

Forms: Jars.

Source: Presumably near an outcrop of Millstone Grit and may therefore have an origin within West Yorkshire.

Drawing No.: 78.

8   The Drawn Pottery

The drawings are arranged in groups according to phase and within each phase group by form and decorative style. As drawing time was limited some types, particularly amphorae, were not represented by drawings for every phase in which they occurred.

Dates for the phases were in general derived from the samian and coin data. This was supplemented by the dating evidence of the other pottery for the later Roman phases.

Phases

Fort Phase I: Catalogue Numbers 1-143.

Fort Phase II: Catalogue Numbers 144-83.

Vicus Phase 1: Catalogue Numbers 184-94.

Vicus Phase 2: Catalogue Numbers 195-232.

Vicus Phase 3: Catalogue Numbers 233-377.

Fort area Phase III: Catalogue Numbers 378-419.

Fort area Phase IV and *vicus* Phase 4: Catalogue Numbers 420-523.

Post-Roman and uncertain phases. Catalogue Numbers 524-54.

Stamped coarse ware. Catalogue Numbers 555-66.

Fort Phase I

Amphorae and amphora type vessels

1* Amphora of Gauloise 5 form (see Peacock and Williams 1986, 148 and fig. 74). The vessel illustrated was the only identifiable example of this type found at Castleford. Fabric 5. *063 T15II; Ic*

2* Amphora, probably of Dressel 28 type as the base is too wide for the normal range of Pelichet 47 (Sealey 1985 and Pelichet 1946, 193 and fig. 5). Fabric 5. *680 T15IV; Ia*

3* Dressel 28 amphora. Fabric 5. *1006 T15V; Ic*

4* Amphora of Dressel 38 form but with a rim resembling Camulodunum form 186A (Hawkes and Hull 1947, 252 and Pl. LXXII). Fabric 2. *706, 704 and 724 T16V; Id*

5* Large amphora type vessel. The fabric is similar to that of Brockley Hill products and this vessel may have been produced there. Amphorae of probable local production have been found at Brockley Hill (Castle 1978) but of apparently dissimilar form to this example. Fabric 56. *985, 995, 1083 and 1150 T15V; Ib*

6* ?Amphora type vessel. Brown colour coat. Fabric 51. *318 T14; Ic*

Flagons

7* Ring-necked flagon. Fabric 43. *108 T14; Ic*

8* Ring-necked flagon. Fabric 32. *007 and 017 T15I; Ib*

9* Ring-necked flagon with slightly flaring neck. Fabric 41. *1162 and 1005 T15V; Ib*

10* Ring-necked flagon with slightly flaring neck. Fabric 41. *1147 T15V; Ib*

11* Ring-necked flagon with flared neck. Traces of pale pink slip survive. Fabric 41. *318 T14; Ic*

12* Small, ring-necked flagon with slightly flared neck. Fabric 41. *329 T12; Ib*

13* Ring-necked flagon with flared rim. Fabric 32. *1161 T15V; Ib*

14* Large, ring-necked flagon. The surface of the vessel was discoloured during firing to black and dark red-brown. Fabric 41. *1139 and 969 T15V; Ic*

15* Flagon with flared rim and undercut lower moulding. This form is a derivation of the continental Haltern 47 form (Hawkes and Hull 1947, 244 and pl. LXI form 143 and 144). Fabric 41. *981 and 982 T15V; Ic*

16* Flagon with flanged rim. Purple-brown colour coat. Fabric 41. *313 T14; Ic*

17* Flagon with flanged rim. Fabric 41. *1146 T15V; Ic*

18* Flagon with flanged rim. Number of handles uncertain. Fabric 41. *017 T15I; Ib*

19* Flagon. Burnished exterior. The process of burnishing has produced ridges on the lower body. Fabric 41. *1006 T15V; Ic*

20* Small flask. Wide impressed grooves. Fabric 41. *007 T15I; Ib*

21* ?Flagon. Rouletted and grooved decoration. Fabric 41. *1145 T15V; Ic*

22* Jug. Spout formed from pinched-in rim. The form is apparently derived from earlier, continental vessels which in turn have metal prototypes (Hawkes and Hull 1947, 246 and pl. LXI and LXII form 159. Fabric 67. *1107 T15V; Id*

Beakers

23* Beaker with everted, internally cupped rim. Rouletted and grooved decoration. Fabric 35. *680, 503, 624, 636 and 660 T15IV; Ia*

24* Beaker. Rouletted bands and grooves, burnished externally. Fabric 33. *1003, 908, 1008 and 1071 T15V; Id*

25* Beaker. Rouletted and grooved decoration. Fabric 63. *995, 950, 992, 1063 and 1131 T15V; Ic*

26* Base of beaker. Fabric 35. *745 T16V; Ib*

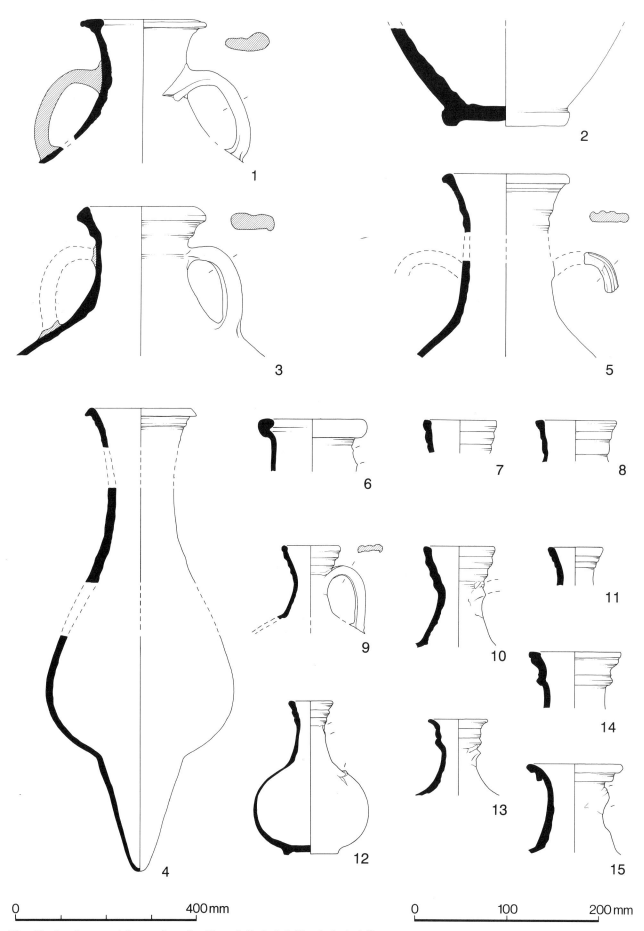

Fig. 43. Amphorae and flagons from fort Phase I. Scale 1:4 (No. 4; Scale 1:8)

0   400 mm

0   100   200 mm

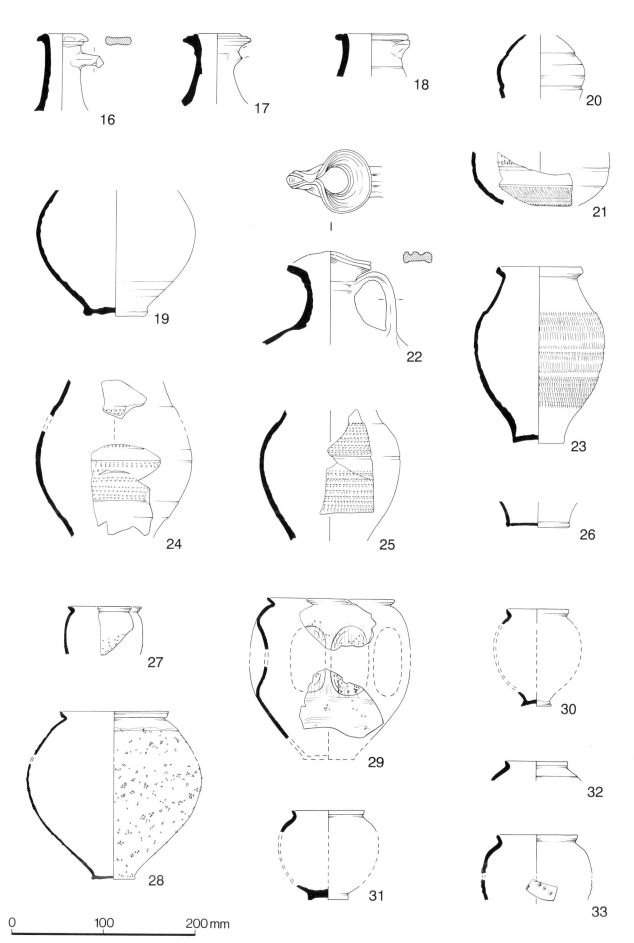

Fig. 44. Flagons and beakers from fort Phase I. Scale 1:4

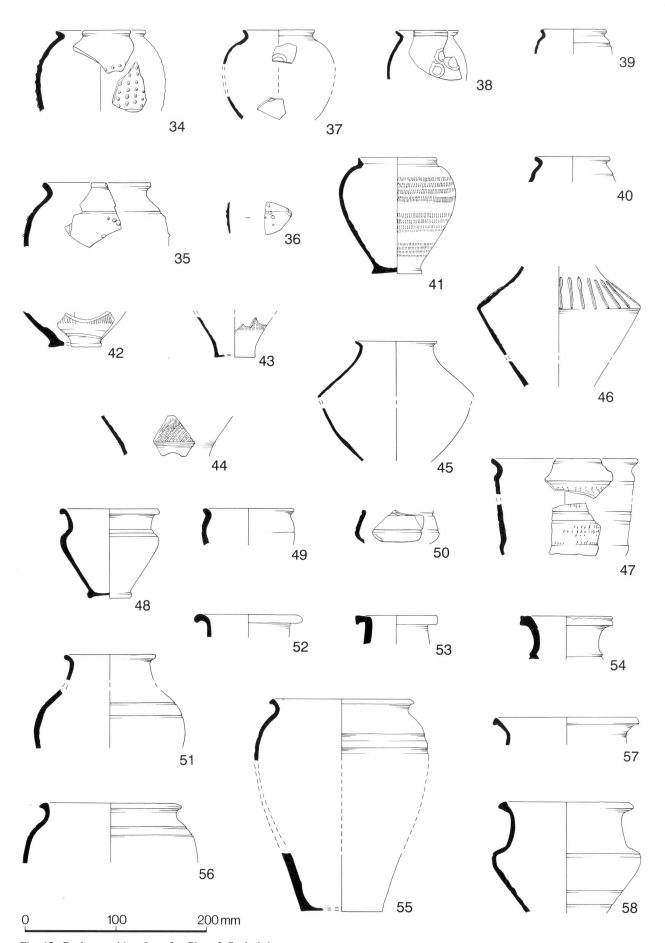

Fig. 45. Beakers and jars from fort Phase I. Scale 1:4

Numbers 23 to 26 are all of forms derived from 'Gallo-Belgic' butt beaker types, cf. forms 113 and 119, Hawkes and Hull 1947, 238-40 and pls LVII and LVIII.

27* Everted rimmed beaker. Rough cast with clay particles and colour-coated dark brown with a slight metallic lustre. Possibly a Central Gaulish product (Greene 1979 43-8 and fig. 19 nos 5 and 6). Fabric 19. *317 T14; Ie*

28* Beaker with everted, grooved rim. Rough cast with stand. Very worn, matt brown colour coat. A Lyon ware vessel, type 20.5 (Greene 1979, 24 and fig. 8). Fabric 8. *743, 704, 712, 719, 722, 723 and 734 T16V; Ib*

29* Indented beaker with everted rim. Rough cast with sand and colour-coated glossy dark brown. A Lyon ware product similar to type 21 but with a different rim (Greene 1979, 24 and fig. 8). Fabric 8. *106 and 129 T14; Ie*

30* Globular beaker with everted rim. Fabric 35. *981 and 1107 T15V; Ic*

31* Globular beaker with everted rim. Fabric 35. *959 and 1033 T15V; Id*

32* Globular beaker with everted rim. Shoulder groove. Fabric 33. *294 and 299 T15III; Ib*

33* Globular beaker with everted rim. External burnish and barbotine dot decoration. Fabric 30. *1149 and 992 T15V; Ib*

34* Large globular beaker with everted rim. Barbotine dot decoration. Fabric 67. *007, 017, 024, 029 and 032 T15I; Ib*

35* Large beaker with everted rim. Shoulder groove and barbotine decoration. Fabric 32. *025 and 029 T15I; Ib*

36* Fragment of beaker or jar. Burnished exterior with barbotine ring and dot decoration. Fabric 41. *023 T15I; Ib*

37* Globular beaker with curved out rim. Part of red slip circle survives. Fabric 32. *997 and 1132 T15V; Ic*

38* Beaker with everted rim. Decoration with circles of thin brown slip. Fabric 33. *318 and 153 T14; Ic*

39* Beaker with everted rim. Wide shoulder groove. Fabric 67. *220 T14; Ic*

40* Beaker with everted rim and step at shoulder. Fabric 67. *318 T14; Ic*

41* Beaker with upright, internally cupped rim. Exterior burnished between rouletted bands. Fabric 72. *984 and 1146 T15V; Ib*

42* Beaker. Burnished and rouletted exterior. Fabric 59. *108 T14; Ic*

43* Beaker. Burnished and rouletted exterior. Fabric 17. *108 T14; Ic*

44* Large beaker. Colour-coated internally red-brown; externally glossy dark brown. Rouletted and grooved. Fabric 18. *333 T12; Ib*

45* Beaker with plain, curved rim and mid-body carination. Fabric 35 *153 and 110 T14; Ie*

46* Beaker with mid-body carination. Vertical lines of red-brown barbotine decoration. Fabric 35. *1139 T15V; Ic*

Numbers 45 and 46 are of a form derived from continental Terra Nigra types. See fig. 52 nos 1-8 (Greene 1979).

47* Large, wide-mouthed beaker with curved out rim. Rouletted and grooved decoration. The form is derived from 'Gallo-Belgic' girth beakers (cf. form 84 Hawkes and Hull 1947 pl. LV). Fabric 49. *1003, 909 and 1085 T15V; Id*

48* Beaker with concave, flared neck and undercut bead rim. Shoulder cordons. Form probably derived from La Tène predecessors (Hawkes and Hull 1947, 259-60 and pl. LXXV, form 218). Fabric 67. *714 T16V; Ic*

49* Wide-mouthed beaker with everted rim and stepped side. Fabric 77. *745 T16V; Ib*

50* ?Beaker. Grooved with traces of red painted decoration. Fabric 33. *1139 T15V; Ic*

Jars

51* Narrow-necked jar with plain, flared rim. Burnished and grooved exterior. Fabric 63. *992 and 1008 T15V; Id*

52* Narrow-necked jar with curved over rim. Fabric 56. *108 T14; Ic*

53* Narrow-necked jar with square-edged, flat rim. Fabric 41. *108 T14; Ic*

54* Narrow-necked jar or, possibly, flagon with square-shaped pulley wheel rim. Cordon on neck. Fabric 56. *108 T14; Ic*

55* Jar with curved, beaded rim. Two wide grooves on shoulder. Fabric 73. *023, 009, 018, 024 and 028 T15I; Ib*

56* Jar with pointed bead rim. Two shoulder grooves. Fabric 59. *055, 061, 065 and 072 T15II; 710 T16V; Ic*

57* Jar with flared, beaded rim. Fabric 67. *024 and 029 T15I; Ib*

58* Carinated, necked jar with flared rim. Grooved. A similar vessel was found associated with kiln 4 at Dragonby (Gregory and May 1996, 576, no. 1412, fig. 20.32). Fabric 67. *321 and 303 T16II; Ib*

59* Jar with everted rim. Two shoulder grooves. Fabric 67. *023, 018, 024, 025, 028 and 029 T15I; Ib*

60* Jar with everted, square-edged rim. Multiple grooves on body. Fabric 67. *108 T14: Ic*

61* Jar with everted rim. Self-coloured slip through which wide grooves have been cut. Circles of brown slip. Fabric 27. *702, 714 and 740 T16V; Ia*

62* Jar with everted rim. Shoulder groove. Fabric 33. *1139, 1132 and 1145 T15V; Ic*

63* Jar with everted rim. Burnished externally and over rim. Fabric 67. *108 T14; Ic*

64* Jar with everted rim. Shoulder groove and incised herringbone style decoration. Fabric 67. *1107 and 1063 T15V; Id*

65* Jar with everted, slightly cupped rim. External burnish. Fabric 63. *1145 T15V; Ic*

66* Jar with everted rim. Shoulder groove. Fabric 67. *220 T14; Ic*

67* Jar with everted rim. Fabric 67. *108 T14; Ic*

68* Jar with everted rim. Shoulder grooves. It has a distorted rim and body, apparently caused by clumsy handling prior to firing. Fabric 68. *321 and 303 T16II; Ib*

69* Jar with everted rim. Rouletted and grooved, externally burnished. Fabric 72. *220 T14; Ic*

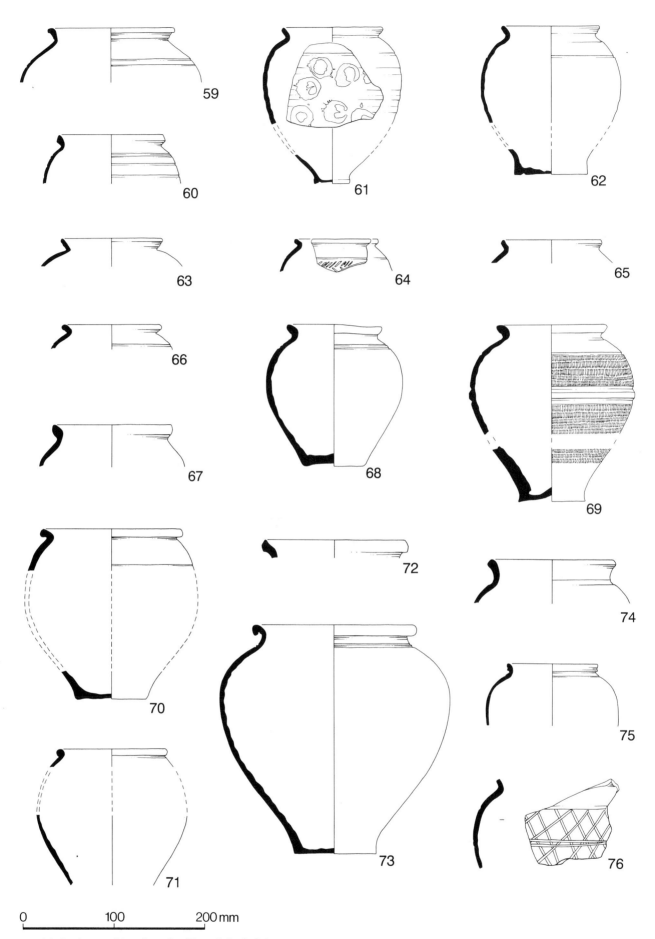

Fig. 46. Beakers and jars from fort Phase I. Scale 1:4

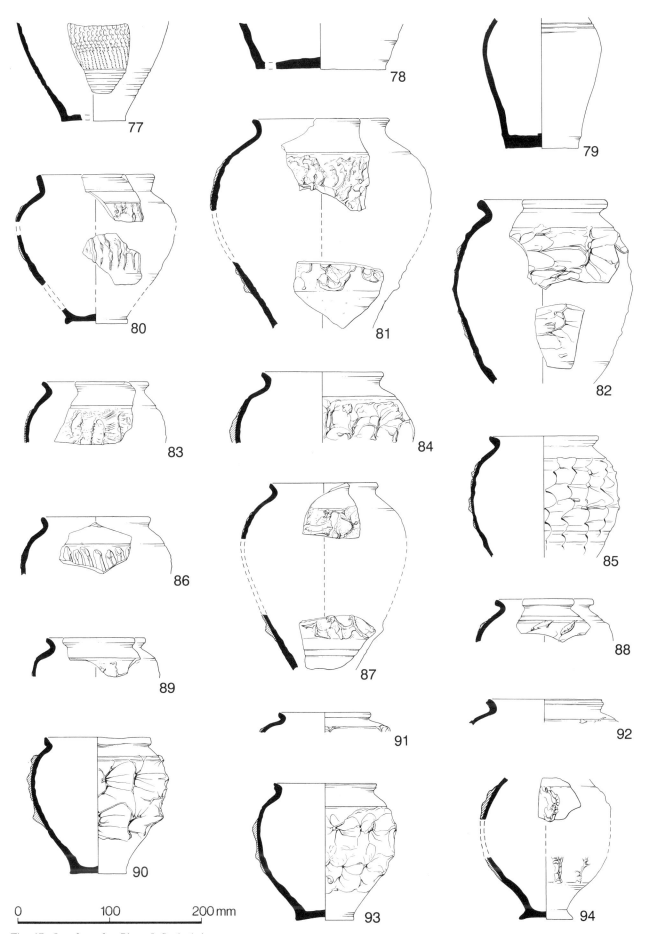

Fig. 47. Jars from fort Phase I. Scale 1:4

0   100   200 mm

105

70* Jar with everted rim. Shoulder groove. Fabric 75. *743 T16V; Ib*

71* Bead rim jar. Fabric 67. *1107 and 1108 T15V; Id*

72* Jar with curved out rim with slight, internal cupping. Fabric 41. *108 T14; Ic*

73* High-shouldered jar with undercut, curved over rim. Fabric 67. *706 T16V; Id*

74* Jar with curved out rim. Fabric 43. *108 T14; Ic*

75* Jar with pulley-wheel rim. Fabric 63. *739 T16V; Id*

76* Jar. Burnished exterior and lattice decoration. Fabric 62. *114, 310 and 312 T14; Ie*

77* ?Jar. Rouletted and grooved decoration. Fabric 67. *1121 and 910 T15V; Id*

78* Jar. Hand made. Fabric 87. *108 T14; Ic*

79* Jar. Shoulder grooves. Fabric 67. *024 T15I; Ib*

80* Jar with everted, straight rim. Vertical linear rustication formed from a layer of coarsely gritted clay giving a pimply finish. Shoulder groove marks the upper limit of rustication. Fabric 72. *106 and 129 T14; Ie*

81* Jar with curved out rim. Random rustication formed from coarsely gritted applied clay similar to No. 80. Shoulder groove. The area below the rustication has been knife trimmed. Fabric 67. *714 T16V; Ic*

82* Jar with everted, curved rim. Shoulder groove and random rustication. Fabric 67. *321 and 303 T16II; 506 T16III; Ib*

83* Jar with slightly curved everted rim. Shoulder groove. Vertical, linear rustication formed from coarsely gritted clay. Fabric 63. *1139, 1144 and 1145 T15V; Ic*

84* Jar with everted rim. Shoulder groove and random rustication. Fabric 67. *108 T14; Ic*

85* Jar with everted rim. Grooved body with regular rustication applied over the grooves. Fabric 67. *300 T15III; Ic*

86* Jar with everted rim. Shoulder groove and vertical linear rustication formed from discrete lines of applied clay. Fabric 63. *997, 992 and 1033 T15V; Ic*

87* Jar with everted rim. Shoulder and lower body grooves. Random rustication formed from coarsely gritted clay. Fabric 63. *024, 018, 027 and 028 T15I; Ib*

88* Jar with curved out rim. Two shoulder grooves. Uncertain style of rustication. Fabric 67. *719 T16V; Ic*

89* Jar with curved out rim. Shoulder groove. Uncertain style of rustication. Fabric 67. *108 T14; Ic*

90* Jar with everted rim. Two shoulder grooves and random rustication. Fabric 67. *984 T15V; Ib*

91* Jar with small, everted rim. Shoulder groove. Uncertain style of rustication. Fabric 67. *108 T14; Ic*

92* Jar with everted, grooved rim. Shoulder groove. Uncertain style of rustication. Fabric 67. *220 T14; Ic*

93* Jar with everted, grooved rim. Shoulder groove and random rustication. Fabric 67. *108 T14; Ic*

94* Jar with solid pedestal base. Shoulder groove. Linear rustication formed from discrete lines of applied clay. The form and the style of rustication are similar to a jar produced at North Hykeham (Thompson 1958, fig. 3 no. 1). Fabric 67. *106 T14; Ie*

95* Two-handled jar with flat-topped rim. Grooved body. Fabric 41. *680 T15IV; Ia*

96* Two-handled jar with everted, flat-topped rim. Fabric 48. *108 T14; Ic*

97* Four-handled jar with everted, square-edged rim. Surface discoloured during firing to streaks of dark red-brown and black. Fabric 59. *969, 1033, 1114 and 1139 T15V; 605 T16IV; Id*

98* Very large jar with everted, horizontal rim. Small neck cordon. One sherd had a scar where a handle had broken off. Number of handles uncertain. Fabric 39. *106 and 121 T14; Ie*

The general form of Numbers 95 to 98 is derived from earlier Continental examples (see Hawkes and Hull 1947, 250 and pl. LXVIII, form 175).

99* Globular jar with upright bead rim. Shoulder groove and externally smoothed. Fabric 77. *603 T15IV; Id*

100* Globular jar with small, upright bead rim. Burnished all over. Hand made. Fabric 81. *021, 023, 024, 028, 029 and 032 T15I; Ib*

101* Globular jar with flat reeded rim, folded onto shoulder. Two grooves at the widest part of the vessel. Fabric 41. *108 T14; Ic*

102* Globular jar with folded down, flat, reeded rim. Decorated with incised grooves and wavy lines. Fabric 41. *1149, 1033, 1063, 1064 and 1083 T15V; Ib*

103* Large globular jar with everted rim and pedestal base. Shoulder decorated with cordon, grooves and impressed marks. Hand made. Fabric 81. *007, 017, 027, 028, 029 and 030 T15I; Ib*

104* Wide-mouthed jar with curved out rim. Cordon and grooves on shoulder. Burnished between top of rim and shoulder. Fabric 71. *108 T14; Ic*

105* Wide-mouthed, necked jar with curved over rim. Fabric 67. *068 and 094 T15II; Ia*

Numbers 104 and 105 are possibly based on earlier La Tène types cf. Hawkes and Hull 1947, 261 and pl. LXXV and LXXVI, forms 220A and 221A.

106* Wide-mouthed jar with plain, curved rim. Two grooves on shoulder. Fabric 41. *055 T15II; Ic*

107* Wide-mouthed jar with everted rim and slight carination at shoulder. Two shoulder grooves. Similar vessels occur at Lincoln and Old Winteringham (e.g. Darling 1984, fig. 15 no. 62; Rigby and Stead 1976, fig. 74 no. 10). Fabric 82. *220 T14; Ic*

108* Wide-mouthed jar with everted rim, internally undercut. Hand made but possibly wheel finished. Fabric 81. *220 T14; Ic*

109* Wide mouthed-jar with everted rim. External burnish. Hand made. Fabric 81. *108 T14; Ic*

110* Jar with plain, everted rim. Hand made. Fabric 81. *743 T16V; Ib*

111* Wide-mouthed jar with thick bead rim. Hand made. Fabric 81. *735 T16V; Ic*

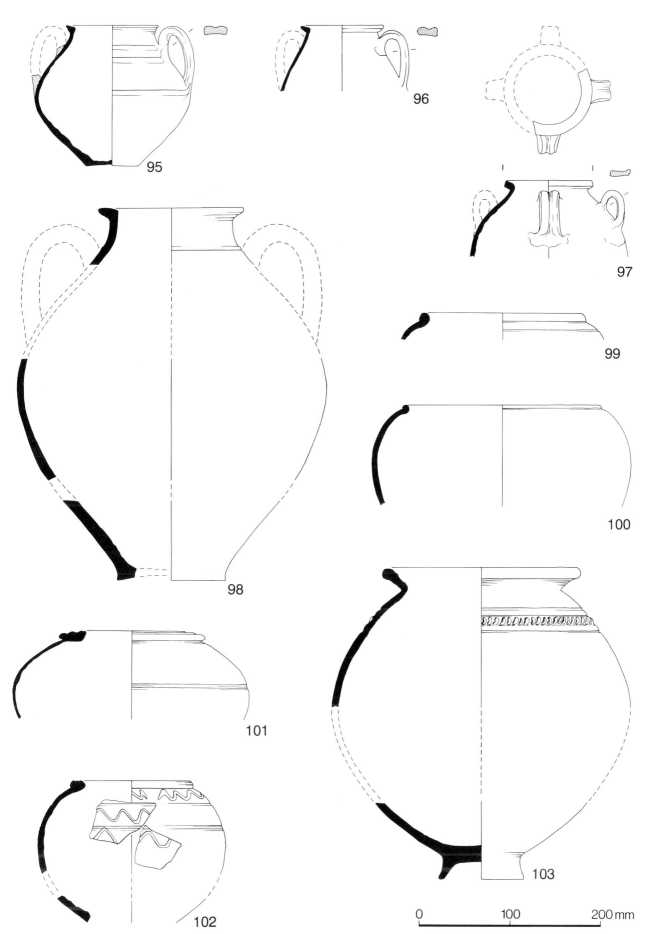

Fig. 48. Jars from fort Phase I. Scale 1:4

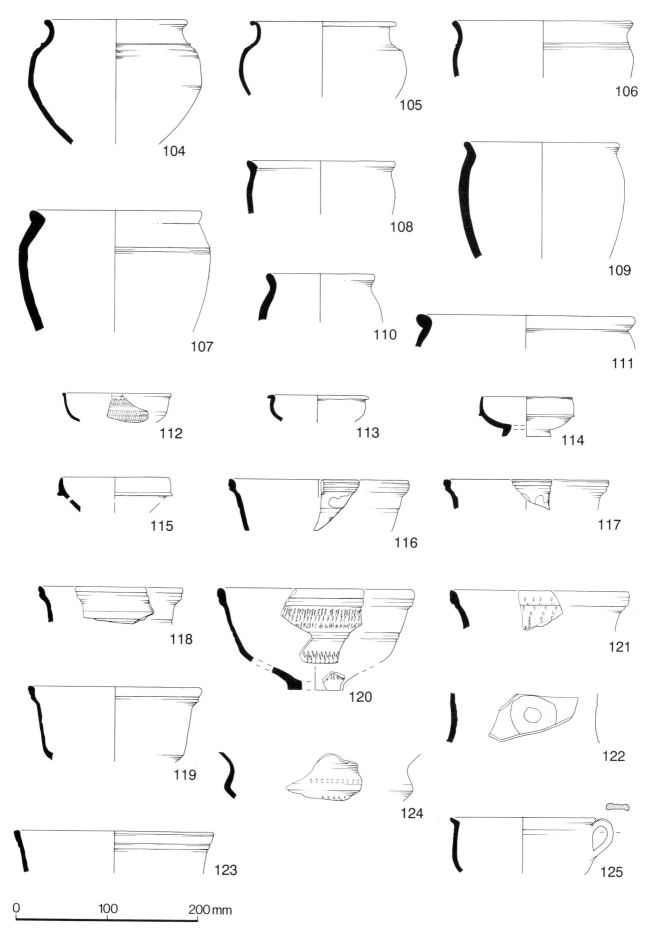

Fig. 49. Jars and bowls from fort Phase I. Scale 1:4

0   100   200 mm

Bowls

112* Bowl with square bead rim. Rouletted. Fabric 41. *108 T14; Ic*

113* Cup. Burnished exterior. Imitation of Dragendorff 27. Fabric 33. *739 T16V; Ia*

114* Flanged bowl or cup. Imitation of Dragendorff 24/25. Fabric 67. *1173 T15V; Ib*

115* Flanged bowl or cup. The form is probably derived from Dragendorff 24/25. Fabric 47. *714 and 735 T16V; Ic*

Numbers 116 to 121 are all derived from the samian form Dragendorff 29.

116* Bowl. Grooved and red-brown painted pattern. Fabric 33. *300 T15III; Ic*

117* Bowl. Grooved and traces of red-brown paint. Fabric 33. *745 T16V; Ib*

118* Bowl. Grooved with orange brown painted stripe. Fabric 33. *1106 and 1073 T15V; Id*

119* Bowl. Groove below rim. Fabric 33. *1145 T15V; Ic*

120* Bowl. Rouletted and grooved decoration. Fabric 41. *981, 1062, 1120, 1123, 1141, 1145 and 1146 T15V; Ic*

121* Bowl. Decorated with deeply incised marks. Fabric 41. *714 and 744 T16V; Ic*

122* Uncertain form but possibly a carinated bowl. Circle of orange-brown slip. Fabric 41. *945 T15V; Id*

123* Bowl. Grooved below rim. Fabric 41. *1145 and 1128 T15V; Ic*

124* Bowl. Rouletted. Fabric 41. *704 T15IV; Ib*

125* Handled bowl with everted rim. Wide groove below rim. Actual number of handles uncertain. Fabric 41. *108 and 177 T14; Ic*

126* Carinated bowl with small, flat topped rim. Evidence of one handle survives. Decorated with grooves and red-brown painted designs. Fabric 41. *743 T16V; Ib*

127* Carinated bowl with everted, square-edged rim. Decorated with grooves and red-brown painted lattice. Similar vessels were produced at Lincoln (Darling 1981 fig. 23.2 nos 16 and 17). Fabric 31. *108 and 112 T14; Ic*

128* Carinated bowl with flat, reeded rim. Grooves on upper body. Fabric 67. *735 T16V; Ic*

129* Carinated bowl with flat, reeded rim. Carination marked by groove. Fabric 56. *313, 314 and 315 T14; Ic*

130* Carinated bowl with flat rim. Groove above slight carination. Fabric 63. *985, 1083, 1093 and 1095 T15V; Ib*

131* Carinated bowl with flat, sloping rim. Groove above slight carination. Fabric 41. *743 and 714 T16V; Ib*

132* Large bowl with hooked, reeded rim. Two grooves on side of body. Rim has distorted during firing. Fabric 67. *313 and 318 T14: Ic*

133* Flanged bowl. Pink-brown colour coat. The exterior has been shaped by trimming. Fabric 33. *079 T15II; Ic*

134* Bowl with flat rim and lid seat. Pouring lip formed from strip of applied clay on top of rim. Fabric 32. *607 T15IV; Id*

135* Tripod bowl with bead rim. Hand made. Fabric 81. *321 and 303 T16II; 501 and 506 T16III; Ib*

136* Tripod bowl with everted rim. Hand made. Fabric 81. *553 and 649 T15IV; Id*

Dishes

137* Convex-sided dish with chamfered rim. Fabric 41. *603 T15IV; Id*

138* Plain-rimmed dish. Wide groove on side. The interior of the base is ridged in the manner of a cheese press but no holes are present. Fabric 67. *235, 276, 277, 281, 300 and 305 T15III; Ib*

Cheese presses

139* Cheese press with grooved rim. Wide grooves on sides. Round holes pierced from inside before firing. Fabric 32. *316 T15III; Id*

Lids

140* Lid with pointed-bead rim. Channel cut on underside of lid, 10mm from edge. Fabric 41. *634 T15IV; Id*

141* Lid with plain rim. Fabric 41. *706, 704 and 722 T16V; Id*

142* Lid with plain rim and pinched up handle. Possibly the lid for a South Gaulish amphora. Fabric 5. *714 T16V; Ic*

143* Lid with squared edge to rim. Fabric 67. *108 T14; Ic*

Fort Phase II

Amphorae

144* Amphora of Dressel 20 form. Fabric 1. *111 Site 1(77); II*

145* Amphora, probably of Camulodunum form 186A (Hawkes and Hull 1947, 252 and pl. LXXII). Fabric 2. *019 T17; II*

Flagons

146* ?Flagon. Impressed grooves and scored line decoration. Fabric 61. *1095 15V; IIa*

147* Ring-necked flagon with flared rim. White slip on exterior and inside neck. Fabric 41. *101 T14; II*

148* Flagon with disc rim. Fabric 56. *289 T15III; IIa*

149* Two-handled flagon with triangular section rim. Fabric 41. *723 T16V; II*

Beakers

150* Beaker with everted rim. Shoulder groove. Fabric 41. *202 T14; II*

151* Beaker. Rough cast with clay particles. Colour-coated brown, matt externally and with metallic lustre internally. The form appears to be close to some Central Gaulish products (e.g. Greene 1978, fig. 2.3 no. 2) but the fabric is similar to Lower Rhineland and Nene Valley material. Fabric 10. *308 and 311 T16II; IIa*

Jars

152* Narrow-necked jar with flared bead rim. Cordon on neck. Fabric 32. *567 T15IV; II*

153* Jar with everted, lid-seated rim. Self-coloured slip. Fabric 34. *1090, 1083 and 1102 T15V; IIa/b*

154* Jar with grooved rim. Fabric 41. *012 T16I; IIa*

155* Large jar with everted, grooved rim. Multiple shoulder grooves. Wheel thrown rim, the body is possibly hand made and wheel finished. Fabric 81. *287 T15III; IIa*

156* Large jar with curved, 'double beaded' rim. Incised grooves and wavy line decoration. Fabric 67. *572, 556, 557 and T15IV; II*

157* Jar with flared rim. Wide shoulder grooves. Hand made and wheel-finished. Fabric 55. *303 T16II; IIa*

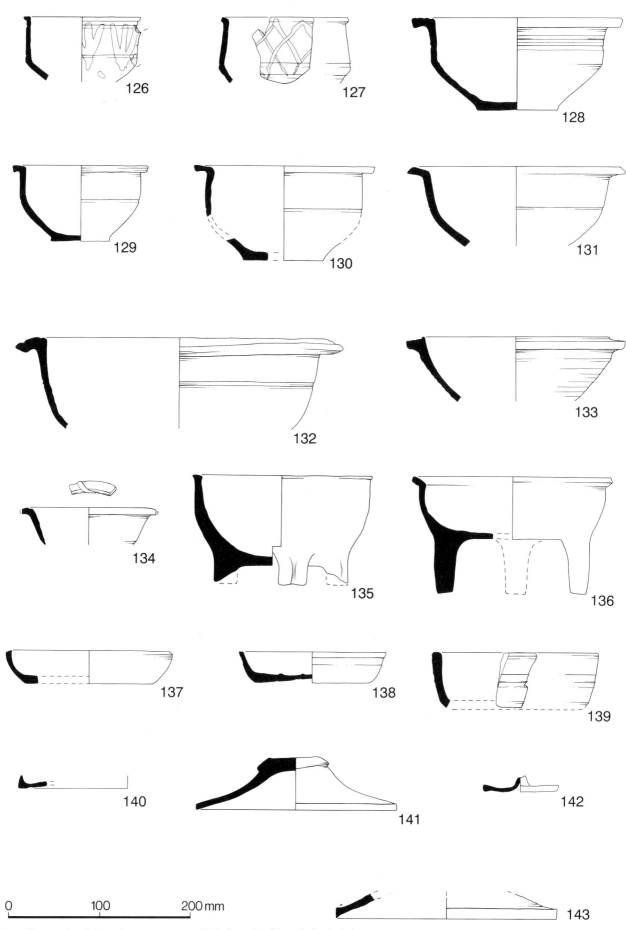

Fig. 50. Bowls, dishes, cheese presses and lids from fort Phase I. Scale 1:4

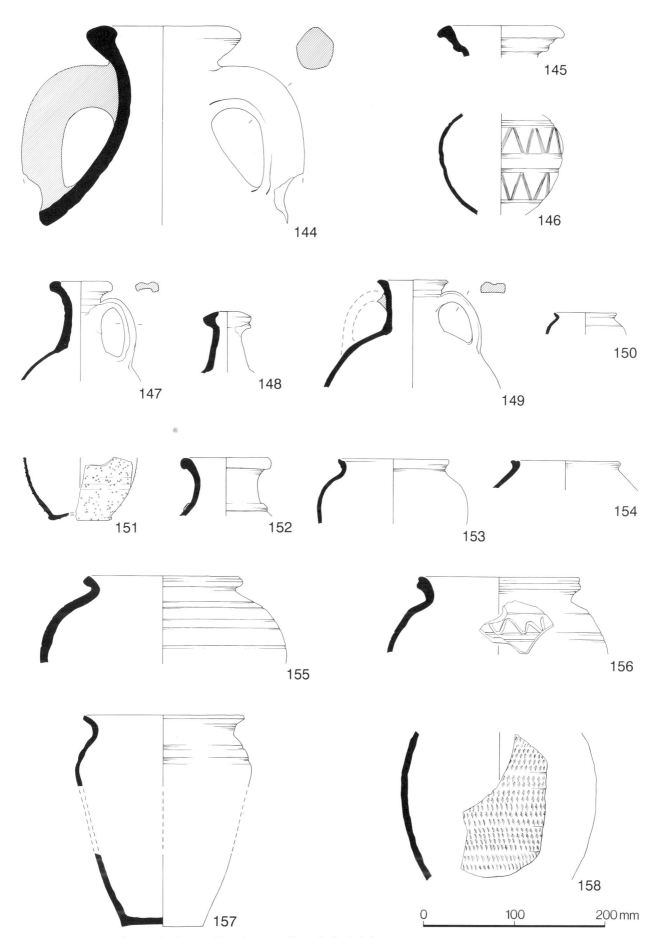

Fig. 51. Amphorae, flagons, beakers and jars from fort Phase II. Scale 1:4

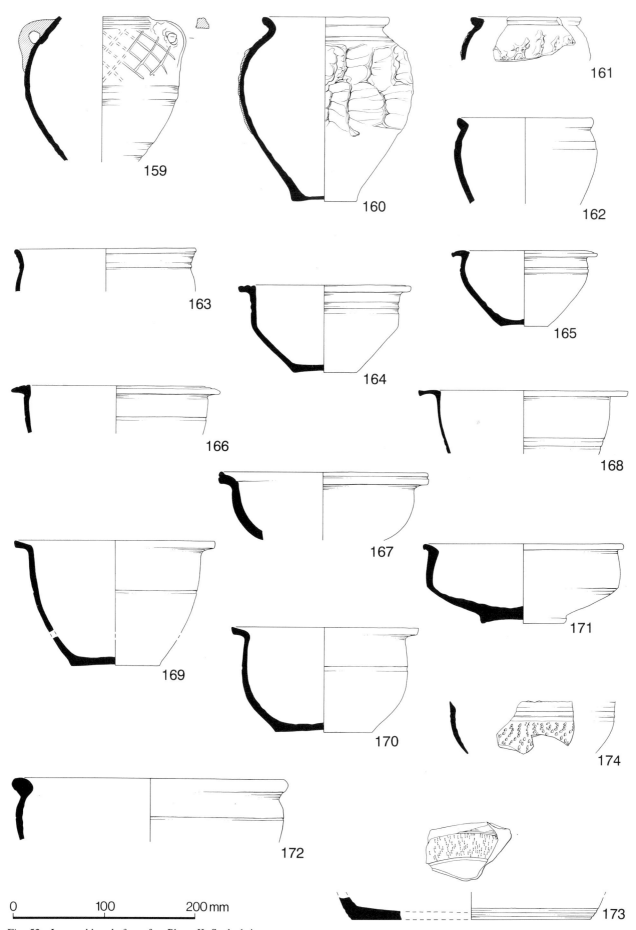

159
160
161
162
163
164
165
166
167
168
169
170
171
172
173
174

0   100   200 mm

Fig. 52. Jars and bowls from fort Phase II. Scale 1:4

112

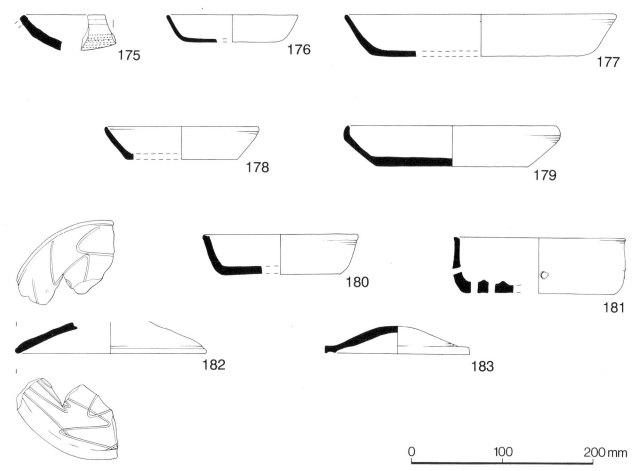

Fig. 53. Dishes, cheese press and lids from fort Phase II. Scale 1:4

158* ?Jar. Rouletted. Fabric 41. *1097 T15V; IIb*

159* Two-handled jar. Burnished lattice and groove decoration. Fabric 73. *253, 278 and 287 T15III; IIa*

160* Jar with curved out rim. Two shoulder grooves. Linear rustication. Fabric 67. *727 T16V; II*

161* Jar with grooved, everted rim. Rustication formed from discrete patches of applied clay. Fabric 67. *008 T17; II*

162* Wide-mouthed jar with everted rim. Stepped shoulder. Fabric 84. *312 T14; II*

163* Wide jar. Grooves below rim. Fabric 44. *586 T15IV; II*

Bowls

164* Carinated bowl with flat, reeded rim. Grooves on upper body. Burnished base and lower 20mm of exterior. Fabric 67. *218, 039 and 201 T14; II*

165* Carinated bowl with grooved rim. Grooves above carination. Fabric 67. *029 T16I; IIb*

166* Bowl with grooved rim. Grooves on side. Fabric 63. *727 T16V; II*

167* Bowl with reeded and grooved rim. Similar vessels were possibly produced at Doncaster (Buckland and Magilton 1986, fig. 34 no. 14). The same rim form also appears on jars (cf. Wacher 1969, fig. 64 no. 289). Fabric 67. *723 T16V; II*

168* Flat-rimmed bowl. Grooved sides and mica dusted. Fabric 50. *315 T14; II*

169* Bowl with flat, sloping rim. Groove on side. Fabric 41. *045, 001, 010 and 032 T18; IIb*

170* Bowl with flat, sloping rim. Groove on side. Fabric 41. *1095 T15V; IIa*

171* Oval carinated bowl with sloping flat rim. Burnished externally. Wheel-thrown but, presumably deliberately, distorted to an oval shape. Long axis illustrated; short axis measures approximately 90mm. Fabric 75. *1095 T15V; IIa*

172* Large bowl with heavy bead rim. Groove at widest point. Fabric 82. *008 T17; II*

173* ?Bowl. Internal rouletted and grooved decoration. Multiple grooves at bottom of exterior sides. Fabric 32. *567 T15IV; II*

174* ?Bowl. Grooved and rouletted decoration. Burnished. Fabric 62. *315 T14; II*

Dishes

175* Dish with carinated sides. Rouletted. Fabric 41. *721 T16V; II*

176* Dish with plain rim. Fabric 41. *931 and 978 T9; II*

177* Dish with plain rim. External burnished bands. Grooves on base interior. Fabric 41. *312 T14; II*

178* Dish with internally grooved rim. Fabric 67. *586 T15IV; II*

179* Carinated dish with plain rim. Fabric 41. *587 and 556 T15IV; II*

180* Dish with moulded-rim top, possibly as lid seat. External burnish. Fabric 41. *043, 001, 034, and 075 T18; IIa*

Cheese Press

181*Cheese press with slightly thickened rim. Internal basal ridges. Round holes pierced from inside through base and sides before firing. Burnished on lower half of exterior. Fabric 43. *102 and 109 T14; II*

Lids

182*Lid with plain rim. Burnished round rim. External and internal wavy line decoration. This decoration has been partly obscured on the exterior by the later addition of more clay. Hand made. Fabric 79. *203 T14; II*

183*Lid with square-edged rim. Channel cut on underside of rim. Fabric 56. *202 T14; II*

Vicus Phase 1

Flagons

184*Large, two-handled flagon or amphora with splayed rim and vestigal ring moulding. Fabric 41. *1048 and 1067 T10; 1*

185*Flagon with flat-topped rim. Fabric 32. *1048 T10; 1*

Beakers

186*Beaker with pointed-bead rim. Groove on side. Possibly a simplified version of a butt beaker cf. Hawkes and Hull 1947, 240 and pl. CVIII form 117. Fabric 41. *471 T10; 1*

187*High shoulder beaker with curved out rim. Apparent uneven grooves may be the result of an attempt at burnishing. Hand built. Fabric 81. *1090 T10; 1*

188*Beaker with everted, grooved rim. Shoulder groove and random rustication. Fabric 67. *1090 T10; 1*

Jars

189*Jar or beaker with bead rim. Grooved shoulder cordon. Fabric 41. *1087 T10; 1*

190*Jar with curved over rim. Groove on upper body. Fabric 41. *471 T10; 1*

191*Bowl, possibly based on Dragendorff 29. Rouletted and grooved decoration. Fabric 41. *783 T10; 1*

192*Large bowl with flat-topped rim. Wavy groove decoration on sides and top of rim. Fabric 41. *Level 7 Site 1(74); 1*

193*Bowl with flat, grooved rim. Fabric 41. *890 T10; 1*

194*Flanged bowl with spout. Grooved flange. Knife trimmed exterior below flange. Fabric 41. *Level 10 Site 1(74); 1*

Vicus Phase 2

Flagons

195*Ring-necked flagon with slightly internally cupped rim. Cream slip, patchy internally. Fabric 44. *495 T10; 2*

196*Ring-necked flagon with internally cupped rim. External thin, pale orange-brown slip. Fabric 34. *495 T10; 2*

197*Ring-necked flagon with flared neck. White slip. Fabric 44. *440 and 445 T10; 2*

198*Large ring-necked flagon with flared neck. White slip on exterior and the interior of the top of the neck. Fabric 41. *503 T10; 2*

199*Ring-necked flagon with flared rim. A possible Brockley Hill - Verulamium product cf. Green 1980, 49 and fig. 24 no. 66; Castle 1978, 211 and fig. 5 no. 4. Fabric 56. *688 T10; 2*

Samian of mostly Hadrianic date was found associated with Numbers 195 to 199. Number 198 was associated with samian that could have been early Antonine in date.

200*Flagon with plain flared rim. Fabric 41. *649 T10; 2*

201*Small flask or *unguentarium*. Fabric 56. *688 T10; 2*

202*Small flask or *unguentarium*. Fabric 41. *835 T10; 2*

Beakers

203*Beaker with everted rim. Shoulder groove. Fabric 41. *1140 T10; 2*

204*Beaker with cornice rim. Matt brown colour coat. Fabric 10. *459 T10; 2*

205*Beaker with cornice rim. Matt black colour coat, patchy on the interior. Associated with samian of AD 110-25 date. Fabric 14. *496 T10; 2*

206*Indented beaker with everted rim. Shoulder groove and self-coloured slip. Fabric 33. *389 T10; 2*

207*Necked beaker with flared rim. Cordon at base of neck. Highly burnished externally, less on the inside of the rim. Associated with Hadrianic samian. Fabric 62. *481 and 495 T10; 2*

208*Beaker with tall neck and flared rim. Dark brown colour coat. External burnish. Fabric 17. *474 T10; 2*

Jars

209*Narrow-necked jar with bead rim. Burnished wavy line and shallow groove decoration. Fabric 67. *495 T10; 2*

210*Narrow-necked jar with bead rim. Shoulder cordon and wide grooves. Fabric 67. *503 and 452 T10; 2*

Numbers 209 and 210 were found associated with Hadrianic and Hadrianic-Antonine samian respectively.

211*Jar with everted beaded rim. Circles of thick orange-brown slip. Associated samian was of Flavian date. Fabric 41. *1075 T10; 2*

212*Jar with thickened everted rim. Fabric 34. *431 T10; 2*

213*Jar with curved out rim. Shoulder cordon above shallow groove. Crude burnished lattice. Associated with Hadrianic samian. Fabric 55. *495, 413 and 452 T10; 2*

214*Jar with hooked rim. Shoulder groove. Associated with Hadrianic to early Antonine samian. Fabric 48. *481 and 448 T10; 2*

215*Jar with bent over rim. Multiple shoulder grooves. Associated with samian dated AD 90-110. Fabric 56. *646 T10; 2*

216*Jar with curved over rim. Two shoulder grooves. Fabric 56. *455 T10; 2*

217*Wide-mouthed, necked jar with flared rim. Small cordon at base of neck. Associated samian is of Flavian date. Fabric 41. *1075 T10; 2*

218*Wide-mouthed, necked jar with flared rim. External burnish. Fabric 74. *656 T10; 2*

219*?Jar. Rouletted, grooved and combed wavy line decoration. Fabric 32. *389 T10; 2*

220*Jar with everted rim. Shoulder groove and linear rustication formed from discrete lines of applied clay. Associated with samian of Hadrianic to early Antonine date. Fabric 67. *462 T10; 2*

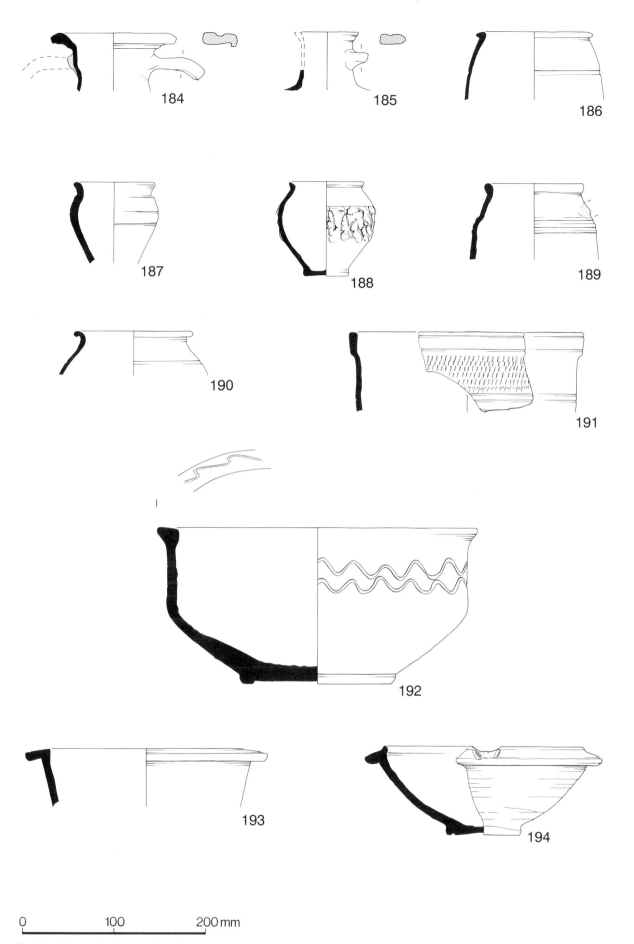

184

185

186

187

188

189

190

191

192

193

194

0   100   200 mm

Fig. 54. Flagons, beakers and jars from *vicus* Phase 1. Scale 1:4

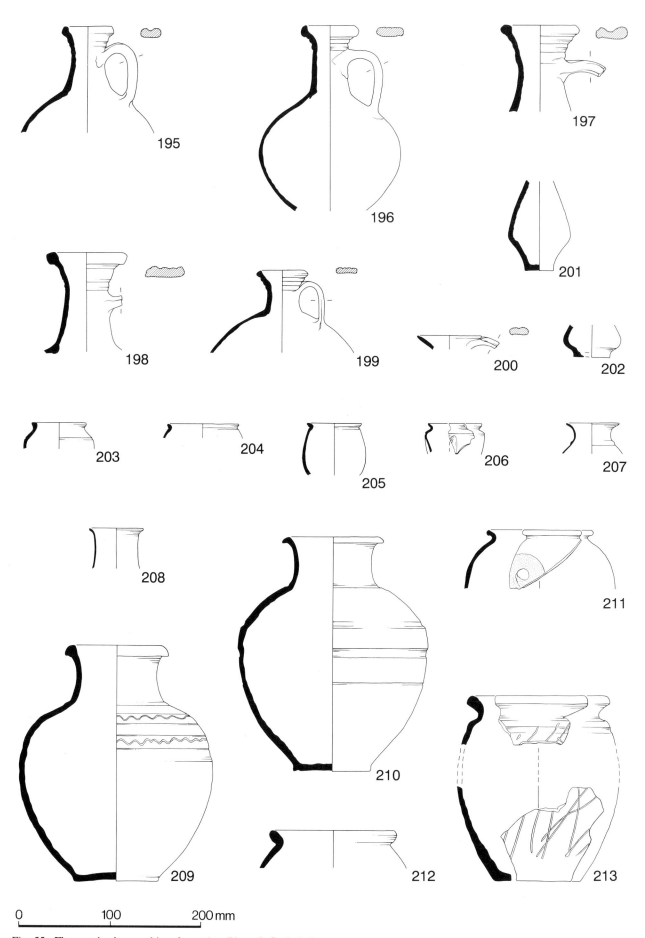

Fig. 55. Flagons, beakers and jars from *vicus* Phase 2. Scale 1:4

0   100   200 mm

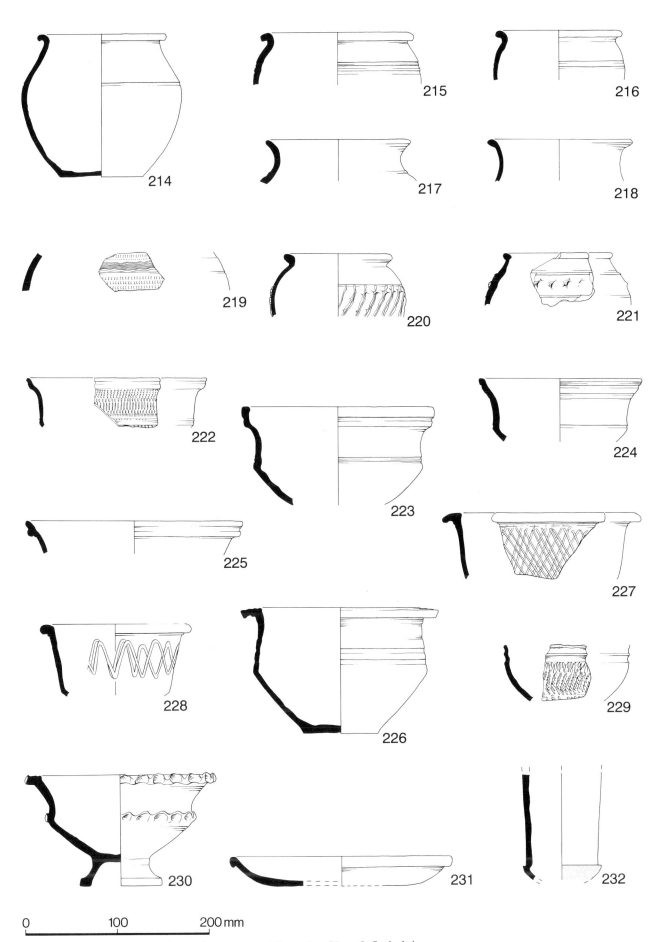

Fig. 56. Jars, bowls, platter and miscellaneous vessel from *vicus* Phase 2. Scale 1:4

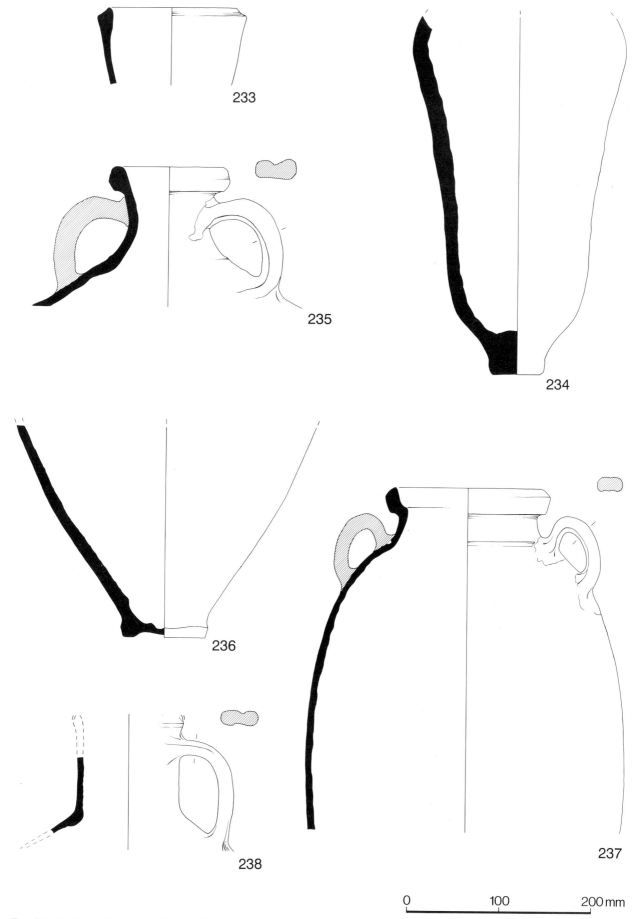

Fig. 57. Amphorae from *vicus* Phase 3. Scale 1:4

0   100   200 mm

221*Jar with bead rim shoulder cordon and grooves. Rustication formed from discrete points of applied clay. Associated with samian dated AD 75-90. Fabric 67. *757 and 825 T10; 2*

Bowls

222*Bowl. Rouletted and grooved. Fabric 41. *389 T10; 2*

223*Bowl. Grooved decoration. Fabric 39. *389 T10; 2*

224*Bowl. Grooved decoration. Fabric 32. *720 and 750 T10; 2*

Numbers 219 to 221 are, more or less, initiations of Dragendorff 29. Associated with samian of early Trajanic or 1st-century date.

225*Bowl with pulley-wheel rim. Fabric 33. *628 T10; 2*

226*Carinated bowl with flat, reeded rim. Grooved above carination. Fabric 41. *481, 129, 443, 448 and 744 T10; 2*

227*Flat-rimmed bowl. Burnished over rim and burnished lattice. Fabric 67. *455 T10; 2*

228*Bowl with heavy bead rim and, probably, chamfered base. Burnished over rim, on lower sides and intersecting wavy lines. Fabric 67. *455 T10; 2*

229*?Bowl. Rouletted and grooved decoration. Fabric 41. *T10 582 T10; 2*

230*Tazza. Two bands of 'pie-crust' decoration. Wheel thrown in three sections; luted together between the pedestal foot and the base of the bowl and at the level of the lower band of decoration. Fabric 41. *481, 129, 244, 301 and 448 T10; 2*

Platter

231*Platter with undercut bead rim. Very worn red-brown slip. A Pompeian red ware vessel. Fabric 26. *474, 472 and 481 T10; 2*

Miscellaneous

232*Unusual shape vessel of unknown function. Colour-coated red on the exterior below the offset. Fabric 34. *743 T10; 2*

Vicus Phase 3

Amphorae

233*Amphora. Evidence of handles missing. Fabric 1. *127 T10; 3*

234*Small amphora. Occurs in Phase 3 and 4 contexts of the *vicus* although never common. One sherd possibly from a similar form occurred in a Phase 1 context. Fabric 1. *952 T10; 3*

235*Amphora of Pelichet 47 form (Pelichet 1946, 193 and fig. 5). Fabric 5. *908, 909 and 910 T10; 3*

236*Amphora base, probably from a Pelichet 47 as the base is too narrow for the normal range of Dressel 28. Sealey 1985. Fabric 5. *298 T10; 3*

237*Amphora. The only identifiable example of this form from Castleford. Fabric 5. *952 T10; 3*

238*?Amphora. Possibly a Brockley Hill-Verulamium product based on Pelichet 47 (Green 1980, 49). Fabric 56. *129 and 244 T10; 3*

239*Dressel 38 amphora. Fabric 2. *129, 198, 295, 298 and 301A T10; 3*

240*Amphorae of Dressel 2 - 4 form. Fabric 4. *946 T10; 3*

Flagons

241*Ring-necked flagon with internally cupped rim. Fabric 32. *452 T10; 3*

242*Ring-necked flagon with internally cupped rim. White slip externally and inside top of neck. Fabric 41. *238 T10; 3*

243*Ring-necked flagon with internally cupped rim. Fabric 32. *951 T10; 3*

244*Ring-necked flagon with internally cupped rim. Fabric 32. *918 T10; 3*

245*Ring-necked flagon with flared neck. Fabric 32. *118, 168 and 169 T10; 3*

246*Ring-necked flagon with flared neck. Fabric 39. *908 T10; 3*

247*Ring-necked flagon with flared neck. White slip. Fabric 44. *535 T10; 3*

248*Bead-rim flagon with vestigal rings on neck. Thin brown slip. Fabric 39. *448 T10; 3*

249*Ring-necked flagon with flared neck. Dark brown slip survives on the inside of the neck and on small areas of the rim. Fabric 32. *952 T10; 3*

250*Ring-necked flagon with flared neck. Fabric 39. *908 T10; 3*

251*Flagon with undercut bead rim and vestigal rings on the neck. White slip externally and to just above the body-neck join internally. Fabric 41. *301A T10; 3*

252*Flagon with internally cupped, bead rim. Wide groove on neck. Fabric 32. *197 T10; 3*

253*Flagon with flared, internally cupped rim. Fabric 41. *908 T10; 3*

254*Flagon with pulley wheel rim. Fabric 41. *420 T10; 3*

255*Flagon with grooved bead rim. Traces of white slip survive on the exterior. Fabric 39. *952 T10; 3*

256*Flagon with pulley-wheel rim. Fabric 51. *081, 118 and 127 T10; 3*

257*Flagon with pulley-wheel rim. Fabric 33. *197 T10; 3*

258*Flagon with collared rim, internally cupped. Burnished on exterior of neck. The burnishing process has left a series of vertical striations on the neck. Impressions at the base of the neck were probably made with the tool used for burnishing. Fabric 41. *448 T10; 3*

259*Flagon with bead and flanged rim. Fabric 32. *910 T10; 3*

260*Two-handled flagon with bead rim. Fabric 41. *129, 224 and 301A T10; 3*

261*Two-handled flagon with bead rim. Fabric 41. *301A T10; 3*

262*Jug. Indented and vertically burnished neck. Hand made. Fabric 79. *425 T10; 3*

263*?*Unguentarium*. The base is too small and rounded for the vessel to be able to stand upright. Multiple grooves on body. Fabric 56. *445 T10; 3*

Beakers

264*Beaker with cornice rim. Matt black colour coat. Fabric 14. *083 T10; 3*

265*Cornice-rimmed beaker. Self-coloured slip. Fabric 16. *022 T10; 3*

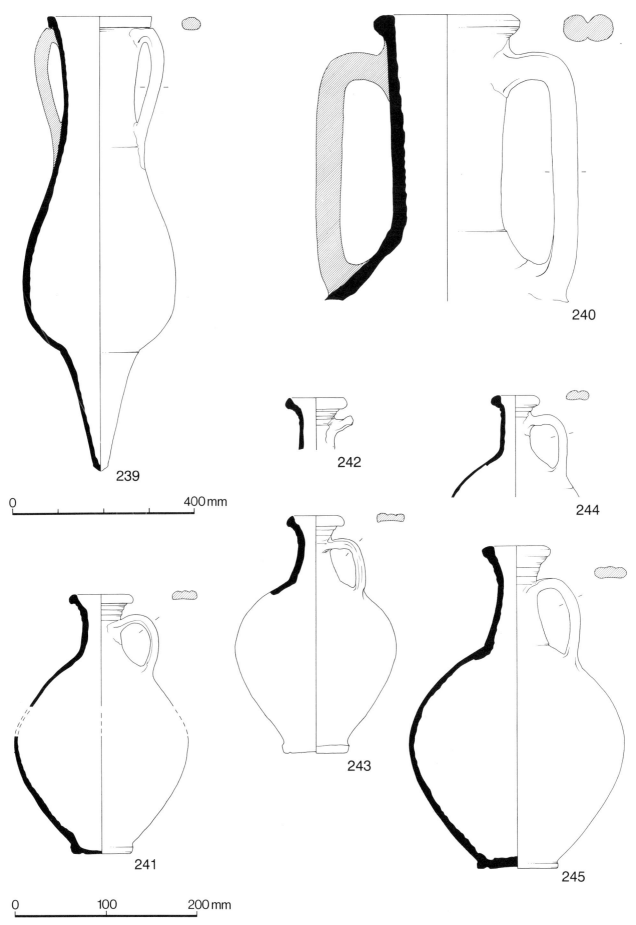

239

0   400 mm

240

242

244

241

243

245

0   100   200 mm

Fig. 58. Amphorae and flagons from *vicus* Phase 3. Scale 1:4 (No. 239; Scale 1:8)

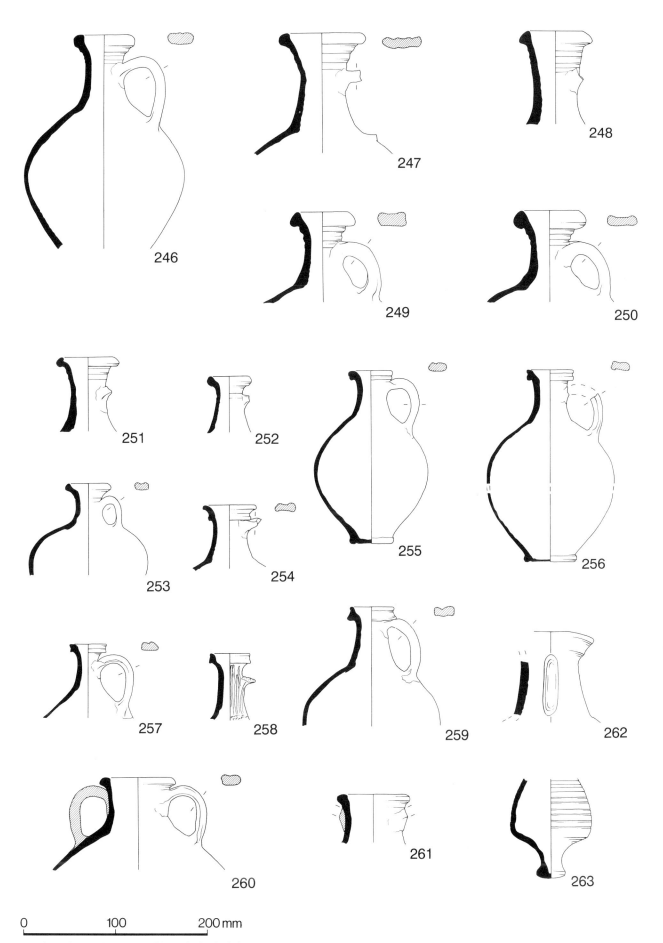

Fig. 59. Flagons from *vicus* Phase 3. Scale 1:4

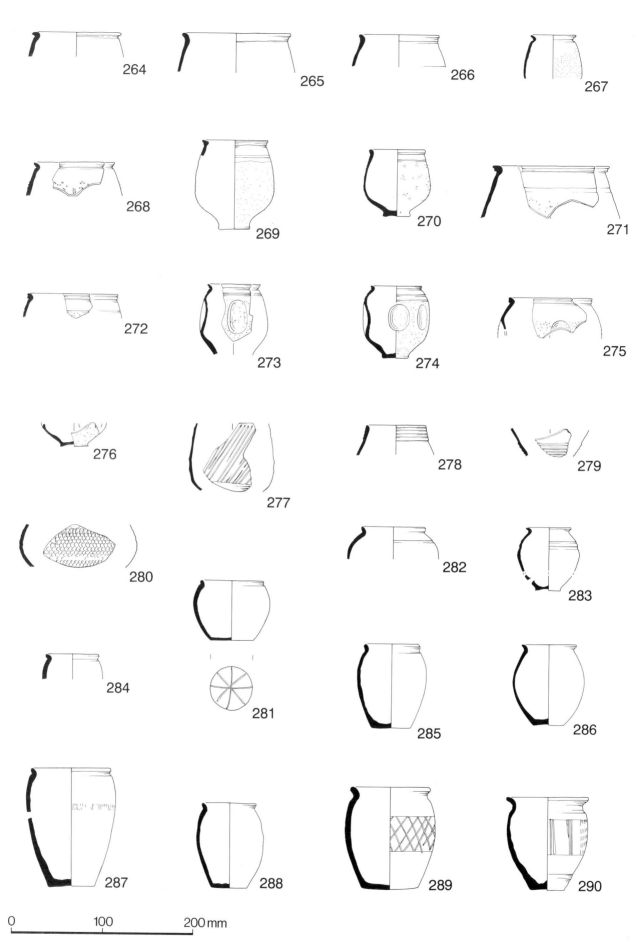

Fig. 60. Beakers from *vicus* Phase 3. Scale 1:4

266* Beaker with cornice rim. Fabric 41. *024 T10; 3*

267* Beaker with cornice rim. Rough cast with clay pellets and colour-coated. The colour of the slip is indeterminate due to burning. Fabric 13. *298 T10; 3*

268* Beaker with cornice rim. Rough cast with clay particles and colour-coated very dark brown/black. Fabric 14. *157 T10; 3*

269* Bag-shaped beaker with grooved cornice rim. Worn dark brown colour coat and rough cast with clay pellets. Fabric 13. *910 T10; 3*

270* Bag-shaped beaker with grooved cornice rim. Self-coloured slip and shoulder groove. Rough cast with clay particles. Fabric 33. *952 T10; 3*

271* Large beaker with grooved cornice rim. Colour-coated dark brown externally and over the rim. Originally rough cast with clay particles which have largely fallen out leaving voids. Fabric 15. *169 T10; 3*

272* Beaker with grooved cornice rim. Rough cast with clay particles. Shoulder groove. Colour-coated matt dark brown. Fabric 10. *420 T10; 3*

273* Bag-shaped, indented beaker with cornice rim. Rough cast with clay pellets. Shoulder groove. Matt black colour coat. Fabric 14. *198 T10; 3*

274* Indented beaker with cornice rim. Two shoulder grooves. Matt black colour coat and clay pellet rough casting. Fabric 12. *908 and 910 T10; 3*

275* Indented beaker with grooved cornice rim. Rough cast with clay particles and colour-coated matt black. Fabric 13. *463 T10; 3*

276* Indented beaker. Clay particle rough casting and colour-coated matt black. Fabric 10, but pale orange-brown rather than the more usual off-white. *900 T10; 3*

277* Beaker. Diagonal ribs of barbotine and matt black colour coat. The fabric is closest to that normally assigned a Lower Rhineland source but Nene Valley production is a possibility (cf. Dannell 1973, 140 and fig. 1 no. 9). Fabric 12. *129 T10; 3*

278* Beaker with multiple grooved rim. Black colour coat. Fabric 14. *129 T10; 3*

279* Beaker. Multiple grooves near base. Black colour coat. Possibly the lower part of Number 276. Fabric 14. *448 and 452 T10; 3*

280* Beaker. Rouletted and very dark brown/black, slightly glossy colour coat. Fabric 12. *908 and 152 T10; 3*

281* Globular beaker with plain rim. Externally burnished and incised line decoration on base. Hand made. Fabric 79. *910 T10; 3*

282* Globular beaker with everted rim. Shoulder groove. Fabric 30. *458 T10; 3*

283* Small beaker with curved out rim. Two shoulder grooves. A small hole was pierced in the side from the exterior before firing. Fabric 67. *196 T10; 3*

284* Small beaker with everted rim. Fabric 41. *448 T10; 3*

285* Beaker with everted rim. Smoothed exterior. Fabric 67. *908 T10; 3*

286* Small beaker with curved out rim. Fabric 67. *255 T10; 3*

287* Beaker with small curved out rim. Band of vertical incised lines. Fabric 67. *908 T10; 3*

288* Beaker with curved out rim. External burnish. Hand made. Marks left by the joining of clay coils are visible on the interior. Fabric 79. *174 T10; 3*

289* Beaker with curved out rim. Burnished externally and over the rim except for the lattice decorated zone. Hand made. Fabric 79. *030 and 083 T10; 3*

290* Beaker with curved out rim. Scored vertical line decoration. Fabric 75. *452 and 482 T10; 3*

291* Handled beaker with everted rim. Burnished on shoulder and over rim and lattice decoration. Hand made. Fabric 79. *298 T10; 3*

292* Beaker with plain everted rim and funnel neck. Fabric 33. *252 T10; 3*

293* Beaker with square-edged bead rim. White slip and cordon. The form is possibly derived from the butt-beaker. Fabric 41. *024 T10; 3*

294* Large beaker or jar with everted rim. Offset at shoulder and barbotine dot decoration. Burnished on the exterior, lower body. Fabric 64. *418, 425, 900 and 908 T10; 3*

295* Large indented beaker with flared, curved rim. Similar vessels were produced at Norton (Hayes and Whitley 1950, fig. 10 no. 9) but this example is not in a Norton fabric. The form is apparently derived from colour-coated vessels (cf. Howe, Perrin and Mackreth 1981, fig. 4 no. 41). The vessel is probably of 3rd-century date and intrusive in this phase. Fabric 67. *028 and 008 T10; 3*

296* ?Beaker. Buff-cream slip on exterior. Hole drilled in centre of base after firing. Fabric 52. *466 T10; 3*

Jars

297* Jar with everted rim. Shoulder groove. Distorted and cracked, a waster. Fabric 78. *028 T10; 3*

298* Small jar with everted rim. Exterior probably burnished. Distorted and cracked, probably a waster. Fabric 78. *174 T10; 3*

299* Jar with turned out rim. Small cordon just below rim. Fabric 34. *104 T10; 3*

300* Jar with turned out rim. Traces of red-brown colour coat are apparent in the wide shoulder groove. Fabric 34. *255 T10; 3*

301* Jar with everted, square-edged rim. Fabric 41. *263 T10; 3*

302* Jar with everted rim. Shoulder groove. Burnished externally and over the rim except for lattice decorated zone. Fabric 78. *169 T10; 3*

303* Jar with curved out rim. Burnished zig-zag line decoration on rim and body of vessel. Burnished on shoulder and over rim. Hand made. Fabric 79. *192 T10; 3*

304* Jar with curved out rim. Burnished over rim and externally except for the lattice decorated zone. Burnished wavy line on rim. Series of small indentations on interior. Hand made. Fabric 79. *910 T10; 3*

305* Large jar with curved out rim. Burnished over the rim and externally except for the lattice decorated zone. Fabric 75. *910 T10; 3*

306* Jar with curved out rim. Burnished over rim and externally except for the lattice decorated zone. Burnished lines on the rim. Hand made. Fabric 79. *083 T10; 3*

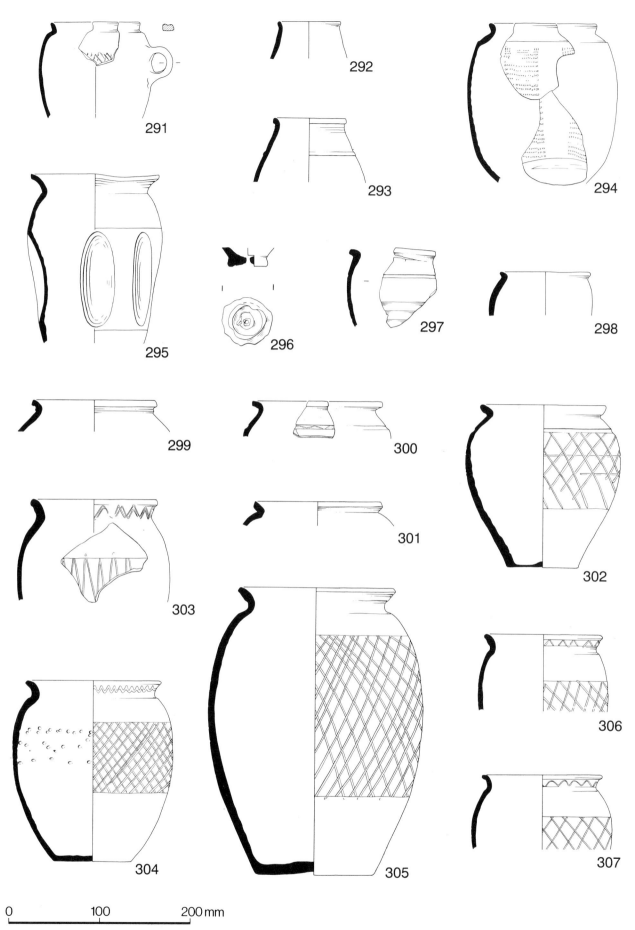

0   100   200 mm

Fig. 61. Beakers from *vicus* Phase 3. Scale 1:4

124

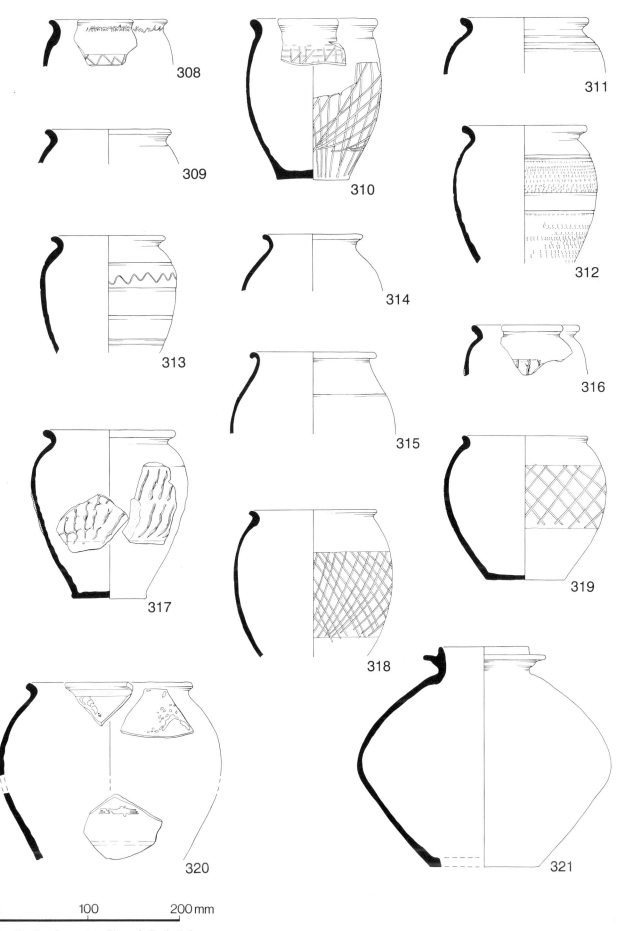

308

309

310

311

312

313

314

315

316

317

318

319

320

321

0   100   200 mm

Fig. 62. Jars from *vicus* Phase 3. Scale 1:4

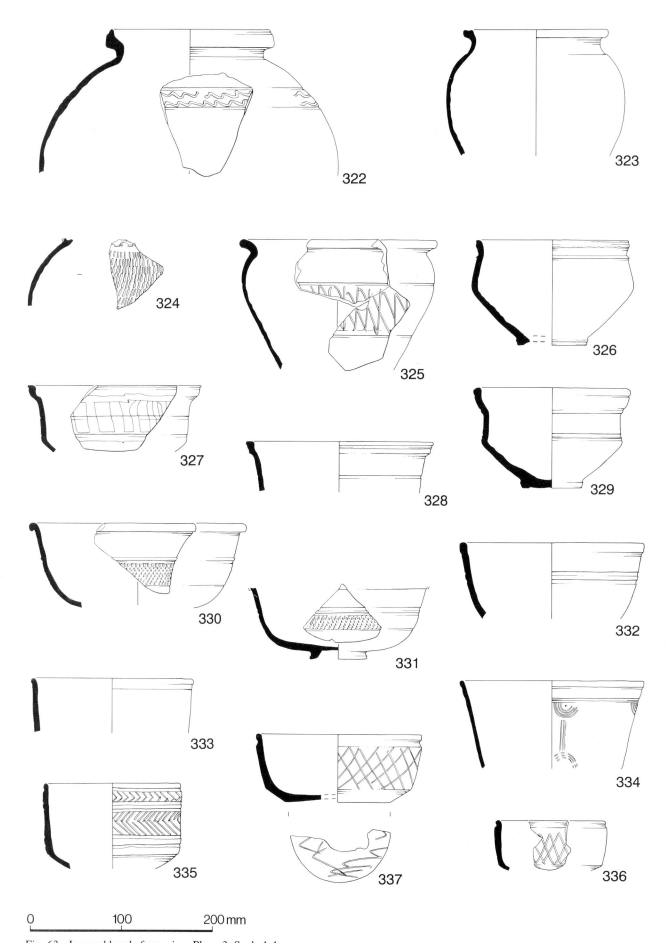

Fig. 63. Jars and bowls from *vicus* Phase 3. Scale 1:4

0   100   200 mm

307* Jar with curved out rim. Burnished over rim and externally except for the lattice decorated zone. Burnished wavy line on the rim. Hand made. Fabric 79. *083 T10; 3*

308* Jar with curved out rim. Burnished over rim and externally except for lattice decorated zone. Burnished 'scribbled' line on rim. Hand made. Fabric 79. *083 and 121 T10; 3*

309* Jar with curved out rim. Burnished over rim and externally. Hand made. Fabric 79. *121 T10; 3*

310* Jar with curved out rim. Smoothed exterior and burnished lattice decoration. Fabric 78. *242 T10; 3*

311* Jar with curved out rim. Multiple shoulder grooves. Fabric 34. *419, 420 and 421 T10; 3*

312* Jar with curved out rim. Grooves and two bands of rouletting. Burnished on shoulder and between rouletted zones. Fabric 67. *169 T10; 3*

313* Jar with curved out rim. Burnished externally. Grooved and burnished wavy line. Fabric 82. *169 T10; 3*

314* Jar with curved out rim. Fabric 41. *129 and 286 T10; 3*

315* Jar with curved over rim. Shoulder groove. Fabric 41. *909 and 913 T10; 3*

316* Jar with curved out rim. Shoulder-groove linear rustication formed from discrete lines of applied clay. Fabric 41. *174 T10; 3*

317* Jar with curved out rim. Shoulder-groove linear rustication formed from discrete lines of applied clay. Burnished externally above and below the rustication. Fabric 74. *118 T10; 3*

318* Globular jar with curved out rim. Burnished externally except for the lattice-decorated zone. Hand made. Fabric 79. *452 T10; 3*

319* Globular jar with curved out rim. Burnished over rim and externally except for lattice decorated zone. Hand made. Fabric 79. *952 T10; 3*

320* Jar with curved out rim. Traces of red painted pattern survive. Fabric 31. *183, 197, 237 and 238 T10; 3*

321* Flanged rim jar. Burnished externally and inside rim. Hand made. Fabric 79. *028, 008 and 078 T10; 3*

322* Very large jar with everted, internally cupped rim. Straight and wavy groove decoration. Fabric 67. *900 T10; 3*

323* Necked globular jar with everted rim. Fabric 63. *129 and 301A T10; 3*

324* ?Jar. Rouletted and frilled decoration. Fabric 41. *420 T10; 3*

325* Wide-mouthed jar with curved over rim. Incised grooves and burnishing intersecting zig-zag line decoration. Burnished externally, over the rim and above and below the grooves. Fabric 74. *169, 196 and 285 T10; 3*

326* Wide-mouthed jar with 'moulded' rim. Burnished externally near the base. Fabric 41. *448 T10; 3*

Bowls

Numbers 327 and 328 are derived from Dragendorff 29. This type is normally dated to before AD 100 and in general the material from Castleford supports this. Hence these may be residual in this phase.

327* Bowl. Grooved and red-brown painted decoration. Fabric 33. *250 T10; 3*

328* Bowl. Grooved. Fabric 44. *226 T10; 3*

329* Carinated bowl with flared rim. Grooved decoration. Conceivably a loose derivation of Dragendorff 29. Fabric 41. *169, 197 and 237 T10; 3*

Numbers 330 to 332 are essentially imitations of Dragendorff 37.

330* Bowl with hooked-bead rim. Grooved and rouletted decoration. Fabric 41. *918 T10; 3*

331* Bowl. Grooved and rouletted decoration. Fabric 41. *452 T10; 3*

332* Bowl with plain rim. Self-coloured slip and grooved decoration. Fabric 43. *127, 164 and 169 T10; 3*

333* Bowl with beaded rim. Faint groove below rim. Fabric 41. *237 T10; 3*

334* Bowl with flared rim and slightly flared sides. Originally burnished but the surface finish has largely worn away. Incised groove decoration. The semi-circular patterns were produced with a compass. Fabric 61. *081, 078, 120 and 448 T10; 3*

335* Carinated bowl with plain rim. Grooved and impressed herringbone decoration. Burnished. Hand made. Fabric 79. *118 and 169 T10; 3*

336* Small bowl with grooved rim and basal chamfer. Burnished and intersecting zig-zag line decoration. Hand made. Fabric 79. *121 T10; 3*

337* Bowl with grooved rim and basal chamfer. Lattice decoration on side and wavy line pattern on base. Burnished. Hand made. Fabric 79. *083 T10; 3*

338* Bowl with slightly curved down, flat rim. Fabric 41. *285 T10; 3*

339* Flat rim bowl. Probably originally burnished but the surface finish has been destroyed by burning. Hand made. Fabric 79. *174 T10; 3*

340* Flat-rimmed bowl with basal chamfer. Burnished with lattice decoration. Hand made. Fabric 79. *493 and 900 T10; 3*

341* Small flat-rimmed bowl with chamfered base. Burnished with zig-zag line decoration. Hand made. Fabric 79. *234 and 250 T10; 3*

342* Flat-rimmed bowl with basal chamfer. Burnished. Intersecting inverted chevron pattern on side and wavy lines on base. Hand made. Fabric 79. *083 and 121 T10; 3*

343* Flat-rimmed bowl with basal chamfer. Burnished with inverted chevron pattern. Hand made. Fabric 79. *083 and 121 T10; 3*

344* Flat-rimmed bowl with basal chamfer. Burnished with crude lattice decoration. Hand made. Fabric 79. *445 T10; 3*

345* Bowl with flat sloping rim. Burnished. Hand made. Fabric 79. *209 T10; 3*

346* Flat-rimmed bowl with lid seating. Burnished with intersecting arc decoration. Probably an early version of the straight-sided flanged bowl cf. Gillam 1977, fig. 3 no. 42. The earliest bowls of this type and with intersecting arc decoration have been previously dated to post AD 180 (Gillam 1977, 68). This bowl, however, would seem to date to before *c.* AD 160. The latest associated samian is of early Antonine date. Hand made. Fabric 79. *535 T10; 3*

347* Bowl with reeded rim. Internal and external grooves. Fabric 56. *341 T10; 3*

348* Hemispherical bowl with flanged rim and footring. Slipped a thin pale orange-brown colour internally and over the flange. Fabric 34. *910 T10; 3*

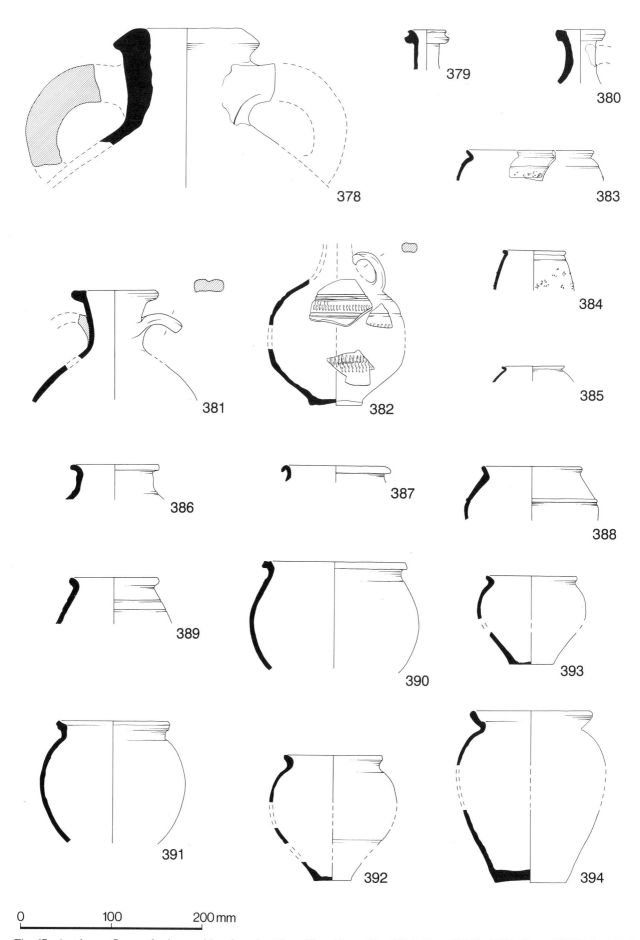

378　379　380　383　381　382　384　385　386　387　388　389　390　393　391　392　394

0　100　200 mm

Fig. 67. Amphorae, flagons, beakers and jars from fort Phase III and later. (No. 382 is Phase IV, No. 386 is Phase III/IV). Scale 1:4

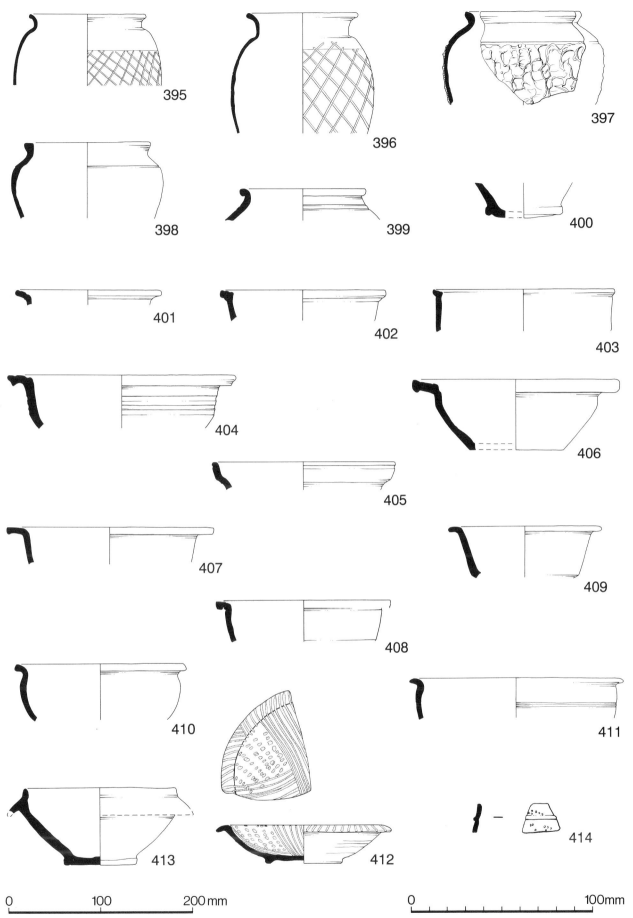

Fig. 68. Jars and bowls from Phase III. Scale 1:4 (No. 414; Scale 1:2)

133

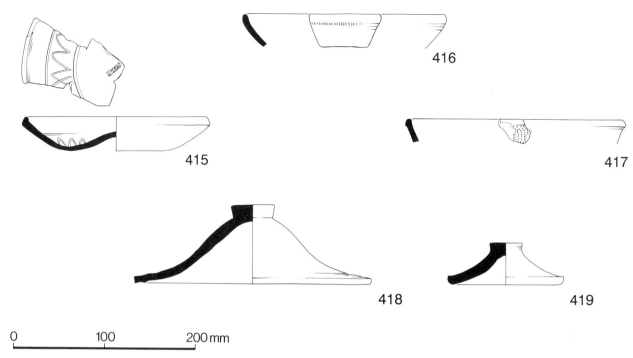

Fig. 69. Dishes and lids from Phase III. Scale 1:4

Later Roman: Phase IV fort area and Phase 4 *vicus* area

Amphora
420* Amphora probably of Dressel 38 form. Fabric 2. *932 T10; 4*

Flagons
421* Ring-necked flagon with flared neck. Probably a 1st-century vessel. Fabric 32. *1036 T15V; IV*

422* Ring-necked flagon with internally cupped rim. Probably of mid to late 2nd-century date. Fabric 32. *056/R T10; 4*

423* Ring-necked flagon with internally cupped rim. Probably mid to late 2nd-century. Fabric 41. *472 T10; 4*

424* Flagon with pulley-wheel rim. Fabric 41. *078 T10; 4*

425* Collared flagon with internal lid seat. Buff colour coat. Fabric 51. *124 Site 1(74); IV*

426* Flagon with pulley-wheel rim and internal bead. Fabric 32. *472 T10; 4*

427* ?Flagon. Decorated with red painted lines and bands of impressed marks. This appears to be a Yorkshire Red Painted Ware vessel (Keen 1970) which are usually dated *c.* AD 75 to *c.* AD 120. Probably residual. Fabric 42. *202 and 211 T15III; IV*

428* Flask with flared rim. Cordon on neck and rouletted and grooved decoration. Fabric 67. *750 T15IV ; IV*

429* ?Flagon. Multiple grooves and externally smoothed. Fabric 41. *078 T10; 4*

Beakers
430* Beaker with bead rim. Colour-coated matt black over barbotine decoration and grooves. Late 2nd or early 3rd century; an associated East Gaulish samian vessel of Dragendorff form 45 supports this date. Fabric 9. *461 T10; 4*

431* Small funnel-necked beaker with flared rim. Decorated with off-white barbotine over a dark grey slip. Probably of 4th-century date cf. Howe, Perrin and Mackreth 1981, fig. 5 no. 54. Fabric 9. *564 T15IV; IV*

432* Fragment of a 'Hunt Cup'. Decorated with a barbotine animal under a dark brown colour coat with a metallic lustre. Probably later 2nd or early 3rd century cf. Howe, Perrin and Mackreth 1981, fig. 3 nos 26 and 27. Fabric 11. *203 T15III; IV*

433* Beaker with grooved rim. Colour-coated matt black externally and red-brown internally. Barbotine decoration under the slip. Fabric 9. *1016 and 1037 T15V; IV*

434* Beaker with cornice rim. Colour-coated matt brown externally and darker brown with a slight metallic lustre internally. Barbotine decoration under the slip. Late 2nd or early 3rd century cf. Howe, Perrin and Mackreth 1981, fig. 3 nos 29 and 30; Dannell 1973, fig. 1 no. 66. Fabric 9. *202, 203 and 211 T15III; IV*

435* ?Beaker. Colour-coated matt black over bands of rouletting and horizontal barbotine dashes. Fabric 12. *709 T16V; IV*

436* Bag-shaped beaker with grooved cornice rim. Rough cast with clay particles and colour-coated matt black. Probably mid to late 2nd century cf. Gillam 1970, fig. 9 no. 75. Fabric 13. *124 T10; IV*

437* Beaker with bead rim. Matt black colour coat. Fabric 12. *202 T15III; IV*

438* Beaker with bead rim. Rouletted and colour-coated matt black. Fabric 12. *202 T15III; IV*

439* Beaker with bead rim. Matt brown colour coat which has largely worn off the exterior. Fabric 9. *079 T10; 4*

440* Folded beaker with a bead rim. Rouletted and colour-coated matt black. ?3rd century. Fabric 9. *461 T10; 4*

441* Folded beaker with bead rim. Rouletted. Colour-coated black/bronze with metallic lustre externally and glossy dark brown internally. A Trier product of late 2nd to mid-3rd-century date cf. Greene 1978, fig. 2.3 no. 5. Fabric 20. *203 and 211 T15III; IV*

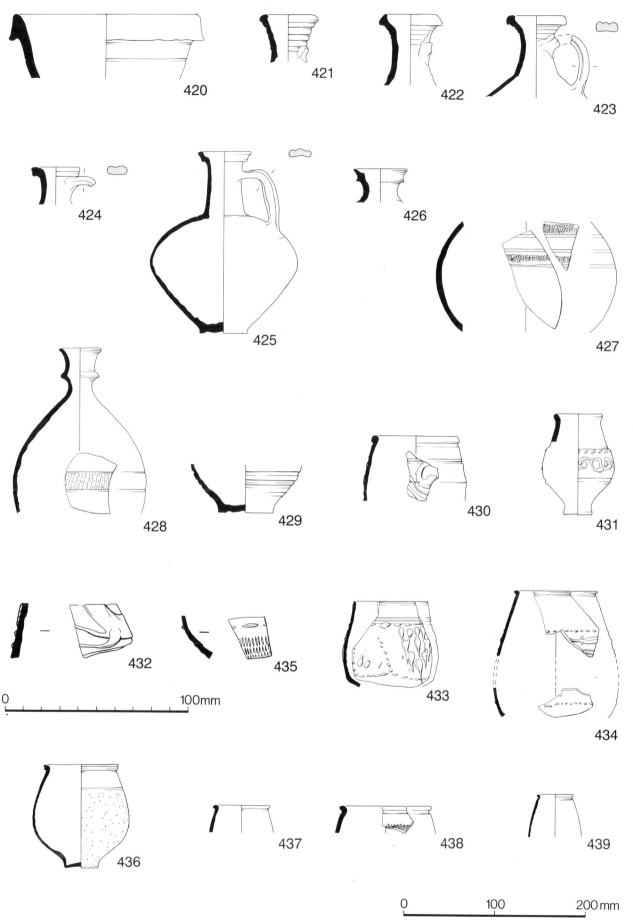

Fig. 70. Amphora, flagons and beakers from fort area Phase IV and *vicus* Phase 4. Scale 1:4 (Nos 432 and 435; Scale 1:2)

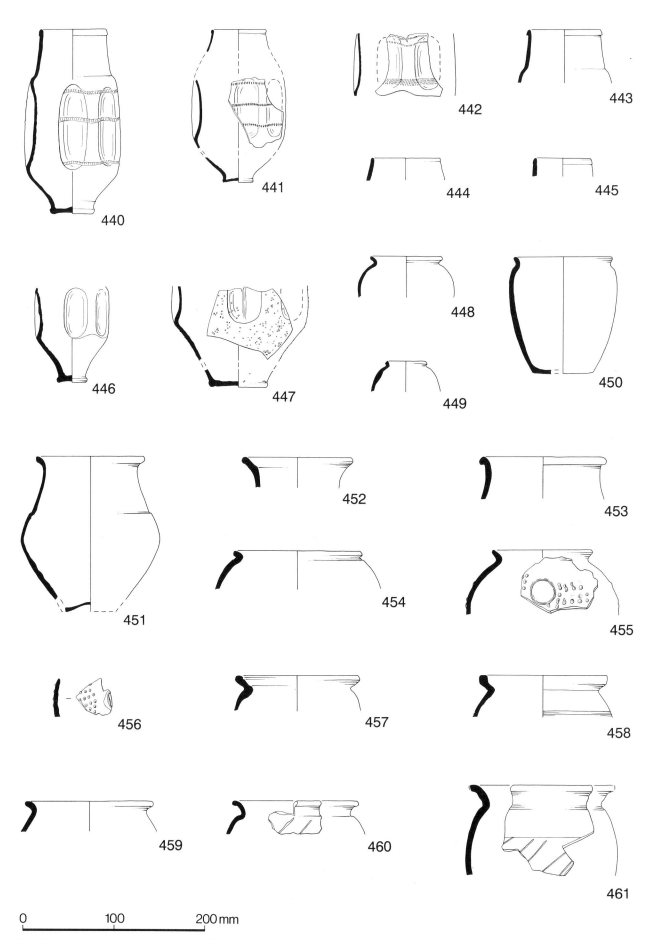

Fig. 71. Beakers and jars from fort area Phase IV and *vicus* Phase 4. Scale 1:4

442*Folded beaker. Rouletted. Colour-coated black externally and orange-brown internally. Probably 3rd century. Fabric 14. *482 T10; 4*

443*Beaker with bead rim. Colour-coated black externally and dark brown and orange-brown internally. ?3rd century. Fabric 14. *482 T10; 4*

444*Beaker with plain rim. Matt black colour coat. Fabric 9. *202 T15III; IV*

445*Beaker with bead rim. Matt black colour coat. Fabric 9. *202 T15III; IV*

446*Folded beaker. Colour-coated orange-brown internally and on the lower 20mm of the exterior; the rest of the exterior is dark brown. Probably 3rd century. Fabric 14. *482 T10; 4*

447*Indented beaker. Self-coloured slip and rough cast with clay particles. The type is more usual in Phase 3 of the *vicus* and is residual in this phase. Fabric 16. *081/R T10; 4*

448*Globular beaker with everted rim. Fabric 41. *078 T10; 4*

449*Beaker with everted rim. Fabric 67. *203 T15III; IV*

450*Beaker with curved out rim. Burnished externally and over rim. Hand made. Fabric 79. *267 T10; 4*

451*Necked beaker with flared rim. Burnished bands on neck. A possible import from North Gaul (Richardson and Tyers 1984) or more probably a copy. Fabric 68. *018 and 004 T18; IV*

Jars

452*Narrow-necked jar or possibly jug with flared rim. Only a small part of the rim circumference actually survives. Burnished horizontally on over-rim and vertically on the neck exterior. Hand made. Fabric 79. *079 T10; 4*

453*Narrow-necked jar with bead rim. Burnished externally. Fabric 65. *078 T10; 4*

454*Jar with everted rim. Fabric 41. *041 T10; 4*

The ring and dot decoration of Numbers 455 and 456 is usually dated late 1st to early 2nd century.

455*Jar with everted rim. Ring and dot barbotine decoration. Fabric 67. *711 T16V; IV*

456*Jar. Dark cream ring and dot barbotine decoration. Fabric 27. *006 T15I; IV*

457*Jar with everted, grooved and lid-seated rim. A possible South Yorkshire product. Fabric 67. *1014 T15V; IV*

458*Jar with lid-seated rim. Shoulder grooves. A probable South Yorkshire product cf. Buckland 1976, fig. 5 no. 46 which is probably of 4th-century date. However, this example may well be earlier. Fabric 67. *1011 T15V; IV*

459*Jar with curved out rim. Fabric 51 *079 T10; 4*

460*Jar with curved out rim. Decorated with faintly impressed diagonal lines. A possible South Yorkshire product cf. Buckland and Dolby 1980, fig.5 nos 64 and 66. Probably late 2nd to mid-3rd century. Fabric 68. *003 and 008 T17; IV*

461*Jar with curved out rim. Burnished over rim and shoulder and burnished line decoration. A possible South Yorkshire product. ?3rd century. Fabric 75. *1016 T15V; IV*

Numbers 462 to 464 are probably of late 3rd-century date, cf. Gillam 1977, fig. 2 no. 10.

462*Jar with curved over rim. Burnished externally and over rim except for the lattice decorated zone. Hand made. Fabric 79. *211 T15III; IV*

463*Jar with curved over rim. Burnished over rim and externally except the lattice decorated zone. Hand made. Fabric 79. *211 T15III; IV*

464*Jar with curved over rim. Burnished over rim and externally except the lattice decorated zone. Hand made. Fabric 79. *211 and 213 T15III; IV*

465*Jar. Burnished below lattice decoration. The angle of the lattice may indicate a date of late 2nd to early 3rd century (Gillam 1977, 63). Hand made. Fabric 79. *006 T15I; IV*

466*Very large jar with hooked rim. Cordons, burnished lattice, wavy and straight line decoration. Fabric 67. *604 and 607 T16IV; IV*

467*Jar with everted rim. Shoulder groove and linear rustication formed from discrete lines of applied clay. Residual in this phase. Fabric 63. *003 T17; IV*

468*Jar with curved out rim. Shoulder groove and linear rustication formed from discrete lines of applied clay. A possible South Yorkshire product probably of mid-2nd-century date cf. Buckland, Magilton and Dolby 1980, fig. 3 no. 19. Fabric 68. *003 T17; IV*

469*Wide-mouthed, carinated jar with bead rim. Groove at carination. ?Late 1st to early 2nd century. Fabric 15. *078 T10; 4*

470*Wide-mouthed jar with grooved bead rim. Rouletted and grooved decoration. Fabric 41. *556 T15IV; IV*

471*Wide-mouthed jar with curved over rim. Grooves on side. Fabric 43. *003 T17; IV*

472*Wide-mouthed jar with flat reeded rim. Wide grooves on side. Fabric 41. *1033 T15V; IV*

473*Very large wide-mouthed jar with heavy flat topped rim. The rim is crudely shaped and the vessel is probably hand made. Prominent wipe marks and fingerprints are visible. Fabric 41. *310 T16II; IV*

474*Part of large jar showing burnished lattice decoration and part of applied face with impressed marks representing a beard. Fabric 67. *202 T15III; IV*

Bowls

475*Bowl with plain rim. Rouletted and grooved decoration. Glossy orange-red slip. African red slip ware vessel of *c.* AD 100 to AD 160 date (Hayes 1972, Form 9 type A, fig. 4 no. 2). Fabric 24. *904 and 901 T15V; IV*

Numbers 476 and 477 are probably derived from Dragendorff form 29 and so would be expected to pre-date AD 100.

476*Bowl with grooved rim. Grooved and brown painted ware pattern. Externally smoothed. Fabric 34. *1030 and 1031 T15V; III*

477*Bowl with finely reeded rim. Fabric 33. *902 T15V; IV*

478*Slightly carinated bowl with flat, grooved rim. Groove at carination. Probably late 1st to early 2nd century. Fabric 41. *053 T15II; IV*

479*Flat-rimmed bowl. Colour-coated brown externally and brown/red-brown internally. Fabric 9, but coarser than usual. *551, 501, 600 and 611 T15IV; IV*

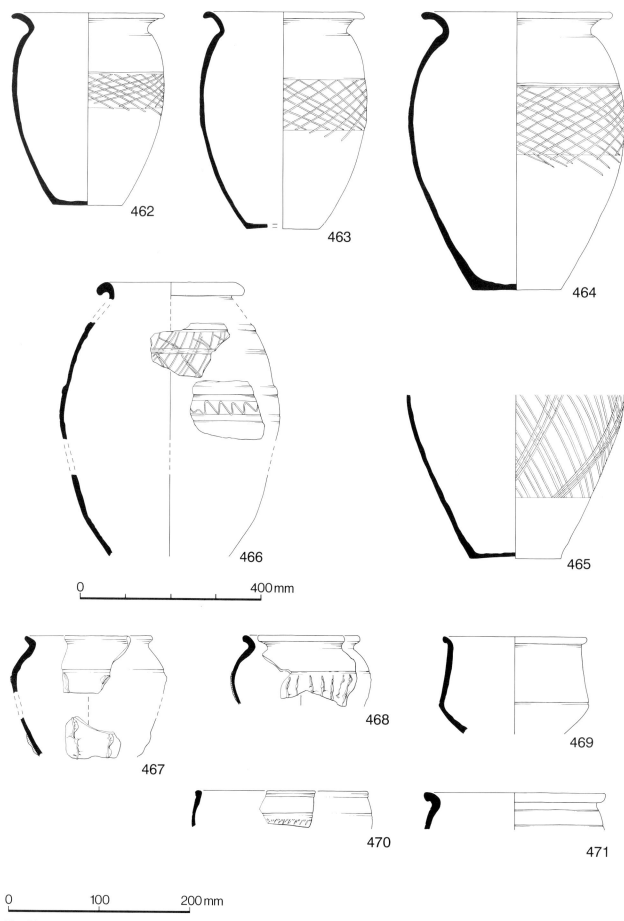

462

463

464

466

0   400 mm

465

467

468

469

470

471

Fig. 72. Jars from fort area Phase IV and *vicus* Phase 4. Scale 1:4 (No. 466; Scale 1:8)

0   100   200 mm

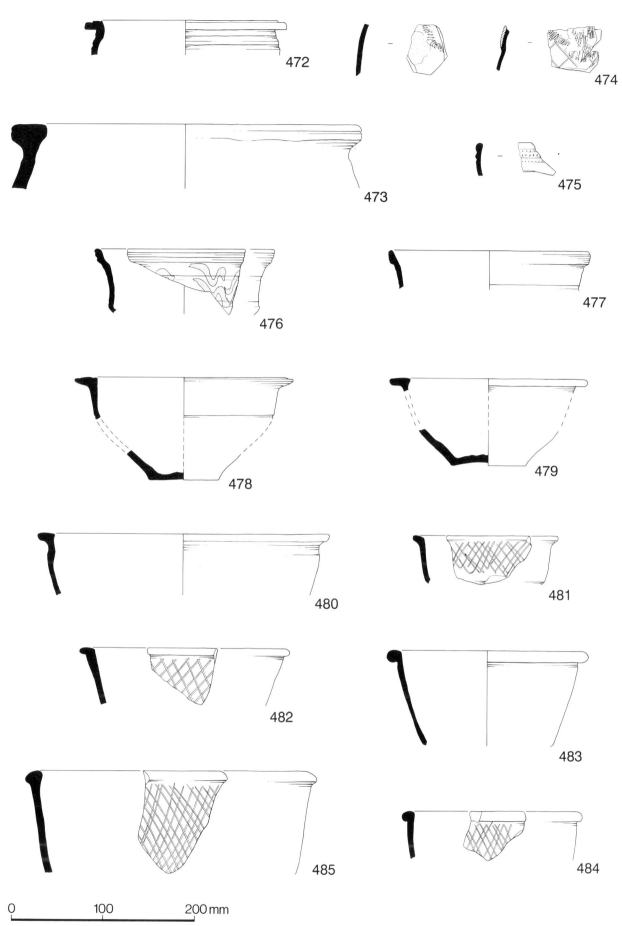

Fig. 73. Jars and bowls from fort area Phase IV and *vicus* Phase 4 (No. 476 is Phase III). Scale 1:4

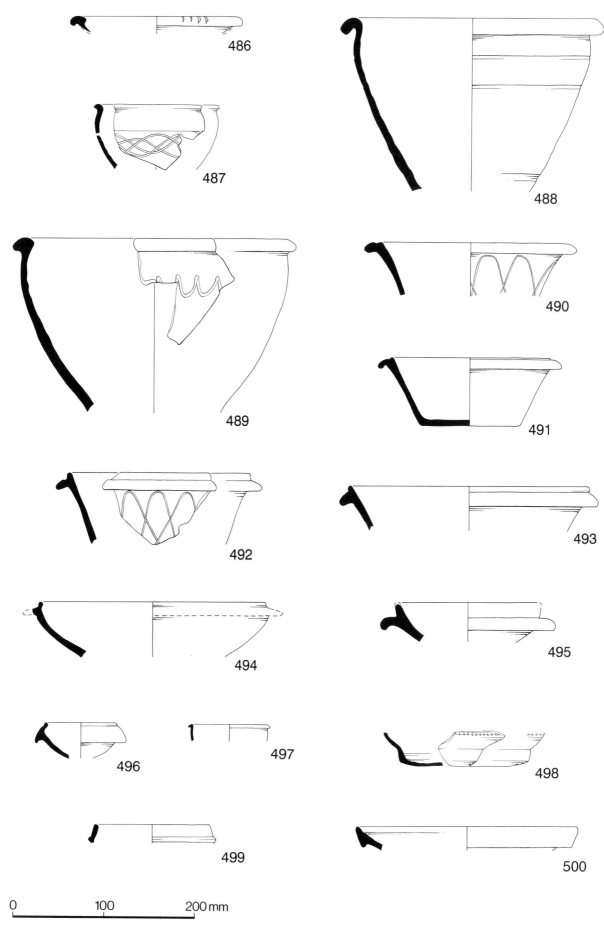

486

487

488

489

490

491

492

493

494

495

496

497

498

499

500

0   100   200 mm

Fig. 74. Bowls from fort area Phase IV and *vicus* Phase 4. Scale 1:4

140

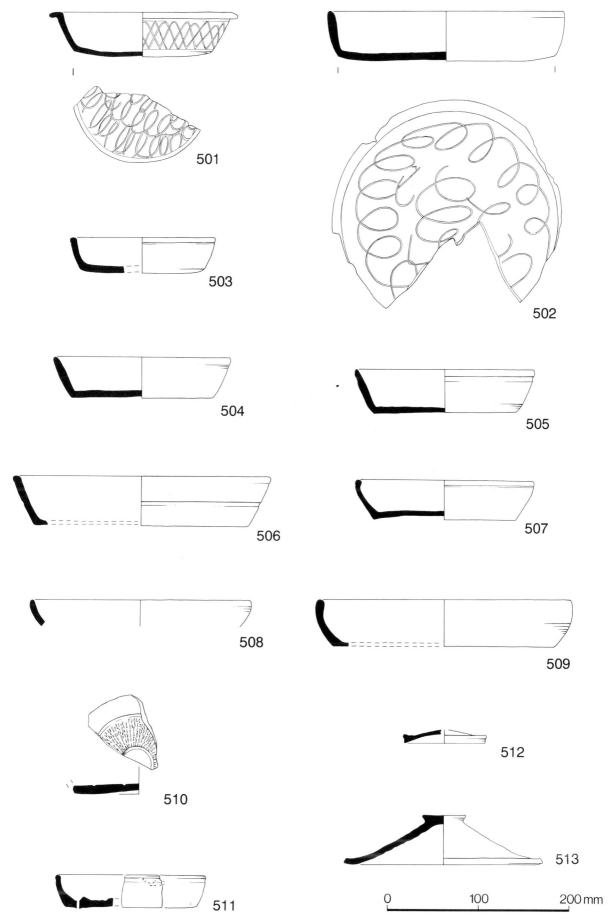

Fig. 75. Dishes and lids from fort area Phase IV and *vicus* Phase 4. Scale 1:4

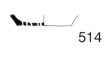

514

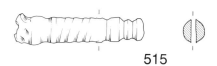

515

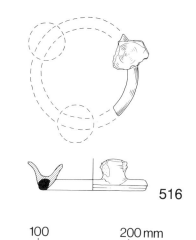

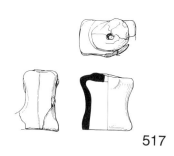

516

517

```
0        100      200 mm
├─────────┼─────────┤
```

Fig. 76. Miscellaneous coarse wares from fort area Phase IV and *vicus* Phase 4. Scale 1:4

480* Large bowl with flat rim. Fabric 41. *018 and 004 T18; IV*

481* Bowl with flat rim and basal chamfer. Burnished and lattice decoration. Hand made. Early to mid-2nd century cf. Gillam 1977, fig. 3 no. 34. Fabric 79. *472 T10; 4*

482* Flat-rimmed bowl. Burnished with lattice decoration. Hand made. 2nd century. Fabric 79. *053 T15II; IV*

483* Bowl with bead rim. Burnished. The vessel has been subjected to intense heat which has caused some rim distortion and surface crazing. Fabric identification uncertain but possibly Fabric 67. *203 and 214 T15III; IV*

484* Bowl with bead rim. Burnished with lattice decoration. Probably mid-2nd to early 3rd century. Fabric 80. *472 T10; 4*

485* Bowl with bead rim. Burnished with lattice decoration. Probably mid-2nd to early 3rd century. Fabric 80. *472 T10; 4*

486* Bowl with hooked rim. The rim is burnished and marked with four lines of white slip. Similar decoration occurs on burnished red ware bowls at Crambeck and similar rim forms are also found there (cf. Corder 1928, pl. 111 nos 67, 68 and 78). However, this vessel appears to match Oxfordshire products more closely (cf. Young 1977, type C48). Probably mid to late 4th century here. Fabric 23. *010 Site 1(77); IV*

487* Bowl with curved over rim. Burnished wavy lines and burnished band below rim. A small hole appears to have been made in the side after firing. Fabric 67. *482 T10; 4*

488* Large bowl with curved over rim. Grooves on body and top of rim is burnished. Probably a South Yorkshire product. Fabric 67. *192 Sg. 15; IV*

489* Large bowl with heavy bead rim. Burnished wavy line decoration. A possible South Yorkshire product cf. Buckland 1976, fig. 7 no. 100. 3rd or 4th century. Fabric 82. *504, 501 and 509 T16III; IV*

490* Flanged bowl. Burnished and with intersecting arc decoration. Hand made. Late 2nd to early 3rd century (cf. Gillam 1977, fig. 3 no. 42). Fabric 79. *1014, 901, 1016 and 1033 T15V; IV*

491* Flanged bowl. Burnished. Hand made. Mid to late 3rd century (Gillam 1977, fig. 3 no. 44). Fabric 79. *932 T10; 4*

492* Flanged bowl. Burnished and intersecting arc decoration. Hand made. Probably late 3rd or 4th century. Fabric 79. *461 T10; 4*

493* Flanged bowl. Probably a Crambeck product cf. Corder 1928, pl. I no. 4. 4th century. Fabric 67. *145 T10; 4*

494* Flanged bowl. Fabric 43. *086 T15II; IV*

495* Flanged bowl. The form is perhaps derived from Dragendorff 38. Fabric 74. *902 T15V; IV*

496* Small flanged bowl. Fabric 67. *472 T10; 4*

497* Small bowl or possibly cup, with turned out rim. Self-coloured slip and a dot of red slip on inside of rim. Fabric 25. *057 T15II; IV*

498* Bowl or possibly a variant of the 'castor box' form. Colour-coated patchy red-brown and rouletted. Fabric 9. *211 T15III; IV*

499* Bowl with plain rim and cordon. Fabric 41. *056/R T10; 4*

500* Shallow bowl with hammerhead style rim. Internal groove below rim. The form is similar to Gillam 1970, fig. 30 no. 300 which is dated AD 80 to AD 100. Fabric 41. *1014 T15V; IV*

Dishes

501* Flat-rimmed dish. Burnished internally over rim and on the exterior corner of the base. Looped decoration on base and intersecting zig-zag lines on side. The base has been deliberately sagged during manufacture. Hand made. Probably early to mid-2nd century. Fabric 79. *267 T10; 4*

502* Plain-rimmed dish. Burnished. Looped decoration on base. Hand made. The form is difficult to date precisely but this example is part of a generally late 3rd-century group of black burnished ware. Fabric 79. *211 and 213 T15III; IV*

503* Dish with grooved rim. Burnished. In some places there is a distinct basal chamfer, in others a rounded edge to the base. A probable South Yorkshire product cf. Annable 1960, fig. 8 no. 7; Buckland and Dolby 1980, fig. 4 no. 6; Buckland 1976, fig. 4 no. 14. Probably mid 2nd to early 4th century. Fabric 67. *1014 T15V; IV*

504* Plain-rimmed dish. Smoothed exterior. A possible Crambeck product (Corder 1928, pl. III no. 50). Fabric 67. *607A T16IV; IV*

505* Plain-rimmed dish. Wide groove below rim. Fabric 67. *607A T16IV; IV*

506* Plain-rimmed dish. Groove on side. Fabric 65. *940 T15V; IV*

507* Dish with grooved rim. The vessel was stored upside down before firing so that the base now appears to sag upwards. Fabric 41. *607 T16IV; IV*

508* Dish or platter with plain rim. Traces of thick red-brown slip survive on the rim. Some thin red-brown colour coat remains on the exterior. Fabric 26. *472 T10; 4*

509* Plain-rimmed dish. Burnished externally except the topmost 10mm. Fabric 52. *715 T9; III/IV*

510* ?Dish. Rouletted interior. Fabric 74. *310 T16II; IV*

511* Cheese press with grooved rim. Square holes pierced from the inside before firing and internal concentric ridges. Fabric 67. *203 T15III; IV*

Lids

512* Lid with pulley-wheel rim. Fabric 32. *609 T15IV; IV*

513* Lid with square-edged rim. Fabric 52. *310 T16II; IV*

Miscellaneous

514* Flat-bottomed strainer. Holes pierced from outside before firing. Fabric 67. *710 T16V; IV*

515* *Patera* handle. Mica dusted. Hole pierced before firing, perhaps to enable the vessel to be hung from a cord for storage. Fabric 41. *078 T10; 4*

516* ?Triple vase. Fabric 67. *203 T15III; IV*

517* ?Figurine base. It appears to have been formed from clay slabs, possibly shaped by pressing into a mould. The hole and oval ring mark on the top are presumably where the figurine was attached. Fabric 33. *079 T10; 4*

Phase IV fort area: the Sondage 23 group

The pottery from the fill of the ditch 260 in Sondage 23 (Fig. 2), although containing some residual material, forms the latest coherent group of vessels from Roman Castleford. The only Roman material of definitely later date is a few isolated sherds of Huntcliff ware.

The general date for the group would appear to be about the first half of the 4th century.

518* Jar with curved out rim. Appears to be hand made with a wheel-finished rim. Fabric 85. *260A Sg. 23; IV*

519* Large jar with thick curved over rim. Rouletted cordon. Burnished over rim and in horizontal bands and oblique lines. The vessel could be a South Yorkshire product (cf. Annable 1960, fig. 13 no. 250; Buckland and Dolby 1980, fig. 6 no 133) or possibly a Norton product. Fabric 67. *260A and 260B Sg. 23; IV*

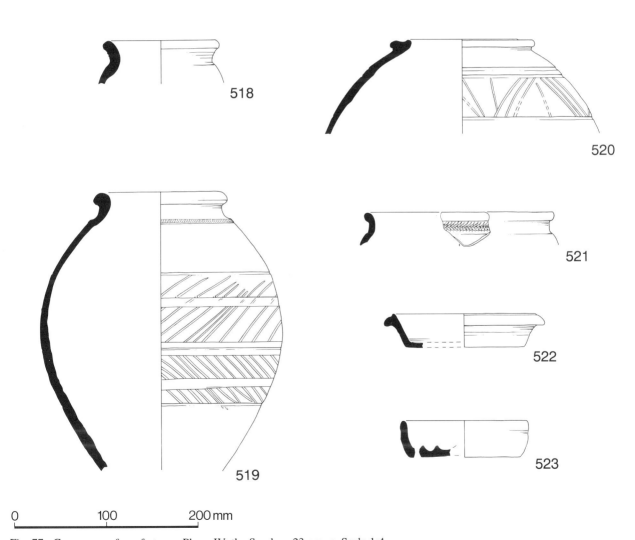

0   100   200 mm

Fig. 77. Coarse ware from fort area Phase IV: the Sondage 23 group. Scale 1:4

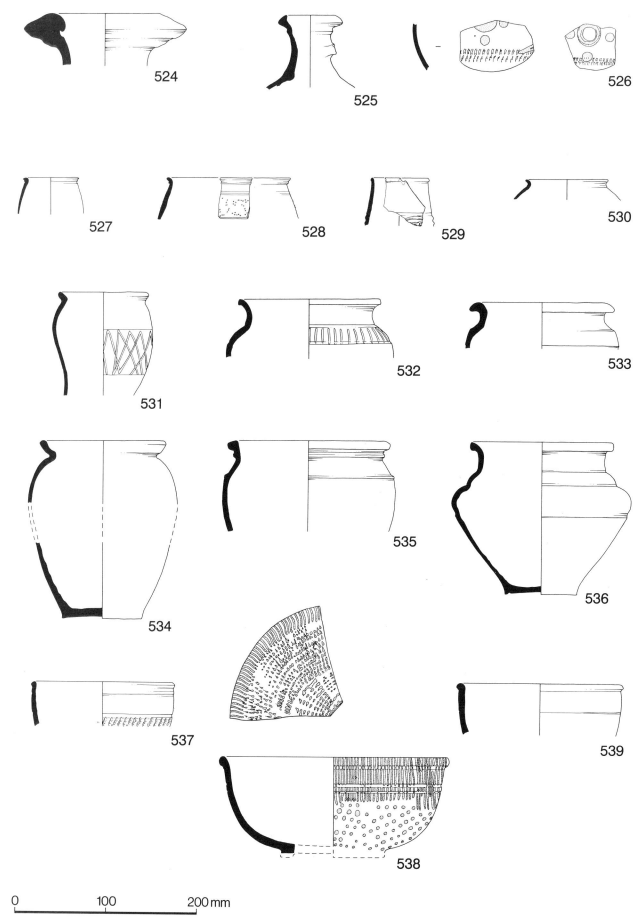

Fig. 78. Amphora, flagons, beakers, jars and bowls from post-Roman, uncertain phases and phases resolved since the preparation of this report. Scale 1:4

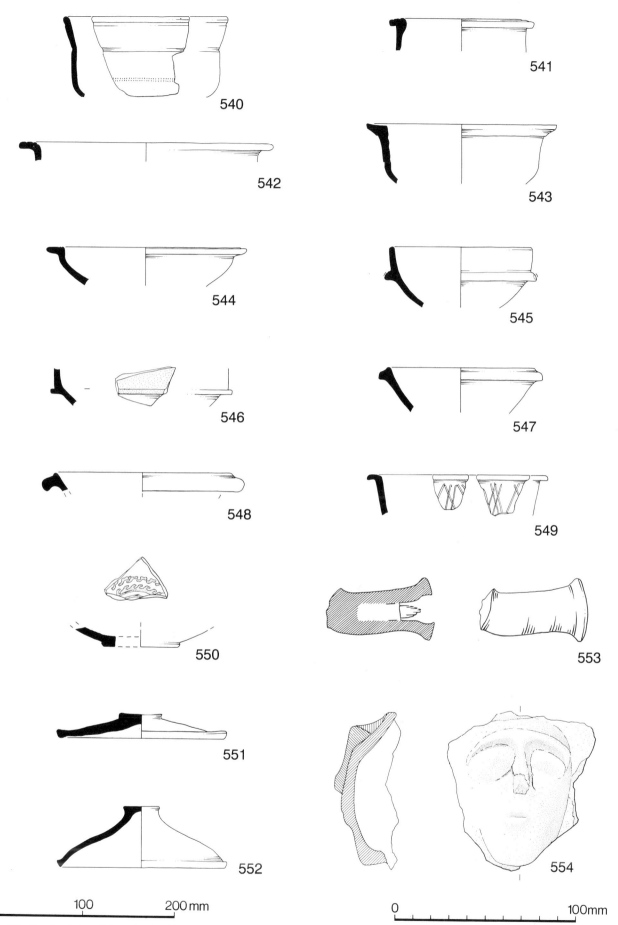

Fig. 79. Bowls, dishes, lids and miscellaneous coarse wares from post-Roman, uncertain phases and phases resolved since the preparation of this report. Scale 1:4 (Nos 553-4; Scale 1:2)

520* Flanged-rim jar. Horizontal grooves and burnished oblique line decoration. A possible Throlam product. Fabric 73. *260A and 260B Sg. 23; IV*

521* Wide-mouthed jar with curved out rim. Rouletted neck and colour-coated orange-brown. A few spots of white slip are present. An Oxfordshire product (Young 1977, fig. 62 types C75.14 and C75.15). Dated AD 325 to AD 400+. Fabric 23. *260 Sg. 23; IV*

522* Flanged dish. Grooves on bottom of interior sides and generally smoothed surface. A Crambeck product (Corder 1928, pl. II no. 43, although this example is only about half the height). 4th century. Fabric 67. *260A Sg. 23; IV*

523* Cheese press with plain rim. Round holes in base pierced from the outside before firing and concentric ridges on the interior. Probably hand made and wheel finished. An unusual form for this fabric. Fabric 85. *260A Sg. 23; IV*

Post-Roman, uncertain phases and phases resolved since the preparation of this report

Amphora
524* Dressel 20 Amphora. Fabric 1. *037 T14; Med.*

Flagons
525* Ring-necked flagon with internally cupped rim. External white slip. Probably mid to late 2nd century. Fabric 41. *006 T10; Mod.*

526* ?Flagon. Rouletted and colour-coated dark brown. Cream barbotine decoration applied over the colour coat. A possible Nene Valley product. ?Late 3rd to 4th century. Fabric 9. *008 T10; Mod.*

Beakers
527* Beaker with cornice rim. Matt brown colour coat. Late 2nd century (cf. Howe, Perrin and Mackreth 1981, fig. 5 no. 46). Fabric 9. *901 T15V; Mod.*

528* Large beaker with cornice rim. Rough cast with clay particles and colour-coated black externally. Two grooves above rough cast zone. 2nd century. Fabric 16. *701 T16V; Mod.*

529* Beaker with bead rim. Colour-coated brown externally and black internally. Barbotine decoration under the slip. ?Late 2nd to 3rd century. Fabric 11. *901 T15V; Mod.*

530* Globular beaker with curved out rim. Externally burnished. Fabric 63. *212 T14; II*

Jars
531* Small jar with everted rim. Burnished zig-zag line decoration. The vessel is distorted and is probably a waster. Fabric 78. *044 T10; Mod.*

532* Jar with curved out rim. Burnished over rim and below the zone decorated with vertical burnished lines. Fabric 73. *052 Site 1(77); II*

533* Jar with curved over rim. Shoulder groove. Probably later 4th century. Fabric 86. *701 T16V; Mod.*

534* Jar with lid seated, everted rim. A South Yorkshire product cf. Buckland and Dolby 1980, fig. 5 no. 110. Fabric 67. *1171 T10; 3*

535* Wide-mouthed jar with 'moulded' rim. Shoulder cordon. Fabric 76. *002 T14; Med.*

536* Wide-mouthed, necked jar with flared rim. Grooved and cordoned shoulder. The form is probably derived from earlier continental La Tène types cf. Hawkes and Hull 1947, 259 and 261 and pl. LXXV forms 218 and 220A. Probably of Flavian date. Fabric 67. *734 T10; 1*

Bowls
537* Bowl with bead rim. Grooved and rouletted. Brown slip and burnished externally. Probably 2nd century (cf. Gillam 1970, fig. 22 no. 197). Fabric 41. *007 T14; Mod.*

538* Bowl with bead rim. grooved and red painted dot and stripe decoration. A Yorkshire red painted ware vessel (cf. Keen 1970, fig. 1 nos 10-12). ?Early 2nd century. Fabric 42. Tr. 13 Site 1(77); ?

539* Bowl with bead rim. Grooved on side and smoothed exterior. Probably 2nd century. Fabric 41. *057 T10; 4*

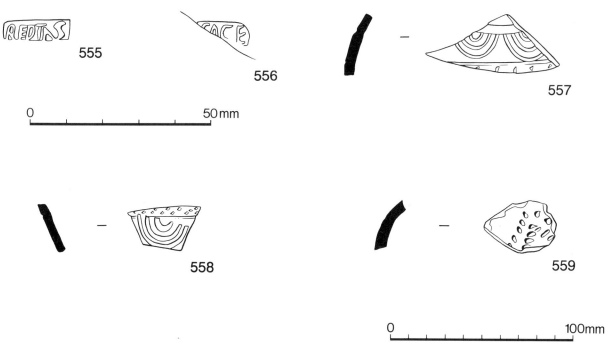

555

556

0   50 mm

557

558

559

0   100 mm

Fig. 80. The stamped coarse ware. Nos 555-6; Scale 1:1, Nos 557-9; Scale 1:2.

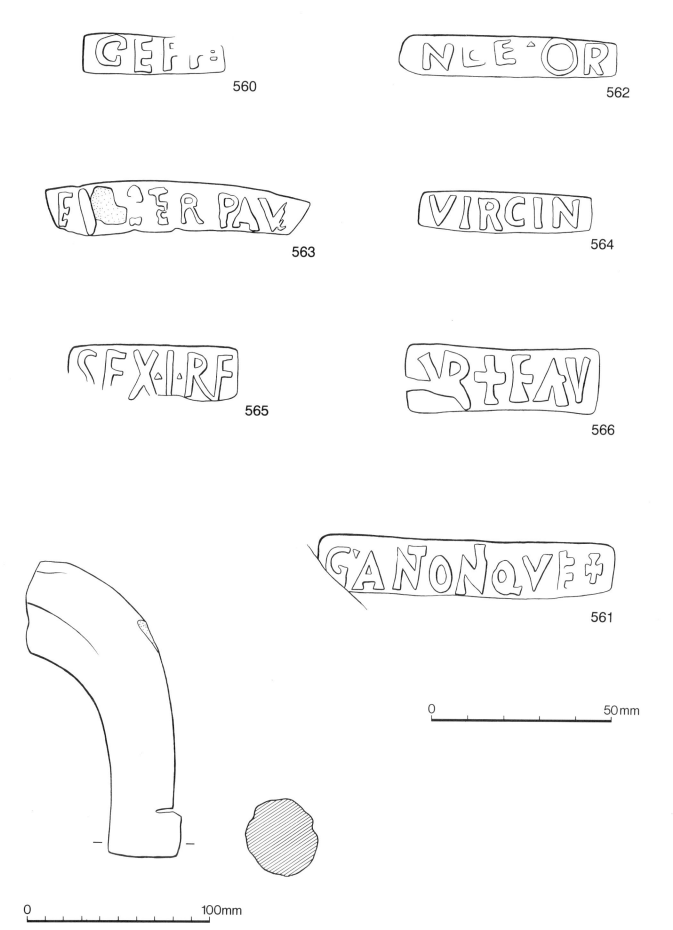

Fig. 81. The amphora stamps. Scale 1:1 (The amphora handle No. 561; Scale 1:2)

Numbers 537 to 539 are probably imitations of the samian form Dragendorff 37.

540* Bowl with flared rim. Grooved and rouletted. Smoothly burnished exterior. The form is perhaps based on Dragendorff 30. Fabric 61. *052 Site 1(77); II*

541* Bowl with flat, reeded rim. Fabric 27. *734 T10; 1*

542* Bowl with flat reeded rim. Fabric 41. *701 T16V; Mod.*

543* Carinated bowl with flat topped rim. Probably early 2nd century (Gillam 1970, fig. 23 no. 217). Fabric 67. *212 T14; II*

544* Flanged bowl. Fabric 32. *212 T14; II*

545* Flanged bowl. Colour-coated brown with a slight metallic lustre. An imitation of Dragendorff 38 (Howe, Perrin and Mackreth 1981, fig. 7 no. 83). Late 3rd to 4th century. Fabric 11. *302 T13; Post-med.*

546* Flanged bowl. Colour-coated red brown on the flange and above externally. The form is probably derived from Dragendorff 38. A Crambeck product (cf. Corder 1928, pl. I no. 22 and pl. II no. 28) 4th century. Fabric 37. *019 T14; Med.*

547* Flanged bowl. Fabric 67. *003 T15I; IV*

548* Flanged bowl. Possibly a Crambeck product and, if so, 4th century in date. Fabric 67. *003 T15I; IV*

Dishes
549* Flat-rimmed dish or, possibly, bowl. Burnished and intersecting line decoration. Probably early to mid-2nd century. Hand made. Fabric 79. *701 T16V; Mod.*

550* Dish or platter. Internal red painted decoration. A Crambeck product (cf. Corder 1928, pl. III no. 64). 4th century. Fabric 37. *501 T16III; Med.*

Lids
551* Lid with thickened rim. Fabric 52. *301 T16II; Med.*

552* Lid with bead rim. Fabric 41. *701 T16V; Mod.*

Miscellaneous
553* Part of *patera* handle. The socket contains the carbonised remains of the wooden part of the handle. Fabric 48. *701 T16V; Mod.*

554* Face probably from the side of a jar. Formed by pushing out from side of pot. Eyebrows and nose formed from applied clay. It appears to be in a South Yorkshire fabric. Fabric 75.) *052 Site 1(77); II*

The stamped coarse ware

555* REDITA S. Stamped on centre of the base interior of the bowl No. 410. A stamp from the same die has been found at Old Winteringham (Rigby 1976, fig. 92 no. 1) and also at Doncaster which has been suggested as the production area of the bowl No. 415. Of 1st-century date and hence residual in this phase. Fabric 74. *704 T16V; III*

556* SACE. From a similar vessel to No. 415. May well have been produced near Doncaster. Of 1st-century date and therefore residual. Fabric 74. *418 T10; 3*

557* ?Jar. Decorated with grooves, triangular impressions and semi-circular stamped designs. Fabric 63. *556 T15IV; IV*

558* Probably part of a bowl. Decorated with a groove, a series of impressed marks and semi-circular stamped design. Fabric 63. *704 T16V; III*

Nos 557 and 558 may be a type of Parisian ware, although the decorative style is unusual (cf. Elsdon 1982).

559* Jar. Stamped decoration. The fabric and the stamp (cf. Elsdon 1982, fig. 5 no. F5) possibly indicate production at Rossington Bridge. Fabric 76. *002 T17; Mod.*

The amphora stamps

All the amphora stamps occurred on the handles of Dressel 20 amphorae in Fabric 1.

560* CEFP . cf. Callender 1965, no. 290, fig. 5 nos 20 and 21, which suggests a date before AD 160. *Level 1 Site 1(74); 4*

561* G·ANT ONI QVIETI . One of the stamps of G. Antonius Quietus (cf Callender 1965, no. 243 fig. 5 no 3) dated to between AD 70 and AD 120. A drawing of the handle is also included. The handle has been completely sawn through at one end, near which a further partial cut can be seen. One possibility is that handle was being sawn up to produce pottery counters. *Level 11 Site (74); 1*

562* NEE . OR . *333 T10; ?*

563* E . . . TER PAV . *448 T10; 3*

564* VIRCIN. A stamp of the firm or figlina Virginesia (Callender 1965, no. 1792). Possibly produced by a branch of firm at Italica, Baetica. Dated to AD 120-60. *952 T10; 3*

565* SEX · I · RF. Similar to Callender 1965 no. 1605. *152 Site1(77); IV*

566* VRIT FAV . A variant of Callender 1965 no. 1751 and fig. no 4. It gives an abbreviated form of the estate owners name Urittius and probably a slaves name represented by the letters FAV. Dated to the 2nd half of the 1st century. Unstratified. A further example of No. 566 was recovered from *931 T9; II*

9 Pottery and Trade in Roman Castleford

Roman pottery was traded both in its own right, an obvious example of which is samian ware, and as containers for other goods. The predominant examples of the latter are found in amphorae although it is possible that some coarse ware vessels, particularly closed forms such as jars and flagons, may have been used in this way as well. These two aspects of ceramic trade or exchange will be considered below.

The dating, provenance and quantification of the pottery all present problems for interpretation. Fortunately most of the Castleford assemblage can be fairly reliably dated stratigraphically and from associated coin and samian evidence. However, the later Roman material is less reliably dated on the basis of comparison to other published pottery.

Whilst for some of the pottery the location of the production area is well known, for many of the different types the source is known only approximately, if at all. This clearly imposes limitations on the extent to which the trade in pottery can be understood.

Quantification is discussed in detail in the introduction and it is only necessary to note here that the amount of pottery recovered from the excavation is but a small fraction of what would have once existed at Roman Castleford. Much of the original assemblage will have been destroyed by post-depositional processes, some will not have been recovered during excavation and some material must, of course, remain in the unexcavated areas of the site. These factors may not have acted upon the assemblage in an unbiased way and may have thereby altered the apparent proportions of different kinds of pottery present.

Tables 12 to 15 show the quantities of the different types of pottery present in the Castleford assemblage. This does not include quantified data for the samian and mortaria assemblages.

Pottery supply to the fort (Phases I and II)

The dominant type of oxidised coarse ware (Type 41) is similar to that known to have been produced in military kilns (e.g. Perrin 1981, 58). The presence of tiles of York, Grimescar and probable local manufacture (Betts 1998) suggests sources for this material, of which local production, probably under military control, may provide the majority.

Local production of the most common grey ware (Type 67) is also possible although grey wares do not generally seem to have been made by potters associated with the Roman army. Early production in the South Yorkshire region, suggested by the distribution of vessels bearing Sace, Reditas and Cen stamps (Swan 1984, 105-106), may have supplied some of this material to Castleford but the major sources were probably to the south.

Types 81-3 and 87 were perhaps of local manufacture and the vessel forms that occur in these wares may have been derived from local Iron Age potting traditions. They do not seem to continue in use after the end of the 1st century AD and are more common in Phase I than Phase II suggesting that perhaps problems of pottery supply to the fort during the earliest occupation period were alleviated by utilising local native pottery.

The fine ware supply was dominated by samian as it was throughout the history of Roman Castleford until the end of Phase 3 on the *vicus* site in the latter half of the 2nd century. However, a small number of other fine wares do appear in the fort assemblages in Phases I and II. These were mainly of Continental origin, the Lower Rhineland probably being the major production area (see Type 10). A small amount of Lyon ware was also found, but as production of this ceased before the fort was established it represents, presumably, material that was brought north by the army rather than being obtained by trade at Castleford.

Most of the rest of the assemblage would appear to have been imported from the south of the province and in a few cases specific sources can be suggested. Some pottery (Type 35) may originate from Colchester and Type 56 was probably made in the Brockley Hill - Verulamium area.

Pottery supply to the early *vicus* (Phases 1 and 2)

In general the assemblage of the early *vicus* is very similar to that of Phases I and II of the fort. The small number of sherds that were recovered from Phase 1 has effectively caused the apparent absence of some of the less common types that were present in the fort assemblage.

The 'native' wares (Types 81-3 and 87) were less common on the *vicus* site but this may be a product of the quantification process. The major difference was the arrival of moderate numbers of BB1 vessels indicating the continuation of Phase 2 of the *vicus* after the military abandonment of the area and into the Hadrianic period. The first appearance of BB1 after the Roman army has left suggests that although military contracts may be involved in the expansion of its market to the north of England (Evans 1985, 374), at Castleford the importation of BB1 was at least partially independent of this.

Pottery supply to the *vicus* (Phase 3)

Phase 3 of the *vicus* appears to have been, initially, a period of expansion during which civilian stone buildings were in use. This expansion was matched by the pottery; the assemblage being far larger than that of the preceding phases.

The most common type of pottery during this phase was BB1 (Type 79) partly due to the presence of one large group of this that was burnt and unused. This group of BB1 vessels was recovered from the make up layers beneath a floor (030, 083 and 121 T10) that had been laid in a burnt out granary prior to re-use. A similar but smaller group of BB1, this time associated with burnt and unused samian and mortaria (c. 600 samian vessels), was recovered from another area of the *vicus* (Level 3 Site 1(74), Phase 3; see Fig. 82). It is possible that the Trench 10 material was derived from this area but was moved after the fire which burnt the pottery to form hardcore beneath a new floor.

This assemblage of BB1, samian, mortaria and, possibly, colour-coated and rough-cast wares would appear to represent the contents of a store of freshly delivered pottery or even the stock of a shop. The pattern of reduction and oxidation on some of the BB1 bowls suggests that at the time of the fire they were being kept in stacks. The location of such a store or shop at Castleford suggests that the pottery was imported by river along the Aire, presumably after having been brought north by sea. Table 16 is a list of the group quantification excluding the samian and mortaria.

Table 12. Quantification of the fort area pottery.

Type	Phase I	Phase II	Phase III	Phase IV	Total
1	487(61)	497(87)	219(28)	201(54)	1959(280)
2	28(13)	14(10)	9(6)	19(9)	78(39)
3	11(3)	4(3)	2(1)	0(0)	17(7)
4	33(9)	4(2)	2(2)	7(5)	46(18)
5	930(49)	205(41)	51(13)	46(21)	1273(142)
6	0(0)	0(0)	0(0)	0(0)	0(0)
7	0(0)	0(0)	2(1)	0(0)	2(1)
8	76(4)	36(6)	12(5)	1(1)	126(17)
9	0(0)	28(19)	3(3)	224(84)	287(129)
11	0(0)	1(1)	0(0)	15(9)	18(11)
12	0(0)	12(6)	3(2)	14(12)	54(21)
13	2(1)	0(0)	15(1)	20(9)	39(13)
14	2(2)	0(0)	6(2)	8(2)	19(7)
15	0(0)	4(2)	0(0)	0(0)	4(2)
16	0(0)	9(5)	2(1)	12(4)	44(27)
17	11(7)	10(6)	0(0)	0(0)	22(14)
18	5(3)	1(1)	0(0)	14(4)	23(10)
19	10(2)	3(2)	5(2)	0(0)	19(7)
20	0(0)	8(1)	2(2)	24(4)	35(7)
21	0(0)	0(0)	0(0)	0(0)	0(0)
22	0(0)	0(0)	0(0)	0(0)	0(0)
23	0(0)	0(0)	0(0)	2(2)	2(2)
24	0(0)	0(0)	0(0)	4(2)	7(3)
25	3(2)	0(0)	0(0)	0(0)	3(2)
26	0(0)	4(3)	0(0)	0(0)	4(3)
27	32(14)	13(7)	1(1)	3(2)	50(25)
28	0(0)	4(2)	0(0)	0(0)	4(2)
29	0(0)	0(0)	3(1)	0(0)	3(1)
30	1(1)	1(1)	0(0)	3(2)	5(4)
31	27(6)	24(2)	5(2)	2(1)	58(11)
32	578(142)	354(157)	132(48)	236(145)	1352(531)
33	294(64)	150(57)	29(13)	84(49)	590(199)
34	59(13)	66(43)	39(17)	23(8)	241(152)
35	119(14)	15(5)	1(1)	0(0)	135(20)
36	2(2)	0(0)	0(0)	2(1)	4(3)
37	0(0)	0(0)	0(0)	0(0)	3(1)
38	32(15)	19(12)	2(2)	1(1)	68(27)
39	222(32)	200(52)	62(22)	29(22)	550(155)
40	4(3)	2(2)	0(0)	0(0)	29(7)
41	1814(696)	1210(638)	466(172)	703(375)	4535(2087)
43	95(52)	43(23)	22(16)	26(23)	234(158)
44	117(30)	30(9)	14(7)	32(19)	214(53)
45	0(0)	1(1)	0(0)	0(0)	1(1)
46	0(0)	4(3)	0(0)	0(0)	5(4)
47	11(4)	60(26)	10(9)	17(14)	167(71)
48	3(3)	14(6)	9(6)	1(1)	36(19)
49	20(11)	65(36)	25(15)	41(14)	166(89)

Table 12 continued. Quantification of the fort area pottery.

Type	Phase I	Phase II	Phase III	Phase IV	Total
50	1(1)	15(5)	3(2)	4(1)	22(10)
51	21(9)	17(7)	9(4)	17(5)	103(38)
52	12(1)	1(1)	2(2)	6(5)	22(16)
53	36(8)	2(2)	1(1)	1(1)	41(13)
54	4(2)	1(1)	0(0)	0(0)	5(3)
55	0(0)	14(1)	0(0)	0(0)	14(1)
56	149(44)	52(28)	119(30)	15(10)	339(116)
57	5(1)	1(1)	0(0)	0(0)	6(2)
58	0(0)	0(0)	24(1)	0(0)	24(1)
59	0(0)	0(0)	0(0)	0(0)	10(3)
60	5(3)	11(5)	1(1)	7(5)	26(16)
61	0(0)	4(3)	1(1)	14(4)	20(9)
62	212(77)	77(49)	57(22)	42(22)	414(181)
63	281(82)	258(124)	78(30)	235(98)	907(364)
64	0(0)	0(0)	0(0)	0(0)	0(0)
65	101(50)	101(51)	48(18)	74(45)	338(171)
66	0(0)	0(0)	0(0)	0(0)	0(0)
67	2819(1114)	1390(775)	705(333)	3037(1386)	8829(4014)
68	42(6)	97(16)	0(0)	38(9)	197(48)
69	0(0)	0(0)	0(0)	1(1)	1(1)
70	22(11)	9(8)	13(7)	2(2)	52(33)
71	13(3)	12(6)	0(0)	3(3)	31(18)
72	78(11)	79(9)	26(7)	11(6)	221(44)
73	78(22)	29(12)	6(4)	8(7)	128(48)
74	13(3)	19(10)	12(8)	11(9)	59(33)
75	15(5)	162(51)	271(78)	233(101)	900(365)
76	27(10)	98(45)	46(29)	58(21)	288(141)
77	42(8)	26(16)	2(2)	9(3)	127(40)
78	0(0)	0(0)	0(0)	0(0)	0(0)
79	8(6)*	289(167)*	205(71)	1334(466)	2031(817)
80	0(0)	0(0)	0(0)	2(1)	2(1)
81	260(73)	94(56)	13(10)	211(90)	619(252)
82	42(8)	10(8)	0(0)	13(5)	75(27)
83	51(16)	33(11)	1(1)	38(8)	140(46)
84	3(2)	8(1)	2(2)	0(0)	13(5)
85	0(0)	1(1)*	0(0)	47(17)	53(22)
86	0(0)	20(2)*	0(0)	2(2)	34(6)
87	46(10)	4(1)	13(1)	13(4)	76(16)
**	49(36)	764(635)	41(28)	271(212)	1530(1152)

* Denotes intrusive pottery and ** unidentified types. The quantities given are sherd numbers with vessel numbers in brackets.
Types 10 and 42 have been combined with Types 9 and 41 respectively, for the purposes of quantification, as they cannot always be distinguished reliably. The column under the 'total' heading includes sherds and vessels from contexts which could not be attributed to a particular phase, and from post-Roman contexts.

Table 13. Quantification of the *vicus* area pottery.

Type	Phase 1	Phase 2	Phase 3	Phase 4	Total
1	94(57)	164(50)	868(315)	299(105)	1570(616)
2	6(4)	16(12)	158(49)	31(12)	230(85)
3	0(0)	4(2)	3(2)	0(0)	7(4)
4	0(0)	10(3)	12(6)	10(3)	32(12)
5	17(13)	183(39)	568(193)	110(52)	993(380)
6	0(0)	1(1)	9(7)	0(0)	10(8)
7	0(0)	0(0)	0(0)	0(0)	0(0)
8	0(0)	0(0)	0(0)	0(0)	0(0)
9	4(4)	15(10)	77(52)	91(55)	258(186)
11	0(0)	6(3)	1(1)	4(4)	20(13)
12	0(0)	1(1)	18(6)	5(4)	25(12)
13	2(2)	40(14)	258(109)	138(54)	463(199)
14	0(0)	37(11)	28(21)	37(18)	106(52)
15	0(0)	2(1)	3(3)	1(1)	6(5)
16	0(0)	2(1)	49(13)	4(3)	59(20)
17	0(0)	1(1)	0(0)	0(0)	1(1)
18	0(0)	0(0)	0(0)	0(0)	0(0)
19	0(0)	2(2)	1(1)	2(2)	5(5)
20	10(1)	0(0)	0(0)	11(8)	27(14)
21	0(0)	0(0)	0(0)	0(0)	1(1)
22	0(0)	0(0)	0(0)	0(0)	1(1)
23	0(0)	0(0)	0(0)	0(0)	0(0)
24	0(0)	0(0)	1(1)	0(0)	1(1)
25	0(0)	0(0)	0(0)	0(0)	0(0)
26	0(0)	0(0)	16(8)	1(1)	17(9)
27	0(0)	0(0)	0(0)	0(0)	5(3)
28	0(0)	2(1)	3(3)	1(1)	6(5)
29	0(0)	0(0)	0(0)	1(1)	1(1)
30	0(0)	18(2)	14(7)	0(0)	35(12)
31	0(0)	2(2)	30(2)	0(0)	34(6)
32	89(38)	438(232)	1407(587)	171(114)	2219(1046)
33	23(16)	90(70)	195(92)	34(21)	358(203)
34	1(1)	100(14)	282(62)	49(8)	445(92)
35	0(0)	0(0)	0(0)	0(0)	0(0)
36	0(0)	0(0)	0(0)	0(0)	0(0)
37	0(0)	0(0)	0(0)	1(1)	1(1)
38	2(2)	0(0)	3(2)	0(0)	6(5)
39	6(5)	47(35)	346(125)	27(18)	460(191)
40	0(0)	0(0)	1(1)	0(0)	1(1)
41	135(78)	502(223)	123(56)	201(111)	2475(1109)
43	1(1)	6(3)	164(10)	23(8)	141(39)
44	21(13)	47(22)	93(47)	42(36)	217(122)
45	1(1)	36(4)	145(19)	9(4)	194(29)
46	1(1)	3(1)	0(0)	0(0)	4(2)
47	0(0)	34(17)	7(6)	29(2)	91(36)
48	0(0)	43(5)	1(1)	0(0)	44(6)

Table 13 continued. Quantification of the *vicus* area pottery.

Type	Phase 1	Phase 2	Phase 3	Phase 4	Total
49	5(3)	15(2)	11(9)	16(9)	59(30)
50	0(0)	7(2)	0(0)	1(1)	8(3)
51	0(0)	5(4)	66(8)	12(7)	89(25)
52	2(2)	19(5)	3(2)	2(1)	26(10)
53	0(0)	3(1)	0(0)	0(0)	3(1)
54	0(0)	0(0)	0(0)	0(0)	0(0)
55	0(0)	21(1)	6(3)	0(0)	27(4)
56	4(4)	42(20)	128(60)	27(11)	227(112)
57	2(2)	10(6)	4(2)	1(1)	18(12)
58	0(0)	0(0)	0(0)	0(0)	0(0)
59	0(0)	0(0)	2(1)	2(1)	8(6)
60	1(1)	0(0)	2(2)	0(0)	3(3)
61	0(0)	27(7)	37(17)	1(1)	67(27)
62	0(0)	14(10)	65(14)	15(7)	94(31)
63	40(16)	212(83)	223(90)	47(23)	542(228)
64	0(0)	5(4)	25(1)	0(0)	43(8)
65	0(0)	3(2)	3(2)	2(1)	8(5)
66	0(0)	0(0)	1(1)	0(0)	1(1)
67	300(127)	1635(639)	2958(1424)	728(524)	6013(2922)
68	0(0)	6(5)	29(17)	4(2)	42(27)
69	1(1)	0(0)	0(0)	0(0)	3(2)
70	1(1)	7(1)	0(0)	0(0)	8(2)
71	4(1)	0(0)	1(1)	0(0)	5(2)
72	0(0)	8(2)	7(5)	1(1)	16(8)
73	0(0)	4(4)	16(4)	0(0)	48(11)
74	2(2)	38(25)	257(87)	24(16)	345(140)
75	1(1)	10(7)	215(70)	29(22)	310(129)
76	1(1)	27(21)	53(31)	2(2)	101(67)
77	0(0)	0(0)	0(0)	0(0)	0(0)
78	0(0)	0(0)	99(21)	6(4)	131(26)
79	7(4)*	197(133)	10568(2083)	1052(904)	12071(3305)
80	0(0)	0(0)	2(2)	3(3)	24(7)
81	20(8)	14(6)	4(4)	2(1)	41(20)
82	3(3)	61(31)	52(19)	3(3)	108(48)
83	1(1)	5(5)	10(7)	0(0)	16(13)
84	0(0)	0(0)	0(0)	0(0)	0(0)
85	0(0)	0(0)	19(9)*	28(20)	64(46)
86	0(0)	0(0)	6(5)*	1(1)	10(8)
87	1(1)	1(1)	13(2)	1(1)	16(5)
**	13(10)	171(121)	992(705)	517(345)	2027(1475)

* Denotes intrusive pottery and ** unidentified types. The quantities given are sherd numbers with vessel numbers in brackets. Types 10 and 42 have been combined with Types 9 and 41 respectively, for the purposes of quantification, as they cannot always be distinguished reliably. The column under the 'total' heading includes sherds and vessels from contexts which could not be attributed to a particular phase, and from post-Roman contexts.

Table 14. Quantification of the fort area pottery (filtered data).

Type	Phase I	Phase II	Phase III	Phase IV
1	394(21)	391(28)	171(5)	104(6)
2	390(1)			6(1)
3	6(1)			
4	14(2)			
5	188(16)	144(8)	23(2)	7(1)
6				
7	26(1)			
8	45(2)	26(2)		
9		6(1)	110(8)	
11				
12				
13			15(1)	
14				7(1)
15				
16				8(1)
17				
18				9(1)
19	6(1)			
20		8(1)		18(1)
21				
22				
23				
24				
25				
26				
27	6(1)			
28				
29				
30				
31	20(2)	23(1)		
32	341(27)	112(8)	59(6)	
33	199(19)	55(5)	8(1)	
34	52(5)		6(1)	7(1)
35	95(5)	10(1)		
36				
37				
38				
39	179(9)	114(4)	21(3)	
40				
41	725(70)	287(27)	190(22)	121(14)
43	6(1)	6(1)		
44	69(7)	19(2)	6(1)	9(1)
45				
46				
47	7(1)	19(1)		
48				

Table 14 continued. Quantification of the fort area pottery (filtered data).

Type	Phase I	Phase II	Phase III	Phase IV
49	7(1)	20(3)	21(1)	
50	10(1)			
51	6(1)		14(2)	
52	12(1)			
53	28(3)			
54				
55		14(1)		
56	89(10)	18(1)	68(7)	
57				
58			6(1)	
59				
60				
61				9(1)
62	86(10)	19(2)	31(4)	17(2)
63	132(14)	63(6)	24(3)	102(5)
64				
65	12(2)	31(3)	18(2)	
66				
67	1061(96)	301(28)	150(15)	576(69)
68	35(2)	75(4)		26(3)
69				
70	9(1)			
71	7(1)			
72	69(3)	66(3)	15(2)	
73	49(3)	12(1)		
74	11(1)	6(1)		
75	10(1)	50(4)	128(14)	52(6)
76	9(1)	31(3)		29(3)
77	15(1)			6(1)
78				
79		42(3)*	129(14)	589(30)
80				
81	151(10)			95(5)
82	12(3)			
83	20(2)	19(1)		25(1)
84		18(2)		
85				21(3)
86		20(2)*		
87	31(2)		13(1)	8(1)

* Denotes intrusive pottery. The quantities given are sherd numbers with vessel numbers in brackets. Types 10 and 42 have been combined with Types 9 and 41 respectively, for the purposes of quantification, as they cannot always be distinguished reliably.

Table 15. Quantification of the *vicus* area pottery (filtered data).

Type	Phase 1	Phase 2	Phase 3	Phase 4
1	6(1)	98(4)	388(18)	67(5)
2			94(7)	16(2)
3				
4		8(1)	6(1)	
5		125(8)	282(25)	26(1)
6				
7				
8				
9			7(1)	23(1)
11				
12				
13		26(3)	105(7)	57(3)
14		14(1)		
15				
16			27(3)	
17				
18				
19				
20	10(1)			
21				
22				
23				
24				
25				
26			6(1)	
27				
28				
29				
30		17(1)		
31		27(1)		
32	42(3)	146(16)	635(35)	6(1)
33			26(4)	
34		87(4)	105(7)	42(2)
35				
36				
37				
38				
39		11(1)	158(16)	6(1)
40				
41	25(3)	165(13)	500(42)	22(2)
43			64(3)	
44		15(2)	19(3)	
45		28(1)	115(5)	
46				
47		17(2)		29(2)
48		36(1)		
49		14(1)		
50				
51			48(2)	
52		12(1)		
53				
54				
55		21(1)		
56		15(2)	41(3)	12(2)
57				
58				
59				
60				
61		16(2)	22(2)	
62			45(4)	
63	14(1)	30(2)	92(7)	8(1)
64			25(1)	
65				
66				
67	92(3)	230(7)	617(49)	26(4)
68				
69				
70		15(2)		
71				
72				
73		16(1)	13(1)	
74		113(7)	6(1)	
75		109(6)		
76		8(1)		
77				
78			68(1)	
79		19(3)	765(71)	11(1)
80				
81	10(1)	7(1)		
82		18(1)	8(1)	
83				
84				
85			12(2)*	
86				
87			12(1)	

* Denotes intrusive pottery. The quantities given are sherd numbers with vessel numbers in brackets. Types 10 and 42 have been combined with Types 9 and 41 respectively, for the purposes of quantification, as they cannot always be distinguished reliably .

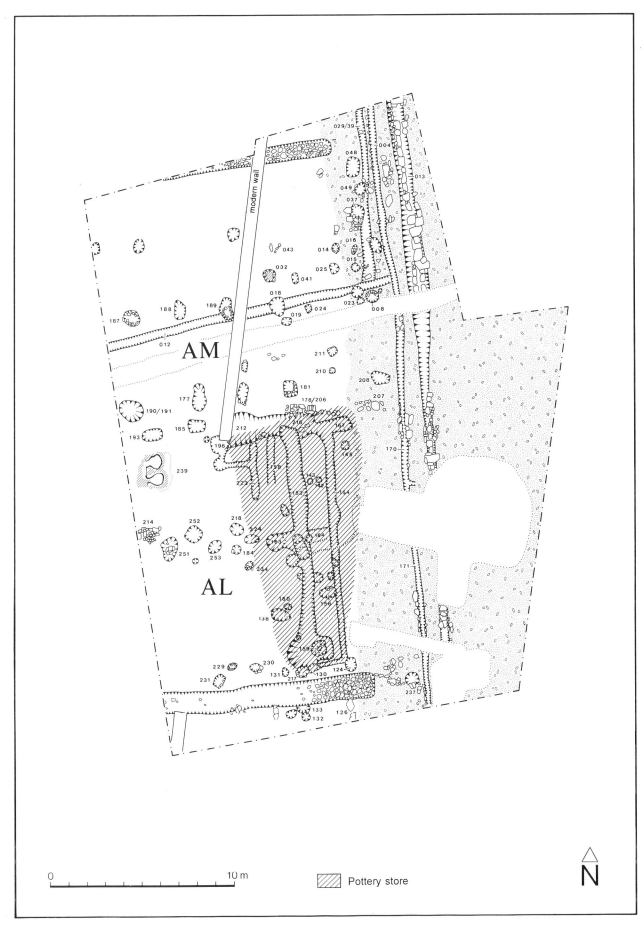

AM

AL

029/39
004
048
013
049
037
016
043 014
015
032 025
041
018
023
019 024 008
012
211
210
208
207
181
177 178/206
190/191
212
193 185 196
148
239
223 143
144
182 154
214 252 218
224
251 253 163 184
184
244
160
156
138
159
229 230
231 131 130 124
133
132 126
237
170
171

0   10 m   ⬚⬚ Pottery store

△
N

Fig. 82. Area of recovery of the 'pottery shop' assemblage (hatched).

Table 16. The 'pottery shop' assemblage.

Level 3 Site 1(74), Phase 3.

	Sherds
BB1 bowl or dish	563
BB1 Jar	232
BB1 uncertain form	53
Colour-coated ware	8
Rough-cast ware	71

030, 083 and 121 Trench 10

	Sherds	Vessels
BB1 beaker	3	2
BB1 bowl or dish	496	135
BB1 jar	1335	413
BB1 uncertain form	6346	?

Vessel numbers are not given for the Site 1(74) material and are less reliable than usual for the Trench 10 material because of the high degree of fragmentation of the vessels in the assemblage. The burning of the pottery made identification of the colour-coated and rough-cast wares difficult but both Type 12 and 13 appear to be present. The samian suggests that the assemblage dates from between AD 140 and AD 150.

The oxidised ware Type 41 became less common, as might be expected for pottery probably produced in military kilns following the departure of the army. However, it is apparent that oxidised ware as a whole was becoming less common and being replaced to a certain extent by both BB1 and coarse grey wares. During this phase the main source of supply of grey wares (Types 67 and 69) were the kilns of the South Yorkshire industry near Doncaster.

The amount of fine colour-coated wares reaching the site in addition to samian increased. These were mainly colour-coated, rough-cast beakers from the Argonne or other Continental sources (Type 13) and a smaller amount of material from the Lower Rhineland (Type 10).

Pottery supply in the later Roman period (Phases IV and 4)

The period from the end of the Phase 3 *vicus*, probably sometime in the last quarter of the 2nd century, to the later 3rd century seems to have been largely devoid of activity and pottery at Castleford. Only a small number of vessels, typically BB1 straight-sided flanged bowls, can be dated to this period suggesting that the site as a whole had been abandoned to a great extent.

In the later 3rd century the increased amount of pottery reflects an increased level of activity on the site of the fort at least. There also appears to have been industrial activity in the form of spoon manufacture shown by the presence of moulds in a rubbish pit in Trench 15III. However, the pottery recovered from this phase on the site of the *vicus* was mainly residual. The fort area ceramic material contained a higher level of contemporaneous pottery although a high proportion of residual material was present.

Until the end of the 3rd century BB1 was one of the main types of coarse ware at Castleford. The group from the fill of a lime kiln and its associated raking pit (211 and 213 T15III) suggests that it may have been the dominant coarse ware in the later 3rd century once residual material has been taken into account for the apparently more numerous grey wares. The Sondage 23 assemblage shows a completely different picture in the 4th century. BB1 has disappeared from the assemblage to be replaced by Dales ware and grey wares from Crambeck and East Yorkshire. Grey wares probably continue to be supplied from the South Yorkshire area as well and some Huntcliff ware occurs in limited amounts across both the former *vicus* and fort sites.

By this period samian had, of course, ceased to be supplied to Castleford and its place has only partially been taken by other fine wares. Nene Valley colour-coated ware was the predominant fine ware, mainly in the form of beakers reflecting a general lack of fine ware bowls.

The amphora trade

Amphorae were imported into Castleford from the earliest phases of the fort and *vicus* through to the end of Phase 3 on the *vicus* site. All of the amphora sherds recovered from later contexts are almost certainly residual, delimiting the period of amphora trading as the AD 70s to the last quarter of the 2nd century.

In considering the relative importance of the different amphora types the main criterion must be the volume of their contents as the contents and not the amphora were the reason for the trade. The volumes given below in Table 8 are derived from Sealey (1985, table 2, Peacock and Williams (1986, table 1) and from calculations based on published drawings.

Table 17. The volume of amphorae.

Type	Form	Mean Volume in Litres
1	Dressel 20	62.83
2	Dressel 38 and Camulodunum 186A	15.71
3	Camulodunum 189	3.15
4	Dressel 2-4	25.2
5	Pelichet 47 and Dressel 28	27.88
6	Dressel 2-4	25.2
7	Dressel 2-4	25.2

Amphora types have been combined where it was not possible to distinguish them reliably. Tables 18 and 19 contain the quantities imported by phase which have been produced by multiplying the vessel numbers given in Tables 12 and 13 by the volumes given above. For details of the contents of the amphora types see *The Type Series* (p. 90).

Table 18. Amphora importation in the fort.

Type	Phase I	Phase II	Total all phases
1	3832.63	5466.21	17592.4
2	204.23	157.1	612.69
3	9.45	9.45	22.05
4	226.8	50.4	453.6
5	1366.16	1143.08	3958.96
6	0.0	0.0	0.0
7	0.0	0.0	25.2

Volume in litres.

Table 19. Amphora importation in the *vicus*.

Type	Phase 1	Phase 2	Phase 3	Total all phases
1	3581.31	3141.5	19791.45	38703.28
2	62.84	188.52	769.79	1335.35
3	0.0	6.3	6.3	12.6
4	0.0	75.6	151.2	302.4
5	362.44	1087.32	5380.84	10594.4
6	0.0	25.2	176.4	201.6
7	0.0	0.0	0.0	0.0

Volume in litres.

The actual quantities imported to Castleford were probably considerably larger but unfortunately it is not really feasible to extrapolate these amounts from the calculated data. However, it is possible to say that throughout the period of importation the most important imports were olive oil from Spain (Type 1), Gallic wine (Type 5) and fish products from the South Spanish Coast (Type 2). Other products seem to have been imported relatively infrequently.

As the duration of the fort occupation can be reliably estimated at approximately 25 years a rate of supply to the fort can be worked out (see Table 20).

The rate of supply appears to suggest a very low level of trade but when the area of the fort remaining unexcavated, the effects of post-depositional processes and the contribution of the *vicus* area towards the total volume of trade are considered it can be seen that the actual level of trade in amphora borne products must have been very much greater.

Table 20. The supply of amphorae to the fort (Phases I and II).

Type	Volume Supplied	No. of Amphorae
1	9298.84	6 per year
2	361.33	1 per year
3	18.9	1 per 4 years
4	277.2	1 per 2 years
5	2509.2	4 per year
Total		**11.75 per year**

Volume in litres, and amphora numbers given to the nearest whole number.

10 Evidence of Pottery Use

The assemblage was examined visually for evidence of the way in which it had been utilised, such as wear marks and sooting. A number of factors make much of the evidence difficult to interpret except in very general terms. For example sooting indicates that a vessel has been heated over a fire but gives no information about the contents of the vessel at the time. Although the cooking of food is often a possibility it is not necessarily the only one.

The way in which many vessels were utilised has apparently not left any trace on the pottery. In some cases the lack of evidence may be due to the incompleteness of a vessel, any evidence of use that may once have existed being located on the missing part. Clearly, this is a factor that affects most of the assemblage.

Some types of vessels were probably used for more than one type of task and individual vessels may have been put to a variety of uses which may have led to the superimposition of patterns of evidence of use. Occasionally this can be shown where a pot has been modified after firing to make it fit for a secondary use. The most common evidence of this is where holes have been drilled in the side of a vessel but unfortunately the purpose of these remain unknown. Other re-use includes the shaping of sherds to make counters and the use of crushed pottery in mortar (Hughes 1989).

Amphorae appear to have been used for a wide range of tasks once their primary function of transport containers had ceased (Callender 1965, 25-36). Number 561 (see Chapter 7) shows an amphora handle sawn through at one end, near to which there is a further sawcut part way across. One possibility is that the handle was being sawn up to produce pottery counters.

Beakers and flagons were generally devoid of sooting marks or other evidence of heating, as might be expected. A few flagons were worn on the rim indicating, perhaps, the use of a lid.

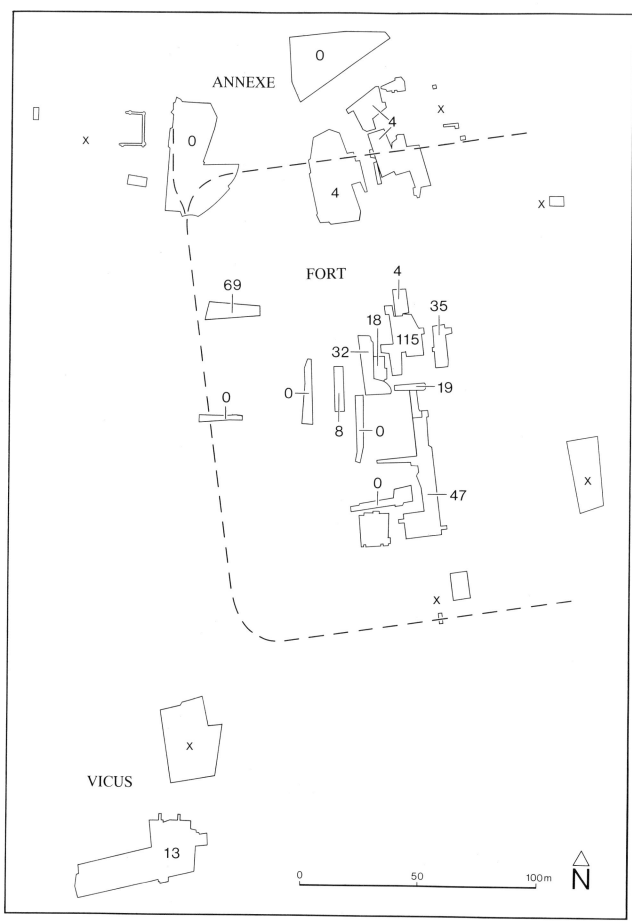

Fig. 83. Pottery distributions: fort Phase I and *vicus* Phase 1.

Jars were probably used for a wide range of tasks including storage and cooking. Where sooting was apparent it occurred most commonly underneath or all over the rim. Sooting occurred less frequently on the sides and rarely on the base. These sooted vessels may have been used for cooking over a fire, generally with the bases protected from the direct heat of the flames. Similar sooting marks appear on some bowls and dishes, particularly those in coarser fabrics and of carinated form with reeded rims or straight-sided form with flanged rims, suggesting similarity of use between these different forms.

Infrequently, wear marks were apparent on the rims of jars indicating the use of a lid but these were not linked to the provision of lid-seating in the jar rim. Wear marks and the occasional sharp internal edge to sooting, on a rim indicates the use of lids on bowls of those types outlined above. A few of the rims of lids also show evidence of sooting, confirming their use in conjunction with jars and bowls whilst they were heated over a fire.

In contrast to the bowls of coarser fabric those that have a finer fabric with few inclusions (e.g. Types 33 and 34) do not exhibit wear or sooting marks. Many of these bowls imitate samian forms and they were presumably used as cheaper alternatives to samian tableware.

Many of the tazze found at Castleford were sooted on the interior. This sooting, together with the evidence of a specialised form and decoration, supports the suggestion that these vessels were used as ritual burners, perhaps of some type of incense.

In general there appears to be a correlation between the presence of sooting marks and the coarseness of a fabric. They are generally absent from vessels with finer fabrics which contain few inclusions.

11 Spatial and Chronological Aspects of the Assemblage

The distribution of the assemblage as it was recovered cannot necessarily be directly related to its distribution in use or to the pattern of original discard for a number of reasons. Post-depositional processes have clearly had a marked effect in some areas; on some trenches the evidence of earlier phases has been destroyed by subsequent activity and hence created a gap in the intra-site pottery distribution for those early phases. An example of this can be seen in the late 3rd or 4th-century ditches that cross Trench 16IV which have completely obliterated Phase I of the fort in this area and yet the neighbouring Trench 16V has produced a substantial number of vessels in this phase.

The location of the excavation trenches may affect the appearance of the pottery distribution through the relationship between the areas excavated and the distribution of surviving archaeological remains. As much of the pottery, particularly when filtered data is used (see introduction), was concentrated in specific pits and layers, the location of the excavation trenches relative

to these localised concentrations can be seen to be important in shaping the apparent pottery distribution.

The distribution of the pottery for the different phases is summarised in Figures 83-6 and the location of the trenches is shown in Figures 1-2. Filtered vessel numbers have been used in an attempt to discriminate against the effects of post-depositional movement on the distribution.

The different wares have not been shown separately, largely because the evidence of the cross-matches between ceramic material recovered from different contexts demonstrated that in the majority of cases the assemblage consists largely of redeposited material. Therefore, the vessels found associated together in a context were neither necessarily discarded in the same place originally nor at the same time, nor were they necessarily used in the same area. The distribution of the pottery in general reflects the use of waste material in the filling of pits, often not dug originally as rubbish disposal pits, and in the levelling of areas on abandonment or prior to re-use.

The concentration of pottery in the central fort area (Trenches 15I, 15II, 15III, 15V, 16II, 16V and 18) in Phase I clearly represents substantial dumping of waste material in this area. This material mainly occurred in the fill of structural features such as wall slots and in layers overlying the structures. It would seem to represent the redisposal of rubbish between sub-phases in Phase I and between Phases I and II and was probably associated with clearance and levelling activity before rebuilding work and changes of use.

A large amount of pottery was recovered from the fill of the ditch of Fort II in Site 1(77) accounting for almost all of the filtered vessel number of 58 shown in Figure 84. This material was clearly associated with the filling of the ditch with rubbish deposits on the abandonment of the fort.

After the abandonment of the fort area by the Roman army the area seems to have generally gone out of use except for rubbish disposal, presumably by the the *vicus* inhabitants. The distribution of this accumulated material is shown in Figure 85 which reflects patterns of rubbish disposal and not activity in the area during Phase III.

The *vicus* in Phase 3 (Trench 10, see Figure 85) contained a large amount of pottery, some 330 filtered vessels. Of these 58 were retrieved from the fills of pits and the rest came from the fills of structural deposits or layers. One of the most significant groups was the large assemblage of burnt but unused black-burnished ware recovered from a levelling layer beneath a floor (see above, p. 149 for a full discussion).

Three associated pits (contexts 908, 909 and 913) of Phase 3 Trench 10 demonstrate the value of the cross-matching technique in deciphering site formation processes. Sherds from some vessels occurred in the fills of all three pits suggesting a common source for some of the material making up the fills and thus indicating the redeposition of rubbish that had been accumulated elsewhere. Similarly, the Phase IV lime kiln and raking pit (contexts 211 and 213) in Trench 15III (see Fig. 86)

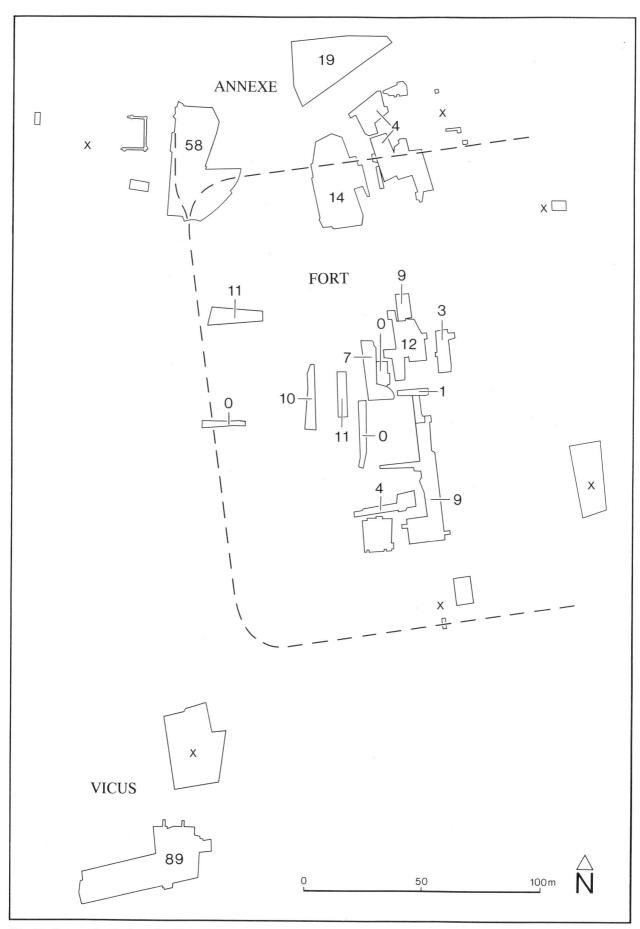

Fig. 84. Pottery distributions: fort Phase II and *vicus* Phase 2.

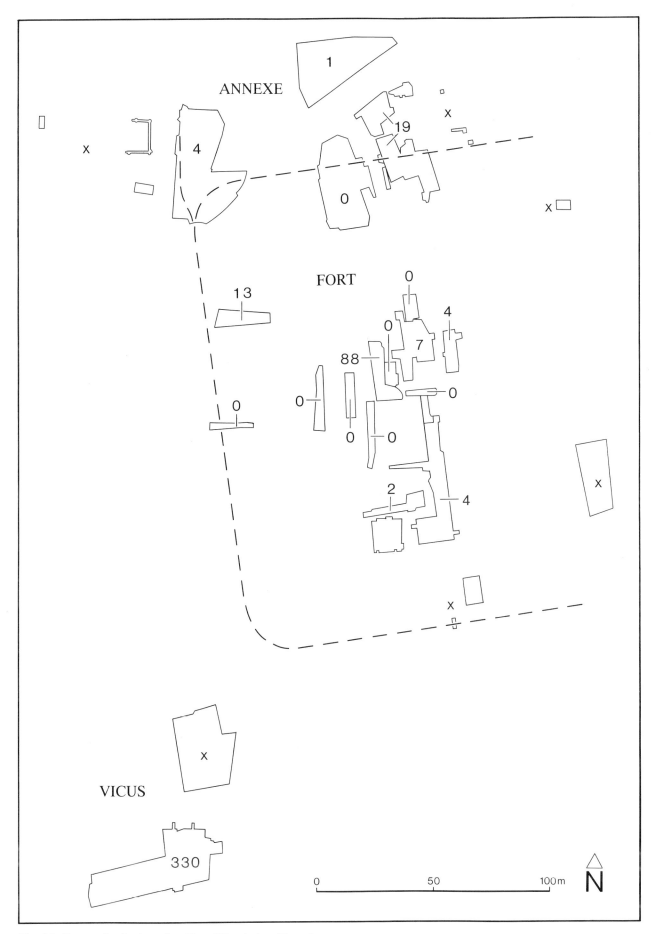

Fig. 85. Pottery distributions: fort Phase III and *vicus* Phase 3.

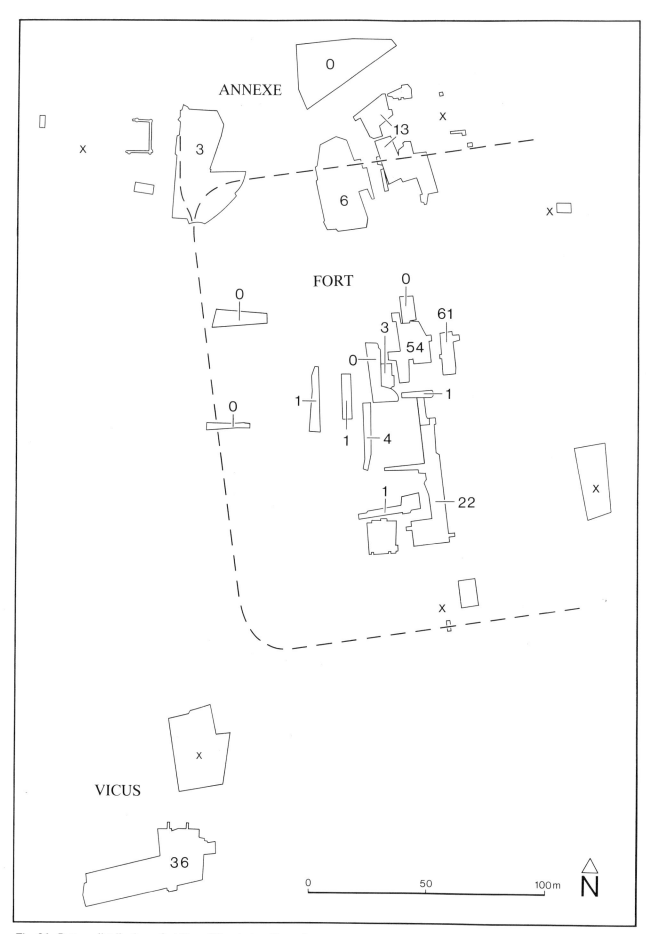

Fig. 86. Pottery distributions: fort Phase IV and *vicus* Phase 4.

Table 21. The pottery forms from the fort area.

Form	Phase I	Phase II	Phase III	Phase IV
Amphora	1144(126)	712(134)	270(45)	268(87)
Beaker	271(76)	187(85)	78(28)	386(159)
Bowl	433(140)	354(185)	181(78)	483(206)
Cheese Press	12(3)	1(1)	1(1)	2(1)
Dish	68(34)	169(114)	51(32)	320(162)
Flagon	2156(731)	1588(647)	649(235)	888(483)
Flask	0(0)	0(0)	0(0)	8(1)
Jar	4967(1719)	3396(1974)	1418(567)	5054(2221)
Jug	2(2)	15(2)	0(0)	4(2)
Lid	120(53)	86(56)	97(45)	57(41)
Platter	8(5)	7(4)	7(6)	5(4)
Strainer	0(0)	1(1)	11(1)	1(1)
Tazza	23(12)	9(5)	3(1)	3(3)
Misc.	0(0)	2(1)	3(2)	21(10)

Quantities are given in sherd numbers with vessel numbers in brackets.

Table 22. The pottery forms from the *vicus* area.

Form	Phase 1	Phase 2	Phase 3	Phase 4
Amphora	116(73)	362(97)	1546(537)	450(172)
Beaker	29(14)	137(63)	611(265)	304(146)
Bowl	28(19)	240(98)	906(402)	196(131)
Cheese press	0(0)	1(1)	0(0)	0(0)
Dish	5(2)	29(16)	515(259)	104(95)
Flagon	159(70)	713(232)	2985(903)	564(259)
Jar	387(164)	2092(788)	6434(2733)	1268(945)
Jug	0(0)	2(1)	7(3)	0(0)
Lid	7(6)	74(47)	132(98)	23(17)
Platter	0(0)	10(1)	9(6)	3(3)
Strainer	0(0)	0(0)	2(1)	0(0)
Tazza	1(1)	13(2)	39(20)	0(0)
Misc.	0(0)	2(2)	5(3)	0(0)

Quantities are given in sherd numbers with vessel numbers in brackets.

Table 23. Relative frequency of selected forms in the fort area.

Form	Phase I	Phase II	Phase III	Phase IV
Amphora	4.3%	4.2%	4.3%	2.6%
Beaker	2.6%	2.6%	2.7%	4.7%
Bowl	4.8%	5.8%	7.5%	6.1%
Dish	1.2%	3.6%	3.1%	4.8%
Flagon	25.2%	20.2%	22.6%	14.3%
Jar	59.3%	61.5%	54.5%	65.7%

Table 24. Relative frequency of selected forms in the *vicus* area.

Form	Phase 1	Phase 2	Phase 3	Phase 4
Amphora	20.9%	7.2%	10.3%	9.7%
Beaker	4.0%	4.7%	5.1%	8.3%
Bowl	5.4%	7.3%	7.7%	7.4%
Dish	0.6%	1.2%	5.0%	5.4%
Flagon	20.1%	17.2%	17.3%	14.6%
Jar	47.0%	58.5%	52.3%	53.5%

appear to have been re-used for the disposal of rubbish which had been kept elsewhere. The evidence for this is cross-matches between pottery from the two contexts.

Only one large group of pottery was recovered from its apparently original discard location. This was the assemblage associated with the midden deposit in Trench 14, Phase I (context 108/C and associated contexts) which consisted of 317 vessels of which 46 were made up of six or more sherds. The full range of pottery types associated with this phase (see Chapter 7, where many of the vessels from this group are represented) was more or less covered by this assemblage, only a few of the rare types being absent. It would therefore seem that the pottery of this assemblage represents general waste disposal and cannot be linked to any particular activity that was perhaps pursued in the vicinity.

In general then, the pottery reveals a consistent pattern of waste disposal at Roman Castleford. Rubbish appears to have been accumulated away from the main areas of occupation and then been periodically used in filling disused pits and levelling over areas, although some direct discard of ceramic material into these contexts may have taken place. As such the bulk of the pottery deposition is not associated with ongoing activities on the site but with discontinuities of use and occupation. The main exception to this is the assemblage of pottery associated with the Phase I midden deposit in Trench 14 which was not redeposited, perhaps suggesting that this area lay outside Fort I

Chronologically, the supply of different types of pottery to Roman Castleford has already been considered

in the preceding chapter and so only variations in the relative amounts of different forms present through time are discussed here. The Tables 21 to 24 show the quantification of the forms.

The percentages are based on the vessel numbers given in Tables 21 and 22. The percentages for Phase 1 of the *vicus* are unreliable due to the small size of the Phase 1 assemblage.

Clearly the occurrence of the various vessel forms differs between the fort and the *vicus* area. Amphorae and beakers were more common on the *vicus* whilst jars and flagons were slightly less frequent. This may reflect differences in pottery utilisation between the two areas. The apparent lower levels of jars and flagons on the *vicus* area may be caused merely by the relatively higher levels of amphorae and beakers compared to the fort area.

The dominant forms throughout the period of Roman occupation at Castleford were the jar and the flagon. The level of jars appears to remain relatively stable but the frequency of flagons does decline with time, particularly in the 3rd and 4th centuries. As some of the later material will be residual the decline may be more pronounced than Tables 23 and 24 show. Beakers, bowls and dishes show a gradual increase over the Roman period suggesting, together with the change in flagon occurrence, change in the pattern of utilisation of pottery. These changes, however, are not independent of each other; a decrease in the total number of flagons will automatically produce an apparent increase in the frequency of occurrence of all the other forms of pottery.

Part Four
The Mortaria

by Peter Rush with contributions by K. F. Hartley

This report was prepared by Peter Rush in 1993 incorporating earlier work by K.F. Hartley, the latter revised her contributions in 1999.

12 Introduction

The methodology applied to this assemblage in terms of identification and quantification was essentially the same as that used for the coarse pottery, which is described in detail on p. 89. In this case, however, it was decided to include all the material from the 1974 *vicus* excavations. The uncertainty of the recording of the stratigraphy on these sites must be borne in mind as demonstrated by the number of apparently intrusive vessels in both the drawn and stamp catalogues. A similar problem would seem to occur for some of the fort contexts, most notably 052 Site 1(77) which includes a number of vessels, both mortaria and coarse ware, too late in date for its phase. This is a minor problem, however, that affects only a small proportion of the assemblage which is as a whole securely stratified.

A large assemblage of burnt and unused mortaria, found in association with samian, black-burnished ware type 1 and possibly rough-cast ware, all in a similar condition, was recovered from the the 1974 *vicus* excavation. This is dealt with in a separate report by K. Hartley. The nature of this material made quantification problematic and as it was not part of the assemblage of pottery in use on the site it has been excluded from the quantification tables given later. Material that was evidently part of this assemblage, usually referred to as the 'pottery shop' assemblage, has been recovered from other areas, particularly 083 and 121 T10 (see The Coarse Wares, pp 149 and 158), but in the case of the mortaria it is not really possible to specify exactly whether or not it belongs to this group. Hence, some 'pottery shop' vessels have almost certainly been quantified with the rest of the assemblage. They affect only the figures for vessels in Fabric 105.

13 The Mortarium Fabrics

The fabric numbers are a continuation of the coarse ware type series.

88 Mancetter-Hartshill cream ware
Tomber and Dore 1998, 188-9.
Fabric: usually fine-textured cream to white fabric. Inclusions of moderate fine colourless and pink tinged quartz and infrequent fragments of orange and red-brown material. Occasional white pieces are also present which may be grog. Blackish pieces are sometimes present which may be grog or sometimes slag.

Trituration grit: after AD 140-50 it consisted of red-brown or black refired pottery fragments. Prior to this date the grit was more variable and included quartz, sandstone, black material and possibly flint, although it could sometimes be made up almost entirely of red-brown material or quartz.

Decoration: red-brown paint.

Source: Mancetter-Hartshill potteries, Warwickshire.

Drawing Nos: 1-21.

89 Verulamium region ware
Hartley 1991, 193; Tomber and Dore 1998, 154-5.
Fabric: grey-cream, cream, pale brown or orange-brown sometimes with a pink or grey core. Inclusions of abundant quartz with occasional red-brown or black iron rich fragments and pieces of flint. The inclusions can vary in frequency and fineness.

Trituration grit: mainly flint with some quartz and occasional iron rich fragments.

Decoration: sometimes has a self-coloured or buff slip.

Source: the known potteries of the Verulamium region: Bricket Wood, Brockley Hill, Radlett and Verulamium.

Drawing Nos: 22-33.

90 Lower Nene Valley tradition ware
Fabric: hard, fine-textured cream fabric with abundant fine quartz inclusions and some mica and red-brown iron rich material.

Trituration grit: black iron slag fragments.

Decoration: red-brown painted designs.

Source: Lower Nene Valley or the north.

Drawing Nos: 34-6.

91 South Yorkshire ware
Tomber and Dore 1998, 194.
Fabric: hard, orange-brown or red fabric sometimes with a grey core. Frequent to abundant quartz inclusions.

Trituration grit: a mixture, in varying proportions, of haematite quartz, sandstone, iron rich material and black slag material. Post-2nd-century vessels usually have trituration grit that consists solely of black iron slag.

Decoration: cream slip.

Source: Rossington Bridge or Cantley near Doncaster, South Yorkshire.

Drawing No.: 37.

92 Swanpool ware

Tomber and Dore 1998, 164.
Fabric: dark red sometimes with grey core. Moderate quartz inclusions with occasional iron rich fragments.

Trituration grit: black iron slag fragments.

Decoration: white to buff slip.

Source: Swanpool near Lincoln.

Drawing Nos: 38-9.

93 Oxidised ware

Fabric: very hard, red or red-brown fabric sometimes with a dark grey core. Inclusions vary but usually consist of frequent medium quartz grains and occasional iron rich red-brown and black material. A fresh fracture under the microscope usually has a vitreous appearance.

Trituration grit: mainly quartz with some sandstone and calcareous material. The grit is often scattered onto the flange as well as internally.

Decoration: matt, self-coloured slip. Very occasionally has a cream slip in addition.

Source: north of England; possibly at Castleford or York. Production probably associated with the army.

Drawing Nos: 40-44.

94 Oxidised ware

Fabric: red or orange fabric sometimes with a grey or brown core and with varying amounts of, but usually abundant, quartz inclusions with some iron rich fragments. Generally not as hard as Fabric 93.

Trituration grit: quartz, sandstone and iron rich material.

Decoration: self-coloured or red-brown slip.

Source: as Fabric 93.

Drawing Nos: 45-51.

95 Oxidised ware

Fabric: hard, red-brown fabric with grey core. Inclusions of frequent small to medium quartz.

Trituration grit: rounded and angular quartz, sandstone and other sedimentary rock fragments and occasional pieces of iron slag.

Decoration: red-brown slip.

Source: as Fabric 93.

Drawing No.: 52.

96 Oxidised ware

Fabric: orange-brown fabric with grey core. Abundant coarse quartz inclusions with some iron rich fragments.

Trituration grit: quartz, sedimentary rock and iron rich fragments.

Decoration: white or red-brown slip.

Source: uncertain.

Drawing No.: 53.

97 Oxidised ware

Fabric: orange-brown fabric with grey or brown core. Occasional quartz and iron rich inclusions.

Trituration grit: small, frequent quartz and iron rich fragments.

Decoration: brown slip.

Source: uncertain.

Drawing No.: none.

98 Pink-slipped ware

Fabric: brown, red-brown or orange-brown sometimes with darker or grey core. Moderate to frequent ill-sorted quartz and occasional iron rich inclusions.

Trituration grit: mainly coarse quartz but some iron rich fragments.

Decoration: pink-cream slip.

Source: uncertain.

Drawing Nos: 55-6.

99 North of England orange-brown ware

Fabric: fairly soft, orange-brown fabric with ill-sorted quartz and opaque black inclusions.

Trituration grit: probably all quartz.

Decoration: cream slip.

Source: north of England, probably fairly local.

Drawing No.: none.

100 North of England brown ware

Fabric: fine textured, light brown fabric with some fine quartz inclusions. Also has inclusions of large quartz grains and red-brown material.

Decoration: cream slip.

Source: north of England, probably fairly local.

Drawing No.: 57.

101 Aldborough cream ware

Tomber and Dore 1998, 193.
Fabric: hard, fine textured cream fabric often with a pink, brown or grey core. Moderate ill-sorted quartz and red-brown slag-like material with sandstone and black iron rich material.

Trituration grit: quartz and sandstone with, possibly, occasional slag fragments.

Decoration: self-coloured or cream slip.

Source: probably Aldborough.

Drawing Nos: 58-9.

102 Aldborough oxidised ware
Fabric: hard, fairly fine, red-brown fabric. Inclusions of fine quartz and red-brown material with occasional larger pieces of slag-like material and quartz.

Trituration grit: quartz, calcareous material, dark red-brown and black slag-like fragments, sandstone and quartz grain clusters.

Decoration: thick cream slip.

Source: Aldborough.

Drawing Nos: 60-62.

103 Aldborough fine cream ware
Fabric: hard, fine cream to pale brown fabric. Moderate to frequent, fine quartz, calcareous and iron rich fragments with occasional larger inclusions in the same materials.

Decoration: self coloured or darker slip.

Source: Aldborough.

Drawing Nos: 63-8.

104 Aldborough or Castleford cream ware
Fabric: similar to Fabric 103 but with a finer texture and a tendency to more frequent but finer inclusions.

Decoration: as Fabric 103.

Source: Aldborough and/or Castleford.

Drawing Nos: 69-71.

Fabrics 103 and 104 share two distinctive types of trituration grits. These are:
a.   Almost all quartz with some red-brown material and limestone pieces.
b.   Mainly red-brown iron rich material with occasional quartz, sandstone and black iron rich fragments.

105 Castleford 'pottery shop' ware
Fabric: there are no surviving fragments which have definitely not been affected by fire but the following description is indicated: probably cream or greyish cream micaceous fabric, perhaps with a pink tinge, and sometimes with a pink core. Inclusions of mica, frequent fine quartz and occasional ill-sorted orange-brown iron rich, larger quartz, sandstone and limestone particles.

Trituration grit: quartz, quartzite, sandstone, orange-brown iron rich material, flint and rare black fragments.

Source: probably local to Castleford.

Drawing Nos: 72-86.

106 Lincoln area cream ware
Fabric: micaceous, fine cream fabric. Moderate fine quartz and red-brown and black iron rich inclusions with rare larger quartz, limestone and iron rich fragments.

Trituration grit: quartz, red-brown iron ore and flint.

Decoration: opaque brown or pink-brown slip.

Source: probably the Lincoln area.

Drawing Nos: 87-8.

107 Lincoln, South Carlton type fabric
Tomber and Dore 1998, 162.
Fabric: grey-white, micaceous fabric sometimes with a pink core. Inclusions of occasional to moderate ill-sorted quartz and flecks of mica with occasional red-brown iron ore and sandstone pieces.

Trituration grit: a variable mixture of colourless and pink quartz, sandstone, haematite, red-brown and black iron rich material and calcareous pieces.

Decoration: yellow-brown slip but can vary in colour.

Source: Lincoln including the South Carlton kilns.

Drawing Nos: 89-91.

108 Northern England orange-brown ware
Fabric: fairly fine, orange-brown fabric with brown core. Moderate to frequent fine quartz and occasional red-brown iron ore and possibly sandstone inclusions.

Trituration grit: quartz, sandstone and dark red slag-like material.

Source: north of England, perhaps York.

Drawing No.: none.

109 Norfolk area ware
Tomber and Dore 1998, 170.
Fabric: soft, fine, cream to cream-brown fabric sometimes with a pink core. Moderate quartz, flint and occasional chalk inclusions.

Trituration grit: mainly flint and occasional quartz.

Source: Norfolk, Brampton and a second source, possibly Caistor St Edmunds.

Drawing No: 92.

110 Cream ware
Fabric: slightly micaceous, fine, cream fabric. Inclusions of occasional large orange-brown iron rich material and fine quartz.

Trituration grit: mainly pinkish quartz with some colourless quartz, orange-brown to dark red-brown and black iron rich material and, perhaps, occasional flint pieces.

Source: probably Gallia Belgica.

Drawing No: 93.

111 Lincolnshire? cream ware
Fabric: cream fabric with thick pink core. Inclusions of quartz and red-brown iron rich material.

Trituration grit: abundant, fine transparent and pink quartz with occasional opaque white, red-brown and grey grits.

Decoration: brown-yellow slip.

Source: probably an army product, made either locally or in Lincolnshire.

Drawing No: 94.

112 Lower Nene Valley ware
Tomber and Dore 1998, 117-19.
Fabric: cream or off-white, sometimes with a pink or grey core. Occasional quartz and red-brown and black iron rich inclusions.

Trituration grit: black iron slag.

Decoration: brown slip.

Source: Lower Nene Valley.

Drawing No: 95.

113 Cream ware
Fabric: pale, with frequent fine quartz and occasional red-brown iron ore and calcareous inclusions.

Trituration grit: none.

Decoration: burnished external surface.

Source: uncertain.

Drawing No: 115.

114 Buff ware
Fabric: buff fabric sometimes with a grey core. Moderate fine quartz with occasional larger iron ore and quartz grains.

Trituration grit: none.

Decoration: pink-buff to cream slip.

Source: uncertain.

Drawing Nos: 116-17.

115 Fine buff ware
Fabric: fine buff fabric with pink-orange core. Occasional quartz inclusions.

Trituration grit: none.

Decoration: brown slip.

Source: uncertain.

Drawing No.: none.

116 Sandy buff ware
Fabric: soft, buff fabric with brown core. Inclusions of frequent ill-sorted quartz and occasional calcareous fragments.

Trituration grit: none survives.

Source: uncertain.

Drawing No.: none.

117 Buff Ware
Fabric: buff fabric with frequent fine quartz and iron ore inclusions and occasional larger fragments.

Trituration grit: milky and transparent quartz.

Source: uncertain.

Drawing No.: none.

118 Brown-slipped buff ware
Fabric: buff fabric with abundant ill-sorted quartz and frequent coarse iron ore inclusions.

Trituration grit: quartz and red-brown iron ore.

Decoration: brown slip.

Source: uncertain.

Drawing No: 96.

119 Brown ware
Fabric: brown fabric with grey core. Inclusions of frequent fine quartz and occasional larger pieces of iron rich material and quartz.

Trituration grit: sparse quartz and iron rich material.

Source: uncertain.

Drawing No: 97.

120 Buff-slipped brown ware
Fabric: brown fabric with very frequent iron rich and quartz inclusions.

Trituration grit: large (up to 10mm) red-brown iron rich fragments and smaller, but still large, quartz grains.

Decoration: buff slip.

Source: uncertain.

Drawing No: 98.

121 Cream-slipped ware
Fabric: red-brown fabric with grey core. Inclusions of ill-sorted quartz, iron ore and calcareous material.

Trituration grit: frequent coarse sub-round milky quartz and larger sandstone pieces with occasional iron ore fragments.

Decoration: cream slip.

Source: uncertain.

Drawing No.: none.

122 Hard cream ware
Fabric: only heavily burnt examples were present and so the fabric description may not be accurate. Hard cream fabric sometimes with pink margins. Inclusions of frequent, ill-sorted iron ore and quartz.

Trituration grit: quartz.

Decoration: possible brown slip.

Source: uncertain.

Drawing No: 99.

123 Cream ware
Fabric: hard, cream fabric with frequent fine to medium quartz and iron rich inclusions.

Trituration grit: moderate medium to coarse quartz and iron ore.

Decoration: dark cream slip.

Source: uncertain.

Drawing No.: none.

124 Pale brown ware
Fabric: pale brown fabric with abundant fine to medium quartz and some iron ore with occasional mica fleck inclusions.

Trituration grit: red-brown iron rich material, quartz and dark brown slag.

Decoration: self-coloured slip.

Source: uncertain.

Drawing No.: none.

125 Brown-slipped buff ware
Fabric: buff fabric with brown core. Frequent small to medium quartz and occasional iron ore inclusions.

Trituration grit: brown iron ore fragments.

Decoration: brown slip.

Source: uncertain.

Drawing No: 100.

126 Soft brown ware
Fabric: soft, brown fabric with moderate coarse quartz inclusions.

Trituration grit: none survives.

Source: uncertain.

Drawing No.: none.

127 Pink ware
Fabric: soft, pink fabric with pink and cream streaked core. Moderate medium quartz and iron ore inclusions.

Trituration grit: red-brown and black iron ore.

Source: uncertain.

Drawing No.: none.

128 Sandy cream ware
Fabric: cream fabric with abundant fine quartz inclusions.

Trituration grit: fine quartz.

Source: uncertain.

Drawing No.: 101.

129 Fine buff ware
Fabric: fine, buff fabric with pink-buff margins. Moderate quartz inclusions.

Trituration grit: quartz.

Decoration: buff slip.

Source: uncertain.

Drawing No.: none.

130 Buff ware
Fabric: buff fabric with pale grey core. Moderate fine quartz and rare large iron ore inclusions.

Trituration grit: black slag.

Source: uncertain.

Drawing No.: none.

131 North France
Tomber and Dore 1998, 75-7.
Fabric: pale brown to cream fabric sometimes with a green tinge and/or a pink core. Inclusions vary but include fine quartz, red-brown and black iron rich material, flint and occasionally chalk.

Trituration grit: flint and quartz.

Source: Oise/Somme area, north France.

Drawing Nos: 102-107.

132 North France
Tomber and Dore 1998, 75-7.
Fabric: hard, fine, cream to brown fabric sometimes with a pink core. Inclusions of fine quartz, medium iron ore fragments and chalk.

Trituration grit: flint and quartz.

Source: Oise/Somme area, north France.

Drawing No.: none, but a similar range of forms to Fabric 131 above.

133 Central France
Tomber and Dore 1998, 68.
Fabric: hard, brown fabric with inclusions of quartz, golden mica and red-brown and black material.

Trituration grit: quartz and some red-brown fragments.

Source: central France.

Drawing No.: 108.

134 Pale brown ware
Fabric: soft, pale brown fabric with frequent coarse quartz and moderate larger red-brown and black iron rich inclusions. The fabric also contains some fine quartz grains.

Trituration grit: never had any grits.

Source: possibly Rhineland.

Drawing No.: 109.

135 Pale buff ware
Fabric: pale buff fabric with infrequent quartz inclusions.

Trituration grit: mainly quartz with some iron ore and occasional golden mica.

Decoration: buff slip.

Source: possibly Gallia Belgica.

Drawing No.: 110.

136 Rhineland ware
Tomber and Dore 1998, 78-80.
Fabric: marbled red-brown and cream fabric as though it is the product of two incompletely mixed clays. Abundant fine quartz inclusions.

Trituration grit: none apparent.

Source: probably the Rhineland.

Drawing No.: 111.

137 Rhineland ware
Tomber and Dore 1998, 78-80.
Fabric: hard, white fabric with very frequent ill-sorted quartz inclusions.

Trituration grit: abundant small translucent white and transparent colourless quartz.

Decoration: white or cream slip.

Source: probably the Rhineland.

Drawing No.: 112.

138 Coarse brown ware
Fabric: brown fabric with frequent medium and coarse quartz and occasional iron rich inclusions.

Trituration grit: quartz.

Source: Gallia Belgica.

Drawing No.: 113.

139 Fine cream ware
Fabric: hard, cream fabric with pale buff core and pink-buff margins. Occasional quartz and red iron rich inclusions.

Trituration grit: never had any grits.

Decoration: buff slip.

Source: uncertain, possibly Rhineland.

Drawing No.: 114.

14 The Drawn Mortaria

The mortaria drawings have been arranged so that vessels in the same fabric are grouped together. Where the date of a vessel is not in conflict with the date of the phase from which it was recovered a specific date range in addition to the phase date has not been assigned. The phase dates are as in Table 1, p. 3.

The dates of stamped vessels and those from the Site 1(74) *vicus* excavations have been taken from K. Hartley's reports. The numbers in brackets are archive identification numbers marked on the sherds. The stamp numbers indicate the entries in the stamp report where further details of the particular stamp may be found.

1* Fabric 88. Stamped. AD 100-150. *Stamp No. 43; (686); 472 T10; 4*

2* Fabric 88. Stamp of Iunius. AD 150-80. *Stamp No. 4; (40 and 83); 170 Site 1 (74); 3*

3* Fabric 88. 2nd century. *(475); 14 T10; Mod.*

4* Fabric 88. Name stamp of G. Attius Marinus and his counter stamp. AD 100-130. *Stamp No. 34a and b; (725); 494 T10; 2*

5* Fabric 88. Stamp of G. Attius Marinus. AD 100-130. *Stamp No. 32; (456); 054 T10; 4*

6* Fabric 88. Produced in the Midlands, perhaps Mancetter-Hartshill. Stamped SEPTV. AD 110-40+. *Stamp No. 48a and b; (803); 704 T16V; III*

7* Fabric 88. AD 90-130. *(482); 43 T10; 4*

8* Fabric 88. Stamp of Loccius Vibo. AD 135-65. Possibly intrusive in this phase. *Stamp No. 5; (39); Level 4 Site 1 (74); 2*

9* Fabric 88. AD 140-80. *(1017); 1081 T15V; III*

10* Fabric 88. Mid-2nd century. *(902, 920, 921, 923, 924 and 927); 214 and 203 T15III; IV*

11* Fabric 88. AD 150-200+, intrusive in this phase. *(389); 052 Site 1(77); II*

12* Fabric 88. AD 150-200+. *(1087, 1088,1089, 1090, 1091, 1092, 1093 and 1094); 1014 T15V; IV*

13* Fabric 88. AD 180-250. *(575); 129 T10; 3*

14* Fabric 88. AD 180-230. Traces of red-brown paint on the flange. *(655); 535 T10; 3*

15* Fabric 88. 3rd century. Red-brown paint on the rim, in stripes on the flange and over the small spout. *(928); 202 T15III; IV*

16* Fabric 88. Late 3rd to early 4th century. Wavy red-brown painted stripes on the flange. *(751); 750 T15V; IV*

17* Fabric 88. Mid-3rd to mid-4th century. *(909); 201 T15III; Mod.*

18* Fabric 88. Mid-3rd to 4th century. *(922 and 929); 202 and 203 T15III; IV*

19* Fabric 88. Mid-3rd to mid-4th century. *(906); 201 T15III; Mod.*

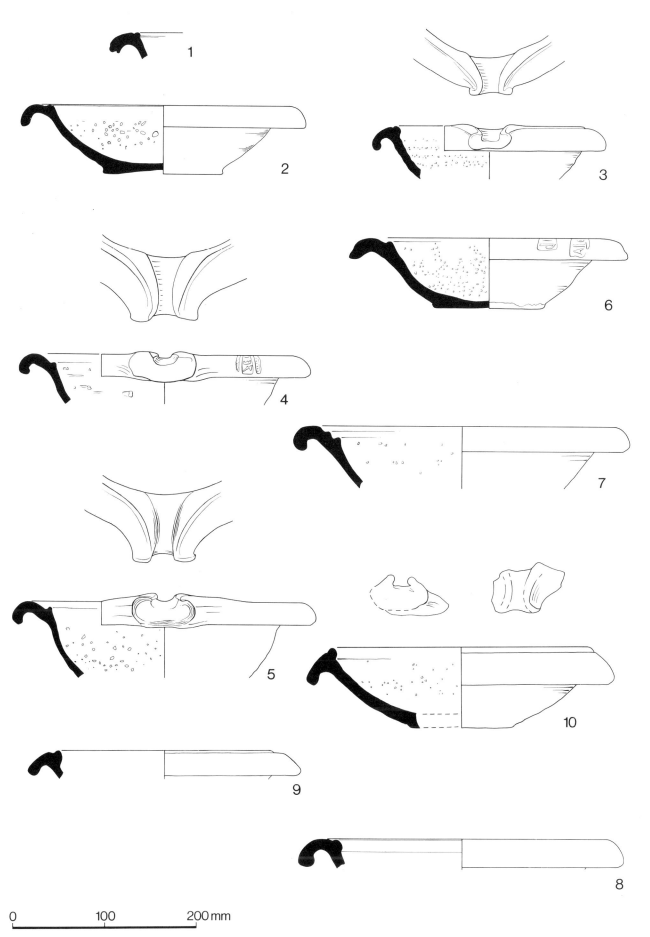

Fig. 87. The mortaria. Scale 1:4

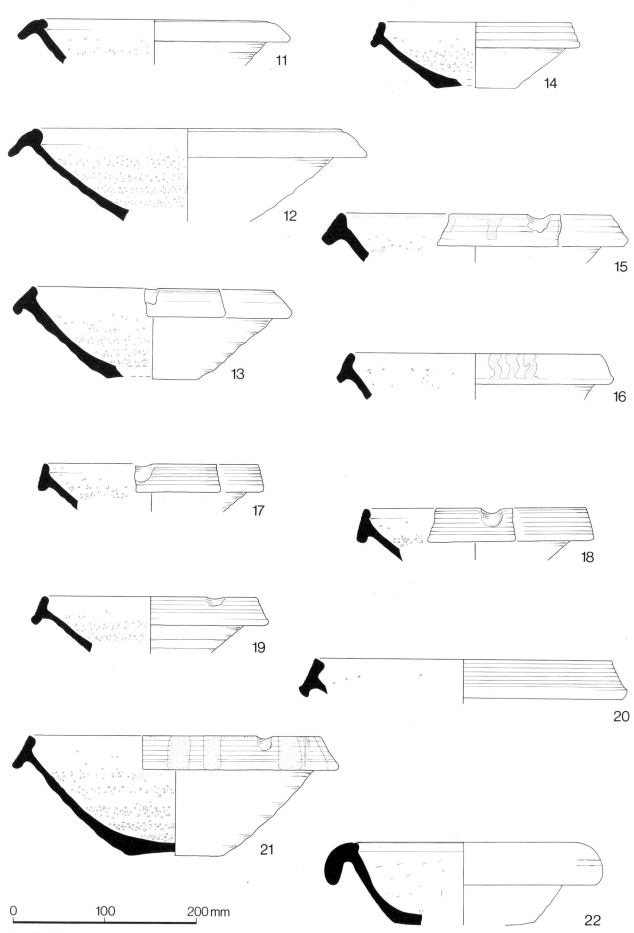

Fig. 88. The mortaria. Scale 1:4

0   100   200 mm

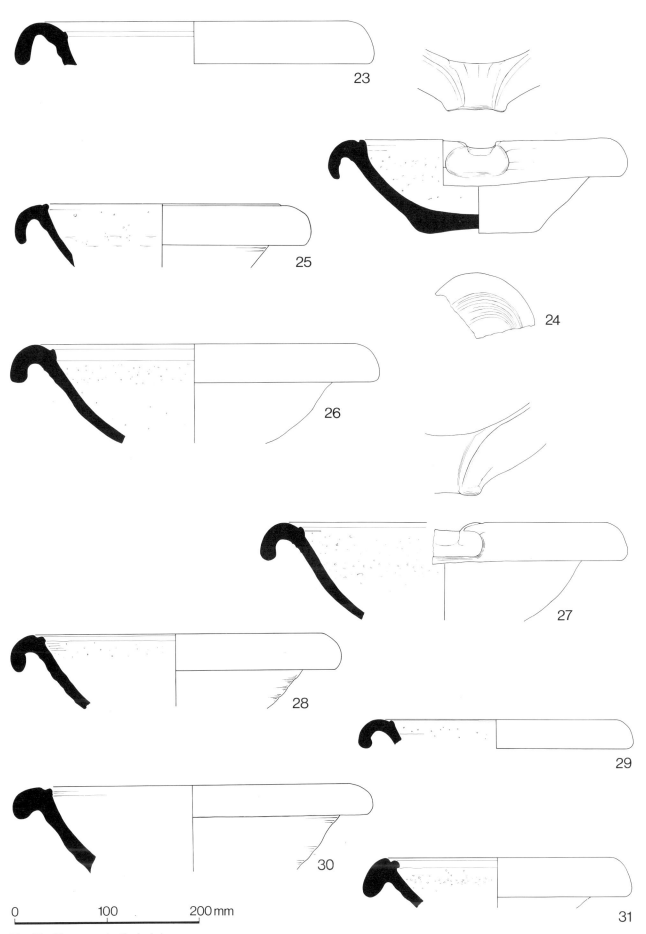

0   100   200 mm

Fig. 89. The mortaria. Scale 1:4

175

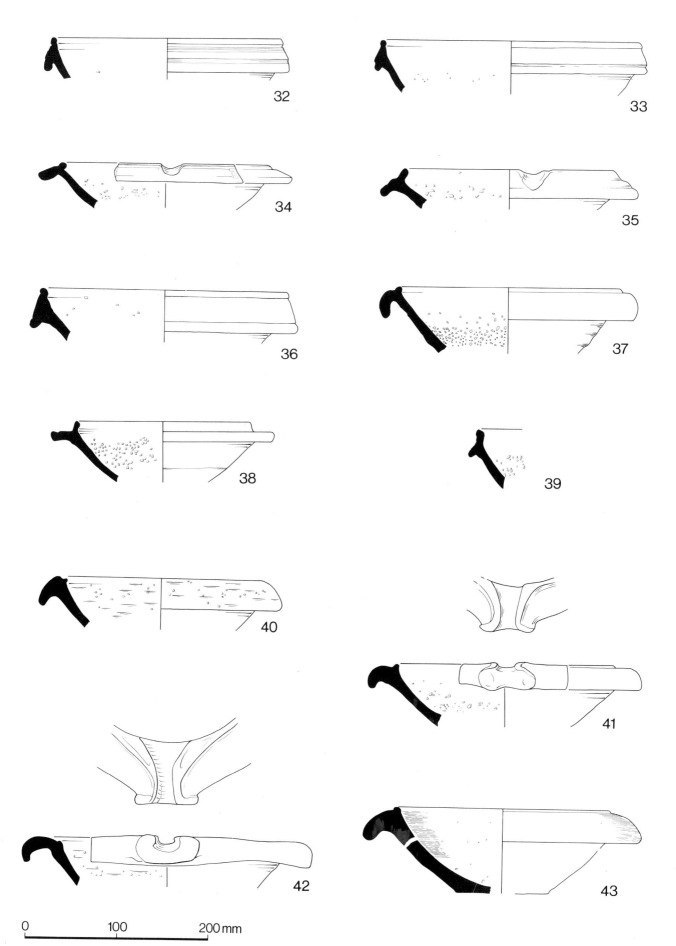

32

33

34

35

36

37

38

39

40

41

42

43

0   100   200 mm

Fig. 90. The mortaria. Scale 1:4

20* Fabric 88. Mid-3rd to mid-4th century. (910); 201 T15II; Mod.

21* Fabric 88. Mid-3rd to mid-4th century. Red-brown paint on the rim, on the flange in stripes and over the spout. (888, 907 and 913); 211 T15III; IV. 201 T15III; Mod.

22* Fabric 89. AD 60-90. (991); 1107 T15V; Id

23* Fabric 89. Stamp of Bruccius, AD 80-110. Stamp No. 28; (524 and 574); 129 T10; 3. 78 T10; 4

24* Fabric 89. Stamp of Doinus AD 70-110. Stamp No. 38; (985, 997, 1000 and 1023); 1073 T15V; IIa. 1066 and 1103 T15V; IIb

25* Fabric 89. Flavian. (385); 121 Site 1(77); IV

26* Fabric 89. AD 70-110. (656 and 726); 431 and 549 T10; 2

27* Fabric 89. Stamp of Doinus AD 70-110. Stamp No. 37; (664, 669 and 728); 783 T10; 1. 431 and 749 T10; 2

28* Fabric 89. Second half of the 1st century. (885); 272 Sg. 24; ?

29* Fabric 89. Stamp of Doinus AD 85-110. Stamp No. 39; (646, 688 and 718); 440 and 700 T10; 2. 414 T10; 3

30* Fabric 89. 1st century. (2029); 989 T9; II

31* Fabric 89. 1st century. (980); 310 T12; III

32* Fabric 89. Mid to late 2nd century. (899); 213 T15III; IV

33* Fabric 89. Mid to late 2nd century. (912); 201 T15III; Mod.

34* Fabric 90. Traces of red-brown paint on the flange and around the spout. (1099); 605 T16IV; IV

35* Fabric 90. (1098); 605 T16IV; IV

36* Fabric 90. Probably a local product, 3rd century. (953); 302 T13; Post-med.

37* Fabric 91. Rossington Bridge or Cantley. 2nd century. Stamp No. 21; (370); U/S Site 1(77)

38* Fabric 92. 3rd or 4th century. Dark cream slip. (1013 and 1084); 1011 T15V; IV. 901 T15V; Mod.

39* Fabric 92. 3rd or 4th century, intrusive in this phase. Brown slip. (832); 011 T16I; II

40* Fabric 93. Flavian. Self slipped. (884); 151 Sg.13; ?

41* Fabric 93. Late 1st to early 2nd century. Self slipped. (864); 715 T9; III/IV

42* Fabric 93. Late 1st to early 2nd century. Self slipped. (704, 707 and 727); 431 T10; 2. 414 and 420 T10; 3

43* Fabric 93. Late 1st century. Cream slip on interior and over flange, no trituration grit but scored internally. Self slipped all over the vessel and under the cream slip. (1027); 1083 T15V; III

44* Fabric 93. Self slipped. (544 and 610); 237 T10; 3

45* Fabric 94? (390); 126 Site 1(77); II

46* Fabric 94. Red-brown slip. (396); 318 T14; Ic

47* Fabric 94. Red-brown slip. (424); 149 T14; Ie

48* Fabric 94. This vessel has a lead rivet still in position. (402, 418 and 427); 149 and 214 T14; Ie. 302 T14; ?

49* Fabric 94? (717); 462 T10; 2

50* Fabric 94? Late 1st to early 2nd century. (617); 244 T10; 3

51* Fabric 94. 1st century. Scored internally and on flange. (679); 1028 T10; 1

52* Fabric 95. Late 1st century to early 2nd century. Scored internally. (977); 302 T12; Med.

53* Fabric 96. Late 1st to 2nd century. Cream slip, worn away from exterior base edge and much of the interior. (967 and 979); 168 and 170 T12; IV

54* Fabric 94?. Red-brown slip. (848 and 854); 052 Site 1(77); II

55* Fabric 98. White slip. (416 and 422); 206 and 215 T14; Ic

56* Fabric 98. Probably 2nd century. Cream slip. (894); 232 T15III; III

57* Fabric 100. Cream slip AD 100-160. (21); 11 Site 1(74); 4

58* Fabric 101. (615); 301 T10 301; 3

59* Fabric 101. (853); 052 Site 1(77); II

60* Fabric 102. Stamp of Viator. AD 100-140. Dark cream slip. Stamp No. 54; (565 and 620); 169 and 299 T10; 3

61* Fabric 102. 2nd century. Cream slip, worn on top of bead and internally. (523); 078 T10; 4

62* Fabric 102. Cream slip. 2nd century. (933); 907 T15V; III

63* Fabric 103b. (421); 206 T14; Ic

64* Fabric 103a. Stamp No. 26; (392); 988 T9; II

65* Fabric 103a. [...]ROMA (MA ligatured), retrograde. Flavian to Trajanic in date. Stamp No. 25; (368) 115 Site 1(77); III

66* Fabric 103. Stamped by Viator AD 100-140. Stamp No. 30; (458, 460 and 604); 118 T10; 3. 081 T10; 4

67* Fabric 103. Stamp of Viator. AD 100-140. Probably produced at Aldborough. Stamp No. 29; (537); 078 T10; 4

68* Fabric 103. Stamped. AD140-80+. Thin brown slip. Stamp No. 50; (1018); 901 T15V; Mod.

69* Fabric 104b. Buff self slip. (716); 462 T10; 2

70* Fabric 104b. Stamp of Viator. AD 100-140. A possible Castleford product. Stamp No. 31; (948); 910 T10; 3

71* Fabric 104. Stamped. AD 90-120. Brown slip. Produced in Lincolnshire, perhaps in Lincoln. Stamp No. 24; (2031); 715 T9; III/IV

Numbers 72 to 86 are types of mortaria that were mainly recovered from a large deposit of burnt unused vessels from a store or shop. They can all be dated from associated samian to the mid-2nd century, probably between AD 140-50. The Type letters refer to the distinct forms identified by K. F. Hartley within this material; see p. 186 for detailed descriptions of these.

72* Fabric 105. Type A. (155); U/S Site 1(74)

73* Fabric 105. Type A. (153); U/S Site 1(74)

74* Fabric 105. Trade-mark stamp Type Bi. Stamp No. 7; (15 and 16); Level 3 Site 1(74); 3

75* Fabric 105. Type Bii. (145); U/S Site 1 (74)

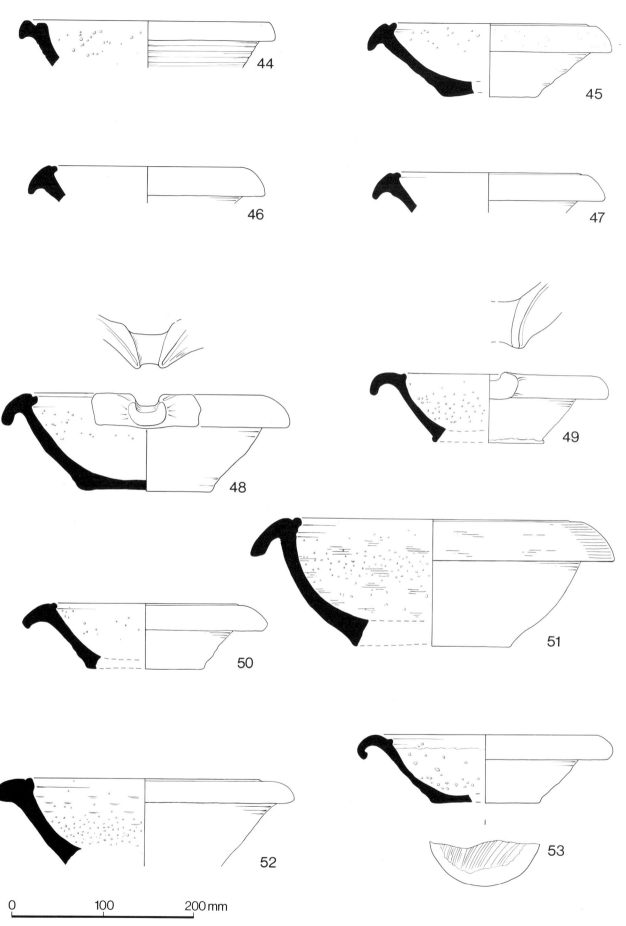

0   100   200 mm

Fig. 91. The mortaria. Scale 1:4

178

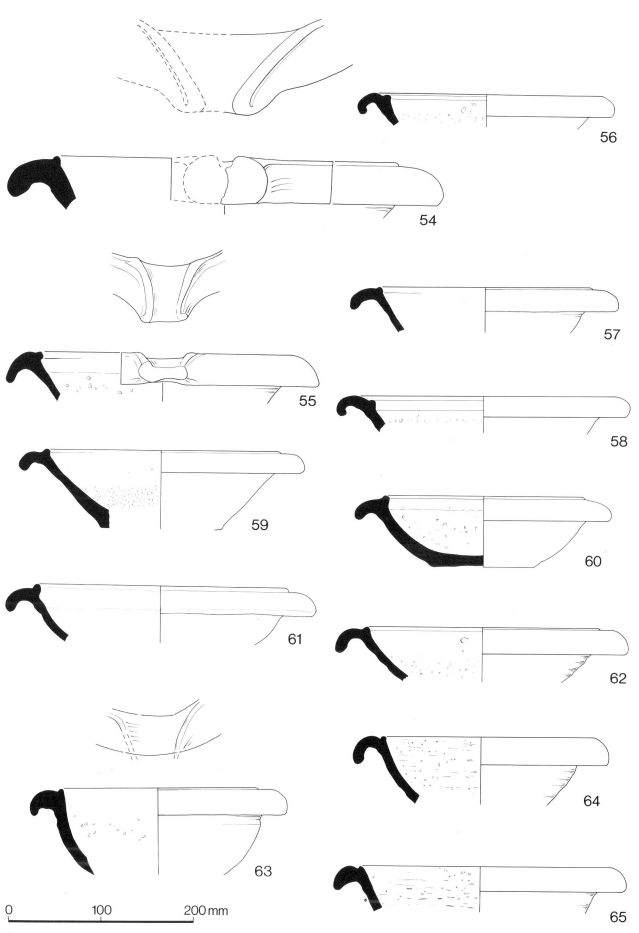

54

55

56

57

58

59

60

61

62

63

64

65

0   100   200 mm

Fig. 92. The mortaria. Scale 1:4

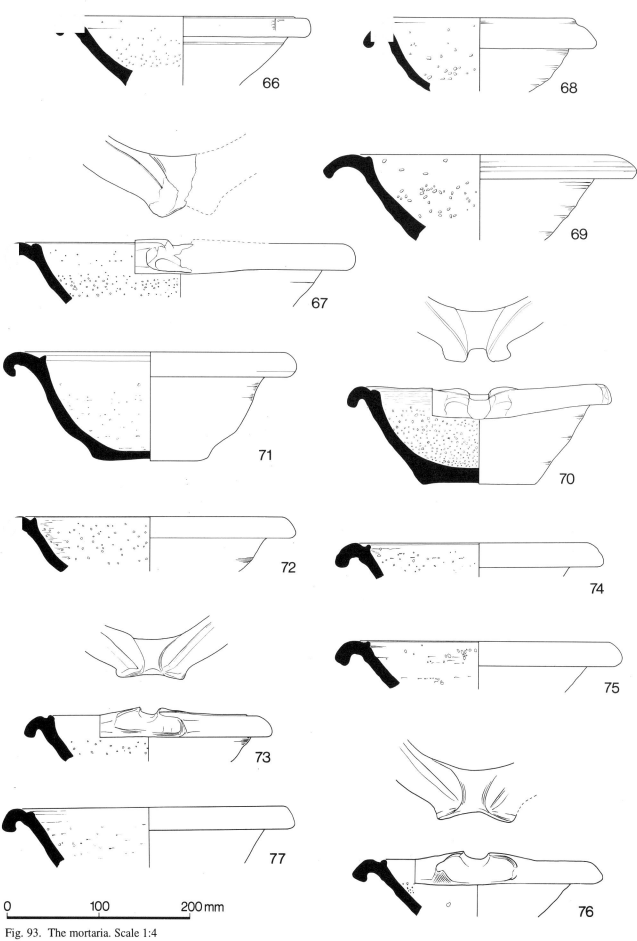

Fig. 93. The mortaria. Scale 1:4

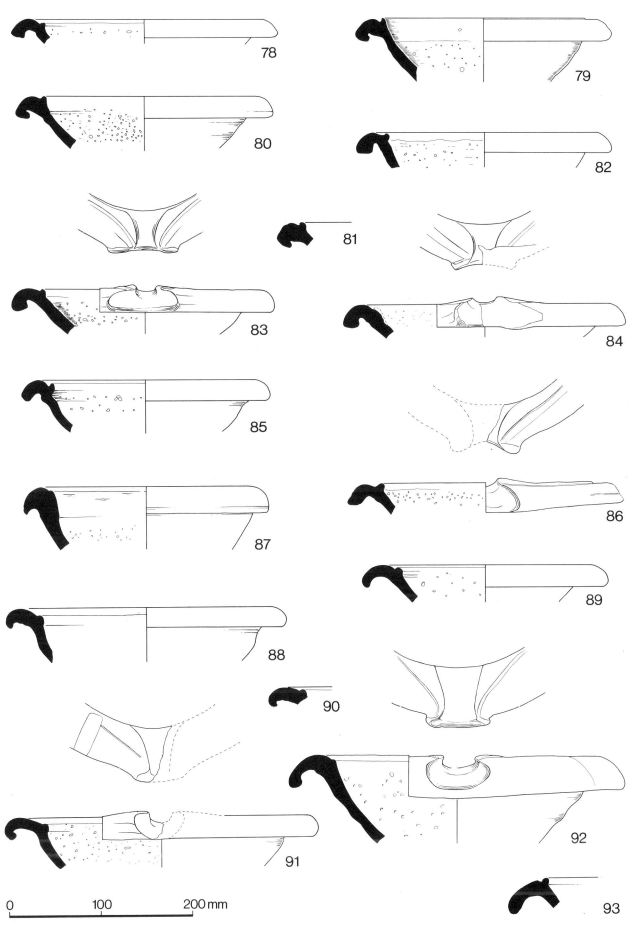

0   100   200 mm

Fig. 94. The mortaria. Scale 1:4

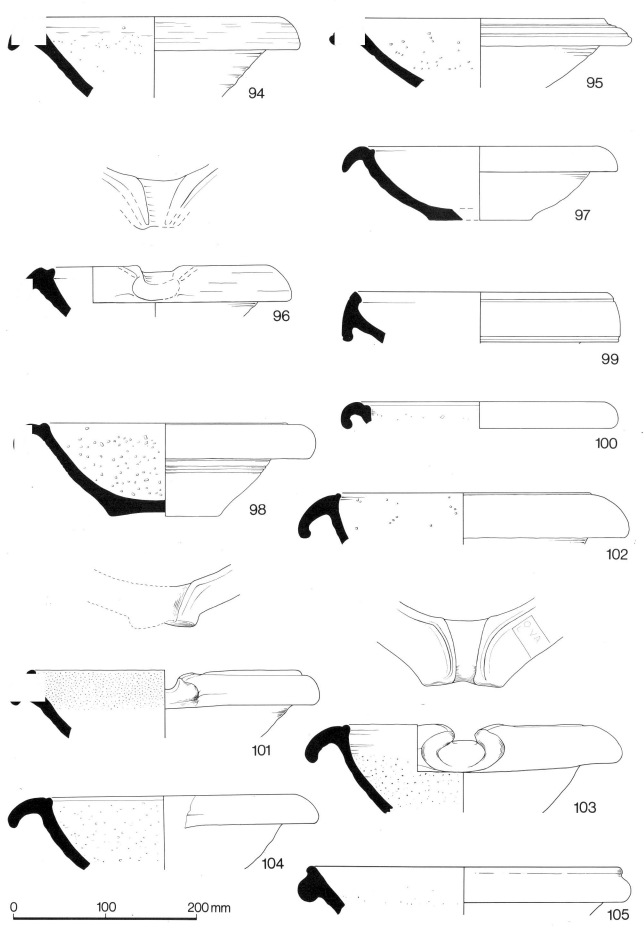

Fig. 95. The mortaria. Scale 1:4

76* Fabric 105. Type C. *(152); U/S Site 1(74)*

77* Fabric 105. Type C. *(154); U/S Site 1 (74)*

78* Fabric 105. Type D. *(142); Level 3 Site 1(74); 3*

79* Fabric 105. Type Ei. *(626); 083 T10; 3*

80* Fabric 105. Type Ei. *(151); U/S Site 1(74)*

81* Fabric 105. Type Eii. *(582); 083 T10; 3*

82* Fabric 105. Type F. *Stamp No. 8; (17); Level 3 Site 1(74); 3*

83* Fabric 105. Type F. *(141 and 165); Level 3 Site 1(74); 3*

84* Fabric 105. Type F with trade-mark stamp. *Stamp No. 6; (13 and 14); 167 Site 1(74); 3*

85* Fabric 105. Type G. *(150); U/S Site 1(74)*

86* Fabric 105. Type H. *(156); Level 3 Site 1(74); 3*

87* Fabric 106. Brown slip. *(414); 196 T14; Ic*

88* Fabric 106. 2nd century. Brown slip. *(938); U/S T10*

89* Fabric 107. Stamped Aesico. Antonine, intrusive in this phase. Produced at or near South Carlton, Lincoln. *Stamp No. 20; (866); 052 Site 1(77); II*

90* Fabric 107. Stamp of Q. Iustius Crescens. AD 100-140. *Stamp No. 36; (691); 388 T10; 3*

91* Fabric 107. Stamp of Q. Iustius Crescens. AD 100-140. *Stamp No. 13; (5); Level 2 Site 1(74); 4*

92* Fabric 109. Stamp of Crispius AD 80-120. *Stamp No. 42; (572 and 737); 127 and 448 T10; 3*

93* Fabric 110. Stamped Boriedo. AD 50-90. *Stamp No. 1; (27, 116, 117, 143 and 144); Levels 6 and 7 Site 1(74); 1. 236 Site 1(74); 2*

94* Fabric 111. AD 60-95. Brown-yellow slip. *(2022); Level 5 Site 1(74); 2*

95* Fabric 112. Probably 3rd-century Lower Nene Valley Ware. Intrusive in this phase. *(519); 028 T10; 3*

96* Fabric 118. Brown slip. *(983, 992, 998, 1002 and 2012); 1115, 1132, 1145 and 1148 15V; I*

97* Fabric 119. *(407 and 429); 108 and 220 T14; Ic*

98* Fabric 120. Late 1st century. *(736); 448 T10; 3*

99* Fabric 122. Heavily burnt, possibly has a brown slip. AD 160-210. *(452, 454 and 522); 028 T10; 3. 008 T10; Mod.*

100* Fabric 125. Brown slip. *(790); 658 T15IV; Id*

101* Fabric 128. *(813 and 819); 739 and 743 T16V; Ia*

102* Fabric 131. North France. *(406); 220 T14; Ic*

103* Fabric 131. North France. Stamped, probably Q. Valerius Esunertus. AD 55-90. *Stamp No. 49 (996 and 1021); 984 T15V; Ib. 936 T15V; IIb*

104* Fabric 131. North France. Stamped Q. Valerius Veranius AD 65-100. *Stamp No. 2; (28); Level 6 Site 1(74); 1*

105* Fabric 131. North France. AD 140-200+.*(33); Level 4 Site 1 (74); 2*

106* Fabric 131. North France. AD 140-200+. *(23); 165 Site 1(74); 3*

107* Fabric 131. North France. AD 140-200+. *(457); 081 T10; 4*

108* Fabric 133. Central France. AD 50-85. *(558); 1179 T15V; Ia*

109* Fabric 134. Possibly Rhineland. Pre-Flavian but at Castleford original deposition must have taken place in the AD 70s at the earliest. *(954); 302 T13; Med.*

110* Fabric 135. Possibly Gallia Belgica AD 80-130. Buff slip which still covers the trituration grit suggesting the vessel has not been used. *(990); 267 T10; 4*

111* Fabric 136. Rhineland AD 150-300. *(627); 952 T10; 3*

112* Fabric 137. Rhineland AD 150-300. Cream slip. *(543); U/S T10*

113* Fabric 138. North France. AD 80-150. *(502); 056 T10; 4*

114* Fabric 139. Possibly Rhineland. Pre-Flavian period, see notes to No. 112. *(665); 749 T10; 2*

Numbers 115 to 117 are spouted bowls rather than mortaria.

115* Fabric 113. Externally burnished. *(1095 and 1096); 1148 T15V; Ib*

116* Fabric 114. *(901); 304 T15II; Ic*

117* Fabric 114. *(951); 378 T13; IIa*

15 The 'Pottery Shop' Mortaria
by K.F. Hartley

The mortarium fragments presented for examination as from this deposit were completely homogeneous in fabric (Fabric 105), trituration grit and in the type of spouts used. The large to tiny trituration grit extends up to the bead, with occasionally a few scraps on top of the flange. The internal surface is sometimes slightly furrowed, probably through application of the grit while the mortarium was turning on the wheel. The short, uneven and broken furrows are caused by the accidental movement of the grits in the clay, not by deliberate scoring. There was some variation in rim-type but only such as one might expect in a group of contemporary products from a single workshop (see Types A-H below). None of the fragments showed any obvious sign of wear.

Virtually all the sherds showed some sign of fire damage, in pale greyish tones, pinkness, blackness or an unusual drab quality, while surface cracking was a normal feature. It was clear from examination of the rest of the mortaria found in the *vicus* excavations that other sherds had derived from this deposit. It is also understood that the layer continued outside the area of the excavations so that this is, in any case, only a portion of the original deposit.

The evidence is entirely consistent with the presence of stacks of mortaria in a store or shop, which suffered destruction through, probably, intense fire, followed by the liberal application of water. This seems to be the

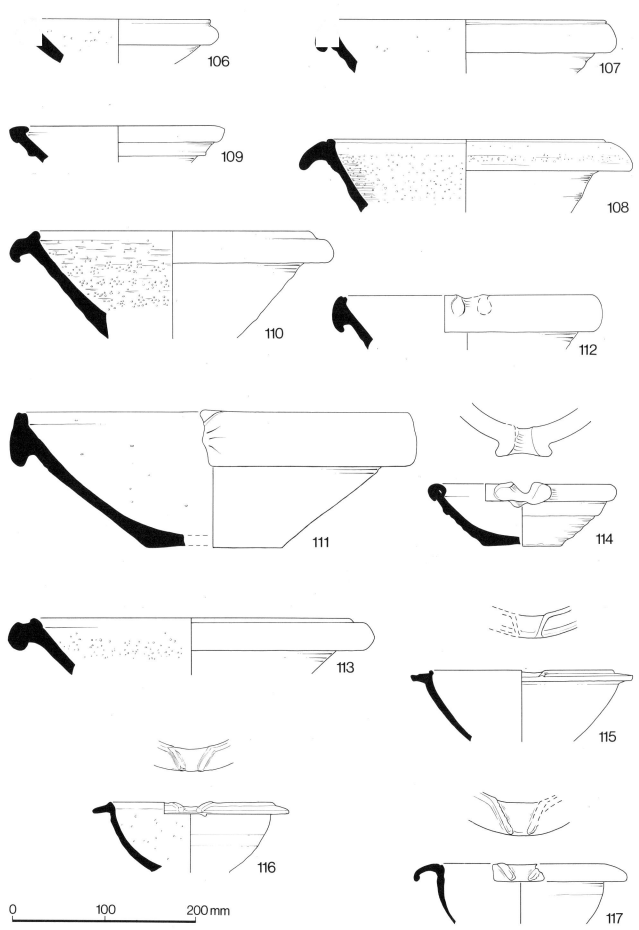

Fig. 96. The mortaria. Scale 1:4

0   100   200 mm

184

likeliest explanation for the extreme degree of cracking and fragmentation. One unusual feature is that all the vessels were broken along the top of the flange, separating the outer half of the flange from the rest, as if roofing material had fallen on top of the mortaria when they were stacked.

Fabric subjected to fire can be difficult or impossible to identify but it was clear that these mortaria were in the same fabric and from a single source, probably a single workshop. Dr D.F. Williams comments:

All the sherds are in a hard, fairly smooth micaceous fabric, normally white (Munsell 10YR 8/2) throughout but with some grey areas. The trituration grits are mainly composed of quartz, quartzite, flint/chert, sandstone and red iron ore. Thin sectioning shows a highly micaceous fabric with frequent quartz grains, average size 0.20mm and under, with a scatter of slightly larger grains, iron ore and some ferruginous sandstone and limestone. Sherd GSSO.74 is a little sandier than the others.

It was also reasonable to assume that they were contemporary and a date in the mid-2nd century, AD 140-50, was provided by the samian in this deposit. It is clear that most of the mortaria in the deposit were never stamped but up to nine of them were stamped with two trademark stamps, probably used by one or two illiterate potters. One die, which has never been recorded elsewhere, was represented only once (Fig. 97, No. 6), while four of the stamps from the other die (Fig. 97, Nos 7-12) were so fragmentary that they could have all been from one vessel. Stamps from the second die have been recorded on two mortaria from Aldborough, both in a red-brown fabric with cream slip, which differs entirely from the 'pottery shop' fabric.

The 'pottery shop' mortaria can be attributed with reasonable confidence to a workshop at or in the vicinity of Castleford or, less likely, Aldborough. There is only one other production centre, at South Carlton, Lincoln, which produced a fabric (Fabric 107), comparable to Fabric 105, especially in its strongly micaceous quality and in the use of vari-coloured trituration grit. There is little doubt that there were other small workshops in Lincolnshire which produced a fairly similar fabric, for example at Newton-on-Trent (Field and Palmer-Brown 1991; updated in Darling and Hartley in preparation). It should be pointed out that many South Carlton mortaria are rather coarser than Fabric 105. The latter is, in fact, closest to the fabric most often used by potters like Q. Iustius Crescens and HDA? (Fabric 106), part or the whole of whose work can be attributed to Lincolnshire, some of it certainly to Lincoln, though their kilns there are not known. Fabric 105, however, never has the type of slip present with Lincoln or Lincolnshire products. The other difficulty is that the rim-forms and the spout-type used do not fit a source in Lincoln.

There is, however, convincing evidence of mortarium production in both off-white fabric and red-brown fabrics at Aldborough, Yorks (Jones 1971). Furthermore, in the work of Viator (see below), there is certainly a very strong indication of a workshop at Castleford as well as at Aldborough. There is no certain evidence to link production of even the mildly micaceous Fabric 104 to Aldborough rather than Castleford. This Fabric 104b is associated with stamps from certain dies of Viator, whose distribution indicates Castleford rather than Aldborough as the source. This fabric is close to Fabric 105. There is absolutely no evidence to link any production by any potter called Viator with the Lincoln area.

Whatever the arguments for and against, the possible sources for the 'pottery shop' mortaria are clear: Castleford, Aldborough or some perhaps unknown site in Lincolnshire. For several reasons, a local source is virtually certain. Recent discoveries at Castleford have established that it has a relatively important status in Roman Britain. Mortarium production, albeit often on a small scale, was very widespread indeed in the 2nd century and the absence of production there would need to be explained, especially when the availability of excellent clay has made Castleford famous for pottery in more recent times. The fact that the only other two stamps known from the two dies represented at Castleford were found at Aldborough, strengthens the idea of a local workshop. Viator's work, in general, points to movement between Aldborough and Castleford or perhaps having workshops at both sites. There is no evidence to suggest that potteries at either site had more than limited regional importance, though Viator's products in Fabric 104 reached Carlisle.

Quantification

All the sherds presented for examination were closely packed and completely covered the surfaces of about five trestle tables. The way the vessels had been fractured along the flange made it difficult to restore rim-sections. However, a rough count of rim fragments was made and an attempt was made to estimate the numbers of vessels and the numbers of different rim-types present (see Types, below). Three means were used for this purpose:

i. Spout fragments from each side of the spouts were assessed separately, according to the associated rim-type.

ii. The rim variants were examined.

iii. It was possible to estimate the diameters of twenty vessels; these ranged between 270-300mm, with a single example measuring 310mm. The rest of the mortaria appeared to be of similar dimensions. The rim-sherds were roughly measured in length and the total obtained was divided by the average circumference.

This gave a minimum of at least 42 mortaria. This is still a minimal estimate; it is likely that there were several more.

Table 25. Rim-profiles associated with the 'pottery shop' mortaria.

Type	No. rim fragments	Minimum no. vessels
A	175	13
Bi-ii	105	8
C	57	6-8
D	7	4
Ei-ii	11	4-5
F	15	3-4
G	3	3
H	1	1
	374	42-6

NB The sub-types i and ii are, in fact, different types but any attempt to separate them now would affect the estimate of numbers of vessels.

Type A: Bead varies in height but is often slightly above the flange; flanges fairly short and rounded, sometimes with concavity behind the bead. Includes a fair amount of variation but the flange is the same thickness throughout. Nos: 72-3.

Type Bi: Bead just below rounded flange, rather deeper than Type A. Similar to Type C but lacks slight concavity in flange.
No.: 74, with cordon like Type G: 85.

Type Bii: Curved flange, thickening towards the distal end.
No.: 75.

Type C: Bead below shallow curved flange, going outwards; wider at distal end. Slight concavity behind the bead and in flange near distal end.
Nos: 76 and 77 variant.

Type D: Bead below wide, very shallow flange; wider at distal end and angled, both internally and externally at distal end.
No.: 78.

Type Ei: Bead marginally above rounded flange, which is quite thick, but thinned near distal end, where it is turned under leaving an obvious gap and making the distal end wide, and flattish underneath.
Nos: 79 and 80 (look as if they should be from 'pottery shop' deposit).

Type Eii: As Ei but thicker flange which is folded right under to join the body making it very stumpy.
No.: 81.

Type F: Bead level with, or below level of, flange. Shallow, rounded flange folded under at distal end to make that part very wide and thick and flat on the underside; angled or squared externally and internally at distal end. Thickish wall.
Nos: 82-4.

Type G: Level of bead varies but never far from that of flange. Differs from A in having what is almost a cordon on the external wall directly below the bead.
No.: 85.

Type H: Bead marginally above flange, which is wide, shallow and splayed, with a slightly projecting distal bead. The only complete rim-section of this type also had a concavity behind the bead.
No.: 86.

All types had distinctive and similar neatly formed spouts, with the wings barely projecting beyond the rim. Nos 73, 76 and 83 are excellent examples.

16 The Mortarium Stamps
by K.F. Hartley

The drawings of the stamps appear in Figures 97-8. Where appropriate, the drawing number indicates the drawing of the vessel from which the stamp came: these drawings appear in Figures 87-96. The numbers in brackets are archive identification numbers marked on the actual vessels.

Stamps from the 1974 *vicus* excavations

1*   Fabric 110. A well-worn mortarium with broken stamp impressed along the flange, [..]EDO F, (DO ligatured), for Boriedo *fecit*. Other mortaria of his have been noted from Ribchester and Elginhaugh. Boriedo was one of several contemporary potters who were active in Gallia Belgica, probably in northern France and probably within the period AD 55-85 (Hartley 1998, 206-8). It is almost certainly from this source (For further details of his work see Hartley in preparation.) *Drawing No. 93; (27, 116, 117, 143 and 144); Levels 6 and 7 Site 1(74); 1. 236 Site 1(74); 2*

2   Fabric 131. A faint two-line stamp partially overlying an earlier impression which shows above the L and R in the upper line. The stamp is from one of the ten basic die-types of Q. Valerius Veranius. Stamps from this die-type appear in three different lengths, perhaps the result of sister dies made from the same matrix (Hartley 1996, 147-8), and this example is the middle length version (see Hartley 1999, 206, fig. 4.25, 197 S5-S7 for a detailed note on this potter and on stamps from the same die). Q. Valerius Veranius's main production can be attributed to the Oise/Somme area of northern France (Hartley 1998, 200-206) within the period AD 65-100. This die had the letters DOGAERIA . FAC in tiny letters between the two lines of the potter's name, presumably indicating where the pottery was made; the name is otherwise unknown. *Drawing No. 104; (28); Level 6 Site 1(74); 1*

3   Fabric 104. Fragmentary stamp of Viator,]OR retrograde. Probably a Castleford product and AD 100-140. It can reasonably be attributed to the same Viator who had a workshop at Aldborough (Jones 1971, 66-7 and fig. 18). *Level 5 Site 1(74); 2*

4* Fabric 88. Stamp of Iunius who had kilns at both Mancetter and Hartshill. AD 150-80, intrusive in this phase. *Drawing No. 2; (40 and 83); 170 Site 1(74); 3*

5* Fabric 88. Stamp of Loccius Vibo. Mancetter-Hartshill. AD 135-65, intrusive in this phase. *Drawing No. 8; (39); Level 4 Site 1(74); 2*

6* Fabric 105. Trade-mark stamp. Probably Castleford. Mid-2nd century. *Drawing No. 84; (13 and 14); 167 Site 1(74); 3*

7* Fabric 105. Trade-mark stamp. Probably Castleford. Mid-2nd century. *Drawing No. 74; (15 and 16); Level 3 Site 1(74); 3.*

8* Fabric 105. Trade-mark stamp, same die as No. 7. Mid-2nd century. *Drawing No. 82; (17); Level 3 Site 1(74); 3*

9* Fabric 105. Fragmentary stamp from the same die as No. 7. Mid-2nd century. *(315); Level 3 Site 1(74); 3*

10* Fabric 105. Corner of stamp from the same die as No. 7. Mid-2nd century. *(314); Level 3 Site 1(74); 3*

11 Fabric 105. Very end of stamp only, same die as No. 7. Mid-2nd century. *Level 3 Site 1 (74); 3*

12* Fabric 105. Stamp from the same die as No. 7. The central part of the stamp is elongated, probably because the die was pulled across the rim when it was being stamped. Mid-2nd century. *(1); Level 2 Site 1(74); 4*

13 Fabric 106. A Lincoln product. Badly damaged stamp attributed to Q. Iustius Crescens. AD 100-140. *Drawing No. 91; (5); Level 2 Site 1(74); 4*

14 Fabric 91? Very hard fabric, overfired to dark blue-grey with some surface cracking but no worse than a second. Unidentified stamp; no other examples from the same die are known. A similar fabric was produced at Rossington Bridge but it cannot be regarded as more than a possible source. 2nd century. If Rossington Bridge is the correct source, it is likely to be early Antonine. *(2); 2 Site 1(74); 4*

15* Fabric 101. Fragmentary stamp from the same die as No. 18. Aldborough. Name of potter unknown. Likely to be first half of the 2nd century. *(125); Level 1 Site 1(74); 4*

16* Fabric 105. Border of stamp from the same die as No. 7. Mid-2nd century. *(316); U/S Site 1(74)*

17* Fabric 105. Border of stamp from the same die as No. 7. Mid-2nd century. *(317); U/S Site 1(74)*

Stamps from the later excavations

18* Fabric 101. Probably Aldborough. Fragmentary stamp from the same die as No. 15. Reading uncertain. Likely to be from the first half of the 2nd century. *(740); 601 T15IV; Mod.*

19* Fabric 109. Diagonally impressed stamp, STNAITO? retrograde (dashed A). Interpretation obscure, perhaps a semi-literate potter. Produced in Norfolk, perhaps at Brampton. Probably 2nd century. *(478); 101 T10; Mod.*

20* Fabric 107. Stamped by Aesico, who worked north-west of Lincoln, at or not far from South Carlton in the Antonine period (see Dore and Gillam 1979, 162 no. 13; his affinities are with Vorolas rather than Crico). AD 140-80, intrusive in this phase. *Drawing No. 89; (866); 052 Site 1(77); II*

21* Variant of Fabric 91. Stamp, probably of an illiterate potter, who can be attributed to Rossington Bridge or Cantley, although the

fabric is unusually fine textured for these potteries. Antonine. *Drawing No. 37; (370); Tr. 4 Site 1(77); ?*

22 Fabric 89. Secundus of Brockley Hill, Middlesex (see Frere 1972, 378 no. 37; Frere 1984, 281 no. 37 for further details). AD 55-85. *(362); 049 Site 1(77); II*

23 Fabric 131. Eroded stamp of Q. Valerius Veranius (see No. 2 for details). AD 65-100. *(373); 049 Site 1(77): II*

24* Fabric 106. Border of a stamp which reads HCA (C reversed) or HDA (HD ligatured). Lincolnshire, perhaps Lincoln. AD 90-120. *Drawing No. 71; (2031); 715 T9; III/IV*

25* Fabric 103a. Retrograde stamp,]ROMA (MA ligatured), impressed along flange. No other stamps of this potter are known. Aldborough or just possibly Castleford. Perhaps Flavian but certainly no later than Trajanic. *Drawing No. 65; (368); 115 Site 1(77); III*

26* Fabric 103a. Stamp reading DEC, followed by strokes which could be interpreted to give Decuma, Decuminus or Decanius. Aldborough or Castleford; probably AD 70-90. There is one other stamp, from Wallsend (Hartley forthcoming), which could have a similar reading, but the die used is different and that mortarium appears to be marginally later in date, while the fabrics, though generally similar, are not identical. Further examples will determine whether they were made by the same potter. *Drawing No. 64; (392); 988 T9; II*

27 Fabric 108. GEN[, stamp of the potter Genialis. There was probably more than one mortarium potter called Genialis, and perhaps three workshops are indicated by the associated fabrics. This is the only fabric that may have been produced at York (Phillips and Heywood 1995, fig. 4.9/7, no. 95 for further comments). AD 100-140. *(507); 058 T10; Mod.*

28 Fabric 89. Poorly impressed stamp of Bruccius. Brockley Hill, Middlesex. See Frere 1984, fig. 118 no. 64 for an example of a stamp from the same die. *Drawing No. 23; (524 and 574); 129 T10; 3. 078 T10; 4*

29* Fabric 103. Two stamps of Viator,]AOR (dashed A), impressed close together. The T was omitted from this die. Fabric suggests Aldborough rather than Castleford. AD 100-140. *Drawing No. 67; (537); 078 T10; 4*

30* Fabric 103. Retrograde stamp of Viator,]TOR, from a different die, but made by the same potter. AD 100-140. *Drawing No. 66; (458, 460 and 604); 118 T10; 3. 081 T10; 4*

31* Fabric 104b. The potter's stamp on each side of the vessel survives, both are incomplete impressions reading VIAT[retrograde. These are from the same die of Viator as No. 30, together with which they give the complete reading for the die. Three other mortaria stamped with the same die are known; all are from Castleford. The distribution of all the mortaria which can be reasonably attributed to this potter links his activity to the Aldborough and Castleford area. This die is, so far, linked only with Castleford but the mortaria are in both Fabrics 103 and 104. The source for Fabric 104 is not certain but is linked with production at Aldborough and it is not unlike Fabric 105, the 'pottery shop' fabric.

It is highly probable that this Viator is to be equated with the potter, who stamped Vator or Nator, and who is known to have worked at Aldborough (Jones 1971, 66-7 and fig. 18). It seems highly likely that he had workshops at both Aldborough and Castleford. He should be considered separately from potters of the same name who worked in the Nene Valley and East Anglia. AD 100-140. *Drawing No. 70; (948); 910 T10; 3*

32* Fabric 88. Corner of a stamp probably of G. Attius Marinus. *Drawing No. 5; (456); 054 T10; 4*

Fig. 97. The mortarium stamps. Scale 1:4

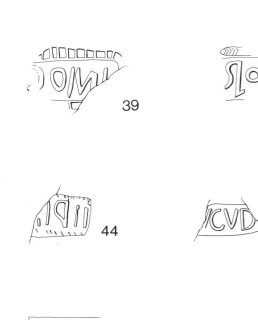

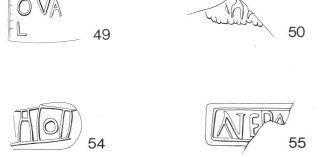

Fig. 98. The mortarium stamps. Scale 1:2

33 Fabric 88. Stamp of G. Attius Marinus. *(595); 127 T10; 3*

34* Fabric 88. Both the name stamp of G. Attius Marinus and his *fecit* counterstamp survive. *Drawing No. 4; (725); 494 T10; 2*

Numbers 32 to 34 are from three different mortaria stamped by G. Attius Marinus within the period AD 100-130. They were probably all made in the Mancetter-Hartshill potteries but it should be remembered that some early 2nd-century potters who are primarily associated with these potteries also had workshops at Little Chester. There is no evidence from the Little Chester kilns to link Marinus with that pottery but the cream fabric produced there is not readily distinguishable in macroscopic examination from the fabric produced at Mancetter at the same date and Marinus would be a prime candidate for activity at both sites. See Wheeler 1985, 126 nos 1-4 for further details of this potter.

35* Fabric 88 with unusual core.]CO[retrograde from a stamp of Icotasgus. AD 130-60. *(560); 119 T10; 3*

36* Fabric 107. QIVSCRES (RE ligatured), stamped twice close together, for Q. Iustius Crescens. Probably Lincoln. AD 100-140. *Drawing No. 90; (691); 338 T10; 3*

37* Fabric 89. Stamp of Doinus. Brockley Hill, Middlesex. AD 70-110. *Drawing No. 27; (664, 669 and 728); 783 T10; 1. 431 and 749; T10; 2*

38* Fabric 89. Stamp of Doinus from the same die as number 37. Brockley Hill, Middlesex. AD 70-110. *Drawing No. 24; (985, 997, 1000 and 1023); 1073 T15V; IIa. 1066 and 1103 T15V; IIb*

39* Fabric 89. Two fragmentary stamps survive, one from each side of the vessel from what is probably the latest die of Doinus. Brockley Hill, Middlesex. AD 85-110. *Drawing No. 29; (646, 688 and 718); 440 and 700 T10; 2. 414 T10; 3*

40 Fabric 89. Border of stamp, probably from the same die of Doinus as No. 39. Probably AD 85-110. *(658); 618 T10; 2*

41* Fabric 104. Flange fragment from a third mortarium with a broken retrograde stamp of Viator,]OR, from the same die as Nos 3 and 29. No mortaria stamped with this die are known from Aldborough but up to four are known from Castleford (including an old find). Only two others are recorded, both from Corbridge. *(735); 448 T10; 3*

42* Fabric 109. One stamp and fraction of another from the other side of the vessel. Crispus. East Anglia, probably Norfolk, perhaps at Caistor St. Edmund. AD 80-120. *Drawing No. 92; (572 and 737); 127 and 448 T10; 3*

43* Fabric 88. Two stamps impressed close together; these are probably the work of a semi-literate potter. He has two dies and the most likely reading for this is ARDS, with the R upside down; Ardusa is a possible but uncertain interpretation. There is a good possibility that he had a workshop at Little Chester, Derbyshire but he may also have worked at the Mancetter-Hartshill potteries. AD 100-150. *Drawing No. 1 (686); 472 T10; 4*

189

44* Fabric 107. Fragmentary retrograde stamp,]IIPA[(A with a dash) can be attributed to Atepacius. Lincoln *c*. AD 90-130. See Stead 1976, 126 no. 29 for further details. *(712); 453 T10; U/S*

45 Fabric 89. Broken stamp,]LB[, almost certainly part of a stamp of Albinus from the same die as Frere 1972, fig. 145 no. 11. Verulamium region. AD 60-90. *763 T10; 2*

46* Fabric 89. A second mortarium of Albinus, with broken counterstamp]GVD[, impressed diagonally, from a die similar to that used for Frere 1972, fig. 145 no. 6 (FLVGVDV). *(433); 101 T14; II*

47* Fabric 101. Fragmentary stamp previously unknown. Probably Aldborough. More likely to be 2nd century than earlier. *(801); 557 T15IV; IV*

48* Fabric 88. Stamped SEPTV, E reversed. Midlands, perhaps Mancetter-Hartshill. The first stamp on one side has been smoothed out and a second impression made; part of the stamp on the opposite side survives. AD 110-140+. *Drawing No. 6; (803); 704 T16V; III*

49* Fabric 131. Poorly preserved stamp almost certainly of Q. Valerius Esunertus. Oise/Somme area, north France (Hartley 1998, 200-206) *c*. AD 55-90. *Drawing No. 103; (996 and 1021); 984 T15V; I. 936 T15V; II*

50* Fabric 103. Fragmentary stamp; no other stamps are known from the same die. Aldborough or Castleford. AD 140-180+. *Drawing No. 68; (1018); 901 T15V; Mod.*

51* Fabric 88. Flange and spout fragment with broken spout reading]STIC[for Aesticus. Mancetter-Hartshill. AD 100-130, intrusive in this phase. *(1051); 077 T18; Ic*

Another sherd (48) from Site 1(74) but otherwise unstratified, has the very edge of a stamp and is probably from the other side of the same vessel.

52 Fabric 89. Fragmentary, unidentifiable stamp. Verulamium region. AD 80-130. *(670); 913 T10; 3*

53 Fabric 89. Edge of unidentified stamp. Verulamium region. AD 70-100+. *(698); 430 T10; 3*

54* Fabric 102. The semi-literate stamp is from the same die as Jones 1971, fig. 18 no. 6. This can best be read as Nator or Vator and is almost certainly from a die of Viator (Jones 1971, 66-7, fig. 18; and notes on Stamp 31 above). Aldborough. AD 100-140. *Drawing No. 60; (565 and 620); 169 and 299 T10; 3*

55* Fabric 107. The stamp is from the same die of Atepacius as Stead 1976, 126 no. 29. Lincoln *c*. AD 90-130. *(799); 556 T15IV; IV*

17 Quantification and Conclusions

The tables below show the amounts of different types of mortaria present in each of the phases of the fort and *vicus*. For the dates of the phases see Table 1. The following tables give numbers of sherds with numbers of vessels in brackets. Intrusive fabrics are indicated with an asterisk. The tables do not include the 'pottery shop' assemblage but the phase and overall totals include vessels that could not be positively attributed to one particular fabric.

Table 26. The mortaria present in the *vicus*

Fabric	Phase			
	1	**2**	**3**	**4**
88	2(2)*	11(9)	16(14)	40(31)
89	14(12)	61(21)	34(20)	13(6)
90	0(0)	0(0)	1(1)*	2(2)
91	0(0)	0(0)	11(6)	3(1)
93	11(8)	7(5)	11(5)	2(2)
94	3(1)	1(1)	5(2)	2(2)
96	1(1)	0(0)	0(0)	0(0)
97	0(0)	0(0)	1(1)	0(0)
98	5(1)	0(0)	4(3)	1(1)
99	0(0)	0(0)	1(1)	0(0)
100	0(0)	0(0)	2(2)	3(2)
101	0(0)	2(2)	2(2)	12(6)
102	0(0)	0(0)	2(1)	0(0)
103	0(0)	2(2)	7(6)	11(4)
104	0(0)	5(4)	23(8)	7(7)
105	0(0)	37(32)	111(38)	17(14)
106	0(0)	1(1)	7(7)	2(2)
107	0(0)	3(3)	1(1)	11(5)
109	0(0)	0(0)	1(1)	0(0)
110	8(1)	1(0)	0(0)	0(0)
111	0(0)	3(1)	0(0)	0(0)
114	0(0)	0(0)	1(1)	0(0)
115	1(1)	0(0)	0(0)	0(0)
118	0(0)	1(1)	0(0)	1(1)
119	0(0)	0(0)	1(1)	0(0)
120	0(0)	0(0)	5(1)	0(0)
122	0(0)	0(0)	10(2)	0(0)
123	0(0)	1(1)	0(0)	0(0)
127	0(0)	0(0)	0(0)	1(1)
131	10(9)	7(4)	19(11)	5(5)
132	0(0)	5(1)	0(0)	0(0)
133	0(0)	1(1)	2(1)	0(0)
135	0(0)	0(0)	0(0)	1(1)
136	0(0)	0(0)	2(1)	0(0)
137	0(0)	0(0)	7(1)	0(0)
138	0(0)	0(0)	0(0)	1(1)
139	0(0)	5(1)	0(0)	0(0)
Total	**59(39)**	**169(97)**	**300(146)**	**147(102)**

Table 27. The mortaria present in the fort.

Fabric	Phase			
	I	II	III	IV
88	1(1)*	5(4)*	32(3)	92(29)
89	11(8)	22(11)	10(9)	11(10)
90	0(0)	0(0)	1(1)*	2(2)
91	0(0)	1(1)	0(0)	5(3)
92	0(0)	1(1)	0(0)	4(1)
93	17(12)	10(7)	5(3)	14(13)
94	18(3)	7(1)	5(1)	2(2)
96	4(4)	3(1)	1(0)	6(2)
97	2(2)	3(3)	3(1)	1(0)
98	7(2)	1(1)	1(1)	4(3)
99	0(0)	1(1)	0(0)	0(0)
100	0(0)	0(0)	0(0)	1(1)
101	0(0)	5(1)	0(0)	2(2)
103	1(1)	1(1)	3(3)	1(1)
104	0(0)	1(1)	0(0)	24(11)
106	2(2)	4(4)	5(1)	7(4)
107	2(1)	3(2)	1(1)	5(5)
112	0(0)	0(0)	0(0)	1(1)
113	3(1)	0(0)	0(0)	0(0)
114	3(2)	0(0)	1(1)	0(0)
119	19(1)	0(0)	0(0)	0(0)
122	1(1)	0(0)	0(0)	0(0)
125	1(1)	0(0)	0(0)	0(0)
126	0(0)	0(0)	0(0)	1(1)
127	0(0)	1(1)	0(0)	0(0)
128	2(1)	0(0)	0(0)	0(0)
129	0(0)	0(0)	0(0)	1(1)
130	0(0)	0(0)	1(1)	0(0)
131	24(13)	16(10)	14(8)	21(18)
132	3(3)	0(0)	1(1)	0(0)
135	1(1)	1(1)	0(0)	0(0)
137	0(0)	1(1)	0(0)	1(1)
Total	**139(71)**	**111(63)**	**90(41)**	**211(118)**

Table 28. Overall totals including unstratified material.

Fabric	Quantity	Fabric	Quantity
88	237(128)	114	19(6)
89	191(111)	115	2(1)
90	9(9)	116	1(1)
91	29(19)	117	1(1)
92	8(4)	118	21(3)
93	93(62)	119	8(2)
94	44(14)	120	5(1)
95	1(1)	121	1(1)
96	18(9)	122	14(4)
97	10(7)	123	1(1)
98	24(13)	124	1(1)
99	2(2)	125	1(1)
100	6(5)	126	1(1)
101	25(15)	127	2(2)
102	2(1)	128	2(2)
103	33(23)	129	1(1)
104	71(43)	130	2(2)
105	205(117)	131	126(83)
106	23(19)	132	9(5)
107	31(22)	133	5(4)
108	1(1)	134	1(1)
109	3(2)	135	3(3)
110	9(1)	136	2(1)
111	3(1)	137	11(5)
112	1(1)	138	1(1)
113	3(1)	139	5(1)
		Total	**1424(837)**

These tables reveal the pattern of supply of mortaria to both the fort and *vicus*. Allowing for the differences in chronology and development between the two areas, it can be seen that the assemblages of mortaria recovered from them are broadly similar. The major difference is in the presence of the 'pottery shop' type, Fabric 105, on the *vicus* site in the 2nd century in large quantities but this must largely be the result of the mid-2nd-century fire that destroyed a substantial quantity of unused pottery.

In the 1st century the supply of mortaria was dominated by three sources; the Verulamium region (Fabric 89), sources in northern France (mainly in the form of Gillam 238 mortaria, from the Oise/Somme area) and military associated production, some of which may have been local. In the 2nd century mortaria continued to be supplied from northern France, the Rhineland and the Verulamium region. The oxidised militarily associated fabrics, particularly 93 and 94, would appear to be present largely on a residual basis.

Although present in small amounts in the last fort phase (Phase II) the products of both the Lincoln area (Fabrics 106 and 107) and Aldborough (Fabrics 101-104) became more common in the 2nd century. Probable local production also appears to become more evident (Fabrics 104 and 105). The bulk of Fabric 105 was recovered as part of the 'pottery shop' assemblage; the suggested local manufacture of Fabric 105 contrasts with the imported nature of the rest of the 'pottery shop' assemblage.

The 3rd and 4th centuries saw the rise to prominence of Mancetter-Hartshill products although these had been reaching Castleford during the 2nd century. A very small amount of Nene Valley wares reached the site.

The evidence of the coarse pottery suggests that most of the ceramic assemblage at Castleford has been redeposited. The occurrence of the bulk of the mortaria assemblage in exactly the same contexts as the coarse pottery suggests that this is the case for the mortaria as well. Hence, an analysis of the spatial distribution of them would not indicate their areas of use on the site and so has not been given here.

Appendix

Concordance of Contexts of Small Finds, Environmental Remains and Pottery by Site, Phase and Context

The following list includes all the catalogued material in Volume I, all of the material in the Archive other than the iron nails from Site 1(74) and the featureless vessel glass fragments, the catalogued pottery in this volume and any environmental remains which are mentioned by context in Volume II. Where no phase is given in the first column, the context is either post-Roman or unstratified. Where a context appears in Volume II in the text and/or in a figure this appears in column four. If a context appears as = to another this is to enable the reader to find the context on a figure e.g. 913=989, indicates that 913 does not appear on a figure but its equivalent 989 appears in Figure 15.

Abbreviations

Vol. 1: *Small Finds*	Lead A.: Lead waste (in archive)	d.: dog
Bone: Bone artefact	Pot. C.: Pottery Counter	h.: horse
Coin	Quern: Quernstone	p.: pig
Cruc.: Crucibles	Quern A.: Quernstone (in archive)	s./g.: sheep/goat
Cu. A.: Copper Alloy artefacts	Sculp.: Sculpture	Bot.: Botanical remains
Cu. Arch.: Copper Alloy (in archive)	Stone: Stone artefact	Hum.: Human remains
Gl. O.: Glass Object	Tex.: Textile	
Gl. V.: Glass Vessel	Wood	Vol. 3: *Pottery*
Graffiti		C. W.: Coarse Ware
Iron: Iron artefacts	Vol. 2: *Environmental*	Dec. Sam.: Decorated Samian
Jewel.: Jewellery	An.: Animal remains	Mort.: Mortarium
Lea.: Leather	ca.: cattle	Mort. St.: Mortarium Stamp
Lead	c.: cat	Sam. St.: Samian Stamp

Part I: The Major Trenches: Excavations of the Fort and Annexe, 1977-85

Site 1(77)

Phase	Context	Description	Page & fig. nos of contexts in Volume II	Catalogued small finds in Volume I, environmental remains in Volume II and catalogued pottery in Volume III
I	50	Slot	P. 21; Fig. 11	
I	116	Slot	P. 21; Figs 11, 13	Sam. St. 87.
I	117	Slot	P. 21; Fig. 11	
I	118	Pit	P. 21; Fig. 11	
I	122	Pit	P. 21; Fig. 11	
I	156	Pit	P. 21; Fig. 11	Dec. Sam. 14.
I	159	Pit	P. 21; Fig. 11	
I	167	Pit/slot	P. 21; Figs 11, 13	
I/II	113	Pit?		Quern A. 60.
II	6	Annexe ditch	P. 21; Figs 12, 13	Coin 74; Cu.A. 60-61, 574, Cu.Arch.; Gl.V. 210, 278; Gl.O. 2; Quern A. 57A; Graffiti 30.
II	21	Latrine	Fig. 12	Gl.V. 209, 211, 276c.
II	46	Rampart	P. 28; Figs 12, 13 S.33	
II	47	Post-hole	P. 28; Fig. 12	
II	48	Post-hole	P. 28; Fig. 12	

Phase	Context	Description	Page & fig. nos of contexts in Volume II	Catalogued small finds in Volume I, environmental remains in Volume II and catalogued pottery in Volume III
II	49	Annexe rampart	P. 28; Figs 12, 13	Cu.A. 130, 354, Cu.Arch.; Quern A. 59A; Dec. Sam. 3-4; Mort. St. 22; Mort. St. 23.
II	52	Latrine	P. 28; Figs 12, 13 S.33	Coin 3, 91, 109; Cu.A. 158, 173, 344, 348, 700; Iron 70, 85; Gl.V. 95, 97; Gl.O. 1, 106, 307; Quern A. 19-22; Shale 2; Stone 2; Bone 7, 33; Dec. Sam. 5-11; Sam. St. 76; C.W. 532, 540, 554; Mort. 11, 54, 59, 89; Mort. St. 20.
II	111	Ditch	P. 21; Figs 12, 13 S.29	Coin 36; C.W. 144.
II	119	Post-hole	P. 28; Fig. 12	
II	120	Post-hole	P. 28; Fig. 12	
II	126	Ditch	P. 21; Figs 12, 13	Lead A. 395; Gl.O. 4; Sam. St. 90; Mort. 45.
II	127	Post-hole	P. 28; Fig. 12	Dec. Sam. 12.
II	130	Layer	P. 28	
II	139	Ditch	P. 21; Fig. 12	
II	153	Ditch	P. 21; Figs 12, 13	
II	154	Ditch	P. 21; Figs 12, 13	Lead A. 396.
II	155	Timber-lined pit	P. 28; Fig. 12	
II	157	Ditch	P. 21; Figs 12, 13	
II	158	Ditch	P. 21; Fig. 12	Sam. St. 68
II	165	Pit recut	P. 28; Fig. 13	
II	166	Pit recut	P. 28; Fig. 13	
III	3	Ditch fill	P. 28	
III	5	Ditch fill	P. 28	
III	42	Ditch fill	P. 28	
III	115	Pit	P. 28	Coin 16, 110; Cu.A. 695; Gl.V. 77b; Sam. St. 109; Mort. 65; Mort. St. 25.
III	148	Ditch fill	P. 28	
IV	7	Pit	P. 28; Fig. 14	
IV	10	Pit		Coin 15, 142; Lead A. 393-4; Iron 69, 89-90; Gl.V. 94, 96; Shale 1; Pot.C. 1; Bone 32; C.W. 486.
IV	54	Pit	P. 28; Fig. 14	Cu.Arch.; Graffiti 2; Sam. St. 74.
IV	121	Road gravel	P. 28; Fig. 14	Mort. 25.
IV	124	Drain	P. 28; Fig. 14	Sam. St. 116; C.W. 425.
IV	125	Drain	P. 28; Fig. 14	
IV	128	Slot	P. 28	
IV	129	Slot	P. 28	
IV	138	Pit	P. 28; Fig. 14	
IV	146	Slot	P. 28; Fig. 14	Coin 112.
IV	151	Pit/grave	P. 28; Fig. 14	Sam. St. 117
IV	152	Drain	P. 28; Fig. 14	C.W. 565.
	0			Coin 67, 107, 111; Cu.A. 105, 270, 448, 573, 575; Gl.V. 36, 77, 208, 276, 276b, e; Quern 13; Stone 73, 74, 98; Bone 128, 180; Dec. Sam. 1-2; Sam. St. 103, 105, 114, 121; Mort. 37.
	1			Stone 100.
	2			Iron 88.
	9			Stone 1.
	17			Quern A. 58A
	19			Coin 99; Cu.A. 642
	56			Coin 5.
	72			Graffiti 3; Sam. St. 73
	74			Cu.A. 416
	76			Cu.A. 152

Phase	Context	Description	Page & fig. nos of contexts in Volume II	Catalogued small finds in Volume I, environmental remains in Volume II and catalogued pottery in Volume III
	110			Cu.A. 501.
	113			Hum.
	140			Dec. Sam. 13.
	156			Cu.A. 320.
	158			Cu.A. 407
	Tr. 4			Pot.C. 2-4; Mort. St. 21.
	Tr. 6			Coin 125; Gl.O. 3; Gl.V. 41.
	Tr. 7			Coin 85.
	Tr. 9			Iron 91.
	Tr. 12			Coin 119, 136.
	Tr. 13			Gl.V. 212; C.W. 538.
	Tr. 15			Sam. St. 144.

Trench 9

Phase	Context	Description	Page & fig. nos of contexts in Volume II	Catalogued small finds in Volume I, environmental remains in Volume II and catalogued pottery in Volume III
I	958	Layer	P. 29	
I	982	Stake-hole	P, 29	
I	983	Ditch	P. 29	
I	996	Beam slot	P. 29	
I	1012	Feature	P. 29	
I	1013	Slot	P. 29	
I	1014	Stake-hole	P. 29	
II	501	Structure B wall	P. 35; Fig. 15	Coin 93; Cu.A. 106, 353; Gl.O. 107; Quern A. 23.
II	504	Structure B furnace/flue	P. 35; Fig. 15	
II	506	Structure B wall	P. 35; Fig. 15	
II	508	Structure B pit	P. 35	
II	701	Bath-house plunge bath	Figs 15-16	Coin 141, 146; Iron 32; Stone 4, 87; Cu.A. 450, 660, 740; Cu.Arch; Sam. St. 67.
II	702	Bath-house wall	P. 32; Figs 15-16	Stone 5, 6; Bone 20.
II	703	Bath-house wall	P. 29; Fig. 15	
II	704	Bath-house drain	P. 32; Fig. 15	
II	705	Pit	P. 37; Fig. 15	Sam. St. 70.
II	706	Central area culvert	Pp 35, 37; Fig. 15	Dec. Sam. 15
II	707	Bath-house wall	Pp 32, 37; Figs 15-16	
II	708	Layer	P. 37; Fig. 15	
II	709	Central area stone setting	P. 35; Fig. 15	
II	711	Central area culvert	P. 35; Fig. 15	
II	712	Bath-house wall	P. 35; Fig. 15	
II	713	Bath-house wall	P. 35; Fig. 15	
II	714	Bath-house extension	Pp 34, 35; Fig. 15	
II	716	Gravel road drain	P. 37; Fig. 16	
II	717	Central area culvert channel	P. 35; Fig. 15	Sam. St. 124.
II	721	Pit	P. 37; Fig. 15	
II	913=989	Structure B wall	P. 35	
II	914	Central area drain	P. 37; Fig. 15	
II	923	Bath-house drain	P. 32; Fig. 15	Coin 145; Lead A. 402; Pot.C. 5.
II	924	Bath-house flue stack	P. 35; Figs 15-16	

Phase	Context	Description	Page & fig. nos of contexts in Volume II	Catalogued small finds in Volume I, environmental remains in Volume II and catalogued pottery in Volume III
II	927	Bath-house floor	Pp 32, 34; Fig. 15	
II	928	Bath-house wall	P. 32; Fig. 15	
II	929	Bath-house wall	Pp 32, 34; Figs 15-16	
II	930	Bath-house wall	P. 32; Fig. 15	Quern A. 30.
II	931	Gravel road	Pp 35, 37; Fig. 15	Coin 25, 65, 73, 92; Cu.A. 131-2, 141, 156, 193, 366, 427, 502-4; Cu.Arch.; Lead 6; Gl.V.1, 43, 78, 98, 100, 279c, 280; Gl.O. 5; 16-19; Sam. St. 118, 123; C.W. 176, 566.
II	935	Bath-house wall	P. 35	
II	936	Bath-house wall	P. 35; Figs 15-16	
II	940	Bath-house drain: limestone	P.32; Fig. 15	
II	941	Bath-house foundation trench	P. 35	
II	943	Bath-house drain	P. 32; Fig. 15	
II	944	Bath-house wall	Pp 29, 32; Fig. 15	
II	945	Bath-house wall	Pp 29, 32; Fig. 15	
II	948	Bath-house layer	P. 35; Fig. 15	
II	957	Layer	P. 37; Fig. 15	
II	959	Bath-house post-hole	P. 35; Fig. 15	
II	960	Bath-house stake-hole	P.35; Fig. 15	
II	961	Bath-house post-hole	P. 35; Fig. 15	
II	962	Bath-house wall	P .32; Fig. 15	
II	965	Bath-house *pilae* stacks	P. 32	
II	967	Bath-house wall	Pp 34,35; Fig. 15	
II	968	Bath-house rubble layer	P. 32	
II	972	Construction trench	P. 37; Fig. 16	
II	973	Construction trench	P. 37; Fig. 16	
II	974	Pit	P. 37; Fig. 15	
II	979=504	Structure B furnace/flue	P. 35	
II	980	Structure B wall	P. 35; Fig. 15	
II	981	Wall	P. 35	
II	984	Gravel road drain	P. 37; Fig. 15	Cu.A. 200, 263.
II	987	Wall	P. 35	
II	988	Structure B	Pp 35, 37; Fig. 15	Cu.A. 101; Gl.V. 214b; Quern 14, Quern A.; 32-3, 61; Mort. 64; Mort. St. 26.
II	989	Structure B wall	P. 35: Fig. 15	Mort. 30.
II	1001	Layer	P. 37; Fig. 15	
II	1024	Bath-house wall	Pp 32, 34, 35; Fig. 15	
II	1025	Bath-house wall	P. 32; Figs 15-16	
II	1026	Bath-house wall	P. 34; Figs 15-16	
II	1027	Bath-house wall	P. 34; Figs 15-16	
II	1028	Bath-house wall	P.p 34, 35; Figs 15-16	
II	1029	*Caldarium*	P. 34	
II	1030	Bath-house floor	P. 34; Figs 15-16	
II	1031	Bath-house floor foundation	P. 34; Fig. 16	
II	1032	Bath-house flue	P. 34; Figs 15-16	
II	1033	Bath-house flue stack	P. 34; Figs 15-16	
II	1034	Bath-house flue stack	P. 34; Figs 15-16	
II	1035	Bath-house *pila*	P. 35; Fig. 16	
II	1036	Bath-house wall	P. 35	
II	1037	Bath-house wall	P. 35	

Phase	Context	Description	Page & fig. nos of contexts in Volume II	Catalogued small finds in Volume I, environmental remains in Volume II and catalogued pottery in Volume III
II	1039	Bath-house stone setting	P. 34; Fig. 15	
II	1040	*Tepidarium*	P. 32	
II	1043	Bath-house wall, robbed	P. 34; Figs 15-16	Stone 101.
II	1044	Bath-house flue stack	P. 35; Figs 15-16	
II	1045	Bath-house flue	Pp 32, 35; Figs 15-16	
II	1046	Bath-house flue	Pp 32, 35; Figs 15-16	
II	1047	Bath-house flue	P. 35; Fig. 16	
II	1048	Bath-house stone setting	P. 34; Fig. 15	
II	1049	Bath-house stone setting	P 35; Fig. 15	
II	1055	Bath-house foundation trench	P. 35; Fig. 15	
II	1056	Bath-house foundation trench	P. 35; Fig. 15	
II	1057	Bath-house foundation trench	P. 35; Fig. 15	
II	1058	Bath-house layer	P. 35; Fig. 15	
II	1062	Bath-house layer	P. 35; Fig. 15	Cu.A. 239.
II	1066	Bath-house layer	P. 35; Fig. 15	
II	1069	Bath-house layer	P. 35; Fig. 15	
II	1071	Bath-house flue	Pp 34, 35	
II	1076	Bath-house layer	P. 35; Fig. 15	
II	1077	Bath-house foundation trench	P. 35	
II	1080	Bath-house stone setting	P. 35; Fig. 15	
II	1081	Bath-house stone setting	P. 35	
II	1082	Bath-house flue	P. 35	
II	1083	Bath-house flue	P. 35	
II	1084	Bath-house flue	P. 35	
II	1085	Bath-house flue	P. 35	
II	1086	Bath-house layer	P. 35	Cu.A. 4.
III/IV	715	Bath-house destruction deposits	P. 37; Fig. 17	Coin 40, 105; Cu.A. 114, 125; Lead A. 400-401; Iron 28; Gl.O. 6-8; Stone 7-8; Bone 75; C.W. 509; Mort. 41, 71; Mort. St. 24.
III/IV	901	Well	P. 37; Fig. 17	
III/IV	902	Post-hole	P. 37; Fig. 17	
III/IV	903	Post-hole	P. 37; Fig. 17	
III/IV	904	Post-hole	P. 37; Fig. 17	
III/IV	905	Post-hole	P. 37; Fig. 17	
III/IV	906	Post-hole	P. 37; Fig. 1·	
III/IV	907	Post-hole	P. 37; Fig. 17	
III/IV	908	Post-hole	P. 37; Fig. 17	
III/IV	918	Post-hole	P. 37; Fig. 17	
III/IV	919	Post-hole	P. 37; Fig. 17	
III/IV	920	Post-hole	P. 37; Fig. 17	
III/IV	922	Post-hole	P. 37; Fig. 17	
III/IV	932	Post-hole	P. 37; Fig. 17	
III/IV	933	Pit	P. 37; Fig. 17	
III/IV	934	Robber trench	P. 37; Fig. 17	
III/IV	942	Robber trench	P. 37; Fig. 17	
III/IV	951	Slot	P. 37; Fig. 17	
III/IV	966	Burnt area	P. 37; Fig. 17	
III/IV	975	Robber trench	P. 37	

Phase	Context	Description	Page & fig. nos of contexts in Volume II	Catalogued small finds in Volume I, environmental remains in Volume II and catalogued pottery in Volume III
III/IV	990	Hearth	P. 37; Fig. 17	Cu.A. 186.
III/IV	998	Clay oven	P. 37; Fig. 17	
III/IV	999	Clay oven	P. 37; Fig. 17	
III/IV	1000	Layer	P. 37	Coin 81; Gl.V. 213.
III/IV	1002	Post-hole	P. 37	
III/IV	1003	Stake-hole row	P. 37; Fig. 17	
III/IV	1004	Cut lining	P. 37; Fig. 17	
III/IV	1006	Post-hole	P. 37; Fig. 17	
III/IV	1007	Post-hole	P. 37; Fig. 17	
III/IV	1008	Stake-hole row	P. 37; Fig. 17	
III/IV	1009	Post-hole	P. 37; Fig. 17	
III/IV	1010	Post-hole	P. 37; Fig. 17	
III/IV	1011	Post/stake-hole	P. 37; Fig. 17	
III/IV	1021	Burnt layer	P. 37; Fig. 17	
III/IV	1050	Bath-house destruction deposits	P. 37; Figs 16-17	Coin 121-2, 127, 132; Cu.A. 360, 451; Lead A. 404-6; Iron 92, 133; Gl.V. 214; Stone 88-9; Pot.C. 6; Bone 23, 129; C.W. 386, 394.
III/IV	1051	Bath-house destruction deposits	P. 37; Figs 16-17	
III/IV	1053	Wall	P. 37; Fig. 17	
III/IV	1065	Hearth	P. 37; Fig. 17	Coin 120.
III/IV	1068	Ditch	P. 37; Fig. 17	Bone 34.
III/IV	1075	Inhumation	P. 37; Fig. 17	Hum.
III/IV	1078	Layer	P. 37; Fig. 17	Cu.Arch.
III/IV	1079	Layer	P. 37; Fig. 17	
	0			Coin 113, 138; Cu.A. 87, 182, 751; Lead 35, Lead A. 397-9A; Gl.V. 101; Quern 2; Stone 86; Graffiti 31.
	401			Stone 3; Sam. St. 104.
	402			Cu.A. 86.
	502			Lead 1, Lead A. 399b.
	503			Coin 32; Quern A. 24-9.
	510			Gl.V. 279.
	925		P. 32	
	937			Cu.A. 183.
	938		P. 32	
	939		P. 32	
	964			Quern A. 31.
	986			Cu.A. 652, 756; Lead A. 403; Stone 9.
	992			Cu.A. 62.
	997			Cu.A. 194.
	1070			Gl.V. 99.

Trench 12

Phase	Context	Description	Page & fig. nos of contexts in Volume II	Catalogued small finds in Volume I, environmental remains in Volume II and catalogued pottery in Volume III
Ib	115	Post-hole	P. 40; Fig. 18	
Ib	116	Post-hole	P. 40	
Ib	117	Pit	P. 40; Fig. 18	
Ib	118	Pit	P. 40	
Ib	131	Post-hole	P. 40; Fig. 18	

Phase	Context	Description	Page & fig. nos of contexts in Volume II	Catalogued small finds in Volume I, environmental remains in Volume II and catalogued pottery in Volume III
Ib	132	Post-hole	P. 40	
Ib	142	Post-hole	P. 40; Fig. 18	
Ib	143	Post-hole	P. 40	
Ib	226	Gully	P. 40; Fig. 18	
Ib	228	Ditch	P. 40; Fig. 18	Cu.A. 201-2; Cruc. 11; Hum.
Ib	229	Slot	P. 40	
Ib	230	Slot	P. 40; Fig. 18	
Ib	234	Post-hole	P. 40; Fig. 18	
Ib	236	Post-hole	P. 40; Fig. 18	
Ib	238	Gully	P. 40; Fig. 18	
Ib	246	Layer	P. 40; Fig. 18	
Ib	250	Layer	P. 40; Fig. 18	
Ib	251	Post-hole	P. 40; Fig. 18	
Ib	252	Post-hole	P. 40; Fig. 18	
Ib	253	Post-hole	P. 40	
Ib	254	Layer	P. 40	
Ib	255	Layer	P. 40	
Ib	256	Slot	P. 40	
Ib	257	Ditch	P. 40; Fig. 18	
Ib	259	Post-hole	P. 40; Fig. 18	
Ib	261	Pit/cistern	P. 40; Fig. 18	
Ib	263	Post-hole	P. 40; Fig. 18	
Ib	264	Post-hole	P. 40; Fig. 18	
Ib	266	Gully	P. 40; Fig. 18	
Ib	268	Post-hole	P. 40; Fig. 18	
Ib	269	Layer	P. 40	
Ib	273	Ditch	P. 40	
Ib	305E	Fort ditch infill	P. 40; Fig. 19	
Ib	306	Levelling	P. 40; Figs 18-19	Cu.A. 507.
Ib	321	Pit	P. 40; Figs 18-19	
Ib	322	Pit	P. 40; Figs 18-19	Cu.Arch.; Dec. Sam. 22.
Ib	323	Pit	P. 40; Figs 18-19	An. ca.
Ib	326	Slot	P. 40; Fig. 18	
Ib	328	Layer	P. 40; Figs 18, 21	Cu.A. 187, 242, 297, 304, 705, Cu.Arch.; Gl.O. 9-11, 219; Bone 161, 163-4; Graffiti 1; An. ca.
Ib	329	Pit	P. 40; Fig. 18	C.W. 12
Ib	333	Layer	P. 40; Figs 18, 21	Cu.A. 335, 681; Gl.O. 11; C.W. 44.
Ib	336	Layer	P. 40; Figs 18, 21	Hum.
Ib	340A-B	Hearth and pit	P. 40; Fig. 18	
Ib	342A-F	Pit	P. 40; Fig. 18	
Ic	218	Levelling	P. 40	
Ic	233	Levelling	P. 40	
IIa	32	Pit	P. 43	
IIa	33	Pit	P. 43	
IIa	46	Military ditch	Pp 40, 43	
IIa	49	Post-hole	P. 40; Fig. 20	
IIa	50	Post-hole	P. 40	
IIa	51	Post-hole	P. 40; Fig. 20	
IIa	52	Post-hole	P. 40	
IIa	53	Pit	P. 40; Fig. 20	
IIa	63	Post-hole	P. 40; Fig. 20	
IIa	64	Post-hole	P. 40	
IIa	67	Well	P. 40; Fig. 20	
IIa	81	Slot	P. 43; Fig. 20	

Phase	Context	Description	Page & fig. nos of contexts in Volume II	Catalogued small finds in Volume I, environmental remains in Volume II and catalogued pottery in Volume III
IIa	82	Slot	P. 43	
IIa	133	Post-hole	P. 40; Fig. 20	
IIa	134	Post-hole	P. 40	
IIa	135	Gully	P. 40; Fig. 20	
IIa	136	Gully	P. 40	
IIa	137	Gully	P. 40; Fig. 20	
IIa	138	Gully	P. 40	
IIa	152	Road gravel	P. 40, Fig. 20	Cu.Arch.
IIa	153	Road foundation	P. 40; Fig. 20	
IIa	154	Road foundation	P. 40; Fig. 20	
IIa	158	Road drain	P. 40; Fig. 20	
IIa	159	Road drain	P. 40; Fig. 20	
IIa	172	Post-hole	P. 43; Fig. 20	
IIa	173	Post-hole	P. 43; Fig. 20	
IIa	188	Pit	P. 43; Fig. 20	
IIa	189	Annexe large pit	P. 40, Fig. 20	Coin 69; Cu.A. 704.
IIa	195	Post-hole	P. 43	
IIa	196	Stake-hole	P. 43; Fig. 20	
IIa	201	Layer	P. 40; Fig. 20	
IIa	204	Layer	P. 40; Fig. 20	
IIa	207	Slot	P. 40	
IIa	208	Layer	P. 40; Fig. 20	
IIa	209	Sand layers	P. 40; Fig. 20	Cu.Arch.
IIa	214	Layer	P. 40; Fig. 20	
IIa	216	Pit	P. 40; Fig. 20	
IIa	217	Annexe large pit	P. 40; Fig. 20	Cu.Arch.
IIa	231	Post-hole	P. 43	
IIa	232	Slot	P. 40; Fig. 20	Lead A. 408.
IIa	237	Layer	P. 43; Fig. 20	
IIa	239	Annexe road	P. 40	Coin 48; Cu.Arch.
IIa	240	Layer	P. 43	
IIa	241	Annexe layer	P. 43; Fig. 20	Coin 47.
IIa	242	Layer	P. 40	
IIa	243	Layer	P. 40	
IIa	244	Slot	P. 40; Fig. 20	
IIa	245	Layer	P. 43	
IIa	247	Layer	P. 43	
IIa	248	Layer	P. 40; Fig. 20	
IIa	249	Layer	P. 40	
IIa	258	Pit	P. 43; Fig. 20	
IIa	260	Layer	P. 43	
IIa	270	Slot	P. 40; Fig. 20	
IIa	271	Pit	P. 43	
IIa	272	Layer	P. 43; Fig. 20	
IIa	303	Rampart	P. 43	
IIa	308	Fort ditch	Pp 40, 43; Figs 19-20	
IIa	309	Well	Pp 40, 43; Fig. 20	
IIa	313	*Intervallum* road	P. 43; Figs 20-21	Cu.A. 334, Cu.Arch.; Gl.V. 281b-c; Gl.O. 221; Sam. St. 137.
IIa	317	Roadside drain ?	P. 43; Figs 20-21	Cu.A. 404, Cu.Arch.
IIa	318	Rampart	P. 43; Fig. 20	
IIa	320	Post-hole	P. 43	
IIa	327	Layer	P. 43; Figs 20-21	

Phase	Context	Description	Page & fig. nos of contexts in Volume II	Catalogued small finds in Volume I, environmental remains in Volume II and catalogued pottery in Volume III
IIa	332	Layer	P. 43	
IIb	47	Slot	P. 45; Fig. 22	
IIb	48	Slot	P. 45	Cu.Arch.
IIb	56	Post-hole	P. 45; Fig. 22	
IIb	57	Post-hole	P. 45	
IIb	106	Structure C: eavesdrip ?	P. 45; Fig. 22	
IIb	107=106	Structure C: eavesdrip ?	P. 45	Cu.A. 607, Cu.Arch.; Gl.O. 230; Cruc. 10.
IIb	161	Str. C: foundation trench	Pp 43, 45; Fig. 22	Cu.A. 653, Cu.Arch.
IIb	162	Structure C: floor slot	P. 43; Fig. 22	Coin 89; Lead A. 407; Cu.A. 703.
IIb	163	Slot	P. 43; Fig. 22	
IIb	165	Str. C foundation trench	P. 43; Fig. 22	
IIb	167	Layer	P. 45	
IIb	176	Str. C foundation trench	Pp 43, 45; Fig. 22	
IIb	182	Layer	P. 45	
IIb	183	Layer	P. 45; Fig. 22	
IIb	185	Slot	Pp 43, 45; Fig. 22	
IIb	186	Gully	P. 45; Fig. 22	
IIb	187	Slot	P. 45; Fig. 22	
IIb	190	Pit	P. 45; Fig. 22	
IIb	194	Annexe pit	P. 43; Fig. 22	Cu.A. 333.
IIb	200	Structure C foundation ?	P. 45	Cu.Arch.
IIb	212	Slot	P. 45	
IIb	219	Structure C stake-hole	P. 43; Fig. 22	
IIb	220	Structure C stake-hole	P. 43; Fig. 22	
IIb	221	Structure C stake-hole	P. 43; Fig. 22	
IIb	222	Structure C stake-hole	P. 43; Fig. 22	
IIb	250	Wall (Trench 8/Sondage 22)	P. 43; Fig. 22	
IIb	267	Structure C slot	P. 43; Fig. 22	
III	26	Annexe well infill	P. 45; Fig. 23	Gl.V. 102; Cruc. 9.
III	34	Fort ditch infill	P. 45; Figs 19, 23	
III	35	Disturbed rampart	P. 45; Figs 19, 23	Cu.A. 63.
III	45	Fort ditch infill	P. 45; Figs 19, 23	Cu.A. 19, Cu.Arch.
III	54B	Well hollow fill	P. 45; Fig. 23	
III	65	Annexe well infill	P. 45	
III	66	Annexe well infill	P. 45	Cu.A. 362; Iron 37.
III	67	Well	P. 45	
III	68	Annexe well infill	P. 45	
III	69	Annexe well infill	P. 45	Cu.A. 20, 675, Cu.Arch.; Iron 38-9; Gl.O. 220; Bot.
III	79	Fort ditch infill	P. 45; Fig. 23	
III	80	Fort ditch infill	P. 45; Fig. 23	
III	109	Fort ditch infill	P. 45; Figs 19, 23	
III	111	Fort ditch infill	P. 45	
III	112	Fort ditch infill	P. 45	
III	113	Fort ditch infill	P. 45; Figs 19, 23	
III	114	Fort ditch infill	P. 45; Figs 19, 23	Coin 49.
III	119	Fort ditch infill	P. 45	
III	120	Fort ditch infill	P. 45	
III	124	Fort ditch infill	Fig. 23	Cu.A. 296.
III	125	Fort ditch infill	P. 45	
III	126	Fort ditch infill	P. 45; Fig. 19	
III	127	Fort ditch infill	P. 45	
III	128	Fort ditch infill	P. 45	
III	166	Structure C: wall robbing	P. 45; Fig. 23	Cu.A. 505.
III	175	Wall rob	P. 45; Fig. 23	

Phase	Context	Description	Page & fig. nos of contexts in Volume II	Catalogued small finds in Volume I, environmental remains in Volume II and catalogued pottery in Volume III
III	181	Layer	P. 45; Fig. 23	
III	202	Layer	P. 45; Fig. 23	
III	203	Layer	P. 45; Fig. 23	
III	206	Hearth	P. 45; Fig. 23	
III	213	Hearth	P. 45; Fig. 23	
III	215	Post-hole	P. 45; Fig. 23	
III	304	Fort ditch infill	P. 45; Figs19, 23	
III	305	Fort ditch infill	P. 45; Fig. 23	Coin 78; Cu.Arch.; Lead 17; Graffiti 26; Sam. St. 108; Hum.
III	310	Accumulation	P. 45; Figs 21, 23	Cu.A. 373; Lead A. 410; Gl.V. 2, 281d; Stone 11; Mort. 31; An. ca., s../g., p.
III	311	Fort ditch infill	P. 45; Figs 19, 23	
III	312	Fort ditch infill	P. 45; Figs 21, 23	
III	314	Disturbed rampart	P. 45; Fig. 23	Coin 41.
III	315B-C	Accumulation	P. 45; Figs 21, 23	Cu.Arch.; Gl.V. 281; An. ca, s./g., p.
III	334	Fort ditch infill	P. 45; Fig. 23	
III	335	Fort ditch infill	P. 45; Fig. 23	
IV	27	Kiln destruction	P. 45; Fig. 24	
IV	54A	Post-hole	P. 45	
IV	55	Post-hole fill	P. 45; Fig. 24	
IV	71	Lime kiln fill	P. 45; Figs 19, 24	Coin 30; Cu.A. 363.
IV	75	Lime kiln fill	P. 45; Fig. 24	
IV	86	Lime kiln: clay	P. 45; Figs 21, 24	
IV	87	Lime kiln fill	P. 45; Fig. 24	
IV	88	Lime kiln: stonework	P. 45; Figs 21, 24	
IV	89	Lime kiln pit	P. 45; Fig. 24	
IV	90	Lime kiln pit	P. 45; Fig. 24	
IV	121	Kiln flue channel	P. 45; Fig. 24	
IV	122	Post-hole	P. 45; Fig. 24	
IV	123	Post-hole	P. 45; Fig. 19	
IV	151	Stonework	P. 45	
IV	160	Stonework	P. 45; Fig. 24	
IV	168	Lime kiln fill	P. 45	Gl.V. 215; Bone 41; Mort. 53.
IV	169	Post-hole	P. 45; Fig. 24	
IV	170	Lime kiln fill	P. 45	Gl.V. 103; Stone 104.
IV	184	Post-hole	P. 45	
IV	191	Lime kiln	P. 45; Fig. 21	
IV	192	Lime kiln	P. 45; Fig. 21	Cu.A. 303.
IV	193	Layer	P. 45	
IV	205	Post-hole	P. 45	
IV	210	Lime kiln fill	P. 45; Fig. 24	
IV	225	Lime kiln fill	P. 45; Fig. 21	
IV	315A	Pit	P. 45; Fig. 24	Sculp. 1.
IV	330	Post-hole	P. 45; Fig. 24	
IV	331	Stake-hole	P. 45; Fig. 24	
	6			Cruc. 12.
	7			Coin 80, 129; Cu.A. 233, 685; Gl.V. 103b; Stone 102-3.
	4			Cu.Arch.
	62			Stone 10.
	70			Bone 203; Dec. Sam. 20.
	301			Cu.A. 153, 506; Quern A. 34; Bone 192; Graffiti 32 Sam. St. 89.
	302			Cu.Arch; Mort. 52.
	308			Lead A. 409.
	316			Dec. Sam. 21.

Trench 13

Phase	Context	Description	Page & fig. nos of contexts in Volume II	Catalogued small finds in Volume I, environmental remains in Volume II and catalogued pottery in Volume III
Ia	202	Pre-fort layer	P. 50	Gl.O. 232.
Ia	225	Pre-fort layer	P. 50	
Ia	351	Pre-fort layer	P. 50	
Ia	382	Pre-fort layer	P. 50	
Ia	401	Pre-fort layer	P. 50	
Ia	404	Pre-fort layer	P. 50	
Ib	25	Post-hole	P. 50; Fig. 25	
Ib	29	Slot	P. 50; Fig. 25	
Ib	328	Slot	P. 50; Fig. 25	
Ib	367	Barrack post-hole	P. 50; Fig. 25	Quern A. 64; Bot. (Appendix 4).
Ib	387	Slot	P. 50; Fig. 25	
Ib	388	Post-hole	P. 50	
Ib	389	Slot	P. 50; Fig. 25	
Ib	390	Layer	P. 50; Fig. 28	
Ib	395	Slot	Figs 25, 28	Coin 7, 9, 11, 52.
Ib	397	Occupation surface	P. 50; Figs 25, 28	Cu.A. 244, Cu.Arch.
Ib	405	Post-hole	P. 50; Fig. 25	
Ib	407	Slot	P. 50; Fig. 25	
Ib	408	Slot	P. 50; Fig. 25	
Ib	409	Slot	P. 50; Fig. 25	
Ib	410	Slot	P. 50; Fig. 25	
Ib	411	Slot	P. 50; Fig. 25	
Ib	412	Slot	P. 50; Fig. 25	
Ib	413	Slot	P. 50; Fig. 25	
Ib	414	Slot	P. 50; Fig. 25	
Ib	415	Slot	P. 50; Fig. 25	
Ib	416	Post-hole	P. 50; Fig. 25	
Ib	417	Post-hole	P. 50; Fig. 25	
Ib	418	Post-hole	P. 50; Fig. 25	
Ib	419	Post-hole	P. 50; Fig. 25	
Ib	431	Slot	P. 50; Fig. 25	
Ib	435	Post-hole	P. 50; Fig. 25	
Ib	437	Slot	P. 50; Fig. 25	
Ic	346	Layer	P. 51	
IIa	7	Rampart	P. 51; Figs 26, 28	
IIa	8	*Intervallum* road foundation	P. 52; Fig. 26	
IIa	10	*Intervallum* road surface	P. 52; Fig. 26	
IIa	15	*Intervallum* road foundation	P. 52; Fig. 26	
IIa	102	Fort ditch	P. 51; Fig. 26	Bot. (Appendix 4).
IIa	203	Rampart revetment trench	P. 51; Fig. 26	Jewel. 1; Cu.A. 686; Gl.V. 282e-f.
IIa	212	Rampart revetment trench	P. 52; Fig. 26	
IIa	215	Rampart revetment trench	P. 51; Fig. 26	
IIa	218	Structure E post-hole	P. 51; Fig. 26	
IIa	219	Structure E wall foundation	P. 51; Fig. 26	
IIa	224	Carriageway	P. 51; Fig. 26	
IIa	226	Structure E post-hole	P. 51; Figs 26-7	
IIa	227	Structure E post-hole	P. 51; Figs 26-7	
IIa	228	Structure E post-hole	P. 51; Figs 26-7	
IIa	229	Structure E post-hole	P. 51; Fig. 26	
IIa	230	Structure E slot	P. 51; Fig. 26	
IIa	231	Structure E post-hole	P. 51; Fig. 26	
IIa	232	Post-hole	P. 52	
IIa	233	Structure E post-hole	P. 51; Fig. 26	

Phase	Context	Description	Page & fig. nos of contexts in Volume II	Catalogued small finds in Volume I, environmental remains in Volume II and catalogued pottery in Volume III
IIa	234	Structure E post-hole	P. 51; Fig. 26	
IIa	235	Structure E post-hole fill	P. 51; Fig. 26	
IIa	240	Structure E post-hole	P. 51; Figs 26-7	
IIa	309	*Intervallum* road foundation	P. 52; Figs 26, 28	
IIa	310	*Intervallum* road surface	P. 51; Figs 26, 28	Sam. St. 126
IIa	313	Rampart	P. 51; Figs 26, 28	
IIa	315	*Intervallum* road foundation	P. 52; Figs 26, 28	Cu.Arch.; Quern A. 62-3.
IIa	316	*Intervallum* road foundation	P. 52; Fig. 26	
IIa	341=440	Structure F post-hole	P. 52	
IIa	347	Layer	P. 52	
IIa	353	Structure F layer	P. 52; Fig. 26	Coin 72; Gl.V. 3; Gl.O. 231.
IIa	354	*Intervallum* road foundation	P. 52	
IIa	360	Structure F post-hole	P. 52; Fig. 26	
IIa	363	Structure F post-hole	P. 52; Fig. 26	
IIa	364	Structure F post-hole	P. 52; Fig. 26	
IIa	366	Layer	P. 52; Fig. 26	
IIa	368	Layer	P. 52; Fig. 26	
IIa	373	Structure F slot	P. 52; Fig. 26	
IIa	374	Post-hole	P. 52; Fig. 26	
IIa	376	Layer	P. 52; Fig. 26	
IIa	378=353	Structure F layer	P. 52	Cu.A. 243; Lead A. 414; Gl.V. 5; Graffiti 27; Mort. 117.
IIa	380	Layer	P. 52	
IIa	384	Post-hole	P. 52; Fig. 26	
IIa	394	Structure F relaid floor	P. 52; Fig. 28	
IIa	396	Structure F post-hole	P. 52; Figs 26, 28	
IIa	398	*Intervallum* road drain	P. 51; Fig. 26	
IIa	400	Structure F slot	P. 52; Fig. 26	
IIa	402	Layer	P. 52; Fig. 26	
IIa	403	Layer	P. 52; Fig. 26	
IIa	406	Structure F post-hole	P. 52; Fig. 26	
IIa	420	*Intervallum* road foundation	P. 52; Fig. 28	
IIa	421A-C	Layer	P. 52; Fig. 28	
IIa	422	Layer	P. 52; Fig. 28	
IIa	423	*Intervallum* road foundation	P. 52; Fig. 28	
IIa	424	Layer	P. 52; Fig. 26	
IIa	425	Structure F hearth	P. 52; Fig. 26	
IIa	426	Structure F post-hole	P. 52; Fig. 26	
IIa	427	Layer	P. 52	
IIa	428	Structure F floor	P. 52; Figs 26, 28	
IIa	429	Structure F hearth	P. 52; Fig. 26	Stone 106.
IIa	430	Structure F slot	P. 52; Fig. 26	
IIa	432	Post-hole	P. 52; Fig. 26	
IIa	433	Structure F post-hole	P. 52; Fig. 26	
IIa	434	Structure F post-hole	P. 52; Fig. 26	
IIa	436	Post-hole	P. 52; Fig. 26	
IIa	438	Structure F post-hole	P. 52; Fig. 26	
IIa	439	Structure F post-hole	P. 52; Fig. 26	
IIa	440	Structure F post-hole	P. 52; Fig. 26	
IIb	20	Structure F floor	P. 53; Figs 28-9	
IIb	26	Layer	P. 53; Fig. 29	
IIb	30	Structure F floor	P. 53; Figs 28-9	Lead A. 411; Stone 75.
IIb	31	Layer	P. 53; Figs 28-9	Gl.V. 282c; Sam. St. 81.
IIb	317	Layer	P. 53; Fig. 29	Cu.A. 768.
IIb	320	Structure F floor	P. 53	

Phase	Context	Description	Page & fig. nos of contexts in Volume II	Catalogued small finds in Volume I, environmental remains in Volume II and catalogued pottery in Volume III
IIb	321	Layer	P. 53	
IIb	322	Structure F floor	P. 53; Figs 28-9	
IIb	323	Structure F hearth	P. 53; Figs 28-9	
IIb	324	Layer	P. 53; Fig. 29	Cu.A. 278.
IIb	325	Layer	P. 53	
IIb	329=323	Structure F hearth	P. 53	
IIb	330=26	Layer	P. 53	
IIb	331	Structure F floor	P. 53; Fig. 29	
IIb	332	Structure F floor	P. 53	
IIb	333	Structure F hearth	P. 53; Fig. 29	Gl.V. 283.
IIb	336	Structure F floor	P. 53; Fig. 29	
IIb	339	Post-hole	P. 53	
IIb	340	Post-hole	P. 53; Fig. 29	
IIb	342	Layer	P. 53; Fig. 29	
IIb	343	Layer	P. 53; Fig. 29	Gl.V. 4.
IIb	352	Layer	P. 53; Fig. 29	
IIb	355	Post-hole	P. 53; Fig. 29	
IIb	357	Post-hole	P. 53; Fig. 29	
IIb	358	Post-hole	P. 53; Fig. 29	
IIb	359	Post-hole	P. 53; Fig. 29	
IIb	361	Hearth	P. 53; Fig. 29	Gl.O. 13; Bot. (Appendix 4).
IIb	362	Hearth	P. 53; Fig. 29	
IIb	369	Layer	P. 53; Fig. 29	
IIb	372	Hearth	P. 53; Fig. 29	
IIb	375	Post-hole	P. 53; Fig. 29	
IIb	377	Post-hole	P. 53; Fig. 29	
IIb	381	Slot	P. 53	
IIb	385=343	Layer	P. 53	Dec. Sam. 24; Sam. St. 91.
IIb	386	Layer	P. 53; Fig. 29	
III	4	Destruction layer	P. 56; Fig. 28	Gl.V. 79, 218.
III	9	Fort ditch infill	P. 53	
III	11	Fort ditch infill	P. 53	Dec. Sam. 23.
III	12	Fort ditch infill	P. 53	
III	13	Layer	P. 56	
III	16	Burnt daub layer	P. 53	
III	19	Burnt daub layer	P. 53; Fig. 28	
III	27	Fort ditch infill	P. 53	
III	102A-B	Fort ditch infill	P. 53	
III	306	Destruction layer	P. 56	Cu.A. 282-4, 305, 772; Stone 16.
III	314	Layer	P. 56	Cu.Arch.; Iron 71.
III	319=019	Destruction layer	P. 53	
III	326	Destruction layer	P. 56	
III	327	Destruction layer	P. 56	
III	334	Destruction layer	P. 56	
III	337	Destruction layer	P. 56	
III	338	Destruction layer	P. 56	Cu.A. 351, Cu.Arch.; Gl.V. 5.
III	345	Destruction layer	P. 56	Coin 87; Cu.A. 21, Cu.Arch.; Stone 17.
IV	17	Post-hole	P. 56; Fig. 30	
IV	18	Slot	P. 56; Figs 28, 30	
IV	21	Hearth	P. 56; Fig. 30	
IV	22	Hearth	P. 56; Fig. 30	
IV	23	Post-hole	P. 56; Fig. 30	
IV	24	Slot	P. 56; Fig. 30	
IV	28	Building post-hole	P. 56; Fig. 30	Gl.V. 282b.

Phase	Context	Description	Page & fig. nos of contexts in Volume II	Catalogued small finds in Volume I, environmental remains in Volume II and catalogued pottery in Volume III
IV	216	Pit	P. 56; Fig. 30	
IV	217	Pit	P. 56	
IV	223	Slot	P. 56; Fig. 30	
IV	237	Post-hole	P. 56; Fig. 30	
IV	238	Post-hole	P. 56; Fig. 30	
IV	312	Pit	P. 56; Fig. 30	
IV	318	Slot	P. 56; Fig. 30	
IV	344	Pit	P. 56; Fig. 30	
IV	348	Pit	P. 56; Fig. 30	
IV	349	Pit	P. 56; Fig. 30	
IV	350	Pit	P. 56; Fig. 30	
IV	365	Hearth	P. 56; Fig. 30	
IV	370	Hearth	P. 56	
IV	371	Hearth	P. 56; Fig. 30	Coin 84.
IV	379	Gully	P. 56; Fig. 30	Coin 42.
	1			Cruc. 13; Stone 90.
	3			Gl.V. 283b.
	200			Stone 12.
	201			Coin 51, 126; Cu.A. 133, Cu.Arch.; Gl.V. 217, 282d; Bone 204.
	236			Cu.Arch.; Gl.O. 12.
	301			Cu.A. 195; Stone 13, 105.
	302			Coin 88, 133, 152; Cu.A. 381, 428, 463, 508-9, 741, 767, Cu.Arch.; Lead A. 412-13; Iron 47; Gl.V. 5, 216, 282; Cruc. 14; Stone 14-15; C.W. 545; Mort. 36, 109.

Trench 14

Phase	Context	Description	Page & fig. nos of contexts in Volume II	Catalogued small finds in Volume I, environmental remains in Volume II and catalogued pottery in Volume III
Ib	239	Structure G clay	Fig.31	Coin 6.
Ib	199	Pit lining	P. 57; Fig. 31	
Ib	200	Pit lining	P. 57; Fig. 31	
Ib	235	Layer	P. 57	
Ib	237	Pit lining	P. 57; Fig. 31	
Ib	238	Pit	P. 56-7, 61; Fig. 31	
Ib	239A	Structure G clay layer	P. 57	
Ib	240	Structure G stake-holes	P. 57; Fig. 31	
Ib	241	Layer	P. 57	
Ib	242	Slot	P. 56-7	
Ib	243	Pit 408 layer	P. 57; Fig. 31	
Ib	244	Pit 408 layer	P. 57; Fig. 31	
Ib	245	Str. G wattle impressions	P. 57; Fig. 31	
Ib	246	Wattle impressions	P. 57; Fig. 31	
Ib	247	Str. G foundation gully	P. 57; Fig. 31	
Ib	401	Pit 408 layer	P. 57; Fig. 31	
Ib	402	Pit 408 layer	P. 57	
Ib	403	Pit 408 layer	P. 57	
Ib	404	Pit 408 layer	P. 57	
Ib	405	Pit 408 layer	P. 57	
Ib	406	Post-hole	P. 57; Fig. 31	
Ib	407	Gully	P. 57; Fig. 31	

Phase	Context	Description	Page & fig. nos of contexts in Volume II	Catalogued small finds in Volume I, environmental remains in Volume II and catalogued pottery in Volume III
Ib	408	Pit	P. 56-7; Fig. 31	
Ic	108	Midden (waterlogged)	P. 57, 61; Figs 32, 36 S.3 & S.35	Coin 1, 4, 12, 17, 39; Jewel. 2; Cu.A. 11, 23-4, 43, 99, 134, 142, 151, 155, 159, 196, 204-6, 209, 219, 223, 226-7, 298, 309, 336, 370, 429-31, 510, 576, 661, 676, 687, 696, Cu.Arch.; Lead A. 416-19; Iron 1, 44-6, 54, 61, 77, 79, 96-7, 106-11, 121, 128; Gl.V. 6, 284, 284b, 285, 288; Gl.O. 16-19, 233, 235; Quern 11-12; Stone 21-3. 83; Bone 156, 165, 172-3, 193-4; Lea. 1-17, 19-34, 40-59, 61-189; Wood 1-5, 11, 14-15, 17-25, 30-43; Tex. 1-8; Graffiti 5-6, 43; Dec. Sam. 27-31; Sam. St. 71, 94-5, 97 107, 129; C.W. 7, 42-3, 52-4, 60, 63, 72, 74, 78, 84, 89, 91, 93, 96, 101, 104, 108, 112, 125, 127, 143; Mort. 97; Bot.; An. ca., s./g., p., h, d.
Ic	112	Midden sealing	P. 61; Fig. 32(ii)	Gl.O. 234; Bone 181; Wood 44; Sam. St. 138.
Ic	172	Midden sealing	P. 61; Fig. 32(ii)	Coin 13, 56; Cu.A. 224, 310; Gl.V. 6, 81.
Ic	175	Turves	P. 61	
Ic	177	Midden sealing	P. 61	Gl.O. 237; Sam. St. 100.
Ic	178	Midden sealing	P. 61	Cu.A. 769.
Ic	182	Structure H hearth	P. 60; Fig. 32(i) & Fig. 36, S.3	
Ic	183	Structure H post-hole	Fig. 32(i)	
Ic	184	Structure H wattle	P. 60; Fig. 32 S.30a	Coin 38; Wood 26.
Ic	186	Structure H wattle	P. 57; Fig. 32 S.30a	Wood 26.
Ic	186B	Structure H wattle infill - clay	P. 60	
Ic	187	Structure H planks	P. 60; Fig. 32(i)	Wood 27.
Ic	189	Layer	P. 61	
Ic	190	Gravel sealing	P. 60; Fig. 32(i)	
Ic	191	Stake-hole	P. 61	
Ic	192	Slot	P. 61	
Ic	193	Clay sealing	P. 60	
Ic	194	Structure H floor (or midden)	P. 60	Cu.A. 511; Lead A. 421; Wood 7.
Ic	195	Layer	P. 61; Fig. 36 S.3	Wood 45.
Ic	196	Structure H floor (or midden)	P. 60;	Wood 8, 12, 16, 46; Mort. 87.
Ic	197	Hearth	P. 60; Fig. 32(i)	
Ic	198	Hearth	P. 60; Fig. 32(i)	
Ic	206=220	Midden (waterlogged)	P. 57	Coin 63; Stone 24; Wood 47; Dec. Sam. 33; Mort. 55, 63; An. ca., s./g., h., d., c.
Ic	215	Turves	P. 61; Fig. 32(ii)	
Ic	216	Clay debris or upcast	P. 61; Fig. 32(i)	
Ic	219	Midden sealing	P. 61; Fig. 32(i)	Gl.V. 221; Sam. St. 102; ca.
Ic	220	Midden (dry)	Pp 57, 61; (i) Fig. 32(i)	Coin 53; Cu.A. 452, 513, 654, Cu.Arch.; Lead 25; Gl.O. 14-15; Bone 122, 143, 195; Lea. 18, 60; Wood 9, 13, 48. Dec. Sam. 35; C.W. 39, 66-7, 69, 92, 107-8; Mort. 102. An. ca., s./g., p., h., d, c.
Ic	232	Turves	P. 61; Fig. 32(ii)	Gl.V. 6; Dec. Sam. 37; Sam. St. 111; ca.
Ic	233	Post-hole	P. 61; Fig. 32(i)	Bone 182.
Ic	236	Post-hole	P. 61; Fig. 32(i)	
Ic	313	Midden (dry)	Pp 57, 61; Fig. 32(i)	Gl.V. 82b; Sam. St. 120; C.W. 16, 129, 132; An. ca., s./g., h., d.; c.

Phase	Context	Description	Page & fig. nos of contexts in Volume II	Catalogued small finds in Volume I, environmental remains in Volume II and catalogued pottery in Volume III
Ic	318	Midden (dry)	Pp 57, 61; Fig. 32(i)	Cu.A. 64; Gl.V. 6, 104; Sam. St. 130; C.W. 6, 11, 38, 40; Mort. 46; An. ca., s./g., h., d., c.
Id	107	Structure I? hearths	P. 62; Fig. 36 S.35	Gl.O. 109.
Id	115	Layer	P. 62; Fig. 36, S.3	
Id	117	Layer	P. 62; Fig. 36, S.3	
Id	118	Layer	P. 62; Fig. 36, S.35	
Id	119	Layer	P. 62; Fig. 36, S.3	
Id	120	Slot	P. 62; Fig. 36, S.3	
Id	122	Layer	P. 62; Fig. 36, S.35	
Id	124	Layer	P. 62	
Id	125	Hearth	P. 62; Fig. 36, S.35	
Id	126	Layer	P. 62	
Id	127	Layer	P. 62	
Id	144	Structure I slot	P. 62; Fig. 33(ii)	Coin 54.
Id	145	Stake-hole	P. 62	
Id	146	Stake-hole	P. 62	
Id	147	Stake-hole	P. 62	
Id	148	Stake-hole	P. 62	
Id	152	Structure I slot	P. 62; Fig. 33(ii)	Gl.O. 21.
Id	154	Structure I gravel layer	P. 62	
Id	155	Structure I hearth area	P. 62; Fig. 33(ii)	Cu.Arch.
Id	156	Structure I hearth	P. 62; Fig. 33(ii)	Cu.Arch.
Id	157	Structure I slot	P. 62; Fig. 33(ii)	
Id	159	Structure I slot	P. 62; Fig. 33(ii)	
Id	160	Structure I slot	P. 62; Fig. 33(ii)	
Id	161	Structure I slot	P. 62; Fig. 33(ii)	
Id	162	Layer	P. 62; Fig. 33(ii)	
Id	164	Charcoal	P. 62	
Id	165	Layer	P. 62	
Id	166	Structure I floor	P. 62; Fig. 33(ii)	
Id	167	Structure I floor	P. 62; Fig. 33(ii)	
Id	168	Structure I relaid floor	P. 62; Fig. 33(ii)	Gl.V. 45, 219.
Id	169	Structure I relaid floor	P. 62; Fig. 33(ii)	An. ca.
Id	170=168	Structure I relaid floor	P. 62	
Id	171	Structure I hearth	P. 62; Fig. 33(ii)	
Id	173	Layer	P. 62	
Id	174	Structure I material on floor	P. 62	Cu.A. 775.
Id	176	Structure I hearth surround	P. 62; Fig. 33(ii)	
Id	179	Structure I floor	P. 61	Gl.V. 82; Dec. Sam. 32.
Id	180	Structure I hearth	P. 62; Fig. 33(i)	
Id	181	Structure I floor	P. 62; Fig. 33(i)	
Id	225	Stake-hole	P. 62; Fig. 33(i)	
Id	226	Slot	P. 62; Fig. 33(i)	
Id	227	Stake-hole	P. 62; Fig. 33(i)	
Ie	106	Hearth	P. 63; Fig; 36	C.W. 29, 80, 94, 98; Hum.
Ie	107	Hearth	P. 63; Fig. 36	
Ie	113	Layer	P. 63; Fig. 36, S.3	
Ie	114	Structure J floor	P. 63; Figs 34, 36 S.3	Gl.O. 20; C.W. 76.
Ie	121	Ash and charcoal	P. 63; Fig. 34	
Ie	123=114	Structure J floor	P. 63	
Ie	130A-S	Structure J post-holes	P. 62-3; Fig. 34	
Ie	132	Structure J floor	P. 63; Fig. 34	Coin 70.
Ie	133	Structure J hearth	P. 63; Fig. 34	

Phase	Context	Description	Page & fig. nos of contexts in Volume II	Catalogued small finds in Volume I, environmental remains in Volume II and catalogued pottery in Volume III
Ie	134	Structure J slot	P. 62-3; Fig. 34	
Ie	135	Structure J wall	P. 62-3; Fig. 34	
Ie	136	Structure J post-hole	P. 62-3; Fig. 34	
Ie	138	Structure J post-hole	P. 62-3; Fig. 34	
Ie	139	Structure J slot	P. 63; Fig. 34	Gl.V. 80.
Ie	140	Hearth	P. 63	
Ie	141	Structure J edge-set plank	P. 63; Fig. 34	
Ie	142	Structure J post-hole	P. 62-3; Fig. 34	
Ie	143	Structure J floor	P. 63; Fig. 34	
Ie	149	Levelling prior to Structure J	P. 62; Fig. 36 S.35	Cu.A. 445; Lead A. 420; Gl.V. 223; 289b; Mort. 47, 48.
Ie	150	Levelling prior to Structure J	P. 62; Fig. 34	
Ie	151	Post-hole	P. 63	
Ie	153=139	Structure J slot	P. 63	Bone 140-41; C.W. 45.
Ie	158	Structure J foundation	P. 62	Gl.V. 289.
Ie	163	Structure J foundation	P. 62	
Ie	185	Structure J foundation	P. 62	
Ie	205	Layer	P. 63	
Ie	214	Layer	P. 63; Fig. 34	Lead A. 423; Sam. St. 106; An. ca.; Hum.
Ie	221	Structure J hearth	P. 63; Fig. 34	
Ie	222	Structure J ash & charcoal	P. 63; Fig. 34	
Ie	223	Post-hole	P. 63	Cu.Arch.
Ie	224	Structure J ash & charcoal	P. 63; Fig. 34	
Ie	228	Layer	P. 63	
Ie	229	Post-hole	P. 63; Fig. 34	
Ie	230	Slot	P. 63; Fig. 34	
Ie	231	Slot	P. 63; Fig. 34	
Ie	234	Structure J post-hole	P. 62-3; Fig. 34	
Ie	317	Pit	P. 63; Fig. 34	Cu.A. 65; Gl.V. 63; Gl.O. 108; C.W. 27; An. ca.
Ie	319	Post-hole	P. 63; Fig. 34	
II	101	Rampart	P. 64; Fig. 35(ii)	Cu.A. 88, 203, 218, Cu.Arch.; C.W. 147; Mort. St. 46; An. ca.; Hum.
II	102	Structure J destruction	P. 64; Fig. 35(ii)	Coin 55; Cu.A. 306, 742, Cu.Arch.; Gl.O. 236; Bone 171; C.W. 181; Hum.
II	103	Rampart core	P. 64; Fig. 35(ii)	
II	104	Rampart	P. 64; Fig. 35(ii)	Bot.
II	105	Rampart	P. 64; Fig. 35(i)	
II	110	Rampart	P. 64; Fig. 35(ii)	Gl.V. 224.
II	137	Stake-hole	P. 65	
II	202	*Intervallum* road	P. 64; Fig. 35(ii)	Cu.A. 197, Cu.Arch.; Gl.V. 82c, 286, 286b; C.W. 150, 183.
II	203	Road drain	P. 64; Fig. 35(ii)	C.W. 182
II	207=308	*Intervallum* road drain fill	P. 64	Cu.A. 697; Dec. Sam. 34.
II	209	*Intervallum* road repair	P. 64	
II	211	*Intervallum* road	P. 64; Fig. 35(i)	Coin 77; Cu.A. 706, Cu.Arch.
II	212=110	Rampart		C.W. 530, 543-4.
II	213	*Intervallum* road	P. 64	Gl.V. 287.
II	217	*Intervallum* road	P. 64; Fig. 35(i)	
II	218	*Intervallum* road	P. 64; Fig. 35(ii)	C.W. 164.
II	270	Rampart	P. 64; Fig. 37	
II	271A	Rampart wash	P. 64; Fig. 37	
II	301	Structure K destruction	P. 64	Gl.V. 37, 222; Graffiti 4.
II	306	Structure K floor	P. 65; Fig. 35(ii)	

Phase	Context	Description	Page & fig. nos of contexts in Volume II	Catalogued small finds in Volume I, environmental remains in Volume II and catalogued pottery in Volume III
II	307	Destruction layer	P. 64	
II	308	*Intervallum* road drain fill	P. 64; Fig. 35(ii)	
II	309	*Intervallum* road	P. 64; Fig. 35(ii)	
II	312	Structure K slot	P. 65; Fig. 35(ii)	Sam. St. 77; C.W. 162, 177.
II	314	Structure K floor	P. 65; Fig. 35(ii)	
II	315	Pit	P. 65	C.W. 168, 174.
II	316	Post-hole	P. 65	
III	36	Layer		Quern A. 36; Stone 109.
III	39	Pit	Pp 65, 68; Fig.38	Cu.A. 245, 329, Cu.Arch.; Lead A. 415; Cruc. 15-16; Stone 20; Bone 1, 174, 205; Lea. 35; C.W. 381, 389, 391, 402-3, 408; Hum.
III	104C	Layer	P. 68; Fig. 36 S.35	
III	110C	Rampart slip	P. 68; Fig.35 (ii)	Gl.V. 64; Hum.
III	129	Rampart deposit	P. 65; Fig. 38	C.W. 383.
III	201	Pit	Pp 65 & 68 Fig. 38 & Fig. 36 S.3	Coin 100; Cu.A. 337, 512, 770-71, Cu.Arch.; Lead A. 422; Gl.V. 286c-d; Stone 110; Bone 131, 142; Sam. St. 139; C.W. 390. 201, 393, 400; C.W. 404, 418.
III	208	Layer	P. 68	
III	210	Hearth	P. 68; Fig. 38	
III	225	Stake-hole	P. 65	
III	226	Slot	P. 65; Fig. 36 S.3	
III	227	Stake-hole	P. 65	
III	310	Pit	Pp 65, 68; Fig. 38	Cu.A. 234; Lead A. 424; Bone 176; Wood 49.
III	311	Slot	P. 68; Fig. 38	Cu.A. 382.
	2		P. 65	Stone 18; Bone 130; Dec. Sam. 25; C.W. 535.
	4			Stone 107-8.
	6			Stone 19, 76-7.
	7			C.W. 537
	12			Quern A. 65.
	19			C.W. 546.
	22			Stone 91-2.
	27			Dec. Sam. 26.
	32			Iron 17; Quern A. 35.
	37			Cu.Arch.; Gl.V. 7; Quern A. 37; C.W. 524.
	192			Slag 32.
	212			Cu.Arch.; Gl.V. 220; Bone 175.
	302			Sam. St. 113

Trench 15I

Phase	Context	Description	Page & fig. nos of contexts in Volume II	Catalogued small finds in Volume I, environmental remains in Volume II and catalogued pottery in Volume III
Ia	35	Pit	P. 68	
Ia	36	Topsoil	P. 68; Fig. 39	
Ib	7	Structure L sealing layer	P. 68; Fig. 39 1b(ii)	Gl.V. 225, 290k; C.W. 8, 20, 34, 103.
Ib	17	Layer	P. 68; Fig. 39 1b(ii)	Cu.A. 25; C.W. 18.
Ib	19	Gully	P. 68; Fig. 39 Ib(ii)	
Ib	21	Structure L floor	P. 68; Fig. 39 1b(ii)	Gl.V. 231; C.W. 100.

Phase	Context	Description	Page & fig. nos of contexts in Volume II	Catalogued small finds in Volume I, environmental remains in Volume II and catalogued pottery in Volume III
Ib	22	Structure L floor	P. 68; Fig. 40	
Ib	23	Structure L floor	P. 68; Fig.40 S.6	Lead 32, Lead A. 425; Gl.V. 11b, 39, 39b, 46; Dec. Sam. 37; C.W. 36, 55, 59.
Ib	24	Structure L floor	P. 68	Cu.A. 264, 577; Lead A. 426; Gl.V. 228; C.W. 57, 79, 87.
Ib	25	Structure L levelling layer	P. 68	Dec. Sam. 38; C.W. 35.
Ib	26	Structure L hearth	P. 68; Fig.40 S.6	Cu.Arch.
Ib	27	Structure L hearth	P. 68	
Ib	28	Structure L eavesdrip gully	P. 68; Fig. 39 Ib(i)	Gl.V. 83.
Ib	29	Structure L slot	P. 68; Fig. 39 Ib(i)	
Ib	30	Structure L slot	P. 68; Fig. 39 Ib(i)	
Ib	31	Structure L slot	P. 68; Fig. 39 Ib(i)	
Ib	32	Ground surface	P. 68; Fig. 39 Ib(i)	
Ib	33	Slot	P. 68; Fig. 39 Ib(i)	
Ib	34	Pit	P. 68; Fig. 40	
Ib	36	Topsoil	P. 68; Fig. 39	
IIa	5	Road	P. 69; Fig. 39	
IIa	15	Road foundation	P. 69; Fig. 40 S.6	
IIa	16	Road	P. 69; Fig. 39	Gl.V. 226.
IIa	18	Road drain	P. 69; Fig. 39	
IV	3	Ditch	P. 72; Fig. 39	Quern A. 38, 66; C.W. 547-8.
IV	6	Cremation pit	P. 72; Fig. 39	C.W. 456, 465; Hum.
IV	8	Pit	P. 72; Fig. 39	Gl.O. 222.
IV	9	Gully	P. 69; Fig. 39	
IV	10	Slot	P. 69	
IV	11	Support wall	P. 69; 72; Fig. 40 S.6	
IV	12	Pit	P. 69; Fig. 39	
IV	13	Pit	P. 69; Figs 39, 40 S.6	
IV	14	Pit	P. 69; Figs. 39, 40 S.6	
	0			Cu.A. 83.
	4			Coin 131.

Trench 15II

Phase	Context	Description	Page & fig. nos of contexts in Volume II	Catalogued small finds in Volume I, environmental remains in Volume II and catalogued pottery in Volume III
Ia	68	Initial slot	P. 72; Fig.41	Gl.O. 110; C.W. 105.
Ia	80	Natural	P. 72; Fig.41	Coin 97; Cu.A. 5; Gl.O. 225; Graffiti 7; Dec. Sam. 40 Sam. St. 82.
Ia	92	Layer	P. 72	
Ia	94	Earliest deposits	P. 72	Iron 80.
Ib	76	Layer	P. 73; Fig. 42	
Ib	88	Layer	P. 73; Fig. 42	Gl.V. 228b.
Ib	93	Post-hole	P. 73; Fig. 42	
Ic	55	Gravel surface	P. 73; Fig. 43	C.W. 56, 106.
Ic	62	Layer	P. 73; Fig. 43	
Ic	63	Floor	P. 73	Gl.V. 11; C.W. 1.
Ic	64	Layer	P. 74	Bone 50; Dec. Sam. 39.
Ic	65	Layer	P. 74; Fig. 43	

Phase	Context	Description	Page & fig. nos of contexts in Volume II	Cataloged small finds in Volume I, environmental remains in Volume II and catalogued pottery in Volume III
Ic	66	Gravel surface	P. 73; Fig. 43	
Ic	73	Floor	P. 73; Fig. 43	Cu.A. 225.
Ic	74	Floor	P. 73; Fig. 43	
Ic	75	Floor bedding	P. 73; Fig. 43	
Ic	77	Floor bedding	P. 73	Gl.V. 65, Quern A. 67.
Ic	78	Floor	P. 73; Fig. 47 S.45 & S.41	Lead A. 428; Gl.V. 66; Quern A. 68-9.
Ic	79	Floor	P. 73; Fig. 47 S.45	C.W. 133.
Ic	84	Pit	P. 74	Gl.V. 38.
Ic	85	Floor	P. 73	Bot. (Appendix 4).
Ic	89	Layer	P. 74	
Ic	91	Slot	P. 74	
Id	58	Destruction	P. 74; Fig. 44	Gl.O. 26.
Id	67	Destruction	P. 74; Fig. 44	
II	83	Structure M slot	P. 74; Fig. 45	
IV	51	Layer	P. 78; Fig. 47 S.45	
IV	52	Floor	P. 78; Fig. 46	
IV	53	Interval tower foundation	P. 78; Fig. 46a	Cu.A. 143, 66; Iron 3, 112; Gl.V. 66b, 291; C.W. 478, 482.
IV	54	Post-hole	P. 78	
IV	56	Post-hole	P. 78	
IV	57	Layer	P. 78	Cu.A. 773, Cu.Arch.; Bone 123; C.W. 497.
IV	59	Wall foundation	P. 78; Fig. 46	Cu.A. 488; Lead 38.
IV	60	Wall robber trench	P. 78	
IV	60A	Wall rob	P. 78; Fig. 47 S.41	
IV	61	Wall footing	P. 78; Fig. 46, 47	
IV	69	Wall footing	P. 78; Fig. 46	
IV	70	Wall footing	P. 78; Fig. 46	
IV	71	Layer	P. 78; Fig. 46	
IV	72	Wall foundation trench	P. 78; Fig. 46a	
IV	81	Foundation trench infill	P. 78	
IV	82	Foundation trench infill	P. 78; Fig. 47 S.45	
IV	86	Initial ditch cut	P. 78; Fig.46a	Slag 34; C.W. 494.
IV	87	Foundation trench infill	P. 78; Figs 46, Fig. 47 S.45	
	51			Coin 130; Cu.A. 355.

Trench 15III

Phase	Context	Description	Page & fig. nos of contexts in Volume II	Cataloged small finds in Volume I, environmental remains in Volume II and catalogued pottery in Volume III
Ia	301	Original topsoil	P. 81; Fig. 48	
Ia	310	Slot	P .81; Fig. 57 S.105	
Ia	311	Slot	P .81; Fig. 57 S.105	
Ib	273	Drain	P. 81; Fig. 49	Graffiti 8.
Ib	282	Gravel strip	P. 81; Fig. 49	
Ib	283	Layer	P. 81; Fig. 57 S.105	
Ib	291	Post-hole	P. 81	
Ib	294	Layer	P. 81; Fig. 57 S.105	C.W. 32.
Ib	295	Surface	P. 81; Fig. 49	Dec. Sam. 42
Ib	297	Layer	P. 81; Fig. 57 S.105	

Phase	Context	Description	Page & fig. nos of contexts in Volume II	Catalogued small finds in Volume I, environmental remains in Volume II and catalogued pottery in Volume III
Ib	298	Layer	P. 81; Fig. 57 S.105	
Ib	299	Curving slot	P .81;Fig. 49	Gl.O. 39.
Ib	302	Drain	P. 81; Fig. 49	Dec. Sam. 44; Sam. St. 85, 140.
Ib	303	Drain	P. 81; Fig. 49	
Ib	306	Structure N floor	P. 81; Fig. 49	Iron 36.
Ib	307	Post-hole	P. 81; Fig. 49	
Ib	308	Post-hole	P. 81; Fig. 49	
Ib	309	Stake-hole	P. 81; Fig. 49	
Ic	271	Gravel/midden	P. 81: Fig. 50	
Ic	281=271	Gravel/midden	P. 81	Cu.Arch.; Bone 196; C.W. 138.
Ic	300	Sand/silt layer	P. 83; Fig. 50	Gl.V. 232; Dec. Sam. 43; C.W. 85, 116.
Ic	304	Sand/silt layer	P. 83; Mort. 116. Fig. 61 S.104	
Ic	305=304	Sand/silt layer	P. 83	
Ic	317	Pit	P. 83; Fig. 61 S.104	
Id	236	Slot in gravel road	P. 87; Fig. 53	Gl.O. 23.
Id	246	Relaid gravel surface	P. 87; Fig. 51	Hum.
Id	247	Structure O destruction	P. 83; Fig. 53	Cu.A. 285, 608-9, Cu.Arch.; Iron 4, 73, 93; Gl.V. 290f, 290l.
Id	252	Structure O destruction	P. 83; Fig. 53	Coin 68, 75.
Id	254	Structure O floor	P. 83; Fig. 51	
Id	257	Slot	P. 87; Fig. 51	Cu.A. 2.
Id	262	Structure O post-hole	P. 87; Fig. 51	Quern 1, 8; Quern A.; 71-5.
Id	264	Structure O destruction	P. 83; Fig. 61 S.104	Cu.A. 453, Cu.Arch.; Iron 20; Gl.O. 96.
Id	265	Structure O ?wattle cladding	P. 83; Fig. 51	
Id	266	Structure O slot	P. 83; Fig. 51	
Id	267	Structure O burnt area	P. 83; Fig. 51	
Id	268	Structure O ? floor	P. 83; Fig. 51	Coin 64; Cu.A. 286, Cu.Arch.; Gl.O. 44, 47; Dec. Sam. .41
Id	269	Structure O stake-hole	P. 83	
Id	270	Structure O slot	P. 83; Fig. 51	
Id	272	Laycr	P. 87; Fig. 61 S.104	
Id	274	Post-hole	P. 87	
Id	275	Road	P. 87; Fig. 61 S. 104	
Id	276	Road foundation	P. 87	
Id	277	Road foundation	P. 87; Fig. 61 S.104	
Id	279	Structure O slot	P. 83; Fig. 51	
Id	290	Layer	P. 87	
Id	296	Structure O levelling	P. 87	
Id	312	Layer	P. 87	
Id	315	Layer	P. 87	
Id	316	Structure O burnt daub	P. 83; Fig. 53	C.W. 139.
IIa	234	Compacted gravel, external	P. 87; Fig. 54	Iron 72.
IIa	239	Granary; surface repair	P. 87; Fig. 54	
IIa	250	Structure P post-hole	P. 89	
IIa	251	Structure P floor slot	P. 87; Fig. 54	
IIa	253	Structure P floor slot	P. 87; Fig. 54	Cu.Arch.; Bone 158; C.W. 159.
IIa	256	Structure P floor slot	P. 87,.89; Fig. 54	Gl.O. 29.
IIa	258	Structure P floor slot	P. 87, 89; Fig. 54	
IIa	260	Stake-hole	P. 91; Fig. 54	
IIa	284	Layer	P. 91	
IIa	285	Structure P slot fill	P. 89	

213

Phase	Context	Description	Page & fig. nos of contexts in Volume II	Catalogued small finds in Volume I, environmental remains in Volume II and catalogued pottery in Volume III
IIa	286	Structure P slot fill	P. 89; Fig. 61 S.104	
IIa	287	Slot	P. 89; Fig. 54	C.W. 155.
IIa	288=286	Structure P slot fill	P. 89	
IIa	289	Structure P slot	P. 89; Fig. 54	C.W. 148.
IIa	293	Structure Q post-hole	P. 91	
IIa	314	Compacted gravel, internal	P. 87; Fig. 54	
IIa	235	Slot	P. 95; Fig. 56	
IIa/b	313/1+2	Structure P/R floor slots	Pp. 87, 91; Figs 54, 56	Gl.O. 34.
IIb	237	Slot south of granary	P. 95; Fig. 56	Cu.A. 322.
IIb	238	Slot south of granary	P. 95; Fig. 56	Cu.A. 70; Iron 48.
IIb	242	Slot	P. 95; Fig. 56	
IIb	245	Structure R wall foundation	P. 91; Fig. 56	
IIb	259	Post-hole	P. 91; Fig. 56	
IIb	278	Slot	P. 95; Fig. 56	
III	215	Wall foundation trench	P. 97; Fig. 59	
III	228	Standstill horizon	P. 95	
III	231	Mortar layer	P. 95	
III	232	Standstill horizon	P. 95; Fig. 58	Coin 101; Cu.A. 246, 578; Lead A. 429; Mort. 56
III	233	Layer	P. 95	
III	240	Robber trench	P. 95; Fig. 58	Cu.A. 388; 432; Quern A. 42.
III	241	Standstill horizon	P. 95; Fig. 57 S.105	
III	243	Post-hole	P. 95	C.W. 378.
III	248	Standstill horizon	P. 95; Fig. 57 S.105	Cu.A. 148, 349; Lead A. 430.
IV	202	Pit at corner of raking pit	P. 97; Fig. 59	Cu.A. 160, 383, Cu.Arch.; Shale 3; Bone 71-2, 145; Spoon moulds; Sam. St. 78, 98; C.W. 427, 434, 437-8, 444-5, 474; Mort. 15.
IV	203	Rubbish deposits	P. 97; Fig. 59	Coin 108; Cu.A. 184, Cu.Arch.; Gl.V. 290j; Cruc.18-19 Sam. St. 93; C.W. 432, 441, 449, 483, 511, 516.
IV	211	Raking pit	P. 97; Fig. 59	Cu.A. 210; Stone 93; Bone 46; Tex. 9; C.W. 462-4, 498, 502; Mort. 21.
IV	212	Layer	P. 99	
IV	213	Kiln	P. 97; Fig. 59	Gl.V. 111; Stone 94-5; Bone 47, 166; Mort. 32.
IV	214	Structure S destruction	P. 95, 97; Fig. 59	Iron 19; Quern 15, Quern A. 39-41; C.W. 382; Mort. 10; Bot.
IV	216	Structure S floor	P. 95; Fig. 59	Gl.O. 45; Lea. 36; Wood 6.
IV	217	Structure S floor	P. 95; Fig. 59	Bone 132.
IV	218	Slot	Pp 95, 97; Fig. 59	
IV	219	Structure S stake-hole	P. 95	
IV	220	Stake-hole	P. 95	
IV	221	Structure S wall	Pp 95, 97; Fig. 59	
IV	222	Layer	P. 99; Fig. 59	
IV	223	Structure S stake-hole	Pp 95, 97	
IV	224	Structure S stake-hole	Pp 95, 97	
IV	225	Layer	P. 99; Fig. 59	
IV	226	Trench	P. 97; Fig. 59	
IV	227	Structure S floor	P. 95; Figs 57 S.105, 61 S.104	Hum.
IV	229=202	Pit at corner of raking pit	P. 97	Stone 111.
IV	230	Wall foundation	P. 97; Fig. 59	Cu.A. 174.
IV	244	Post-hole	P. 99	
IV	249	Structure S stake-hole	P. 95	
IV	280	Robber trench	P. 97; Fig. 59	

Phase	Context	Description	Page & fig. nos of contexts in Volume II	Catalogued small finds in Volume I, environmental remains in Volume II and catalogued pottery in Volume III
IV	292	Post-hole	P. 99	
	0			Coin 20; Gl.O. 32; Bone 144
	201			Coin 117; Cu.A. 207; Cruc. 17; Bone 45; Mort. 17, 19, 20, 33.
	210			Coin 10.

Trench 15IV

Phase	Context	Description	Page & fig. nos of contexts in Volume II	Catalogued small finds in Volume I, environmental remains in Volume II and catalogued pottery in Volume III
Ia	670	Layer	P. 102; Fig. 62	Dec. Sam. 48
Ia	672	Slot	P. 102; Fig. 62	
Ia	677	Slot	P. 102; Fig. 62	Gl.V. 290i.
Ia	680	Slot	P. 102; Fig. 62	Cruc. 22; Dec. Sam. 49; C.W. 2, 23, 95.
Ia	682	Slot	P. 102; Fig. 62	
Ia	686	Slot	P. 102; Fig. 62	
Ia	687	Slot	P. 102; Fig. 62	
Ia	689	Slot	P. 102	
Ia	690	Slot	P. 102; Fig. 62	
Ia	701	Pit	P. 102; Fig. 62	
Ia	706	Slot	P. 102; Fig. 62	Sam. St. 125
Ia	708	Slot	P. 102; Fig. 62	
Ia	710	Slot	P. 102; Fig. 62	
Ia	711	Slot	P. 102; Fig. 62	
Ia	712	Slot	P. 102; Fig. 62	
Ia	713	Timber staining	P. 102	
Ia	715	Pit	P. 102; Fig. 62	
Ia	716	Slot	P. 102; Fig. 62	
Ia	718	Post-hole	P. 102; Fig. 62	
Ia	719	Slot	P. 102; Fig. 62	
Ia	720	Pit	P. 102; Fig. 62	
Ia	764	Slot	P. 102; Fig. 62	Coin 21.
Ia	765	Slot	P. 102; Fig. 62	
Ib	577	Slot	P. 102; Fig. 63	
Ib	671	Structure V post-hole	P. 102; Fig. 63	
Ib	673	Structure W slot	P. 102; Fig. 63	
Ib	674	Slot	P. 102; Fig. 63	
Ib	675	Structure V slot	P. 102; Fig. 63	
Ib	676	Structure V slot	P. 102; Fig. 63	
Ib	678	Pit	P. 102; Fig. 63	Lead A. 437.
Ib	679	Structure V slot	P. 102; Fig. 63	
Ib	681	Pit/post-hole	P. 102; Fig. 63	
Ib	684	Post-hole	P. 102; Fig. 63	
Ib	685	Post-hole	P. 102; Fig. 63	
Ib	688	Post-hole	P. 102; Fig. 63	
Ib	691	Structure U slot	P. 102; Fig. 63	
Ib	692	Structure U slot	P. 102; Fig. 63	
Ib	693	Structure U slot	P. 102; Fig. 63	
Ib	694	Structure U slot	P. 102; Fig. 63	
Ib	695	Structure U slot	P. 102; Fig. 63	
Ib	696	Slot	P. 102; Fig. 63	
Ib	697	Structure V post-hole	P. 102; Fig. 63	

Phase	Context	Description	Page & fig. nos of contexts in Volume II	Catalogued small finds in Volume I, environmental remains in Volume II and catalogued pottery in Volume III
Ib	698	Structure V post-hole	P. 102; Fig. 63	
Ib	700A-E	Structure U stake-hole	P. 102; Fig. 63	
Ib	702	Structure W slot	P. 102; Fig. 63	Cu.A. 610, 612.
Ib	703	Structure W slot	P. 102; Fig. 63	
Ib	704	Structure W slot	P. 102; Fig. 63	C.W. 124.
Ib	705	Structure U slot	P. 102; Fig. 63	
Ib	709	Structure V pit/post-hole	P. 102; Fig. 63	
Ib	714	Post-hole	P. 102; Fig. 63	
Ib	717	Structure V pit/post-hole	P. 102; Fig. 63	
Ib	721	Structure V post-hole	P. 102; Fig. 63	
Ib	725	Structure W slot	P. 102; Fig. 63	
Ib	726	Structure W slot	P. 102; Fig. 63	
Ib	727	Structure W slot	P. 102; Fig. 63	
Ib	728	Structure W slot	P. 102; Fig. 63	
Ib	768	? Structure W slot	P. 102; Fig. 63	
Ic	568	Destruction	P. 102; Fig. 64	Sam. St. 141.
Ic	624	Destruction	Fig. 64	Cu.Arch.; Lead A. 435; Gl.V. 291b; Cruc. 20.
Ic	655	Destruction	P. 102; Fig. 64	
Ic	660	Destruction	P. 102; Fig. 64	Cu.A. 287, 514, Cu.Arch.; Lead 36, Lead A. 436; Cruc. 21.
Id	553	Destruction	P. 106; Fig. 65	Coin 94; Cu.A. 311, Cu.Arch.; Lead 18-19, Lead A. 432; Stone 26; Graffiti 9; Sam. St. 83; C.W. 136.
Id	554	Gravel strip	P. 106; Fig. 65	Cu.A. 779; Gl.O. 48.
Id	585	Pit	P. 106; Fig. 65	
Id	596	Destruction	P. 106; Fig. 66	
Id	603	Destruction (Phase II floor?)	P. 106; Fig. 65	Cu.A. 666, Cu.Arch.; Gl.O. 36; C.W. 99, 137.
Id	607	Structure X slot	P. 106; Fig. 65	C.W. 134.
Id	615	Structure X slot	P. 106; Fig. 65	
Id	616	Structure X slot	P. 106; Fig. 65	Cu.A. 47, 782.
Id	626	Gravel corridor	P. 106	
Id	633	Structure X clay floor	P. 106; Fig. 65	
Id	634	Structure X slot	P. 106; Fig. 65	Dec. Sam. 47; Sam. St. 119; C.W. 140.
Id	635	Structure X slot	P. 106; Fig. 65	
Id	636	Structure X clay floor	P. 106; Fig. 65	
Id	637	Structure X slot	P. 106; Fig. 65	
Id	638	Structure X clay floor	P. 106; Fig. 65	
Id	641	Structure X clay floor	P. 106; Fig. 65	
Id	642	Structure X partition slot	P. 106; Fig. 65	
Id	643	Structure X hearth	P. 106; Fig. 65	
Id	644	Structure X hearth	P. 106; Fig. 65	
Id	649	Rubbish pit north of Str. Y	P. 106; Fig. 65	Quern A. 78-9.
Id	651	Structure X clay layer	P. 106; Fig. 65	
Id	652	Structure Y slot	P. 106; Fig. 65	Cu.A. 405; Bot.
Id	653	Structure Y clay floor	P. 106; Fig. 65	
Id	658	Structure Y slot	P. 106; Fig. 65	Mort. 100.
Id	659	Post-hole	P. 106; Fig. 65	
Id	661	Pit	P. 106; Fig. 65	
Id	666	Structure Y partition slot	P. 106; Fig. 65	
Id	667	Post-hole	P. 106; Fig. 65	
Id	668	Structure Y partition slot	P. 106; Fig. 65	
II	567	Road	P. 109; Fig. 67	Cu.A. 758; Stone 113-15; Dec. Sam. 45; C.W. 152, 173.
II	571	Structure Z clay floor	P. 106; Fig. 67	
II	572	Road drain	P. 109; Fig. 67	Cu.A. 175; C.W. 156.
II	573	Structure Z surface	P. 109; Fig. 67	

Phase	Context	Description	Page & fig. nos of contexts in Volume II	Catalogued small finds in Volume I, environmental remains in Volume II and catalogued pottery in Volume III
II	574	Post-hole	P. 109; Fig. 67	
II	575	Structure Z slot	P. 106, 109; Fig. 67	Cu.Arch.
II	576	Structure Z slot	P. 106; Fig. 67	Cu.Arch.
II	578	Structure Z slot	P. 106; Fig. 67	
II	579	Structure Z slot	P. 106; Fig. 67	Cu.Arch.; Stone 116.
II	580	Structure Z partition slot	P. 106; Fig. 67	
II	582	Structure Z relaid floor	P. 106; Fig. 67	
II	583	Structure Z relaid floor	P. 106; Fig. 67	
II	584	Structure Z occupation layer	P. 106; Fig. 67	
II	586	Road drain	P. 109; Fig. 67	Cu.A. 247; Dec. Sam. 46; C.W. 163, 178.
II	587	Layer	P. 109; Fig. 67	C.W. 179.
II	588	Destruction	P. 106	Cu.A. 162.
II	589	Structure Z hearth	P. 109; Fig. 67	
II	590	Structure Z pit	P. 106; Fig. 67	Hum.
II	591	Structure Z clay floor	P. 106; Fig. 67	
II	592	Structure Z clay floor	P. 106; Fig. 67	
II	593	Road surface	P. 109; Fig. 67	Lamp 4.
II	594	Structure Z slot	P. 106; Fig. 67	Cu.Arch.
II	595	Structure Z slot	P. 106; Fig. 67	
II	603	Destruction	P. 109; Fig. 66	
II	604	Structure AB slot	P. 109; Fig. 67	Cu.A. 655, Cu.Arch.
II	605	Structure AB slot	P. 109; Fig. 67	Gl.V. 230, 290m.
II	606	Structure AB slot	P. 109; Fig. 67	
II	608	Layer	P. 109	
II	610	Structure AB interior	P. 109; Fig. 67	Coin 57; Cu.A. 185; Gl.V. 229; Stone 27.
II	617	Structure Z slot	P. 106; Fig. 67	
II	618	Structure Z slot	P. 106; Fig. 67	
II	619	Layer	P. 109	
II	621	Structure Z occupation layer	P. 106; Fig. 67	
II	622	Structure Z clay floor	P. 106; Fig. 67	
II	623	Structure AB slot	P. 109; Fig. 67	
II	625	Structure AB slot	P. 109; Fig. 67	Gl.O. 28.
II	627	Structure Z clay floor	P. 106; Fig. 67	
II	628	Structure Z slot	P. 106; Fig. 67	
II	629	Structure AB slot	P. 109; Fig. 67	
II	630	Structure AB slot	P. 109; Fig. 67	
II	631	Structure AB post-hole	P. 109; Fig. 67	Cu.A. 338.
II	632	Structure AB slot	P. 109; Fig. 67	
II	645	Slot	P. 109	
II	646	Road drain	P. 109; Fig. 67	
II	654	Structure Z slot	P. 106; Fig. 67	
II	656	Structure AB post-hole	P. 109; Fig. 67	
II	657	Structure AB post-hole	P. 109; Fig. 67	
II	662	Structure Z post-hole	P. 109; Fig. 67	
II	663	Structure Z slot	P. 109; Fig. 67	
II	664	Structure Z post-hole	P. 109; Fig. 67	
II	665	Structure Z partition slot	P. 106; Fig. 67	Sam. St. 131
II	683	Structure Z slot	P. 106; Fig. 67	
II	767	Road drain	P. 109; Fig. 67	
II	770	Road drain	P. 109; Fig. 67	
II	772	Slot	P. 109; Fig. 67	
III	613	Slot	P. 109	
III	647	Slot	P. 109	

Phase	Context	Description	Page & fig. nos of contexts in Volume II	Catalogued small finds in Volume I, environmental remains in Volume II and catalogued pottery in Volume III
III	648	Slot	P. 109	
IV	503	Ditch	P. 109; Fig. 68	Cu.A. 265; Gl.V. 290c.
IV	550	Bank	P. 110	Quern A. 76.
IV	551	Rubbish dumping	P. 113; Fig. 68	Coin 115; Cu.Arch.; Sam. St. 143; C.W. 479.
IV	555	Inhumation grave	P. 110; Fig. 68	Lead 22; Hum.
IV	556	Rubbish dumping	P. 113; Fig. 68	Coin 114, 116, 135, 140, 143, 147-8, 150; Cu.A. 91, 135, 161, 188, 323, 374, 389, 422, 464, 579, 611, 644, 743, 757, 790, Cu.Arch.; Lead A. 433-4; Gl.V. 108, 108b; Gl.O. 25, 27, 31, 37, 43, 46; Lamp 3; Quern A. 77; C.W. 470, 557; Mort. St. 55; Hum.
IV	557	Bank	P. 110	Coin 139; Stone 96; Mort. St. 47; Hum.
IV	558=565	Ditch	P. 110; Fig. 68	Coin 134; Gl.O. 35; Hum.
IV	559	Inhumation grave	P. 110; Fig. 68	Hum.
IV	560	Inhumation grave	P. 110; Fig. 68	Iron 29; Hum.
IV	561	Stone setting	P. 113; Fig. 68	
IV	562	Grave	P. 110; Fig. 68	Quern A. 43.
IV	563	Grave	P. 110; Fig. 68	
IV	564	Grave	P. 110; Fig. 68	C.W. 431; Hum.
IV	565	Ditch	P. 110; Fig. 68	Gl.O. 38.
IV	566	Ditch	Pp 109-110, 113; Fig. 68	
IV	566A-B	Primary fills of ditch 566	P. 110; Fig. 68	
IV	570	Grave	P. 110; Fig. 68	
IV	564	Grave	P. 110; Fig. 68	
IV	581	Robber trench	P. 110; Fig. 68	Quern A. 44.
IV	597	Wall rob	P. 110	
IV	598	Wall rob	P. 110	
IV	600	Wall rob	P. 110	
IV	602	Fill	P.113	Cu.A. 384.
IV	609	Structure AC foundation	Pp 110, 113; Fig. 68	Cu.A. 271; Slag 38; C.W. 512.
IV	611	Structure AC foundation	P. 110; Fig. 68	Cu.A. 774.
IV	611A-B	Wall rob	P. 113	
IV	612A/B	Wall foundation	P. 110	
IV	614	Structure AC foundation	Pp 110, 113; Fig. 68	Coin 22, 149; Gl.V. 107.
IV	669	Cremation	P. 110; Fig. 68	Hum.
IV	724	Gully	P. 113; Fig. 68	
IV	750	Ditch	P. 109, 113; Fig. 68	Cu.A. 797; Gl.V. 106, 109, 234; Gl.O. 22, 240; Stone 117; C.W. 428; Mort. 16.
IV	751	Shallow cut	P. 113	
IV	771	Structure AC post setting	P. 113; Fig. 68	
	501			Cu.A. 69, 121; Lead A. 431; Gl.O. 223; Stone 25, 112; Bone 2.
	601			Cu.A. 777, Cu.Arch; Mort. St. 18.
	723			Stone 28.

Trench 15V

Phase	Context	Description	Page & fig. nos of contexts in Volume II	Catalogued small finds in Volume I, environmental remains in Volume II and catalogued pottery in Volume III
Ia	1010=1179	Levelling layer	P. 81	
Ia	1170	Hearth	P. 81; Fig. 48	
Ia	1179	Levelling layer	P. 81; Fig. 48	Mort. 108.
Ia	1180	Stone setting	P. 81; Fig. 48	
Ia	1181	Stake-holes	P. 81; Fig. 48	
Ia	1186	Levelling layer	P. 81; Fig. 48	
Ia	1191	Slot	P. 81; Fig. 48	
Ia	1192	Slot	P. 81; Fig. 48	
Ia	1193	Slot	P. 81; Fig. 48	
Ia	1194	Stake-holes	P. 81; Fig. 48	
Ia	1197	Levelling layer	P. 81	
Ia	1198	Hearth	P. 81	
Ia	1199	Original topsoil	P. 81	
Ib	984	Drain	P. 81; Fig. 49	Cu.A. 212, Cu.Arch.; Bone 207; Graffiti 10; Sam. St. 72 Sam. St. 112, 132; C.W. 41, 90; Mort. 103; Mort. St. 49.
Ib	985	Structure N slot	P. 81; Fig. 49	Cu.Arch.; Graffiti 11; Dec. Sam. 50; C.W. 5, 130.
Ib	1147	Structure N slot	P. 81; Fig. 49	Coin 43; C.W. 10.
Ib	1148	Drain	P. 81; Fig. 49	Mort. 96, 115.
Ib	1149	Sealing layer	P. 81	Cu.A. 515; Stone 31; C.W. 33, 102.
Ib	1150	Floor to north of gravel	P. 81; Fig. 49	Gl.V. 8.
Ib	1151	Structure N hearth	P. 81; Fig. 49	
Ib	1152	Post-hole	P. 81; Fig. 49	
Ib	1153	Post-hole	P. 81; Fig. 49	
Ib	1154	Post-hole	P. 81; Fig. 49	
Ib	1155	Sealing layer	P. 81; Fig. 49	
Ib	1157	Stake-hole	P. 81; Fig. 49	
Ib	1158	Drain	P. 81; Fig. 49	
Ib	1159	Structure N gravel surface	P. 81; Fig. 49	
Ib	1160	Stake-holes	P. 81; Fig. 49	
Ib	1161	Gravel strip	P. 81; Fig. 49	Coin 14; Cu.A. 760; Cu.Arch; Sam. St. 122; C.W. 13.
Ib	1162	Structure N surface	P. 81; Fig. 49	Cu.A. 361; Lead A. 446; Gl.O. 33; Stone 32; C.W. 9.
Ib	1163	Slot	P. 81; Fig. 49	
Ib	1164	Slot	P. 81; Fig. 49	
Ib	1165	Hearth	P. 81; Fig. 49	
Ib	1166	Slot	P. 81; Fig. 49	
Ib	1167	Slot	P. 81; Fig. 49	
Ib	1168	Gravel strip	P. 81; Fig. 49	Coin 151.
Ib	1169	Gravel strip	P. 81; Fig. 49	Sam. St. 84
Ib	1171	Layer	P. 81; Fig. 49	
Ib	1172	Layer	P. 81	
Ib	1173	Layer	P. 81	Sam. St. 136; C.W. 114.
Ib	1174	Layer	P. 81	Cu.A. 745.
Ib	1175	Layer	P. 81	
Ib	1176	Layer	P. 81	Cu.A. 761.
Ib	1177	Structure N floor	P. 81; Fig. 49	
Ib	1178	Structure N hearth	P. 81; Fig. 49	
Ib	1182	Structure N post-hole	P. 81; Fig. 49	
Ib	1183	Pit	P. 81; Fig. 49	
Ib	1184	Stake-holes	P. 81; Fig. 49	
Ib	1185	Stake-holes	P. 81; Fig. 49	
Ib	1187	Stake-holes	P. 81; Fig. 49	
Ib	1188	Post-hole	P. 81; Fig. 49	
Ib	1189	Post-hole	P. 81; Fig. 49	

Phase	Context	Description	Page & fig. nos of contexts in Volume II	Catalogued small finds in Volume I, environmental remains in Volume II and catalogued pottery in Volume III
Ib	1190	Gravel sealing layer	P. 81; Fig. 49	
Ib	1195	Post-hole	P. 81; Fig. 49	
Ib	1196	Stake-holes	P. 81; Fig. 49	
Ic	972	Sealing layer	P. 81; Fig. 50	
Ic	979	Gravel and sand strip	P. 81; Fig. 50	
Ic	981	Gravel/midden	P. 81; Fig. 50	Gl.V. 235; Gl.O. 243; C.W. 15, 30, 120.
Ic	982	Gravel/midden	P. 81; Fig. 50	Stone 69.
Ic	995	Gravel/midden	P. 83; Fig. 50	Lead A. 439; Graffiti 12; Sam. St. 133; C.W. 25.
Ic	997	Silt sealing Ib	P. 81; Fig. 50	Coin 71; Cu.A. 6; Sam. St. 128; Sam. St. 134; C.W. 37, 86.
Ic	998	Gravel and sand strip	P. 81; Fig. 50	
Ic	1005	Layer	P. 83; Fig. 50	
Ic	1006	Layer	P. 83; Fig. 50	Lead A. 440; Iron 27; C.W. 3, 19.
Ic	1109	Pit	P. 81; Fig. 50	
Ic	1127	Pit	P. 81; Fig. 50	
Ic	1139=1006	Layer	P. 83	Coin 34; Bone 147, 209; C.W. 14, 46, 50, 62, 83.
Ic	1143	Layer	P. 83; Fig. 52 S.209	
Ic	1145=979	Gravel/midden	P. 81	Coin 86; Cu.A. 215-16, 421, 456, Cu.Arch.; Gl.V. 9; Gl.O. 241; Dec. Sam. 57; Sam. St. 142; C.W. 21, 65, 119, 123.
Ic	1146	Gravel/midden	P. 81; Fig. 50	Cu.A. 261, 467, 689, Cu.Arch.; Iron 21; Bone 177; Sam. St. 69; Sam. St. 110; C.W. 17.
Ic	1156	Layer	P. 83	
Id	918	Structure O post-hole	P. 87; Fig. 51	
Id	938	Structure O stake-hole	P. 87; Fig. 51	
Id	939	Structure O stake-hole	P. 87; Fig. 51	
Id	945	Stucture O destruction	P. 83	C.W. 122.
Id	946	Structure O destruction	P. 83; Fig. 53	Cu.A. 454; Lead A. 438; Quern A. 83.
Id	950	Structure O floor	P. 83, 87; Fig. 51	
Id	951	Structure O post-hole	P. 87	
Id	952	Structure O stake-hole	P. 87; Fig. 51	
Id	953	Structure O stake-hole	P. 87	
Id	954	Structure O stake-hole	P. 87	
Id	955	Structure O floor	P. 83, 87; Fig. 51	
Id	955A	Structure O floor	P. 87	
Id	956	Structure O slot	P. 87; Fig. 51	
Id	957	Road	P. 87; Fig. 51	
Id	958	Road foundation	P. 87; Fig. 51	
Id	959	Layer	P. 87; Fig. 51	Cu.A. 68, Cu.Arch.; Gl.V. 44, 227, 234b, 290; C.W. 31.
Id	962	Structure O stake-hole	P. 87; Fig. 51	
Id	963	Structure O stake-hole	P. 87; Fig. 51	
Id	964	Structure O stake-hole	P. 87	
Id	965	Post-hole	P. 87	
Id	967	Slot	P. 87; Fig. 51	Gl.O. 42.
Id	968	Slot	P. 87; Fig. 51	
Id	969	Slot	P 87; Fig. 51	Cu.A. 189; C.W. 97.
Id	970	Structure O layer	P. 83; Fig. 60 S.207	
Id	971	Layer	P. 87	
Id	974	Structure O layer	P. 87; Fig. 51	
Id	975	Layer	P. 87	
Id	976	Slot	P. 87	
Id	977	Structure O floor	P. 83, 87	

Phase	Context	Description	Page & fig. nos of contexts in Volume II	Catalogued small finds in Volume I, environmental remains in Volume II and catalogued pottery in Volume III
Id	978	Structure O grooves	P. 87; Fig. 51	
Id	980	Road foundation	P. 87; Fig. 51	
Id	987	Structure O stake-hole	P. 87; Fig. 51	
Id	988	Structure O stake-hole	P. 87; Fig. 51	
Id	989	Structure O stake-hole	P. 87	Gl.O. 30.
Id	990	Structure O plank slot	P. 87; Fig. 51	
Id	991	Structure O plank slot	P. 87; Fig. 51	
Id	992	Structure O floor	P. 87; Fig. 51	Coin 76; Quern A. 47; C.W. 51.
Id	993	Structure O relaid floor	P. 87; Fig. 51	
Id	996	Stake-holc	P. 87	
Id	994	Layer	P. 87; Fig. 51	Cu.A. 614.
Id	999	Structure O construction	P. 83; Fig. 51	Bone 183.
Id	1000	Structure O slot	P. 87; Fig. 51	
Id	1002	Structure O sealing layer	P. 87	
Id	1003	Structure O sealing layer	P. 87	C.W. 24, 47.
Id	1007	Structure O surface	P. 87	
Id	1008	Structure O occupation	P. 87	Coin 58; Gl.O. 40.
Id	1009	Structure O occupation	P. 87	Coin 58; Gl.O. 40.
Id	1105	Structure O courtyard	P. 87; Fig. 51	Graffiti 15.Cu.A. 18; Gl.V. 11c; Gl.O. 41; Quern A. 49 Sam. St. 135.
Id	1106	Structure O courtyard	P. 87; Fig. 51	C.W. 118.
Id	1107	Structure O courtyard	P. 87; Fig. 51	Cu.A. 18; Gl. V. 11c; Gl.O. 41; Quern A. 49; Dec. Sam. 53-4; Sam. St. 79; C.W. 22, 64, 71; Mort. 22.
Id	1108	Structure O courtyard	P. 87; Fig. 51	
Id	1009	Structure O occupation		Cu.A. 466, Cu.Arch.
Id	1110	Structure O levelling layer	P. 87	
Id	1111	Structure O courtyard	P. 87; Fig. 51	Cu.Arch.
Id	1112	Structure O courtyard	P. 87; Fig. 51	
Id	1113	Layer	P. 87; Fig. 51	
Id	1114	Clay feature	P. 83	
Id	1115	Structure O foundation	P. 83; Fig. 51	Gl.V. 291c; Dec. Sam. 56.
Id	1116	Layer	P. 87; Fig. 52 S.209	
Id	1117	Structure O stake-holes	P. 83; Fig. 51	
Id	1118	Structure O stake-holes	P. 83; Fig. 51	
Id	1119	Structure O stake-holes	P. 83; Fig. 51	
Id	1120	Structure O stake-holes	P. 83; Fig. 51	Dec. Sam. 55
Id	1121	Structure O destruction	P. 83; Fig. 52 S.209	Cu.Arch.; Iron 94; Gl.O. 238; Bone 146; C.W. 77.
Id	1122	Structure O floor	P. 83; Fig. 52 S.209	
Id	1123	Structure O slot	P. 83; Fig. 51	
Id	1124	Structure O hearth	P. 83; Fig. 51	Gl.V. 290g.
Id	1125	Pit	P. 87; Fig. 51	
Id	1128	Structure O surface	P. 83; Fig. 51	Gl.V. 234c, 290h, 291d; Gl.O. 24, 239.
Id	1129=1131	Structure O foundation	P. 83	
Id	1130	Layer	P. 87	Cu.A. 190.
Id	1131	Structure O foundation	P. 83; Fig. 51	Gl.V. 233.
Id	1132	Structure O slot	P. 83; Fig. 51	Cu.A. 208, 581, Cu.Arch.
Id	1133	Structure O relaid floor	P. 83; Fig. 51	Lead A. (pewter) 527; Gl.O. 242.
Id	1134	Structure O layer	P. 83; Fig. 52; S.209	
Id	1135	Fill	P. 87	
Id	1136	Structure O floor	P. 83	Stone 30.
Id	1137	Structure O floor	P. 83	

Phase	Context	Description	Page & fig. nos of contexts in Volume II	Catalogued small finds in Volume I, environmental remains in Volume II and catalogued pottery in Volume III
Id	1138	Structure O floor	P. 83	
Id	1140	Structure O slot	P. 83	
Id	1141	Structure O slot	P. 83; Fig. 51	Lead A. 445; Bone 184.
Id	1142	Pit	P. 87	Hum.
Id	1144	Structure O slot	P. 83; Fig. 51	Stone 121.
Id	1145	Structure O layer	P. 83; Fig. 52 S.209	
IIa	902	Drain	P. 89; Fig. 55 S.208	
IIa	909	Road drain	P. 89; Fig. 54	Cu.A. 136, 433-4; Cruc. 23.
IIa	927	Drain	P. 89; Fig. 55 S.208	
IIa	929	Drain	P. 89; Fig. 55 S.208	
IIa	931	Road	P. 89; Fig. 54	Coin 66; Cu.A. 67, 645, Cu.Arch.
IIa	947	Structure P post-hole	P. 87; Fig. 54	
IIa	948	Structure P slot	P. 89; Fig. 54	
IIa	949	Post-hole	P. 91	
IIa	960	Structure P slot	P. 89; Fig. 54	
IIa	961	Structure P slot	P. 89; Fig. 54	
IIa	966	Structure P slot	P. 89; Fig. 54	
IIa	973	Post-hole	P. 91; Fig. 54	
IIa	983	Structure P post-hole	P. 89; Fig. 54	
IIa	1065	Structure P slot	P. 87, 89; Fig. 54	Cu.A. 213, 615; Quern A. 89-90.
IIa	1067	Structure P slot	P. 87; Fig. 54	Cu.A. 455, Cu.Arch.; Bone 152.
IIa	1068	Compacted gravel (internal)	P. 87; Fig. 54	Gl.V. 290e.
IIa	1069	Compacted gravel (internal)	P. 87; Fig. 54	Cu.A. 688; Gl.V. 84.
IIa	1070	Compacted gravel (internal)	P. 87; Fig. 54	Dec. Sam. 52
IIa	1073	Structure P slot	Pp 87, 89; Fig. 54	Mort. 24; Mort. St. 38.
IIa	1074	Compacted gravel (internal)	P. 87; Fig. 54	
IIa	1075	Structure P slot	P. 87; Fig. 54	
IIa	1078	Compacted gravel (internal)	P. 87; Fig. 54	
IIa	1085	Compacted gravel (internal)	P. 87; Fig. 54	
IIa	1087	Compacted gravel (internal)	P. 87; Fig. 54	
IIa	1089	Compacted gravel (internal)	P. 87; Fig. 54	
IIa	1091	Compacted gravel (internal)	P. 87; Fig. 54	
IIa	1093	Structure P/R floor slot	P. 89; Fig. 54	Quern A. 96.
IIa	1094	Pit	P. 91; Fig. 54	Vessel moulds.
IIa	1095	Pit (fill of 1094)	P. 91	Cu.A. 102, 656; Lead A. 442-3; Sam. St. 101; C.W. 146, 170-71.
IIb	905	Structure R post setting	P. 91; Fig. 56	
IIb	906	Structure R post setting	P. 91; Fig. 56	
IIb	918B	Structure R post-hole	P. 91; Fig. 56	
IIb	935	Structure R post setting	P. 91; Fig. 56	
IIb	936	Structure R post setting	P. 91; Fig. 56	
IIb	937	Structure R slot	P. 91; Fig. 56	
IIb	941	Structure R post setting	P. 95; Fig. 56	
IIb	943	Structure R post-hole	P. 91; Fig. 56	
IIb	944	Slot	P. 91; Fig. 56	
IIb	1004	Layer	P. 91	
IIb	1062	Structure R butress	P. 91; Fig. 56	
IIb	1064	Structure R slot	P. 91; Fig. 54	Quern A. 87-8.
IIb	1066	Structure R slot	P. 91; Fig. 56	Quern A. 91.
IIb	1071	Structure R wall foundation	Pp 89, 91; Fig. 56	

Phase	Context	Description	Page & fig. nos of contexts in Volume II	Catalogued small finds in Volume I, environmental remains in Volume II and catalogued pottery in Volume III
IIb	1076	Structure R post-hole	P. 91; Fig. 56	Stone 120.
IIb	1079	Structure R slot	P. 91; Fig. 56	Cu.A. 708.
IIb	1082	Structure R wall foundation	P. 91; Fig. 56	
IIb	1097	Structure R post-hole	P. 91	C.W. 158.
IIb	1098	Structure R butress	P. 91; Fig. 56	
IIb	1099	Structure R post-hole	P. 91	Quern A. 97.
IIb	1100	Structure R post-hole	P. 91; Fig. 56	Quern A. 98.
IIb	1101	Structure R post-hole	P. 91	
IIb	1102	Slot	P. 95	
IIb	1103	Structure R post-hole	P. 91	Quern A. 48, 99
IIb	1104	Post-hole	P. 95	
II	910	Compacted gravel	Pp 87, 95; Figs 54, 56	Coin 45; Cu.A. 248, 346, 465, 613; Gl.V. 290d; Quern A. 82; Bone 159.
II	930	Road	P. 89; Figs 54, 56	Cu.Arch.; Gl.O. 111.
II	1063	Structure P slot	Pp 87, 89, 91; Figs 54, 56	Cu.A. 331; Lead A. 441; Gl.O. 224; Bone 168; Graffiti 14.
II	1088	Structure P/R floor slots	Pp 87, 91; Figs 54, 56	Cu.Arch.; Gl.V. 10; Quern A. 94-5.
II	1086	Structure P/R slot	P. 87, 91; Figs 54, 56	
II	1090	Structure P/R slot	P. 87, 91; Fig. 54, 56	C.W. 153.
II	1092	Structure P/R slots	P. 87, 91, Figs 54 56	
III	909A-B	Road drain fill	Pp 95, Fig. 58	Coin 106; Cu.A. 330; Gl.V. 290b; Quern A. 81; Stone 118-19; Sam. St. 86; C.W. 380, 413, 419.
III	907	Robber trench	P. 95; Fig. 58	Coin 46; Cu.A. 272, 707; Bone 51; C.W. 414; Mort. 62.
III	908	Robbing	P. 95; Fig. 58	Coin 37.
III	925	Oven destruction	P. 95	
III	926	Oven destruction	P. 95; Fig. 58	
III	927	Oven destruction	P. 95; Fig. 58	
III	928	Oven	P. 95; Fig. 58	
III	1001	Post-hole	P. 95; Fig. 58	
III	1013	Standstill horizon	P. 95	
III	1028	Standstill horizon	P. 95	
III	1029	Standstill horizon	P. 95	Stone 70.
III	1030	Standstill horizon	P. 95; Figs 52, 58 S.209	Cu.A. 1, 290; Stone 29; C.W. 476.
III	1061	Wall robbing	P. 95; Fig. 58	Cu.A. 744; C.W. 405.
III	1081	Robber trench	P. 95; Fig. 58	Cu.A. 250, 759; Mort. 9.
III	1083	Standstill horizon	P. 95	Cu.Arch.; Mort. 43
III	1084	?Dcstruction	P. 95	
IV	902	Roadside drain	P. 98; Fig. 59	Quern A. 80; Sculp. 4; C.W. 477, 495, 495.
IV	903	Paving setting	P. 98	
IV	904	Gully	P. 98; Fig. 59	C.W. 475.
IV	911	Roadside drain	P. 98; Fig. 59	
IV	912	Roadside drain	P. 98	
IV	913	Post-hole	P. 99	
IV	914	Layer	P. 99	
IV	915	Post-hole	P. 98; Fig. 59	Coin 28; Cu.A. 580.
IV	916	Paving setting	P. 98; Fig. 59	
IV	917	Paving	P. 98; Fig. 59	
IV	920	Robber trench	P. 98; Fig. 59	Cu.Arch.; Bone 206.

Phase	Context	Description	Page & fig. nos of contexts in Volume II	Catalogued small finds in Volume I, environmental remains in Volume II and catalogued pottery in Volume III
IV	921	Layer	P. 98; Fig. 59	
IV	922	Layer	P. 99; Fig. 59	
IV	923	Ditch infill	P. 98; Fig. 59,	
				Fig. 60 S.207
IV	924	Layer	P. 99; Fig. 59	Sam. St. 147.
IV	930	Paving setting	P. 98	
IV	932	Layer	P. 99	
IV	933	Post-hole	P. 98; Fig. 59	
IV	940	Ditch	P. 98; Fig. 59	Cu.A. 211, Cu.Arch.; Quern 18, Quern A. 45-6; C.W. 506.
IV	942	Slot	P. 99	
IV	1011	Structure T destruction	P. 97	Cu.A. 289; Spoon mould; Lamp 5; Quern A.84; Bone 3; C.W. 458; Mort. 38.
IV	1012	Structure T construction trench	P. 97; Fig. 59	Coin 44.
IV	1013	Occupation deposit	P. 97; Fig. 52 S.209	
IV	1014	Structure T construction trench	P. 97; Fig. 59	Gl.V. 110b; C.W. 457, 490, 500, 503; Mort. 12.
IV	1015	Structure T floor	P. 97; Fig. 59	Cu.A. 249.
IV	1016	Structure T floor	P. 97; Fig. 59	Cu.A. 489; Graffiti 13; C.W. 433, 461.
IV	1017	Structure T post setting	P. 97; Fig. 59	
IV	1018	Structure T post setting	P. 97; Fig. 59	
IV	1019	Structure T post setting	P. 97	
IV	1020	?Structure T ?hearth	P. 97; Fig. 59	
IV	1022	?Structure T post-hole	P. 97; Fig. 59	
IV	1023	Post setting	P. 97; Fig. 59	
IV	1024	Post setting	P. 97; Fig. 59	
IV	1025	Post setting	P. 97; Fig. 59	
IV	1026	Post setting	P. 97; Fig. 59	
IV	1027	Post setting	P. 97; Fig. 59	
IV	1028	Occupation layer	P. 97; Fig. 52 S.209	
IV	1032=1034	Cobbling north of Structure T	P. 97	Cu.Arch.; Bone 35; Dec. Sam. 51.
IV	1033	Occupation north of Structure T	P. 97; Fig. 59	Coin 59; Gl.V. 105; Gl.O. 112; Amber 1; Quern A. 85-6; Bone 167; Sam. St. 127; C.W. 472.
IV	1034	Cobbling north of Str. T	P. 97	
IV	1036	Layer	P. 99	Bone 208; C.W. 421.
IV	1037	Pit	P. 99	Gl.V. 110.
IV	1038	Burial	P. 99	
IV	1039	Structure T post setting	P. 97; Fig. 59	
IV	1040	Structure T post setting	P. 97; Fig. 59	
IV	1126	Post-hole	P. 99; Fig. 59	
	901			Coin 103; Cu.A. 17, 413; Stone 78; C.W. 527, 529; Mort. 68; Mort. St. 50.
	919			Cu.A. 288.
	1031			Coin 137, 153.
	1076			Quern A. 92-3.

Trench 16I

Phase	Context	Description	Page & fig. nos of contexts in Volume II	Catalogued small finds in Volume I, environmental remains in Volume II and catalogued pottery in Volume III
Ia	37	Layer	P. 113; Fig. 71	
Ia	39	Fill	P. 113; Fig. 71	
Ia	40	Stake-hole	P. 113; Fig. 71	
Ia	41	Stake-hole	P. 113; Fig. 71	
Ia	42	Stake-hole	P. 113; Fig. 71	
Ia	48	Layer	P. 113; Fig. 71	
Ia	51	Post-hole	P. 113; Fig. 71	
IIa	11	Road drain	P. 116; Fig. 72	Gl.V. 68;Mort. 39; h.
IIa	12	Gravel north of drain	P. 116; Fig. 72	Coin 50; Dec. Sam. 58; Sam. St. 145; C.W. 154.
IIa	22	Gravel metalling	P. 116; Fig. 72	
IIa	23	Road	P. 116	Gl.V. 88.
IIa	24	Gravel north of drain	P. 116; Fig. 72	
IIa	25	Layer below road	P. 116; Fig. 72	Gl.V. 67; Sam. St. 115.
IIa	26	Layer	P. 116	
IIa	28	Slot	P. 116	
IIa	32	Gravel north of wall	P. 116; Fig. 72	
IIa	33	Layer	P. 116	Cu.A. 163.
IIa	34	Slot	P. 116; Fig. 72	
IIa	45	Layer	P. 116; Fig. 72	
IIa	46	Layer	P. 116; Fig. 72	
IIa	47	Pit	P. 116; Fig. 72	Bone 133.
IIa	49	Pit	P. 116; Fig. 72	
IIa	52	Pit	P. 116; Fig. 72	
IIb	2	Clay oven	P. 116; Fig. 73	
IIb	3	Clay oven	P. 116; Fig. 73	Coin 98.
IIb	4	Burnt material from ovens	P. 116; Fig. 73	
IIb	5	Burnt material from ovens	P. 116; Fig. 73	
IIb	6	Burnt material from ovens	P. 116; Fig. 73	
IIb	7	Road	P. 116; Fig. 73	Quern A. 100.
IIb	9	Road	P. 116; Fig. 73	Stone 122.
IIb	10	Burnt material from ovens	P. 116; Fig. 73	
IIb	29	Ditch	P. 116;Fig. 73	Stone 79-80; C.W. 165.
IIb	30	Slot	P. 116; Fig. 73	
IIb	31	Layer	P. 116; Fig. 73	
IIb	50	Slot	P. 116; Fig. 73	
IV	14A-B	Robber trench fill	P. 116; Fig. 74	Gl.V. 114.
IV	17	Layer	P. 119	
IV	18	Robber trench	P. 116; Fig. 74	
IV	35	Ditch	P. 116; Fig. 74	Bone 38.
IV	53	Ditch	P. 116; Fig. 74	
IV	54	Ditch	P. 119	
IV	55	Ditch	P. 116; Fig. 75 S.2	
	1			Cu.A. 414; Stone 33.
	8			Stone 34; Graffiti 16-17.
	20			Cu.A. 516.

Trench 16II

Phase	Context	Description	Page & fig. nos of contexts in Volume II	Catalogued small finds in Volume I, environmental remains in Volume II and catalogued pottery in Volume III
Ib	321	Rubbish pit	P. 113; Fig. 71	Cu.A. 273; Gl.V. 12; Quern 3; Bone 149; Sam. St. 92; C.W. 58, 68, 82, 135.
Ib	322	Pit	P. 113; Fig. 71	
IIa	303	Levelling layer	P. 116; Fig. 72	Cu.A. 103, 423; Gl.V. 53, 53b, 54, 56b; Bone 148; Dec. Sam. .59; Sam. St. 88; C.W. 157.
IIa	308	Gravel beyond drain	P. 118; Fig. 72	Gl.V. 85; C.W. 151.
IIa	309	Road	P. 116; Fig. 72	Coin 33.
IIa	312	Slot	P. 116; Fig. 72	
IIa	313	Layer	P. 116; Fig. 72	Gl.V. 53c, 56c, 292i.
IIa	316	Drain	P. 116; Fig. 72	
IIa	317	Slot	P. 116	
IIa	318	Layer below road	P. 116; Fig. 72	Coin 26.
IIa	320	Pit	P. 116	
IV	302	Hearth	P. 119	
IV	304	Wall foundation	P. 119; Fig. 74	
IV	305	Wall foundation	P. 119; Fig. 74	Gl.O. 97.
IV	306	Wall rob	P. 119; Fig. 74	
IV	307	Wall rob	P. 119; Fig. 74	
IV	310	Layer	P. 119; Fig. 74	Gl.V. 55, 239c, 292f, 292h; Sam. St. 96; C.W. 473, 510, 513.
IV	311	Pit	P. 119; Fig. 74	
IV	319	Ditch	P. 119; Fig. 74	
	301			C.W. 551.

Trench 16III

Phase	Context	Description	Page & fig. nos of contexts in Volume II	Catalogued small finds in Volume I, environmental remains in Volume II and catalogued pottery in Volume III
I	512	Clay	P. 123; Fig. 76	Coin 8.
II	515	Wall rob	P. 123; Fig. 76	
IV	504	Ditch fill	P. 123	Cu.A. 517; Gl.V. 293; Stone 72.
IV	505	Ditch	P. 123	Graffiti 19.
IV	511	Ditch	P. 123; Fig. 76	
IV	513	Ditch	P. 123; Fig. 76	Lead A. 447-8; Gl.V. 115, 295, 295b; Cruc. 24; Bone 198; Lea. 37; Wood 10, 50-53; Bot.
IV	514	Ditch recut	P. 123	
	501			Coin 128; Graffiti 18; C.W. 550.
	509			Coin 24.

Trench 16IV

Phase	Context	Description	Page & fig. nos of contexts in Volume II	Catalogued small finds in Volume I, environmental remains in Volume II and catalogued pottery in Volume III
I/II	602	Pit	P. 123; Fig. 77	
I/II	603	Slot	P. 123; Fig. 77	
I/II	608	Pit	P. 123; Fig. 77	
IV	604=607	Ditch	P. 123	C.W. 466.

Phase	Context	Description	Page & fig. nos of contexts in Volume II	Catalogued small finds in Volume I, environmental remains in Volume II and catalogued pottery in Volume III
IV	605	Ditch	P. 123; Fig. 77	Coin 60; Gl.V. 296; Stone 35, 81; Lea. 38-9; Mort. 34-5.
IV	606	Ditch fill	P. 123	
IV	607	Ditch	P. 123; Fig. 77	Stone 123; C.W. 504-5, 507; Hum.

Trench 16V

Phase	Context	Description	Page & fig. nos of contexts in Volume II	Catalogued small finds in Volume I, environmental remains in Volume II and catalogued pottery in Volume III
initial a	717	Natural	P. 72; Fig. 41	Cu.A. 13
initial a.	739	Slot	P. 72; Fig. 41	C.W. 75, 113; Mort. 101.
initial a.	740	Slot	P. 72; Fig. 41	C.W. 61.
initial a.	741	Slot	P. 72; Fig. 41	
initial a.	742	Slot	P. 72; Fig. 41	Stone 124.
initial a.	746	Layer		Bot. (Appendix 4).
initial a.	747	Post-hole	P. 72; Fig. 41	
initial a.	748	Post-hole	P. 72; Fig. 41	Coin 23.
initial a.	749	Post-hole	P. 72; Fig. 41	
initial a.	750	Post-hole	P. 72; Fig. 41	
initial a.	751	Post-hole	P. 72; Fig. 41	
initial a.	752	Post-hole	P. 72; Fig. 41	
initial a.	753	Post-hole	P. 72; Fig. 41	
initial a.	754	Post-hole	P. 72; Fig. 41	
Ib	743	Gravel road	P. 73; Fig. 42	Cu.A. 72, 667, Cu.Arch.; Gl.V. 239; 292d; Gl.O. 113; Quern A. 108; Bone 185; Dec. Sam. 64-5; Sam. St. 146; C.W. 28, 70, 110, 126, 131.
Ib	745	Gravel	P. 73	C.W. 26, 49, 117.
Ic	707	Floor	P. 73; Fig. 43	
Ic	708	Floor	P. 73; Fig. 43	Cu.A. 71; Gl.O. 246-7.
Ic	713A	Resurfacing	P. 73; Fig. 43	
Ic	713B	Resurfacing	P. 74; Fig. 43	
Ic	714	Gravel road edge	P. 73; Fig. 43	Coin 29, 31; Cu.A. 776, Cu.Arch.; Gl.V. 40, 236, 292e; Gl.O. 52; C.W. 48, 81, 115, 121, 142.
Ic	719=713A	Resurfacing	P. 73	C.W. 88.
Ic	720	Gravel road	P. 73; Fig. 43	Coin 27, 35, 90; Cu.A. 7, 49; Gl.V. 292b; Quern A. 107; Dec. Sam. .60-61.
Ic	732=713B	Resurfacing	P. 74	Cu.A. 122.
Ic	733	Building slot	P. 73; Fig. 43	Cu.A. 48.
Ic	734	Resurfacing	P. 73; Fig. 43	Cu.A. 291, 299; Lead A. 449; Iron 22; Gl.O. 245, 249; Stone 39; Bone 134, 160.
Ic	735	Occupation surface	P. 73; Fig. 43	Dec. Sam. 63; C.W. 111, 128.
Ic	736	Slot	P. 73; Fig. 43	Gl.V. 292c.
Ic	738	Post-hole	P. 74; Fig. 43	
Ic	744	Slot	P. 73	
Id	706	Building slot	P. 74; Fig. 44	Cu.A. 312; Gl.V. 112; Gl.O. 51, 251; Quern A. 50; C.W. 4, 73, 141.
II	712	Southern road	P. 75; Fig. 45	Quern A. 106; Bone 187.
II	715	Layer	P. 75	
II	716	Road drain	P. 75	
II	718	Structure M slot	P. 74; Fig. 45	Cu.A. 27.
II	719	Gravel road	P. 75; Fig. 45	Cu.Arch.; Gl.O. 53, 244, 248; Stone 37.
II	721	Structure M slot	P. 74; Fig. 45	Iron 13; Dec. Sam. 62; C.W. 175.
II	722	Structure M slot	P. 74; Fig. 45	Cu.A. 646.

Phase	Context	Description	Page & fig. nos of contexts in Volume II	Catalogued small finds in Volume I, environmental remains in Volume II and catalogued pottery in Volume III
II	723	Gravel road drain	P. 75	Gl.V. 240; C.W. 149, 167.
II	724	Structure M slot	P. 74; Fig. 45	
II	725	Structure M slot	p. 74; Fig. 45	Coin 83.
II	726	Structure M slot	P. 74; Fig. 45	
II	727	Structure M slot	P. 74; Fig. 45	C.W. 160, 166.
II	730	Layer	P. 75; Fig. 45	Stone 38.
II	731	Post-hole	P. 75; Fig. 45	
II	737	Southern road	P. 75; Fig. 45	
III	704	Abandonment/rubbish	P. 75	Coin 2, 61, 79, 95; Cu.A. 126, 137, 350, 390, 518, 798, Cu.Arch.; Lead 37; Iron 12; Gl.V. 113, 238, 239b, 292, 294, 297; Gl.O. 49-50, 250, 308; Quern 6, Quern A. 102; Stone 36; Bone 157, 197: Graffiti 20, 29; C.W. 379, 384-5, 387-8, 395-9, 406-7, 409-12, 415-17, 555, 558; Mort. 6; Mort. St. 48; An. ca.
IV	702	Wall rob	P. 78; Fig. 45	
IV	703	Wall foundation	P. 78; Fig. 46	Coin 104; Gl.V. 237; Hum.
IV	705	Southern road	P. 78; Fig. 45	
IV	709	Ditch fill	P. 78; Fig. 46	C.W. 435; Hum.
IV	710	Ditch fill	P. 78; Fig. 46	Gl.V. 19, 86-7; Quern A. 103-5; C.W. 514; Hum.
IV	711	Ditch fill	P. 78; Fig. 46	Cu.A. 26; Quern A. 51; C.W. 455.
	701			Coin 82, 124; Cu.A. 112, Cu.Arch.; Iron 42; Gl.V. 292g; Quern A. 101; Graffiti 28; C.W. 528, 533, 542, 549, 552, 553.

Trench 17

Phase	Context	Description	Page & fig. nos of contexts in Volume II	Catalogued small finds in Volume I, environmental remains in Volume II and catalogued pottery in Volume III
Id	10	Structure Y layer	P. 106; Fig. 65	
II	4A-B	Foundation layer	P. 109; Fig. 67	Cu.A. 339.
II	8	Road drain	P. 109; Fig. 67	Graffiti 33; Sam. St. 99; C.W. 161, 172.
II	9	Road drain	P. 109; Fig. 67	
II	13	Structure AA slot	P. 109; Fig. 67	
II	14A-B	Structure AA floor	P. 109; Fig. 67	Quern A. 109.
II	15	Structure AA slot	P. 109; Fig. 67	Quern A. 110-11; Sam. St. 80.
II	16	Structure AA slot	P. 109; Fig. 67	
II	17	Layer	P. 109	
II	18	Structure AA slot	P. 109; Fig. 67	
II	19	Road drain	P. 109; Fig. 67	C.W. 145.
II	20	Structure AA slot	P. 109; Fig. 67	
II	21	Structure AA slot	P. 109; Fig. 67	
II	22	Structure AA slot	P. 109; Fig. 67	
II	25	Gully	P. 109	
III	11	Pit	P. 109	
III	12	Pit	P. 109	
III	24	Pit	P. 109	
IV	3	Rubbish dumping	P. 113; Fig. 67	Cu.A. 307; Gl.O. 54; C.W. 460, 467-8, 471.
IV	6A	Robber trench	P. 110; Fig. 68	Gl.V. 47.
IV	7	Cremation	P. 109; Fig. 68	Hum.
	2			Dec. Sam. 66; C.W. 559.

Trench 18

Phase	Context	Description	Page & fig. nos of contexts in Volume II	Catalogued small finds in Volume I, environmental remains in Volume II and catalogued pottery in Volume III
Ib	54	Post-hole	P. 81; Fig. 49	
Ib	60	Slot	P. 81; Fig. 49	
Ib	71	Post-hole	P. 81; Fig. 49	
Ib	73	Post-hole	P. 81; Fig. 49	
Ib	78	Post-hole	P. 81	
Ib	79	Levelling layer	P. 81; Fig. 49	Coin 18.
Ib	82	Slot	P. 81; Fig. 49	
Ib	83	Levelling layer	P. 81; Fig. 49	
Ib	86	Levelling layer	P. 81; Fig. 49	
Ic	77	Mould pit upper fill	P. 83; Fig. 50	Vessel moulds; Mort. St. 51.
Ic	81	Gravel strip	P. 83; Fig. 50	
Ic	85	Layer	P. 83; Fig. 50	
Ic	88	Slot	P. 83; Fig. 50	
IIa	43	Compacted gravel	Pp 87, 91; Fig. 54	Vessel moulds; C.W. 180.
IIa	44	Layer	P. 91	
IIa	49	Layer	P. 91	
IIa	50	Layer	P. 91	
IIa	51	Layer	P. 91	
IIa	65	External gravel	P. 87	
IIa	67	External gravel	P. 87, 91; Fig. 54	
IIa	68	Slot	P. 91	
IIa	69	External gravel	P. 91; Fig. 54	
IIa	72	Mould pit	P. 91; Fig. 54	Gl.V. 72; Vessel moulds.
IIa	49	Layer	P. 91	
IIa	50	Layer	P. 91	
IIa	51	Layer	P. 91	
IIa	65	External gravel	P. 87; Fig. 54	
IIa	67	External gravel	P. 87, 91	
IIa	68	Slot	P. 91	
IIa	69	External gravel	P. 87	
IIa	72	Fill	P. 91	
IIa	74	Structure Q slot	P. 91; Fig. 54	
IIa	75	Structure Q slot	P. 89; Fig. 54	Cu.A. 709; Cu.Arch.
IIa	75C	Structure Q slot	P. 89; Fig. 54	
IIa	76	Structure Q slot	P. 91; Fig. 54	
IIa	87	Mould pit upper fill	P. 91; Fig. 54	Cruc. 28.
IIa/b	66	Structure R slot	P. 91; Fig. 56	
IIb	24	Structure R buttress	P. 91; Fig. 56	
IIb	25	Structure R buttress	P. 91; Fig. 56	
IIb	27	Structure R levelling	P. 91; Fig. 56	
IIb	34	Structure R foundation	P. 91; Fig. 56	Cu.A. 391; Cruc. 26.
IIb	37	Structure R foundation	P. 91; Fig. 56	
IIb	38	Post-hole	P. 95; Fig. 56	
IIb	39	Post-hole	P. 95; Fig. 56	Bot. (Appendix 4).
IIb	40	Post-hole	P. 95	Bot. (Appendix 4).
IIb	41	Post-hole	P. 95; Fig. 56	
IIb	42	Layer	P. 95; Fig. 56	
IIb	45	Layer	P. 95; Fig. 56	Vessel moulds; C.W. 169.
IIb	46	Post-hole	P. 95; Fig. 56	Vessel moulds.
IIb	47	Structure Q demolition	P. 91; Fig. 56	
IIb	48	Structure Q demolition	P. 91	
IIb	52	Structure Q demolition	P. 91; Fig. 56	Cu.Arch.; Gl.V. 89b.
IIb	53	Structure Q demolition	P. 91; Fig. 56	

Phase	Context	Description	Page & fig. nos of contexts in Volume II	Catalogued small finds in Volume I, environmental remains in Volume II and catalogued pottery in Volume III
IIb	55	Structure Q demolition	P. 91; Fig. 56	Vessel moulds
IIb	56	Structure Q demolition	P. 91; Fig. 56	
IIb	57	Structure Q demolition	P. 91; Fig. 56	Gl.V. 89c; Bone 178.
IIb	58	Structure Q demolition	P. 91; Fig. 56	
IIb	62	Stake-hole	P. 95	
IIb	64	Levelling layer	P. 91; Fig. 56	
IIb	70	Structure Q demolition	P. 91	Bot. (Appendix 4).
IIb	80	Layer	P. 95	
III	21	Robber trench	P. 95; Fig. 58	
III	23	Robber trench	P. 95; Fig. 58	Cu.A. 345; Stone 40.
III	24A	Butress robber trench	P. 95; Fig. 58	
III	25A	Butress robber trench	P. 95; Fig. 58	
III	26	Standstill horizon	P. 95	
III	31	Layer	P. 95; Fig. 58	Cruc. 27; Vessel moulds; Bone 189.
III	32	Standstill horizon	P. 95; Fig. 58	Cu.A. 519, Cu.Arch.; Gl.V. 89, 89d, 298, 298b; Cruc. 25; Vessel moulds.
III	33	Standstill horizon	P. 95	
III	35	Robber trench	P. 95	
III	36	Robber trench	P. 95	
IV	5	Post-hole	P. 99; Fig. 59	
IV	6	Hearth	P. 99; Fig. 59	
IV	7	Wall	P. 99; Fig. 59	
IV	8	Tile layer	P. 99; Fig. 59	
IV	10	Sealing layer	P. 98; Fig. 59	
IV	11	Wall	P. 99; Fig. 59	
IV	12	Wall	P. 99; Fig. 59	
IV	14	Layer	P. 99; Fig. 59	
IV	15	Layer	P. 99; Fig. 59	
IV	16	Layer	P. 99; Fig. 59	
IV	17	Tile layer	P. 99	
IV	18	Tile layer	P. 99	C.W. 451, 480.
IV	19	Tile layer	P. 99; Fig. 59	
IV	20	Layer	P. 99; Fig. 59	
IV	22	Tile layer	P. 99	
IV	26	Levelling	P. 98	
IV	28	Tile layer	P. 99	
IV	29	Layer	P. 99; Fig. 59	
IV	30	Layer	P. 99; Fig. 59	
IV	32	Levelling	P. 98; Fig. 59	
IV	33	Levelling	P. 98	
	1			Sam. St. 75.
	9			Bone 52.

Trench 19

Phase	Context	Description	Page & fig. nos of contexts in Volume II	Catalogued small finds in Volume I, environmental remains in Volume II and catalogued pottery in Volume III
II	3	Daub	P. 123; Fig. 80 S.1	Gl.V. 299.
II	4	Layer	P. 123; Fig. 80 S.1	
II	8	Depression	P. 123; Fig. 80 S.1	
II	10	Compacted gravel	P. 123; Fig. 80 S.5	
II	12	Drain	P. 123; Fig. 80 S.5	

Phase	Context	Description	Page & fig. nos of contexts in Volume II	Catalogued small finds in Volume I, environmental remains in Volume II and catalogued pottery in Volume III
II	13	Compacted gravel	P. 123; Fig. 80 S.2	
II	14	Drain	P. 123; Fig. 80 S.1	
II	15	Drain	P. 123; Fig. 80 S.3	
II	16	Gravel strip	P. 126; Fig. 80 S.3	
III/IV	5	Slot	P. 126; Fig. 79	
III/IV	6	Slot	P. 126; Fig. 79	
III/IV	7	Slot	P. 126; Fig. 79	
III/IV	11	Layer	P. 126	
	0			Gl.V. 299b-c.

Part II: The Major Trenches: Excavations of the *Vicus*, 1974 and 1980-82

Site 1 (74)

Phase	Context	Description	Page & fig. nos of contexts in Volume II	Catalogued small finds in Volume I, environmental remains in Volume II and catalogued pottery in Volume III
1	Level 6			Coin 173, 179, 199, 240, 281, 284; Cu.A. 31, 123, 252, 280, 293, 459, 471, 522-5, 677, 684; Lead 23, 31, Lead A. 472-5; Gl.V. 13-14, 20, 92b, 121, 247, 256, 301c,g; Gl.O. 60-61, 71, 73-4, 79, 99, 114-15, 117, 253; Quern A. 53, 155-8; Stone 48-9; Bone 85-6; Dec. Sam. 168, 171, 184-5, 188, 193; Sam. St. 538, 541, 544; Mort. 104; Mort. St. 2.
1	Level 7			Coin 167, 202, 216; Cu.A. 28, 100, 108, 228, 340, 371, 447, 623, 720-21; Lead A. 476; Iron 8, 35; Gl.V. 13, 15b, 92, 129, 253, 253b, 301k; Gl.O. 57, 100-102, 226-7, 254-5; Quern A. 54; Dec. Sam. 150, 152-3, 156-7, 159, 165, 172-3, 175-8, 189; Sam. St. 533, 540, 542; C.W. 192; Mort. 93; Mort. St. 1.
1	Level 8			Coin 186; Cu.A. 144, 176, 281, 669; Lead A. 477; Gl.O. 252; Quern A. 159-60; Bone 135.
1	Level 9			Cu.A. 44, 54, 415, 784; Lead A. 478; Gl.V. 15, 93, 301l, 306; Quern 4-5, Quern A.161-2; Dec. Sam. 149, 158,169 180; Sam. St. 534, 539.
1	Level 10			Cu.A. 51, 692; Iron 9; Quern A. 163; Dec. Sam. 148, 155, 166; C.W. 194.
	Level 11			Sam. St. 535, 543; C.W. 561.
1	99	Structure AD hearth	P. 126, 128; Fig. 81	
1	105	Beam slot	P. 128	Cu.A. 386.
1	110	Drain lining stakes	P. 126; Fig. 81	
1	111	Timber-lined drain	P. 126; Fig. 81	Cu.A. 375; Dec. Sam. 154; Sam. St. 536-7.
1	113	Slot running into drain	P. 128; Fig. 81	Cu.A. 220.
1	114	Slot/depression	P. 128; Fig. 81	
1	120A	Drain	Pp 126, 128; Fig. 81	
1	249	Timber-lined drain	P. 126; Fig. 81	
1	250	Timber-lined drain	P. 126; Fig. 81	
1	256	Drain	P. 126	

Phase	Context	Description	Page & fig. nos of contexts in Volume II	Catalogued small finds in Volume I, environmental remains in Volume II and catalogued pottery in Volume III
1	268	Hearth	P. 128; Fig. 81	
1	275	Structure AD slot	Pp 126, 128; Fig. 81	
1	277	Structure AE slot	P. 128; Fig. 81	
1	293	Structure AF wall	P. 128; Fig. 81	Cu.A. 275-6.
1	303	Hearth	P. 128; Fig. 81	
1	?			Dec. Sam. 151, 160-64, 167, 170, 174, 179, 181-3, 186-7, 190-92.
2	Level 4			Coin 169, 196, 248, 253-5, 275; Cu.A. 50, 139, 462, 470, 589, 622, 698, 717; Lead 12; Iron 84, 100, 105, 119; Gl.V. 69, 91, 305, f; Gl.O. 274-5; Quern A. 145-6; Stone 82; Dec. Sam. 247; Sam. St. 545, 551-3; Mort. 8, 105; Mort. St. 5.
2	Level 5			Coin 178, 198, 201, 207, 211, 219, 225, 282-3; Cu.A. 3, 29, 32, 52-3, 89, 107, 251, 436-7, 520-21, 590, 691, 718-19, 762, 780; Lead 3,; Iron 98; Gl.V. 15c, 20, 21c, 250, 301, 301i, n, p; Gl.O. 276; Quern A. 147-54; Sam. St. 547-8, 550, 554; Mort. 94; Mort. St. 3.
2	27	Structure AH post-hole	P. 129; Fig. 82	
2	28	Structure AH slot	P. 129; Fig. 82	
2	40	Structure AI slot	P. 129; Fig. 82	
2	44	Structure AH post-hole	P. 129; Fig. 82	
2	52	Post-hole		Gl.V. 254
2	53	Post-hole	P. 129	Lead A. 479; Dec. Sam. 206.
2	62	Structure AH post-hole	P. 129; Fig. 82	
2	64	Ditch		Dec. Sam. 205
2	68	Structure AH post-hole	P. 129; Fig. 82	Cu.A. 364.
2	71	Ditch		Coin 238; Cu.A. 527.
2	72	Post-hole	P. 129; Fig. 82	
2	75	Post-hole	P. 129; Fig. 82	Quern A. 164.
2	86	Structure AH post-hole	P. 129; Fig. 82	
2	102	Hearth	P. 129; Fig. 82	
2	104	Structure AG slot	P. 129; Fig. 82	
2	107	Post-hole	P. 129; Fig. 82	
2	118	Structure AH slot	P. 129; Fig. 82	
2	199	Structure AJ post-hole	P. 131; Fig. 82	
2	200	Structure AJ post-hole	P. 131; Fig. 82	
2	215	Structure AK post-hole	P. 131; Fig. 82	
2	219	Structure AK slot	P. 131; Fig. 82	
2	220	Structure AK slot	P. 131; Fig. 82	Coin 234; Bone 87.
2	226	Structure AK slot	P. 131; Fig. 82	
2	227	Structure AI floor repair	P. 129	Lead A. 483.
2	228	Structure AJ slot	P. 131; Fig. 82	
2	236	Structure AK post-hole	P. 131; Fig. 82	
2	238	Layer	P. 131	Coin 159.
2	248	Structure AK oven	P. 131; Fig. 82	
2	254	Post-hole		Lead 13.
2	258	Pit/cistern	P. 129; Fig. 82	Cu.A. 438; Gl.V. 249.
2	259	Layer	P. 131	Stone 84.
2	266	Structure AI slot	P. 129; Fig. 82	Dec. Sam. 195
2	269	Structure AJ post-hole	P. 131; Fig. 82	
2	271	Structure AI slot	P. 129; Fig. 82	
2	272	Structure AI post-hole	P. 129; Fig. 82	
2	273	Structure AI post-hole	P. 129; Fig. 82	

Phase	Context	Description	Page & fig. nos of contexts in Volume II	Catalogued small finds in Volume I, environmental remains in Volume II and catalogued pottery in Volume III
2	274	Structure AI slot	P. 129; Fig. 82	
2	281	Structure AJ post-hole	P. 131; Fig. 82	
2	283	Structure AK slot	P. 131; Fig. 82	
2	286	Structure AJ slot	P. 131; Fig. 82	Cu.A. 753.
2	287	Structure AJ post-hole	P. 131; Fig. 82	
2	289	Structure AJ post-hole	P. 131; Fig. 82	
2	291	Structure AK slot	P. 131; Fig. 82	
2	292	Structure AJ post-hole	P. 131; Fig. 82	
2	304	Post-hole		Quern A. 170.
2	306	Pit/cistern	P. 131; Fig. 82	Cu.A. 473, 678.
2	?			Dec. Sam. 194, 196-204, 207-46, 248-9; Sam. St. 546, 549, 555.
3	Level 3			Coin 161, 208, 212, 261, 268, 280, 298, 304; Jewel. 4; Cu.A. 109-10, 116, 165, 198, 332, 385, 393, 446, 468-9, 490-95, 587, 617-21, 714-16, 752, 778; Lead 2, 9-11, 24, Lead A. 454-70; Iron 7, 34, 53, 57-8, 68, 78, 101, 103, 118, 120, 127, 136-7; Gl.V. 21b, 25, 50, 50b, 62, 90, 116-17, 120, 122-3, 128, 131, 242b, 243-4, 246, 251-2, 252c, 255, 255b, 256b, 301b, 301d-f, h, j, o, r, s, 304, 305b-e; Gl.O. 56, 58, 64-7, 69-70, 75-6, 98, 119-78, 191-202, 277-86; Quern A. 125-44; Stone 44-7; Bone 54, 79-84; Dec. Sam. 266, 275-8, 282, 285-525; Sam. St. 559-996; Mort. 74, 82-3, 86; Mort. St. 7-11.
3	4	Stone-capped drain	Pp 132, 134; Fig. 83	
3	5	Drain construction trench	P. 132	
3	6	Stake-hole		Sam. St. 556.
3	8	Structure AM post-hole	P. 134; Fig. 83	
3	12	Slot	P. 134; Fig. 83	
3	13	Stone-capped drain	P. 132; Fig. 83	
3	14	Post-hole	P. 134; Fig. 83	
3	15	Post-hole	P. 134; Fig. 83	
3	16	Post-hole	P. 134; Fig. 83	
3	18	Structure AM post-hole	P. 134; Fig. 83	
3	19	Post-hole	P. 134; Fig. 83	
3	23	Post-hole		Cu.A. 526.
3	24	Post-hole	P. 134; Fig. 83	
3	25	Post-hole	P. 134; Fig. 83	
3	29	Drain	P. 134; Fig. 83	Cu.A. 763.
3	32	Hearth	P. 134; Fig. 83	C.W. 401.
3	37	Post-hole/pit	P. 134; Fig. 83	
3	39	Slot	P. 134; Fig. 83	Coin 217.
3	41	Post-hole	P. 134; Fig. 83	
3	43	Post-hole	P. 134; Fig. 83	Sculp. 5.
3	47	Pit		Cu.A. 177.
3	48	Post-hole/pit	P. 134; Fig. 83	
3	49	Post-hole/pit	P. 134; Fig. 83	Dec. Sam. 252, 257.
3	124	Structure AL post-hole	P. 134; Fig. 83	
3	126	Edge-set stones	P. 134; Fig. 83	
3	130	Structure AL post-hole	P. 132; Fig. 83	
3	131	Structure AL post-hole	P. 132 Fig. 83	
3	132	Post-hole	P. 134; Fig. 83	
3	133	Post-hole	P. 134; Fig. 83	
3	138	Structure AL pit	P. 134; Fig. 83	

Phase	Context	Description	Page & fig. nos of contexts in Volume II	Catalogued small finds in Volume I, environmental remains in Volume II and catalogued pottery in Volume III
3	142	Structure AL post-hole	P. 132; Fig. 83	
3	143	Structure AL post-hole	P. 132; Fig. 83	
3	145	Post-hole	P. 134; Fig. 83	
3	153	Structure AL drain	Pp 132, 134; Fig. 83	Quern A. 166; Graffiti 41.
3	154	Structure AL slot	P. 132, 134; Fig. 83	Cu.A. 624; Sam. St. 558.
3	156	Structure AL post-hole	P. 132; Fig. 83	
3	158	Structure AL slot	P. 134; Fig. 83	
3	159	Structure A L post-hole	P. 132; Fig. 83	
3	160	Structure AL post-hole	P. 134; Fig. 83	
3	163	Structure AL post-hole	P. 132; Fig. 83	
3	164	Structure AL slot	P. 132; Fig. 83	
3	165	Drain		Mort. 106
3	167	Structure AL slot	P. 132; Fig. 83	Mort. 84; Mort. St. 6.
3	170	Stone capped drain	Pp 132, 134; Fig. 83	Mort. 2; Mort. St. 4.
3	171	Stone capped drain	Pp 132, 134; Fig. 83	
3	177	Structure AM post-hole	P. 134; Fig. 83	Cu.A. 746.
3	178	?Revetment	P. 132; Fig. 83	Bone 21.
3	181	Structure AM post-hole	P. 134; Fig. 83	Quern A. 167.
3	184	Structure AL post-hole	P. 132; Fig. 83	
3	185	Structure AL post-hole	P. 132; Fig. 83	
3	187	Structure AM post-hole	P. 134; Fig. 83	
3	188	Structure AM post-hole	P. 134; Fig. 83	
3	189	Structure AM post-hole	P. 134; Fig. 83	
3	190	Structure AM post-hole	P. 134; Fig. 83	
3	191	Structure AM post-hole	P. 134; Fig. 83	
3	193	Structure AL post-hole	P. 132; Fig. 83	
3	196	Structure AL post-hole	P. 134; Fig. 83	
3	201		Fig. 83	Cu. A. 352
3	206	Revetment	P. 132; Fig. 83	
3	207	Structure AL stone setting	P. 136; Fig. 83	
3	208	Structure AM post-hole	P. 134; Fig. 83	
3	210	Structure AM post-hole	P. 134; Fig. 83	
3	211	Structure AM post-hole	P. 134; Fig. 83	
3	212	Structure AL slot/gully	P. 132; Fig. 83	Cu. A. 588.
3	214	Structure AM ?post pad	P. 132; Fig. 83	
3	216	Structure AL slot/gully	P. 132; Fig. 83	
3	217	Structure AL post-hole	P. 132; Fig. 83	
3	218	Structure AL post-hole	P. 132; Fig. 83	
3	223	Structure AL slot	P. 134; Fig. 83	
3	224	Structure AL post-hole	P. 132; Fig. 83	
3	229	Structure AL post-hole	P. 132; Fig. 83	Quern A. 168-9.
3	230	Structure AL post-hole	P. 132; Fig. 83	
3	231	Structure AL post-hole	P. 132; Fig. 83	
3	232	Drain fill		Gl.O. 273
3	234	Structure AL post-hole	P. 134; Fig. 83	
3	237	Structure AL post-hole	P. 136; Fig. 83	
3	239	Double oven	P. 134; Fig. 83	
3	251	Structure AL post-hole	P. 132; Fig. 83	
3	252	Structure AL post-hole	P. 132; Fig. 83	
3	253	Structure AL post-hole	P. 132; Fig. 83	

Phase	Context	Description	Page & fig. nos of contexts in Volume II	Catalogued small finds in Volume I, environmental remains in Volume II and catalogued pottery in Volume III
3	?			Dec. Sam. 250-51, 253-6, 258-65, 267-74, 279-81, 283-4, 526-9; Sam. St. 557.
4	Level 1			Coin 185, 262, 265, 287; Cu.A. 111, 115, 279, 583-4, 616, 668, 690, 799; Iron 14, 59, 60, 104, 117; Gl.V. 57, 124-7, 251b, 252b; Gl.O. 63, 77-8, 103, 118, 288; Quern A. 114-16; Bone 76; C.W. 560; Mort. St. 15.
4	Level 2			Coin 232, 300, 303; Cu.A. 127, 164, 313, 458, 585-6, 713, 785; Lead A. 453; Iron 99, 126, 132; Gl.V. 21-2, 24, 49-50, 118, 242, 248, 302; Gl.O. 179-84, 287, 289-99; Quern A. 117-24; Bone 4, 53, 77-8, 124; Mort. 91; Mort. St. 12-13.
4	Levels 1-2			Dec. Sam. 530-32.
4	Levels 1-3			Gl.V. 119
4	2	Ditch		Mort. St. 14.
4	11	Drain fill	P. 136	Coin 267; Lead 5; Mort. 8.
4	125	Wall robbing		Coin 162, 218, 279; Cu.A. 387, 472; Lead A.480-81, (pewter) 528; Quern A. 165; Bone 24.
4	138			Lead A. 482.
4	140	Slot	P. 136	Cu.A. 591.
4	145			Cu.A. 253.
4	146		P. 136	Cu.A. 130.
	0			Coin 157-8, 164, 166, 168, 170, 177, 183, 187-8, 190, 193-5, 213, 215, 243, 299; Cu.A. 12, 45, 73, 104, 138, 266, 292, 300, 356, 392, 435, 457, 582, 682-3, 710-12; Lead 4, 7-8, 16, Lead A. 450-52; Iron 56, 67, 102;Gl.V. 245, 300, 301q, 303, 305g; Gl.O. 300-301; Quern A. 52; Mort. 72-3, 75-8, 80, 85; Mort. St. 16-17; Hum.

Trench 10

Phase	Context	Description	Page & fig. nos of contexts in Volume II	Catalogued small finds in Volume I, environmental remains in Volume II and catalogued pottery in Volume III
1	471	Layer	P. 138; Fig. 85	Cu.A. 76, 606, 748; Iron 124; Gl.V. 175b; Quern A. 178-9; Bone 15-16; Hum.; Sam. St. 1155; C.W. 186, 190.
1	471	Layer	P. 138; Fig. 85	
1	578	Structure AS post-hole	P. 137; Fig. 85	
1	583=471	Layer	P. 138	
1	611	Layer	P. 138	
1	612	Layer	P. 138	
1	734	Structure AO layer	P. 137; Fig. 85	Cu.A. 486; Gl.V. 258, 313b, 322b; C.W. 536, 541.
1	759	Ditch fill	P. 137	
1	760	Ditch fill	P. 137	
1	764	Structure AN destruction	P. 137	
1	783	Structure AO destruction	P. 137	C.W. 191; Mort. 27; Mort. St. 37.
1	802	Post-hole	P. 137	
1	823	Structure AO destruction	P. 137	Cu.A. 570.
1	824	Structures AP, AQ, AR sealing	P. 137	
1	826	Structures AP, AQ, AR sealing	P. 137; Fig. 85	Cu.A. 380.
1	836	Post-hole	P. 137; Fig. 85	

Phase	Context	Description	Page & fig. nos of contexts in Volume II	Catalogued small finds in Volume I, environmental remains in Volume II and catalogued pottery in Volume III
1	837	Post-hole	P. 137; Fig. 85	
1	840	Ditch fill	P. 137	
1	842	Structure AO destruction	P. 137	Cu.A. 651.
1	843	Post-hole	P. 137; Fig. 85	
1	844	Post-hole fill	P. 137	
1	845	Post-hole fill	P. 138	
1	847	Stake-hole	P. 137	
1	848=920	Structure AS slot	P. 137	Cu.A. 750.
1	849	Boundary ditch fill	P. 137	Cu.A. 487.
1	851	Layer	P. 137	
1	856	Gully	P. 137; Fig. 85	Gl.V. 312u.
1	862	Stake-hole	P. 137	
1	863	Stake-hole	P. 137	
1	864	Stake-hole	P. 137	
1	865	Post-hole	P. 137: Fig. 85	
1	867	Gully	P. 137; Fig. 85	
1	872	Structure AP, AQ, AR sealing	P. 137	Cu.A. 789; Cu.Arch.; Dec. Sam. 1038-9.
1	879	Structure AO destruction	P. 137	
1	881	Layer	P. 137; Fig. 85	
1	882	Structure AO layer	P. 137	Cu.A. 325; Gl.V. 273b.
1	883	Structure AO layer	P. 137	Cu.A. 34.
1	884	Post-hole	P. 137	
1	886	Slot	P. 137; Fig. 85	
1	888	Post-hole	P. 137; Fig. 85	
1	889	Structure AO destruction	P. 137	
1	890	Slot	P. 137; Fig. 85	C.W. 193.
1	892	Slot	P. 137; Fig. 85	
1	893	Post-hole	P. 137; Fig. 85	
1	895	Slot	P. 137	
1	896	Hearth	P. 137	
1	897	Structure AO destruction	P. 137	
1	898	Layer	P. 137	
1	919	Structure AS slot	P. 137; Fig. 85	
1	920	Structure AS slot	P. 137; Fig. 85	
1	926	Stonework	P. 138	
1	927	Structure AS slot	P. 137; Fig. 85	
1	928	Ditch	P. 137; Fig. 85	
1	930	Structure AS post-hole	P. 138; Fig. 85	
1	931	Structure AS post-hole	P. 138; Fig. 85	
1	933	Structure AS post-hole	P. 138; Fig. 85	
1	936	Slot	P. 138; Fig. 85	
1	937	Slot	P. 138; Fig. 85	
1	941	Slot	P. 138; Fig. 85	
1	942	Slot	P. 138; Fig. 85	
1	954	Slot area of Structure AS	P. 138; Fig. 85	Stone 68.
1	1000	Post-hole	P. 137; Fig. 85	
1	1001	Hearth	P. 137; Fig. 85	
1	1002	Gully	P. 138; Fig. 85	
1	1003	Sealing deposit	P. 137	
1	1004	Hearth	P. 137; Fig. 85	
1	1005	Layer	P. 137; Fig. 85	
1	1006	Sealing deposit	P. 137; Fig. 85	

Phase	Context	Description	Page & fig. nos of contexts in Volume II	Catalogued small finds in Volume I, environmental remains in Volume II and catalogued pottery in Volume III
1	1007	Gully area of Structures AP-AQ	P. 137	Gl.V 329b.
1	1008	Sealing deposit	P. 137	
1	1009	Stake-hole	P. 137	
1	1010	Stake-hole	P. 137	
1	1011	Stake-hole	P. 137	
1	1012	Stake-hole	P. 137	
1	1013	Stake-hole	P. 137	
1	1014	Stake-hole	P. 137	
1	1022	Layer	P. 137; Fig. 85	
1	1026	Post-hole	P. 137; Fig. 85	
1	1028	Layer	P. 137; Fig. 85	Mort. 51.
1	1029	Structure AO layer	P. 137; Fig. 85	Gl.V. 264; Quern A. 198.
1	1030	Stake-hole	P. 137	
1	1031	Stake-hole	P. 137	
1	1032	Stake-hole	P. 137	
1	1033	Stake-hole	P. 137	
1	1035	Slot	P. 137; Fig. 85	
1	1036	Slot	P. 137; Fig. 85	
1	1037	Slot	P. 137; Fig. 85	
1	1038	Structure AO stake-hole	P. 137	
1	1039	Structure AO stake-hole	P. 137	
1	1040	Structure AO stake-hole	P. 137	
1	1041	Structure AO stake-hole	P. 137	
1	1042	Structure AO stake-hole	P. 137	
1	1043	Structure AO stake-hole	P. 137	
1	1044	Structure AO stake-hole	P. 137	
1	1045	Structure AO stake-hole	P. 137	
1	1047	Structure AO rubbish	P. 137	
1	1048	Structure AO rubbish	P. 137	Cu.A. 308, 572, 766; C.W. 184-5.
1	1049	Sealing deposit	P. 137	
1	1050	Sealing deposit	P. 137	
1	1051	Sealing deposit	P. 137	
1	1052	Sealing deposit	P. 137	
1	1053	Post-hole	P. 137; Fig. 85	
1	1054	Stake-hole	P. 137	
1	1055	Stake-hole	P. 137	
1	1056	Stake-hole	P. 137	
1	1057	Stake-hole	P. 137	
1	1058	Stake-hole	P. 137	
1	1059	Post-hole	P. 137	
1	1060	Sealing deposit	P. 137	
1	1061	Sealing deposit	P. 137	
1	1062	Gully	P. 137	
1	1063	Sealing deposit	P. 137	
1	1064	Gully	P. 137; Fig. 85	
1	1065	Sealing deposit	P. 137	
1	1066	Sealing deposit	P. 137; Fig. 85	
1	1067	Structure AO rubbish	P. 137	Coin 228; Cu.A. 145, 181, 328, 739, Cu.Arch.; Gl.O. 92 Sam. St. 1118.
1	1068	Structure AO hearth	P. 137; Fig. 85	
1	1069	Structure AO hearth	P. 137; Fig. 85	
1	1070	Structure AO hearth	P. 137; Fig. 85	
1	1071	Structure AO hearth	P. 137; Fig. 85	

Phase	Context	Description	Page & fig. nos of contexts in Volume II	Catalogued small finds in Volume I, environmental remains in Volume II and catalogued pottery in Volume III
1	1072	Structure AO hearth	P. 137; Fig. 85	
1	1073	Structure AO hearth	P. 137; Fig. 85	
1	1074	Structure AO hearth	P. 137; Fig. 85	Bot. (Appendix 5).
1	1076	Structure AO stake-hole	P. 137	
1	1077	Structure AO stake-hole	P. 137	
1	1078	Structure AO stake-hole	P. 137	
1	1079	Post-hole	P. 137; Fig. 85	
1	1080	Structure AO stake-hole	P. 137	
1	1081	Structure AO stake-hole	P. 137	
1	1082	Structure AO stake-hole	P. 137	
1	1083	Structure AO post-hole	P. 137; Fig. 85	
1	1084	Structure AO gully	P. 137; Fig. 85	
1	1086	Structure AO rubbish	P. 137; Fig. 85	
1	1087	Structure AO topsoil	P. 137; Fig. 85	Coin 192, 214; Cu.A. 199, 222; Quern A. 199; Sam. St. 1180; C.W. 189.
1	1088	Structure AO post-hole	P. 137	
1	1089	Structure AO post-hole	P. 137; Fig. 85	
1	1090	Structure AO hearth	P. 137; Fig. 85	C.W. 187-8.
1	1091	Structure AO post-hole	P. 137; Fig. 85	
1	1092	Structure AO post-hole	P. 137	
1	1093	Structure AO post-hole	P. 137; Fig. 85	
1	1094	Structure AO post-hole	P. 137; Fig. 85	
1	1095	Slot	P. 137	
1	1096	Structure AO post-hole	P. 137	
1	1097	Slot	P. 137	
1	1098	Structure AO layer	P. 137	
1	1099	Structure AO post-hole	P. 137	
1	1100	Structure AO pit	P. 137; Fig. 85	
1	1101	Structure AO post-hole	P. 137; Fig. 85	
1	1102	Structure AO slot	P. 137; Fig. 85	
1	1103	Natural	P. 137	
1	1104	Structure AO stake-hole	P. 137	
1	1105	Structure AO stake-hole	P. 137	
1	1106	Structure AO stake-hole	P. 137	
1	1107	Structure AO stake-hole	P. 137	
1	1108	Structure AO stake-hole	P. 137	
1	1109	Structure AO stake-hole	P. 137	
1	1110	Structure AO stake-hole	P. 137	
1	1111	Structure AO stake-hole	P. 137	
1	1112	Structure AO stake-hole	P. 137	
1	1113	Structure AO stake-hole	P. 137	
1	1114	Structure AO stake-hole	P. 137	
1	1115	Structure AO stake-hole	P. 137	
1	1016	Structure AO stake-hole	P. 137	
1	1017	Structure AO stake-hole	P. 137	
1	1018	Structure AO stake-hole	P. 137	
1	1119	Structure AO stake-hole	P. 137	
1	1120	Structure AO stake-hole	P. 137	
1	1121	Structure AO stake-hole	P. 137	
1	1122	Structure AO stake-hole	P. 137	
1	1123	Structure AO stake-hole	P. 137	
1	1124	Structure AO stake-hole	P. 137	
1	1125	Structure AO stake-hole	P. 137	
1	1126	Structure AO stake-hole	P. 137	

Phase	Context	Description	Page & fig. nos of contexts in Volume II	Catalogued small finds in Volume I, environmental remains in Volume II and catalogued pottery in Volume III
1	1127	Structure AO stake-hole	P. 137	
1	1128	Structure AO stake-hole	P. 137	
1	1129	Structure AO stake-hole	P. 137	
1	1130	Structure AO stake-hole	P. 137	
1	1131	Structure AO stake-hole	P. 137	
1	1132	Structure AO stake-hole	P. 137	
1	1133	Structure AO stake-hole	P. 137	
1	1134	Structure AO stake-hole	P. 137	
1	1135	Structure AO stake-hole	P. 137	
1	1136	Structure AO stake-hole	P. 137	
1	1137	Structure AO stake-hole	P. 137	
1	1138	Structure AO stake-hole	P. 137	
1	1139	Structure AO hearth	P. 137; Fig. 85	
1	1141	Layer	P. 137	Cu.A. 192.
1	1142	Topsoil	P. 137	
1	1143	Layer	P. 137	
1	1144	Structure AN slot	P. 136; Fig. 85	
1	1145	Structure AN slot	P. 136, 137; Fig. 85	
1	1146	Structure AN slot	P. 136	
1	1147	Structure AN hearth	P. 136; Fig. 85	Cu.A. 408.
1	1148	Structure AN hearth	P. 136; Fig. 85	
1	1149	Boundary ditch	P. 137; Fig. 85	Cu.A. 358.
1	1144	Structure AN slot	P. 136	
1	1151	Natural surface	P. 136	Gl.V. 310b.
1	1152	Structure AN floor	P. 136; Fig. 85	
1	1153	Structure AN post-hole	P. 136; Fig. 85	
1	1154	Structure AN slot	P. 136; Fig. 85	
1	1156	Structure AN slot	P. 136	
1	1157	Structure AP slot	P. 137; Fig. 85	
1	1158	Structure AP slot	P. 137; Fig. 85	
1	1159	Structure AP slot	P. 137; Fig. 85	
1	1160	Hearth	P. 137; Fig. 85	
1	1163	Structure AQ slot	P. 137; Fig. 85	
1	1164	Structure AQ slot	P. 137; Fig. 85	
1	1165	Structure AQ slot	P. 137; Fig. 85	
1	1166	Structure AR slot	P. 137; Fig. 85	
1	1167	Structure AR slot	P. 137; Fig. 85	
1	1169	Structure AR slot corner	P. 137	
1	1170	Pit	P. 138	Dec. Sam. 1046.
1	1173	Structure AR floor	P. 137; Fig. 85	Dec. Sam. 1047-9.
1	1174	Structure AQ slot	P. 137; Fig. 85	
1	1175	Structure AR floor	P. 137; Fig. 85	
2	62	Bye-road	P. 139	Sam. St. 1146.
2	64	Layer	P. 139	
2	65	Layer	P. 139	
2	70	Bye-road	P. 139	
2	293	Bye-road	P. 139	
2	327	Structure AV oven	P. 140	
2	389	Rubbish over Structure AT	P. 138	Cu.A. 237, 257, 341, 369, 378, 481, 552, 635, 754, Cu.Arch; Lead A. 508-9; Iron 114, 135; Gl.V. 71, 267, 269b, 272; Gl.O. 80, 105, 257, 268; Cruc. 2, 4; Sam. St. 1083, 1085, 1109; C.W. 206, 219, 222-3; An. ca., s./g., h., d., c.; Hum.

Phase	Context	Description	Page & fig. nos of contexts in Volume II	Catalogued small finds in Volume I, environmental remains in Volume II and catalogued pottery in Volume III
2	431	Structure AU destruction	P. 139	Cu.A. 555; Lead A. 510-11; Gl.V. 132; Quern A. 177; Stone 71; C.W. 212; Mort. 26, 42.
2	432	Structure AU abandonment	P. 139	
2	433	Structure AU abandonment		Cu.A. 403.
2	434	Structure AU abandonment	P. 139	
2	440	Bye-road	P. 139; Fig. 86	Cu.A. 15, 93, 124, 149, 268, 357, 365, Cu.Arch; Dec. Sam. .1026; Sam. St. 1133; C.W. 197; Mort. 29; Mort. St. 39.
2	455	Slot in vicinity of bye-road	P. 139	Cu.Arch.; Lead A. 513; Gl.V. 155, 191f, 312af, 329f; C.W. 216., 227-8
2	459	Bye-road drain	P. 139; Fig. 86	Cu.A. 342, 460, 765; Gl.V. 272c; Gl.O. 265, 269; Bone 65; C.W. 204.
2	460	Bye-road	P. 139; Fig. 86	Iron 25
2	462	Rubbish over Structure AT	P. 138;	Cu.A. 238, 258, 277, 547-9, 558, 636, Cu.Arch.; Lead A. 516; Gl.V. 312v; C.W. 220; Mort. 49, 69.
2	469	Structure AV *opus signinum*	P. 140; Fig. 86	
2	473=440	Bye-road	P. 139	Cu.Arch..
2	474	Pit	P. 139	Coin 271; Cu.A. 319; Gl.V. 312z, 318; C.W. 208, 231.
2	475	Bye-road drain	P. 139	Sam. St. 1139.
2	476	Hearth	P. 139	
2	477	Post-hole	P. 139	
2	478	Post-hole	P. 139	
2	479=609	Structure AV hearth ash	P. 140; Fig. 86	Cu.A. 500; Iron 125.
2	480	Structure AV slot	P. 140; Fig. 86	Cu.A. 560; Sam. St. 1095.
2	481	Pit	P. 140;	Cu.A. 117, 637; Lead A. 517; Gl.V. 191g, ac; C.W. 207, 214; C.W. 226, 230.
2	484	Structure AV oven	P. 140	
2	487	Slot	P. 139	
2	490	Structure AT abandonment	P. 139	
2	491	Structure AT slot	P. 138; Fig. 86	Cu.A. 58, 90, 561-2.
2	492	Slot fill	P. 138	
2	494	Structure AV hearth	P. 139; Fig. 86	Mort. 4; Mort. St. 34.
2	495	Structure AV slot	P. 140; Fig. 86	Gl.V. 165; Dec. Sam. 1031; Sam. St. 1160, 1163; C.W. 195-6, 209, 213.
2	496	Structure AV floor	P. 140	Jewel. 72; C.W. 205.
2	497	Structure AV floor	P. 140	
2	498	Structure AV floor	P. 140	Gl.V. 73b.
2	499	Structure AV hearth ash (external)	P. 140	Cu.A. 483, Cu.Arch.; Lead A. 520; Gl.V. 143
2	500	Structure AV slot	P. 140; Fig. 86	
2	501	Structure AV floor	P. 140	Cu.A. 75; Iron 15; Bone 103.
2	502	Structure AV slot	P. 140; Fig. 86	
2	503	Structure AV floor	P. 140	Jewel. 9; Gl.O. 258; C.W. 198, 210.
2	504	Structure AV slot	P. 140; Fig. 86	
2	505	Structure AV slot	P. 140: Fig. 86	
2	506	Structure AV floor	P. 140	Cu.A. 634; Gl.V. 262b; Gl.O. 263, 266; Bone 106-21.
2	527	Structure AT layer	P. 138; Fig. 86	Cu.A. 269; Iron 82.
2	528	Structure AT slot	P. 138: Fig. 86	
2	529	Structure AT layer	P. 138; Fig. 86	
2	530	Structure AT layer	P. 138; Fig. 86	Iron 139-40.
2	533	Structure AV floor	P. 140; Fig. 86	Cu.A. 259.
2	534	Structure AV ?oven flue	P. 140; Fig. 86	
2	543	Structure AU pit/post-hole	P. 139	
2	544	Structure AU pit/post-hole	P. 139	

Phase	Context	Description	Page & fig. nos of contexts in Volume II	Catalogued small finds in Volume I, environmental remains in Volume II and catalogued pottery in Volume III
2	545	Structure AU pit/post-hole	P. 139	
2	546	Structure AU abandonment	P. 139	
2	547	Structure AU post-hole	P. 139	Gl.V. 312ag.
2	548	Structure AU abandonment	P. 139	
2	549=440	Bye-road	P. 139	Cu.A. 396.
2	550	Structure AU abandonment	P. 139	
2	551	Structure AU abandonment	P. 139	
2	552	Structure AU abandonment	P. 139	
2	564	Structure AU abandonment	P. 139	
2	569	Bye-road	P. 139	
2	571	Structure AU abandonment	P. 139	
2	574	Structure AU abandonment	P. 139	
2	579	Structure AU abandonment	P. 139	Cu.A. 674; Gl.V. 175c. 183; Amber 2; Shale 4; Sam. St. 1149.
2	580	Structure AU sealing	P. 139	
2	581	Structure AU sealing	P. 139	
2	582	Structure AU abandonment	P. 139	Graffiti 42; C.W. 229.
2	584	Structure AV hearth	P. 140; Fig. 86	
2	589	Structure AU abandonment	P. 139	Cu.A. 735; Gl.V. 310e; Dec. Sam. 1032.
2	590	Structure AU stake-hole	P. 138	
2	591	Structure AU stake-hole	P. 138	
2	592	Structure AU stake-hole	P. 138	
2	593	Structure AU stake-hole	P. 138	
2	594	Structure AU stake-hole	P. 138	
2	595	Structure AU stake-hole	P. 138	
2	596	Structure AU stake-hole	P. 138	
2	597	Structure AU stake-hole	P. 138	
2	598	Structure AU stake-hole	P. 139	
2	600	Structure AT layer	P. 138	Cu.A. 10.
2	601	Structure AV hearth	P. 140	
2	602	Structure AV hearth	P. 140	Cu.A. 793.
2	603	Structure AV hearth	P. 140	
2	604	Structure AT layer	P. 138	
2	606	Structure AV floor	P. 140; Fig. 86	Cu.A. 92.
2	607	Structure AV hearth debris	P. 140	
2	608	Structure AV floor	P. 140	
2	609	Structure AV hearth ash	P. 140; Fig. 86	Bone 68.
2	616	Structure AV oven ash pit	P. 140	
2	617	Pit	P. 139	
2	618	Structure AT destruction	P. 138	Gl.V. 312w; Mort. St. 40.
2	619	Structure AT destruction	P. 138	Cu.A. 461; Gl.V. 268.
2	620	Bye-road	P. 139	Coin 182; Cu.A. 39, 295.
2	620A	Bye-road	P. 139	Dec. Sam. 1034.
2	621	Bye-road	P. 139	Gl.O. 260.
2	622	Slot	P. 140	
2	624	Bye-road	P. 139	Coin 154.
2	625	Structure AV layer	P. 140	Cu.Arch.
2	626	Bye-road	P. 139	
2	627=616	Oven ash pit	P. 140	
2	628	Bye-road	P. 139	Dec. Sam. 1035; Sam. St. 1099-1100; C.W. 225.
2	629=440	Bye-road	P. 139	
2	630	Structure AV slot	P. 140; Fig. 86	
2	631	Hearth	P. 140; Fig. 86	
2	632	Structure AV floor	P. 140; Fig. 86	

Phase	Context	Description	Page & fig. nos of contexts in Volume II	Catalogued small finds in Volume I, environmental remains in Volume II and catalogued pottery in Volume III
2	633	Structure AV stake-hole	P. 140	
2	634	Structure AV slot	P. 140; Fig. 86	
2	635	Layer	P. 140; Fig. 86	
2	636=632	Structure AV floor	P. 140	
2	637	Structure AV floor	P. 140	
2	638	Structure AV floor	P. 140; Fig. 86	
2	639	Structure AV layer	P. 140	Bone 105.
2	643	Pit/post-hole	P. 139	
2	646	Structure AU post-hole	P. 139	Gl.V. 313i; C.W. 215.
2	647	Layer	P. 139	Cu.A. 444, 736, Cu.Arch.
2	648	Structure AU post-hole	P. 139	Gl.V. 321.
2	649	Structure AU post-hole	P. 139	Quern A. 55-6, 180; C.W. 200.
2	650	Structure AU ash pit	P. 139; Fig. 86	Cu.A. 221, 563-5, Cu.Arch.; Lead 21, Lead A. 523; Gl.O. 271.
2	651	Pit/post-hole	P. 139	
2	652	Pit/post-hole	P. 139	
2	653	Pit/post-hole	P. 139	
2	654	Pit/post-hole	P. 139	
2	656	Structure AU abandonment	P. 139	C.W. 218.
2	657	Structure AU sealing	P. 139	
2	658	Structure AU abandonment	P. 139	
2	659	Pit/post-hole	P. 139	
2	670	Structure AT burnt daub	P. 138; Fig. 86	
2	671	Structure AT layer	P. 138	Cu.A. 484.
2	672	Structure AT stake-hole	P. 138	
2	673	Structure AT stake-hole	P. 138	
2	674	Structure AT stake-hole	P. 138	
2	675	Structure AT stake-hole	P. 138	
2	679	Structure AV hearth ash (external)	P. 140	
2	688	Structure AV hearth ash (external)	P. 140	Coin 226, 233; Cu.A. 41, 232, 419; Gl.V. 169-70, 174, 194, 312ah; Quern A.181; Bone 212; Sam. St. 1060, 1167, 1171; C.W. 199, 201.
2	689	Structure AU slot	P. 139	Cu.Arch.
2	690	Structure AU pit/post-hole	P. 139	
2	691	Structure AT stake-hole	P. 138	
2	692	Bye-road	P. 139	Cu.A. 33; Bone 127.
2	694=440	Bye-road	P. 139	Cu.A. 749, Cu.Arch.
2	695	Slot in vicinity of bye-road	P. 139;	Gl.V. 261; Quern A. 182.
2	696=745/ 758/831	Structure AU floor	P. 139; Fig. 86	Cu.A. 737.
2	697	Slot in vicinity of bye-road	P. 139	
2	698	Bye-road	P. 139	
2	699	Bye-road	P. 139	Cu.Arch.
2	700	Structure AU abandonment	P. 139	Coin 229; Cu.A. 420, 567, 738; Cu.Arch.; Stone 139.
2	701	Structure AU stake-hole	P. 139	
2	702	Structure AU stake-hole	P. 138	
2	703	Structure AT stake-hole	P. 138	
2	704	Structure AT stake-hole	P. 138	
2	705	Structure AU stake-hole	P. 139	
2	706	Structure AU stake-hole	P. 139	
2	707	Structure AU stake-hole	P. 139	
2	708	Structure AU pit/post-hole	P. 139	Sam. St. 1112.
2	709	Structure AU stake-hole	P. 139	

Phase	Context	Description	Page & fig. nos of contexts in Volume II	Catalogued small finds in Volume I, environmental remains in Volume II and catalogued pottery in Volume III
2	710	Structure AU stake-hole	P. 139	
2	711	Structure AU stake-hole	P. 139	
2	712	Structure AU pit/post-hole	P. 139	
2	714	Structure AU stake-hole	P. 139	Gl.V. 317.
2	715	Structure AU stake-hole	P. 139	
2	716	Structure AU stake-hole	P. 139	
2	717	Structure AU pit/post-hole	P. 139	
2	718	Structure AU pit/post-hole	P. 139	
2	719	Structure AT stake-hole	P. 138	
2	720	Structure AT stake-hole	P. 138	C.W. 224.
2	721	Structure AT stake-hole	P. 138	
2	722	Structure AT stake-hole	P. 138	
2	723	Structure AT stake-hole	P. 138	
2	724	Structure AT stake-hole	P. 138	
2	725	Structure AT occupation	P. 138; Fig. 86	
2	726	Structure AT occupation	P. 138; Fig. 86	
2	727	Structure AT floor	P. 138; Fig. 86	
2	728	Structure AT floor	P. 138; Fig. 86	Cu.A. 397, 485,Cu.Arch.; Gl.V. 71a, 139; Quern A. 183; Bone 6.
2	729	Structure AT floor	P. 138; Fig. 86	Lead A. 524; Iron 16; Quern A. 184.
2	730	Structure AT floor	P. 138; Fig. 86	
2	731	Structure AT floor	P. 138; Fig. 86	
2	732	Structure AT floor	P. 138; Fig. 86	
2	733	Structure AU stake-hole	P. 138; Fig. 86	
2	735	Structure AU slot	P. 139; Fig. 86	
2	736	Structure AU slot	P. 138; Fig. 86	
2	737	Structure AU slot	P. 138; Fig. 86	Quern A. 185.
2	737/1	Bye-road	P. 139; Fig. 86	
2	738	Layer	P. 139	Cu.Arch.
2	738/1	Bye-road hoof marks	P. 139	
2	739	Structure AU abandonment	P. 139	Gl.O. 86; Sam. St. 1078.
2	740	Structure AU slot	P. 138; Fig. 86	
2	741	Bye-road wheel ruts	P. 139	
2	742	Bye-road wheel ruts	P. 139	
2	743	Bye-road	P. 139	Cu.A. 217, 566, 568, 638-9; Iron 83; Gl.O. 83; C.W. 232
2	744	Bye-road	P. 139	
2	745	Structure AU floor	P. 139	
2	746	Structure AU floor	P. 139; Fig. 86	
2	747	Structure AU floor	P. 139	Cu.Arch.; Iron 10.
2	748	Structure AU abandonment	P. 139	
2	749	Structure AU abandonment	P. 139	Cu.A. 551; Sam. St. 1084; Mort. 114.
2	750	Structure AU pit/post-hole	P. 139	
2	771	Structure AU stake-hole	P. 139	
2	751	Structure AU abandonment	P. 139	
2	752	Structure AU hearth/oven	P. 139; Fig. 86	
2	753	Structure AU stake-hole	P. 138	
2	754	Structure AU stake-hole	P. 138	
2	755	Structure AU stake-hole	P. 138	
2	756	Structure AU stake-hole	P. 138	Cu.Arch.
2	757	Structure AU abandonment	P. 139	Cu.A. 35, 74, 343, 569, Cu.Arch; Gl.V. 307c; Quern A. 186-7; C.W. 221.
2	758	Structure AU floor	P. 139: Fig. 86	
2	761	Structure AU slot	P. 138; Fig. 86	Quern A. 57, 188-9.
2	762	Structure AU slot	P. 138; Fig. 86	Cu.A. 398, 425; Quern 16-17, Quern A. 58-9; Stone 141.

Phase	Context	Description	Page & fig. nos of contexts in Volume II	Catalogued small finds in Volume I, environmental remains in Volume II and catalogued pottery in Volume III
2	763	Structure AU abandonment	P. 139	Lead 14; Mort. St. 45.
2	765	Bye-road drain	P. 139; Fig. 86	
2	768	Structure AU pit/post-hole	P. 139	
2	769	Structure AU pit/post-hole	P 139	
2	770	Structure AU stake-hole	P. 138	
2	771	Structure AU stake-hole	P. 139	
2	772	Structure AU stake-hole	P. 139	
2	773	Structure AU stake-hole	P. 139	
2	774	Structure AU stake-hole	P. 139	
2	775	Structure AU stake-hole	P. 139	
2	776	Structure AU stake-hole	P. 139	
2	777	Structure AU oven ash pit	P. 139; Fig. 86	
2	778	Structure AU slot	P. 139; Fig. 86	
2	779	Structure AU slot	P. 139; Fig. 86	
2	780	Slot	P. 139	Cu.Arch.
2	781	Structure AU stake-hole	P. 139	
2	782	Structure AU hearth/oven	P. 139; Fig. 86	
2	784	Structure AU floor	P. 139; Fig. 86	Cu.A. 401.
2	785	Structure AU floor	P. 139; Fig. 86	Cu.Arch.
2	786	Structure AU hearth/oven	P. 139; Fig. 86	
2	787	Layer	P. 139	Cu.Arch.
2	788	Bye-road	P. 139	
2	789	Bye-road	P. 139	
2	790	Structure AT slot	P. 138; Fig. 86	
2	791	Structure AT stake-hole	P. 138; Fig. 86	
2	792	Structure AT ?drain	P. 138; Fig. 86	
2	793	Structure AT layer	P. 138	
2	794	Structure AT layer	P. 138	
2	795	Structure AT floor	P. 138; Fig. 86	Gl.V. 311; Quern A. 191.
2	796	Structure AT slot	P. 138; Fig. 86	Lead A. 525; Quern A. 192; Dec. Sam. 1036.
2	797	Structure AV oven	P. 140	
2	798	Structure AT oven	P. 140	
2	799	Structure AU pit/post-hole	P. 139	
2	800	Structure AV oven	P. 140	Sam. St. 1148.
2	801	Structure AV floor	P. 140	Gl.V. 264b.
2	803	Slot	P. 139	Cu.Arch.
2	804	Structure AT layer	P. 138	
2	805	Structure AU stonework	P. 139	Stone 142.
2	806	Structure AU stake-hole	P. 139	
2	807	Structure AU stake-hole	P. 138	
2	808	Bye-road	P. 139	
2	809	Structure AU abandonment	P. 139	Cu.Arch.
2	811	Structure AU hearth	P. 139; Fig. 86	
2	812	Bye-road	P. 139	Gl.V. 329c.
2	813	Structure AV slot	P. 140; Fig. 86	
2	814	Structure AV hearth	P. 140	
2	815	Structure AU abandonment	P. 139	Cu.A. 260.
2	816	Bye-road	P. 139	
2	817	Structure AV layer	P. 140	
2	818	Structure AV layer	P. 140	
2	819	Layer	P. 140	
2	820	Pit cut into bye-road foundation	P. 139; Fig. 86	

Phase	Context	Description	Page & fig. nos of contexts in Volume II	Catalogued small finds in Volume I, environmental remains in Volume II and catalogued pottery in Volume III
2	821	Pit cut into bye-road foundation	P. 139; Fig. 86	
2	822	Structure AU slot	P. 138	Dec. Sam. 1037.
2	825	Bye-road	P. 139	Cu.A. 699; Sam. St. 1161.
2	827	Structure AU abandonment	P. 139	Cu.A. 571, Cu.Arch.
2	828=440	Bye-road	P. 139	Cu.A. 172, Cu.Arch.
2	829	Bye-road	P. 139	
2	831	Structure AU floor	P. 139; Fig. 86	
2	832	Structure AU slot	P. 138; Fig. 86	
2	833	Structure AU abandonment	P. 139	
2	834	Structure AU abandonment	P. 139	Cu.A. 412, Cu.Arch.; Gl.V. 269.
2	835	Bye-road	P. 139	Cu.A. 80; C.W. 202.
2	838	Post-hole cut into bye-road foundation	P. 139; Fig. 86	
2	839	Structure AU post-setting	P. 138; Fig. 86	
2	846	Structure AU pit/post-hole	P. 139	
2	850	Structure AU hearth sealing	P. 139	
2	852	Bye-road	P. 139	
2	853	Bye-road wheel-ruts	P. 139	
2	854	Bye-road hoof marks	P. 139	
2	855	Bye-road	P. 139	
2	857	Structure AV slot	P. 140; Fig 86	
2	858=440	Bye-road	P. 139	
2	866	Structure AU abandonment	P. 139	Cu.A. 399.
2	868	Structure AU pit/post-hole	P. 139	
2	869	Structure AU abandonment	P. 139	
2	870	Structure AU hearth bowl	P. 139	
2	871	Bye-road	P. 139	
2	873	Structure AU abandonment	P. 139	Cu.A. 8; Quern A. 193.
2	874	Structure AU stake-hole	P. 139	
2	875	Structure AU stake-hole	P. 139	
2	876	Structure AU stake-hole	P. 139	
2	877	Structure AU stake-hole	P. 139	
2	878	Structure AU post-setting	P. 138; Fig. 86	
2	880	Structure AU abandonment	P. 139	
2	885	Structure AU slot	Pp 138, 139; Fig. 86	
2	887	Structure AU pit/post-hole	P. 139	
2	891	Structure AU slot	P. 139	Cu.A. 82, 326, 640.
2	894	Structure AU post-hole	P. 139; Fig. 86	Quern A. 194; Stone 143.
2	899	Structure AU slot	P. 138	
2	925	Slot	P. 140	
2	929	Structure AV hearth ash (external)	P. 140	Cu.A. 46.
2	934	Structure AV hearth ash (external)	P. 140	
2	943	Bye-road	P. 139	
2	1015	Structure AU stake-hole	P. 139	
2	1016	Structure AU stake-hole	P. 139	
2	1017	Structure AU stake-hole	P. 139	
2	1018	Structure AU stake-hole	P. 139	
2	1019	Structure AU stake-hole	P. 138	
2	1020	Structure AU pit/post-hole	P. 139	
2	1021	Structure AU pit/post-hole	P. 139	

Phase	Context	Description	Page & fig. nos of contexts in Volume II	Catalogued small finds in Volume I, environmental remains in Volume II and catalogued pottery in Volume III
2	1024	Structure AU abandonment	P. 139	
2	1025	Structure AU post-hole	P. 139; Fig. 86	Quern A. 196-7.
2	1034	Structure AU pit/post-hole	P. 139	
2	1075	Structure AT preparatory level	P. 138	Cu.A. 9; Sam. St. 1162; C.W. 211, 217.
2	1085	Structure AU slot	P. 139	
2	1140	Structure AU pit/post-hole	P. 139	C.W. 203.
2	1155=528	Structure AT slot	P. 138	
2	1168=480	Structure AV slot	P. 140	
3	16	Structure AW wall	P. 140; Fig. 87	Iron 62; Gl.O. 216.
3	17	Structure AW wall	P. 140; Fig. 87	Cu.A. 530, Cu.Arch; Sam. St. 1098.
3	18	Structure AW wall	P. 140; Fig. 87	Coin 291; Cu.A. 150, 230, 235; Lead A. 491; Iron 5, 63-5, 113; Bone 36, 89; Graffiti 23; C.W. 352.
3	19	Structure AW wall	P. 140; Fig. 87	
3	20	Structure AW foundation trench	P. 141	Cu.A. 409.
3	21	Structure AW slot	P. 143; Fig. 87	
3	22	Structure AW wall	P. 140; Fig. 87	C.W. 265.
3	23	Structure AW ?foundation trench	P. 141	
3	24	Structure AW wall	P. 140; Fig. 87	Stone 52; Dec. Sam. 1003; C.W. 266, 293.
3	25	Structure AW wall	P. 140; Fig. 87	
3	26	Structure AW wall	P. 140; Fig. 87	Coin 205, 301; Bone 58.
3	27	Structure AW surface	P. 141	Cu.A. 670-71, Cu.Arch.; Gl.V. 323; Bone 29; Hum.
3	28	Structure AW late slot	P. 143	Cu.Arch.; Gl.V. 311e, 312ai, 320, 325, 327d; Stone 53, 130; Dec. Sam. 1002, 1004; Sam. St. 1156, 1175; C.W. 295, 297, 321, 354, 357; Mort. 95, 99.
3	29	Structure AW *opus signinum*	P. 143; Fig. 87	
3	30	Structure AW; grain store gravel	P.141	Cu.A. 531, Cu.Arch; C.W. 289.
3	31	Structure AW courtyard floor	P. 141	Cu.A. 592, 725; Bot. (Appendix 4).
3	33	Structure AW layer	P. 143	Pot.C. 10.
3	34	Structure AW wall	P. 140; Fig. 87	
3	35	Structure AW wall	P. 140; Fig. 87	
3	56	Structure AW slot	Pp 143, 144; Fig. 87	Dec. Sam. 1005; Hum.
3	59=131	Structure AX wall	P. 143	
3	60=131	Structure AX wall	P. 143	
3	61	Layer	P. 144	Hum.
3	63=299	Structure AX floor	P. 144	
3	66=245	Structure AX wall	P. 143	
3	74	Structure AX layer	P. 150	Cu.A. 440, Cu.Arch.; Gl.V. 27.
3	75=909	Structure AX rubbish pit	P. 147	Gl.V. 31, 153, 315c, 325b; Sam. St. 1134, 1177.
3	76=908	Structure AX rubbish pit	P. 147	
3	81	Structure AX wall	Pp 143, 144	Cu.Arch.; Lead A. 493-4; Gl.V. 72, 179, 193, 260, 260b; Sam. St. 1075, 1113; C.W. 256, 334.
3	83	Structure AW; grain store gravel	P. 141	Coin 231; Cu.A. 167, 255, 314, 497, 533, 727, Cu.Arch.; Iron 43; Gl.V. 30, 34, 168, 191h-i, 312h; Sam. St. 1128 C.W. 264, 306-8, 337, 342-3, 358, 361-3; Mort. 79,81.
3	84	Structure AW courtyard floor	P. 141	Cu.A. 85, Cu.Arch.
3	85	Structure AW foundation	P. 143	

Phase	Context	Description	Page & fig. nos of contexts in Volume II	Catalogued small finds in Volume I, environmental remains in Volume II and catalogued pottery in Volume III
3	86	Structure AW foundation	P. 143	
3	87	Structure AW foundation	P. 143	
3	88	Structure AW foundation	P. 143	
3	89	Structure AW foundation	P. 143	
3	90	Structure AW courtyard floor	P. 141	
3	91	Structure AW courtyard	P. 141	Cu.A. 376, 394, 534, Cu.Arch.; Lead 20, 27, Lead A. 495-6; Bone 30; Sam. St. 1051.
3	92	Structure AW courtyard floor	P. 141; Fig. 87	Cu.Arch.; Gl.V. 71b; Dec. Sam. 1010.
3	93	Structure AW floor foundation	P. 141	
3	94A/B	Structure AW pit	P. 143	Cu.A. 400, 417.
3	95	Structure AW floor foundation	P. 141	
3	96	Structure AW layer	P. 143	
3	98	Structure AW layer	P. 143	
3	102	Structure AW floor foundation	P. 141	
3	103	Structure AW floor foundation	P. 141	
3	104	Structure AW floor foundation	P. 141	C.W. 299.
3	105	Structure AW floor foundation	P. 141	
3	106	Structure AW deposit	P. 141	
3	108	Structure AW layer	P. 143	
3	109	Structure AW layer	P. 143	
3	110	Structure AW layer	P. 143	
3	111	Structure AW layer	P. 143	
3	118	Gap between structures	P. 143	Cu.A. 231, Cu.Arch.; Iron 123; Gl.V. 28, 165, 191c; Pot.C. 14; Graffiti 35; Sam. St. 1106, 1117, 1120, 1182; C.W. 245, 317, 335; Mort. 66; Mort. St. 30.
3	119	Structure AW layer	P. 143;	Cu.Arch; Mort. St. 35.
3	121	Structure AW; grain store floor	P. 141	Coin 258; Cu.A. 14, 315-16, 535-7, 593, 627-8, 647, 672, 801, Cu.Arch.; Lead A. 497-500; Iron 86-7; Gl.V. 166; Quern 10, Quern A. 172-3, Bone 90-91; C.W. 309, 336; Bot.
3	125	Gap between structures	P. 143; Fig. 89 S.13	Cu.Arch.; Gl.V. 191j; Stone 132.
3	126	Gap between structures	P. 143; Fig. 89 S.13	
3	127	Gap between structures	P. 143; Fig. 89	Gl.V. 178, 191k, 312c, n, x; Dec. Sam. 1012; C.W. 233, 332; Mort. 92; Mort. St. 33, 42.
3	129	Structure AX floor	P. 144	Jewel. 8; Cu.Arch.; Gl.V. 133, 180-81, 198b, 205, 264c, 265, 307d, 309-10; Quern A. 174-5; Stone 55, 133; Graffiti 36; Sam. St. 1094; C.W. 238-9, 260, 277-8, 314, 323, 360; Mort. 13, 23; Mort. St. 28; Hum.
3	131	Structure AX wall	Pp 143,144; Fig. 87	Cu.A. 538, Cu.Arch.; Lead 28; Gl.V. 260d.
3	133	Structure AX post-hole	P. 144	Cu.Arch.
3	134	Structure AX destruction	P. 144	Cu.A. 594-5, 764, Cu.Arch.; Iron 33, 50; Bone 92, 125.
3	135	Structure AX destruction	P. 144; Fig. 87	
3	136	Structure AX pit	P. 144	Bone 93; Sam. St. 1147.

Phase	Context	Description	Page & fig. nos of contexts in Volume II	Catalogued small finds in Volume I, environmental remains in Volume II and catalogued pottery in Volume III
3	137	Structure AX post-hole	P. 144	
3	138	Structure AX post-hole	P. 144	
3	139	Structure AX post-hole	P. 144	
3	140	Structure AX post-hole	P. 144	
3	141	Structure AX layer	P. 144	Sam. St. 1127.
3	142	Structure AX destruction	P. 144	
3	144	Drain west of Structure AX	P. 150	
3	147	Structure AX floor	P. 144	Coin 171, 223, 242; Cu.A. 424; Sam. St. 1055, 1102.
3	148	Structure AX relaid surface	P. 141	
3	149	Layer between buidings	P. 143; Fig. 87	
3	150	Structure AW destruction deposit	P. 141	
3	151	Structure AX floor	P. 144	Coin 224; Cu.A. 648; Cu.Arch.; Gl.V. 146b; Gl.O. 87; Bone 94.
3	153	Structure AW courtyard floor	P. 141	Cu.A. 630; Cu.Arch.; Iron 55.
3	155	Well pit lining	P. 150	Sam. St. 1081.
3	157	Structure AW courtyard floor	P. 141	Cu.Arch.; Gl.O. 267; C.W. 268.
3	160	Structure AX floor	P. 144; Fig. 87	
3	162	Structure AX floor	P. 144	Cu.A. 178, 539-41, 596, 792, 796, Cu.Arch.; Gl.V. 191l, 201b, 312s, 313, 324b; Gl.O. 302-3, 306; Bone 190, 201 Dec. Sam. 1013; C.W. 367.
3	166	Structure AW debris	P. 141	Bot.
3	167	Structure AX courtyard pit	P. 144	Coin 272, 307; Cu.A.477, 729, Cu.Arch.; Jewel. 5; Gl.V. 191ad, 192b; Bone 95.
3	168	Structure AX layer	P. 144	Cu.A. 262; Stone 56.
3	169	Gap between structures	P. 143; Fig. 89	Gl.V. 175g, 191ae, af; C.W. 271, 302, 312-13, 325, 329; Mort. 60; Mort. St. 54.
3	170	Structure AX floor	P. 144	Lead A. 503; Bone 59.
3	171	Structure AW debris	P. 141	
3	172	Structure AW slot	P. 143	Bot.
3	173	Structure AW floor foundation	P. 141	Cu.Arch.
3	174	Structure AW slot	P. 143; Fig. 87	Cu.A. 317-18; Cu.Arch.; Iron 23, 51; Gl.V. 191m, 324; Stone 57; Bone 210; Dec. Sam. 1014-17; Sam. St. 1057, 1090, 1119, 1131; C.W. 288, 298, 316, 339.
3	175	Structure AW slot fill	P. 143	
3	176	Structure AX pit	P. 144	
3	177	Structure AW wall	P. 140; Fig. 87	
3	178	Structure AW layer	P. 143	
3	179	Structure AW floor	P. 141; Fig. 87	
3	180	Structure AW layer	P. 143	
3	181=305	Structure AW wall	P. 140	
3	182	Structure AW pit	P. 143	
3	183	Structure AW courtyard floor	P. 141	Cu.Arch.; Bone 170, 211; C.W. 320.
3	184	Structure AW wall	P. 141; Fig. 87	Gl.V. 185.
3	185=184	Structure AW wall	P. 141	
3	186	Structure AW post-hole	P. 143	
3	187	Structure AW post-hole	P. 143	
3	188	Structure AW surface	P. 141	Gl.O. 218.
3	189	Structure AW pit	P. 143	
3	190	Structure AW foundation	P. 143	

Phase	Context	Description	Page & fig. nos of contexts in Volume II	Catalogued small finds in Volume I, environmental remains in Volume II and catalogued pottery in Volume III
3	191	Structure AX layer	P. 144	
3	192	Structure AW slot fill	P. 143	C.W. 303.
3	193	Structure AW post-hole	P. 141	
3	194	Structure AW pit	P. 143	
3	195	Structure AX post-hole	P. 144	Cu.Arch.
3	196	Structure AW pit	P. 143	C.W. 283.
3	197	Structure AX floor	P. 144	Coin 189; Cu.A. 498; Lead 34; Gl.V. 312y, 327; Sam. St. 1087; C.W. 252, 257.
3	198	Structure AX courtyard rubbish	P. 144	Cu.A. 347, 406, 597-8, Cu.Arch.; Lead A. 504 C.W. 273.
3	199	Structure AW post-hole	P. 143	
3	200	Structure AW post-hole	P. 143	
3	201	Structure AW post-hole	P. 143	
3	202	Structure AW floor foundation	P. 141	
3	203	Structure AX ?wheel ruts	P. 144	
3	205	Structure AW courtyard floor	P. 141	
3	206	Structure AW destruction deposit	P. 141	Cu.A. 94.
3	209	Fill of slot 021/174	P. 143	C.W. 345.
3	210	Structure AW post-hole	P. 143	
3	211	Structure AW post-hole	P. 143	
3	212	Structure AW post-hole	P. 143	C.W. 212.
3	213	Structure AX pit fill	P. 144	
3	215	East of Structure AW	P. 143	
3	217	Structure AW pit	P. 143	
3	218	East of Structure AW	P. 143	
3	220	Structure AW post-hole	P. 143	
3	221	Structure AW layer	P. 143	
3	222	Structure AW layer	P. 143	
3	223	Structure AW debris	P. 141	
3	226	Structure AX floor	P. 144	Gl.V. 16; Stone 58; Sam. St. 1164.; C.W. 328
3	227	Structure AX pit	P. 144	
3	230	Structure AW layer	P. 143	
3	231	Structure AX layer	P. 144	Gl.V. 175f; Bone 12.
3	232	Structure AX layer	P. 144	
3	233	Structure AX layer	P. 144	
3	234	Structure AW grain store floor	P. 141	Cu.A. 154, 168, 236, 542-5, 631-2, 662, 680, Cu.Arch.; Gl.V. 29; Gl.O. 93, 215, 217; Bone 31, 97-9; Sam. St. 1079; C.W. 341.
3	235	Structure AW layer	P. 143	
3	236	Structure AX floor	P. 144	Bone 100.
3	237	Structure AX floor	P. 144	Coin 160, 174-6, 181, 209, 222, 247, 250, 270; Cu.A. 599, 730, Cu.Arch.; Gl.V. 61c, 73-4, 159b, 160, 167, 172b, 191b, n, o, 271, 315; Gl.O. 259; Stone 59-60, 134 Sam. St. 1110; C.W. 333; Mort. 44.
3	238	Structure AX floor	P. 144	Cu.A. 57, 426, Cu.Arch.; Iron 40; Gl.V. 158, 188-9, 263, 311d, 316, 322; Bone 126; C.W. 242; Hum.
3	239	Structure AW layer	P. 143	Cu.A. 95; Dec. Sam. 1018.
3	240	Structure AW floor	P. 141	
3	241	Structure AW grain store debris	P. 141	Coin 241.
3	242	Structure AW layer	P. 143	C.W. 310.
3	243	Structure AW layer	P. 143	

Phase	Context	Description	Page & fig. nos of contexts in Volume II	Catalogued small finds in Volume I, environmental remains in Volume II and catalogued pottery in Volume III
3	244	Structure AX floor	P. 144	Coin 260; Cu.A. 146, 179, 649, 731, Cu.Arch.; Iron 75; Gl.V. 159e, 270; Sam. St. 1140; Mort. 50.
3	245	Structure AX wall	P. 143; Fig. 87	Cu.A. 663; Iron 130; Gl.V. 59; 190; Bone 150
3	247	Structure AX foundation	P. 144	
3	248=184	Structure AW wall	P. 141	
3	249	Structure AW floor	P. 141	
3	250	Structure AW courtyard	P. 141	Gl.V. 260c; C.W. 327.
3	251	Structure AW floor	P. 141	
3	252	Structure AX courtyard ash	P. 144	C.W. 292.
3	253	Structure AW pit	P. 143	
3	254	Structure AW courtyard	P. 141; Fig. 87	Cu.A. 664; Gl.O. 85; Dec. Sam. 1019.
3	255	Structure AX floor	P. 144	Coin 156, 172, 235-6, 256-7, 259, 264, 285; Jewel. 6; Cu.A. 81, 96, 169-71, 256, 267, 301, 372, 418, 441-2, 546, 600-601, 650, 657, Cu.Arch.; Iron 6, 52; Gl.V. 159c, 177, 182b, 188a, 312d, 319; Gl.O. 91; Bone 60-61; Sam. St. 1111; C.W. 286, 300.
3	256	Structure AW layer	P. 143	
3	257	Structure AW foundations	P. 143	
3	258	Structure AX layer	P. 144	Cu.A. 499, Cu.Arch.; Gl.V. 191p; Stone 61, Graffiti 25. Sam. St. 1070, 1125.
3	259	Structure AX layer	P. 144	Cu.A. 602.
3	260	Structure AX pit	P. 144	
3	261	Structure AW layer	P. 143	
3	262	Structure AW floor	P. 141	
3	263	Structure AW layer	P. 143	Cu.A. 377, 411, 478; C.W. 301.
3	264	Structure AW pit	P. 143	Cu.A. 368; Sam. St. 1058.
3	265	Structure AW courtyard	P. 141	Cu.A. 180.
3	266	Structure AW floor	P. 141	
3	268	Structure AW floor	P. 141	
3	269	Structure AW layer	P. 143	Cu.Arch.; Gl.V. 312o
3	270	Structure AW layer	P. 143	Cu.A. 732.
3	271	Structure AW layer	P. 143	
3	272	Structure AW slot	P. 143	Cu.A. 97, Cu.Arch.; Lead 29; Graffiti 37.
3	273	Structure AW floor	P. 141	
3	274	Structure AW floor	P. 141	
3	275	Structure AW floor	P. 141	
3	276=325	Structure AX courtyard rubbish	P. 144	Lead A. 505; Iron 24; Gl.V. 177, 191ag; Stone 136; Bone 42; Sam. St. 1173.
3	277	Structure AW courtyard stone setting	P. 141; Fig. 87	
3	278	Structure AW floor	P. 141	
3	279	Structure AW courtyard	P. 141	Cu.A. 550; Gl.O. 89.
3	281	Structure AW floor	P. 141; Fig. 87	
3	282	Structure AW floor	P. 141; Fig. 87	
3	283	Structure AW floor	P. 141	
3	284	Structure AW foundation	P. 143	
3	285	Structure AW foundation	P. 143	Dec. Sam. 1020; C.W. 338.
3	286	Structure AX foundation	P. 144	Bone 74.
3	290	Structure AW floor	P. 141	
3	291	Structure AW wall	P. 141; Fig. 87	
3	292	Structure AW surface	P. 141; Fig. 87	
3	294	Structure AW layer	P. 143	
3	295	Structure AX layer	P. 144	
3	296	Structure AW layer	P. 143	

Phase	Context	Description	Page & fig. nos of contexts in Volume II	Catalogued small finds in Volume I, environmental remains in Volume II and catalogued pottery in Volume III
3	297	Structure AW post-hole	P. 143	Cu.A. 240.
3	298	Structure AX floor foundation	P. 144; Fig. 87	Cu.A. 157, 395, Cu.Arch.; Iron 31, 66; Gl.V. 52, 144, 147, 151, 154, 159, 161, 175d, 191q, r, ah, ai, aj, 192, 307b, 312aj, 326; Stone 63, 138; Dec. Sam. 1021; C.W. .236, 267, 291, 368-9; Hum.
3	299	Structure AX floor foundation	P. 144; Fig. 87	Iron 122; Gl.V. 133, 265b; Gl.O. 212; Bone 43, 49. Dec. Sam. 1022; C.W. 374.
3	300	Structure AW floor	P. 141	
3	301	Structure AX layer	P. 144; Fig. 87	Cu.Arch.; Gl.V. 60, 182, 191s, 198; C.W. 373; Mort. 58.
3	301/A	Structure AW layer	P. 143	C.W. 251, 261, 370.
3	302	Structure AW layer	P. 143	
3	303	Structure AX courtyard rubbish	P. 144	Sam. St. 1166.
3	304	Structure AW floor	P. 141	
3	305	Structure AW wall	P. 140; Fig. 87	
3	306	Structure AW courtyard floor	P. 141	Cu.A. 479, 633, Cu.Arch.; Lead 30; Gl.V. 26.
3	307	Structure AW layer	P. 143	
3	308	Structure AW layer	P. 143	
3	309=335	Structure AX floor	P. 144	C.W. 366.
3	311	Structure AW stone setting	P. 141	
3	312	Structure AX layer	P. 144	
3	313	Structure AX courtyard rubbish	P. 144; Fig. 87	
3	314	Structure AX courtyard rubbish	P. 144; Fig. 87	Cu.A. 603.
3	315	Structure AX courtyard rubbish	P. 144; Fig. 87	
3	316	Structure AX foundation	P. 144; Fig. 87	
3	317	Structure AX floor	P. 144; Fig. 87	Gl.V. 312j.
3	318	Structure AX layer	P. 144	Cu.A. 673; Dec. Sam. 1023.
3	319	Structure AX courtyard rubbish	P. 144; Fig. 87	
3	320A-B	Structure AX stone settings	P. 144; Fig. 87	
3	321	Structure AW floor	P. 141	
3	322	Structure AX courtyard rubbish	P. 144; Fig. 87	
3	323	Structure AX courtyard rubbish	P. 144; Fig. 87	
3	324	Structure AX courtyard rubbish	P. 144; Fig. 87	
3	325	Structure AX courtyard rubbish	P. 144; Fig. 87	Cu.A. 443, Cu.Arch.; Gl.V. 272b.
3	326	Structure AX courtyard rubbish	P. 144	Gl.V. 329
3	328	Structure AX courtyard rubbish	P. 144	
3	329	Structure AX courtyard rubbish	P. 144; Fig. 87	
3	330	Structure AW layer	P. 143	
3	331	Structure AW layer	P. 143	
3	334	Structure AW pit	P. 143	
3	335	Structure AX floor	P. 144; Fig. 87	Coin 251; Gl.V. 175e.
3	336	Structure AX burning	P. 144; Fig. 87	

Phase	Context	Description	Page & fig. nos of contexts in Volume II	Catalogued small finds in Volume I, environmental remains in Volume II and catalogued pottery in Volume III
3	330	Structure AW layer		Cu.Arch.
3	337	Structure AX hearth	P. 144; Fig. 87	Gl.V. 33.
3	338	Structure AX hearth debris	P. 144; Fig. 87	
3	339	Structure AW layer	P. 143	
3	340	Structure AX post-hole	P. 144	
3	341=299	Structure AX floor foundation	P. 144	Gl.V. 142; C.W. 347.
3	343	Structure AX stake-hole	P. 144	
3	344	Structure AW pit	P. 143;	Cu.A. 40.
3	345	Structure AX ?floor	P. 144	
3	346	Structure AX wall	P. 143; Fig. 87	
3	347	Structure AX foundation	P. 143	
3	348	Structure AX foundation	P. 143	C.W. 376.
3	349	Structure AX foundation	P. 143	
3	350	Structure AW layer	P. 143	
3	351	Structure AW floor	P. 141	
3	352	Structure AW floor foundation	P. 141	Gl.O. 104.
3	353	Structure AW layer	P. 143	
3	354	Structure AX floor foundation	P. 144; Fig. 87	Cu.Arch., Gl.V. 73e.
3	355	Structure AW courtyard floor	P. 141;	Cu.A. 77; Lead A. 506; Gl.O. 81, 88, 264; C.W. 351.
3	356	Structure AX post-hole	P. 144	
3	357	Structure AX post-hole	P. 144	
3	358	Structure AX stake-hole	P. 144	
3	359	Structure AX stake-hole	P. 144	
3	360	Structure AX stake-hole	P. 144	
3	361	Structure AX stake-hole	P. 144	
3	362	Structure AX stake-hole	P. 144	
3	363	Structure AW floor	P. 141	
3	364	Structure AX slot	P. 144	
3	365	Structure AX slot	P. 144	
3	366	Structure AX post-hole	P. 144	
3	367	Structure AX post-hole	P. 144	
3	368	Structure AX post-hole	P. 144	
3	369	Structure AX post-hole	P. 144	
3	370	Structure AX stake-hole	P. 144	
3	371	Structure AX post-hole	P. 144	
3	372	Structure AX post-hole	P. 144	
3	373	Structure AX slot	P. 144	
3	374	Structure AX post-hole	P. 144	
3	375	Structure AX stake-hole	P. 144	
3	376	Structure AX stake-hole	P. 144	
3	377	Structure AX post-hole	P. 144	
3	378	Structure AW layer	P. 143	Gl.O. 256.
3	379	Structure AW floor	P. 141; Fig. 87	
3	380	Structure AX post-hole	P. 144	
3	381	Structure AX stake-hole	P. 144	
3	382	Structure AX stake-hole	P. 144	
3	383	Structure AX layer	P. 144	
3	384	Structure AX layer	P. 144	
3	385	Structure AX post-hole	P. 144	
3	386=254	Structure AW floor	P. 141	

Phase	Context	Description	Page & fig. nos of contexts in Volume II	Catalogued small finds in Volume I, environmental remains in Volume II and catalogued pottery in Volume III
3	387	Structure AW floor foundation	P. 141; Fig. 87	Cu.A. 16, 480, Cu.Arch.; Lead A. 507.
3	388	Structure AW courtyard floor	P. 141; Fig. 87	Mort. 90; Mort. St. 36.
3	390	Structure AW floor foundation	P. 141	
3	391	Structure AW floor	P. 141	
3	393	Structure AW floor	P. 141	
3	394	Structure AW foundation	P. 143	Cu.A. 38, Cu.Arch.
3	395	Structure AX stake-hole	P. 144	
3	396	Structure AX stake-hole	P. 144	
3	397	Structure AX post-hole	P. 144	
3	398	Structure AX post-hole	P. 144	
3	399	Structure AX stake-hole	P. 144	
3	400	Structure AX stake-hole	P. 144	
3	401	Structure AX slot	P. 144	
3	402	Structure AX post-hole	P. 144	
3	403	Structure AX post-hole	P. 144	Gl.V. 312ak.
3	404	Structure AX slot	P. 144; Fig. 87	
3	405	Structure AX post-hole	P. 144; Fig. 87	
3	406	Structure AX post-hole	P. 144; Fig. 87	
3	407	Structure AX slot	P. 144; Fig. 87	
3	408	Structure AX stake-hole	P. 144; Fig. 87	
3	409	Structure AX stake-hole	P. 144; Fig. 87	
3	410	Structure AX stake-hole	P. 144; Fig. 87	
3	411	Structure AX post-hole	P. 144	
3	412	Structure AX post-hole	P. 144	
3	413	Structure AW foundation	P. 143	Gl.V. 136.
3	414	Structure AW layer	P. 143	Gl.V. 262d.
3	415	Structure AW floor foundation	P. 141	Cu.A. 79, Cu.Arch.
3	416	Structure AW floor foundation	P. 141; Fig. 87	
3	417	Structure AW floor foundation	P. 141; Fig. 87	
3	418=299	Structure AX floor foundation	P. 144	Cu.A. 604; Stone 64; C.W. 556.
3	419	Structure AW floor foundation	P. 141; Fig. 87	Coin 210; Cu.A. 553-4; C.W. 311.
3	420	Structure AW floor foundation	P. 141; Fig. 87	Cu.A. 55, 140, 482, 747, Cu.Arch.; Gl.V. 175, 269e; C.W. 254, 272, 324.
3	421	Structure AW floor foundation	P. 141	Cu.Arch.; Gl.V. 134; Gl.O. 270; Graffiti 38; C.W. 350.
3	422	Structure AX courtyard rubbish	P. 144	Cu.A. 402; Gl.O. 213.
3	423	Structure AX courtyard rubbish	P. 144	
3	424	Structure AX courtyard rubbish	P. 144	Coin 244; Cu.Arch.
3	425=298	Structure AX floor foundation	P. 144	Cu.Arch.; Iron 81; Gl.V. 310c; C.W. 262, 353, 372; Hum.

Phase	Context	Description	Page & fig. nos of contexts in Volume II	Catalogued small finds in Volume I, environmental remains in Volume II and catalogued pottery in Volume III
3	426	Structure AX courtyard rubbish	P. 144	
3	427	Structure AX courtyard rubbish	P. 144	
3	428	Structure AW foundation	P. 143	
3	429	Structure AX courtyard rubbish	P. 144	
3	430	Structure AW floor foundation	P. 141	Cu.Arch; Mort. St. 53.
3	435	Structure AX courtyard rubbish	P. 144	
3	436	Structure AW pit	P. 143	
3	437	Structure AX floor foundation	P. 144	
3	438	Structure AW layer	P. 143	
3	439=335	Structure AX floor	P. 144	
3	441	Structure AW pit	P. 143	
3	442	Structure AW pit	P. 143	
3	443	Structure AW pit	P. 143	
3	445	Structure AX layer	P. 144	Coin 237; Cu.A. 556; Lead A. 512; Sam. St. 1054; C.W. 263, 344.
3	446	Structure AX layer	P. 144	Bone 14.
3	447	Structure AX layer	P. 141	
3	448=299	Structure AX floor foundation	P. 144	Cu.A. 37, 379, 557, 641, 659, Cu.Arch.; Iron 131; Gl.V. 138, 171, 176, 180, 191ak, 206a, 257, 274, 312an, 325c; Graffiti 39; Dec. Sam. 1027-8; Sam. St. 1068, 1097, 1105; C.W. 248, 258, 279, 284, 326, 377, 563; Mort. 98; Mort. St. 41.
3	450	Structure AX courtyard rubbish	P. 144	
3	451	Structure AX courtyard rubbish	P. 144	
3	452	Structure AX floor foundation	P. 144; Fig. 87	Cu.Arch.; Iron 18; Gl.V. 162, 191t, 203-4, 266, 273, 312k; Stone 65; Bone 13, 62-4, 139; Sam. St. 1064, 1074; C.W. 241, 290, 318, 331.
3	454	Structure AX layer	P. 144	
3	456=298	Structure AX floor foundation	P. 144	
3	457	Structure AX courtyard rubbish	P. 144; Fig. 87	Coin 286; Lead A. 514; Gl.V. 73f, 145, 307; Sam. St. 1056, 1143.
3	458	Structure AW floor	P. 141; Fig. 87	C.W. 282.
3	463	Pit fill	P. 150	C.W. 275.
3	464	Pit fill	P. 150	
3	465	Pit fill	P. 150	
3	466	Western rubbish pit	P. 150; Fig. 87	Gl.V. 310d, 312e; Bone 66; C.W. 296, 371; An. ca.
3	483	Structure AW earliest deposits	P. 141	Cu.Arch.; Gl.V. 58, 262c.
3	493	Western rubbish pit	P. 150; Fig. 87	Lead A. 518-19; Gl.V. 191u, 312aa; Cruc. 8; Bone 162 C.W. 340; An. ca.
3	535	Western rubbish pit	P. 150	Gl.V. 61b, 329d; Bone 67, 104; C.W. 247, 346; Mort. 14; An. ca.
3	536	Pit fill	P. 147	
3	537	Western rubbish pit	P. 147	Cu.A. 302. Cu.Arch.; Lead A. 522; Cruc. 3.
3	539	Outside E wall Str. AW	P. 143	

Phase	Context	Description	Page & fig. nos of contexts in Volume II	Catalogued small finds in Volume I, environmental remains in Volume II and catalogued pottery in Volume III
3	540	Outside E wall Str. AW	P. 143	
3	541	Outside E wall Str. AW	P. 143	
3	542	Outside E wall Str. AW	P. 143	Cu.A. 734.
3	576=900A	Pit fill	P. 147	
3	577	Pit fill	P. 150	
3	585	Outside E wall Str. AW	P. 143	
3	586	Structure AW foundation	P. 143	
3	587	Outside E wall Str. AW	P. 143	
3	605	Outside E wall Str. AW	P. 143	Cu.A. 241; Dec. Sam. 1033.
3	641	Structure AW layer	P. 143	
3	642	Structure AX courtyard rubbish	P. 144	
3	676	Pit	P. 143	Cu.Arch.; Gl.V. 48.
3	680=683	Layer	P. 150	Gl.V. 312ab.
3	681=684	Layer	P. 150	
3	682	Layer	P. 150	Stone 140.
3	683	Layer	P. 150; Fig. 87	Cu.Arch.; Gl.V. 141.
3	684	Layer	P. 150; Fig. 87	
3	685=683	Layer	P. 150	Coin 155.
3	686	Grave ? Western area	P. 150	Cu.Arch.; Iron 95; Gl.V. 191v; An. ca.
3	687=684	Layer	P. 150	
3	693	Outside E wall Str. AW	P. 143	Gl.O. 90.
3	767	Outside E wall Str. AW	P. 143	
3	830	Western rubbish pit	P. 150	
3	860	Outside E wall Str. AW	P. 143	
3	861	Outside E wall Str. AW	P. 143	
3	900	Western rubbish pit	P. 147; Fig.92	Cu.A. 755; Gl.V. 76, 191am, 262; Gl.O. 228, 229; Cruc. 6-7; Bone 151, 188; C.W. 276, 322, 365.
3	900A	Western rubbish pit fill	P. 147; Fig. 92	
3	901=921	Western rubbish pit fill	P. 147	
3	902	Western rubbish pit	P. 147; Fig. 87	Cu.A. 120.
3	904	Western rubbish pit	P. 147; Fig. 87	
3	908	Western rubbish pit	P. 147; Fig. 87	Cu.A. 781, Cu.Arch.; Gl.V. 70, 75-6, 173, 187, 196, 312g, 313h, 314, 327b; Quern A. 195; Bone 155, 202 Dec. Sam. 1040-41; Sam. St. 1050, 1073, 1121, 1136-8; C.W. 908, 246, 250, 253, 274, 280, 285, 287, 359, 375; An. ca.
3	909	Western rubbish pit	P. 147; Fig. 87	Gl.V. 201, 313e; Cruc. 5; Lamp 6; Dec. Sam. 1042 Sam. St. 1183; C.W. 315, 364; An. ca.
3	910	Western rubbish pit	P. 147; Fig. 91	Coin 269; Gl.V. 191al, 200, 313c; Dec. Sam. 1043 Sam. St. 1052-3, 1107-8, 1122; C.W. 259, 269, 281, 304-5, 348; Mort. 70; Mort. St. 31; Bot; An. ca.
3	911	Western rubbish pit fill	P. 147; Fig. 91	Bot.
3	912	Western rubbish pit fill	P. 147; Fig. 91	Bot.; Hum.
3	913	Western rubbish pit	P. 143; Fig. 87	Stone 66; C.W. 355; Mort. St. 52.
3	915	Post-hole in western rubish pit	P. 147	Bot.
3	916	Western rubbish pit packing	P. 147; Fig. 91	
3	917	Post-hole	P. 150	
3	918	Western rubbish pit	P. 150; Fig. 87	C.W. 244., 330.
3	921	Western rubbish pit fill	P. 147; Fig. 92	
3	922	Western rubbish pit	P. 147; Fig. 90	Wood 28; Bot.
3	923	Layer	P. 150	Coin 221.
3	924	Layer	P. 150	

Phase	Context	Description	Page & fig. nos of contexts in Volume II	Catalogued small finds in Volume I, environmental remains in Volume II and catalogued pottery in Volume III
3	935	Western rubbish pit	P. 150; Fig. 87	An. ca.
3	944	Well packing	P. 150; Fig. 93	
3	945	Well fill	P. 150; Fig. 93	
3	946	Well west of Structure AX	Pp 147, 150; Fig. 93	Gl.V. 157; Stone 144; C.W. 240.
3	947	Well west of Structure AX	P. 150; Fig. 87	Wood 29.
3	950	Western rubbish pit	P. 150; Fig. 87	Stone 67.
3	951	Western rubbish pit	P. 150; Fig. 87	Coin 200; Gl.V. 51, 163, 186, 188b, 206, 312l; Dec. Sam. 1044-5; Sam. St. 1176; C.W. 243.
3	952	Western rubbish pit	P. 150	Gl.V. 152, 191w, 262e; Sam. St. 1061, 1063, 1071, 1091 1093; Sam. St. 1150; C.W. 234, 237, 249, 255, 270, 319, 356, 564; Mort. 111.
3	1171=902	Western rubbish pit	P. 147	Lead A. 526; Gl.V. 191a, 195, 312ae; C.W. 534; Hum.
3/4	56	Structure AX foundation and robber trench	Fig. 87 & 95	Coin 292; Cu.A. 191, 693, 726, Cu.Arch.; Iron 129; Gl.V. 73g, 137, 197, 269f, 312f; Gl.O. 261; Pot.C. 11.
4	9	Destruction Structures AW and AX	P. 151; Fig. 95	
4	11	Fragmentary human bone	P. 151	Gl.O. 204-10; Hum.
4	32	Wall rob	P. 151	
4	37	Destruction Structures AW and AX	P. 151	
4	38	Destruction Structures AW and AX	P. 151	Coin 249.
4	39	Destruction Structures AW and AX	P. 151	
4	40	Dark earth	P. 151	
4	41	Dark earth	P. 151	C.W. 454.
4	43	Fragmentary human bone	P. 151	Sam. St. 1089; Mort. 7; Hum.
4	52	Destruction Structures AW and AX	P. 151	Cu.A. 496.
4	53	Dark earth	P. 151	
4	54	Dark earth	P. 151	Gl.V. 329e, 269f, 312f; Gl.O. 261; Pot.C. 11; Mort. 5; Mort. St. 32.
4	56R	Wall rob	P. 151	C.W. 422, 499; Mort. 113; Hum.
4	57	Structure AY slot	P. 151	C.W. 539.
4	68	Dark earth	P. 151	Gl.V. 327c, 328; Bone 5.
4	78	Dark earth	P. 151	Coin 204, 276; Cu.A. 118, 367, 475, 625, 787, 791, Cu.Arch.; Gl.V. 156, 198d, 269c, 311c, 312, 312i, p; Stone 54; Dec. Sam. 1007; Sam. St. 1123, 1151-2; C.W. 424, 429, 448, 453, 469, 515; Mort. 61, 67; Mort. St. 29; Hum.
4	79	Dark earth	P .151; Fig. 95	Coin 289-90; Cu.A. 36, 78; Cu.Arch.; Gl.V. 149-50, 191d-e, 311b, 312ac; Gl.O. 203, 211, 304; Stone 131; Bone 11, 18, 137; Dec. Sam. 1008-9; Sam. St. 1077, 1154, 1168; C.W. 439, 452, 459, 517; Hum.
4	81R	Structure AX robber trench	P. 151; Fig. 95	Coin 297, 305; Cu.A. 294, 324, 788, 795; Pot.C. 13; C.W. 447; Mort. 107.
4	97	Disturbed human remains	P. 151	Cu.A. 694; Dec. Sam. 1011; Hum.
4	107	Wall rob	P. 151	
4	114	Human remains	P. 151; Fig. 95	Hum.
4	115	Grave fill	P. 151	Gl.V. 259.
4	116	Goat	P. 151	An. s./g.
4	117	Goat	P. 151	

Phase	Context	Description	Page & fig. nos of contexts in Volume II	Catalogued small finds in Volume I, environmental remains in Volume II and catalogued pottery in Volume III
4	123	Dark earth	P. 151	
4	124	Dark earth	P. 151	Cu.Arch.; Gl.V. 184, 313g; Sam. St. 1116, 1170; C.W. 436.
4	128	Wall rob	P. 151	Bot. (Appendix 4).
4	131	Wall rob	P. 151; Fig. 95	
4	132	Human remains	P. 151; Fig. 95	Hum.
4	143	Dark earth	P. 151	Cu.A. 476, Cu.Arch.
4	145	Well fill	P. 151; Fig. 95	Coin 293; Cu.A. 84, 629, Cu.Arch.; Gl.O. 272; Cruc. 1; Bone 10; Sam. St. 1082; C.W. 493.
4	146	Well fill	P. 151	Cu.A. 800; Gl.V. 198c; Sam. St. 1130.
4	152	Well fill	P. 151	Gl.V. 188c; Bone 48.
4	154	Well fill	P. 151	Bone 138.
4	156	Well fill	P. 151	
4	158	Human remains	P. 151: Fig. 95	Hum.
4	159	Human remains	P. 151: Fig. 95	Hum.
4	161	Well fill	P. 151	Gl.V. 148.
4	163	Well fill	P. 151	
4	164	Well fill	P. 151	Iron 74.
4	165	Destruction Structures AW and AX	P. 151	Cu.A. 728; Lead A. 501-2.
4	207	Pit	P. 151; Fig. 95	
4	208	Pit	P. 151	
4	214	Wall rob	P. 151	
4	216	Wall rob	P. 151	
4	224	Pit	P. 151; Fig. 95	
4	228	Pit	P. 151; Fig. 95	
4	229	Pit fill	P. 151	
4	267	Well fill	P. 151	Coin 180, 191; Cu.A. 658; Iron 41; Gl.V. 73c-d, 267b, 308-9, 311f, 313d, 315b; Stone 62, 135; Bone 101, 153, 191; Sam. St. 1072, 1092, 1101, 1144-5, 1153; C.W. 450, 501; Mort. 110.
4	280	Inhumation	P. 151; Fig. 95	Cu.A. 119, Stone 137; Hum.
4	287	Robber trench	P. 151; Fig. 95	Gl.V. 165, 191y-z; Hum.
4	288	Robber trench	P. 151; Fig. 95	Gl.V. 35b, 191aa.
4	289	Wall rob	P. 151; Fig. 95	
4	332	Disturbed human remains	P. 151	Dec. Sam. 1024; Hum.
4	392	Robber trench	P. 151; Fig. 95	
4	393	Robber trench	P. 151	
4	461	Pit western area	P. 151; Fig. 95	Coin 278; Lead A. 515; Bone 37; C.W. 430, 440, 492.
4	467=461	Pit	P. 151	
4	468	Structure AY stonework	P. 151; Fig. 95	
4	470	Inhumation	P. 151; Fig. 95	Hum.
4	472	Dark earth	P. 152	Coin 206; Cu.A. 559, 733, Cu.Arch.; Iron 115-16; 138; Gl.V. 199, 202, 313j; Bone 102, 154; Graffiti 24 Dec. Sam. 1029-30; Sam. St. 1132, 1165, 1174, 1179, C.W. 423, 426, 481, 484-5, 496, 508; Mort. 1; Mort. St. 43.
4	482	Pit western area	P. 151; Fig. 95	Cu.Arch.; Gl.V. 191; Stone 97; Bone 17; Sam. St. 1158; C.W. 442-3, 446, 487; Hum.
4	485	Pit fill	P. 151	
4	486	Pit fill	P. 151	
4	489	Inhumation	P. 151; Fig. 95	Cu.Arch.; Iron 76; Hum.
4	507	Structure AY post-hole	P. 151; Fig. 95	
4	508	Structure AY post-hole	P. 151; Fig. 95	Sam. St. 1065-7.

Phase	Context	Description	Page & fig. nos of contexts in Volume II	Catalogued small finds in Volume I, environmental remains in Volume II and catalogued pottery in Volume III
4	509	Structure AY post-hole	P. 151; Fig. 95	
4	511	Structure AY post-hole	P. 151	
4	512	Structure AY post-hole	P. 151; Fig. 95	
4	513	Structure AY post-hole	P. 151; Fig. 95	
4	514	Structure AY post-hole	P. 151; Fig. 95	
4	515	Structure AY post-hole	P. 151; Fig. 95	
4	516	Structure AY post-hole	P. 151; Fig. 95	
4	517	Structure AY post-hole	P. 151; Fig. 95	
4	518	Structure AY post-hole	P. 151; Fig. 95	
4	519	Structure AY post-hole	P. 151; Fig. 95	
4	520	Structure AY post-hole	P. 151; Fig. 95	
4	521	Structure AY post-hole	P. 151; Fig. 95	
4	522	Structure AY post-hole	P. 151; Fig. 95	
4	523	Structure AY post-hole	P. 151	
4	524	Structure AY post-hole	P. 151; Fig. 95	
4	525	Structure AY post-hole	P. 151; Fig. 95	
4	526	Structure AY post-hole	P. 151; Fig. 95	
4	531	Structure AY stonework	P. 151; Fig. 95	
4	538	Dark earth	P. 151	
4	553	Structure AY post-hole	P. 151; Fig. 95	
4	554	Structure AY post-hole	P. 151	Gl.V. 74a, 312q, 313f; Gl.O. 228, 305; Hum.
4	555	Structure AY post-hole	P. 151; Fig. 95	
4	556	Structure AY post-hole	P. 151; Fig. 95	
4	557	Structure AY post-hole	P. 151; Fig. 95	
4	558	Structure AY post-hole	P. 151; Fig. 95	
4	559	Structure AY post-hole	P. 151; Fig. 95	
4	560	Structure AY slot	P. 151; Fig. 95	Gl.V. 71c.
4	561	Structure AY slot	P. 151; Fig. 95	
4	562	Structure AY post-hole	P. 151; Fig. 95	
4	563	Structure AY post-hole	P. 151; Fig. 95	Cu.Arch.
4	565	Structure AY post-hole	P. 151; Fig. 95	
4	566	Structure AY post-hole	P. 151; Fig. 95	
4	567	Structure AY post-hole	P. 151; Fig. 95	
4	568	Structure AY post-hole	P. 151; Fig. 95	
4	570	Structure AY post-hole	P. 151; Fig. 95	
4	575	Structure AY post-hole	P. 151; Fig. 95	
4	613	Structure AY post-hole fill	P. 151	Sam. St. 1141.
4	614	Disturbed human remains	P. 151	Hum.
4	615	Structure AY post-hole	P. 151; Fig. 95	
4	640	Structure AY post-hole	P. 151	
4	644	Structure AY post-hole	P. 151; Fig. 95	
4	645	Structure AY post-hole	P. 151; Fig. 95	
4	677	Structure AY post-hole	P. 151; Fig. 95	Iron 26.
4	678	Structure AY post-hole	P. 151; Fig. 95	
4	810	Dark earth	P. 151	Cu.A. 665, Cu.Arch.
4	841	Robber trench	P. 151	
4	903	Dark earth	P. 151; Fig. 95	Gl.V. 262f.
4	905	Structure AY post-hole/slot	P. 151	
4	906	Structure AY post-hole/slot	P. 151	
4	907	Dark earth	P. 151	
4	932	Western rubbish pit	P. 151; Fig. 95	C.W. 420, 491.
4	940	Western rubbish pit	P. 151	

Phase	Context	Description	Page & fig. nos of contexts in Volume II	Catalogued small finds in Volume I, environmental remains in Volume II and catalogued pottery in Volume III
	0			Coin 163, 245, 273, 302, 308; Cu.A. 129, 166, 214, 528-9, 722-3, 794; Lead 26, 33, Lead A. 484-9; Stone 50, 128-9; Pot.C. 7-8; Gl.V. 146, 269d, 312t, ad; Bone 22, 25-8, 55-7, 73, 88; Graffiti 22; Dec. Sam. 1000, 1025; Sam. St. 1052, 1059, 1062, 1076, 1080, 1086, 1126, 1142, 1157, 1169, 1172; C.W. 333; Mort. 88, 112.
	2			Coin 274; Sam. St. 1088.
	4			Coin 252, 263, 266, 277, 288, 294-6; Cu.A. 724, 786, Cu.Arch.; Gl.V. 35, 312am; Gl.O. 82, 214; Stone 85; Bone 200; Sam. St. 1124.
	5			Coin 246; Cu.A. 254; Lead A. 490; Gl.V. 275; Stone 51 Dec. Sam. 1001; Sam. St. 1181.
	6			Cu.Arch.; C.W. 525.
	7			Coin 220; Cu.A. 679.
	8			Coin 184; Pot.C. 9; C.W. 526.
	10			Cu.A. 439; Sam. St. 1178; Mort. St. 19.
	13			Gl.V. 172.
	14			Mort. 3.
	44			C.W. 531.
	55			Cu.A. 474; Gl.V. 177.
	57/1			Cu.A. 59
	58			Coin 230; Cu.A. 56, 359; Gl.V. 135, 191ab; 312r; Pot.C. 12; Bone 9; Dec. Sam. 1006; Mort. St. 27.
	72			Coin 165.
	80			Cu.A. 532; Lead A. 492.
	100			Cu.Arch.; Iron 134.
	112			Cu.A. 626.
	219			Coin 306; Cu.A. 410; Gl.V. 264d, 312m; Quern A. 176; Bone 96.
	444			Sam. St. 1159.
	449			Cu.A. 605.
	453			Gl.V. 140; Sam. St. 1069; Mort. St. 44.
	859			Gl.O. 262.

Part III: The Minor Trenches and Sondages

Phase	Context	Description	Page & fig. nos of contexts in Volume II	Catalogued small finds in Volume I, environmental remains in Volume II and catalogued pottery in Volume III

Trench 3
Phase	Context	Description	Page & fig.	Catalogued
	0			Coin 102

Trench 8
Phase	Context	Description	Page & fig.	Catalogued
IIb	250	Wall	P. 43; Fig. 22	
	0			Cu.A. 321, 643, 701-2; Lead 15; Stone 99; Bone 8, 19, 39-40, 44, 69-70, 136, 179, 186,

Trench 11
Phase	Context	Description	Page & fig.	Catalogued
	9			Iron 11;
	12			Iron 30

Phase	Context	Description	Page & fig. nos of contexts in Volume II	Catalogued small finds in Volume I, environmental remains in Volume II and catalogued pottery in Volume III
Sondage 2				
	11			Cu.A. 783
Sondage 4				
	3			Stone 41
	4			Gl.O. 94
Sondage 10				
IIa/b	102	North gate post-hole	P. 43; Fig. 20	
IIa/b	106	North gate post-hole	P. 43; Fig. 20	Tile 41
IIa/b	107	North gate post-hole	P. 43; Fig. 20	
	103			Stone 42
Sondage 11A				
IIa	121	Military ditch terminal	Fig. 20	
Sondage 12				
	131			Coin 123
Sondage 13				
	151			Bone 169; Mort. 40.
Sondage 14				
IIa	190	Structure P floor slot	P. 87; Fig. 54	
	189			Cu.A. 147
Sondage 15				
IV	192	?Post-hole		C.W. 488.
Sondage 17				
	214/B			Gl.V. 330
Sondage 21				
	247		P. 159; Fig. 98	
	351		P. 159	
	352		P. 159; Fig. 98	
	353		P. 159; Fig. 98	
	354		P. 154; Fig. 98	
	355		P. 159; Fig. 98	
	356		P. 159; Fig. 98	
	357		P. 159; Fig. 98	
	358		P. 159; Fig. 98	
	359		P. 159; Fig. 98	
	360		P. 159; Fig. 98	
	361		P. 159; Fig. 98	
	362		P. 159; Fig. 98	
	363		P. 159; Fig. 98	
	364		P. 159; Fig. 98	
	365		P. 159; Fig. 98	
	366		P. 159; Fig. 98	

Phase	Context	Description	Page & fig. nos of contexts in Volume II	Catalogued small finds in Volume I, environmental remains in Volume II and catalogued pottery in Volume III
	367		P. 159; Fig. 98	
	368		P. 159; Fig. 98	
	369		P. 159; Fig. 98	
	370		P. 159; Fig. 98	

Sondage 22

Phase	Context	Description	Page & fig. nos of contexts in Volume II	Catalogued small finds in Volume I, environmental remains in Volume II and catalogued pottery in Volume III
IIb	250	Wall	P. 43; Fig. 22	
	0			Coin 19

Sondage 23

Phase	Context	Description	Page & fig. nos of contexts in Volume II	Catalogued small finds in Volume I, environmental remains in Volume II and catalogued pottery in Volume III
IV	260(A-B)		Pp 109, 113; Figs 68, 70	Gl.V. 207; Jewel. 3; Sculp. 3, Stone 43, 125-6; Bone 199; C.W. 518-523; Hum.
IV	262		P. 113; Fig. 68	
	0			Coin 118

Sondage 24

Phase	Context	Description	Page & fig. nos of contexts in Volume II	Catalogued small finds in Volume I, environmental remains in Volume II and catalogued pottery in Volume III
II	273		P. 64; Fig. 35	
	272			Mort. 28.

Sondage 26

Phase	Context	Description	Page & fig. nos of contexts in Volume II	Catalogued small finds in Volume I, environmental remains in Volume II and catalogued pottery in Volume III
	300			Gl.V. 18; Quern 7, 9; Graffiti 21, 40

Sondage 27

Phase	Context	Description	Page & fig. nos of contexts in Volume II	Catalogued small finds in Volume I, environmental remains in Volume II and catalogued pottery in Volume III
	0			Coin 62

Bibliography

Abbreviations

D., figure type in Déchelette, J., 1904, *Les Vases céramiques ornés de la Gaule romaine* (Paris)

O., figure type in Oswald, F., 1936-7, *Index of Figure-Types on Terra Sigillata ("Samian Ware")*

O. & P. 1920, Oswald, F. and Pryce, T.D., 1920, *An Introduction to the Study of Terra Sigillata*

ORL, *Der obergermanisch-raetische Limes des Römerreiches*

Rogers, motif in Rogers, G.B., 1974, *Poteries sigillées de la Gaule centrale,* Gallia Suppl. 28 (Paris)

S. & S., Stanfield, J.A. and Simpson, G., 1958, *Central Gaulish Potters*

References

Abramson, P., Berg, D.S. and Fossick, M.R., 1999, *Roman Castleford Excavations 1974-85. Volume II: The Structural and Environmental Evidence,* Yorkshire Archaeol. 5

Allgaier, D., 1992, *Die glatte Sigillata der Grabungen Schoppas 1955-67 aus den Südvicus des Steinkastells Hofheim am Taunus* (doctoral thesis, Freiburg).

Anderson, A.C., 1980, *A Guide to Roman Fine Wares,* Vorda Res. Ser. 1

Anderson, A.C., Fulford, M.G., Hatcher, H. and Pollard, A.M., 1982, 'Chemical analysis of hunt cups and allied wares from Britain', *Britannia* 13, 229-38

Annable, F.K., 1960, *The Romano-British Pottery at Cantley Housing Estate, Doncaster: kilns 1-8,* Doncaster Mus. Art Gallery Pub. 24

Atkinson, D.A., 1914, 'A hoard of samian ware from Pompeii', *J. Roman Stud.* 4, 27-64

Atkinson, D.A., 1942, *Report on Excavations at Wroxeter, 1923-1927*

Baatz, D., 1973, *Kastell Hesselbach,* Limesforschungen 12, (Berlin)

Betts, I.M., 1998, 'The Roman tile' in Cool and Philo, (eds)

Birley, E., 1930, 'The pottery', in Richmond, I.A. and Birley, E., 'Excavations on Hadrian's Wall, in the Birdoswald-Pike Hill sector, 1929', *Cumberland Westmorland Antiq. Archaeol. Soc.* 30, 175-98

Birley, E., 1946, in Birley, E. and Gillam, J.P. 'The pottery from the Roman fort at Carzield', *Trans. Dumfriesshire Galloway Nat. Hist. Antiq. Soc.,* 3rd ser., 24, 67-78

Birley, E., 1948, 'The samian ware', in Simpson, F.G. and Hodgson, K.S., 'The coastal mile-fortlet at Cardurnock', *Cumberland Westmorland Antiq. Archaeol. Soc.* 47 (for 1947), 98-108

Bishop, M.C., 1999, 'The Historical and Archaeological context of the *Castra* at Castleford' in Abramson *et al.,* 307-12

Bosanquet, R.C., 1904, ' Excavations on the site of the Roman wall in Northumberland. The Roman camp at Housesteads', *Cumberland Westmorland Antiq. Archaeol. Soc.* 25, 193-300

Buckland, P.C., 1976, 'A Romano-British pottery kiln site at Branton near Doncaster', *Yorkshire Archaeol. J.* 48, 69-82

Buckland, P.C. and Dolby, M.J., 1980, *A Roman Pottery Kiln Site at Blaxton Quarry near Doncaster,* Archaeol. Doncaster 4/1

Buckland, P.C. and Magilton, J.R., 1986, *The Archaeology of Doncaster 1: The Roman Civil Settlement,* Br. Archaeol. Rep. Br. Ser. 148

Buckland, P.C., Magilton, J.R. and Dolby, M.J., 1980, 'The Roman pottery industries of South Yorkshire: A Review', *Britannia* 11, 145-64

Bushe-Fox, J.P., 1913, *Excavations on the Site of the Roman Town at Wroxeter, Shropshire, in 1912,* Rep. Res. Comm. Antiq. London 1

Bushe-Fox, J.P., 1928, *Second report on the excavations of the Roman Fort at Richborough, Kent,* Rep. Res. Comm. Soc. Antiq. London 7

Bushe-Fox, J.P., 1932, *Third report on the excavations of the Roman Fort at Richborough, Kent,* Rep. Res. Comm. Soc. Antiq. London 10

Bushe-Fox, J.P., 1949, *Fourth report on the excavations of the Roman Fort at Richborough, Kent,* Rep. Res. Comm. Soc. Antiq. London 16

Callender, M.H., 1965, *Roman Amphorae*

Castle, S.A., 1976, 'Roman pottery from Brockley Hill, Middlesex, 1966 and 1972-4', *Trans. London Middlesex Archaeol. Soc.* 27, 206-27

Castle, S.A., 1978, 'Amphorae from Brockley Hill 1975', *Britannia* 9, 383-392

Cool, H.E.M., 1998a, 'Introduction', in Cool and Philo (eds), 1-10

Cool, H.E.M., 1998b, 'Life in Roman Castleford', in Cool and Philo (eds), 355-73

Cool, H.E.M., 1999a, 'Building AX and the *vicus* in Phase 3: a further discussion', in Abramson *et al.,* 300-304

Cool, H.E.M., 1999b, 'Appendix 2: Concordance of Contexts discussed in Part Two', in Abramson *et al.,* 317-29

Cool, H.E.M. and Philo, C. (eds), 1998, *Roman Castleford Excavations 1974-85. Volume I: The Small Finds,* Yorkshire Archaeol. 4

Corder, P., 1928, *The Roman Pottery at Crambeck, Castle Howard*, Roman Malton Dist. Rep. 1

Corder, P., 1930, *The Defences of the Roman Fort at Malton*, Roman Malton Dist. Rep. 2

Curle, J., 1911, *A Roman Frontier Post and its People: the Fort of Newstead in the Parish of Melrose*

Dannell, G.B., 1971, ' The samian pottery', in Cunliffe, B.W., *Excavations at Fishbourne, 1961-1969. Volume II: The Finds*, Rep. Res. Comm. Soc. Antiq. London 27, 260-318

Dannell, G.B., 1973, 'The potter indixivixus', in Detsicas, A.P. (ed.), *Current Research in Romano-British Coarse Pottery*, Counc. Br. Archaeol. Res. Rep. 10, 139-42

Dannell, G.B., 1990, 'The decorated samian', in Neal, D.S., Wardle, A. and Hunn, J., *Excavation of the Iron Age, Roman and Medieval Settlement at Gorhambury, St Albans*, Engl. Heritage Archaeol. Rep. 14, 196-200

Dannell, G.B. and Dickinson, B. 1994, 'The samian', in Williams, R.J. and Zeepvat, R.J., *Bancroft: a late Bronze Age/Iron Age settlement, Roman villa and temple-mausoleum,* Buckinghamshire Archaeol. Soc. Monogr. Ser. 7, Vol. 2, 507-512

Darling, M.J., 1981, 'Early red slipped ware from Lincoln', in Anderson, A.C. and Anderson, A.S., *Roman Pottery Research in Britain and North-West Europe*, Br. Archaeol. Rep. Int. Ser. 123, part 2, 397-416

Darling, M.J., 1984, 'Roman Pottery from the Upper Defences', *Archaeol. Lincoln* 16 pt 2, 43-100

Darling, M.J. and Hartley, K.F., in preparation, *Lincolnshire Hist. Archaeol.*

De Laet, S.J. and Thaen, H., 1969, Études sur la ceramique de la Necropole Gallo-Romaine de Blicquy (Hainaut) IV. La Ceramique "a enduit rouge Pompeien", *Helinium* 9, 28-38

de Schaetzen, P. and Vanderhoeven, M., 1964, *De Terra Sigillata te Tongeren* II (Tongeren)

Dickinson, B.M., 1984, 'The samian ware', in Frere, S.S., *Verulamium Excavations: Volume III,* Oxford Univ. Comm. Archaeol. Monogr. 1, 175-197

Dickinson, B.M., 1986a, 'Samian pottery from the civil settlement, Doncaster', in Buckland, P.C. and Magilton, J.R., *The Archaeology of Doncaster 1: The Roman Civil Settlement*, Br. Archaeol. Rep. Br. Ser. 148

Dickinson, B., 1986b, 'Potters' stamps and signatures on samian', in Miller, L., Schofield, J. and Rhodes, M., *The Roman Quay at St Magnus House, London,* London Middlesex Archaeol. Soc. Spec. Pap. 8, 186-98

Dickinson, B., 1990, 'The samian ware', in McCarthy, M.R,. *A Roman, Anglian and Medieval site at Blackfriars Street, Carlisle,* Cumberland Westmorland Antiq. Archaeol. Soc. Res. Ser. 4, 213-236

Dickinson, B., 1996, 'Samian Pottery' in May, J., *Dragonby: Report on Excavations at an Iron Age and Romano-British Settlement in North Lincolnshire, Volume 2*, Oxbow Monogr. 61

Dickinson, B.M. and Hartley, K.F., 1971, 'The evidence of potters' stamps on samian ware and on mortaria for the trading connections of Roman York', in Butler, R.M. (ed.), *Soldier and civilian in Roman Yorkshire*

Dickinson, B.M. and Hartley, B.R., 1992, 'The samian ware (Figs 14-19)', in Hinchliffe, J., Williams, J. and Williams, F., *Roman Warrington. Excavations at Wilderspool 1966-9 and 1976*, Brigantia Monogr. 2, 31-41

Dickinson, B.M. and Hartley, B.R., 1993, 'Samian ware', in Monaghan, J., *Roman pottery from the fortress: 9 Blake Street*. Archaeol. York. 16/7, 722-5, 745-69.

Durand-Lefebvre, M., 1963, Durand-Lefebvre, *Marques de Potiers gallo-romains trouvées à Paris* (Paris)

Elsdon, S.M., 1982, *Parisian Ware: a study of the stamped wares of the Roman period in Lincolnshire, Humberside and South Yorkshire*, Vorda Res. Ser. 4

Ettlinger, E., 1978, 'Stempel auf römischer Keramik von der Engehalbinsel Bern', *Jahrbuch des Bernischen Historischen Museums* 55-8 (1975-8), 115-28

Evans, J., 1985, 'Aspects of later Roman pottery assemblages in northern England', unpubl. PhD Thesis, Univ. Bradford

Field, F.N. and Palmer-Brown, C.P.H., 1991, 'New evidence for a Romano-British greyware pottery industry in the Trent valley', *Lincolnshire Hist. Archaeol.* 26, 40-56

Forrer, R., 1911, *Die römischen Terrasigillata-Töpfereien von Heiligenberg-Dinsheim und Ittenweiler im Elsass* (Stuttgart)

Frere, S.S, 1972, *Verulamium Excavations, Volume I*

Frere, S.S., 1984, *Verulamium Excavations, Volume III*

Gillam, J.P., 1970, *Types of Roman Coarse Pottery Vessels in Northern Britain* (3rd ed.)

Gillam, J.P., 1977, 'Coarse fumed ware in northern Britain and beyond', *Glasgow Archaeol. J.* 4, 57-80

Glasbergen, W., 1948, 'Pottenbakkersstempels op Terra Sigillata van Valkenburg Z.H. (1942)', *Jaarverslag van de Vereniging voor Terpenonderzoek*, 25-28 (Groningen)

Glasbergen, W., 1955, 'Pottenbakkersstempels op Terra Sigillata van Valkenburg Z.H. (1942)', *Jaarverslag van de Vereniging voor Terpenonderzoek* 33-7, 1948-53, (Groningen)

Glasbergen, W., 1972, *De Romeinse Castella te Valkenburg Z.H. Opgravingen 1962* (Groningen)

Green, C., 1980, 'The Roman pottery', in Jones, D.M. (ed.), *Excavations at Billingsgate Buildings 'Triangle', Lower Thames Street, London, 1974*, London Middlesex Archaeol. Soc. Spec. Pap. 4, 39-79

Greene, K., 1978, ' Imported fine wares in Britain to AD 250: a guide to identification', in Arthur, P. and

Marsh, G. (eds), *Early fine wares in Roman Britain*, Br. Archaeol. Rep. Br. Ser. 57, 15-30

Greene, K., 1979, *Report on the excavations at Usk, 1965-76: the pre-Flavian fine wares*

Gregory, A.K. and May. J., 1996, 'The pottery from Kiln 4' in May, J., *Dragonby: Report on Excavations at an Iron Age and Romano-British Settlement in North Lincolnshire, Volume 2*, Oxbow Monogr. 61

Grimes, W.F., 1930, 'Holt, Denbighshire: The works-depot of the twentieth legion at Castle Lyons', *Y Cymmrodor* 41, 1-235

Guéry, R., 1979, 'Les Marques de Potiers sur *Terra Sigillata* découvertes en Algérie', *Antiquités Africaines* 13, 23-97

Hartley, B.R., 1957, 'The samian pottery', in Pickering, E.E., 'Roman Walton-le-Dale', *Trans. Hist. Soc. Lancashire Cheshire* 109, 25-37

Hartley, B.R., 1961, 'The samian ware', in Steer, K.A., 'Excavations at Mumrills Roman fort 1958-60', *Proc. Soc. Antiq. Scotl.* 94, 100-110

Hartley, B.R., 1970, 'The dating evidence for the end of the Saalburg Erdkastell', in Schönberger, H., 'Die Namenstempel auf glatter Sigillata aus dem Erdkastell der Saalburg', *Saalburg Jahrbuch* 27, 28-30

Hartley, B.R., 1972a, 'The samian ware', in Frere, S.S., *Verulamium Excavations: Volume I*, Rep. Res. Comm. Soc. Antiq. London 28, 216-62

Hartley, B.R., 1972b, 'The Roman occupations of Scotland: the evidence of samian ware' *Britannia* 3, 1-55

Hartley, B.R., 1972c, 'Samian', in Fox, A. and Ravenhill, W., 'The Roman Fort at Nunstallon, Cornwall' *Brittania* 3, 100-102

Hartley, B.R., 1974, 'The samian', in Frere, S.S. and St Joseph, J.K., 'The Roman fortress at Longthorpe', *Britannia* 5, 91-96

Hartley, B.R., 1983, 'Samian ware', in Webster, G. and Smith, L., 'The excavations of a Romano-British rural establishment at Barnsley Park, Gloucestershire 1961-1971', *Trans. Bristol Gloucestershire Archaeol. Soc.* (1982), 169-74

Hartley, B.R., 1985, 'The samian ware', in Pitts, L.F. and St Joseph, J.K., *Inchtuthil: The Roman Legionary Fortress Excavations 1952-65*, Britannia Monogr. Ser. 6, 314-22

Hartley, B.and Dickinson, B., 1981, 'The samian stamps', in Partridge, C., *Skeleton Green. A late Iron Age and Romano-British site*, Britannia Monogr. Ser. 2

Hartley, B., Pengelly, H. and Dickinson, B., 1994, 'Samian ware', in Cracknell, S. and Mahany, C., (eds), *Roman Alcester: southern extramural area: 1964-1966 excavations*, Roman Alcester Ser. 1 Pt 2, Counc. Br. Archaeol. Res. Rep. 97, 93-119

Hartley, K.F., 1977, 'Two major potteries in the first century A.D.', in Dore, J. and Greene, K., *Roman Pottery Studies in Britain and Beyond*, Br. Archaeol. Rep. Suppl. Ser. 30, 5-17

Hartley, K.F., 1991, 'Mortaria', in Holbrook, N. and Bidwell, P., *Roman Finds from Exeter*, Exeter Archaeol. Rep. 4, 189-215

Hartley, K.F., 1996, 'Procuratorial mortarium stamps' in Bird, J., Hassall, M. and Sheldon, H., (eds) *Interpreting Roman London: Papers in memory of Hugh Chapman*, Oxbow Monogr. 58, 147-51

Hartley, K.F., 1998, 'The incidence of stamped mortaria in the Roman Empire with special reference to imports to Britain', in Bird, J. (ed.), *Form and Fabric: studies in Rome's material past in honour of B.R. Hartley*, Oxbow Monogr. 80, 199-217

Hartley, K.F., 1999, 'The stamped mortaria' in Symonds, R. P. and Wade, S., *Roman Pottery from excavations in Colchester, 1971-86* , Colchester Archaeol. Trust, 195-211

Hartley, K.F., in preparation, in Hanson, W.S., *Elginhaugh: a Flavian fort and its annexe,* Britannia Monogr. ser.

Hawkes, C.F.C. and Hull, M.R., 1947, *Camulodunum: first report on the excavations at Colchester 1930-1939*, Rep. Res. Comm. Soc. Antiq. London 14

Hayes, J.W., 1972, *Late Roman Pottery: a catalogue of Roman fine wares*

Hayes, R.H. and Whitley, E., 1950, *The Roman Pottery at Norton, East Yorkshire*, Roman Malton Dist. Rep. 7

Hermet, F., 1934, *La Graufesenque (Condatomago)* (Paris)

Howe, M.D., Perrin, J.R. and Mackreth, D.F., 1981, *Roman pottery from the Nene Valley: A guide*, Peterborough City Mus. Occas. Pap. 2

Hughes, D.C., 1989, 'The History of Cement', Lecture given for the Inst. Civil Engineers 21 February 1989

Jacobs, J., 1913, 'Sigillatafunde aus einem römischen Keller zu Bregenz', *Jahrbuch für Altertumskunde* 6te Band 1912 (Vienna)

Juhász, G., 1935, *Die Sigillaten von Brigetio,* Dissertationes Pannonicae 3, 2nd ser., (Budapest)

Jones, M.U., 1971, 'Aldborough, West Riding, 1964: Excavations at the South Gate and Bastion and at extra-mural sites', Yorkshire Archaeol. J. 43, 39-78

Karnitsch, P., 1959, *Die Reliefsigillata von Ovilava* (Linz)

Keen, L., 1970, 'Roman red-painted ware from Yorkshire', *Antiq. J.* 50, 88-93

Kenyon, K.M., 1948, *Excavations at the Jewry Wall Site, Leicester*, Rep. Res. Comm. Soc. Antiq. London 15

Knorr, R., 1905, *Die verzierten Terra-Sigillata-Gefässe von Cannstatt und Köngen-Grinario* (Stuttgart)

Knorr, R., 1907, *Die verzierten Terra-sigillata Gefässe von Rottweil* (Stuttgart)

Knorr, R., 1910, *Die verzierten Terra-Sigallata Gefässe von Rottenburg-Sumelocenna (Stuttgart)*

Knorr, R., 1912a, *Die verzierten Terra-sigillata-Gefässe von Aislingen* (Dillingen)

Knorr, R., 1912b, *Südgallische Terra-sigillata-Gefässe von Rottweil* (Stuttgart)

Knorr, R.,1913, *Die Terra-Sigillata-Gefässe von Aislingen* (Dillingen).

Knorr, R., 1919, *Töpfer und Fabriken verzierter Terra-sigillata des ersten Jahrhunderts* (Stuttgart)

Knorr, R., 1921, 'Terra sigillata-Gefässe', in Goessler, P. and Knorr, R., *Cannstatt zur Römerzeit*, 33-70 (Stuttgart)

Knorr, R., 1952, *Terra-sigillata-Gefässe des ersten Jahrhunderts mit Töpfernamen* (Stuttgart)

Laubenheimer, F., 1979, 'La collection de céramiques sigillées gallo-romaines estampillées du Musée de Rabat', *Antiquités Africaines* 13, 99-225.

Loughlin, N., 1977, 'Dales ware: a contribution to the study of Roman coarse pottery' in Peacock, D.P.S. (ed.), *Pottery and Early Commerce: Characterization and Trade in Roman and Later Ceramics*, 85-146

Ludowici, W., 1927, *Stempel-Namen und Bilder römischer Töpfer, Legions-Ziegel-Stempel, Formen von Sigillata und anderen Gefässen aus meinen Ausgrabungen in Rheinzabern 1901-1914* (München)

Marsh, G., 1978, 'Early second century fine wares in the London area', in Arthur, P. and Marsh, G. (eds), *Early fine wares in Roman Britain*, Br. Archaeol. Rep 57, 119-223

May, T., 1916, *The Pottery found at Silchester*

May, T., 1930, *Catalogue of the Roman Pottery in the Colchester and Essex Museum*

May, T. and Hope, L.E., 1917, 'Catalogue of the Roman pottery in the museum, Tullie House, Carlisle', *Cumberland Westmorland Antiq. Archaeol. Soc.* 17 (1916-17), 114-97

Mees, A.W., 1995, *Modelsignierte Dekorationen auf sudgallischer Terra Sigillata* (Stuttgart)

Moorhouse, S., 1986, 'Non-dating uses of medieval pottery', *Medieval Ceramics* 10, 85-123

Morren, C.G.A., 1966, 'Een Terra-sigillata-handelaar te Nijmegen?', *Numaga* 13, 4, 223-32

Nash-Williams, V.E., 'The samian potters' stamps found at Caerwent (Venta Silurum) in Monmouthshire', *Bull. Board. Celtic Stud.* 5, 166-185

Newstead, R., 1928, 'Records of archaeological finds at Chester', *J. Chester Archaeol. Soc. new ser.* 27, 59-162

Newstead, R., and Droop, J.P., 1939, 'Excavations at Chester, 1939. The Princess Street clearance area', *J. Chester Archaeol. Soc. new ser.* 34, 5-47

Nieto Prieto, J., 1989, *Excavacions arqueòlògiques subaquàtiques a Cala Culip 1* (Girona)

Orton, C.R., 1975, 'Quantitative pottery studies: some progress, problems and prospects', *Sci. Archaeol.* 16, 30-35

Oswald, F., 1945, 'Decorated ware from Lavoye', *J. Roman Stud.* 35, 49-57

Oswald, F., 1948, *Terra Sigillata ("Samian Ware") of Margidunum*

Oswald, F., 1951, 'The volute in late-Arretine ware, and its adoption in early South Gaulish Terra Sigillata in the Tiberius-Claudius period', *Antiq. J.* 31, 149-53

Peacock, D.P.S., 1971, 'Roman amphorae in pre-Roman Britain', in Jesson, M. and Hill, D. (eds), *The Iron Age and its Hillforts*, 161-88

Peacock, D.P.S., 1977, 'Pompeian Red Ware', in Peacock, D.P.S. (ed.), *Pottery and Early Commerce: characterisation and trade in Roman and later ceramics*, 147-62

Peacock, D.P.S. and Williams, D.F., 1986, *Amphorae and the Roman Economy: an introductory guide*

Pelichet, P.E., 1946, A propos des amphores Romaines trouvées a Nyon, Zeit Schweiz Archaeol. und Kunstgeschicht 8, 189-209

Perrin, J.R., 1981, *Roman pottery from the colonia: Skeldergate and Bishophill*, Archaeol. York. 16/2, 45-111

Phillips, D. and Heywood, B., 1995, *Excavations at York Minster Volume I. Part 2 The Finds*

Pryce, T.D., 1941, 'Decorated samian ware', in Fox, A., *The Roman Legionary Fortress at Caerleon in Monmouthshire: report on the excavations carried out in Myrtle Cottage Orchard in 1939*

Richardson, B. and Tyers, P.A., 1984, 'North Gaulish pottery in Britain', *Britannia* 15, 133-41

Ricken, H., 1934, 'Die Bilderschüsseln der Kastelle Saalburg und Zugmantel', *Saalburg Jahrbuch* 8, 130-82

Ricken, H., 1939, 'Die Bilderschüsseln der Kastelle Saalburg und Zugmantel II. Teil', *Saalburg Jahrbuch* 9, 87-96

Ricken, H. and Fischer, C., 1963, *Die Bilderschüsseln der Römischen Töpfer von Rheinzabern* (Bonn)

Rigby, V., 1976, 'Gallo-Belgic and other imported wares', in Stead, I.M., *Excavations at Winterton Roman Villa and other Roman sites in North Lincolnshire 1958-67*, Dep. Environ. Archaeol. Rep. 9, 127-135

Rigby, V and Stead, I.M., 1976, 'The coarse pottery', in Stead, I.M., *Excavations at Winterton Roman Villa and other Roman sites in North Lincolnshire 1958-67*, Dep. Environ. Archaeol. Rep. 9, 136-90

Ritterling, E., 1913, *Das frührömische Lager bei Hofheim im Taunus. Annalen des Vereins für Nassauische Altertumskunde und Geschichtsforschung* 4

Rivet, A.L.F. and Smith, C., 1979, *The Place-names of Roman Britain*

Rogers, G. and Laing, L.R., 1966, *Gallo-Roman Pottery from Southampton*, City Mus. Pub. 6

Rouquette, D., Richard, J-C. and Soyris, P., 'Les estampilles sur céramique sigillée de Murviel-lès-Montpellier (Hérault)', *Revue Archaeol. de Narbonnaise* 22, 287-31.

Schiffer, M.B., 1987, *Formation Processes of the Archaeological Record* (Alburquerque)

Schönberger, H. and Hartley, B.R., 1970, 'Die Namenstempel auf glatter Sigillata aus dem Erdkastell der Saalburg', *Saalburg Jahrbuch* 27, 21-30

Sealey, P.R., 1985, *Amphoras from the 1970 excavations at Colchester Sheepen*, Br. Archaeol. Rep. Br. Ser. 142

Simon, H-G., 1962, 'Terra Sigillata aus Köngen', *Saalburg Jahrbuch* 20

Simon, H-G., 1978, 'Fundkatalog C: Terra Sigillata', in Schönberger, H., *Kastell Oberstimm, die Grabungen von 1968 bis 1971*, Limesforschungen 18, 227-258

Simpson, G., 1953, 'The figured samian ware', in Richmond, I.A. and Gillam, J.P., 'Buildings of the first and second centuries north of the Granaries at Corbridge', *Archaeol. Aeliana* 4th ser., 31, 242-53

Simpson, G., 1982, 'The samian pottery, in Wedlake, W.J., *The Excavation of the Shrine of Apollo at Nettleton, Wiltshire, 1956-1971*, Rep. Res. Comm. Soc. Antiq. London 40, 154-74

Simpson, G. and Rogers, G., 1969, 'Cinnamus de Lezoux et quelques potiers contemporains', *Gallia* 27, 3-14

Stead, I.M., 1976, *Excavations at Winterton Roman Villa*, Dep. Environ. Archaeol. Rep. 9

Swan, V.G., 1984, *The Pottery Kilns of Roman Britain*, R. Comm. Hist. Monuments (England)

Symonds, R.P., 1987, Le probleme des gobelets ovoides sables, SFECAG Actes du Congrès de Caen

Terrisse, J.R., 1968, *Les céramiques sigillées des Martres-de-Veyre (Puy de Dôme)*, Gallia Suppl. 19 (Paris)

Thompson, F.H., 1958, 'A Romano-British pottery kiln at North Hykeham, Lincolnshire; with an appendix on the typology, dating and distribution of 'rustic' ware in Great Britain', *Antiq. J.* 38, 15-51

Tomber, R. and Dore, J., 1998, *The National Roman Fabric Collection*, Mus. London Archaeol. Serv.

Ulbert, G., 1959, *Die römischen Donau-Kastelle Aislingen und Burghöfe*, Limesforschungen 1

Vanderhoeven, M., 1975, *De Terra Sigillata te Tongeren* IV (Tongeren)

Vanderhoeven, M., 1976, *Funde aus Asciburgium*, Heft 6 (Duisburg)

Vernhet, A., 1981, 'Un four de la Graufesenque (Aveyron). La cuisson des vases sigillées', *Gallia* 39, 25-43.

Wacher, J.S., 1969, 'The coarse pottery', in Wacher, J.S., *Excavations at Brough-on-Humber 1958-1961*, Rep. Res. Comm. Soc. Antiq. London 25, 133-205

Walke, N., 1965, *Das Römische Donaukastell Straubing-Sorviodurum*, Limesforschungen 3 (Berlin)

Wheeler, H.M., 1985, 'North-west sector excavations 1979-80', *Derbyshire Archaeol. J.* 105, 38-153

Wild, F.C., 1985, 'Samian ware', in Hurst, H.R., *Kingholm*, Gloucester Archaeol. Rep. 1, 56-111

Young, C.J., 1977, *The Roman Pottery Industry of the Oxford Region*, Br. Archaeol. Rep. Br. Ser. 43

Indexes
compiled by H.E.M. Cool

Notes on the index

Numbers in **bold** are either catalogue numbers or fabric types as appropriate. Forms have only been indexed by fabric for samian vessels. Details of the forms found in all other fabrics will be found on pages 90-99 and 167-72. Details of pottery from particular sites, sondages and trenches will be found in the Appendix. The counties and unitary authorities given for the United Kingdom reflect the situation at January 1998.

General index

Cambridge (Cambs.), samian from, 39
Camelon (Falkirk), samian from, 5, 18-20, 27, 33, 39, 41, 56-7, 73, 79, 80, 81, 82
Campania (Italy), amphora source, 90 **4**
Cannstatt (Germany), samian from, 31, 32, 83
Cantley (S. Yorks.), mortaria from, 168
Cardiff (Cardiff), samian from, 20
Carlisle (Cumbria), mortaria from, 185
    samian from, 19-20, 47, 59, 73, 75, 79
Carmarthen (Carmarthens.), samian from, 19
Carthage (Tunisia), samian from, 25
Carzield (Dumfries and Galloway), samian from, 19, 33, 43, 81
Castlecary (N. Lanarks.), samian from, 80
Castleford (W. Yorks.), coarse pottery source, 98 **78**
    Dixon Street, 3, 52, 56
    fort dating evidence, 21-2
    mortaria source, 168-9 **93-5**, **104-5**; 185
    site phases, 3
    vicus dating evidence, 22, 30, 33, 55-6, 63-4, 84-5
Castle Hill (Notts.), samian from, 73
Castor (Cambs), samian from, 82
'Castor box', 130 **354**
Catalonia (Spain), amphora source, 90 **6**
Catterick (N. Yorks.), samian from, 19, 56, 80, 81
Central Gaulish samian *see* Drag. Form 18/31, 18/31R, 27, 30, 30/37, 31, 31R, 33, 37-8, 38/44, 42, 44/81, 81; Les Martres-de-Veyre, Lezoux, Toulon sur Allier
Cerialis see *Q. Petilius Cerialis*
cheese press, 109 **139**; 114 **181**; 143 **5**, **11**; 146 **523**
Chester (Cheshire), samian from, 15, 18-20, 27, 40, 41, 43, 51, 56-7, 59, 67, 81
Chesterholm (Northumberland), samian from, 80, 82
Chesters (Scottish Borders), samian from, 41, 47, 80
Cirencester (Glos.), samian from, 55
Clermont-Ferrand (France), samian from, 27, 79
coarse wares, black, 97-8 **73-4**, **81**
    brown, 95 **46**, **54-5**
    buff ware, 94 **44**
    cream ware, 94 **38**
    grey, 97-8 **71**, **75-7**, **81**
    grey-white ware, 92-3 **32**, **36**
    grog-tempered, 98 **84**
    millstone grit, 99 **87**
    oxidised, 95-6 **52**, **56**
Cologne (Germany), samian from, 73
Colchester (Essex), black-burnished ware, 98 **80**
    colour-coated ware, 91 **14**
    samian from, 20, 21, 35, 82
colour-coated wares, Argonne, 91 **13**
    Colchester, 91 **14**
    brown, 92 **17**
    buff, 92 **19**
    in pottery shop, 158
    Lower Rhineland, 91 **10**, **12**
    Lyon ware, 91 **8**
    Nene Valley, 91 **9**, **11**
    Oxfordshire, 92 **23**

red, 92 **18**
    rough cast, 91-2 **15-16**
Corbridge (Northumberland), samian from, 5, 7, 15, 18, 20, 36, 55-6, 63-4, 73, 79, 81-3
Crambeck (N. Yorks.), coarse pottery source, 94 **37**; 99 **86**; 142, 146, 148, 158
cream wares, coarse pottery, 93-6 **29-31**, **33-4**, **38-40**, **57**
    mortaria, 168-72 **101**, **103-4**, **106**, **110-111**, **113**, **122-3**, **128**, **139**
Croft Ambrey (Hereford), samian from, 32
cross-matches, 89, 161
cup, 131 **414**
Curle Form 11, 54-5, 64
Curle Form 21, 64
Curle Form 23, 55, 64
Dales ware, 98 **85**; 158
    survival of, 90
Déchelette Form 72, 54-5
de Meern (The Netherlands), samian from, 11, 80
dish, 109 **137-8**; 113 **175-180**; 130 **359-67**; 131 **415-17**; 142 **501-510**; 146 **522**; 148 **549-50**
    evidence for use, 161
Dixon Street *see* Castleford
Doncaster (S. Yorks.), bowl from, 113, 148
    coarse pottery source, 91, 158
    samian from, 51, 73, 75, 84
    stamp from, 148
Dorchester (Dorset), samian from, 41, 67
Drag. Form 15/17, 19 **81**, **83-4**, **89**, **96-7**; 20 **107-111**, **113-15**, **125**, **127**, **133**, **138**; 21 **140-41**
Drag. Form 15/17R, 64
Drag. Form 15/17 or 18, 20 **122-3**; 56 **534**, **538**; 57 **546**, **549**, **555**; 81 **1078**, **1083**, **1085**; 82 **1110-11**; 83 **1164**
Drag. Form 15/17R or 18R, 82 **1118**; 83 **1159**
Drag. Form 18, 18 **71**, **79**, 19 **81-4**, **89-90**, **92**, **96-7**; 20 **107-111**, **113-15**, **125**, **127**, **133-4**, **138**; 21 **140-41**; 56 **540**; 57 **544**; 57 **548**, **553**; 81 **1098**; 83 **1162**
Drag. Form 18R, 56 **539**
Drag. Form 18/31, 18 **76**, **80**; 19 **105**; 20 **124**; 56 **1**, **4**; 57 **547**, **550**, **563-4**, **576-81**, **588-93**; 59 **601-14**, **616-17**, **622-5**, **628-52**, **654**, **694-9**, **782-7**, **790-92**, **794-813**, **818-29**, **831-3**, **837-44**, **852-3**, **869-77**, **943-54**; 61 **956-8**, **974-6**, **983-91**; 80 **1050-51**, **1054**, **1060-61**, **1064**, **1067**, **1072**; 81 **1077**, **1079**, **1087**, **1089-90**; 82 **1109**, **1116**, **1121-2**, **1128**, **1131**; 83 **1138**, **1141**, **1143**, **1148**, **1156-7**, **1169**, **1171**
    in Dixon Street assemblage, 56
    in pottery shop, 54
Drag. Form 18/31R, 18 **73**, **77**; 57 **545**, **565-81**; 59 **595-6**, **626**, **773-9**, **793**, **830**, **867-8**; 61 **959-73**, **978**; 63 **993-4**; 80 **1057**; 81 **1082**, **1094**, **1101**; 82 **1107-8**, **1127**; 83 **1142**, **1145**, **1170**, **1172**
    in Dixon Street assemblage, 56
    in pottery shop, 54
Drag. Form 27, Central Gaulish, 57 **551**, **554**, **557**, **582-7**; 59 **615**, **655-76**, **691**, **700-723**, **788-9**, **814-17**, **834**, **850-51**, **854-61**, **878-915**; 61 **919-20**; 63 **995**;

64 **997**; 80 **1056, 1058, 1065-6, 1068**; 81 **1076, 1102**; 82 **1113-15, 1134-5**; 83 **1139-40, 1152-3, 1166-7**
   in Dixon Street assemblage, 56
   in pottery shop, 54
   South Gaulish, 18 **67-9, 72**; 19 **85, 99, 101, 104, 106**; 20 **112, 116-18, 129, 131-2, 135-6, 139**; 21 **142-3**; 56 **533, 537**; 57 **542-3**; 81 **1084, 1095-7, 1099-1100, 1103-4, 1106, 1123**; 83 **1146, 1150-51, 1160-61, 1163, 1165**
Drag. Form 29, 5 **3, 5**; 7 **14**; 9 **19, 21, 23**; 11 **24, 26-9**; 13 **30-33, 35, 37, 40**; 15 **43, 47-50, 53-4, 56**; 16 **57, 60-61**; 18 **63-4**; 19 **91, 94, 100**; 20 **119-20, 126, 128, 137**; 25 **148-51**; 27 **152-65**; 29 **184**; 30 **194-8**; 33 **250**; 56 **535-6**; 57 **541**; 75 **1034**; 79-80 **1037-8, 1047-9**; 82 **1133**
Drag. Form 30, Central Gaulish, 7 **12**, 32 **226, 241**; 35 **262, 266, 284** (?); 36 **285-91**; 39 **292, 338, 388**; 41 **418, 421-5, 429, 434, 436**; 43 **437-44, 446-9**; 49 **489, 492**; 51-2 **514, 516-18**; 69 **1016**
   Southern Gaulish, 33 **256**
Drag. Form 30 or 37, 39 **295-337, 346-87, 392-417**
Drag. Form 31, Central Gaulish, 18 **75**, 19 **98**; 21 **144**; 57 **558**; 80 **1074**
   East Gaulish, 82 **1132**
   in Dixon Street assemblage, 56
Drag. Form 31R, Central Gaulish, 83 **1158**
   East Gaulish, 64 **999**; 82 **1124**
   present in Trench 10, 64
Drag. Form 33, Central Gaulish, 18 **70, 74**; 19 **86, 93**; 20 **121**; 56 **2-3**; 57 **552, 556, 560-62**; 59 **597-9, 618-21, 627, 653, 677-90, 724-72, 780, 845-7, 849, 863-6**; 61 **921-42, 978-81, 992**; 64 **998**; 80 **1055, 1062, 1069-71**; 81 **1075, 1080-81, 1086, 1088, 1091-3**; 82 **1105, 1117, 1119-20, 1125, 1129**; 83 **1144-5, 1147, 1154-5, 1168**
   in pottery shop, 54
   South Gaulish, 19 **95, 102**; 20 **130**; 80 **1059**; 82 **1106**; 83 **1149**
Drag. Form 35/36, in pottery shop, 54
Drag. Form 37, Central Gaulish, 5 **2, 6**; 7 **7-11, 13, 15**; 11 **25**; 15 **45-6**; 18 **66**, 19 **103**, 21 **147**; 32-3 **233-49**; 33 **259-60**; 35 **261, 263-5, 267, 270-82**; 39 **293-4, 338-45, 389-91**; 41 **419-20, 426-8, 430-3, 435**; 43 **445, 450-62**; 47 **463-81**; 49 **482-8, 490-91, 493-503**; 51 **504-13, 515**; 52 **519-25**; 55 **526-9**; 57 **559**; 59 **600, 836, 848**; 63 **996**; 64-9 **1000-1016**; 73-5 **1017-28**; 75 **1030-31, 1033, 1036**; 80 **1052-3, 1063, 1073**; 82 **1126, 1130**; 84 **1177-9, 1181-3**
   East Gaulish, 15 **51**, 18 **78**; 35 **283**
   South Gaulish, 5 **1, 4**; 9 **16-8, 20, 22**; 13 **34, 36, 38-9**; 15 **41-2, 44, 52, 55**; 16 **58** = 21 **145**; 16 **59**; 18 **62**; 19 **88**; 27 **166-70**; 29 **171-83, 185-9**; 30 **190-92**; 31 **199-214, 216-23**; 32 **224-5, 227-32**; 33 **251-5, 257**; 75 **1029, 1032**; 79 **1039-48**; 84 **1180**
Drag. Form 38, Central Gaulish, 83 **1137**
   in Dixon Street assemblage, 56

   in pottery shop   54
Drag. Form 38 or 44, 82 **1112, 1136**
Drag. Form 42, 64
Drag. Form 43, 64
Drag. Form 44, 56
Drag. Form 44/81, 57 **576-81**; 59 **692-3, 781, 835**; 61 **982**
   in pottery shop, 54-5
Drag. Form 46, 83 **1173**
Drag. Form 67, 18 **65** = 21 **146**; 30 **193**; 33 **258**
Drag. Form 81, Central Gaulish, 57 **572-5, 594**; 61 **955**
   in Dixon Street assemblage, 56
   in pottery shop, 54-5
Dragonby (N. Lincs), coarse pottery from, 103
   samian from, 49
Dramont Wreck G, samian from, 56
East Gaulish samian *see* Drag. Forms 31, 31R, 37, 43; Argonne, Heiligenberg, La Madeleine, Rheinzabern, Trier
East Studdal (Kent), samian from, 69
Ebchester (Co. Durham), samian from, 81
Elginhaugh (Midlothian), mortarium from, 186
   samian from, 81
Epfach Dorf (Germany), samian from, 56
Epinal (France), samian from, 29
Espalion (France), source of samian, 31
fabric descriptions, 90-99, 167-72
face jar, 148 **554**
figurine, 143 **517**
filtered record, definition of, 90
Fishbourne (W. Sussex), samian from, 27, 29
fish products, 159
   see also amphora form Dr 38 and Camulodunum 186A
flagon, 19 **7-21**; 109 **146-9**; 114 **184-5, 195-200**; 119 **241-91**; 131 **379-82**; 134 **422-7, 429**; 146 **525-6**
   decline of, 166
   evidence of use, 159
flask, 99 **20**; 114 **201-2**; 119 **263**; 134 **428**
Framlingham (Suffolk), samian from, 15
France, mortaria from, 171 **132-3**; 192
Frontinus see *S. Iulius Frontinus*
Gallia Belgica, possible mortaria source, 169, 172
Gauting (Germany), samian from, 56, 82
Gloucester (Glos.), samian from, 11
Gorhambury (Herts), samian from, 49
green-glazed wares, 92 **21-2**
Great Chesters (Northumberland), samian from, 20, 32, 55
grey wares, 96-8 **58, 62-72, 75-8, 82**
grey-white wares, 93-4 **32, 36**
Grimescar (W. Yorks.), tiles from, 149
grog-tempered ware, 93 **28**; 98 **84**
Günzburg (Germany), samian, 31
Halton Chesters (Northumberland), samian from, 18, 57
Hayton (E. Yorks.), samian from, 57
handle, 131 **374-7**
Hardknott (Cumbria), samian from, 35
Heddesdorf (Germany), samian from, 56

272

Index of samian potters mentioned in text

Entries for individual named potters relate to their stamps found at Castleford unless otherwise stated.

Cettus, as comparanda, 5; 33 **246**; 35 **280**
    as dating evidence, 33, 84
    present in Trench 10, 64, 67, 75, 79
Cinnamus, as comparanda, 35 **276**; 52 **525**; 55 **532**
Cinnamus ii, 5 **6**; 18 **76**; 80 **1070**
    as comparanda, 7 **13**; 18 **66**; 39 **292, 295-338,**
    340, 342-3, 390; 47 **466**; 55 **526-7**; 67 **1005**;
    69 **1013**; 73 **1023**
    present at Dixon Street, 56
Cintusmis i, 59 **625-6**
    as dating evidence, 64
Ciriuna, as comparanda, 35 **283**
Cobnertus, 18 **77**
Cobnithus, as comparanda, 29 **170**
Coelus, as comparanda, 13 **31**; 18 **63**; 27 **155**; 29 **172,**
    184; 79 **1037**
Comitialis, 18 **78**
Comitialis-Latinnus, as dating evidence, 85
Cosius Rufinus, 18 **79**
    as comparanda, 13 **37**; 27 **167**; 31 **200**
L. Cosius, as comparanda, 29 **184**; 75 **1029**
L Cosius Virilis, 18 **80**
    as comparanda, 31 **203**; 32 **232**
Cotto, as comparanda, 29 **181**; 31 **200**
Cotto ii, as comparanda, 13 **35**
Cracissa, 59 **627**
Cracuna I, attested by stamp, 59 **628-30**
Crestio, 19 **81**
    as comparanda, 5 **3**, 27 **161**
M. Crestio, as comparanda, 5 **5**; 9 **16, 20**; 29 **176, 181**;
    31 **208-9**
Crestus, 19 **82**
Criciro, as comparanda, 51 **505**; 67 **1003**
Criciro v, 80 **1071**
    as comparanda, 7 **12**; 11 **25**; 15 **45**; 52 **520**;
    73 **1017**
    attested by signature, 84 **1178**
    present in Trench 10, 64
Crucuro, as comparanda, 29 **181**
Crucuro i, as comparanda, 75 **1032**
Curmillus, as comparanda, 67 **1001, 1006**
Dagomarus, 59 **631-2**; 63 **993**; 80 **1072**
    present in pottery shop, 53
Divicatus, 59 **633-52**
Divicus, 59 **653**
Divixtus, as comparanda, 73 **1017**
    as dating evidence, 55
Divixtus i, as comparanda, 55 **528**; 67 **1003**
    as dating evidence, 84
Doccalus, 59 **654-90**
    present at Dixon Street, 56
Docilis i, 80 **1073**
    as comparanda, 7 **15**; 41 **435**
Donatus ii, 80 **1074**
Donnaucus, as comparanda, 32 **238-9**; 35 **270**; 69 **1016**
Dov(e)ccus i, as comparanda, 7 **9**; 64 **1000**
    as dating evidence, 21
Drusus I, as comparanda, 32 **236**; 33 **260**; 35 **261**
    present in Trench 10, 67, 75

Drusus ii, as comparanda, 15 **46**; 32 **241**; 36 **291**;
    43 **448**; 49 **492**; 51-2 **514-18**
    as dating evidence, 22
    attested by signature, 84 **1179**
    present in pottery shop, 52
    present in Trench 10, 64, 67, 75
Episus, 59 **691-3**
Fabianus ii, attested by stamp, 81 **1075**
Falana, 81 **1076**
Fedotus, as comparanda, 25 **148**
Felicio i, 19 **83**
Felix i, 19 **84**
Felix ii, 59 **694-5**; 81 **1077**
Frontinus, 81 **1078**
    as comparanda, 25 **151, 158**; 29 **171**; 30 **190-91,**
    194; 31 **219, 222**
Fuscus ii, 81 **1079**
Gallicanus, as comparanda, 5 **5**; 25 **151**
Gallus ii, 19 **85**
Geminus iv, as comparanda, 41 **423, 426-8**; 73 **1022**
    as dating evidence, 22
    present in Trench 10, 67, 75
Geminus vi, 59 **696-8**
Germanus i, as comparanda, 13 **40**; 29 **184, 186**; 30 **195**;
    31 **200, 206, 213-4**; 32 **231**; 33 **255**
Gnatius, present in Trench 10, 67
Gnatius ii, 59 **699-772**; 81 **1080**
Gongius, 81 **1081**
Granio, 56 **1**; 57 **547**
Gratus ii, 19 **86**
Icttiama, 81 **1082**
Igocatus, as comparanda, 35 **262**
Illixo, as comparanda, 39 **390**; 79 **1044**
Immunus, as comparanda, 33 **247**; 35 **281**
    as dating evidence, 33
Ingenuus ii, 19 **87**
Ioenalis, 63 **994**
    as comparanda, 32 **235, 237, 239**; 35 **266**; 36 **287**
Iucundus iii, 81 **1083**
    as comparanda, 31 **222**; 57 **548**
Iulius ii, 81 **1084**
C. Iulius Sabinus, as comparanda, 27 **168**; **172**
Iullinus i, 81 **1085**
Iullinus ii, 81 **1086**
Iustus i, 16 **59** = 19 **88**
    as comparanda, 11 **24**; 13 **36**; 15 **49**; 16 **58-9**; 27
    156, 168; 31 **200**; 80 **1049**
Labio, 19 **89-90**
    as comparanda, 13 **30**
Littera i, 59 **773-9**; 81 **1087**
Litugenus i, as comparanda, 9 **22**
Logirnus, 11 **24** = 19 **91**; 19 **92**; 56 **540**
    as comparanda, 11 **24**
Lollius ii, 81 **1088**
Lupoisucus, 59 **780-81**
Macrinus ii, 81 **1089**
Maiudilus, 59 **782-5**
Malliacus, 59 **786-9**; 81 **1090**
Malluro, 57 **556**

Mallus, 59 **790-93**

Manduilus, as comparanda, 7 **14**; 27 **156**; 29 **170**

Mapillus, as comparanda, 43 **452**; 52 **524**

Marcus v, 81 **1091**

Martinus iii, 19 **93**

Masclus i, as comparanda, 25 **156**

Masc(u)lus i, as comparanda, 25 **158**

Maternus iii, 81 **1092**

Matugenus, as comparanda, 27 **158**

Matugenus ii, as comparanda, 11 **28**; 13 **30**, 16 **60**;
    27 **156**

Meddillus, 19 **94**
    as comparanda, 9 **18**; 13 **36**, **39**; 15 **56**; 16 **58-9**;
        25 **150**; 27 **154**, **161**, **166**; 29 **170**; 30 **195**, 31 **199**;
        32 **225**; 33 **251**; 75 **1034**; 79 **1037**; 80 **1049**
    attested by signature, 13 **39**, 16 **58** = 21 **145**

Medetus, as comparanda, 18 **66**; 32 **240**; 35 **267-8**;
    36 **285**

Medetus-Ranto, present in Trench 10, 69

Medi *see* Meddillus

Memor, as comparanda, 5 **1**; 27 **162**, **166**; 29 **175**, **181**,
    184

Mercator i, as comparanda, 11 **25**, 13 **34**, 27 **167**;
    29 **175**, **181**, **183**, **187-8**; 31 **210**, **217**; 32 **229-30**;
    33 **251**, **253**; 79 **1039**; 80 **1048**

Mettius, 81 **1093**

Miccius, 81 **1094**

Modestus I, 81 **1095-6**
    as comparanda, 5 **3**, **5**; 25 **151**

Mommo, 19 **95**,
    as comparanda, 5 **1**; 7 **14**; 9 **23**; 15 **41**; 15 **55**,
    18 **63**; 25 **151**; 27 **165-6**, **170**; 29 **173**, **184**;
    31 **222**; 32 **224**, **229**
    attested by signature, 84 **1180**

Mon- ii, 81 **1097**

Montanus i, 19 **96**

Monti- Cres-, 19 **97**; 81 **1098**
    as comparanda, 13 **35**

Murranus, 81 **1099-1100**
    as comparanda, 11 **28**; 25 **148**, **157**; 79 **1047**

Muxtullus, 59 **794-808**; 81 **1101**
    as dating evidence, 64

Namilianus, 19 **98**

Natonus, 57 **557**; 63 **995**

Nicephor ii, 81 **1102**

Niger ii, as comparanda, 5 **5**

Ovidius, 19 **99**; 81 **1103-4**

Pacatus iii, 82 **1102**

Pass(i)enus, 19 **100-102**; 57 **549**; 82 **1106**
    as comparanda, 13 **35**; 30 **189**, **198**; 79-80 **1047-9**

Pater ii, 57 **550**

Pateratus, 59 **809-11**; 82 **1107-8**

Paterclus, as comparanda, 35 **274**; 82 **1109**

Paternus ii, 57 **551**

Paternus iii, 59 **812-16**

Paternus iv, as comparanda, 5; 49 **498-5**; 52 **519**, **525**;
    67 **1005**; 73 **1018**
    as dating evidence, 22
    present at Dixon Street, 56

Paternus v, 19 **103**
    as comparanda, 7 **7**; 55 **530**
    as dating evidence, 21
    present in Trench 10, 69

Patricius i, 19 **104**; 82 **1110-11**
    as comparanda, 13 **37**, 15 **42**; 29 **188**

Patricius ii, 56 **2-3**; 82 **1112**
    as dating evidence, 64

Paullus, as comparanda, 36 **289**; 47 **466**

Paullus iii, as comparanda, 30 **190-91**; 31 **219**

Paullus iv, 59 **817-30**; 82 **1113-16**
    as comparanda, 36 **288**; 39 **292**, **295-337**, **339**;
    73 **1023**
    present in Trench 10, 67

Paullus vi, as comparanda, 33 **247**

Peculiaris i, 19 **105**

Perrus, 19 **106**

Pinna, 82 **1117**

Pontheius, 20 **107**

Pontus, 20 **108-111**
    as comparanda, 25 **161**; 31 **217**

Potter A-10, present in pottery shop, 52

Potter of the large S, as comparanda, 7 **13**; 52 **521-3**; 69
    1015
    as dating evidence, 84

Potter of the rosette, as comparanda, 32 **234**; 35 **263**,
    265; 75 **1036**

Potter X-2, as comparanda, 32 **233**; 33 **259**

Potter X-3, present in Trench 10, 67

Potter X-4, as comparanda, 35 **262**

Potter X-5, as comparanda, 5; 32 **244**; 35 **273**; 47 **465**;
    75 **1031**; 79 **1042**
    as dating evidence, 22
    present in Trench 10, 67, 69, 75

Potter X-6, as comparanda, 5, 35 **275**; 41 **421**; 43 **446**,
    450-62; 47 **464-6**, **468**, **474-5**; 67 **1007**; 73 **1024**
    present at Dixon Street, 56
    present in Trench 10, 64, 67, 69

Potter X-7, as comparanda, 52 **525**

Potter X-8, present in Trench 10, 64

Potter X-9. as comparanda, 36 **285**

Potter X-12, as comparanda, 36 **287**

Potter X-13, as comparanda, 69 **1016**

Primigenius ii, 59 **831-3**

Primulus i, 20 **112-14**; 56 **534**

Primulus i-Pater, 82 **1118**

Primus iii, 20 **115-17**
    as comparanda, 5 **5**; 11 **29**; 30 **195**

Priscinus, 59 **834**
    as comparanda, 67 **1001**, **1004**, **1006**; 79 **1046**

Pudens, as comparanda, 79 **1037**

Pugnus ii, 59 **835**; 59 **837**; 82 **1119-20**
    as comparanda, 5; 36 **289**; 41 **425**, **435-6**; 43 **437**,
    443, **447**, **452-3**, **462**; 47 **464-7**, **475**; 52 **524-5**;
    67 **1007**; 73 **1024**; 75 **1027-8**, **1031**, **1033**
    as dating evidence, 64
    attested by signature, 59 **836**
    present at Dixon Street, 56

Putrimus, 59 **838**

Quartus iii, 20 **118**
Quintilianus i, 59 **839-42**
    as comparanda, 41 **423**; 41 **430-31, 433**; 49 **491**
Quintilanus i group, as comparanda, 32 **243**; 41 **429-34**;
    43 **440**; 47 **466**; 69 **1011-12**
    as dating evidence, 22
    present in pottery shop, 52
    present in Site 1(77), 5
    present in Trench 10, 64, 67
Quintio i, 15 **47** = 20 **119**; 20 **120**
Ranto, as comparanda, 18 **66**; 32 **240**; 35 **267-8**; 36 **285**
Reburrus ii, 20 **121**
Regenus, as comparanda, 16 **61**
Regullus, 82 **1121-22**
Regulus, 82 **1123**
Rentus, as comparanda, 36 **289**
Restutus, 82 **1124**
Rogers' P-3, as comparanda, 41 **418**
Rogers' P-8, as comparanda, 73 **1019**
Rogers' P-14, *see* Pugnus ii
Rogers' P-15, as comparanda, 5
Rogers' P-16, as comparanda, 79 **1044**
Roppus ii, 59 **843-4**
Ruffus ii, 59 **845-7**
Rufinus, as comparanda, 27 **165**
Rufinus iii, 20 **137**; 57 **544**
    as comparanda, 13 **35**, 27 **152, 163**, 29 **184**
Sabinus, as comparanda, 33 **252**
Sabinus iv, as comparanda, 31 **212**; 75 **1032**
Sacer, as comparanda, 35 **276-7**; 39 **338**; 49 **490, 494-7,
    502**; 51 **504, 507-13**; 52 **525**; 55 **532**
    attested by signature, 59 **848**
Sacer group, as comparanda, 39 **390**; 49 **489-90, 492,
    501**
Sacer i, 63 **996**
    as comparanda, 7 **13**; 15 **45**; 18 **66**; 32 **228**;
    35 **270**; 49 **493**; 67 **1005**; 73 **1016**
    present in Trench 10, 75
Sacer i group, as dating evidence, 22
    present at Dixon Street, 56
    present in Trench 10, 69
Sacer i - Attianus ii group, as comparanda, 69 **1009**
Sacisamo, 59 **849**; 82 **1125**
Sacr(i)emus, 59 **850-51**
    as dating evidence, 64
Sacroticus, 59 **852-66**; 67 **1006** = 82 **1126**;
Secundus ii, 57 **541**
    as comparanda, 13 **37**; 43 **445**; 47 **466**
    present at Dixon Street, 56
Secundus v, 57 **552**; 59 **867-8**; 82 **1127**
    as comparanda, 35 **276**; 55 **529**
Secundinus ii, as comparanda, 75 **1033**
Sedatus iv, 56 **1**; 82 **1128-9**
Senea, 82 **1130** (?)
Senila, 82 **1130** (?)

as comparanda, 49 **491**; 69 **1012**
    present at Dixon Street, 56
Senilis ii, 82 **1131**
Severianus ii, 82 **1132**
Severus iii, 20 **122-3**; 82 **1133**
    as comparanda, 11 **26**; 27 **169**; 29 **170**
Severus v, 59 **869-913;** 82 **1134-5**
Sextus ii, 59 **914-20**
Sextus v, 82-3 **1136-7**
Silvanus i, as comparanda, 15 **43**
Silvanus iv, 83 **1138**
Silvinus iv, 83 **1139**
Silvius ii, 83 **1140**
Sissus ii, as comparanda, 35 **282**; 41 **425**; 67 **1006**;
    79 **1042**
    attested by signature, 84 **1181**
    present at Dixon Street, 56
    present in Trench 10, 64, 75
Sissus I-Pr-, 20 **124**
Sollemnis i, 61 **921-41**
    as dating evidence, 64
Sulp-Certus, 61 **942-3**
Sulpicius, 57 **553**
Suobnus, 57 **558**
Suservio-Cer-, 61 **944-54**
Tarvillus, 57 **554**
Tasgillus ii, 83 **1141**
Taurianus, 83 **1142**
Taurinus, 83 **1143-5**
L. Ter— Secundus, 83 **1146**
Tertullus ii, 61 **955**
Tetturo, as comparanda, 33 **247-8**; 35 **281**; 73 **1025**
    as dating evidence, 33
    present at Dixon Street, 56
Tintirio, 61 **956-70**
Tittius, 61 **971-3**; 83 **1147**
    as comparanda, 41 **434**; 43 **453**
Tittius-Cassia, as comparanda, 41 **434**; 47 **475**
L. Tr- Masculus, as comparanda, 32 **226**
Trim-/Prim, as comparanda, 5 **1**
Urbicus ii, 64 **999**
C. Valerius Albanus, as comparanda, 9 **16**; 27 **168**
Vanderio, as comparanda, 9 **23**; 15 **55**; 18 **63**; 27 **168**;
    29 **175**
Vegetus iii, as comparanda, 41 **421-5**; 43 **438 440**
    see also Avitus-Vegitus
Vespo, 61 **974-82**
Viducus ii, 83 **1148**
Virthus, 20 **125**
Virtus i, 20 **126-8**
Vitalis ii, 56 **535**
    as comparanda, 13 **36**; 16 **58**; 18 **65**; 27 **159, 161,
    167**; 31 **216**; 32 **224**; 80 **1049**
    attested by signature, 18 **65** = 21 **146**
Vonus, 56 **537**